Comparative Approaches to Cognitive Science

Complex Adaptive Systems
John H. Holland, Christopher Langton, and Stewart W. Wilson, advisors

Adaptation in Natural and Artificial Systems: An Introductory Analysis with Applications to Biology, Control, and Artificial Intelligence, John H. Holland

Toward a Practice of Autonomous Systems: Proceedings of the First European Conference on Artificial Life, edited by Francisco J. Varela and Paul Bourgine

Genetic Programming: On the Programming of Computers by Means of Natural Selection, John R. Koza

From Animals to Animats 2: Proceedings of the Second International Conference on Simulation of Adaptive Behavior, edited by Jean-Arcady Meyer, Herbert L. Roitblat, and Stewart W. Wilson

Intelligent Behavior in Animals and Robots, David McFarland and Thomas Bösser

Advances in Genetic Programming, edited by Kenneth E. Kinnear, Jr.

Genetic Programming II: Automatic Discovery of Reusable Programs, John R. Koza

Turtles, Termites, and Traffic Jams: Explorations in Massively Parallel Microworlds, Mitchel Resnick

From Animals to Animats 3: Proceedings of the Third International Conference on Simulation of Adaptive Behavior, edited by Dave Cliff, Philip Husbands, Jean-Arcady Meyer, and Stewart W. Wilson

Artificial Life IV: Proceedings of the Fourth International Workshop on the Synthesis and Simulation of Living Sytems, edited by Rodney A. Brooks and Pattie Maes

Comparative Approaches to Cognitive Science, edited by Herbert L. Roitblat and Jean-Arcady Meyer

Dynamic Patterns: The Self-Organization of Brain and Behavior, J. A. Scott Kelso

Comparative Approaches to Cognitive Science

edited by Herbert L. Roitblat and Jean-Arcady Meyer

A Bradford Book
The MIT Press
Cambridge, Massachusetts
London, England

This book was set in Palatino by Compset, Inc. and was printed and bound in the United States of America.

Library of Congress Cataloging-in-Publication Data

Comparative approaches to cognitive science / edited by Herbert L.
  Roitblat and Jean-Arcady Meyer.
      p. cm. — (Complex adaptive systems)
  "A Bradford book."
  Includes bibliographical references and index.
  ISBN 0-262-18166-5
  1. Human information processing. 2. Psychology, Comparative.
3. Cognitive science. I. Roitblat, H. L. II. Meyer, Jean-Arcady.
III. Series.
BF444.C64   1995
156'.3—dc20   95-11946
                                                            CIP

Contents

Preface   ix

Introduction   1

I   Introductory Issues   11

1   Comparative Approaches to Cognitive Science   13
     Herbert L. Roitblat

2   The Animat Approach to Cognitive Science   27
     Jean-Arcady Meyer

3   Creative Creatures   45
     Margaret A. Boden

II   Intentions and the Organization of Behavior   67

4   Animal Behavior in Four Components   69
     Bartlett W. Mel

5   Intentionality: Natural and Artificial   93
     Colin Allen

6   Do Animals Have Beliefs?   111
     Daniel C. Dennett

7   Cognitive Ethology and the Explanation of Nonhuman   119
     Animal Behavior
     Marc Bekoff

8   Perceptual Control Theory   151
     W. Thomas Bourbon

III	Representation	173
9	Natural and Relational Concepts in Animals *Roger K. R. Thompson*	175
10	The Integration of Content with Context: Spatiotemporal Encoding and Episodic Memories in People and Animals *Julie J. Neiworth*	225
11	Spatial Information Processing in Animals *Catherine Thinus-Blanc*	241
12	Complex Adaptive Systems as Intuitive Statisticans: Causality, Contingency, and Prediction *Patricia W. Cheng and Keith J. Holyoak*	271
IV	Memory and Attention	303
13	A Model of the Brain and the Memory System *J. Delacour*	305
14	Factors in Visual Attention Eliciting Manual Pointing in Human Infancy *George Butterworth*	329
V	Communication	339
15	Language and Animal Communication: Parallels and Contrasts *Christopher S. Evans and Peter Marler*	341
16	Toward the Acquisition of Language and the Evolution of Communication: A Synthetic Approach *Michael G. Dyer*	383
VI	Motivation and Emotion	413
17	Opportunity versus Goals in Robots, Animals, and People *David McFarland*	415
18	Animal Motivation and Cognition *Frederick Toates*	435
19	Cognition and Emotion in Animals and Machines *J. R. P. Halperin*	465

20   Emotions in Robots   501
     Nico H. Frijda

     Contributors   517
     Author Index   519
     Subject Index   531

Preface

This book is the end product of an International Summer School held in the Ecole d'Art d'Aix-en-Provence, France, July 6–17, 1992, within the framework of Differentiel(s)92, a meeting that brought together scientists and artists interested in animals and robots. The school was attended by 75 students. They came from Europe (56), from North America (16), from Japan (2), and from Australia (1). Mornings were devoted to lectures, many of which are presented and elaborated in this book. Afternoons were spent in discussion of the issues that confront this growing field. The Ecole d'Art provided a wonderful venue for these activities, including a number of discussions between artists and scientists on the nature of art and representation and a number of artistic ''manifestations'' illustrative of the themes of Differentiel(s)92.

This school would not have been possible without the assistance of many people and organizations. We are especially grateful to our leading instructors. We also wish to acknowledge the staff of the Ecole d'Art for their efficient cooperation and good humor, as well as the members of the Groupe de BioInformatique de l'Ecole Normale Supérieure, who worked long and hard to make the school a success.

Finally, we are greatly indebted to the sponsors of the school:

Programme Cognisciences CNRS

Réseau régional CogniSeine

Ministère de la Recherche

Ministère de l'Education Nationale et de la Culture

Ministère de la Défense, DGA/DRET

Electricité de France

Introduction

There is an old Chinese folktale about a man who envied his rich neighbors and their two-story houses. He hired a builder and asked for a house as tall as those of his neighbors. When he visited the building site he was appalled to find that the builder was framing in the lower level of the house. The angry man cursed the builder for wasting money on a ground floor when what he wanted was a second floor.

It would be something of an exaggeration to claim that cognitive science is like the Chinese man, concerned with high-level cognitive activities at the cost of attention to the fundamental problems of intelligence. There nevertheless remains some small truth in the analogy. The ground floor has not been wholly neglected, but the emphasis has certainly been on the second story.

Cognitive science has been dominated by a computationalist approach, according to which cognition is symbolic computation consisting of "the manipulation of physical 'symbol tokens' on the basis of syntactic rules that operate only on the 'shapes' of the symbols (which are arbitrary in their relation to what the symbols can be interpreted as meaning), as in a digital computer or its idealization, a Turing machine manipulating, say, '0's and '1's" (Harnad 1993, p. 12). A physical symbol system is assumed to be the architecture of intelligent systems, both a necessary and sufficient mechanism for producing intelligent performance (Newell and Simon 1976).

Given this approach to cognition, it should come as no surprise that cognitive science has concerned itself largely, and quite successfully, with modeling the performance of tasks that are readily describable in terms of a well-specified set of symbols and an articulated set of rules for operating on those symbols. These tasks, such as planning, problem solving, chess playing, and the like, are typical of the highest level of human achievement. In contrast, there remains a very large domain of problems that have resisted solution by standard cognitive science methods. These problems involve modeling tasks, such as perception, categorization, motor control, and the like, which are not uniquely human, but rather are shared by many or all animals.

It is unlikely that the development of an effective artificial chess player or scientific problem solver would yield a generally intelligent artificial human. A physical symbol system operates on the symbols it is given and produces additional symbols. For example, given a symbolic representation of a chess board, a chess program (modeling perhaps an expert chess player) can determine which symbols to produce in order to describe an effective subsequent chess position. The program does not include, however, a mechanism by which a chess configuration on an arbitrary chess board can be recognized (although there are exceptions that use special-purpose algorithms designed to discriminate chess pieces). The computational approach to cognitive science does very well at processing symbols, but it largely neglects the problem of how those symbols are related to the environment. This is the problem of symbol grounding (Harnad 1990)—how the symbols come to have the interpretation that they do.

Some of the investigators in the field address the symbol-grounding problem by avoiding the use of symbols insofar as possible (see, e.g., several chapters in the books resulting from the meetings on simulation of adaptive behavior: Meyer and Wilson 1991; Meyer, Roitblat, and Wilson 1993; Cliff et al. 1994). Rather than conceiving of the mind as a symbol-processing device, these approaches view the mind as a hierarchically organized collection of simple behavioral mechanisms that interact with one another to produce intelligent action. Unlike the symbol system view, in which organisms are seen as syntactic symbol processors, this view sees organisms as collections of interacting agents. Some of the agents are directly responsible for transducing environmental variables into system variables (such as sonar return times into distances) that are maintained as analog quantities and function to influence other agents. The structure of these agents determines the causal relations between the environmental variables and the influence they have on other agents. No system of these agents has yet been developed that can play a sophisticated game of chess, but they could, in principle, be developed to do so. Rather, these systems have concentrated on the solution of more mundane behavioral problems, such as navigating through a cluttered environment. Just because the behaviors are more mundane, they are not necessarily more trivial. No one, for example, has yet modeled a fly landing on a ceiling, but there is no reason to believe that this problem should be intrinsically any more difficult than modeling the heuristics used by Hans Krebs in his discovery of the urea cycle (Kulkarni and Simon 1988). Nevertheless, it has so far received relatively little attention.

It is impossible to know whether cognitive scientists have focused on solving complex intellectual problems because their tools have been better suited to such problems or whether they have developed tools to suit what they think are more interesting problems. One possible explanation of why scientists have concentrated on tasks that are most amenable to symbolic description and emulation is the apparent belief that if the complex problems indicative of human sophistication can be solved, then the solution of simple problems will follow. The same mechanisms that operate in the solution of complex problems will prove effective in solving the mundane.

An alternative approach notes that evolutionary continuity implies that human intelligence rests on a foundation of long evolutionary history, some of which is shared by other extant organisms. Many of the contributors to this volume argue that there is much to be learned from investigating the mechanisms employed by those other species to solve the kinds of problems that our species shares with them (e.g., searching, navigation, pattern recognition, and others). The investigation of these mechanisms has been largely ignored because animals are incapable of the kinds of tasks that have been favored as subjects for computational modeling and because many investigators have believed that they know the mechanisms of animal behavior and that these mechanisms are necessarily too simple to be useful in explaining advanced human cognitive performance. Many investigators have thought that animal behavior is governed solely by stimulus-response mechanisms.

More recently, however, a perspective on animal behavior has been emerging that views animals not as passive reflex devices, but as active information processors seeking information in their environment, encoding it, and using it for their benefit in flexible and intelligent ways (e.g., Roitblat 1987). Investigation of animal behavior and the brain mechanisms that produce it provides important insight into the operation of fundamental cognitive processes. Although the gulf is often still quite wide, much is known about the neural processes of animal behavior, and a great deal of this information is potentially useful in developing models of the behavior and the mechanisms that implement it.

Animals provide a useful comparative basis for testing the development of cognitive theories. We are all so intimately familiar with our own cognitive processing that it is difficult to discriminate what is difficult from what is simple. Our intuitions regarding our own cognitive complexity are not typically reliable indicators. Processes that seem automatic and natural to us are often based on highly complex mechanisms and processes. By examining related processes in other organisms with whom we are less familiar, we can more objectively assess the processes and more skeptically entertain alternative accounts of them.

Partly as a reflection of this new-found interest in animals as a legitimate venue for investigation of cognitive processing, some investigators have begun attempts to simulate or build adaptive "animats" that are able to cope with unpredictable and more or less threatening environments. An animat (Wilson 1991) is an artificial organism, either a simulated animal or an animal-like robot. Its structure and functionality are based substantially on mechanisms observed in biological animals. Animals provide a kind of existence proof in that they can demonstrably perform the functions for which they are adapted. Our knowledge of those functions and of the mechanisms that produce them is an invaluable resource for the development of related functions in artificial autonomous systems.

A related benefit of the animat approach is that it makes it more difficult to conceal ad hoc special solutions. Many difficult problems can be made simple once the necessary information is represented in an appropriate format. A model may easily succeed in solving a problem if it is given information about its environment in the form of "predigested" representations. If these representations must be provided by the investigator, however, then the system cannot provide a model for the intelligence necessary to solve the problem because the intelligence resides in the investigator who formulated the representation.

The "mutilated checkerboard" problem provides one example of a problem that is easy to solve with the correct representation and difficult to solve without it. Imagine a checkerboard with 64 alternating black and white squares (an 8-by-8 square). Mutilate this checkerboard by removing two white squares, one at the upper left corner of the board and the other at the lower right. The board now contains 62 squares. Is there an arrangement of 31 dominoes, each of which exactly covers 2 squares, that can cover the board exactly (i.e., no dominoes overlap and none extend beyond the board)? Because there are 31 dominoes and 62 squares, one might think that this is an easy problem and that the task can be performed, but one would be wrong. Most people trying to solve this problem attempt to lay down dominoes on the board (perhaps using imaginary dominoes and an imaginary board) one by one until they cover the board (and find that they do not fit exactly). Nevertheless, although the number of arrangements of 31 dominoes is large, these people think perhaps some arrangement can be found, so they continue their attempts at solving the problem. Only after attempting all arrangements can a problem solver using this method be sure that the dominoes cannot exactly cover the board.

Using an alternative representation, however, the problem clearly appears as insoluble. Any domino must cover exactly one black square and one white square, because a black square is never adjacent to a black square. There are 32 black squares on the board, but only 30 white squares. Therefore, no arrangement of dominoes can cover the board exactly. Humans are capable (at least some of them, at any rate) of changing from a visual representation of the problem to another form of representation. A computer given the appropriate representation could easily be programmed to solve this problem. The difficult task for the computer would be to take the raw information as given and determining which representation was best suited to solving it. This task of switching representations is probably not impossible for a computer, but those who work within the animat approach argue that this kind of metatask (i.e., adopting appropriate representations) will more robustly and more quickly be performed by developing systems that can adapt themselves and their representations to the problems they solve rather than relying on preprogrammed strategies. These investigators argue that (a) one should model whole organisms that (b) obtain their information about the environment directly from sensors and (c) have internal mechanisms for evolving representations appropriate to the environment and the problems it presents to the artificial organism. Success in explaining human performance may depend a great deal on understanding the operation of the basic processes that produce representations. These processes constrain and support the operations of so-called higher cognitive functions.

The first group of chapters in this book addresses general issues in comparative approaches to cognitive science. Roitblat outlines a conceptual program for the endeavor. He draws an important distinction between cognitive science as it has traditionally been implemented via serial processors following explicitly described rules and what he calls a biomimetic approach based more on connectionist principles and constraint satisfaction than on explicit rules. He does not argue that traditional approaches to cognitive science have no place; rather, he argues that progress will be made faster when multiple approaches are exploited by the field, each of which is specially suited to particular classes of problems.

Meyer describes the animat approach in more detail. He describes a number of systems that have been developed and behave in ways that were not specifically programmed into them. This work demonstrates that some of the adaptive capacities of an insect can be generated in an animat endowed with a very simple nervous system featuring fewer than 100 neurons and fewer than 200 connections. Meyer further offers examples of how one can successfully design animats with nonsymbolic subsumption architectures that are quite capable of dealing with uncertain, difficult-to-predict environments without using symbolic or world model representations. These systems are capable of adaptation and of learning.

Boden addresses the epistemological question of when an organism (or a robot) can be said to be creative. Adaptation plays an essential role in intelligence, but how such adaptations are achieved often depends on creativity (or chance). A system that could exploit creativity to derive suitable adaptations would have an advantage over competing organisms that had to rely on chance. Boden explicitly compares humans, animals, computers, and robots in her exploration of the nature of creativity.

The second section of the book presents a set of five chapters concerned with intentionality and the organization of behavior. Mel describes a scheme for decomposing animal behaviors into sets of more or less independent components based on the kind of computational machinery necessary to implement that behavior. He argues that these four kinds of behavioral components provide a conceptual framework in which we can understand the continuity of cognitive/behavioral evolution linking the simplest brains to the most complex.

One of the most important and contentious issues in cognitive science is the role played by intentionality in controlling behavior. A number of critics, most notably Searle (1980), have argued that machines cannot have intentionality because they lack the proper mental states and are purely syntactic—that is, they merely follow rules without any knowledge of what those rules are about. Part of the support for intentionality as an important factor in behavior is our own introspection: It is immediately apparent to us that we know what our ideas are about, but machines apparently have no way of knowing what their symbols are about. A parallel problem exists concerning intentionality in animals. We have no way to know whether animals know what their representations are about. Biological continuity suggests that animals are likely to be intentional, but it does not demand that they be. Allen argues that a comparison among animals, machines, and humans provides grounds for understanding the nature of intentionality and the role it plays in behavior.

Intentionality in its philosophical usage refers to the idea that symbols are about something. Dennett explores a series of criteria for the presence of beliefs in animals. For Dennett, "belief" is a generic term for a cognitive state. Such a cognitive state is necessarily an intentional state (because it is about items, events, etc.), so by understanding animal beliefs we necessarily also gain understanding of animal intentionality. Dennett argues that animals can truly be said to have beliefs because their behavior can be sensibly understood only when described in belief-assuming terms (or technical translations of those terms, such as semantic information terms). He further argues, in contrast to Fodor, that beliefs are not like sentences—that is, they need not be expressed in some underlying mentalese in order to be intentional. Instead, Dennett argues that systems of related beliefs are more like maps than like sentences.

Bekoff continues the conceptual investigation of intentionality in animals by arguing that naturalistic—that is, ethological—investigations are essential in order to investigate what animals actually do. He outlines an agenda for cognitive ethology and for the kinds of data that are essential to understanding cognition in animals.

In thorough contrast to the emphasis on intentionality as an essential feature of behavior is Bourbon's emphasis on control theory. In his view, behavior is not the object of control; rather, it is the means by which organisms routinely achieve and maintain control over their perceptions and incidentally over parts of the environment. He argues that control of behavior need not depend on prior plans, commands, or solutions of problems in inverse kinematics; rather, patterned coordinated actions occur when independent systems (agents, body parts) control their own sensations of local variables.

The topic of the third section of the book is representation. The preceding section has been concerned with whether animals have beliefs and the nature of those beliefs. The chapters in this section explore the content of those beliefs. A representation is a cognitive structure that stands for something else. Some representations are symbols, but, as Dennett has pointed out in the preceding section, other forms of representation are also possible. In this section, Thompson explores the content of concepts and beliefs in animal behavior. He describes a series of experiments that have been used to investigate conceptual representations (i.e., representations about open-ended classes of items) in a variety of species and uses these experiments to inform a discussion of alternative theories of representation (see also Roitblat 1982).

Neiworth addresses the problem of representation from a more biological perspective by considering the role that neuropsychological evidence plays in the formation and exploitation of representations in people and in animals. She considers features of amnesia-related memory deficits, brain lesions, and behavioral data to investigate spatiotemporal processing and memory.

Thinus-Blanc continues the investigation of spatial representations and information processing in the next chapter. By "spatial information processing" she means retrieval and use of environmental knowledge in order to reach goals. She describes some data concerning exploration by animals and a psychological model for the formation and exploitation of cognitive maps.

Cheng and Holyoak also explore conceptual representations in humans and animals, but their concern is more with how organisms represent causality and contingency. Even the simplest classical conditioning seems to depend on some form of causal representation in the animal's ability to use a conditioned stimulus as a predictor of an unconditioned stimulus and to make a response that is appropriate to that prediction. The authors argue that inductions concerning causes cannot be explained simply on the basis of associative mechanisms, but rather require a mechanism based on contingency for extracting causation.

The chapters in the next section of the book concern memory and attention. Delacour describes a view of memory that integrates neurophysiological findings with behavioral data to describe an integrated model of brain/memory functioning. His model consists of three subsystems. The R subsystem consists of the primary sensory and motor structures of the brain. The A system has no precise relation to the sensory or motor mechanisms, but its activity is correlated with arousal or motivational states. Finally, the S subsystem consists of the prefrontal cortex and some related areas and is responsible for supervision of the activity of the other subsystems. The three systems interact to produce organized behavior.

Butterworth explores the means by which one organism, in this case a human infant, comes to coordinate its attentional focus with that of another. Such coordination of action is essential when independent agents must cooperate in order to complete a task. By investigating the development of this process in human infants, Butterworth suggests, we can gain a better understanding of the precursors of thought and language and of situated action.

The next section concerns communication and its evolution. Humans use a system of communication that is far more complex and flexible than that of any other animal. It seems obvious, however, that humans' language capacity evolved just as every other biological capacity evolved. By comparing animals and humans, we can potentially learn a great deal about the nature of language, but also about its precursors and their functionality. These precursors may have important implications for understanding intelligence and important applications in the development of communication systems for robots and similar devices.

Evans and Marler explore the commonalties among human language and animals' communication systems. They describe three cognitive abilities that had once been held to be essential to language production or perception: (a) the ability to partition continuous variation into discrete categories, (b) the ability to designate external events or objects, and (c) the ability to be responsive to an audience in planning and executing one's communication.

Dyer takes a more formal approach to the evolution of language by investigating the roles that evolution and learning play in the acquisition of communication systems by artificial organisms. He describes two projects, one of which involves the acquisition of primitive subsets of human language through association of simple sequences with moving shapes on an artificial retina. The second project describes the evolution of animal-like signaling among interacting and evolving populations of simple-connections animats.

The final section of the book concerns motivation and emotion. MacFarland notes that robots will evolve over the coming years. Instead of natural selection, their evolution will depend on the demands of the marketplace. Successful robots will have to evolve appropriate motivations to sustain themselves and meet the selection criteria of their customers. A self-sufficient robot must have appropriate motivations for maintenance of its viability. An autonomous robot must have some degree of motivation and cognition in order to maintain its functionality.

Toates points out the essential nature of motivation in cognition and argues that motivation has so far largely been ignored in cognitive science. An organism requires motivation in order to be goal-oriented, employ attentional mechanisms, guide its inferences during learning, and perform many other functions. Toates argues that motivation and cognition are so intimately intertwined that, in reality, it is impossible to study one without the other. That we have failed to do so is detrimental to the field.

The last two chapters of the book take up the relation between emotion and cognition. Despite the folk-psychological position that emotion and cognition are polar opposites, Halperin and Frijda argue that they are actually intimately linked to one another and have important adaptive value. Halperin shows how a comparative approach that considers relevant evidence from animals and machines can be productive. She outlines a neurobiologically based connectionist model for integrating emotion and cognition that could be implemented as part of the control architecture for a robot.

Frijda extends this discussion of emotion in robots. He argues that emotions have been neglected because of the focus on their subjective and affective values, but that emotions also serve a number of other functions for an organism, including appraisal and action readiness. He describes a model, ACRES, that incorporates a functional theory of emotion that provides a system for monitoring and safeguarding the organism's or robot's concerns.

We hope that this book will provide a foundation on which to build an emerging approach to cognitive science. We do not believe that the approach we describe should be the only way of investigating issues in cognitive science, but we do believe that such investigations are essential to continuing success in the field. The approach is novel, not yet fully formed, but we think that it is potentially quite powerful.

REFERENCES

Cliff, D., Husbands, P., Meyer, J. A. and Wilson, S. W. (eds.) (1994). *From Animals to Animats 3: Proceedings of the Third International Conference on Simulation of Adaptive Behavior*. Cambridge, MA: MIT Press.

Harnad, S. (1990). The symbol grounding problem. *Physica D,* 42, 335–346.

Harnad, S. (1993). Grounding symbols in the analog world with neural nets: A hybrid model. *Think,* 2 (June), 12–20.

Kulkarni, D., and Simon, H. A. (1988). The processes of scientific discovery: The strategy of experimentation. *Cognitive Science,* 12, 139–175.

Meyer, J. A., and Wilson, S. W. (eds.) (1991). *From Animals to Animats: Proceedings of the First International Conference on Simulation of Adaptive Behavior*. Cambridge, MA: MIT Press.

Meyer, J. A., Roitblat, H. L., and Wilson, S. W. (eds.) (1993). *From Animals to Animats 2: Proceedings of the Second International Conference on Simulation of Adaptive Behavior*. Cambridge, MA: MIT Press.

Newell, A., and Simon, H. A. (1976). Computer science as empirical enquiry. In J. Haugeland (ed.), *Mind Design*. Cambridge, MA: MIT Press.

Roitblat, H. L. (1982). The meaning of representation in animal memory. *The Behavioral and Brain Sciences,* 5, 353–406.

Roitblat, H. L. (1987). *Introduction to Comparative Cognition*. New York: W. H. Freeman.

Searle, J. R. (1980). Minds, brains, and programs. *Behavioral and Brain Sciences,* 3, 417–424.

Wilson, S. W. (1991). The Animat Path to AI. In J. A. Meyer and S. W. Wilson (eds.), *From Animals to Animats: Proceedings of the First International Conference on Simulation of Adaptive Behavior*. Cambridge, MA: MIT Press.

I Introductory Issues

1 Comparative Approaches to Cognitive Science

Herbert L. Roitblat

COGNITIVE SCIENCE

Standard Cognitive Science

A major focus in cognitive science has been on modeling the performance of tasks that are characteristic of advanced human intelligence, such as planning, problem solving, scientific creativity, and the like, tasks that characterize the achievement of intelligent, educated, language-using humans. These tasks are apparently performed through conscious and deliberate effort. People perform them badly and slowly relative to fluent and apparently automatic sensory and perceptual motor tasks (Clark 1990).

Language is an important component of the performance of these tasks. In fact, language is such an obvious and important characteristic of human cognitive performance that a number of theorists, at least since Descartes, have considered language to be the defining feature of human cognition. Language is the skill that putatively separates people from other animals. Language use is so central to our conceptualization of what it means to be human, and so tied to our intellectual achievements, that it may actually be the cause of our achievements (Bickerton 1990). If language is the cause of our intelligence, then it makes sense to endow our models with internal structures that correspond to our own use of language (Bolles 1975; Fodor 1975). In other words, one possibility is that humans are as intelligent as we are precisely because we have language; therefore, language is likely to be an essential mechanism of that intelligence.[1] If our models are to be similarly effective, then they must use similar structures. As a result, a great deal of effort has been expended in the development of models of human cognitive performance that parallel language use through the expression of rules and symbolic tokens.

Although such verbal-like systems have been found effective in solving a number of problems, the problems they address tend to be rather small portions of the whole of human performance and tend to operate on the basis of a limited range of inputs that are often a restricted set of simple assertions abstracted from real data by the human investigators. That is, many of these systems operate on descriptions of data rather than on the data themselves. These descriptions are typically abstracted and prepared by the experimenters, thus freeing the model from the perceptual problems.

In contrast to cognitive science's success with rule-based models in a number of domains, such verbal-like systems have not proved as effective in solving an important set of problems that involve fundamental processes of perception, categorization, and the like. Although tasks such as chess playing and circuit routing have been effectively modeled using standard techniques, tasks that humans find easy and automatic, such as recognizing the face of a friend, have not been modeled with anywhere near the same level of success. Furthermore, there is no clear demarcation between perception and reasoning. Perception is affected by beliefs and expectations (from the top down), and reasoning is necessarily affected by perception (from the bottom up). Therefore, it may be unclear whether the success of a model is the result of the experimenter's intelligence in abstracting and representing data or whether it is the result of an intelligent model.

The verbal-type systems emphasize reasoning and logic, which they can exercise well in a language-like way. The success of chess-playing programs, for example, has come largely from perfecting algorithms for effectively evaluating potential chess moves and extrapolating board configurations on several subsequent moves. In contrast, human intelligence often seems to depend on the operation of perception more than on any particular ability to reason. For example, one difference between expert and novice chess players seems to be the number of board configurations that can be recognized and categorized by the player rather than any ability to think more or fewer moves ahead in the game (Charness 1989; de Groot 1966).

The Biomimetic Perspective of Cognitive Science

Many of the processes that have resisted successful cognitive modeling using verbal-like rule following are those that humans share with other organisms. Hence, understanding nonhuman organisms, about whom we are less inclined to infer the use of verbal-like systems, can yield critically important information about fundamental cognitive processes that are essential to truly understanding how the mind works.

Evolutionary continuity clearly implies that human intelligence rests on a foundation of long evolutionary history, some of which is shared by other extant organisms. It is perhaps parochial to view chess playing and similar activities as the most important aspects of human achievement. It is probably misleading to assume that the development of an effective artificial chess player or scientific problem solver would yield a generally intelligent artificial human. Without denying the usefulness of an artificial Bobby Fisher, an Albert Einstein, or the other systems modeled using these techniques, these achievements represent only a small fraction of the intelligence displayed by humans and other organisms. Much everyday behavior, although technologically rather mundane, nevertheless appears on closer examination to require rather sophisticated processes. Some of these include speech recognition, spatial navigation, sensorimotor coordination and balance, recognition of objects, path planning, obstacle avoidance, learning from experience, selective attention, anticipation, and effective response to changing environmental conditions. The success in modeling these skills and others like them has been much more limited. In some ways it is a curious inversion that several successful systems exist that solve chess problems with world-class success, but few if any systems can walk across a crowded room on two legs.

There is no reason to believe that modeling a fly landing on a ceiling should be intrinsically more difficult than modeling a scientist. Differences in our ability to address these two problems are more likely to be due to differences in the effort allocated to their solution and differences in the mechanisms exploited than to differences in the difficulty of the problems. Both would seem to involve some kind of intelligence, though the kinds may be extremely different from one another.

In fact, there are a number of good historic reasons for the neglect of animals as worthy targets of cognitive modeling. Among these are the equation between language use and mind, the conceptualization of animals as mere mechanical reflex devices, and ignorance about animal behavior. These latter two factors are simply the result of the previous dominance of behaviorism in psychology enquiry. More recently, however, a perspective on animal behavior has been emerging that views animals as active information processors seeking information in their environment, encoding it, and using it for their benefit in flexible and intelligent ways. Investigation of animal behavior and the brain mechanisms that produce it provide important insight into the operation of fundamental cognitive processes. Animals provide a useful comparative basis for testing the development of cognitive theories. Similarly, recent approaches in computer science and robotics seek to simulate or build adaptive "animats" (Wilson 1991) that are able to cope with unpredictable and more or less threatening environments.

The mechanisms of real intelligence may be revealed by investigation of animals and animats (simulated animals). Success in explaining human performance may depend a great deal on understanding the operation of fairly basic processes, because these processes constrain and support the operations of those so-called higher cognitive functions. There is likely to be much to gain from attempting to model the performance of whole organisms behaving according to real needs in a real environment. The solution of circumscribed problems may be deceptive in that there may be simple special-purpose solutions to the particular problem being modeled that cannot be generalized to a broader domain. Human intelligence, as a whole, may simply be too complex to model until we have a more complete understanding of more fundamental processes.

The investigation of animals and animats also helps us gain a perspective on intelligence. We are all so intimately familiar with our own cognitive processes that it is very easy to gloss over apparently simple, but actually complex, problems. Steps in a familiar process are easy to miss, and introspection is a notoriously unreliable, although compelling, source of data. When human cognition is viewed as just one cognitive system among many, it becomes easier to imagine alternative processes and to increase the rigor of analysis.

As a result of such considerations, a number of investigators have suggested the possibility of a comparative approach to cognitive science. Rather than modeling toy problems from the larger domain of human expert behavior, this approach advocates modeling whole, albeit simple, organisms in a real environment that are performing real biological tasks (surviving, exploring, mating, feeding, escaping predators, etc.). The goal of this approach is to develop coherent incremental models out of functionally complete components. My colleagues and I have labeled this the "biomimetic" approach, because we seek to design models that mimic the function of biological life forms.

Achieving this goal requires that we investigate animal performance and the mechanisms they use as the basis for our growing models. This comparative approach is not a replacement for more conventional investigations, but it may serve a useful purpose in the development of true understanding of cognitive processing.

ON THE DISTINCTION BETWEEN THE TWO APPROACHES

The comparative, or biomimetic, approach I am describing is intended to complement, rather than compete with, more typical approaches to cognitive science. Neither approach is necessarily better in any absolute sense than the other, but each approach is likely to be better suited to deal with certain kinds of problems than the other. Although the two approaches have a great deal in common, it may be useful to highlight their differences in order to better understand the relation between them. These differences are listed in table 1.1.

The Symbol System Approach

The standard quasi-verbal method can be described as the physical symbol system approach after Newell and Simon (1976; see also Newell 1980, Harnad 1990). A physical symbol system is a set of physical tokens or patterns—such as marks on paper, punches on computer tape, or patterns

Table 1.1 Comparison of the physical symbol and biomimetic approaches

Feature	Physical symbol system approach	Biomimetic approach
Example tasks	Problem solving, theorem proving, grammatical competence	Navigation, object recognition, motor control, animal survival and function in uncertain environment
Characteristics of paradigm tasks	Specialized, often abstracted fragments of human achievement	Focus on performance of whole organism, including sensorimotor tasks
Sources of conceptual inspiration	Conscious descriptions of human expert performance	Observation of basic animal performance
Representation	Discrete, semantically transparent formal systems	Semantically opaque continuity-preserving systems
Representation	Compositional symbols with combinatorial syntax and semantics	Analog/continuous representations
Processes	Defined functionally in implementation-independent, computationally equivalent terms	Defined functionally in implementation-constrained terms
Paradigm process	Rule following	Constraint satisfaction
Methodological approach	Ahistorical, design-oriented perspective	Incremental-evolutionary, biologically guided
Problems	Well structured	Ill structured

of magnetic domain orientation—and a set of explicit rules. The tokens can be strung together to yield a structure or expression. The rules describe how to manipulate the symbol tokens—for example, how to substitute one token or token string for another. The rules can also be coded as symbolic structures. The symbol tokens and rules can be implemented on a real physical artifact, such as a computer, which could be built to carry out the manipulations that the rules describe. The symbols can be given a systematic semantic interpretation, but the operation of the system does not demand that the symbols be interpretable. The rules are defined relative to the characteristics of the symbols (called their form or shape) rather than relative to the things the symbols might stand for. The notion of a physical symbol system as an information-processing device is derived from Turing's (1937) notions of a universal machine.

A Turing machine is an abstract concrete computing device or process whose states can vary according to a small number of denumerable rules.

The device consists of an external memory or tape, holding symbols that the machine can read and write, a finite set of internal states, and a set of rules relating states and symbols (both those read and those written). Any computable problem can be computed by one of these machines operating on symbols. Turing (1937) showed that there could be a universal machine that could simulate any mechanism describable in the machine's formalism. Similar formulations were proposed by Church (1936) and by Post (1936).

To derive the results of universality required the development of a completely formal, mechanical, content-free approach based on the manipulation of symbols that was independent of what those symbols stood for. Logic was to be interpreted syntactically, that is, exclusively in terms of the symbols' form and the rules for transforming them. The symbols could be interpreted to represent sets and their relations, for example, and the transformations of the system could be interpreted to correspond to proofs or inferences, but the rules of transformation are defined relative to the shape or form of the symbols rather than on the basis of what the symbols might represent. Turing's machine provided a concrete basis for characterizing abstract mental phenomena and showed how a symbol-manipulating device with a few very specific and carefully defined processes could be constructed to perform very general operations. The Turing machine is abstract in its ability to perform logical operations on symbols that could stand for practically anything and in the sense that it could be built from many different kinds of hardware. It is concrete, however, in that its description specifies exactly the operation of the machine. The abstract nature of the Turing machine highlighted the issue of equivalent devices. Two Turing machines, built out of different components, but implementing the same rules, would be considered equivalent because they are computationally identical. The notion of computational equivalence suggested that issues surrounding the implementation of the machine (e.g., what parts it used and the specifics of their operation could be separated from the computational performance of the device.

The Strong Physical Symbol System Hypothesis

Newell, Shaw, and Simon (1958) recognized the potential similarity between the mind and a universal Turing machine. They proposed that the mind is an example of a general symbol-manipulating system, just as the computer can be seen as an example of a general symbol-manipulating machine. This recognition became the basis for most investigations in cognitive psychology and artificial intelligence for more than two decades (with a few notable exceptions). Newell and Simon (1976) asserted that their conceptualization of a physical symbol system is *the* architecture of intelligent systems—that is, that a physical symbol system is both a necessary and a sufficient mechanism for producing intelligent performance. This assertion can be called the strong physical symbol hypothesis, or SPSS (Clark 1990).

Semantic Transparency

One of the key assumptions of the SPSS is that the symbols are semantically transparent. Each of the symbols has an independent, directly translatable meaning. In the case of a computer program, for example, one could describe the meaning of any symbol in the program. Roughly speaking, one could define the object in the world outside the program to which each symbol corresponds. The operations of the semantically transparent system are easy to understand and easy to describe. When the process goes astray, it is relatively easy to determine which counterfactual assertions have slipped inadvertently into the program.

Semantic transparency has some disadvantages as well, however. It forces the world to be broken into discrete units, because the tokens are discrete and each must correspond to some unit in the world. Similarly, because the tokens are only arbitrarily related to the objects they represent, the similarity between tokens bears no resemblance to the similarity between represented items. Similarity must be specifically encoded within token strings rather than being inherent in the tokens.

The arbitrary relation between the symbol and its referent in SPSS also allows the system to operate with a combinatorial syntax and semantics. Expressions within an SPSS are compositional and systematic. A combinatorial syntax provides rules for combining tokens into strings. The rules of the syntax partially determine the semantics of the string. Different combinations of symbols have different meanings. The rules for combining strings depend on the formal properties of the symbols that make them up, but in order for a system to be effective, the rules that combine symbols must preserve the systematic relations among the symbols. More specifically, if the symbols are associated with a semantic interpretation, then any transformations of symbol strings must not violate the interpretations of the symbols. For example, the sequence of tokens $2 + 3 = 5$ might be interpretable as an expression that 2 apples plus 3 more apples yields a total of 5 apples. That is, the symbol "2" is interpreted to correspond to "2 apples," the symbol "+" is interpreted to indicate summation, and so forth. Certain transformations of that string yield systematic interpretations (e.g., $3 + 2 = 5$), but capricious combinations do not (e.g., $* 5 + 2 = 3$).[2]

In order to describe the relations among items, an SPSS must use a string of tokens, each of which describes some property or some relation among properties. The description of an object is composed of elements, each of which is semantically interpretable. Compositionality implies that strings of symbols can be broken into substrings of symbols and can be recombined into other strings. The recombination of tokens is systematic in that it preserves the semantic values of the tokens. The rules for recombining strings of tokens must systematically preserve the meanings of the symbols. There must be a consistent relation between the state transitions of the system and the intended interpretation of the symbols. For example, if one of the operations the computer performs is intended to be addition, then every time that operation occurs, the symbol that is the output of the addition function must stand for a number that equals the sum of the two numbers used as inputs.

An intelligent system, furthermore, consists not of unrelated expressions, but rather of expressions that are related by virtue of the shared use of symbols in a consistent manner. In language, sentences are constructed by combining meaningful parts in particular ways. Sentences consisting of the same parts in different arrangements can express different relations among those parts. Different constructions of symbol strings can similarly correspond to different meanings. An SPSS utilizing compositional semantics that is capable of representing that John loves Mary is also capable of representing that Mary loves John (Fodor and Pylyshyn 1988). "This sort of systematicity follows automatically from the use of structured symbolic expressions to represent knowledge and to serve as the basis for inference" (Pylyshyn 1989, p. 62).

The SPSS view, in other words, argues for a "language of thought" (Fodor 1975) in which internal symbol strings correspond to sentences that might be uttered in a human language. The meaning of the internal symbols corresponds to the meaning of morphemes or groups of morphemes in a human language, and the internal combination rules correspond to the syntax of the human language.

Comparison with the Biomimetic Approach

The biomimetic approach recognizes that systematicity of behavior is a frequently observed phenomenon, but it does not attribute such systematicity to a corresponding semantically transparent compositionality of the underlying representation. Instead it emphasizes a holistic representational system. The systematicity of behavior may result from similarity in the way in which items are represented rather than from a systematic recombination of discrete representational elements. Some representations may be discrete, but unlike the language-of-thought hypothesis, such representations are not required for all cognitive processing.

The Relevance of Language

The correspondence assumption inherent in the language-of-thought hypothesis (and SPSS generally) implies too narrow a range of possible representational systems. Although it would be convenient to, for example, identify activity of a certain brain area with having a certain idea,

limited perspective. The comparative biomimetic approach provides a different set of tools, representational assumptions, and expectations from the standard approach. There are many situations in which these alternatives may be very useful.

NOTES

1. Another possibility, of course, is that humans use language precisely because we are so intelligent.

2. The symbol * indicates that this string is invalid.

REFERENCES

Bickerton, D. (1990) *Language & Species*. Chicago: University of Chicago Press.

Bolles, R. C. (1975) Learning, motivation and cognition. In W. K. Estes (ed.), *Handbook of Learning and Cognitive Processes* (pp. 249–280). Hillsdale, NJ: Lawrence Erlbaum Associates.

Brooks, R. A. (1991) Intelligence without representation. *Artificial Intelligence,* 47, 139–159.

Charness, N. (1989) Expertise in chess and bridge. In D. Klaahr and K. Kotovsky (eds.), *Complex Information Processing: The Impact of Herbert A. Simon* (pp. 183–208). Hillsdale, NJ: Lawrence Erlbaum Associates.

Church, A. (1936) An unsolvable problem of elementary number theory. *American Journal of Mathematics,* 58, 345–363.

Clark, A. (1990) *Microcognition: Philosophy, Cognitive Science, and Parallel Distributed Processing.* Cambridge, MA: MIT Press.

de Groot, A. D. (1966) Perception and memory versus thought: Some old ideas and recent findings. In B. Kleinmuntz (ed.), *Problem Solving: Research, Method, and Theory.* New York: Wiley.

Fodor, J. A. (1975) *The Language of Thought.* New York: Thomas Y. Crowell.

Fodor, J. A., and Pylyshyn, Z. (1988) Connectionism and cognitive architecture: A critical analysis. *Cognition,* 28, 3–71.

Harnad, S. (1990) The symbol grounding problem. *Physica D,* 42, 335–346.

Hopfield, J. J., and Tank, D. (1985) "Neural" computation of decisions in optimization problems. *Biological Cybernetics,* 52, 141–152.

McClelland, J. L. (1986) The programmable blackboard model of reading. In J. L. McClelland and D. E. Rumelhart (eds.), *Parallel Distributed Processing: Explorations in the Microstructure of Cognition. Vol. 2, Psychological and Biological Models* (pp. 122–169). Cambridge, MA: MIT Press.

Newell, A. (1980) Physical symbol systems. *Cognitive Science,* 4, 135–183.

Newell, A., Shaw, J. C., and Simon, H. A. (1958) Elements of a theory of human problem solving. *Psychological Review,* 65, 151–166.

Newell, A., and Simon, H. A. (1976) Computer science as empirical enquiry. In J. Haugeland (ed.), *Mind Design.* Cambridge, MA: MIT Press.

Payton, D. W. (1990) Internalized plans: A representation for action resources. In P. Maes (ed.), *Designing Autonomous Agents: Theory and Practice from Biology to Engineering and Back* (pp. 89–103). Cambridge, MA: MIT Press.

Post, E. (1936) Finite combinatory processes, formulation I. *The Journal of Symbolic Logic*, 1, 103–105.

Pylyshyn, Z. (1989) Computing in cognitive science. In M. I. Posner (ed.), *Foundations of Cognitive Science* (pp. 49–92). Cambridge, MA: MIT Press.

Roitblat, H. L., and von Fersen, L. (1992) Comparative cognition: Representations and processes in learning and memory. *Annual Review of Psychology*, 43, 671–710.

Turing, A. (1937) On computable numbers, with an application to the Entscheidungsproblem. *Proceedings of London Mathematical Society*, 42, 230–265.

Turing, A. (1950) Computing machinery and intelligence. *Mind*, 59, 433–460.

Waltz, D. (1975) Understanding line drawings of scenes with shadows. In P. H. Winston (ed.), *The Psychology of Computer Vision*, pp. 19–91. New York: McGraw Hill.

Wilson, S. W. (1991) The Animat Path to AI. In J. A. Meyer and S. W. Wilson (eds.), *From Animals to Animats: Proceedings of the First International Conference on Simulation of Adaptive Behavior*. Cambridge, MA: MIT Press.

2 The Animat Approach to Cognitive Science

Jean-Arcady Meyer

INTRODUCTION

Recently, a major focus in cognitive science has been on modeling the performance of tasks that are characteristic of human intelligence, such as problem solving, planning, logical reasoning, and understanding of natural language. Most often, such models are implemented by computer programs that receive input data that have been carefully selected by the programmer. They also concern extremely limited fields of application in which heterogeneity and unpredictability are kept to a minimum.

On the other hand, several investigators have recently suggested the possibility of a complementary comparative approach to cognitive science that seeks to determine in what respect faculties found only in man can be traced to the simplest adaptive processes inherited from animals. Such research is inclined to favor the animat approach (Meyer and Wilson 1991; Meyer, Roitblat, and Wilson 1993; Cliff et al. 1994), which relies on the conception of simulated animals or of robots capable of surviving in more or less unpredictable and more or less dangerous environments. Such animats are modeled as whole, albeit simple, organisms in real environments that are performing real biological tasks like exploring, mating, feeding, or escaping predators. They are capable of actively seeking the information they require and of selecting those behaviors that allow them to profit from their interactions with the environment. What is more, they often can improve their adaptive capacities through individual learning or by means of an evolutionary process involving several successive generations.

The objectives of the animat approach have been summarized by Wilson (1991) as follows:

Obviously, we can't yet simulate human intelligence holistically. But the basic hypothesis of the animat approach is that by simulating and understanding complete animal-like systems at a simple level, we can build up gradually to the human. At each point we will be careful to include full connection with a sensory environment, together with maximum use of perception, categorization, and adaptation. Thus when we reach the human level these crucial abilities will not be missing. We hope to reach human intelligence "from below," instead of piecemeal through high-level competences as in Standard AI.

A detailed comparison of the animat approach and Standard AI from the triple standpoint of the questions studied, the solutions adopted, and the criteria used to define success are to be found in Maes (1993).

The applications of the animat approach can be divided into three categories (Meyer and Guillot 1990) according to whether they concern animats whose behaviors have been entirely preprogrammed by their creator or animats whose behaviors may be altered to a certain extent by processes that mimic individual learning or collective evolution. In the remainder of this chapter, some examples of such applications will be described and the significance and limitations of the whole approach will be discussed.

ANIMATS WITH PREPROGRAMMED BEHAVIORS

Most of the work pertaining to this category proposes to determine which cognitive architecture can ensure which adaptative faculty in a given environment. Should this architecture be more complicated as the problems the animat is called upon to solve become harder? Should it be centralized or distributed? What elementary components should it mobilize?

The work of Beer (1990) belongs to what is known as the *neuroethological approach* to adaptive behavior, which aims at reproducing available knowledge about neuron operation and about the architecture of animal nervous systems as faithfully as possible. This work has resulted in the elaboration of a model enabling an artificial insect to display a variety of behaviors— locomotion, wandering, edge-following, and feeding—ensuring its survival in a simulated environment.

The neural network in figure 2.1a, for instance, provides the insect's locomotion and governs the rhythmic motion of its legs. It involves artificial neurons that are more realistic than those traditionally used in artificial neural network research (McClelland and Rumelhart 1986), because they can exhibit rhythmic activities or temporally extended responses to brief stimuli. This network calls upon three motor neurons: The neurons involved with stance and swing determine how forcefully the leg is propelled forward or backward, while the foot motor neuron determines whether the foot is set down. The motion's periodicity is taken care of by a pacemaker neuron P, and the force applied in each stance phase, together with the periodicity of P's discharges, depend on a general level of excitation governed by the command neuron C. The sensors essential to the proper operation of such a network are comprised of two neurons that emit a signal whenever a leg reaches an extreme angle. A central connection between the pacemakers (figure 2.1b) synchronizes the movements of the insect's six legs, thus guaranteeing its stability. In addition,

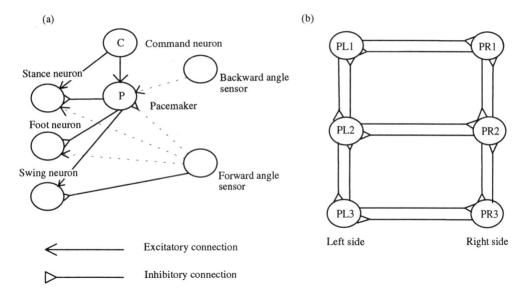

C   Command neuron

Stance neuron

Backward angle
sensor

P   Pacemaker

Foot neuron

Swing neuron

Forward angle
sensor

⟵_____ Excitatory connection

▷_____ Inhibitory connection

PL1   PR1

PL2   PR2

PL3   PR3

Left side   Right side

Figure 2.1 Beer's artificial insect circuits: (*a*) A leg controller, (*b*) Central coupling between pacemakers.

other neurons not described here allow the animat to use its motor equipment for specific purposes, such as avoiding obstacles or exploring.

Another neural network enables the insect to reach food when it is hungry (figure 2.2a). The odors detected by the chemical sensors located on each antenna (ACS) are compared by two neurons (LOS and ROS). The difference of odor strengths is used to trigger rotation of the insect toward the strongest odor, which is caused by the excitation of the appropriate interneuron (LT or RT) governing the lateral extension of the front legs. Furthermore, when the internal energy of the insect runs low, the activity of an energy sensor neuron (ES) also diminishes, disinhibiting a feeding arousal neuron (FA) that otherwise would be spontaneously active. This neuron then excites a search command neuron (SC) that will decide whether the insect should head for food.

Still another network (figure 2.2b) governs food ingestion. When the chemical (MCS) and tactile (MTS) sensors in the mouth indicate that food is present (FP) and when the insect is motivated enough to feed (FA), the consummatory command neuron (CC) is activated and forces the pacemaker neuron (BP) to produce rhythmic signals that make the motor neuron (MO) open and shut the insect's mouth. When the animat's internal energy rises, the activation level ES does, too, inhibiting FA, which in turn suppresses the activity of BP and terminates the feeding. Moreover, a positive feedback loop between FA, BP, and MO realistically modulates the frequency of chewing movements during a meal.

Considering that the same neurons are involved in the initiation and control of these behaviors, it is evident that proper organization must

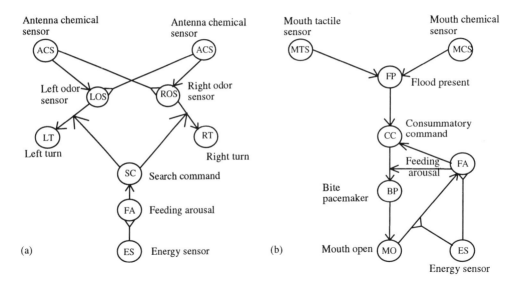

Figure 2.2 Beer's artificial insect circuits: (*a*) Appetitive controller, (*b*) Consummatory controller.

preclude the simultaneous occurrence of incompatible acts—that is, those calling upon the same motor units. The solution adopted (Beer and Chiel 1991) is a hierarchical organization (figure 2.3) in which the consummatory part of feeding behavior takes precedence over the orientation-toward-food behavior and edge-following behavior takes precedence over wandering behavior. The interaction between edge following and the appetitive phase of feeding depends on the context and, more specifically, on whether the direction of greatest odor strength is on the same side of the body as the obstacle encountered. If it is, the animat must edge-follow around the obstacle. If it does not, the animat must ignore the obstacle and continue to orient to the food patch. Such controls are implemented by means of appropriate neural connections, which can be very simple or quite complex. Whatever the case, according to this overall organization, exploration is the behavior engaged in by default, while locomotion is activated in the course of every behavior entering into the corresponding hierarchy.

This research demonstrates that some of the adaptive capacities of an insect can be generated in an animat endowed with a very simple nervous system featuring fewer than 100 neurons and fewer than 200 connections. These connections must, however, be judiciously conceived. The corresponding cognitive architecture is totally distributed, but not at all uniform. On the contrary, it is obvious that it must be highly structured to ensure an adapted alternation between one type of behavior and another in response to changes in the animat's external or internal environment.

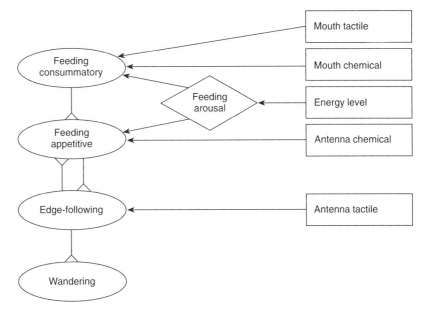

Figure 2.3 The behavioral control organization of Beer's artificial insect. Ellipses represent behaviors, boxes represent sensory stimuli, and the diamond represents a motivational state governing feeding.

Many other creations presuppose a more elaborate cognitive architecture (Albus 1991; Iyengar and Elfes 1991; Maes 1990; Meystel 1991). More particularly, various studies of robot navigation rely on explicit models of the outer world, the corresponding robots being run by appropriate planning programs that determine what path should be followed to go from one point to another (Giralt, Chatila, and Vaisset 1984; Koch et al. 1985; Lin et al. 1989; Nilsson 1984).

To solve the problems that can arise from such an approach when an unforeseen obstacle hinders the normal operation of the plan, Arkin proposes a type of architecture referred to as AuRA (autonomous robot architecture), which is based both on an a priori world model and on mechanisms allowing rapid and effective reaction to changes occurring within the world (Arkin and Taylor 1990). This architecture mobilizes five major subsystems that are responsible, respectively, for perception, cartography, planning, path execution, and homeostatic control.

The perception subsystem fields the incoming sensor data and presents it to the cartographer and path executor. The cartographer maintains both long-term and short-term memory representations of the world model. The former is based on a priori knowledge and is used for path planning and for providing perceptual expectations for navigation. The latter is dynamically adjusted according to incoming sensor data and is used when motor schema-based navigation fails. The planning subsystem incorporates a hierarchical planner that produces a path through the world that is subject to the robot's mission constraints. The planning subsystem is likewise in charge of selecting the motor behaviors and perceptual strategies necessary to accomplish the mission.

Path execution depends upon motor schemas, which are the basic control units of motor behavior in AuRA. They are multiple concurrent processes that contribute independently to the overall concerted action of the robot. These processes call on concepts that originated in psychology and neurology (Arbib 1989; Arkin 1987) and also on the work of Krogh (1984) on potential fields. They are associated with various motor activities, such as MOVE-TO-GOAL, MOVE-AHEAD, STAY-ON-PATH, or AVOID-OBSTACLES, and each produces a vector derived from its goal and the currently perceived state of the world. These vectors are summed, subject to certain constraints, and the result determines the current direction and velocity of the robot. Perceptual schemas are embedded within each motor schema and provide only information that is of value to it, thus exploiting the concept of action-oriented perception.

The homeostatic control subsystem is concerned with maintaining a safe internal environment for the robot. It provides feedback directly to the motor schemas, thus affecting the ultimate path taken by the robot and the speed at which it runs (Arkin 1989).

For Brooks (1991a, 1991b, 1991c), the use of a world model is not essential to the generation of intelligent behavior, even for a robot carrying out navigational tasks. This viewpoint is illustrated by the construction of ten or so autonomous robots of widely varying sizes and missions (Flynn and Brooks 1988), but all characterized by the same *subsumption architecture* (Brooks 1986). This architecture represents a parallel and distributed computational formalism for connecting sensors to actuators in robots. Instead of fusing sensory data into an internal world model of the robot's environment and using this model to plan intelligent action, subsumption architecture provides an alternative way of writing intelligent control programs for robots in which sensors are more directly linked to action-suggestion modules. Fusion happens at the actuator-planning level rather than at the sensor-perception level.

One writes a subsumption program by specifying layers of networks of finite-state machines augmented with various timers and registers. Each layer connects sensors to actuators and implements a control system which achieves a certain level of competence. Higher-level layers can subsume the roles of lower-level layers by suppressing their outputs. However, lower-level layers continue to function as higher-level layers are added and higher levels of competence are achieved. The result is a robust and flexible robot control system that requires much less computation than in more traditional approaches. For example, this architecture makes it possible for the robot Genghis to chase infrared sources over rough terrain (Brooks 1989). Likewise, it permits Squirt, "the world's largest one cubic inch robot" (Flynn et al. 1989), to act as a "bug," hiding in dark corners and venturing out in the direction of noises only after the noises are long gone.

ANIMATS WITH LEARNED BEHAVIORS

Many models within the framework of the animat approach call upon the reinforcement learning situation, which prompts an animat to discover which actions it must perform in order to maximize an external gain or a reinforcement signal. The Barto and Sutton (1981) model, for example, allows an animat to learn to use odorous landmarks to orient itself in a two-dimensional environment. In this environment, a central landmark is surrounded by four others, and each landmark emits an odor whose strength decreases with distance. The goal of the animat is to learn how the peripheral odor gradients are associated with the spatial location of the goal so that it can reach this location even if the goal ceases to emit its odorous signal.

This task is carried out by means of a neural network endowed with special neurons drawn from the theories of Klopf (1980). This network receives as an input a combination of four sensory signals, XN ... XW, associated with peripheral landmarks and furnishes as an output a combination of motor signals, YN ... YW, associated with the four spatial directions. The reinforcement signal, Z, corresponds to the odor of the central landmark, a signal that the animat seeks to maximize (figure 2.4).

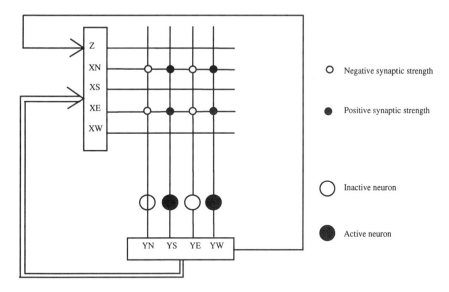

Figure 2.4 Neural network controller of Barto and Sutton's animat. In a position near N and E landmarks, inputs XN and XE are activated. Due to the actual values of the corresponding synaptic strengths, outputs YS and YW are activated, causing the animat to move in the SW direction.

The activation of each neuron depends not only on the signals it receives, but also on a random component, which confers on the animat exploration and exploitation faculties essential to its learning.

Learning takes place when the animat moves about in its environment and when the synaptic strengths of its neurons are updated so that, if the activation of a motor neuron at a given spot brings about a motion in a direction in which Z increases, this neuron will have a better chance of being activated on the same spot in the future. Conversely, a motion in a direction in which Z decreases will occasion a decrease in the probability of activation of the corresponding neuron.

Living in such an environment, the animat gradually learns what direction it must move in from any given point so as to approach its goal. It thus becomes capable of reaching this goal from any starting point by selecting the correct displacement at each intermediate point. Furthermore, it can easily get back on the right route should it accidentally depart from it. Adaptive capacities of this kind characterize most animals and pertain to what is known as the route-navigation metaphor (Gallistel 1990).

The work of Mataric (1991) implements a more elaborate variety of navigation, which resorts to the metaphor of cognitive maps (Gallistel 1990). This metaphor concerns the way in which biologists conceive certain animals' mode of memorizing the information they gain about the spatial organization of their environments and how they make use of this information to navigate from one point to another. It is thought that these maps contain both topological and metric information about several landmarks that an animal has learned to distinguish in its environment.

Mataric's animat is a real robot equipped with 12 sonar sensors that report the distance to the nearest obstacle, with a flux-gate compass and a series of sensors that can detect stalling, providing information that prevents the robot from pushing helplessly against environmental barriers. This robot is also equipped with motors that permit forward and backward motion, right or left turns, and stopping. Such a combination of sensors and actuators allows the robot to wander around office environments building a cognitive map based on landmarks, then use that map to navigate from one location to another. Control of the robot is ensured by a subsumption architecture that presupposes a hierarchy of three competence layers (figure 2.5).

In the lowest layer, simple reflex-like rules combine into emergent collision-free motion behavior and allow the robot to wander around following boundaries (such as walls and furniture clutter) in an indoor environment. The middle layer profits from the motion of the robot while it is tracing boundaries to dynamically extract landmarks in the environment. Such landmarks are selected as large, permanent, robustly detectable environmental features like walls and corridors, and the method is

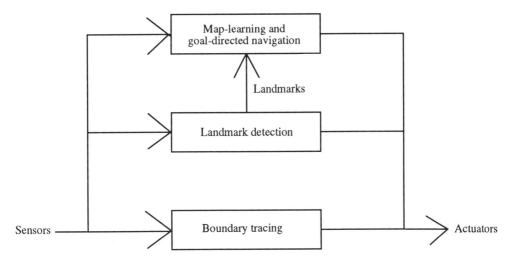

Figure 2.5 The three layers of competence in Mataric's robot.

based on continuous updating of confidence levels associated with features detected as the robot is moving. To allow disambiguation, landmark descriptors are augmented with estimated positions (provided by integrated compass bearings) and size.

The top layer constructs a distributed map of the world from the landmarks and uses it to find paths. The map is represented internally as a graph with nodes that are computational elements, each representing a landmark unique in the world (figure 2.6). Such elements receive inputs from the landmark detectors, as well as from the sensors, and can communicate by sending messages to and receiving them from neighbors in the graph. The robot's location in the environment is indicated by a single active graph node corresponding to that location. The active node performs lateral inhibition by spreading deactivation. It also spreads expectation to its neighbor in the direction of travel as a means of facilitating graph verification and landmark disambiguation.

In order to make the robot navigate to an arbitrary landmark in the known environment, one presses a combination of three buttons on its top, exciting the corresponding goal node in the map. This excitation is spread through the map following its topological links, estimating total path length and arriving at the node corresponding to the robot's current position. The direction from which the incoming excitation arrives is the direction of desired motion, and pursuing it will lead the robot toward the next landmark on the path to the goal.

Such a navigation system—as in the case of the route-navigation system described above—gives the robot knowledge about the optimal direction in which to pursue travel toward the goal, regardless of where it is located. This eliminates the need for replanning if the robot strays from the desired path or becomes lost.

The Animat Approach to Cognitive Science

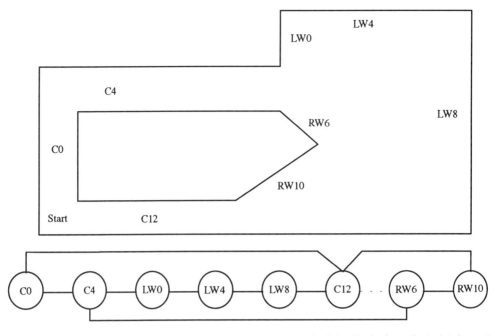

Figure 2.6 An example of an environment and of the kind of topological information stored in the cognitive map of Mataric's robot in a given environment. Eight landmarks are stored in the map and ordered left to right by discovery time. Each landmark is characterized by a type and a compass bearing (e.g., C0 = corridor going north; LW8 = left wall going south; RW10 = right wall going southwest).

From the standpoint of cognitive science, it is interesting to note, as Brooks (1991c) has done, that this work shows Mataric's animat is much more than purely reactive, insofar as it can (1) make predictions about what will happen in the world and have expectations; (2) make plans, although they are somewhat different from traditional AI plans (Agre and Chapman 1990); and (3) have goals, although it is entirely devoid of central representations, manipulatable representations, or symbolic representations.

In the work of Sutton (1991), Lin (1991), or Peng and Williams (1993) are to be found examples of animats with cognitive architectures that include learned internal models of the world. By intermixing conventional trial and error in the real world with hypothetical trial and error using the world model, these animats can plan and learn optimal behavior very rapidly. Likewise, Riolo (1991) gives an example of another animat with a cognitive architecture that relies on the use of a world model and exhibits look-ahead planning and latent learning properties.

ANIMATS WITH EVOLVED BEHAVIORS

The genetic programming technique invented by Koza (1992a) is based on the biological metaphor of natural selection. It simulates an evolving process during which the operation laws of a population of animats, coded as computer programs that determine the dynamic interaction of the sensors and the actuators of each animat, are improved over successive generations. During such a process, these operation laws are managed like genotypes that are inherited from the behavior programs of both parents and more or less altered under the influence of mutation and crossing-over operators. At each generation, the adaptive value of each phenotype—its *fitness*—is evaluated by means of a test of the aptitude of each program to generate the behavior or behaviors sought by the experimenter. The programs that perform best are allowed to reproduce from one generation to the next, while the programs that perform most poorly are eliminated.

This technique has enabled Koza (1992b) to evolve a series of control programs that render an autonomous robot capable of following the walls of an irregularly shaped room, thus reaching the first level of competence of Mataric's robot, described above. These programs use data supplied by the robot's 12 sonars to decide in which direction the robot should move. The fitness of each program is estimated in the course of simulated experiments (figure 2.7) by the number of times it causes the robot to touch one of the 56 tiles arranged at the periphery of the room within a given time span.

Under these conditions, although the behavior programs of the individuals of the first generation are drawn at random and do not perform very well, with fitnesses that may be 0 (figure 2.8a) or 1 (figure 2.8b), it appears that a program capable of reaching a perfect score of 56 can nevertheless be discovered in under 60 generations, with each generation composed

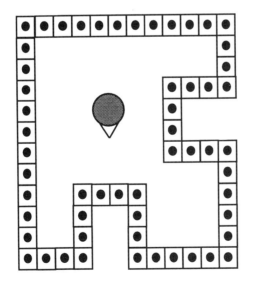

Figure 2.7 Room with 56 tiles on the periphery showing Koza's robot at its starting position.

The Animat Approach to Cognitive Science

(a)   (b)

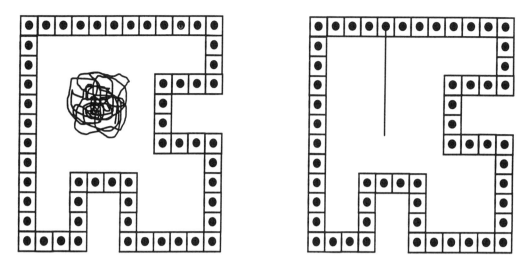

Figure 2.8 (*a*) Individual of the first generation scoring 0. (*b*) Individual of the first generation scoring 1. (After Koza 1992b.)

of 1,000 individuals and the corresponding fitnesses evaluated after 400 time steps (figure 2.9).

Instead of generating explicit control programs expressed in a sophisticated programming language, Cliff, Harvey, and Husbands (1993) prefer to directly evolve the architecture of neural networks linking the sensors and the actuators in a simulated robot. This robot is equipped with two forward and two backward whiskers, a front and a back bumper, and two photoreceptors. It has two wheels and a trailing rear castor. The wheels have independent drives, allowing the robot to turn on the spot and giving it fairly unrestricted motion across a flat floor.

The architecture of this robot's nervous system is quite general. The corresponding neurons are noisy linear threshold devices and are variable in number. If eight of them are input neurons (one neuron per sensor) and four of them output neurons (two neurons per motor), the number of intermediate neurons is variable and is determined genetically. Likewise, if certain connections may interconnect two neurons, other connections result in temporarily preventing any transfer of information along specific direct connections, the number and nature of these various connections being likewise determined genetically. The genotype of each robot consists of two chromosomes. One codes for the neural architecture, and the other for the properties of the visual sensors—i.e., the angle of acceptance and the eccentricity of the robot's two photoreceptors.

The first results obtained by Cliff, Harvey, and Husbands (1993) show that it is possible to cause the robot's nervous system to evolve in such

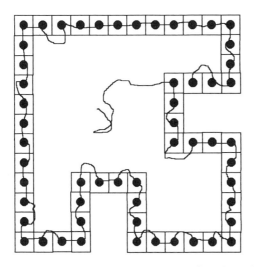

Figure 2.9 Wall-following trajectory of the best-of-generation individual (scoring 56 out of 56) from generation 57. (After Koza 1992b.)

a way as to enable it to use its visual perception capabilities to avoid collisions with the wall of an empty cylindrical room prior to making physical contact with the wall via one of its tactile sensors. In other words, a robot can evolve that is able to predict, from visual data alone, that a collision is likely in the near future and will take appropriate evasive action.

Examination of the evolved networks that generate such behavior reveals a complicated connectivity with numerous redundancies. In earlier generations, the tactile sensors are widely used. Later, over a number of generations, vision becomes dominant, and the tactile sensor input units are essentially used as internal neurons that process visual information (figure 2.10).

Such results indicate that an evolutionary process, even a very simple one, is able to profit from its opportunistic assets to discover solutions to control problems that may be relatively complex. These solutions are not necessarily either as elegant or as straightforward as those sought or understood by engineers, and any attempt to model the nervous system of an animal, let alone that of a human being, on the basis of a network of homogeneous neurons accordingly appears totally unrealistic. This is a point that has been clearly illustrated in the work of Beer described above.

More elaborate cognitive faculties can be developed through an evolutionary process, as has been evidenced by the work of MacLennan (1992) or Werner and Dyer (1992) on the evolution of communication between

The Animat Approach to Cognitive Science

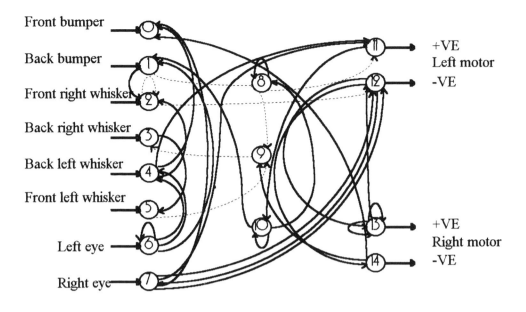

(a)

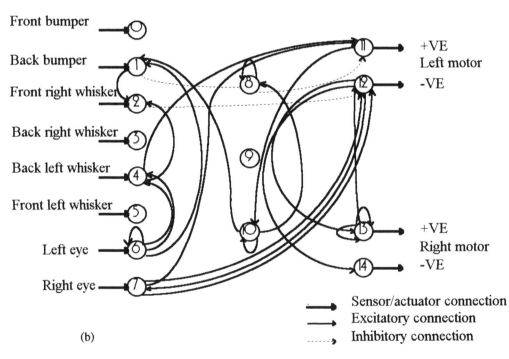

→	Sensor/actuator connection
→	Excitatory connection
⌁⤑	Inhibitory connection

(b)

Figure 2.10 (*a*) The evolved nervous system of the robot of Cliff, Harvey, and Husbands. (*b*) Same reduced system. +VE and −VE are velocity signals in the range [0, 1] that are paired and differenced to give two motor signals in the range [−1, 1]. After Cliff, Harvey, and Husbands (1993).

animats. An example is also to be found in the work of Deugo and Oppacher (1993) on the application of various "genetic operators" to the sorts of symbolic structures used in traditional AI systems, thus giving rise to an evolutionary variant of case-based reasoning termed evolution-based reasoning.

DISCUSSION AND PROSPECTS

The primary advantage of work inspired by the animat approach is obviously that it affords proof of the principle that complex functionalities can arise out of interactions among simple elements. It is now admitted, for instance, that a few hundred neurons can suffice to control the motivational system and the behavioral sequences of an artificial insect. It is also recognized that a system of symbolic representations need not be managed in order for a robot to be conferred cognitive aptitudes that go far beyond simple stimulus-response associations. A second advantage of such studies is that they make it possible to analyze problems that are more or less out of reach of traditional observational and experimental methods, particularly when they implement an evolutionary process.

Nevertheless, the animat approach, or at least its current expressions, present severe limitations. The proof of principles that they yield are rarely used to best avail. Indeed, virtually never has research been conducted to ascertain whether a given simple solution to a problem is actually the simplest one possible. Nor has it been demonstrated that any given adaptive capacity can be expressly ascribed to a specific global architecture rather to a particular operational detail.

Furthermore, there is no doubt that there has been insufficient comparison of these solutions and problems. Nothing short of a systematic comparison of several different implementations of a single type of solution with as wide as possible a range of problems is liable to reveal the generic properties of the solution considered. Conversely, only a systematic comparison of several different versions of the same problem with as varied as possible a range of solutions can allow the respective advantages and the degree of originality of these solutions to be effectively evaluated.

More generally, it can be seen that the animat approach is essentially empirical in nature and that it would have everything to gain from a broadening of its theoretical perspective. From this viewpoint, the work of Wilson (1991) or Horswill (1992) on the characterization of environments and the adaptational problems to which they give rise, that of Agre (1991) or Chapman (1992) on the theory of interactions between organisms and environments, the work of Kiss (1991) or Gallagher and Beer (1993) on the dynamics of complex systems, and the work of Steels (1991) on the theory of emerging functionalities indisputably constitute a valuable groundwork.

REFERENCES

Agre, P. E. (1991). *The Dynamic Structure of Everyday Life.* Cambridge, Britain: Cambridge University Press.

Agre, P. E., and Chapman, D. (1990). What are plans for? In Maes, P. (ed.), *Designating Autonomous Agents: Theory and Practice from Biology to Engineering and Back.* Cambridge, MA: The MIT Press.

Albus, J. S. (1991). Outline for a theory of intelligence. *IEEE Transactions on Systems, Man, and Cybernetics,* 21: 473–509.

Arbib, M. A. (1989). *The Metaphorical Brain 2: Neural Networks and Beyond.* New York: Wiley.

Arkin, R. C. (1987). Motor schema based navigation for a mobile robot: An approach to programming by behavior. *Proceedings of the IEEE Conference on Robotics and Automation.* Raleigh, NC.

Arkin, R. C. (1989). Dynamic replanning for a mobile robot based on internal sensing. *Proceedings of the 1989 IEEE International Conference on Robotics and Automation.* Scottsdale, AZ.

Arkin, R. C., and Taylor, D. T. (1990). Reactive behavioral support for qualitative visual navigation. *Proceedings of the IEEE Conference on Intelligent Motion Control.* Istanbul, Turkey.

Barto, A. G., and Sutton, R. S. (1981). Landmark learning: An illustration of associative search. *Biological Cybernetics,* 42: 1–8.

Beer, R. D. (1990). *Intelligence as Adaptive Behavior: An Experiment in Computational Neuroethology.* New York: Academic Press.

Beer, R. D., and Chiel, H. J. (1991). The neural basis of behavioral choice in an artificial insect. In Meyer, J. A., and Wilson, S. W. (eds.), *From Animals to Animats: Proceedings of the First International Conference on Simulation of Adaptive Behavior.* Cambridge, MA: The MIT Press.

Brooks, R. A. (1986). A robust layered control system for a mobile robot. *IEEE Journal of Robotics and Automation.* RA-2: 14–23.

Brooks, R. A. (1989). A robot that walks: Emergent behaviors from a carefully evolved network. *Neural Computation,* 1: 253–262.

Brooks, R. A. (1991a). Challenges for complete creature architectures. In Meyer, J. A., and Wilson, S. W. (eds.), *From Animals to Animats: Proceedings of the First International Conference on Simulation of Adaptive Behavior.* Cambridge, MA: The MIT Press.

Brooks, R. A. (1991b). Intelligence without reason. *Proceedings of the Twelfth International Joint Conference on Artificial Intelligence.* Sydney, Australia.

Brooks, R. A. (1991c). Intelligence without representation. *Artificial Intelligence,* 47: 139–159.

Chapman, D. (1992). *Vision, Instruction and Action.* Cambridge, MA: The MIT Press.

Cliff, D., Harvey, I., and Husbands, P. (1993). Explorations in evolutionary robotics. *Adaptive Behavior,* 2: 71–108.

Cliff, D., Husbands, P., Meyer, J. A., and Wilson, S. W. (eds.) (1994). *From Animals to Animats 3: Proceedings of the Third International Conference on Simulation of Adaptive Behavior.* Cambridge, MA: The MIT Press.

Deugo, D., and Oppacher, F. (1993). An evolutionary approach to cognition. In Meyer, J. A., Roitblat, H. L., and Wilson, S. W. (eds.), *From Animals to Animats 2: Proceedings of the Second International Conference on Simulation of Adaptive Behavior.* Cambridge, MA: The MIT Press.

Flynn, A. M., and Brooks, R. A. (1988). MIT mobile robot: what's next? *Proceedings of the IEEE Conference on Robotics and Automation.* Philadelphia.

Flynn, A. M., Brooks, R. A., Wells, W. M., and Barrett, D. S. (1989). Intelligence for miniature robots. *Sensors and Actuators,* 20: 187–196.

Gallagher, J. C., and Beer, R. D. (1993). A qualitative dynamical analysis of evolved locomotion controllers. In Meyer, J. A., Roitblat, H. L., and Wilson, S. W. (eds.). *From Animals to Animats 2: Proceedings of the Second International Conference on Simulation of Adaptive Behavior.* Cambridge, MA: The MIT Press.

Gallistel, C. R. (1990). *The Organization of Learning.* Cambridge, MA: The MIT Press.

Giralt, G., Chatila, R., and Vaisset, M. (1984). An integrated navigation and motion control system for autonomous multisensory mobile robots. In Brady and Paul (eds.), *Proceedings of Robotics Research: The First International Symposium.* Cambridge, MA: The MIT Press.

Horswill, I. (1992). Characterizing adaptation by constraint. In Varela, F. J., and Bourgine, P. (eds.), *Toward a Practice of Autonomous Systems: Proceedings of the First European Conference on Artificial Life.* Cambridge, MA: The MIT Press.

Iyengar, S. S., and Elfes, A. (1991). *Autonomous Mobile Robots, Vols. I and II.* Los Alamitos, CA: IEEE Computer Society Press.

Kiss, G. (1991). Autonomous agents: AI and chaos theory. In Meyer, J. A., and Wilson, S. W. (eds.), *From Animals to Animats: Proceedings of the First International Conference on Simulation of Adaptive Behavior.* Cambridge, MA: The MIT Press.

Klopf, A. H. (1980). *The Hedonistic Neuron: A Theory of Memory, Learning and Intelligence.* New York: Hemisphere.

Koch, E., Yeh, C., Hillel, G., Meystel, A., and Isik, C. (1985). Simulation of path planning for a system with vision and map updating. *Proceedings of the IEEE International Conference Robotics and Automation.* St. Louis.

Koza, J. R. (1992a). *Genetic Programming: On the Programming of Computers by Means of Natural Selection.* Cambridge, MA: The MIT Press.

Koza, J. R. (1992b). Evolution of subsumption using genetic programming. In Varela, F. J., and Bourgine, P. (eds.), *Toward a Practice of Autonomous Systems: Proceedings of the First European Conference on Artificial Life.* Cambridge, MA: The MIT Press.

Krogh, B. (1984). *A Generalized Potential Field Approach to Obstacle Avoidance Control.* Technical Report SME-RI MS84-484. Dearborn, MI: Society of Manufacturing Engineers.

Lin, L. J. (1991). Self-improving reactive agents: Case studies of reinforcement learning frameworks. In Meyer, J. A., and Wilson, S. W. (eds.), *From Animals to Animats: Proceedings of the First International Conference on Simulation of Adaptive Behavior.* Cambridge, MA: The MIT Press.

Lin, L. J., Mitchell, T. M., Philips, A. R., and Simmons, R. (1989). *A Case Study in Robot Exploration.* Technical Report CMU-RI-TR-89-1. Pittsburgh: Carnegie Mellon University.

MacLennan, B. (1992). Synthetic ethology: An approach to the study of communication. In Langton, C. G., Taylor, C., Farmer, J. D., and Rasmussen, S. (eds.), *Artificial Life II.* Reading, MA: Addison-Wesley.

Maes, P. (ed.) (1990). *Designing Autonomous Agents: Theory and Practice from Biology to Engineering and Back.* Cambridge, MA: The MIT Press.

Maes, P. (1993). Behavior-based artificial intelligence. In Meyer, J. A., Roitblat, H. L., and Wilson, S. W. (eds.), *From Animals to Animats 2: Proceedings of the Second International Conference on Simulation of Adaptive Behavior.* Cambridge, MA: The MIT Press.

Mataric, M. J. (1991). *A Distributed Model for Mobile Robot Environment-Learning and Navigation.* Technical Report 1228. Cambridge, MA: The MIT AI Lab.

McClelland, J. L., and Rumelhart, D. E. (1986). *Parallel Distributed Processing: Explorations in the Microstructure of Cognition.* Cambridge, MA: The MIT Press.

Meyer, J. A., and Guillot, A. (1990). *From Animals to Animats: Everything You Wanted to Know about the Simulation of Adaptive Behavior.* Technical Report BioInfo-90-1. Ecole Normale Supérieure, Paris.

Meyer, J. A., and Wilson, S. W. (eds.) (1991). *From Animals to Animats: Proceedings of the First International Conference on Simulation of Adaptive Behavior.* Cambridge, MA: The MIT Press.

Meyer, J. A., Roitblat, H. L., and Wilson, S. W. (eds.) (1993). *From Animals to Animats 2: Proceedings of the Second International Conference on Simulation of Adaptive Behavior.* Cambridge, MA: The MIT Press.

Meystel, A. (1991). *Autonomous Mobile Robots. Vehicles with Cognitive Control.* Singapore: World Scientific.

Nilsson, N. J. (1984). *Shakey the Robot.* Technical Report 323. Palo Alto, CA: SRI AI Center, Stanford University.

Peng, J., and Williams, J. W. (1993). Efficient learning and planning within the dyna framework. *Adaptive Behavior,* 1: 437–454.

Riolo, R. L. (1991). Lookahead planning and latent learning in a classifier system. In Meyer, J. A., and Wilson, S. W. (eds.), *From Animals to Animats: Proceedings of the First International Conference on Simulation of Adaptive Behavior.* Cambridge, MA: The MIT Press.

Steels, L. (1991). Towards a theory of emergent functionality. In Meyer, J. A., and Wilson, S. W. (eds.), *From Animals to Animats: Proceedings of the First International Conference on Simulation of Adaptive Behavior.* Cambridge, MA: The MIT Press.

Sutton, R. S. (1990). Integrated architectures for learning, planning, and reacting based on approximating dynamic programming. *Proceedings of The Seventh International Conference on Machine Learning.* San Mateo, CA: Morgan Kaufmann.

Sutton, R. S. (1991). Reinforcement learning architectures for animats. In Meyer, J. A., and Wilson, S. W. (eds.), *From Animals to Animats: Proceedings of the First International Conference on Simulation of Adaptive Behavior.* Cambridge, MA: The MIT Press.

Werner, G. M., and Dyer, M. G. (1992). Evolution of communication in artificial organisms. In Langton, C. G., Taylor, C., Farmer, J. D., and Rasmussen, S. (eds.), *Artificial Life II.* Reading, MA: Addison-Wesley.

Wilson, S. W. (1991). The animat path to AI. In Meyer, J. A., and Wilson, S. W. (eds.), *From Animals to Animats: Proceedings of the First International Conference on Simulation of Adaptive Behavior.* Cambridge, MA: The MIT Press.

3 Creative Creatures

Margaret A. Boden

INTRODUCTION

Cognitive science seeks explanations of how intelligence is possible. Intelligence has many aspects, one of which creativity is. Indeed, one might argue that "true" intelligence necessarily involves creativity. However that may be, creativity—as an aspect of at least some intelligences, some minds—is something that cognitive science should, in principle, be able to explain. Moreover, since cognitive science is not concerned only with human beings, it should be able to explain the presence—or the absence—of creativity in many different creatures.

Let us agree that many creatures have minds. Many are even intelligent. But which of them are creative? "Creatures" include animals, humans, and machines. Animals range from the amoeba to the chimpanzee, humans from you and me to Mozart, and machines from coffee mills, through VDUs and teletypes to mobile robots. So the class of creative creatures may be highly diverse. Cognitive science should be able to tell us whether this class includes bowerbirds and chimpanzees or whether all nonhuman animals are barred. It should show us whether only superhuman humans like Mozart are creative or whether we all are. And it should help us to decide whether the class of creative creatures includes any computer programs or any robots—and if so, which ones.

To answer such questions, we first need to know what creativity is—that is, how it is to be defined. I discuss this in the next section of this chapter. We shall see that even with respect to human beings, whose creativity we would not normally doubt, what counts as creativity is problematic because of differences in the way the term is used. However, one crucial use denotes novel ideas that (in a sense made clear later in this chapter) *could not* have arisen before. In the third section of this chapter, I ask what sorts of psychological processes could be involved in this type of creativity. My examples concern only the human species. But the argument I present applies, in principle, to *any* instance of creativity. This being so, in the fourth section I turn to the discussion of nonhuman animals. I ask what they would need to be able to do in order to be creative. I ask, too, whether there actually are any examples of creative animals. I conclude that there are not, because the sorts of processes outlined in the previous section do not occur in nonhuman animals.

In the fifth section I turn from animals to artifacts. I ask whether there are any persuasive computer models of creativity—and, if not, whether any current programs could be modified so as to give us a creative computer. These questions can be considered in detail with respect to specific computer models and generative processes (for example, "evolutionary" algorithms). They are relevant not only to computers, but also to cognitive science in general, for they concern the nature of creativity as such. They can therefore help us to clarify our ideas about the psychology of creativity in human beings.

Finally, in the sixth section I turn to robots. I ask whether there could be a creative robot—and if so, whether we would know it was creative. And I explain that certain issues of importance to cognitive science are raised by considering robots that are not raised by thinking only of "teletyping" computer programs. The argument in this section is not primarily concerned with "tin cans." On the contrary, it is relevant to the differences between animal and human intelligence. Specifically, it focuses on the role of embodiment in molding the thought processes of the creature concerned.

One preliminary caveat: The question of whether a human, an animal, or an artifact could be creative may be asked in a spirit of scientific enquiry focusing on the psychological processes going on in the creatures concerned and the behavioral evidence of these processes. Or especially if artifacts are in question, it may be asked in a more philosophical spirit. In the latter case, the empirical evidence—no matter how strong—is set aside. The question now is "Yes, but even so, is it *really* creative?" Various arguments may be made to prove, for example, that no computer—irrespective of its actual performance—could be really creative, since its program must have been written by a human being, or that no computer could really understand any idea at all (whether creative or not), because computers can be concerned only with meaningless syntactic manipulations of semantically empty formal symbols.

Here I shall ignore the second form of the question, which I have discussed elsewhere (Boden, 1990, chap. 11). In this volume, concerned as it is with cognitive science as an empirical, comparative enquiry, I shall concentrate instead on the first. That is, in what D. C. Dennett (1992) calls the heterophenomenological spirit, I shall ask whether any animals or computer systems *appear* to be creative, given the definition of creativity offered in the section that follows. If so, what sorts of psychological (computational) processes would they need, and how could we know that those processes were actually occurring?

THE CONCEPT OF CREATIVITY

Creativity is often said, in ordinary conversation, to be the ability to use intuition, or insight, to produce new ideas. But this definition will not do. Creative ideas are not only new, but deeply surprising, though some also appear surprisingly obvious once they have occurred. (We often say to ourselves, "Of course! Why didn't I think of that?" This fact in itself requires an explanation.) As for intuition, this term marks the fact that artists and scientists typically have their creative ideas unexpectedly, with little if any conscious awareness of how they have arisen. But to mark a fact is not to explain it. To include "intuition" in the definition of creativity is to multiply mysteries.

The philosophical challenge, then, is to distinguish creativity from mere novelty—preferably in a way that helps us to understand both the surprise value of creative ideas and their sometimes startling obviousness. The psychological challenge is to explain creativity in scientifically intelligible terms. If we knew how intuition works, we might be able to say whether animals or computers could be intuitive, too.

People of a scientific cast of mind often try to define creativity in terms of novel combinations of old ideas. If that were the case, the surprise caused by a creative idea would be due to the improbability of the combination, and purely statistical tests (such as those used by some experimental psychologists) could identify creativity. Combination theorists typically leave at least two things unsaid. The "novel combinations" have to be not only new, but interesting: To call an idea creative is, in part, to say that it is valuable. This fact is recognized by accounts of creativity that describe it in terms of "generate and test," the test being the evaluation. But combination theorists usually omit value from their definition of creativity. Also, they fail to explain how the novel combination comes about. They take it for granted that we can associate similar ideas, or recognize more distant analogies, without asking just how such feats are possible (see the section of this chapter entitled "Could a Computer Be Creative?").

These cavils aside, what is wrong with the combination theory? Many ideas we regard as creative are indeed based, at least in part, on unusual combinations. Much of Coleridge's enchanting imagery in "The Ancient Mariner," for example, draws together diverse ideas scattered throughout his eclectic reading (Livingston Lowes 1951; Boden 1990, chap. 6). And Harvey's vision of the heart as a pump is just one case in which a novel comparison of ideas led to important scientific discoveries.

Combination theory, to be sure, is not wholly irrelevant to creativity. But it cannot explain, or even adequately describe, the most intriguing cases. Creativity is not a natural kind. Accordingly, there cannot be one single theory that explains all instances of it. There are two main reasons why creativity fails to be a natural kind. One is that its definition essentially involves an aspect of evaluation, which depends on a host of sociocultural factors, some of which are arbitrary. (Donne's poetry and Mozart's music have not been applauded in all historical periods since their production; and what the latest pop star is wearing in a paparazzo's photograph can influence judgments of "creativity" concerning fashion). Quite apart from the many, and untidily various, criteria used in evaluating candidate ideas, creative "novelties" are of significantly different types—the most interesting of which lie beyond combination theory.

Many creative ideas are surprising not because—as combination theory claims—they involve unusual juxtapositions of familiar ideas, but in a deeper way. They concern novel ideas that not only *did* not happen before, but—in a sense that must be made clear (and that combination theory cannot express)—*could* not have happened before.

Before we can consider just what this seemingly paradoxical "could not" means, we must distinguish two senses of this (deep, or impossibilist) type of creativity. One is psychological (P creativity), the other historical (H creativity). An idea is P creative if it is valuable and if the individual person in whose mind it arises could not, in the relevant sense, have had it before; it does not matter how many times other people have already had the same idea. By contrast, an idea is H creative if it is P creative *and* no one else has ever had it before.

There can be no systematic explanation of H creativity. Whether an idea survives, whether it is lost for a while and resurfaces later, and whether historians at a given point in time happen to know about it (and happen to value it) depend on a wide variety of unrelated factors, including fashion, flood, and fire. It follows that there can be no psychological explanation of H creativity as such. But all H creative ideas, by definition, are P creative, too. So an explanation of P creativity would apply to H creative ideas as well.

Before trying to explain P creativity (in the next section, where we shall consider the psychological processes that give rise to it), we must first define it intelligibly. What does it mean to say that an idea "could not" have arisen before? Unless we know that, we cannot make sense of P creativity (or H creativity either), for we cannot distinguish radical originality from mere first-time newness.

Noam Chomsky (1957), discussing what he called the "creativity" of natural language, reminded us that language is an unending source of novel (even H novel) sentences. But, in my terms, these sentences are novelties that clearly *could* have been produced before, generated by the same rules by which other sentences in the language can be generated. Any native speaker (and many computers, too) could produce novel sentences using the relevant grammar. In general, to come up with a new sentence is not to do something P creative.

The "coulds" in the previous paragraph are computational "coulds." That is, they concern the set of structures described and/or produced by one and the same set of generative rules. Sometimes we want to know whether a particular structure is describable by a specific schema or set of abstract rules: Is this a sonnet, and is that a sonata? Is a benzene ring a molecular structure describable by early nineteenth-century chemistry? To ask whether an idea is creative (as opposed to how it came about) is to ask this sort of question. But whenever a particular structure is produced in practice, we can also ask what generative processes actually went on in the computational system concerned: Was the sonata composed by following a textbook on sonata form? Did Kekulé rely on the then-familiar principles of chemistry to generate his idea of the benzene ring, and if not how did he come up with it? To ask how an idea (creative or otherwise) actually arose is to ask this type of question.

We can now distinguish first-time novelty from radical originality. A merely novel idea is one that can be described and/or produced by the same set of specified generative rules as are other familiar ideas within the same domain. A genuinely original, or creative, idea is one that cannot. It follows that constraints, far from being opposed to creativity, make creativity possible. To throw away all constraints would be to destroy the capacity for creative thinking. Random processes alone can produce only first-time curiosities, not radical surprises, although randomness may contribute to creativity (Boden 1990, chap. 9).

To justify calling an idea creative, then, one must specify the particular set of generative principles—what one might call the conceptual space—with respect to which it is impossible. Accordingly, literary critics, musicologists, and historians of art and science have much to teach the psychologist. But their knowledge of the relevant conceptual spaces must be made as explicit as possible to clarify just which structures can, and which cannot, be generated within them.

However, it now begins to look as though even humans—never mind other creatures—cannot be creative. To be sure, all of us can juggle ideas in our heads, sometimes coming up with interesting improbabilities. But, with respect to the familiar structures in the relevant domain (chemistry, poetry, music and so on), a "deeply" creative idea is not just improbable, but impossible. How can it arise, then, if not by magic? And how can one impossible idea be more surprising, more creative, than another? How can creativity happen?

EXPLORING AND TRANSFORMING CONCEPTUAL SPACES

A generative system defines a certain range of possibilities: molecules, for example, or jazz melodies. These structures are located in a conceptual space whose limits, contours, and pathways can be mapped, explored, and transformed in various ways.

The "mapping" of a conceptual space involves the representation, whether at conscious or unconscious levels, of its structural features

(Boden 1990, chap. 4). These features include such things as the articulation of the space into different parts, any hierarchical relations between different levels within the space, whether certain aspects of the space are represented by constants or by variable parameters, and so on. The more such features are represented in the mind of the person concerned, the more power (or freedom) the person has to navigate and negotiate these spaces. Much as a real map helps a traveler to find—and modify—his route, so mental maps enable us to explore and transform our conceptual spaces in imaginative ways.

Detailed evidence of this view is available from recent work in developmental psychology (Karmiloff-Smith 1986, 1990, 1993). In various domains, implicit knowledge becomes increasingly available in explicit form, providing the ability to change one's behaviour in creative ways. For example, young children may be able to draw a man, or a house, with perfect fluency. But this lower-level skill must be represented in some explicit (though not necessarily conscious) way within their minds if they are to be able to modify it so as to draw imaginatively. The extent to which a child can P create a picture of a one-armed man, for instance, or a seven-legged dog depends on the development of higher-level representations of specific (and order-invariant) aspects of the conceptual space, or skill, concerned. Before such "representational redescriptions" emerge, the child simply *cannot* draw a one-armed man (and finds a two-headed man extremely difficult even to copy).

Comparable evidence has been found with regard to other skills, such as language and piano playing in adults as well as children. In general, explicit articulation of various aspects of a skill-space enables them to be adapted in specific ways (e.g., by varying variables) and manipulated independently of other aspects. To understand Mozart's creativity, then, we would need to know his (many-leveled) mental maps of musical space, and what processes he employed to alter them. A crucial difference—probably *the* crucial difference—between Mozart and the rest of us is that his cognitive maps of musical space were very much richer, deeper, and more detailed than ours. In addition, he presumably had available many more domain-specific processes for exploring them.

What counts, in this context, as "exploration"? One interesting example is the development of post-Renaissance Western music, which is based on the generative system known as tonal harmony. Each piece of tonal music has a "home key" from which it starts, from which (at first) it did not stray, and in which it must finish. Reminders and reinforcements of the home key are provided (chords, arpeggios, and fragments of scales). As the years passed, the range of possible home keys became increasingly well defined. J. S. Bach's *Forty-Eight* was specifically designed to explore, and clarify, the tonal range and basic dimensions of this conceptual space.

Traveling along the path of the home key alone soon became insufficiently challenging. Modulations from one key into another within the body of the composition then appeared. But all possible modulations did not appear at once. The range of harmonic relations implicit in the system of tonality became apparent only gradually. At first, only a small number within one composition were tolerated, and these early modulations were only between keys very closely related in harmonic space. With time, the modulations became more daring and more frequent. By the late nineteenth century there might be many modulations within a single bar, not one of which would have appeared in early tonal music.

Eventually, the very notion of the home key was undermined. With so many, and so daring, modulations within the piece, a "home key" could be identified not from the body of the piece, but only from its beginning and end. Inevitably, someone (it happened to be Schoenberg) suggested that the convention of the home key be dropped altogether, since it no longer made sense in terms of constraining the composition as a whole.

The introduction and proliferation of modulations counts as exploration of the space of tonal harmony. That there were 12 different possible home keys was always known, but not always fully exploited. Similarly, the possibility of moving from one key to another was recognized long before every possible example was actually realized.

The criteria establishing the identity of a given conceptual space are not always clear. In general, if a domain's rules for dealing with a conceptual space include mechanisms for changing some of those rules, then one may argue over whether the space is "closed" over all of the rules and all of their mutations. (If we substitute "cognitive system" for "domain," then of course the system—the mind in question—must include all the rules and their variations. Creative ideas do not arise by magic: something in the mind is generating them. But that "something" is not part of what is conventionally accepted as the domain in question. Conventions change over time, as past novelties become socially accepted and even required, so what counts as "the domain" changes too.)

Accordingly, one may regard this modulation example as the continuing exploration of one and the same musical space. Or one may prefer to think of it as a continual enlarging of the space by making minimal changes ("tweakings" rather than "transformations") to the rules of composition involved. In either case, the creativity involved is less fundamental, less surprising, than that involved in creative transformation.

What is it to transform a conceptual space? One example has just been mentioned: Schoenberg's dropping the home-key constraint to create the space of atonal music. Dropping a constraint is a general heuristic for transforming conceptual spaces. Non-Euclidean geometry, for instance, resulted from dropping Euclid's fifth axiom, about parallel lines meeting at infinity.

Another very general way of transforming conceptual spaces is to consider the negative: that is, to negate a constraint. Like other domain-general heuristics, this may exist in specialized forms—musical inversion in fugues, for instance. But there are many cases in which constraint-negation is apparently used in a domain-general way, even if the *value* of the resulting idea can be recognized only by means of domain-specific expertise.

One well-known instance of constraint-negation concerns Kekulé's discovery of the benzene ring. He described it like this:

I turned my chair to the fire and dozed. Again the atoms were gambolling before my eyes. . . . [My mental eye] could distinguish larger structures, of manifold conformation; long rows, sometimes more closely fitted together; all twining and twisting in snakelike motion. But look! What was that? One of the snakes had seized hold of its own tail, and the form whirled mockingly before my eyes. As if by a flash of lightning I awoke.

This vision was the origin of his hunch that the benzene molecule might be a ring, a hunch which turned out to be correct.

Prior to this experience, Kekulé had assumed that all organic molecules are based on strings of atoms (he himself had produced the string theory some years earlier). But for benzene, the valencies of the constituent atoms did not fit.

We can understand how it was possible for him to pass from strings to rings as plausible chemical structures if we assume three things (for each of which there is independent evidence): first, that snakes and molecules were already associated in his thinking; second, that the topological distinction between open and closed curves was present in his mind; and third, that the "consider the negative" heuristic was also present. Together these three factors could transform string into ring.

A string molecule is an open curve. If one considers the negative of an open curve, one gets a closed curve. Moreover, a snake biting its tail is a closed curve that one had expected to be an open one. For that reason, it is surprising, even arresting ("But look! What was that?"). Kekulé might have had a similar reaction if he had been out on a country walk and happened to see a snake with its tail in its mouth. Likewise, he might have been arrested by a cooper making barrel staves or a blacksmith making hoops out of bars. But there is no reason to think that he would have been stopped in his tracks by seeing a Victorian child's hoop: no topological surprises there.

Finally, the change from open curves to closed ones is a topological change, which by definition will alter neighbor relations. And Kekulé was an expert chemist who knew that the behavior of a molecule depends partly on how the constituent atoms are juxtaposed. A change in atomic neighbor relations is very likely to have some chemical significance. So it is understandable that he had a hunch that this vision of a tail-biting snake molecule might contain the answer to his problem.

Hunches are common in human thinking (mathematicians often describe them in terms of an as-yet-unproven "certainty"). An adequate theory of creativity must be able to explain them. The theory must show how it is possible for someone to feel (often correctly) that a new idea is promising even before he can say just what its promise is. The example of Kekulé suggests that a hunch is grounded in appreciation of the structure of the space concerned, and some notion of how the new idea might fit into it. (This structural appreciation, too, accounts for those cases in which the "impossible" idea, once it has arisen, seems obvious.)

A creative animal or computer would benefit from having hunches, as people do. (An example of a program capable of having "hunches," of regarding some of its new ideas as potentially "interesting," is mentioned in the section entitled "Could a Computer Be Creative?") Without them, the creature would waste a lot of time in following up new ideas that "anyone could have seen" would lead to dead ends. Some of its hunches, some of its intuitions, would doubtless turn out to be mistaken (as some of ours do, too). But that is not to say that it would be better off without them. This remark, however, prejudges the main issue. Animals with insights, computers with hunches . . . could there actually be such things?

IMAGINATIVE ANIMALS?

On the face of it, people who define creativity in terms of (valuable) novel combinations should allow that some animals can be creative. The chimpanzee Washoe, for instance, came up with a number of new sign combinations that were not only found interesting by her human keepers, but helped her to achieve her own goals. One example is her signing of "water bird" on first seeing a duck. And bowerbirds, it seems, can build nests of startling originality and beauty. No two nests are alike, and a bower might combine sparkling objects of such delicately balanced shades of blue as to stop the young Picasso in his tracks.

However, these examples are not persuasive. Each item paired in Washoe's surprising combination was potentially directly triggered by the environment: there was a bird present, and there was water present. We do not need to infer that the new sign combination resulted from the creature's autonomous imaginative processes. Likewise, the bowerbird uses what scraps it can find. Our surprise is based on the unlikelihood of a chimp's using sign language at all or of a bird's raw materials happening to be harmoniously colored. Other signing chimps and other bowerbirds would very likely produce much the same behavior in similar circumstances.

By contrast, the improbability of valued novel combinations in humans is due to the rich idiosyncracy of individual human minds and to our ability to muse about our ideas in the absence of direct external stimulus. Indirect stimulus, of course, there may be: a single environmental cue (such as Fleming's dirty petri dish) may lead into a richly diverse semantic net.

If any animals have interconnected semantic nets comparable to ours, then external cues might lead them, by indirect paths, to behave in startling (yet sometimes appropriate) ways. They might even come up with interesting new combinations independent of external cues. Such animals could be credited with a relatively autonomous, or imaginative, form of "combinatorial" creativity. But the examples of Washoe and bowerbirds do not fit the bill.

Suppose, contra Chomsky, that psychologists found that Washoe or Sarah or some cherished vervet monkey or dolphin could learn syntax and generate novel English sentences. Would that mean the animal was creative? Chomsky himself would have to say so, given his definition of linguistic creativity. But earlier we saw that the generation of novel structures of a familiar type is not enough for "deep" creativity. For that, the preexisting generative system must be somehow transformed. I know of no example of animal behavior that I would want to describe in this way.

The discussion of mental maps in the previous section suggested that human creativity depends on our developing reflexive representations of our own skills on various levels. The implication is that any creative creature that is capable of transforming as well as exploring its conceptual spaces would likewise need many-leveled representations of them. If animals do not have these metarepresentations, that could explain why they do not appear to be (deeply) creative.

Human beings often use language to describe—and even to constitute—their conceptual spaces. That is, they use linguistic resources to map conceptual spaces in complex and explicit ways. Animals, lacking language, cannot do this. However, the earliest representational redescriptions in children are prelinguistic in the sense of not being verbally reportable. If they are prelinguistic also in the sense of not depending on linguistic cues for development, then the absence of animal language cannot fully explain the apparent absence of animal creativity. Again, many adults "explain" their creativity in terms of visual or musical imagery (consider Kekulé's diary entry, for example, or Mozart's remarks about hearing music in his mind). Does the development of visual and musical imagery depend, at least in part, on natural language? If not, why cannot chimpanzees draw men, and one-armed men as well?

These matters are not well enough understood to allow us to answer such questions. We do not know just what computational resources are required for individuals to transform their skills in flexible ways, nor how representations of different types are related. Forget Kekulé and Mozart: even the very young child's imaginative abilities are not understood.

Some suggestions have been made as to how a connectionist system might construct "symbolic" models of the activity of another such system, but these ideas are still sketchy (Clark and Karmiloff-Smith 1993). Thornton (1993) has argued that a certain type of constructive induction (exploring compositions on a set of base functions) might be a plausible computational model for a sort of representational redescription. However, he points out that this implies that even sea slugs should be capable of higher-level, reflexive thinking, so constructive induction is not enough.

For whatever reason, animals seemingly cannot develop higher-level maps of their lower-level skills. They do not produce imaginative combinations of ideas free of environmental cues. Nor do they explore complex conceptual spaces in systematic ways. Above all, they do not transform such spaces so as to do things that they could not have done before. Animals, in short, are not creative.

COULD A COMPUTER BE CREATIVE?

A computer could be creative (that is, it could at least appear to be creative) if the ideas conveyed metaphorically in the section entitled "Exploring and Transforming Conceptual Spaces" could be expressed in terms of functioning computer systems. Conceptual spaces would have to be precisely identified and mapped, and ways (some general, some domain-specific) of exploring and changing them explicitly defined. In addition, the system would need a computational model of analogical thinking, since analogy plays a large part in "combinatorial" creativity and sometimes contributes to "impossibilistic" creativity, too (as in the example of Kekulé, described earlier).

Some relevant AI work has already been done. In some cases, a conceptual space has been effectively mapped without any intention to model creativity as such. Models specifically focused on creativity are still relatively uncommon, and they usually deal with space exploration rather than space transformation. As for analogy, we shall see that some work in this area suggests that a creative computer could emerge only after a fundamental change in current AI methodology.

Computational work on musical perception, for example, has helped to advance the theory of harmony as well as to show how listeners manage to find their way around the space of tonal harmony (Longuet-Higgins 1987). This account of the musical interpretation of key, modulation, and meter has been applied to compositions by many composers, from baroque to romantic. If a computer model were to appreciate Brahms, or even recognize a waltz as being in $3/4$ tempo almost as soon as it has begun (as we can), it would have to inhabit this musical space, as we do.

Closely related work on jazz has shown that very simple computational processes that make only minimal demands on short-term memory can generate acceptable (and unpredictable) improvisations. By contrast, the generation of the underlying chord sequence requires a much more powerful grammar, so it cannot be done on the fly by human musicians (Johnson-Laird 1988, 1993). The rules for improvisation take account of melodic contours, harmony, meter, tempo, and playing (and passing between) the chords schematically described in the underlying chord sequence.

In both these cases (only one of which was intended as a study of creativity), musical "intuition" has been, in part, anatomized. Indeed, a computerized jazz musician has been developed that is capable of improvising *Tea for Two* in a pleasing manner (Hodgson, in preparation). In both cases, too, detailed psychological and musicological questions have arisen from specific aspects of the model. A heuristic that is helpful in interpreting Bach cantatas, for example, may or may not be helpful in dealing with other music by Bach, or with pieces by Vivaldi or Brahms. Given that different composers (or the same composer at different times) have different compositional habits, distinct musical signatures, one's expectations (heuristics) will not be the same in every case. Just what these musical differences are may be difficult to divine. Much as computer modeling helps to clarify and test psychological theories, so it could help clarify these delicate matters of musical interpretation.

Recent research by H. C. Longuet-Higgins (1994) has begun to anatomize the expressive space that characterizes, say, a Chopin waltz. The human pianist does not play a piece "deadpan," but interprets expressive terms in the score such as *legato, staccato, piano, forte, sforzando, crescendo, diminuendo, rallentando, accelerando, ritenuto,* and *rubato.* But how? Only if we could formulate this musical sensibility precisely could a computer system play Chopin expressively. Longuet-Higgins has provided rules for all these expressive terms (and for the use of the two pedals). That is, he has added to a program capable merely of sounding the notes correctly (in the correct tempo) a set of rules that enable the program to modify its playing by taking account of the terms of expression provided in the score. Told to play *rubato,* it plays *rubato* by following the relevant rule for interpreting this term—and it does the same for the other terms listed.

Formulating and applying such rules is not a straightforward matter, and Longuet-Higgins has come up with some counterintuitive results. He shows that the conceptual space of a *crescendo,* for instance, is more complex than one might think. A constant increase in the loudness of the relevant passage (the program must work out what is "the relevant passage") does not sound like a *crescendo,* but like someone turning up the volume knob on a radio. Instead he uses a nonlinear rule based on the velocity of a ball rolling on a hill. Many terms of expression, including *crescendo,* require the player to "parse" the music. Decisions must be made, on structural grounds, just where the effect in question should start and just where it should stop. The interpretive rules provided by Longuet-Higgins to the program enable it to do this.

Since this program plays Chopin's *Minute Waltz* fairly acceptably (and a *Fantaisie Impromptu* very acceptably), one could say that there is already a computer that can play Chopin. Whether it can cope equally well with all of Chopin's piano music is a different—and very interesting—question. But the current program has, to some degree, the appreciation of musical space that is required to distinguish "mechanical" from "expressive" performance of these two pieces.

This is not to say that the program is creative. Longuet-Higgins was not attempting to model creativity. What he was trying to do, in the terms of our discussion, was to discover the conceptual space of "expressiveness" in this form of music. Pianists who try to play a familiar composition in a new way, however, typically explore and modify the aspects of performance (among others) that Longuet-Higgins has begun to delineate in detailed terms.

A conceptual space of a very different sort has been modeled by Harold Cohen's AARON (McCorduck 1991). This program, in one of its incarnations, generates aesthetically acceptable line drawings of human acrobats. The drawings are individually unpredictable, but all lie within the pre-assigned genre. This genre is defined, in part, by AARON's "body grammar," which specifies not only the anatomy of the human body (two arms, two legs), but also how the various body parts appear from different points of view or in different bodily attitudes.

The program can draw acrobats with only one arm visible (because of occlusion), but it cannot draw one-armed acrobats. Its model of the human body does not allow for the possibility of there being one-armed people. They are, one might say, unimaginable. If, as a matter of fact, the program has never produced a picture showing an acrobat's right wrist occluding another acrobat's left eye, that is a mere accident of its processing history: it could have done so at any time. But the fact that it has never drawn a one-armed acrobat has a deeper explanation: Such drawings are, in a clear sense, impossible.

If Cohen's program were capable of "dropping" one of the limbs (as a geometer may drop Euclid's fifth axiom or Schoenberg the notion of the home key), it could then draw one-armed or one-legged figures. A host of previously unimaginable possibilities, only a subset of which might ever be actualized, would have sprung into existence at the very moment of dropping the constraint that there must be (say) a left arm.

A superficially similar, but fundamentally more powerful, transformation might be effected if the numeral "2" had been used in the program to denote the number of arms. For "2," being a variable, might be replaced by "1" or even "7." A general-purpose tweaking-transformational heuristic—whether in a human mind or a computer—might look out for numerals and try substituting varying values. Kekulé's chemical successors employed such a heuristic when they asked whether any ring molecules could have fewer than six atoms in the ring. (They also treated carbon as a variable—as a particular instance of the class of elements—when they asked whether molecular rings might include nitrogen or phosphorus atoms). A program that (today) drew one-armed acrobats for the first time by employing a "vary-the-variable" heuristic could (tomorrow) be in a position to draw seven-legged acrobats as well. A program that merely "dropped the left arm" could not.

At present, only Cohen can change the constraints built into the program, enabling it to draw pictures of a type that it could not have drawn before. But some programs, perhaps including some yet to be written by Cohen, might do so for themselves. To be able to transform its style, a program would need maps of its own conceptual spaces: metarepresentations of the lower-level constraints it uses. The creative potential of a self-transforming system depends on how it represents its current skills (drawing "a left arm and a right arm" or drawing "two arms") and on what heuristics are available to modify those representations and thereby enlarge its skills. We have already seen that, if Cohen's program had an explicit representation of the fact that it normally draws four-limbed people, and if it were given very general "transformation heuristics" (like "drop a constraint," "consider the negative," or "vary the variable"), it might sometimes omit, or add, one or more limbs.

The program's evaluative criteria would have to "pass" the results, of course. AARON cannot evaluate its ideas post hoc. All its evaluations are implicit in its drawing procedures. Human beings can judge their new ideas in both ways. To some extent, we can evaluate our novel ideas in the very process of generating them, so that most or all of them are at least plausible. But we can also look back at them once they have arisen, and ask ourselves whether they are satisfactory.

We saw earlier that explicit representation of a lower-level drawing skill is required if a child is to generate P creative drawings. Without such representations, the child (like Cohen's program in its current form) cannot draw a one-armed man. In general, imaginative flexibility requires the development of generative systems that explicitly represent lower-level systems. This applies to computers, if computers are creative creatures. The proverbial all-singing, all-dancing robot, for instance, would need high-level representations of its verbal, musical, and motor skills.

A few existing computer models of creativity can indeed transform their own spaces to some extent. Douglas Lenat's AM (Automatic Mathematician) and EURISKO are well-known examples (Lenat 1983). AM generates and explores mathematical ideas, coming up with new concepts and hypotheses to think about. It starts out with 100 primitive concepts drawn from set theory concerning such matters as sets, lists, equality, and operations. These concepts do not include any of the concepts of arithmetic—not even "addition" or "integer." It starts out, also, with about 300 heuristics that can examine, combine, and transform its concepts in many ways, some general and some domain-specific. Concepts built up by AM's use of its heuristics are fed back into the pool, and so are available for further exploration. The heuristics include ways of comparing concepts, ways of finding examples of concepts, and ways of generalizing or specializing concepts. Some ask about the operations that can be performed on a given concept or can result in it. Yet others search for potential theorems involving the concept. One heuristic can generate the inverse of a function (this is a mathematical version of "consider the negative").

Earlier we asked whether computers could have hunches. Well, AM does: Some of its heuristics suggest which sorts of concept are likely to be the most interesting, and AM concentrates on exploring them accordingly. AM finds it interesting, for instance, that the union of two sets has a simply expressible property that is not possessed by either of them (an instance of the notion that emergent properties, in general, are interesting). AM also finds it interesting if a property is conserved when two sets are combined or if it notices that a single operation (for instance, multiplication) has been defined in several different ways.

AM's hunches, like human hunches, are sometimes wrong. Nevertheless, it has come up with some powerful mathematical notions. These include prime numbers, square roots, Goldbach's conjecture, and an H novel theorem concerning maximally divisible numbers, which were not described until the 1920s and which Lenat himself had never heard of. (AM cannot prove theorems, or do sums either; it can only suggest possible concepts and theorems.) In short, AM appears to be significantly P creative, and slightly H creative, too.

However, critics have suggested that some heuristics were specifically included to make certain mathematical discoveries (such as prime numbers) possible and that the use of LISP provided AM with some mathematically relevant structures "for free" (Ritchie and Hanna 1984; Lenat and Seely-Brown 1984). The precise extent of AM's creativity, then, is unclear. But we do have a sense of what questions we should ask in order to judge.

EURISKO, unlike AM, has heuristics for changing heuristics, as well as for changing concepts. Consequently, it can explore and transform not only its stock of concepts, but also its own processing style. For example, one heuristic asks whether a rule has ever led to any interesting result. If it has not (given that it has been used several times), it will be less often used in future. If the rule has occasionally been helpful, though usually worthless, it may be specialized in one of several different ways. (Because it is sometimes useful and sometimes not, the specializing heuristic can be applied recursively, to itself). Other heuristics work by generalizing rules in various ways or by creating new rules by analogy with old ones. There are various ways in which generalizations, or analogies, can be constructed. EURISKO is able to keep track of the differential success of these ways of doing things and concentrate on the ones that have been most useful.

With the help of domain-specific heuristics to complement these general ones, EURISKO has generated H novel ideas concerning (for instance) genetic engineering and VLSI design. One of its VLSI suggestions has even been granted a U.S. patent (the U.S. patent law insists that the new idea must not be "obvious to a person skilled in the art"). This was a three-dimensional computer chip that enabled one and the same unit to carry out two different logical functions simultaneously (namely, "Not-And" and "Or"). EURISKO came up with this patentable idea by using its symmetry heuristic: "If you have a valuable structure, try to make it more symmetric." Human designers favor symmetry, too. But they had not thought of it in this particular case, nor had they envisaged the possibility that a single unit could perform two different functions. The heuristic principles embodied in EURISKO have nothing specifically to do with science. They could be applied to artistic spaces, too. So some future acrobat-drawing program, for example, might be able to transform its graphic style by using similar methods.

A different type of self-transforming program is seen in systems using genetic algorithms (Holland et al. 1986). These heuristics are inspired by the genetic mutations underlying biological evolution. For example, two chromosomes may swap their left-hand sides or their midsections (the point at which they break is largely due to chance). Repeated mutations over many generations result in unexpected combinations of genes drawn from many different sources. GA programs produce novel structures by means of similar sorts of (partly random) transformations.

In general, the usefulness of the new structures is increased if the swapped sections are coherent minisequences (like the alternative bars allowed at every bar line in eighteenth-century "dice music"). However, identifying the "coherent minisequences" is not a trivial matter. For one thing, they do not function in isolation: Both genes and ideas express their influence by acting in concert with many others. Moreover, coherent minisequences are not always sequences: co-adapted genes tend to occur on the same chromosome, but may be scattered over various points within it; similarly, potentially related ideas are not always located close to each other in conceptual space. Finally, a single unit may enter more than one group: a gene can be part of different co-adaptive groups, and an idea may be relevant to several kinds of problems.

GA programs help to explain how plausible combinations of far-distant units can nevertheless occur. They can identify the useful parts of individual rules and the significant interactions between rule parts, even though a given part may occur within several rules and even though a "part" need not be a sequence of juxtaposed units (it may be two sets of three units separated by an indefinite number of unspecified units). Rules are "selected" by assigning a strength to each one according to its success and gradually eliminating the weaker rules. Over time, the most useful rules are identified, even though they act in concert with many others. A GA system may transform an initial set of randomly generated rules into a rule set that solves the relevant problem even better than human experts do.

Creative computers could rely (in part) on combinatorial methods like these. Indeed, some interactive systems for computer graphics already use the mutation capabilities of genetic algorithms (e.g., Todd and Latham 1992). In these systems, the images are generated by automated random mutations. But the selection is not done by the program: at each generation, a human being makes the aesthetic choice as to which images should be used as the seeds of the next generation. If evaluative rules (defining aesthetic "success") were added to such a program, it could carry out its own "natural selection" by making the aesthetic judgments itself. (However, to be true to human artistic creativity, the evaluative rules themselves should also evolve.)

Psychologists favoring the combination theory described earlier might posit processes akin to GA mechanisms within human minds. But in explaining many "creative" combinations, they would also need to appeal to analogy. A creative computer would need to be able to identify analogies, for seeing a new analogy is often important in art and science. Various computational models of analogical thinking have been developed (e.g., Holyoak and Thagard 1989; Falkenhainer, Forbus, and Gentner 1990). One of the most interesting is Douglas Hofstadter's Copycat (Hofstadter et al. 1994).

Hofstadter reminds us that seeing a new analogy is often much the same as perceiving something in a new way. It is hard to say where perception ends and analogizing begins, since perception itself is informed by high-level concepts. The Copycat project takes these psychological facts seriously. The program allows for the generation of many different analogies, favoring appropriate comparisons over inappropriate ones. It does not rely on ready-made, fixed representations, but constructs its own representations in a context-sensitive way.

Copycat's "perceptual" representations of the input patterns are built up dialectically, each step influenced by (and also influencing) the type of analogical mapping that the current context seems to require. A part-built interpretation that seems to be mapping well onto the nascent analogy is maintained and developed. A part-built representation that seems to be heading for a dead end is abandoned, and an alternative one is started that exploits different aspects of the target concept.

The domain actually explored by Copycat is a highly idealized one, namely, alphabetic letter strings. But the computational principles involved are relevant to analogies in any domain. Copycat considers letter strings such as *ppqqrrss*, which it can liken to strings such as *mmnnoopp*, *tttuuuvvvxxx*, and *abcd*. Its self-constructed "perceptual" representations describe strings in terms of descriptors like *leftmost*, *rightmost*, *middle*, *same*, *group*, *alphabetic successor*, and *alphabetic predecessor*. It is a parallel

processing system in that various types of descriptors compete simultaneously to build the overall description.

The system's sense of analogy is expressed by its producing a pair of
letter strings that it judges to be like some pair provided to it as input.
If, for instance, it is told the string *pqr* changes into *stu* and is then
asked what the string *def* will change into, it will probably (though not
necessarily) produce the string *ghi*. If, on this occasion, it is not looking
for the most obvious analogy but for a somewhat more creative one, it
may produce *gghhii* instead.

The mapping functions used by Copycat at a particular point in time
depend on the representation that has already been built up. Looking for
successors or for repetitions, for instance, will be differentially encouraged
according to the current context. So the two letters *m* in the string *ffmmtt*
will be mapped as a sameness pair, whereas in the string *abcefgklmmno* they
will be mapped as parts of two different successor triples, *klm* and *mno*.

Even in the highly idealized domain of alphabetic letter strings, interesting problems arise. Suppose, for instance, that Copycat is told that *abc*
changes into *abd* and it must decide what *xyz* changes into. Its initial
description of the input pair, couched in terms of alphabetic successors,
has to be destroyed when it comes across *z*, which has no successor.
Different descriptors then compete to represent the input strings, and the
final output depends partly on which descriptors are chosen. On different
occasions, Copycat comes up with *xyd* and *wyz*. Each of these is a consequence of different internal representations and mapping functions. The
line of thought, and of redescription, that led to *wyz*, for instance, involved
moving backwards through the alphabet instead of forwards, and so
seeing the head of the input string as the place where some substitution
should take place, instead of the tail. Notice that the initial description
here is not merely adapted, but destroyed. It is no longer available for
describing this particular input. Hofstadter compares this example with
conceptual revolutions in science.

In Kuhnian revolutions, of course, many people failed to appreciate
the creativity involved. To recognize a creative idea requires one to understand the relevant conceptual space and to locate the new structure with
reference to it. One must be able to distinguish explorations of various
types and transformations of various depths. In art as in science, we
cannot always recognize the transformations involved; even if we do, we
do not always value them.

Nor could we always recognize creativity in a computer. If the program
was specifically built in by us, we would have a better chance of doing
so. But even so, we might be temporarily "trapped" within certain thought
structures, and so fail to understand the computer's potentially intelligible
ideas. Or we might be defeated by its speed and storage. A computer
could have a larger short-term memory than human jazz musicians, and
so use musical rules of greater computational complexity. Not only could

it (unlike us) compose new chord sequences on the fly, but it could produce improvisations that we could neither mimic nor even fully appreciate.

Moreover, just how specific might a program "specifically built in by us" be? A program allowing for quasirandom transformations (perhaps using genetic algorithms) might produce ideas that we would value because they solved a class of problems in which we were interested, but could not understand.

If creative computers were willing and able to explain to us how their novel ideas related to the preexisting conceptual spaces, that would help. But a computer might not have much better access to its own thought processes than we do. Despite its greater speed and storage capacity, it might not be able, in real time, to reflect on all its internal processes. Its introspection might be limited for much the same reasons as ours is. If so, it could not always initiate us (or itself) into the mysteries of its own creativity.

WHAT ABOUT ROBOTS?

Robots are computer creatures. So the arguments in the previous section about computers or programs apply to robots, too. But robots are mobile creatures with sensorimotor capacities that physically negotiate a material environment. This physical embodiment might involve significant differences in their conceptual spaces. If there were creative robots, exploring and transforming their conceptual spaces in what they regarded as valuable ways, the bodily differences between them and us might prevent us from recognizing their creativity.

To the extent that our own understanding is grounded in our human embodiment, androids might well share some understanding with us. Language, for example, has many characteristics arguably due to the fact that we are bodily creatures moving face-forward in a material world. Countless linguistic expressions are metaphors, living or dead, grounded in our bodily experience. Conceptual "spaces," and their "exploration" and "mapping," are obvious examples. Even "transformation" recalls, for instance, the potter's clay. Indeed, some have argued that our oppositional conceptual schemes, and our rhetoric and argument, are fundamentally shaped by the bilateral symmetry of our bodies (Turner 1991).

If these admittedly speculative hypotheses are sound, the Archangel Gabriel—a purely immaterial, disembodied being—simply *could not* have conversed with Mary in her native Aramaic (Boden 1981). Moreover, an embodied robot shaped like an amoeba or a jellyfish could be expected to have a conceptual architecture significantly unlike ours. A genuine android, on the other hand *(sic)*, might structure its concepts in a more humanlike way, largely as a result of its bilateral symmetry.

This assumes, of course, that the robot's conceptual architecture developed spontaneously along with its sensorimotor skills, as opposed to being built in by a human roboticist. Perhaps a human roboticist could build all manner of oppositional thought structures into a jellyfish robot, which (if this argument is correct) could not be expected to develop them "naturally" for itself. After all, our body-grounded categories are, to some extent at least, provided to current programs in nonrobotic computers.

In sum, our own conceptual spaces are fundamentally molded by very general features of our biology—features that are often ignored by people investigating the nature of thought. The same applies, presumably, to animals and robots—and Martians. Our mutual understanding, including our appreciation of other people's creativity, is grounded in the structures of our shared conceptual spaces. Without shared spaces, mutual understanding is compromised. This is why we could not imagine, in any detail, what it is like to be a bat (Nagel 1974; see also Dennett 1992).

Bats, like other animals, appear to lack language and high-level reasoning power. But robots, up to a point, could be provided with these. The upshot is that some instances of creativity in robots might remain, in principle, unknown to us. Wittgenstein said, "If a lion could speak, we would not understand it." A robot (if it were a man-made lion or an android) could be much more intelligible. But it need not be.

NOTE

This paper is largely based on two other sources: M. A. Boden, *The Creative Mind: Myths and Mechanisms* (London: Weidenfeld & Nicolson, 1990) and M. A. Boden, "Could a Robot Be Creative—And Would We Know?" in K. M. Ford and P. J. Hayes (eds.), *Android Epistemology: Advances in Human and Machine Cognition, Vol. 2* (Greenwich, Connecticut: JAI Press, in press).

REFERENCES

Boden, M. A. (1981). "Implications of Language Studies for Human Nature." In M. A. Boden, *Minds and Mechanisms: Philosophical Psychology and Computational Models*. Ithaca: Cornell University Press. Pp. 174–190.

Boden, M. A. (1990). *The Creative Mind: Myths and Mechanisms*. London: Weidenfeld and Nicolson. (Expanded edition, London: Abacus, 1992.)

Boden, M. A. (in press) "Could a Robot Be Creative—And Would We Know?" In K. M. Ford and P. J. Hayes (eds.), *Android Epistemology: Advances in Human and Machine Cognition, Vol. 2*. Greenwich, CT: JAI Press.

Chomsky, N. (1957). *Syntactic Structures*. The Hague: Mouton.

Clark, A., and Karmiloff-Smith, A. (1993). "The Cognizer's Innards: A Psychological and Philosophical Perspective on the Development of Thought." *Mind and Language*, 8, 487–519.

Dennett, D. C. (1992). *Consciousness Explained*. London: Allen Lane.

Falkenhainer, B., Forbus, K. D., and Gentner, D. (1990). "The Structure-Mapping Engine: Algorithm and Examples." *Artificial Intelligence*, 41, 1–63.

Hodgson, P. (in preparation) *A Cognitive Model of Musical Creativity*.

Hofstadter, D. R., and Fluid Analogies Research Group Staff (1994). *Fluid Concepts and Creative Analogies: Computer Models of Mental Fluidity and Creativity*. New York: Basic.

Holland, J. H., Holyoak, K. J., Nisbett, R. E., and Thagard, P. R. (1986). *Induction: Processes of Inference, Learning, and Discovery.* Cambridge, Mass.: The MIT Press.

Holyoak, K. J., and Thagard, P. (1989). "Analogical Mapping in Constraint Satisfaction." *Cognitive Science,* 13, 295–356.

Johnson-Laird, P. N. (1988). *The Computer and the Mind: An Introduction to Cognitive Science.* London: Fontana.

Johnson-Laird, P. N. (1993). "Jazz Improvisation: A Theory at the Computational Level." In P. Howell, R. West, and J. Cross (eds.), *Representing Musical Structure.* London: Academic Press. Pp. 291–326.

Karmiloff-Smith, A. (1986). "From Meta-processes to Conscious Access: Evidence from Children's Metalinguistic and Repair Data." *Cognition,* 23, 95–147.

Karmiloff-Smith, A. (1990). "Constraints on Representational Change: Evidence from Children's Drawing." *Cognition,* 34, 57–83.

Karmiloff-Smith, A. (1993). *Beyond Modularity: A Developmental Perspective on Cognitive Science.* Cambridge, MA: The MIT Press.

Lenat, D. B. (1983). "The Role of Heuristics in Learning by Discovery: Three Case Studies." In R. S. Michalski, J. G. Carbonell, and T. M. Mitchell (eds.), *Machine Learning: An Artificial Intelligence Approach.* Palo Alto, CA: Tioga.

Lenat, D. B., and Seely Brown, J. (1984). "Why AM and EURISKO Appear to Work." *Artificial Intelligence,* 23, 269–294.

Livingston Lowes, J. (1951). *The Road to Xanadu: A Study in the Ways of the Imagination.* 2nd edition. London: Constable.

Longuet-Higgins, H. C. (1987). *Mental Processes: Studies in Cognitive Science.* Cambridge, MA.: The MIT Press.

Longuet-Higgins, H. C. (1994). "Artificial Intelligence and Musical Cognition." *Philos. Trans. Royal Society, London: Series A,* 349, 103–113.

McCorduck, P. (1991). *Aaron's Code.* San Francisco: W. H. Freeman.

Nagel, T. (1974). "What Is It Like to Be a Bat?" *Philosophical Review,* 83, 435–457.

Ritchie, G. D., and Hanna, F. K. (1984). "AM: A Case Study in AI Methodology." *Artificial Intelligence,* 23, 249–268.

Thornton, C. (1993). "Representational Redescription for Sea Slugs." *Proc AAAI Symposium on AI and Creativity.* Stanford, CA, March 1993.

Todd, S., and Latham, W. (1992). *Evolutionary Art and Computers.* London: Academic Press.

Turner, M. (1991). *Reading Minds: The Study of English in the Age of Cognitive Science.* Princeton, NJ: Princeton University Press.

II Intentions and the Organization of Behavior

4 Animal Behavior in Four Components

Bartlett W. Mel

INTRODUCTION

One of the most important bridges that must be built in the brain sciences and cognitive sciences is the bridge linking human and animal behavior to underlying neural hardware. We might, for example, wish to know what set of interacting brain systems underlies nest-building behavior in birds. How is the basic sensorimotor coordination achieved? What causes the bird to perform one action before another? How much of the nest-building is genetically "canned," where are the canned parts stored in the brain, and how are the noncanned parts of the behavior acquired and neurally represented? In a more global vein, how is a bird's intelligence similar to that of a human, and how is it different? How many fundamentally different kinds of animal behavior are there? How does the evolutionary progression in the power and flexibility of behavior depend on the expansion of underlying nervous system structures?

One difficulty encountered in approaching such questions is that most interesting behaviors are also complex, consisting of interactions among motivational components, sensorimotor components, learning and memory components, and sequential planning components. In a standard textbook on the subject, animal behavior is typically classified according to its ecological function, such as feeding, nest building, communication, or reproduction. In this chapter, by contrast, we explore the utility of a scheme for behavior classification based on properties of the computing machinery needed for the performance of the behavior. The advantage of classifying behavior in this way is that algorithmic and representational regularities, where they may be observed, seem most likely to lead to links between behavior and the underlying structure and function of nervous tissue.

We begin by identifying four qualitative modes of processing that superpose nonhierarchically in the control of behavior, corresponding to (1) motivation management, (2) sensorimotor computation, (3) memory-based computation, and (4) internal simulation. Within this breakdown, an animal's behavioral repertoire—even a single behavior—will in general consist of more than one component. The goal of this decomposition scheme is thus to make explicit which aspects of the animal's behavior are attributable to which component and how each component contributes to the power—e.g., efficiency, reliability, and generalizability—of the associated behavioral capacity. For purposes of concrete illustration, we trace a single behavioral function—the search for food—through a sequence of four increasingly powerful pseudoneural implementations.

After discussing practical and theoretical aspects of each of the four components of behavioral control, we take up the question of evolution in the final part of this chapter. We first consider the biological relevance of the four-component breakdown. We argue that, while all organisms may include all four behavioral components at least to a limited degree, the evolutionary progression from simple invertebrates through vertebrate and mammalian species may be roughly characterized as a sequence of explosions in behavioral capacity, first within the realm of component 2, then component 3, and then component 4. The concepts of "generalized sensorium," "generalized motorium," and "generalized behavior" are introduced, which help to make explicit certain fundamental commonalities among the nervous systems and behavioral repertoires of animals with widely divergent physical structures and behavioral niches.

FOUR COMPONENTS OF BEHAVIOR

The main thesis of this chapter is that the range of behaviors that spans from animals with very simple nervous systems, such as nematodes, to those with very complex nervous systems, such as humans, may be usefully decomposed into contributions from four pseudoindependent modes of processing. To illustrate this idea in the following sections, we rely on block diagrams specifying the organization of an organism's "brain." Certain graphical conventions are used throughout (figure 4.1). Sensors are depicted as square boxes, and they always appear in a row at the top of the organism's schematic. They are defined as subsystems that provide information whose readout represents some aspect of the state of the environment or of the organism itself. In the simplest case, sensors are driven directly by external or internal transducers. In an extension to this basic physical measurement/recoding role, they may also be activated or modulated by other sensory, motor, or motivational subsystems within the organism's brain. Motors are depicted as diamonds, and they always appear in a row at the bottom of the organism's schematic. They are defined as subsystems that cause actions to be performed. In the simplest case, the actions are effected via direct connections to muscles or secretatory systems or through central pattern generators that act on muscles or other effector systems. Motors may also act on sensors directly—for example, to internally retune or "reorient" sensors to changing stimulus conditions. Motivational variables are depicted as circles, and they always

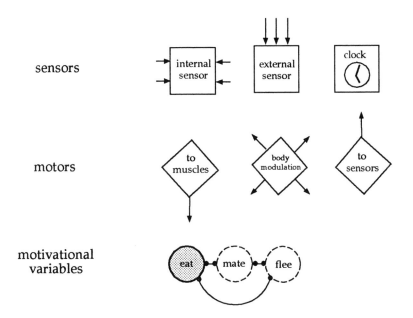

sensors

motors

motivational
variables

Figure 4.1 (A) Sensors are represented as square boxes. They may "sense" and recode external or internal quantities, including the states of other brain areas. (B) Motors are represented as diamonds. They may contain pattern generators and can act directly on locomotory muscles; cause the emission of chemical, auditory, or other communication signals; reorient the body or the sensory receptor surfaces; cause secretion of modulatory signals within the body; or act directly to modulate internal sensory systems. (C) Motivational state variables are represented as circles, here shown with mutually inhibitory interconnections. They may receive input from external or internal sensors reflecting the state of the environment, the body, or the brain. The function of the motivational system is to select which sensors, motors, and their interconnections are to be active at any point in time.

appear in a column at the left of the organism's schematic. They are defined as those internal state variables, correlated with the physiological or mental state of the organism, that cooperate and compete among themselves to select which actual behavioral control routines are operational at any given moment. The dividing lines between the functions performed by sensory, motor, and motivational subsystems are in many cases arbitrary. Classification of a subsystem as one category or another depends on its judged conceptual proximity to afferent measuring or recoding functions; efferent muscular, attentional, or secretory functions; or internal motivational state management functions.

Component 1: Motivation Management

The core neural machinery underlying animal behavior is that which manages the motivational state variables. The concept of motivation in animal behavior is complex and highly loaded (e.g., see Hinde 1970, chaps. 8, 9, and 12 for a general discussion). Motivational variables are assumed here to individually manipulate the organism's computing circuitry in ways appropriate for their own regulation (homeostasis). Thus, a hunger-related internal variable might act to modulate the responsivity of the sensory system to food-like stimuli and activate sensorimotor programs that tend to bring the organism into the proximity of food.

A component 1 process controls the selection, superposition, and/or sequencing of elemental behaviors as suits the biological needs of the organism. For purposes of the present classification, an important characteristic of a component 1 process is that its internal computations are confined to motivation management; other computations—for example, those involving direct interactions between sensory and motor units—are excluded from this component.

Many behavioral patterns in animals belie the interaction of two or more motivational states. For example, mating behavior in certain male birds has been characterized as a competition between underlying sexual-advance and fear-withdrawal motivational states (Hinde 1953). The underlying motivational competition in this case reveals itself as the mating season progresses; a gradual alteration in the bird's internal hormonal environment sways the competition away from fear and withdrawal and in favor of sexual advance. Likewise, adults of some fish species, while in their parenting phase, may protect or lead another species of smaller fish, normally their favorite food, as if they were their offspring (Baerends 1957). Such "inappropriate" behavior is again evidence of competition between internal motivational states, in this case parenting vs. predation.

It is unlikely that the behavior of any real organism is governed exclusively by component 1 mechanisms. However, for purposes of exposition, an example of a "pure" component 1 schematic is shown in figure 4.2. Two mutually exclusive motivational states are possible in this organism, corresponding to eating vs. mating. As indicated by shading, the organism is depicted in the motivational state labelled "eat." In this state, two independent fixed action pattern "motors" superpose to produce forward crawling with the mouth open. If a sex pheromone is detected externally at the appropriate point in the organism's reproductive cycle and hunger is not too great, the internal motivational state is switched to "mate" and the organism stops crawling and lays eggs. Behavior in this imaginary component 1 organism is unguided by sensory input, though it may be triggered by sensory input. A hypothetical feeding trajectory for this organism is shown in figure 4.2, where its accidental encounters with food are guaranteed only by the abundance of food in its environment.

Much more complex component 1 processing is possible than is present in this example. An organism can, for example, be driven by a dozen competing and cooperating motivational state variables, each influenced by different external and internal stimuli, and each with different internal time constants. Intricate and unpredictable behavioral switching can result from such a process (see Beer 1990 for a discussion along these lines). To

Component 1: Motivation Management

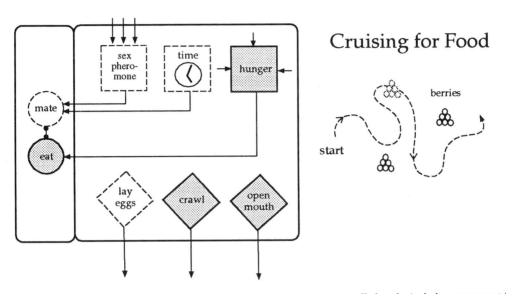

Figure 4.2 Schematic for a hypothetical organism controlled exclusively by component I mechanisms. Organism alternates between laying eggs and foraging for berries. Sensors lie at top (squares), motors at bottom (diamonds), and motivational state variables at left (circles). Active subsystems are shaded. When internal hunger sensor dominates sex-related stimuli, motivational state labeled "eat" is activated. Two feeding-related motor subsystems are activated, causing organism to crawl forward with mouth open. Since eating behavior is unguided by sensory input in this organism, search trajectory for food (piles of berries) is random and consumption accidental.

reiterate, the behavior of any real animals is unlikely to be controlled by component 1 mechanisms exclusively. It is nonetheless useful to consider the general characteristics of component 1 computation so that they may be recognized when embedded in more realistic organisms at much greater levels of behavioral complexity.

Component 2: Sensorimotor Computation

We define a component 2 process as one that contains explicit sensorimotor interactions that are distinct from those mediated indirectly by motivational (component 1) subsystems. We identify five types of sensorimotor interaction (figure 4.3). (1) Sensory input can drive motor subsystems reflexively, as in a knee-jerk reflex, or can reflexively modulate motor programs in progress, as in proprioceptive modulation of gait during walking. (2) Motor subsystems that drive muscles can map an "efference

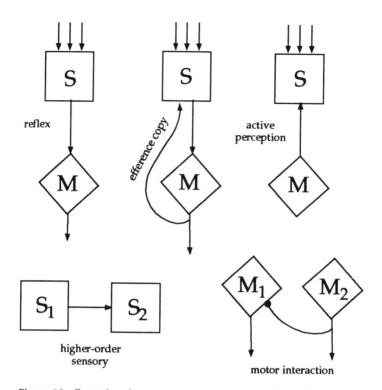

Figure 4.3 Examples of sensorimotor interaction possible within component II, including sensorimotor reflexes, efference copy, modulation of sensory selectivity (active perception), higher-order sensory processing, and intermotor competition.

copy" back onto a sensory area in order to cancel the effects of "reafferent," or self-induced, stimulation. A canonical neurobiological example of an efference copy mechanism is the lateral line system of the fish (Russel 1976). The hair cells of the "lateral line" sensory system, which are sensitive to small water displacements along the length of the body, are actively inhibited by the central nervous system when the fish is about to execute a violent movement that would overload the fish's own sensory system. (3) In a role similar to that of efference copy, a motor subsystem can have as its principal target a sensory subsystem, so it enhances the selectivity of the sensory system for behaviorally significant stimuli. (4) Sensory subsystems can project to other sensory subsystems for higher-order feature extraction, as is seen, for example, throughout multiple levels of the primate visual system (DeYoe and Van Essen 1988). Finally, (5) motor subsystems can inhibit each other as a mechanism for behavioral sequencing or alternation.

Component 2 processing thus includes a wide range of possible sensorimotor computations. A component 2 process allows an organism to swim up a food gradient, follow a pheremone trail to its nest, generate directed escape responses, identify and attack rivals, and orient to and capture prey using vision. Figure 4.4 shows an organism that includes component

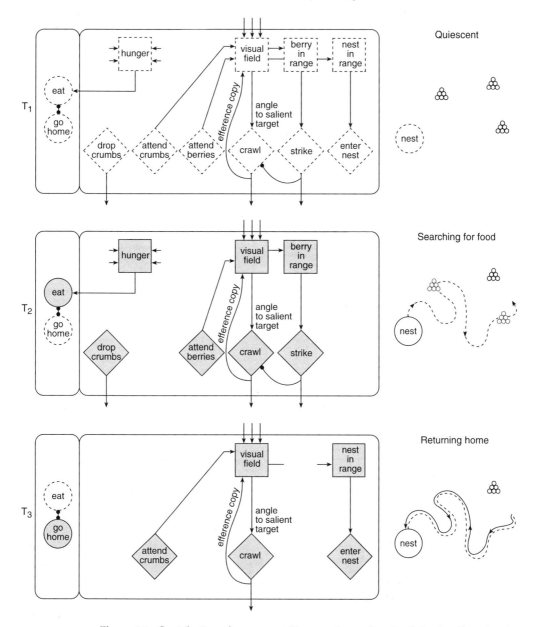

Figure 4.4 Contribution of component II processing to foraging behavior. Organism in sequence of three motivational states: quiescent (T_1), searching for food (T_2), and returning home (T_3). When active (shaded), a motivational state variable functionally enables a subset of the organism's internal circuitry through connections not shown. Disabled or inactive subsystems are omitted for clarity in T_2 and T_3. In T_2 four motors superpose their activities such that organism attends, approaches, and strikes at berries during exploration while marking its outbound journey with a trail of crumbs. After feeding has satisfied hunger, organism follows trail of breadcrumbs back to nest (T_3). Example illustrates use of sensorimotor reflex, higher-order sensory processing, selective perception, efference copy, and behavioral chaining via "consummatory" stimuli (see text).

2 mechanisms in a sequence of three motivational states: quiescent, searching for food, and returning to its nest. The organism is shown first in the quiescent state (T_1). When the internal hunger sensor is active, the "eat" motivational state enables a subset of the organism's internal circuitry (T_2). Four motors function simultaneously in this state: (1) the "attend berries" motor enhances visual selectivity for berries via a direct projection to the visual system, (2) the "crawl" motor causes the animal to locomote in the direction of the nearest salient visual stimuli—a berry if within visual range, (3) the "strike" motor causes the organism to grab a berry when one appears in central vision within striking range, and (4) the "drop crumbs" motor causes a constant stream of trail-marking particles to be dropped during foraging. When the motivation to eat subsides, the motivation to return home becomes dominant (T_3). In this case, the "attend crumbs" motor enhances visual perception for crumb-like stimuli, the crawl motor causes the animal to locomote down the crumb trail, and the "enter nest" motor causes the appropriate fixed action pattern to be executed when the nest is perceived at the proper range and orientation.

In contrasting the roles of components 1 and 2 in the foraging behavior portrayed in figure 4.4, we note that component 1 processing is responsible for regulating the competition among the various active and quiescent motor behaviors, while component 2 processing is responsible for guiding the currently selected motor behavior based on direct sensory measurement. Each component could exist without the other. If the organism were deprived of its component 1 mechanisms, it would appear reactive but motivationally inert, whereas, if selectively deprived of its component 2 processing, it would appear industrious but rather stupid.

In spite of the relatively discrete partitioning of function across components 1 and 2, we note that both are capable of controlling the sequencing of behavior, though in quite different ways. Thus, the sequential alternation of behavioral states—for example, resting vs. foraging vs. returning home—was in figure 4.4a component 1 process governed by competition among internal motivational state variables. A second, entirely different, means of sequencing behaviors can occur within the realm of component 2 processing. For example, the alternation of crawling vs. striking during the foraging sequence of figure 4.4 is controlled by "consummatory" stimuli—i.e., sensory stimuli that result from the organism's previous actions and stimulate performance of its next action. The behaviors are in this case sequenced based on external state variables rather than internal state variables. Many examples of this type of behavioral chaining are known in both invertebrates and vertebrates. For example, according to Hinde (1970, p. 610), "The zig-zag dance of the male three-spined stickleback [fish] is elicited by stimuli from the female. When the female swims towards him, he turns and leads her to the nest. She follows, and this stimulates the male to point his head at the nest entrance. His behavior causes the female to enter the nest. Stimuli from the female elicit 'trembling' from the male which induces the female to spawn. The male is then stimulated to fertilize the eggs, and stimuli from the eggs produce a decrease in his tendency to show further courtship behavior."

Component 3: Memory

Component 3 processing involves memory in any form. A precise definition of memory is elusive. For example, should an innate search image for a specific type of nesting location be considered memory? It functions as a rich internal data structure that is of use to the animal, but it does not contain "remembered" information—that is, information extracted from experience. Another uncertain case concerns an internal state variable within, say, a central pattern generator. While it functions in part to "remember" the state of the motor subsystem and is dependent on past states of the motor subsystem, its representational scope is entirely confined to the internals of the motor subsystem, uninfluenced by sensory experience. A third ambiguous case is that of a memory that is richly representational of some learned aspect of the environment, but can never be brought to bear on future behavior. In lieu of a precise definition, therefore, we identify instead three heuristic criteria that must be satisfied in order for an internal representation to qualify as memory for the purposes of present discussion. The internal state must be (1) in systematic correspondence to some aspect of the state of the environment, body, or brain; (2) modifiable by sensory experience, directly or indirectly; and (3) usable for the modulation of future behavior or brain state.

The availability of memory, in addition to pure sensory state, enables more powerful behaviors than are possible in a memoryless organism. Examples include habituating to an uninformative repetitive stimulus, acquiring a conditioned fear response to a previously neutral cue, recording times of the day at which foraging is most richly rewarded, encoding the location of a food source so that it may be later communicated to conspecifics, imprinting the visual pattern in field of view during an early critical period for later use in social behavior, maintaining a list of several actions to carry out in order of priority, and imitating a behavioral sequence previously observed in another organism. The organism with memory may be said to have access to a "generalized sensorium" consisting of information available at the sensors and information available in the internal state variables that were computed based on earlier sensor values. For example, the organism that remembers the locations of active food sources (or depleted food sources) encountered during exploration may be said to "see" the food sources in its memory though the food sources are physically out of view. The search for food is much more efficient in such an organism, since food sources known to be depleted may be avoided in subsequent foraging activities and food sources known to be active may be revisited directly in time of future need, without further unnecessary search effort.

Figure 4.5 illustrates the contribution of a component 3 process to foraging behavior. In this case, an internal map of food sources in the vicinity of the organism's nest is constructed. A small white square inside a component block denotes the presence of memory. The "current location" sensor integrates the outgoing locomotory commands of the organism to keep a running estimate of the organism's location relative to a known starting point—in this case, the nest. This type of navigation is called "dead reckoning" (see Gallistel 1989). The berry map encodes the locations of berries encountered during exploration. The behavioral sequence proceeds as follows: The initial exploratory trajectory is punctuated by two encounters with berry patches (T_1). When berries are within range, the organism picks up a berry, stores the current location in the map, and continues its search. When the organism is fully loaded with berries, the motivational balance is tipped in favor of the "go home" state. The current-location sensory component then steers a straight-line trajectory back to the nest based on a simple hard-wired geometric calculation (T_2). On subsequent foraging trips, the berry map steers the organism directly to the previously visited berry patches in sequence (T_3). Exploration then resumes as before. The berry map qualifies as "memory" in that it systematically represents the locations of berries in the environment, is directly modifiable by sensory experience, and is usable for the modulation of future behavior or brain state. The current-location register is also a form of memory in that it represents location relative to the nest, is initialized based on sensory information, and is useful for guiding future behavior—i.e., returning home.

The biological relevance of spatial maps is well known (Gallistel 1989). With regard to the integration of body position, certain species of ants have been shown to dead reckon with astonishing accuracy along highly convoluted outbound paths, as evidenced by their ability to return to their nest on a straight course. The return path to the nest of certain desert ants was found to be accurate to within 1 to 2 degrees directionally and to within 10 percent in straight-line distance from a starting point 20 to 40 meters from the nest (Wehner and Srinivasan 1981).

In comparing the internal mechanisms underlying component 2 vs. component 3 processing in figures 4.4 and 4.5, we note strong similarities. A visual field map within component 2 steers the organism based on immediately available sensory cues. Within component 3, the organism is steered by a visuospatial map that "remembers" the locations of earlier stimuli. Thus, with the addition of a small amount of memory, relatively minor changes in the underlying sensorimotor architecture lead to greatly improved efficiency of foraging.

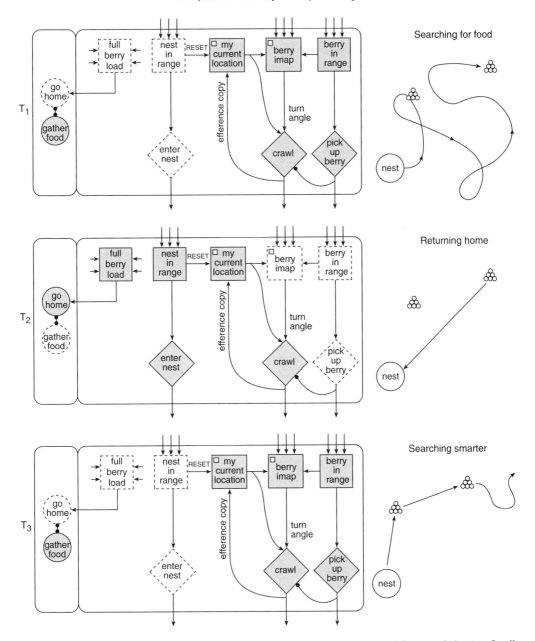

Figure 4.5 Addition of component 3 processing in context of foraging behavior. Small white squares denote subsystems containing internal representational state. Organism initially explores for food, integrates its own motion trajectory, collects berries, and records berry patch locations in its internal map (T_1). When a full load of berries is achieved, organism returns home in a straight-line path based on direction provided by current-location sensor (T_2). On a subsequent foraging trip, organism returns directly to previously visited food sources before continuing exploration (T_3).

Component 4: Simulation

Component 4 processing is that which permits the organism to run internal simulations. An internal simulation is a sequence of brain states that represents a sequence of environmental states, body states, or other brain states. The same representational criteria apply here as did in the case of memory, so that the contents of the internal simulations must be (1) in systematic correspondence to some aspect of the state of the environment, body, or brain; (2) modifiable by sensory experience, either directly or indirectly; and (3) usable for the modulation of future behavior or brain state. Simulations are run within a "mental model" that captures relationships between actions and their consequences (James 1890; Craik 1943; Rumelhart et al. 1986). A true simulation capacity entails that the internally driven sequences of states must have the possibility of being decoupled from overt behavior. This condition rules out the simple component 3 motion integration system illustrated in figure 4.5: the sequence of internally driven states within the integration component represents the organism's location through time, but the sequence cannot be decoupled in this implementation from the organism's actual movement through space.

One important form of simulation would involve prediction and evaluation of the sensory outcome of a sequence of actions. A "decision"—i.e., a choice between several candidate actions—can be based on the outcomes of such simulations. A capacity for simulation thus enables behaviors that involve reasoning and planning. Other examples of simulation-based behaviors include flexibly avoiding obstacles or dead ends during exploration using look-ahead capability, mentally rotating a novel view of an object in order to compare it to a previously stored view, chaining logical inferences to arrive at novel conclusions, and internally rehearsing a telephone number in order to commit it to long-term memory.

The power of search during foraging is again amplified at this level in that it may now be carried out first in simulation when necessary, saving time and energy or avoiding risk (James 1890; Craik 1943). An example of a component 4 foraging process is shown in figure 4.6. In this environment, the organism can see over, but not crawl over, the obstacles, and must thus circumvent the obstacles in order to reach the berries. The basic circuitry for crawling toward berries and striking at them when in range is present as before. When the organism is in the "plan" state, however, physical crawling and striking movements are inhibited. Exploration thus continues only in simulation, where the crawling motor component drives the internal visual mental model predictively—i.e., into the future. When a berry is encountered during the course of this simulated exploration process, the organism is thrown back into "eat" mode, physical crawling and striking are once again enabled, and the visual mental model is temporarily disabled. Memory within the crawling motor component causes a "replay" of the successfully planned trajectory, pruned of dead

Component 4: Internal simulation

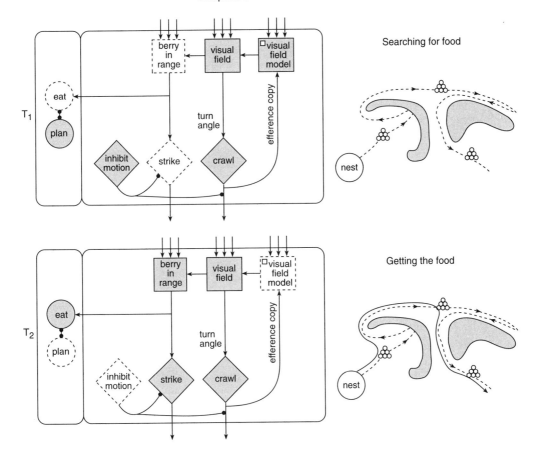

Figure 4.6 Contribution of component 4 processing to foraging behavior. In "plan" mode (T$_1$), crawling and striking are physically inhibited. Crawling motor component simulates search for berries by acting on the internal visual field of mental model. This mental model component simultaneously integrates the organism's crawling commands to maintain an estimate of the organism's location and orientation and updates visual field representation to reflect the organism's changing viewpoint relative to the fixed layout of berries and obstacles. When berries are detected within striking range in the course of this covert planning process, the motivational mode is switched to "eat," and crawling and striking are physically disinhibited. The crawling component then guides the organism directly to berries based on the planned trajectory, pruned of wasteful excursion (pruning operation not shown here). Trajectory during planning is shown as a dashed line, actual trajectory as a solid line.

ends and other wasteful excursions. The simulated (T_1) vs. actual (T_2) trajectories of the organism are shown as it forages for berries among obstacles.

Behaviors indicative of a true internal simulation capacity are most commonly ascribed to human beings, to a lesser extent to other mammals, and to a very limited degree or not at all to nonmammalian vertebrates and invertebrates. What are the defining characteristics of a simulation-based behavior? It is first essential to notice that any finite simulation process can in principle be mimicked by a nonsimulation process with the same input-output behavior, though the resulting direct input-output mechanism may be an exceedingly clumsy representation of the behavior. For example, an internal simulation process such as mental arithmetic, a common human practice, could in principle be mimicked by a mental process that directly maps visual images of numbers and arithmetic operators into a representation of the final result. How, then, may the existence of a true simulation process be inferred through observation of external behavior alone? The hallmarks of an internal simulation process are that the time to carry out the simulation grows in direct relation to the length of the process being simulated and that the intermediate states of the simulation are in meaningful correspondence to the intermediate states of the process being simulated. Thus, the time necessary to complete an arithmetic problem using an internal simulation should grow in a regular fashion with the number of digits, operations, carries, and so on. Mental ''chronometry'' has in fact been used as a powerful experimental tool—for example, in the study of mental rotation and other internal visual transformations (Shepard and Cooper 1982), as well as in the study of covert motor planning (Henry 1960). The time course of a simulation may also be probed and characterized—for example, by plotting a subject's changing sensitivity to stimuli corresponding to the presumed sequence of intermediate states of their internal simulations (Shepard and Cooper 1982). A crucial neurophysiological correlate of an internal simulation process is the presence of activity in components of the ''motor'' system during the covert planning of a behavior (see Mel 1991 for a discussion of some of these issues).

DISCUSSION: LEARNING FROM THE FOUR-LEVEL BREAKDOWN

Braitenberg (1984) has previously described a series of *gedanken* automata that can exhibit a wide range of interesting animal-like behaviors. As was done by Braitenberg, the sequence of automata presented in this chapter may be classified as ''experiments in synthetic psychology.'' The implication of this label is that the act of constructing automata using biologically inspired mechanisms, followed by an analysis of their behavior, can provide intuitions concerning both the internal workings of real biological organisms and the design stages that produce behaviorally more complex biological organisms from simpler ones. One important difference between Braitenberg's sequence of 14 "vehicles" and the four-component breakdown discussed here is that Braitenberg's vehicles are defined in some cases in terms of their external behavior (e.g., "aggressive," "fearful"), in other cases in terms of specific internal computations (e.g., "motion-sensitive" or "map-building"), and in still other cases in terms of their high-level algorithmic/representational niche ("trains of thought," "foresight"). In contrast, the goal in the present case was to identify the minimum set of biologically significant information processing modes without reference to the specific contents of internal representations or specific functionally defined external behaviors.

The present proposal of a four-component decomposition of behavior is also different in spirit from the idea of a "subsumption" architecture (Brooks 1991), which has emerged as a powerful new methodology within the field of robotics. In this latter work, complex behaviors are assumed to be decomposable in terms of a network of simple autonomous processors, augmented finite state machines (AFSMs), each of which is devoted to a single straightforward task. The evolution of "nervous systems" within this framework proceeds through the incremental construction of successively more elaborate networks of AFSMs. The explicit representation of information, such as might be contained in a map of an organism's extrapersonal environment, is strongly deemphasized as a fundamental feature of the approach. In contrast, the four-component decomposition under discussion here specifically allows for explicit representation of information, such as maps, lists, mental images, planning sequences, etc. Secondly, as discussed below, the evolution of nervous systems within the present breakdown is viewed as a process of building successively richer generalized sensors and generalized motors without significantly altering the relatively flat basic system architecture.

An Analogy of Evolution?

What is the evolutionary relevance, if any, of the four-component breakdown of behavior presented in this chapter? One possible hypothesis holds that most animals exhibit most of the behavioral components, at least in rudimentary forms, but that the evolutionary path from primitive to highly evolved nervous systems is characterized by a series of explosions, first in the realm of sensorimotor processing (component 2), then in terms of representational memory systems (component 3), and finally in terms of simulation capacity (component 4).

In support of this view, we observe that even very simple animals have internal motivational state variables that modulate the probabilities associated with each of their behaviors, at least some sensorimotor computation, and usually an identifiable, if highly limited, memory capacity. For example, a nematode can locomote and eat food and lay eggs, and it has a few chemical sensing neurons, a few mechanoreceptors, and a crude temperature-sensing capability (Wood 1988). It can crawl up a food gradient, recoil from mechanical stimulation to the head or tail, and, as evidence of its nonzero memory capacity, learn simple conditioned locomotory responses (Wood 1988). According to current definitions, therefore, the nematode exhibits behavioral components of type 1, 2, and 3, although in crude forms. In making the leap to higher invertebrates, however, such as insects, we are struck primarily by the enormous expansion of their sensorimotor processing capacity (component 2), permitting, for example, high-speed visually guided airborne pursuit of another flying object, rapid directional escape responses, and sophisticated prey-catching sequences. At this level, however, memory systems, even when clearly in operation, as in ants and bees (see Gallistel 1989), remain crude and inflexible in comparison to those present in higher animals.

Thus, in the progression to birds and mammals, the expansion of central nervous system hardware is not associated with yet another dramatic leap in sensorimotor performance, but rather with the capacity, flexibility, and generality of internal representational memory that the animal is able to load and manipulate (component 3). For example, nutcrackers, relatives of the crows and jays, have been observed to make on the order of 10,000 separate caches of pine seeds buried in the ground or stashed into crevices to provide for winter's sustenance. It was calculated that approximately 1,000 of the caches must be relocated in order for the nutcracker to survive, a nontrivial task given the chances in vegetation and landscape (e.g., the presence of snow) associated with the winter months (VanderWall and Balda 1981). In a further manifestation of the highly flexible role of memory in the control of behavior in mammals, Pierrel and Sherman (1963) showed that a rat may be operantly conditioned to successively climb spiral stairs, push down and cross a drawbridge, climb a ladder, pull in and pedal a car through a tunnel, climb stairs, run through a tube, and take an elevator down to an area where finally, when a buzzer sounds, pressing a level produces food.

If the expansion of memory-intensive behavioral control is associated with the generic growth of forebrain structures in birds and mammals, it is less clear where in phylogeny a true internal simulation capacity first emerges (component 4). It is tempting to link such a capacity to the rapid expansion of prefrontal cortex, cerebellum, and basal ganglia seen in primate evolution (Passingham 1975). The prefrontal cortex in particular is commonly suggested to be the structure where planning and other preparatory mental activities are carried out (Goldman-Rakic 1987), though there is considerable evidence that the neocerebellum, much enlarged in humans relative to nonhuman primates (Passingham 1975), plays an important role as well in the control of higher cognitive functions (analogous to its traditionally assumed role in overt motor control (see Schmahmann 1991; Leiner, Leiner, and Dow 1986).

Generalized Behavior

The concept of a "generalized sensorium" was introduced earlier to highlight the equivalence of internal representational memory systems and direct sensory systems. We shall take up this issue here in greater detail, and we shall also introduce the analogous idea of a "generalized motorium." Finally, we shall illustrate how combined internal and external interactions between a generalized motorium and a generalized sensorium lead to the concept of "generalized behavior." The utility of this concept lies in its ability to place the most rudimentary and most elaborate animal behaviors on the ends of a single continuum.

We shall begin by reiterating that a "direct" sensory subsystem is driven by a physical measuring device or transducer that provides access to information about the state of the organism's external environment or some aspect of the physical state of the body. The information provided by a direct sensor is used in the control of behavior. Several ways in which direct sensors could interact with the motor system for the control of behavior have been discussed in previous sections. We have also seen that under some conditions an internal representational memory variable has all of the properties of a sensor except the connection to a physical transducer: it provides access to information about the state of the organism's external or internal environment and is used in the control of behavior. Unlike a direct sensor, however, an internal memory variable, which may be called a "generalized sensor," can represent information about a past state of the environment, a possible future state of the environment, or a past, present, or possible future state of another component of the brain—or of itself. The example of figure 4.5 illustrated how an internal map of the locations of multiple food sources is, in effect, a generalized sensory structure that allows the organism to "see" food that is physically concealed. In this case, the memory structure serves something like the function of an imaginary long-range x-ray vision system. A generalized sensor can also allow the organism to "see" stimuli in the past—that is, information concealed by the passage of time. This analogy between memory and sensing immediately leads to the concept of a generalized sensorium, which we define to consist of all effective sensory structures, both direct and memory-based.

The idea of a "generalized motorium" is analogous. Motors were heuristically defined as subsystems that cause actions to be performed. A "direct motor" operates on muscles or via central pattern generators that in turn act on physical effector systems. Another important type of action, in analogy with the production of overt orienting responses, consists of the internal modulation of the filtering properties of a sensory subsystem, such as for the establishment of a state of selective attention. A neural component that modulates a sensory subsystem may therefore be classified as a "modulatory motor." Another type of "generalized motor" is one that does not simply modulate a sensor's response to an incoming stimulus, but rather fully drives the sensory component through a sequence of states corresponding to an internal simulation. We may call this type of component a "mental motor." Central motivational states (component 1) may thus dispatch behavior either via direct motors that drive the musculature and cause physical movement or via generalized motors that act on sensory areas. When a direct motor component is driven, something moves, and the effects are registered as changes in sensor values—a physical consequence of the overt motor behavior. When a modulatory motor is driven, the effects are again registered as changes in sensor values, this time due to the altered filtering properties of the modulated sensory component. When a mental motor is driven, the effects are registered as changes in internal representational state variables, which we have previously classified as generalized sensors. Based on this underlying functional similarity, we group direct motors, modulatory motors, and mental motors together as the elements of a "generalized motorium."

From the perspective of system operation, therefore, the control of behavior remains virtually unchanged along the evolutionary line: in each case, actions are commanded via the generalized motorium, and the consequences are extracted, recoded, and made available at the generalized sensorium. In an organism dominated by component 2 processing, actions are mediated almost exclusively by direct motors and information about sensory state is provided almost exclusively by direct sensors. In an organism with highly developed component 4 processing, actions can in some cases be mediated exclusively by mental motors and their effects registered exclusively at generalized sensors. The running of internal simulations using mental motors may be viewed as fundamentally similar to the overt performance of motor behavior, the two differing only in that one entails movement of body parts, the other "movement" or change of internal representations. Given this essential equivalence, it is convenient to describe the combined internal and external interactions between the generalized motorium and the generalized sensorium as the performance of "generalized behavior."

The utility of the concept of generalized behavior is that it suggests a continuous design path linking simple and complex nervous systems. Along this path, the basic type of sensory, motor, and motivational interactions are preserved. As the continuum is traced from simpler to more complex brains, generalized sensors and motors become increasingly dominant over direct sensors and motors in the control of behavior. Mental motors become the most powerful motor effectors available to the organism, while generalized sensors overwhelm in importance the relative "trickle" of state information provided by the direct sensory stream. In the most highly evolved nervous systems, a preponderance of an animal's behavior may be internal, no longer primarily mediated by the external musculature. However, from the limited viewpoint of an individual neural component participating in the control of behavior, the distinction between commands sent to direct motors vs. mental motors is on a par with the distinction between commands set to the right leg vs. the left leg: the choice of one or the other has different generalized sensory consequences that are more or less desirable with respect to the organism's current behavioral objectives. Whether physical movement is generated is thus not of fundamental importance. A component 2–dominated organism whose nervous system commands intermittent bouts of feeding vs. scouting for predators is the primitive cousin of a component 4–dominated organism whose internal behavioral dispatch gives rise to intermittent bouts of feeding vs. planning the path to its next meal.

What might generalized sensors and motors actually look like in a brain, and how might they evolve? The example in figure 4.5 illustrates one type of generalized sensor—a map that stores the locations of significant entities in the organism's external space. A more elementary example of a generalized sensor is that which results from the learning of a sensory association. In an imaginary bird, for example, an auditory and a visual area of the brain are interconnected via a modifiable synaptic pathway. On one occasion the bird learns that a specific rustling noise is associated with the visual image of a cat lurking nearby. This association is learned via modification of the association synapses according to standard connectionist principles (Hertz, Krogh, and Palmer 1991). Later, in the dark, the bird encounters this same auditory stimulus, which produces a crude mental image of the cat in the associated visual area of the bird's brain. Since no actual visual stimulus is present at the direct sensors, the availability of the image in the brain is due, effectively, to a memory-based generalized sensor. In this way, a capacity for sensory association may be viewed as the basis for construction, during normal behavior, of an increasingly powerful generalized sensorium. The above example illustrates how a generalized sensor can be more powerful than a direct sensor in that it can "see in the dark"; however, it is also less reliable: the inference that the rustling sound is due to a feline predator may simply be incorrect.

For an example of the development of a mental motor, let us assume that an imaginary cat has an association pathway connecting a motor area that controls walking to a visual area that encodes the pattern of optic flow in the visual field. In addition to driving the leg musculature, the motor area's synaptic projection to the visual area is modified during learning in such a way as to capture the relationship between the state of the walking program and the resulting states of optic flow. Thus, as the cat fixates and circles a nesting bird off its right flank, the bird's image rotates continuously to the right. Once this relationship is learned, the cat possesses a rudimentary capacity for "mental rotation": if direct motor action is disabled during the execution of a walking program and direct sensory input is properly attenuated, then the cat may internally drive a mental image of the bird or some other object through a smooth rotation sequence without actually moving (see Mel 1986). In this way, the cat has developed a novel generalized motor subsystem, much like an extra limb, that it may now use in coordination with its direct motor systems to more capably pursue its goals.

The transition from direct behavioral control to generalized behavioral control could thus depend on relatively simple rewiring of the nervous system during evolution. A tantalizing instantiation of this idea has been proposed elsewhere in the suggestion that the cerebellum, nearly three times larger in humans than in other primates (Passingham 1975), may have turned its motor learning functionality inward to act on the brain in addition to the musculature (Leiner, Leiner, and Dow 1986; Schmahmann 1991). Leiner, Leiner, and Dow point out that input to the large, relatively new lateral zone of the cerebellum does not come from the spinal cord, as is the case for phylogenetically older spinocerebellum, but consists of a massive projection from a number of neocortical association areas via the pons. This projection has been estimated to contain 20 million fibers (Tomasch 1969; see also Schmahmann 1991) and is nearly an order of magnitude larger than all of the brain's direct sensory input pathways combined. The output of the neocerebellum is likewise directed not to the periphery via the brain stem and spinal cord, but to the motor thalamus, which projects to promotor and prefrontal areas of the neocortex (see Leiner et al. 1986). A long, though sometimes poorly controlled, history of clinical evidence strongly suggested a link between damage to the cerebellum and a variety of severe mental disorders (for a review see Schmahmann 1991). More recent clinical studies have shown deficits in mental imagery, anticipatory planning, visuospatial skills, abstract thinking, concept formation, paired word association, word and pattern discrimination, and naming (Schmahmann 1991).

In further considering possible substrates for "mental motoria," converging lines of evidence have suggested that the prefrontal cortex, which has also undergone great expansion in primates (Brodmann 1925), is in part responsible for the neural commands that allow an animal to "hold" a representation of a stimulus in short-term memory, in the sense that a limb might be used to hold an object suspended in air (see Goldman-Rakic 1987). Both this and the example of the neocerebellum thus appear consistent with the notion that the evolution of intelligent animal behavior has progressed along an architectural design continuum characterized by progressive generalization of direct motor control subsystems to permit control of other parts of the brain.

CONCLUSIONS

The main thesis of this chapter is that complex animal behavior may be usefully broken down into contributions from four pseudo-independent categories of computation, consisting of motivation management, sensori-motor computation, memory-based computation, and the capacity for internal simulation. The lines that divide the functionality of these four components are not especially clean, and their neural instantiations are unlikely to be wholly distinct. Nonetheless, the four behavioral components considered here are ecological in their constitution and can help to some degree in the disentanglement of the elements of animal behavior. In support of their ecological relevance, it has been observed that the evolution of biological intelligence from simple invertebrates through vertebrates and mammalian species appears to have consisted of a series of dramatic expansions of initially crude capacities first at the level of sensorimotor processing, then at the level of flexible memory systems, and finally at the level of internal simulation capacity. In support of this conjecture, it has been pointed out through examples from invertebrate and vertebrate phyla that prodigious sensorimotor processing preexisted substantial or flexible memory capacity, while prodigious learning and memory capacity preexisted substantial or flexible internal simulation processes (e.g., reasoning, planning, and natural language).

Finally, based on the fundamental similarity of sensory function to memory function and of motor action to "mental" action, the concept of "generalized behavior" has been introduced. The concept of generalized behavior entails the assumption that the behavior of more complex organisms differs from that of simpler organisms only in the richness of the generalized sensorium and motorium available to it, but not in terms of the basic intercomponent (e.g., sensorimotor) interactions. Clearly, an organism with x-ray vision, all else being equal, is likely to act much more intelligently than an organism without x-ray vision in the search for food. Memory, a generalized sensory mechanism, is like x-ray vision in that it allows an organism to "see" food where it is presently indetectable. Organisms with access to memories of locations of food sources will thus act more intelligently than organisms without such access. In this light, humans, like other mammals, should be regarded as possessing not five senses and four limbs, but rather 100 generalized senses and an equal number of generalized limbs in which the preponderance of sensation and action transpires internally, and thus covertly.

Should it prove to be true that the behavioral control principles of the simplest and most complex organisms are fundamentally similar, as suggested by the idea of generalized behavior, by far the most difficult questions remain those regarding the specific construction of the generalized sensors and generalized motors that interact within each different type of brain. Much work remains to be done in order to understand how more complex and more abstract mental sensors and motors can be constructed from experience that permit, for example, abstract reasoning or production of natural language.

ACKNOWLEDGMENTS

Thanks to Ken Miller, Ernst Niebur, Marius Uscher, Herb Roitblat, and Jean-Arcady Meyer for their many helpful comments on the manuscript. Thanks also to Steve Omohundro for the late-night discussion that sparked my interest in these ideas. I am indebted to Christof Koch for his role in providing an excellent working environment and to the ONR and Pew Charitable Trusts for material support.

REFERENCES

Baerends, G. P. (1957). The ethological analysis of fish behavior. In *The Physiology of Fishes.* M. E. Brown (Ed.). New York: Academic Press.

Beer, R. D. (1990). *Intelligence as Adaptive Behavior.* Cambridge, MA: Academic Press.

Braitenberg, V. (1984). *Vehicles.* Cambridge, MA: The MIT Press.

Brodmann, K. (1925). *Vergleichende Lokalisationslehre der Grosshirnrinde.* Leipzig, Germany: Barth.

Brooks, R. A. (1991). New approaches to robotics. *Science,* 253, 1227–1232.

Craik, K. (1943). *The Nature of Explanation.* Cambridge University Press.

DeYoe, E. A., and Van Essen, D. C. (1988). Concurrent processing streams in monkey visual-cortex. *Trends in Neuroscience,* 11, 219–226.

Gallistel, C. R. (1989). Animal cognition: The representation of space, time and number. *Annual Review of Psychology,* 40, 155–189.

Goldman-Rakic, P. S. (1987). Circuitry of primate prefrontal cortex and regulation of behavior by representational memory. In *Handbook of Physiology: The Nervous System V.* Bethesda, MD: American Physiological Society.

Henry, F. M., and Rogers, D. E. (1960). Increased response latency for complicated movements and a "memory drum" theory of neuromotor control. *Research Quarterly,* 31, 448–458.

Hertz, J., Krogh, A., and Palmer, R. G. (1991). *Introduction to the Theory of Neural Computation.* Redwood City, CA: Addison-Wesley.

Hinde, R. A. (1953). The conflict between drives in the courtship and copulation of the Chaffinch. *Behavior,* 5, 1–31.

Hinde, R. A. (1970). *Animal Behavior.* New York: McGraw-Hill.

James, W. (1890/1983). *The Principles of Psychology.* Cambridge, MA: Harvard University Press.

Leiner, H. C., Leiner, A. L., and Dow, R. S. (1986). Does the cerebellum contribute to mental skills? *Behavioral Neuroscience,* 100, 443–454.

Mel, B. W. (1986). A connectionist learning model for 3-d mental rotation, zoom, and pan. In *Proceedings of the 8th Annual Conference of the Cognitive Science Society,* 562–571.

Mel, B. W. (1990). Connectionist robot motion planning: A neurally-inspired approach to visually-guided reaching. Cambridge, MA: Academic Press.

Mel, B. W. (1991). A connectionist model may shed light on neural mechanisms for visually guided reaching. *Journal of Cognitive Neuroscience,* 3, 273–292.

Passingham, R. E. (1975). Changes in the size and organisation of the brain in man and his ancestors. *Brain, Behavior, and Evolution,* 11, 73–90.

Pierrel, R., and Sherman, J. G. (1963). Barnabus, the rat with college training. *The Brown Alumni Monthly,* Brown University.

Rankin, C. H., Beck, C. D. O., and Chiba, C. M. (1990). *Caenorhaditis elegans:* A new model system for the study of learning and memory. *Behavioural Brain Research,* 37, 89–92.

Rumelhart, D. E., Smolensky, P., McClelland, J. L., and Hinton, G. E. (1986). Schemata and sequential thought processes in PDP models. In *Parallel Distributed Processing: Explorations in the Microstructure of Cognition, Vol. 2.* D. E. Rumelhart, J. L. McClelland (Eds.). Cambridge, MA: The MIT Press.

Russell, I. J. (1976). Central inhibition of lateral line input in the medulla of the goldfish by neurones which control active body movements. *Journal of Comparative Physiology,* 111, 335–358.

Schmahmann, J. D. (1991). An emerging concept: The cerebellar contribution to higher function. *Archives of Neurology,* 48, 1178–1187.

Shepard, R. N., and Cooper, L. A. (1982). *Mental Images and Their Transformations.* Cambridge, MA: The MIT Press.

Tomasch, J. (1969). The numerical capacity of the human cortico-ponto-cerebellar system. *Brain Research,* 13, 476–484.

Vander Wall, S. B, and Balda, R. P. (1981). Ecology and evolution of food-storing behavior in conifer-seed-caching corvids. *Z. Tierpsychol.,* 56, 217–242.

Wehner, R., and Srinivasan, M. V. (1981). Searching behavior of desert ants, genus *Cataglyphis* (Forrmicidae, Hymenoptera). *Journal of Comparative Physiology,* 142, 315–338.

Wood, W. B. (1988). *The Nematode Caenorhaditis elegans.* Cold Spring Harbor, NY: Cold Spring Harbor Press.

5 Intentionality: Natural and Artificial

Colin Allen

INTRODUCTION

Our common-sense theory of human minds involves the attribution of mental states that have "content." For example, to have a belief one must have a belief about something, and to have a desire one must have a desire for something. Philosophers label such states "intentional." The term "intentional" and its cognates have both an ordinary sense and a philosophical sense. The ordinary sense of "intentional" connotes purpose; this is the sense in which *actions* can be said to be intentional. In this chapter, however, the term is used in its philosophical sense, which is concerned with the idea that certain mental states are representational, or "about" other states of affairs. Intentionality is not limited to folk-psychological notions like belief and desire. Notions like mental representation and information, which are widely used by cognitive scientists, are also intentional in the philosophical sense (Allen 1992a; Allen and Hauser 1993).

Philosophers do not agree about the correct way to define "intentionality." Nor do they agree that it can be defined in a way that makes questions about the mind empirically tractable. If intentionality cannot be treated empirically, then much of our common-sense view of minds will not find a place in cognitive science (e.g., see Churchland 1986), so this topic is of utmost importance to cognitive science. The gridlock caused by philosophical controversies about intentionality often causes empirical scientists to turn away from philosophical theorizing about this issue, but I will attempt to show that this would be a mistake and that cognitive science can proceed without a precise definition of intentionality. I will not presuppose familiarity with the philosophical literature on intentionality, so the next section contains a brief introduction. For the remainder of this section, it will be adequate to think of intentionality as "aboutness," in the way that one's thoughts, for example, can be about Provence.

Comparative approaches to cognitive science (CACS) provide the best hope for relieving the philosophical gridlock surrounding intentionality.

Both philosophers and cognitive scientists stand to benefit from the perspectives that arise when one attempts to compare cognitive abilities across species and outside the biological realm. CACS will involve the synthesis of perspectives from humans (cognitive psychology), nonhuman organisms (cognitive ethology), and computers (artificial intelligence). Foundational questions for CACS include whether terms that involve intentionality provide an appropriate theoretical framework for the explanation of behavior and whether intentionality is appropriately attributed to (nonhuman) animals or to computational models of cognition.

Philosophers often attempt to provide conceptual grounds for the view that intentional states are not appropriately attributed to animals or to computers. Such arguments start with a conception of intentionality and then attempt to show how the given conception applies (or fails to apply) to animals or to computers. For example, some authors have argued that language is a prerequisite for intentionality and that nonhuman animals thus lack intentionality. Davidson (1975) argues that a creature must have the concept of belief in order to have a belief and that one cannot have the concept of belief unless one has the capacity for interpreting linguistic utterances. Davidson's position is based on a philosophically sophisticated argument about the nature of interpretation that cannot, for reasons of space, be addressed here. However, the upshot is clear: language use provides a criterion for the application of intentional terms. Leahy (1991) uses language in a less sophisticated way to get to the same point. He argues that, lacking a language, animals do not have the kind of behavioral capacities that underpin talk about human beliefs and that it is therefore inappropriate to describe animals as having beliefs. Whether or not language use is as important as these authors believe, it nonetheless provides one criterion for comparative judgments about cognitive abilities.

Other authors have suggested different criteria. Searle (1980) is notorious among computer scientists for arguing, on conceptual grounds, that a program capable of passing the Turing test need not possess intentionality. His criterion hinges on a notion of "understanding" that is not entirely clear. He thinks that human mental states always involve understanding, and as a result they are intrinsically intentional. Searle argues that, in contrast, execution of a program sophisticated enough to pass the Turing test can occur without understanding, so attribution of intentional states to computers by virtue of program execution are, at best, metaphorically derived from the intentionality of those who use them. Searle's view will be discussed in more detail later in this chapter. Dennett (1969) has also argued that the intentionality of computers is derived, not intrinsic. More recently, Dennett (1987) has argued that not even the intentionality of humans is intrinsic, that it is derived from the role of the human body as survival machine for its genes (Dawkins 1976). The argument, roughly, is that we cannot say what our mental states are about without knowing what they are for, in evolutionary terms. Dennett's view is influenced by

Millikan (1984), who bases attributions of intentionality on a biological notion of function. Millikan's view is discussed later in this chapter.

In this chapter, I shall argue that cognitive science in general and CACS in particular need not be committed to any particular philosophical view of the nature of intentionality (despite the exhortations of various philosophers to jump on their respective bandwagons). This does not mean that cognitive scientists should ignore philosophical work on intentionality. In fact, to ignore the arguments of someone like Searle could be perilous, since funding and publishing decisions are often affected by conceptual arguments such as his. Secondly, I shall attempt to show how the various philosophical conceptions of intentionality can provide starting points for comparative, empirical investigations. In doing so, I hope to address criticism such as that by Heyes (1987), who knocks Dennett for suggesting too little in the way of experimentation for cognitive scientists to do. While Heyes may be too harsh on Dennett, who has suggested specific experiments (see Dennett 1983 and Cheney and Seyfarth 1990), the general point is well taken; philosophical work will be most useful to cognitive science when it can be used to suggest empirical research. Even Searle's work, which seems antithetical to the objectives of many artificial intelligence researchers, can be useful in this way. Finally, it will be seen that the approach to cognitive science that naturally emerges from these considerations is a comparative approach.

INTENTIONALITY

Most contemporary philosophical work on intentionality is influenced by Chisholm's (1957) discussion of work by Brentano (1924). Brentano borrowed the notion of intentionality from medieval philosophers and was interested in what they called the "intentional inexistence" of mental objects, as opposed to the existence of the objects of physical actions. For example, a person cannot ride a horse unless the horse exists, but a person can desire to ride a unicorn or believe in the existence of unicorns even though there are no unicorns. In this way, the objects of beliefs, desires, and certain other mental states are unlike the objects of actions such as kicking, riding, or eating. Beliefs, desires, and the other intentional states can represent or be about things that do not exist. (Intentions, in the ordinary sense of "purposes," are intentional in the philosophical sense. The fact that one intends to capture a unicorn does not entail the existence of a unicorn.) Brentano's thesis was that only psychological phenomena exhibit intentionality and that intentionality is thus a distinguishing characteristic of mentality. His characterization of the intentionality of mental states was "relation to a content" or "direction upon an object" (Brentano 1924 as quoted by Chisholm 1957, p. 168). A problem with this characterization is that it does not give a clear test for intentionality.

Chisholm sought to clarify Brentano's thesis by focusing on the language used to describe mental phenomena. He proposed to regard intentionality as a property of sentences instead of mental states, and he proposed three logical tests to determine whether a given sentence is an intentional sentence. One of these logical properties—failure of substitutivity—will suffice to illustrate the idea. In most sentences, if a given phrase can be substituted for another phrase with the same referent, the truth value of the resulting sentence will be the same as that of the original. For example, given that the name "Margaret Thatcher" and the description "the first female British prime minister" have the same referent (i.e., Margaret Thatcher = the first British prime minister), then the sentence "Margaret Thatcher was deposed" has the same truth value as the sentence "The first female British prime minister was deposed." This principle of substitutivity is known as "substitutivity of identicals." In some contexts substitutivity appears to fail. For example, the sentence "John believes that Margaret Thatcher was deposed" need not have the same truth value as "John believes that the first female British prime minister was deposed"; even though Margaret Thatcher was the first female British prime minister, John might not know it. Chisholm proposed to reformulate Brentano's thesis as the claim that psychological phenomena need to be described using intentional sentences, whereas nonpsychological phenomena can always be described using nonintentional sentences.

If Chisholm's test worked, it would provide a clear criterion for demarcating psychological phenomena from other phenomena. Unfortunately, substitutivity appears to fail in contexts that are not psychological. For example, although the number of planets is nine, and nine is necessarily greater than seven, it is not true that the number of planets is necessarily greater than seven; there could have been fewer planets (Quine 1953). In the face of examples like these, failure of substitutivity seems to be an inadequate criterion for psychological intentionality, and Chisholm himself came to this view (Chisholm 1967), although there are philosophers who believe that the apparent counterexamples are not genuine and that the criterion can be saved (Jacquette 1986).

Nowadays, failure of substitutivity is seen as an aspect of the intensionality (with an "s") of meaning. (It is easy to confuse the terms "intentional" and "intensional," so from here on, where "intenTion" and "intenSion" appear in the same or adjacent sentences, I will capitalize the distinguishing letter as shown.) The major contemporary use of the term "intenSion" has been by those who have attempted to develop a formal theory of meaning. Frege (1892) was driven by considerations (including failure of substitutivity) to postulate two components of meaning—sense and reference. Set theory, which Frege helped to develop, provides a powerful apparatus for modeling the referential aspect of meaning. For example, given a domain of individuals, the referent of a proper name, if it has one, is an element in the domain. The referential component of the meaning of a predicate is just the subset of members of the domain to which the predicate applies, called the extension of the predicate. In other words, the extension of the predicate "is green" in a given domain is just the subset of green objects from the domain. On this account, a sentence such as "a is green" is true just in case a is in the extension of the predicate "is green."

Extensional accounts of meaning are incomplete. For example, the predicate "is a member of a species that has evolved kidneys" has exactly the same extension as the predicate "is a member of a species that has evolved hearts"; the same entities belong to each set. Despite their extensional equivalence, they do not have the same meaning. Since the referential component of meaning cannot account for all semantic phenomena, Frege postulated a second component to meaning, which he called "sense." Carnap (1928) is generally credited with introducing the term "intension" to contrast the second component of meaning with "extension."

Quine is a notorious critic of intensions. As he once put it, "Intensions are creatures of darkness, and I shall rejoice with the reader when they are exorcised" (Quine 1966, p. 186). The argument for the existence of intensions is theoretical: they appear to be needed to account for certain phenomena surrounding meaning, but there is little agreement about what exactly they are. Whether intenSions can be made philosophically respectable and how they might be relevant to intenTionality remain areas of active philosophical research. The suggestion that there is a connection is tempting: the fact that a person believes he is a member of a species that has evolved hearts does not entail that he believes he is a member of a species that has evolved kidneys, despite the extensional identity of the two predicates. The failure of substitutivity in the context of an individual's belief (an inTensional context) might be accounted for by the difference in intenSion of the two predicates if we only had an adequate account of intenSions.

To nonphilosophers, lack of agreement among philosophers about intenTionality and intenSionality may seem to make these notions unsuitable for empirical study. In the rest of this paper I shall focus on intenTionality and argue that, despite the philosophical controversy, cognitive scientists can make use of the theories that have been proposed.

METHODOLOGY

Rather than seeing disagreement about intentionality as a problem for cognitive science, I see it as an opportunity for developing an empirical account of intentionality. This attitude may seem to present a problem. We are a long way from being able to give an uncontroversial definition of intentionality, but many behavioral scientists believe it is not possible to study a given phenomenon without a rigorous (preferably operational) definition of that phenomenon. That this idea is false should be made obvious by considering early investigation of the chemical nature of elements like gold or carbon. Prior to understanding atomic structure, overt properties such as density, hardness, color, and reactivity were used to determine whether a given specimen was indeed gold. It would have been premature to define gold in terms of those kinds of properties, since gold could have turned out to occur, like carbon, in more than one form. A precise definition of "gold" prior to comparative work on numerous putative examples of gold would have begged certain questions about the nature of gold, since by definition things that shared the overt properties would have been gold and things that lacked the properties would not have been gold. Rough characterizations in terms of overt properties are not properly regarded as definitions, although they do provide an initial classificatory scheme that is then revised by careful comparative work. The comparative work revised the concept of gold to include ideas about atomic structure, thus legitimizing the concept by fitting it into an empirically productive theoretical framework. (See Kripke 1972 for a general account of scientific terms on which these considerations are based.)

The motivation for a comparative approach to the study of intentionality should now be clear. The empirical utility of a notion of intentionality will depend on whether it can be fitted into an appropriate theoretical framework. This cannot be decided a priori by philosophers any more than philosophers could have decided whether gold, carbon, etc., was a better classification scheme than earth, air, fire, and water. This suggests that cognitive scientists would be ill advised to look to philosophers for a crisp and empirically rigorous definition of intentionality (even if some philosophers promise to provide it). Philosophical conceptions of intentionality distinguish a certain class of phenomena from others. Given a particular classification scheme based on a particular philosophical conception, further investigation may show whether there is a scientifically useful theoretical basis for including all the phenomena initially characterized in this way. Phenomena initially included may come to be dropped from the categorization scheme, and some phenomena initially omitted may be usefully included. Or the phenomena picked out by the philosophical categories may turn out to be so heterogeneous that no useful theory can be built around them. From this perspective, the variety of philosophical views about intentionality is a good thing insofar as they suggest different bases for comparative studies.

Empirical investigation of a philosophical classification scheme need not commit one to the entire position of the philosopher who developed it.[1] For example, the question of whether to treat intentionality as a property of sentences or as a property of minds is less significant from this perspective. Both Brentano and Chisholm provide criteria for distinguishing some phenomena (intentional ones) from others (the nonintentional). The resulting categorization schemes may not precisely overlap, but both can provide starting points for more detailed comparisons of the phenomena. The results of the comparative work may lead to refinements in the notion of intentionality, or to its abandonment, but this cannot be predicted reliably without doing the empirical work. The main point here, though, is that choosing to start from a particular categorization scheme does not commit one to accepting that it is the correct scheme. Indeed, investigation of conflicting categorization schemes might even hasten convergence on a more useful one.

INTENTIONALITY AND SCIENCE

Some critics think that there are good philosophical arguments against the possibility of a scientific theory of intentionality. Before addressing some specific criticisms, let us forestall a range of possible arguments. Any valid argument against the possibility of giving a scientific account of intentionality will rely on particular features of a conception of intentionality, so the argument will be, at best, an argument against conceptions that share those features. If there is no guarantee that a scientific theory of intentionality will incorporate those features, then such arguments can show only the unsuitability of a particular conception of intentionality for scientific development, but they cannot constitute an argument against scientific accounts of intentionality in general.

Thus it may be possible to respond to some arguments that they rely on too narrow a conception of intentionality. This response strategy, in effect, shifts the target away from the initial criticism and is reasonable up to a point. There are, however, some features of philosophical conceptions of intentionality that may be deemed crucial in the sense that any account of intentionality that abandoned those features would be using the same name for something else (as happened in the appropriation of the ancient Greek term "atom" by modern physics). If there are central features to the notion of intentionality and if philosophical arguments against a science of intentionality can be based on those features, then those arguments must be responded to directly.

If there is one feature of intentionality that falls into this category, it is Brentano's notion that philosophical states involve content. In English we specify the content of mental states such as beliefs with embedded propositional clauses (as in "John believes that Mary is coming to dinner"). Dennett (1969), Stich (1983), and Rosenberg (1990) have all objected to basing cognitive science on the notion of mental content on the grounds that in many cases content cannot be specified precisely enough, particularly when considering nonhuman animals. These authors draw attention to the unsuitability of using a human language to describe the contents of a dog's "beliefs" on the grounds that the human words used will refer to distinctions that humans make, but dogs do not. For example, the concept of "squirrel" has associations for humans that a dog may be insensitive to—that squirrels are phylogenetically close to rats, for example. Dennett, Stich, and Rosenberg attempt to use considerations like this to call into question the scientific value of attributions such as "Fido believes that a squirrel ran up the tree" to dogs. But the arguments are really quite weak. Given good comparative data on the discriminative abilities of dogs and humans, there is no principled reason to think that we cannot use human language in some (perhaps) long-winded way to specify the content of a dog's beliefs.[2]

Comparative approaches are particularly relevant here. Careful comparison of the cognitive mechanisms of dogs and humans will enable us to say how similar their conceptual schemes are to ours with respect, for example, to associations between various perceptual categories. Without such comparisons, the use of the term "squirrel" in the description of Fido's belief is anthropomorphic. With such comparisons in hand, it is possible to describe Fido's beliefs in a way that is not overly anthropomorphic since our descriptions can explicitly cancel connotations that the concept of "squirrel" has for normal speakers of English. Once again, the utility of doing this ought not to be decided on philosophical grounds alone. CACS provides the best approach to deciding the utility of such attributions.

I have not exhausted the challenges to incorporating intentional language into science. One particularly pressing problem is the apparent circularity of attributing beliefs and desires on the basis of actions and then using those belief and desire attributions to predict or explain action. While actions are predictable given knowledge of the contents of beliefs and desires, the contents of beliefs and desires can be attributed only on the basis of actions. If the action explained by a particular set of beliefs and desires is the same action used to justify attributing those beliefs and desires, then there is a circle. But in general our attributions and explanations of behavior are not so tightly linked. If the fact that Joe is carrying his umbrella is our only evidence that he thinks it is going to rain, it is obviously circular to explain his carrying an umbrella by citing his belief that it is going to rain. Usually, however, we have independent evidence that Joe believes it is going to rain, such as his words of warning to his friends, his setting houseplants out in the yard, and so on, and in such circumstances it is not obviously circular to explain his picking up his umbrella by his belief that it will rain.

Some critics resort to pointing out that any belief can be used in the explanation of any action, no matter how bizarre the connection, since other beliefs and desires can always be attributed to fill the gap. Here is an example from Rosenberg (1988, p. 34): "Someone might light a cigarette because, say, he believed that the theory of relativity is false. How is this possible? Well, suppose he believed that someone was asking him whether the theory of relativity was true and he also believed that the way to signal dissent in the language of the questioner was to light up and that he wanted to so signal." Clearly this is possible, but just as clearly we would not take this one action as compelling evidence that the person had the beliefs mentioned.

Here, too, a comparative approach to intentionality is helpful. Ethological and neuroethological work is capable of revealing what features of the environment a given organism's sense organs and nervous system can respond to. Given this kind of knowledge, the range of intentional states that may plausibly be attributed to an organism is constrained. Rosenberg's point that beliefs and desires do not predict anything in isolation is well taken. But this does not justify his pessimistic continuation: "The number of specific beliefs and desires that lead to actions is so large, and the difficulty of identifying them exactly is so great, that our explanations of action cannot help but be seriously incomplete. . . . And our predictions must be equally weak, for they rest on nothing but guesswork about the vast number of specific beliefs and desires that are needed for a precise prediction" (Rosenberg 1988, p. 34). The range of beliefs that may be attributed to an organism, including a human, is constrained by what we know about its cognitive capacities. In most cases, it is not simply guesswork to discount the idea that someone believes that the appropriate way to signal dissent to a question is to light a cigarette. Such a belief can be held only by an organism with certain perceptual and cognitive abilities, and it would be held only as the result of some specific experiences. If we have evidence that either of these conditions has not been met, then it is not guesswork to withhold the attribution of such a belief.

NATURALIZING INTENTIONALITY

I shall presuppose that a scientifically useful notion of intentionality must be naturalistic. In other words, it should not require the adoption of any kind of dualism of mental and physical substance. This presupposition provides a tension for attempts to develop a theory of intentionality. On the one hand, there is a tendency to want to assimilate intentionality to physical or biological mechanisms in order to show there is nothing special about it (e.g., Dretske 1981; Millikan 1984; Dennett 1987). On the other hand, we are faced with intuitions about qualitative differences in intro-spective experiences associated with our mental capacities and the functional capacities of other organisms (e.g., Nagel 1974) and artifacts, such as computers and vending machines (e.g., Searle 1980). Various degrees of obviousness attach to the claims made about such qualitative differences, particularly where other organisms are concerned. Nonetheless, such considerations provide a source of intuitions about the specialness of human cognition and provide a basis for objections to the use of folk psychological terms to describe computers (Searle 1980) and animals (Leahy 1991). CACS has the potential to alleviate the unease arising from the interaction of these intuitions and naturalism if, against a background of detailed comparison of humans to other organisms and artifacts, neither the similarities nor the differences provide grounds for blanket declarations about the uniqueness, or lack thereof, of human minds. Thus, for example, worries about lack of language in animals seem less significant when language is seen as just one dimension along which comparisons can be made.

REPRESENTATIONS AND INTENTIONALITY

The notion of representation is ubiquitous in the various sciences making up the cognitive sciences (Allen 1992a). This suggests that CACS should exploit this common ground in making comparisons between humans, other organisms, and computers. Comparison of the role of representation in these various systems can ground useful theoretical claims about them all. The basic notion underlying representation is that of a mapping from the features of one structure to the features of another. Roitblat (1982) has developed what he calls a "metatheory" of representation that usefully analyzes the basic notion of a mapping as having four components: a domain (what the representation is used for), content (what is represented), code (the mapping rules), and medium (the physical basis for representation). From a different perspective, Swoyer (1991) gives a useful account of the logical properties of structural representations.

The basic idea of a mapping is widely applicable. In a connectionist network, for example, there may be a mapping between connection strengths and the frequencies with which inputs to the network are correlated. However, not every mapping that exists is of interest to cognitive science. For example, ridges in sand underwater near the shore represent wave patterns because there is a mapping from ridge orientation to average wave direction. But there is no need to think of the ocean floor as a cognitive device or of its displaying intentionality. The same point can be put in terms of information. In the sense of "information" defined by Shannon and Weaver (1949), the ridges in the sandy ocean floor are a source of information about the waves. Cognition is often characterized as information processing, but clearly not all information-bearing structures are cognitive. Philosophers are interested in developing notions of information that are richer than the Shannon and Weaver notion and that can be used to suggest empirical work for comparative cognitive science (Dretske 1981; Allen and Hauser 1993).

Although the tasks of developing cognitively interesting notions of representation and information are related, to pursue both topics would take us too far afield here (but see Allen and Hauser 1993). The remainder of this section focuses on the question of how to extend the basic notion of representation in a way that can be applied to questions about intentionality.

Intentionality and Control

The first suggestion is that a representation is intentional if it is used by a system to control behavior. The idea that behavioral control is a key feature of cognitive representation is implicit in Roitblat's (1982) characterization of the domain of a representational system as the "class of situations or tasks in which it is used and to which it applies" (p. 353). Roitblat does not discuss intentionality explicitly, but the notion of representation he develops is an intentional notion in the sense that representations are about features of the represented world. (Reader exercise: Are they intenSional?)

The idea that the intentionality of a representation derives from what it does in that system is "functionalist" in the sense of Cummins (1989, ch. 9). In a functionalist account of representation, the functional role of a given representation may be specified either causally (i.e., by the role the representations play in the causal network between environmental stimuli and behavior), or computationally (i.e., by the role such representations play in a Turing machine characterization of the system). But, as Cummins points out, it is convenient to use the term "functionalism" generically without specifying in which way functional roles are to be attributed.

Functionalism underlies a common view that the mechanisms underlying human intentionality are just very complicated versions of those found in common artifacts. Thus, for example, McCarthy (1980) argues that it is appropriate to attribute beliefs to thermostats, and Dretske (1980) argues that it is appropriate to attribute intentionality to similar devices. Thermostats contain mechanical parts (e.g., metal coils) whose properties (e.g., coil tension) map the temperature of the environment and directly control the heating and cooling devices. Coil tension maps onto ambient temperature, thus representing the temperature. Other features of the thermostat may also represent the temperature (such as the degree of expansion of the plastic housing) but, whereas coil tension figures in the causal story about furnace switching, expansion of the housing does not. Thus, according to this suggestion, it is the role of a representation in producing behavior that constitutes its intentionality.

This approach is obviously compatible with the desire to naturalize intentionality. However, the approach also seems to run afoul of intuitions against attributing mental properties to pieces of metal and plastic commonly found on walls. Thus, for example, Searle (1980) vehemently disagrees that intentional descriptions of thermostats are comparable to belief attributions in humans. My purpose here does not include adjudicating this dispute. Models of human cognitive performance that focus on the representational requirements of brain mechanisms provide an obvious domain of comparison with similar models of animal competence or with artificial intelligence models. CACS can make use of such comparisons without prior commitment to the correctness of one philosophical position over another.

Biofunctional Intentionality

The second suggestion (Millikan 1984) is that a representation is intentional if similar mappings have historically played a role in the survival of ancestral systems. Millikan's account of intentionality is perhaps the most detailed attempt to put intentionality into a biological framework, and it is beginning to attract attention from ethologists (e.g., Beer 1991; Bekoff and Allen 1992). On Millikan's view, intentionality is a biological property derived from the biological functions of those things that possess it. She uses bee dances as examples of what she calls "intentional icons." According to her account, bee dances are about the location of nectar, because the adaptive value of bee dances for ancestors of current bees is explained by a representational mapping between features of the dance and the location of nectar.

Millikan's account is historical in the sense that a thing's intentionality depends not on present characteristics, but on its being the product of a selective process that allows us to say what the thing is for. This leads her to claim that an exact duplicate of a human being produced by a random process (e.g., an extremely unlikely quantum accident), while it might be conscious or have other mental states, would not have any intentional states such as beliefs, desires, etc., since, initially at least, representational properties of these states have nothing to do with their existence (Millikan 1984, p. 93). It is important to realize that the sense of "function" invoked by Millikan is very different from that inherent in the functionalism of the previous suggestion. In most functionalist accounts, it does not matter what the history of a system is; all that counts is its current Turing machine description. If it has certain functional capabilities according to this description, then it has intentionality. According to Millikan's account, however, it is the historical role of similar states in adapting other systems to their environments that determines function and thus intentionality. This is why she thinks two devices can be identical in all physical respects, yet differ in that one has intentionality and the other does not.

Applying Millikan's account of intentionality, even trees can exhibit it. For example, in work on African acacia trees it has been found that individual trees will increase tannin production in their leaves in response to predation by kudu antelope to a level that can kill the antelope. In addition to this primary response, acacias undergoing predation release ethylene into the air, causing downwind acacias up to 50 yards away to step up their tannin production within 5 to 10 minutes. The adaptive significance of ethylene release is easily imagined and has led at least one science journalist to call it an "alarm system" (Hughes 1990).[3] If, for acacias, ethylene has historically played the role of adapting downwind trees to the environmental condition of predation by herbivores, then ethylene released by the trees is an intentional icon according to Millikan's account.

These examples point out the distance between Millikan's account and Brentano's view that intentionality is the distinguishing mark of the mental. She admits that an entity might be conscious while lacking intentionality. On the other hand, on the plausible assumption that acacia trees do not have minds, her account allows intentionality to occur in conjunction with nonpsychological phenomena. I am not arguing here whether it is a good thing or a bad thing that Millikan's account of intentionality diverges so much from Brentano's or whether CACS should adopt one view rather than another. Instead, I wish again to emphasize my point that divergence between philosophers on the subject of intentionality need not be considered a hindrance to cognitive scientists. Whether or not one thinks that Millikan's account of intentionality is correct, its focus on historical antecedents suggests a line of comparison that other accounts would not.[4] According to Millikan's view, intentional content is specified not by looking inside the system in question, but by looking at how the system is adapted to its environment. Insofar as this perspective can be applied to organisms, robots, or other entities, it provides a basis for comparison.

Is this the right basis for a comparative approach to intentionality? By now it should be clear that I will not answer this question on the grounds that such questions should be addressed empirically. Conceptual arguments have their place, but the real test of an approach is in its application. The question also contains a problematic presupposition—namely, that there is a single correct basis for comparing the cognitive abilities of diverse organisms and machines. This presupposition may be unwarranted, since the purposes of different scientists, even within the various cognitive sciences, are divergent. Given my exact physical constitution at this moment, whether I came together as a quantum accident two seconds ago or whether I came to be typing this paper by a more normal route does not bear on the probability of my ending this sentence with a period. A theory that focuses on predictive aims such as this one might have little use for categorizing things in terms of their evolutionary history. For other purposes, comparison on the basis of this history might well turn out to be significant. Different sciences with different purposes can coexist. It might even turn out to be useful for some purposes to categorize the behavior of trees with the behavior of humans, animals, and computers.

Intentionality and Detection of Error

The third suggestion is that a representation is intentional if the system in which it plays a role is capable of discriminating content from reality. According to this test, thermostat coils fail to be intentional representations of temperature since the thermostat cannot distinguish circumstances in which tension is manually applied to the coil (and thus does not correspond to the ambient temperature) from those in which the coil tension properly represents ambient temperature. In comparison, humans and some organisms are capable of treating their own perceptual states as misleading. I would suggest that how this capability is realized is of major interest for comparative cognitive science.

This suggestion, like that two sections earlier, is functionalist because it looks to the role representations play in the present capabilities of the system in question. However, it differs from the earlier suggestion by requiring a more sophisticated role for the representations to play. In doing so it avoids some of the pitfalls of Searle's challenge to the possibility of realizing artificial intentionality via a computer program. He has a conception of intentionality as a property of mental states directly, but precisely what property is not entirely clear from his account. According to Searle, intentionality requires "some awareness of the causal relation between the symbol and the referent" (Searle 1980, p. 454), but it is unclear what this awareness amounts to. He also suggests that intentionality inherently depends on the specific biochemical properties of brains (Searle 1980, p. 424). Searle gives no indication which biochemical properties of brains are necessary, nor does he give any idea why biochemistry might be important to intentionality. He develops a vague analogy with digestion, but in the case of digestion it is clear why biochemical properties are important. Furthermore, Searle rejects all forms of the Turing test as evidence of intentionality. Thus, absolutely nothing an artificial intelligence (AI) system could do would convince him that the system possessed intentionality. This has the unfortunate consequence of removing the question of the intentionality of AI systems from the empirical realm.

This idea that intentionality requires not just a causal or computational connection between symbol and referent, but awareness of that connection, is compatible, however, with the suggestion at the beginning of this section. We can use a comparative approach to cognitive science to demystify the notion of awareness here by considering what it is about humans that makes us attribute such awareness to each other and then trying to build similar capabilities into computers and trying to find those capabilities in other organisms. One of the things that convinces us of this awareness, I believe, is that humans are sometimes skeptical of the veracity of their immediate perceptual stimuli. What other organisms are capable of similar skepticism and over what range of their potential stimulations they are capable of such skepticism is a prime question for empirical research.

An observation involving vervet monkeys can be used to illustrate the point. Subordinate male vervets isolated with an infant behaved less aggressively toward the infant when they could see that they were being watched by the infant's mother, who was isolated behind a clear piece of glass, than when the same female was hidden behind a piece of sheet metal or behind a one-way mirror. When the females were subsequently released to interact with the males, female aggression toward the males correlated with what they had seen through the glass or the one-way mirror (Keddy-Hector, Seyfarth, and Raleigh 1989). After only a few experiences, males placed in a cage with a one-way mirror spent more time inspecting the mirror than interacting with the infant (Keddy-Hector, reported in conversation). This anectodal evidence is suggestive, since it appears to indicate that vervets can distinguish the appearance of not being watched from the actuality of not being watched. This kind of observation makes it plausible to include beliefs about whether they are being watched as part of the explanation of the behavior of the males toward the females. The possibility of discovering this kind of capability in different species further illustrates how it is possible to address Rosenberg's worry about the guesswork involved in attributing the background beliefs needed to explain an action.

The suggestion of this section also makes the variety of sensory modalities found in cognitively sophisticated organisms particularly interesting. Humans can use one sensory modality—e.g., touch—as a test of their perceptions in another modality—e.g., vision—and also use perceptions in a given modality to test earlier perceptions from that same modality. Apparently the human brain produces a model of the world and then tests its perceptions against that model. Investigating the computational requirements for such a capability is a challenging task for AI that, as far as I know, has not been attempted. The degree to which organisms can question their immediate perceptions is a topic whose empirical investigation is relevant to the conception of intentionality considered in this section.

SUMMARY

No one of the accounts of intentionality that I have presented here is suggested as a full analysis of intentionality. Instead, each indicates avenues of research, both for observation of animals and for development of computational models. Cognitive scientists should not look to philosophers for a prepackaged concept of intentionality. Rather, the different philosophical theories that are available can be used to motivate various empirical lines of enquiry. By using a particular philosophical theory in this way, one is not committed to all of the philosophical baggage that comes with that theory. In the end, it may turn out that intentionality is not a useful concept for cognitive science, or it may turn out that it is a useful concept. In either case, the decision should not be made on conceptual grounds alone, such as lack of language, lack of a particular biochemical makeup, or lack of an appropriate history, despite what some philosophers may think. Furthermore, different conceptions of intentionality may be useful for different scientific goals. Only a fully empirical comparative approach to cognitive science is adequate to deal with the topic of intentionality.

ACKNOWLEDGMENTS

I would like to thank the organizers of CACS 92, particularly Jean Arcady-Meyer and Herb Roitblat, for their invitation and their efforts to make the summer school a success. I am grateful to the French CNRS for its financial support of CACS 92. Marc Bekoff and I have spent many hours discussing these and other issues. He, Dale Jamieson, Ruth Millikan, and Herb Roitblat all provided helpful comments on the manuscript.

NOTES

1. This point is made in detail with respect to cognitive ethology and Millikan's analysis of intentionality, in Bekoff and Allen 1992. Millikan's account is also discussed later in this chapter.

2. The argument against Dennett and Stich is presented in much greater detail in Allen 1992b.

3. Hughes reports that this phenomenon was discovered by Wouter Van Hoven after the sudden death of approximately 3,000 kudu. She also reports his observation that giraffes feeding on acacias graze on only about one tree in ten and avoid downwind trees.

4. Bekoff and Allen (1992) discuss the application of Millikan's theory to canid play behavior.

REFERENCES

Allen, C. (1992a). "Mental content and evolutionary explanation." *Biology and Philosophy* 7: 1–12.

Allen, C. (1992b). "Mental content." *British Journal for the Philosophy of Science* 43: 537–553.

Allen, C., and Hauser, M. (1993). "Communication and cognition: Is information the connection?" *PSA 1992*, vol. 2: 81–91.

Beer, C. G. (1991). "From folk psychology to cognitive ethology." In C. A. Ristau (ed.) *Cognitive Ethology: The minds of other animals. Essays in Honor of Donald Griffin*, 19–34. Hillsdale, NJ: Lawrence Erlbaum.

Bekoff, M., and Allen, C. (1992). "Intentional icons: Towards an evolutionary cognitive ethology." *Ethology* 91: 1–16.

Brentano, F. (1924). *Psychologie vom empirischen Standpunkte*. Leipzig: F. Meiner.

Carnap, R. (1928/1967). *The Logical Structure of the World: Pseudoproblems in Philosophy*. Trans. by R. A. George. Berkeley, CA: University of California Press.

Cheney, D. L., and Seyfarth, R. M. (1990). *How Monkeys See the World: Inside the Mind of Another Species*. Chicago: University of Chicago Press.

Chisholm, R. M. (1957). *Perceiving: A Philosophical Study*. Ithaca, NY: Cornell University Press.

Chisholm, R. M. (1967). "Intentionality." In P. Edwards (ed.). *The Encyclopedia of Philosophy*, vol. 4: 203. New York: Macmillan and The Free Press.

Churchland, P. S. (1986). *Neurophilosophy: Toward a Unified Science of the Mind/Brain.* Cambridge, MA: The MIT Press.

Cummins, R. (1989). *Meaning and Mental Representation.* Cambridge, MA: The MIT Press.

Davidson, D. (1975). "Thought and talk." In S. Guttenplan (ed.). *Mind and Language.* Oxford: Oxford University Press.

Dawkins, R. (1976). *The Selfish Gene.* Oxford: Oxford University Press.

Dennett, D. C. (1969). *Content and Consciousness.* London: Routledge and Kegan Paul.

Dennett, D. C. (1983). "Intentional systems in cognitive ethology. The 'Panglossian paradigm' defended." *Behavioral and Brain Sciences* 6: 343–345.

Dennett, D. C. (1987). *The Intentional Stance.* Cambridge, MA: The MIT Press.

Dretske, F. I. (1980). "The intentionality of cognitive states." In P. A. French, T. E. Uehling Jr., and H. K. Wettstein (eds.). *Midwest Studies in Philosophy*, vol. 2: 281–294. Minneapolis: University of Minnesota Press.

Drestske F. I. (1981). *Knowledge and the Flow of Information.* Cambridge, MA: The MIT Press.

Frege, G. (1892/1948). "Über Sinn und Bedeutung." Trans. as "On Sense and Reference" by M. Black. *Philosophical Review* 57: 209–230.

Heyes, C. (1987). "Contrasting approaches to the legitimation of intentional language within comparative psychology." *Behaviorism* 15: 41–50.

Hughes, S. (1990). "Antelope activate the acacia's alarm system." *New Scientist* 127: 19.

Jacquette, D. (1986). "Intentionality and intensionality: Quotation contexts and the modal wedge." *The Monist* 69: 598–608.

Keddy-Hector, A. C., Seyfarth, R. M., and Raleigh, M. J. (1989). "Male parental care, female choice and the effect of an audience in vervet monkeys." *Animal Behavior* 38: 262–271.

Kripke, S. A. (1972). *Naming and Necessity.* Cambridge, MA: Harvard University Press.

Leahy, M. P. T. (1991). *Against Liberation: Putting Animals in Perspective.* London: Routledge.

McCarthy, J. (1980). "Beliefs, machines, and theories." *Behavioral and Brain Sciences* 3: 435.

Millikan, R. G. (1984). *Language, Thought, and Other Biological Categories.* Cambridge, MA: The MIT Press.

Nagel, T. (1974). "What is it like to be a bat?" *Philosophical Review* 83: 435–450.

Quine, W. V. O. (1953). *From a Logical Point of View.* Cambridge, MA: Harvard University Press.

Quine, W. V. O. (1966). "Quantifiers and propositional attitudes." In *The Ways of Paradox and Other Essays*, 185–196. Cambridge, MA: Harvard University Press.

Roitblat, H. L. (1982). "The meaning of representation in animal memory." *Behavioral and Brain Sciences* 5: 353–406.

Rosenberg, A. (1988). *Philosophy of Social Science.* Boulder, CO: Westview Press.

Rosenberg, A. (1990). "Is there an evolutionary biology of play?" In M. Bekoff and D. Jamieson (eds.). *Interpretation and Explanation in the Study of Animal Behavior. Vol. 2, Explanation, Evolution, and Adaptation*, 180–196. Boulder, CO: Westview Press.

Searle, J. R. (1980). "Minds, brains and programs." *Behavioral and Brain Sciences* 3: 417–424.

Shannon, C. E., and Weaver, W. (1949). *The Mathematical Theory of Communication.* Urbana, IL: University of Illinois Press.

Stich, S. (1983). *From Folk Psychology to Cognitive Science: The Case Against Belief.* Cambridge, MA: The MIT Press.

Swoyer, C. (1991). "Structural representation and surrogative reasoning." *Synthese* 87: 449–508.

6 Do Animals Have Beliefs?

Daniel C. Dennett

According to one more or less standard mythology, behaviorism, the ideology and methodology that reigned in experimental psychology for most of the century, has been overthrown by a new ideology and methodology: cognitivism. Behaviorists, one is told, did not take the mind seriously. They ignored—or even denied the existence of—mental states such as beliefs and desires, and mental processes such as imagination and reasoning; behaviorists concentrated exclusively on external, publicly observable behavior and the (external, publicly observable) conditions under which such behavior was elicited. Cognitivists, in contrast, take the mind seriously and develop theories, models, and explanations that invoke, as real items, these internal, mental goings-on. People (and at least some other animals) have minds after all; they are *rational agents*.

Like behaviorists, cognitivists believe that the purely physical brain controls all behavior without any help from poltergeists or egos or souls, so what does this supposedly big difference come to? When you ask a behaviorist what the mind is, the behaviorist retorts, "What mind?" When you ask a cognitivist, the reply is, "The mind is the brain." Since both agree that it is the brain that does all the work, their disagreement looks at the outset to be merely terminological. When, if ever, is it right, or just perspicuous, to describe an animal's brain processes as thinking, deciding, remembering, imagining? This question suggests to some that the behaviorists may have been right about lower animals—perhaps about pigeons and rats, and certainly about frogs and snails; these simple brains are capable of nothing that should be dignified as properly "cognitive." Well, then, where do we "draw the line" and why?

Do animals have beliefs? One of the problems with this question, which has provoked a lot of controversy among animal researchers and the ideologues of cognitive science, is that there is scant agreement on the meaning of the term "belief" as it appears in the question. "Belief" has come to have a special, nonordinary, sense in the English of many (but not all) of these combatants: it is supposed by them to be the generic, least-marked term for a cognitive state. Thus, if you look out the window and *see* that a cow is in the garden, you ipso facto have a belief that a cow is in the garden. If you are not ignorant of arithmetic, you believe the proposition that $2 + 2 = 4$ (and an infinity of its kin). If you *expect* (on whatever grounds) that the door you are about to open will yield easily to your tug, then you have a belief to that effect, and so on. It would be more natural, surely, to say of such a person, "He thinks the door is unlocked" or "He is under the impression that the door is open" or, even less positively, "He does not know the door is locked." "Belief" is ordinarily reserved for more dignified contents, such as religious belief, political belief, or—sliding back to more quotidian issues—specific conjectures or hypotheses considered. But for Anglophone philosophers of mind in particular, and other theoreticians in cognitive science, the verb "believe" and the noun "belief" have been adopted to cover all such cases; whatever information guides an agent's actions is counted under the rubric of belief.

This particularly causes confusion, I have learned, among non-native speakers of English; the French term "*croyance*," for instance, stands even further in the direction of "creed" or "tenet," so that the vision my title question tends to conjure up for Francophones is an almost comical surmise about the religious and theoretical convictions of animals—not, as it was meant to be understood, a relatively bland question about the nature of the cognitive states that suffice to account for the perceptuoloco-motory prowess of animals. But even those Anglophones who are most comfortable with the artificially enlarged meaning of the term in their debates suffer, I think, from the same confusion. There is much less agreement than these theorists imagine about just what one would be asserting in claiming, for instance, that dogs have beliefs.

Consider the diversity of opinion. Do animals have beliefs? I have said yes, supporting my claim by pointing to the undeniable fact that animals' behavior can often be predicted (and explained and manipulated) using what I call the intentional stance (Dennett 1971, 1987)—the strategy of treating animals as rational agents whose actions are those they deem most likely to further their "desires" given their "beliefs." One can often predict or explain what an animal will do by simply noticing what it notices and figuring out what it wants. The raccoon wants the food in the box-trap, but knows better than to walk into a potential trap where it cannot see its way out. That is why you have to put two open doors on the trap—so that the animal will dare to enter the first, planning to leave by the second if there is any trouble. You will have a hard time getting a raccoon to enter a trap that does not have an apparent "emergency exit" that closes along with the entrance.

I take it that this style of explanation and prediction is uncontroversially valuable: it works, and it works *because* raccoons (for instance) are that smart. That fact suffices, given what I mean by "belief," to show that raccoons have beliefs—and desires, of course. One might call the latter preferences or goals or wants or values, but whatever you call them, their specification involves the use of intentional (mentalistic) idioms. This guarantees that translating between "desire" talk and "preference" or "goal" talk is trivial, so I view the connotational differences between these terms as theoretically irrelevant. The same thing holds for beliefs, of course: you might as well call the state of the raccoon a belief, since if you call it a "registration" or a "data-structure" in the "environmental information store" or some other technical term, the logic you use to draw inferences about the animal's behavior, given its internal states, will be the standard, "intentionalistic" logic of belief. For more on the logic of intentionality, see Dennett (1969, 1971, 1983, 1987) or the article on intentionality in the *Oxford Companion to the Mind* (Gregory 1987).

When called upon to defend this indifference to terminological niceties, I like to point out that when economists, for example, consider the class of *purchases* and note the defining condition that the purchaser believes he is exchanging his money for something belonging to the seller and desires that item more than the money he exchanges for it, the economist is not requiring that the purchaser engage in any particularly salient act of creed endorsing (let alone suffer any spasms of *desire*). A purchaser can meet the defining "belief-desire" conditions while daydreaming, while concentrating on some other topic, while treating the seller almost as if he/it were a post stuck in the ground. All that has to be the case is that the purchaser has somehow or other come into a cognitive state that identifies a seller, a price, and an opportunity to exchange and has tipped the balance in favor of completing the transaction. This is not nothing; it would be a decidedly nontrivial task to design a robot that could distinguish an apple seller from an apple tree while not becoming a money pump when confronted by eager salesmen. But if you succeeded in making a successful purchaser-robot, you would ipso facto have made a robot believer, a robot desirer, because belief and desire, in this maximally bland (but maximally useful!) sense are logical requirements of purchasing behavior.

Others do not approve of this way with words. Donald Davidson (1975), for instance, has claimed that only creatures with the concepts of truth and falsehood can properly be said to have beliefs and, since these are metalinguistic concepts (I am simplifying his argument somewhat), only language-using animals such as human beings can have beliefs. And then there are those who have some other criterion for belief, according to which some animals do have beliefs and others do not. This criterion must be an empirical question for them, presumably, but which empirical question it is—which facts would settle it one way or the other—is something about which there is little agreement. David Premack (1988) has claimed that chimpanzees—and perhaps only chimpanzees—demonstrate belief, while Jerry Fodor (1990) has suggested that frogs—but not paramecia—have beliefs. Janet Halperin (at the conference that resulted in this book) expressed mixed feelings about the hypothesis that her

Siamese fighting fish have beliefs; on the one hand, they do seem richly amenable (in some regards) to intentional interpretation, while on the other hand she has a neural net–like model of their control systems that seems to lack any components with the features beliefs are often supposed to have.

The various assumptions tacitly made about how to use these words infects other controversies as well. Does it follow from the hypothesis that there is something it is like to be a bat (Nagel 1974) that bats have beliefs? Well, could it be the case that there is indeed something it is like to be a bat, but no bat knows what it is like? But could the bat know what it is like without having any beliefs about what it is like? If knowledge entails belief, as philosophical tradition declares, then a bat must have beliefs about what it is like to be it—if it is like anything at all to be a bat. But philosophers have different intuitions about how to answer all these questions, so of course they also have clashing opinions on whether robots could have beliefs.

The maximal leniency of the position I have recommended on this score is notoriously illustrated by my avowal that even lowly thermostats have beliefs. John McCarthy (1979) has joined me in this provocative stance, and he proposes just the right analogy in defense, I think. Is zero a number? Some people were outraged when the recommendation was first made that zero be considered a number in good standing. What kind of a number is zero? It stands for no quantity at all! But the number system you get if you include zero is vastly more perspicuous and elegant than the number system you get if you exclude zero. A thermostat, McCarthy and I claim, is one of the simplest, most rudimentary, least interesting systems that should be included in the class of believers—the class of intentional systems, to use my term. Why? Because it has a rudimentary goal or desire (which is set, dictatorially, by the thermostat's owner, of course), which it acts on appropriately whenever it believes (thanks to a sensor of one sort or another) that its desire is unfulfilled. Of course, you don't have to describe a thermostat in these terms. You can describe it in mechanical terms, or even molecular terms. But what is theoretically interesting is that if you want to describe the set of all thermostats (cf. the set of all purchasers) you have to rise to this intentional level. Any particular purchaser can also be described at the molecular level, but what purchasers—or thermostats—all have in common is a systemic property that is captured only at a level that invokes belief talk and desire talk (or their less colorful but equally intentional alternatives—semantic information talk and goal registration talk, for instance).

It is an open empirical question which other things, natural and artificial, fall into this class. Do trees? The case can be made—and in fact was made (or at least discussed in the appropriate terms) by Colin Allen in the symposium. One can see why various opponents of this view have branded it as ''instrumentalism'' or ''behaviorism'' or ''eliminative materialism." But before accepting any of these dismissive labels, we should look at the suggested alternative, which is generally called "realism" because it takes seriously the questions Which animals *really* have beliefs and, of those that do, what do they *really* believe? Jerry Fodor (1990), John Searle (1992), and Thomas Nagel (1986) are three prominent philosophical realists. The idea that it makes sense to ask these questions (and expect that, in principle, they have answers) depends on a profound difference of vision or imagination between these thinkers and those who see things my way. The difference is clearest in the case of Fodor, as we can see by contrasting two pairs of propositions:

1. Fodor: *Beliefs are like sentences.* Beliefs have structure, are composed of parts, and take up room in some spatial or temporal medium. Any finite system can contain only a finite number of beliefs. When one claims that Jones believes *that the man in the blue suit is the murderer,* this is true if and only if the belief in Jones's head really is composed of parts that mean just what the words in the italicized phrase mean, organized in a structure that has the same syntactic—and semantic—analysis as that string of words.

1A. Dennett: *Beliefs are like dollars.* Dollars are abstract (unlike dollar bills, which are concrete). The system of dollars is just one of many possible systems for keeping track of economic value. Its units do not line up "naturally" with any salient differences in the economic value of goods and services in the world, nor are all questions of intersystemic translation guaranteed to be well founded. How many U.S. dollars (as of July 4, 1994) did a live goat cost in Beijing on that date? One has to operationalize a few loose ends to make the question meaningful: Do you take the exchange rate from the black market or use the official rate, for instance? Which should you use, and why? Once these loose ends are acknowledged and tied off, this question about the dollar value of goats in Beijing has a relatively satisfactory answer. That is, the various answers that might be reasonably defended tend to cluster in a smallish area about which disagreement might well be dismissed as trivial. How many U.S. dollars (as of July 4, 1994) was a live goat worth in ancient Athens? Here any answer you might give would have to be surrounded by layers of defense and explanation.

Now, no one doubts that a live goat really had value in ancient Athens, and no one doubts that dollars are a perfectly general, systematic system for measuring economic value, but I do not suppose anyone would ask, after listening to two inconclusive rival proposals about how to fix the amount in dollars, "Yes, but how many dollars did it *really* cost back then?" There may be good grounds for preferring one rival set of auxiliary assumptions to another (intuitively, one that pegs ancient dollars to the price per ounce of gold then and now is of less interest than one that pegs ancient dollars to assumptions about "standard of living," the cost per year of feeding and clothing a family of four, etc.), but that does not imply that there must be some one translation scheme that "discovers the truth." Similarly, when one proposes and defends a particular scheme for expressing the contents of some agent's beliefs via a set of English sentences, the question of whether these sentences—supposing their meaning is fixed somehow—describe what the agent *really* believes betrays a certain naivete about what a belief might be.

2. Fodor: *Beliefs are independent, salient states.*

2A. Dennett: *There are independent, salient states that belief talk "measures" to a first approximation.*

What is the difference between these two propositions? We both agree that a brain filled with sawdust or jello could not sustain beliefs. There has to be structure; there have to be elements of plasticity that can go into different states and thereby secure one revision or another of the contents of the agent's beliefs. Moreover, these plastic elements have to be to some considerable extent independently adjustable to account for the productivity (or, less grandly, the versatility) of beliefs in any believer of any interest (of greater interest than the thermostat).

The difference is that Fodor stipulates that the ascribing language (the sentences of English or French, for instance) must have much the same degrees of freedom, the same planes of revision, the same joints, as the system the sentences describe. I disagree. Consider the information contained in a map drawn on some plane surface according to some mapping rules and utilizing some finite set of labeling conventions. Imagine a robot that locates itself by means of such a system, moving a symbol for itself on its own map as it moves through the world. At any moment, its system contains lots of information (or misinformation) about its circumstances—e.g., *that* it is nearer point A than point B, *that* it is within the boundary of region C, *that* it is between F and G, *that* it is fast approaching agent D, who is on the same path but moving slower, etc. (Notice that I have captured this limited selection of information in a series of "that"-clauses expressed in English.) Some of this information will be utilizable by the robot, we may suppose, and some not. Whatever it can use, it believes (I would say); whatever it cannot use, it does not believe, since although the information is *in* the system, it is not *for* the system: it cannot be harnessed by the system to modulate behavior in ways that are appropriate to the system. Perhaps the fact *that* J, K, and L all lie on a straight line is a fact that we can see from looking at the robot's map, but that the robot would be unable to extract from its map using all the map-reading apparatus at its disposal.

There is a temptation here to think of this map reading or extraction as a process having the map as its "input" and some sentence expressing one or more of these propositions or "that"-clauses as its "output." But no such sentence formation is required (though it may be possible in a talking robot). The information extraction might just as well consist of the generation of locomotory control signals sufficient for taking some action appropriate to the state of affairs alluded to by the "that"-clause (appropriate, that is, given some assumptions about the agent's current "desires"). That locomotory recipe might not be executed; it might be evaluated and discarded in favor of some option deemed better under the circumstances. But since its generation as a candidate is dependent on the map's containing the information that-p, we can attribute the belief that-p to the system. All this is trivial if you think about the beliefs a chess-playing computer has about the location and value of the pieces on the chess board and the various ways it might utilize that information in generating and evaluating move candidates. Belief talk can do an acceptable job of describing the information storage and information revision contained in a map system.

Are map systems as versatile as "propositional" systems? Under what conditions does each flourish and fail? Are there other data structures or formats that are even better for various tasks? These are good empirical questions, but if we are going to raise them without confusing ourselves, we will need a way of speaking—a level of discourse—that can neutrally describe what is in common between different robot implementations of the same cognitive competence. I propose the intentional stance (and hence belief talk) as that level. Going along with that proposal means abjuring the inferences that depend on treating belief talk as implying a language of thought.

Alternatively, one could reserve belief talk for these more particular hypotheses and insist on some other idiom for describing what information-processing systems have in common whether or not they utilize beliefs (now understood as sentences in the head). I am not undivorcibly wed to the former way of speaking, though I have made out the case for its naturalness. The main thing is not to let misinterpretations cloud the already difficult arena of theoretical controversy.

There are important and interesting reasons, for example, for attempting to draw distinctions between different ways in which information may be utilized by a system (or organism). Consider the information that is "interwoven" into connectionist nets (as in Janet Halperin's example). As Clark and Karmiloff-Smith (1994) say, "It is knowledge *in* the system, but it is not yet knowledge *to* the system." What must be added, they ask, (or what must be different) for information to be knowledge *to* the system? (See also Dennett 1994.) This is one of the good questions we are on the brink of answering, and there is no reason why we cannot get clear about preferred nomenclature at the outset. Then we shall have some hope of going on to consider the empirical issues without talking past each other. That would be progress.

Do animals have beliefs, then? It all depends on how you understand the term "belief." I have defended a maximally permissive understanding of the term, having essentially no specific implications about the format or structure of the information structures in the animals' brains, but simply presupposing that whatever the structure is, it is sufficient to permit the sort of intelligent choice of behavior that is well predicted from the intentional stance. So yes, animals have beliefs. Even amoebas—like thermostats—have beliefs. Now we can ask the next question: what structural and processing differences make different animals capable of having more sophisticated beliefs? We find that there are many, many differences, almost all of them theoretically interesting, but none of them, in my opinion, marking a well-motivated chasm between the mere mindless behavers and the genuine rational agents.

REFERENCES

Clark, A., and Karmiloff-Smith, A., 1994. "The Cognizer's Innards." *Mind and Language,* 8: 487–519.

Davidson, D., 1975. "Thought and Talk." In *Mind and Language: Wolfson College Lectures, 1974.* Oxford: Oxford Univ. Press.

Dennett, D., 1969. *Content and Consciousness.* London: Routledge & Kegan Paul.

Dennett, D., 1971. "Intentional Systems." *J. Phil.,* 68: 87–106.

Dennett, D., 1983. "Intentional Systems in Cognitive Ethology: The 'Panglossian Paradigm' Defended." *Behavioral and Brain Sciences,* 6: 343–90.

Dennett, D., 1987. *The Intentional Stance.* Cambridge, MA: The MIT Press/A Bradford Book.

Dennett, D., 1994. "Labeling and Learning." *Mind and Language,* 8: 540–48. "Learning and Labeling" (comments on Clark and Karmiloff-Smith, *Mind and Language*).

Fodor, J., 1990. *A Theory of Content.* Cambridge, MA: The MIT Press/A Bradford Book.

Gregory, R. L., 1987. *Oxford Companion to the Mind.* Oxford: Oxford Univ. Press.

McCarthy, J., 1979. "Ascribing Mental Qualities to Machines." In M. Ringle, ed. *Philosophical Perspectives in Artificial Intelligence.* Atlantic Highlands, NJ: Humanities Press.

Nagel, T., 1974. "What Is It Like to Be a Bat?" *Philosophical Review,* 83: 435–50.

Nagel, T., 1986. *The View from Nowhere.* Oxford: Oxford Univ. Press.

Premack, D., 1988. "Intentionality: How to Tell Mae West from a Crocodile." *Behavioral and Brain Sciences,* 11: 522–23.

Searle, J., 1992. *The Rediscovery of the Mind.* Cambridge, MA: The MIT Press.

7 Cognitive Ethology and the Explanation of Nonhuman Animal Behavior

Marc Bekoff

COGNITIVE ETHOLOGY AS A SCIENCE

Cognitive ethology, broadly defined as the evolutionary and comparative study of nonhuman animal (hereafter animal) thought processes, consciousness, beliefs, or rationality, is a rapidly growing field that is attracting the attention of researchers in numerous and diverse disciplines.[1] Because behavioral abilities have evolved in response to natural selection pressures, ethologists favor observations and experiments on animals in conditions that are as close as possible to the natural environment where the selection occurred, and because cognitive ethology is a comparative science, cognitive ethological studies emphasize broad taxonomic comparisons and do not focus on a few select representatives of limited taxa. In addition to situating the study of animal behavior in an evolutionary and comparative framework, cognitive ethologists maintain that field studies of animals that include careful observation and experimentation can inform the study of animal cognition; cognitive ethology will not necessarily have to be brought into the laboratory in order to make it respectable. Cognitive psychologists, in contrast to cognitive ethologists, typically work on related topics in laboratory settings and do not emphasize evolutionary or comparative aspects of animal cognition. When cognitive psychologists do make cross-species comparisons, they are typically interested in explaining different behavior patterns in terms of common underlying mechanisms; ethologists, in common with other biologists, are often more concerned with the diversity of solutions that living organisms have found for common problems.

Many different types of research fall into the category "cognitive ethology," and it is currently pointless to try to delimit the boundaries of cognitive ethology; because of the enormous amount of interdisciplinary interest in the area, any stipulative definition of cognitive ethology is likely to rapidly become obsolete (Allen 1992a). Although cognitive ethology can trace its beginnings to the writings of Charles Darwin and some of his contemporaries and disciples, the modern era of cognitive ethology is usually thought to have begun with the appearance of Donald R. Griffin's

(1976, 1981) book *The Question of Animal Awareness: Evolutionary Continuity of Mental Experience.* Thus, cognitive ethology as most of us know it is really a young science with great aspirations, and, like many other fields in their infancy, cognitive ethology also suffers from various sorts of growing pains. While there are those who are presently willing to let cognitive ethological research take its course and wait to see how these sorts of investigations deal with current problems and inform and motivate future research, there are some who want to dispense with cognitive ethology because some of its ideas seem muddled and difficult to study or because other minds are never fully accessible to outsiders. The latter position seems to be short-sighted and narrow-minded. To claim that some of the basic tenets of cognitive ethology are unfalsifiable and thus not worthy of study is simply too cavalier (Sober 1983); there should be enough flexibility for alternative explanations, especially in developing fields. Some patience is needed. Imagine if other fields were ignored or terminated because their early thinking seemed confused or because "final answers" were not immediately available.

THREE VIEWS OF COGNITIVE ETHOLOGY

For cognitive ethology, the major problems are those that center on methods of data collection and analysis and on the description, interpretation, and explanation of animal behavior (Bekoff and Jamieson 1990a, b; Jamieson and Bekoff 1993; see also Purton 1978). Because cognitive ethology deals with animal minds and mental states, there is also some debate about whether a science of cognitive ethology is even possible (Yoerg and Kamil 1991; for a discussion see Jamieson and Bekoff 1993). Based on published reviews of some of Griffin's works and other clearly stated opinions concerning animal cognition, Bekoff and Allen (1996) divided those with different views of cognitive ethology into three major categories, *slayers, skeptics,* and *proponents;* unfortunately, all views of cognitive ethology could not be covered in their survey. The views of some members of these groups can be summarized as follows.

Slayers

Slayers deny any possibility of success in cognitive ethology. They sometimes conflate the difficulty of doing rigorous cognitive ethological investigations with the impossibility of doing so. Slayers also often ignore specific details of work by cognitive ethologists and frequently mount philosophically motivated objections to the possibility of learning anything about animal cognition. They do not see that cognitive ethological approaches can lead, and have lead, to new and testable hypotheses. They often pick out the most difficult and least accessible phenomena to study (e.g., consciousness) and then conclude that, because we can gain little detailed knowledge about these subjects, we cannot do better in other areas. Slayers also appeal to parsimony in explanations of animal behavior, but they dismiss the possibility that cognitive explanations can be more parsimonious than noncognitive alternatives, and they deny the utility of cognitive hypotheses for directing empirical research. Some specific examples of the slayers' position are as follows.

Zuckerman (1991), in his review of Cheney and Seyfarth's (1990) book *How Monkeys See the World: Inside the Mind of Another Species,* exemplifies the unargued view of those who dismiss the field of cognitive ethology because they make little effort to consider available evidence. He writes, "Some of the issues they do raise sound profound as set out but, when pursued, turn out to have little intellectual or scientific significance" (Zuckerman 1991, p. 46). Zuckerman does not tell us what types of data would have intellectual or scientific significance; this does not seem too much to ask of a student of primate behavior.

Heyes (1987a), who is a laboratory psychologist, advises cognitive ethologists to hang up their field glasses and turn to laboratory research if they want to understand animal cognition. She writes, "It is perhaps at this moment that the cognitive ethologist decides to hang up his field glasses, become a cognitive psychologist, and have nothing further to do with talk about consciousness or intention" (Heyes 1987a, p. 124). Thus, Heyes denies that evidence gained by observing animals in natural settings, an activity that usually involves using some sort of visual aid such as field glasses, is particularly relevant to understanding animal minds. Other slayers, who claim that they need more convincing evidence from the field, rarely tell what evidence would be convincing (Colgan 1989, p. 67). Heyes and these other critics generally simply assume that no evidence that could be collected from the field would provide convincing support for attributions of mental states.

Unlike Heyes, who thinks that animal cognition can at least be studied in the laboratory, some slayers argue against the study of animal cognition on the basis of a philosophical view about the privacy of the mental (for a well-developed counterargument see Whiten 1993) or the related "other minds" problem. These critics typically do not give specific critiques of actual empirical investigations carried out by cognitive ethologists; rather, they try to dismiss such investigations on philosophical grounds alone. Thus, the renowned evolutionary biologist George C. Williams (1992, p. 4), writes, "I am inclined merely to delete [the mental realm] from biological explanation, because it is an entirely private phenomenon, and biology must deal with the publicly demonstrable." Williams' argument goes like this: (1) Mental events are private phenomena. (2) Private phenomena cannot be studied biologically. (3) Therefore, mental events cannot be studied biologically. (4) Cognitive ethology is possible only if mental events can be studied biologically. (5) Therefore, cognitive ethology is not possible. When analyzed in this way, Williams' argument is seen to depend on a contentious philosophical premise (1).

Slayers often base their arguments on claims about the privacy of the mental or skepticism about other minds. It is ironic that these premises, which can be defended only in nonempirical, philosophical fashion, are produced by critics who would typically regard themselves as hard-nosed empiricists. Cognitive ethologists do empirical work, yet slayers who argue on such philosophical grounds rarely analyze that empirical work to see what it is designed to show and whether it in fact shows what it is designed to show. Instead, they base their arguments on claims that are at least as fraught with interpretive difficulty as the cognitive conclusions they wish to deny. This unwillingness to engage in debate about the actual empirical work of cognitive ethologists gives the impression that many slayers simply barge in, declare victory, and get out without genuinely engaging cognitive ethologists in a dialogue about their work. Williams does not stand alone. For example, McFarland (1989, p. 146) wonders if we are designed by natural selection to assume that deceitful acts are intentional, and Kennedy (1992, p. 167) claims that the sin of anthropomorphism is programmed into us genetically.[2] If either or both is the case, how are we to know? These claims make for empirical questions that require detailed study.

Other tactics used by some slayers involve grounding their criticisms on very narrow bases. Cronin thinks that Griffin, a "sentimental softy," and other cognitive ethologists are only concerned with demonstrating cleverness, and hence consciousness. In her recent review of Griffin's *Animal Minds* (1992) she writes:

"A Griffin bat is a miniature physics lab. So imagine the consternation among behavioristic ethologists when Mr. Griffin came out a decade ago, with "The Question of Animal Awareness," as a sentimental softy. . . . For Mr. Griffin, all this [cleverness] *suggests* consciousness. He's wrong. If such cleverness were enough to *demonstrate* consciousness, scientists could do the job over coffee and philosophers could have packed up their scholarly apparatus years ago. (p. 14; my emphases)

Even McFarland (1989), who is categorized as a slayer by Bekoff and Allen (1996), recognizes that there are indicators of cognition other than the ability to produce clever solutions to environmental problems. Furthermore, not only is Cronin wrong about slaying the field of cognitive ethology because of the difficulty of dealing with the notion of consciousness (think about all of the other fields of inquiry that would suffer if it were appropriate to base rejection of those fields on singling out their most difficult issues), but she is also wrong to think that demonstrating cleverness is a simple matter. Certainly the difficult work needed to demonstrate cleverness could not be done over coffee! Cronin also conveniently slides from claiming that for Griffin cleverness *suggests* consciousness to claiming that his view is that cleverness is "enough to *demonstrate* consciousness" (my emphasis).

Even Heyes (1987b) notes that it is not Griffin's program to *prove* that animals are conscious. Cronin later goes on to claim that at least chimpanzees are conscious and tells us why. She concludes her scathing review with the following statement: "Well, I know that I am conscious, I know a mere 500,000 generations separate me from my chimpanzee cousin, and I know that evolutionary innovations don't just spring into existence full-blown—certainly not innovations as truly momentous as our hauntingly elusive private world." Cronin places herself on a slippery slope here. Why did she stop with chimpanzees? After all, if evolutionary innovations do not spring into existence full-blown, where did chimpanzee consciousness come from? Her phylogenetic argument cannot be assessed directly; behavioral evidence is needed to help it along.

Skeptics

Skeptics are often difficult to categorize. They are a bit more open-minded than slayers, and there seems to be greater variation among skeptical views of cognitive ethology than among slayers' opinions. However, some skeptics recognize some past and present successes in cognitive ethology and remain cautiously optimistic about future successes; in these instances they resemble moderate proponents. Many skeptics appeal to the future of neuroscience and claim that, when we know all there is to know about nervous systems, cognitive ethology will be superfluous. (Griffin [1992] also makes strong appeals to neuroscience, but he does not fear that increased knowledge in neurobiology will cause cognitive ethology to disappear.) Like slayers, skeptics frequently conflate the difficulty of doing rigorous cognitive ethological investigations with the impossibility of doing so but, when it is shown that some light can be shed on the nature of animal cognition, they often hedge their skepticism. Skeptics find folk psychological, anthropomorphic, anecdotal, and cognitive explanations to be off-putting, but they are not as forcefully dismissive as slayers. Some specific examples of the skeptics' position are as follows.

With respect to the types of explanations that are offered in studies of animal cognition, many slayers and some skeptics favor noncognitive explanations because they believe them more parsimonious and more accurate than cognitive alternatives, and also less off-putting to others who do not hold the field of cognitive ethology in high esteem. Snowdon (1991, p. 814) claims that "it is possible to explore the cognitive capacities of nonhuman animals without recourse to mentalistic concepts such as consciousness, intentionality, and deception. Studies that avoid mentalistic terminology are likely to be more effective in convincing other scientists of the significance of the abilities of nonhuman animals." Beer (1992, p. 79) also thinks that, if cognitive ethology limited its claims for animal awareness to sensation and perception, a practice that could change the vocabulary used in cognitive ethological studies, then "even tough-minded critics would be more receptive." Griffin (1992, p. 11) actually agrees with this point, but even a consideration of simple forms of consciousness is contentious to many slayers and skeptics (Bekoff 1993a; Bekoff and Allen 1996). Michel (1991, p. 253) is also concerned about folk psychological explanations. He writes, "folk psychological theory pervades human thinking, remembering, and perceiving and creates a very subtle anthropomorphism that *can* corrupt the formation of a science of cognitive ethology" (my emphasis).

Some skeptics simply make vacuous claims about the supposed parsimoniousness of noncognitive explanations and move on. Thus, Zabel et al. (1992, p. 129), in their attempts to explain redirected aggression is spotted hyenas *(Crocuta crocuta) before* quantitatively analyzing it, are of the opinion that "one must be cautious about inferring complex cognitive processes when simpler explanations will suffice." They do not tell us why they believe this to be so, and it should be noted that even they admit that the other noncognitive explanations they offer are questionable. Appeals to parsimony on a case-by-case basis do not take into account the possibility that cognitive explanations might help scientists come to terms with larger sets of available data that are difficult to understand and also help in the design of future empirical work. (For further discussion of the weakness of the idea that the simplest explanation is always the most parsimonious, see Bennett [1991]. For a comparison of different perspectives of cognitive "versus" more parsimonious explanations, see proponent de Waal's [1991] consideration of the views of skeptics Kummer, Dasser, and Hoyningen-Huene [1990] on parsimony.)

With respect to the difficulties in studying consciousness, Alcock (1992) is a notable example in that he does not find the inaccessibility of consciousness grounds for dismissing the study of animal cognition (as does Cronin [1992]; see also Whiten's 1993 discussion of the importance of studying observable events in studies of animal cognition). Alcock writes:

We need ways in which to test hypotheses in a convincing manner. In this regard *Animal Minds* disappoints, because it offers no practical guidance on how to test whether consciousness is an all-purpose, problem-solving device widely distributed throughout the animal kingdom. . . . And there are alternative approaches to consciousness not based on the behavioristic principle that thinking cannot be studied because it does not exist. (Alcock 1992, p. 63)

Others find the intractability of the problems of studying intentionality, awareness, and conscious thinking to be prohibitive for establishing the importance of mental experiences in determining animal behavior (Yoerg and Kamil 1991, p. 273).

Proponents

Proponents keep an open mind about animal cognition and the utility of cognitive ethological investigations, (e.g., Cheney and Seyfarth 1990, 1992; Allen and Hauser 1991; Burghardt 1991; de Waal 1991; Ristau 1991a; Allen 1992a, b; Bekoff and Allen 1992; Bekoff 1993a; Bekoff, Townsend, and Jamieson 1994; Jamieson and Bekoff 1993; Whiten 1993).[3] They claim that there are already many successes, and they see that cognitive ethological approaches have provided new and interesting data that also can inform and motivate further study. Proponents also accept the cautious use of folk psychological and cognitive explanations to build a systematic explanatory framework in conjunction with empirical studies, and they do not find anecdote or anthropomorphism thoroughly off-putting. While proponents recognize that Griffin has not made detailed suggestions for experimental studies, this does not discourage them from seeking ways to make ideas like Griffin's empirically rigorous (Allen and Hauser 1991; de Waal 1991; Ristau 1991a; Allen 1992a, b; Whiten 1992; Bekoff 1993a). Proponents are critical, but patient, and they do not want prematurely to doom the field; if cognitive ethology is to die, it will be of natural causes and not as a result of hasty slayings.

This quotation of William Mason (1976, p. 931) from his review of Griffin's (1976) *The Question of Animal Awareness* is a good place to start with respect to proponents' views. Mason writes, "That animals are aware can scarcely be questioned. The hows and the whys and wherefores will occupy scientists for many years to come." Mason's claim is a strong one. Note that, in his endorsement of the field, Mason does not qualify his statement by writing, "That *some* animals are aware. . . ." However, he does recognize that animals may differ with respect to levels of development of their cognitive abilities, and at a later date he noted that "on the basis of findings such as those reviewed in this paper, I am persuaded that apes and man have entered into a cognitive domain that sets them apart from all other primates" (Mason 1979, pp. 292–293). Mason's inclusive statement about animal awareness is typical of those who narrowly focus their attention only on primate cognition (Beck 1982; Bekoff 1993a; Bekoff, Townsend, and Jamieson 1994).

Proponents are more optimistic in their views about the contributions that the field of cognitive ethology and its reliance on field work and on comparative ecological and evolutionary studies can make to the study of animal cognition in terms of opening up new areas of research and reconsidering old data. Ristau (1991b, p. 102) notes that, in her attempts to study injury feigning under field conditions, the cognitive ethological perspective "led me to design experiments that I had not otherwise thought to do, that no one else had done, and that revealed complexities in the behavior of the piping plover's distraction display not heretofore appreciated." The challenge of using ethological ideas in the study of animal cognition is reflected in the following quotation:

At this point, . . . cognitive ethologists can console themselves with the knowledge that their discipline is an aspect of the broader field of cognitive studies and conceptually may not be in any worse shape than highly regarded, related fields such as cognitive psychology. We are a long way from understanding the natural history of the mind, but in our view this amounts to a scientific challenge rather that grounds for depression or dismissal. (Jamieson and Bekoff 1992a, p. 81)

Proponents also share some of the concerns of the slayers and skeptics with respect to problems associated with the use of anecdote, anthropomorphism, and folk psychological explanations. However, proponents claim that the careful use of anthropomorphic and folk psychological explanations can be helpful in the study of animal cognition, and they also maintain that anecdotes can be used to guide data collection and to suggest new experimental designs (Dennett 1987, 1991, pp. 446ff). Thus, other proponents write:

Cognitive ethology, rescued from both behaviorism and subjectivism, has much to say about what the life of the animal is really like. It is silent on what it is like to have that life. (Gustafson 1986, p. 182)

I have advocated use of a critical anthropomorphism in which various sources of information are used including: natural history, our perceptions, intuitions, feelings, careful behavioral descriptions, identifying with the animal, optimization models, previous studies and so forth in order to generate ideas that may prove useful in gaining understanding and the ability to predict outcomes of planned (experimental) and unplanned interventions. (Burghardt 1991, p. 73)

When a number of anecdotal examples, each with a possible alternative explanation, collectively point to the likelihood of intentional deception, and this is supported by more rigorous tests in the laboratory . . . I would argue that it adds up to a strong case. (Archer 1992, p. 224)

Perhaps some would assume that Griffin is the strongest proponent of cognitive ethology. However, toward the end of *Animal Minds* Griffin (1992, p. 260) writes, "Contrary to the widespread pessimistic opinion that the content of animal thinking is hopelessly inaccessible to scientific inquiry, the communicative signals used by many animals provide empirical data on the basis of which much *can reasonably be inferred* about their subjective experiences" (my emphasis). Note that Griffin counters some slayers' and skeptics' concerns about the inaccessibility of animal minds, but he does not make a very strong claim that he or others can ever know the content of animal minds. Rather, Griffin, like other proponents, remains open to the possibility that we can learn a lot about animal minds by carefully studying communication and other behavior patterns. He and other proponents want to make the field of cognitive ethology more rigorous on theoretical and empirical grounds.

In summary, as a field of inquiry, cognitive ethology need not model itself on other scientific fields such as physics or neurobiology in order to gain some credibility or to acquire status as a respectable branch of science. Physics (or hard science) envy is what led to the loss of animal minds (Rollin 1990; Bekoff 1992a) in the early part of the 20th century. Now, after a successful battle against those who were content to study behavior in the absence of animal minds, there are ample data that strongly support the idea that many nonhuman animals do have minds. Thus, we should continue studying animal minds and not have to begin to search for them once again. Those who believe that cognitive ethology is not worthy of being called a science seem to have an impoverished conception of science; many different types of activity fall under the umbrella "science."

FOLK PSYCHOLOGY, COGNITIVE ETHOLOGY, AND BELIEFS ABOUT THE FUTURE OF NEUROSCIENCE

Because folk psychological explanations are so off-putting to slayers and some skeptics, a bit more needs to be said about these sorts of explanations and how they are related to cognitive ethological research. Folk psychological explanations, usually referred to as the ways in which common folk talk about the world in their daily dealings with one another, can be useful parts of cognitive ethological explanations. Folk psychological explanations that appeal to beliefs and desires of and about things, while not necessarily true, often help to provide the best explanation (*sensu* Harman 1965) of observed behavior (see below; see also Cling 1991). I fully agree with Mason (1986) that common sense is not a serious risk for contemporary behavioral science. Thus, while folk psychological explanations play a role in the successful prediction of animal behavior and in many cases do the explanatory work, they do not replace detailed empirical studies concerning the content of animal beliefs and desires; rather, folk psychological explanations need to be used along with these endeavors. Thinking about different levels of analysis and explanation might be useful for seeing how different sorts of explanations are related to one another (figure 7.1).

With respect to cognitive ethology, it is those who are skeptical regarding whether nonhumans (and even humans) have beliefs and desires of or about things—that is, behave intentionally—who are very critical of folk psychological explanations. One name that is frequently associated with a strong skepticism concerning the role of folk psychology in explaining animal beliefs is Stephen Stich (1979, 1983; for further discussion see M. A. Levvis 1992). Stich provides detailed arguments for his views,

Different Levels of Analysis and Explanation of Nonhuman Behavior (Jethro is a dog)

1. **Observations and descriptions of behavior**$_{\text{Jethro (J)}}$ inform us about the possibility of there being
2. **mental states**$_J$ **and beliefs**$_J$ (*cognitive ethology*) that lead to attempts to ascribe
3. **content to beliefs**$_J$ (*folk psychological explanations*) that lead to attempts to discover more about the
4. **neural bases of beliefs**$_J$ (*mature neuroscientific explanations*) that lead to attempts to learn more about the
5. **molecular biology of beliefs**$_J$ (*more mature explanations*).

Some Questions

A. How do we go from 1 to 5 and from 5 to 1?

B. Is there some sort of orderly mapping of environmental and mental events in the nervous system?

C. Is 5 "better" than 1? Do we gain more control and increase the certainty with which we can offer more precise causal explanations as we deal with smaller pieces of the puzzle?

D. Why should we wait for a mature neuroscience? Why can we not also expect to learn more if we wait for a mature cognitive ethology?

Figure 7.1

but in some sense he really does not see folk psychological explanations as problematic to cognitive ethology, since we cannot precisely ascribe content to the beliefs of animals, they have no beliefs at all. Thus, there is nothing for folk psychology to explain, because we cannot fill in the blank in the following statement: "Jethro believes that———." However, Stich is not as unequivocal as he often is said to be. For example, he concludes his 1979 paper entitled "Do animals have beliefs?" as follows (p. 28): "Do animals have beliefs? To paraphrase my young son: 'A little bit they do. And a little bit they don't'." While Stich believes that folk psychology does not play a role in a mature and empirical cognitive science, the conclusion of his 1979 paper, which is cited as supporting the claim that animals do not have beliefs, seems to leave at least a little room for interpretation.

Beer (1992) also does not think that Stich's case against folk psychology is necessarily compelling. However, Beer is concerned with the framing and grounding of questions in cognitive ethology in folk psychology because of the weakness of some of the philosophical underpinnings of folk psychology. For the reasons given above, I do not think that Beer should be as troubled as he is (see also Sober 1983).

Like folk psychological explanations, "scientific" explanations also enjoy successes and failures. For example, scientists still disagree, even with hard data, over whether global warming has occurred and, if so, whether global warming can be explained by what is called the greenhouse effect (e.g., Lindzen 1990). Scientists also disagree about whether vitamin C is useful in treatment of the common cold. Nonetheless, folk psychological explanations of nonhuman behavior are often viewed as scientifically weak or even ascientific. Generally, the theory of folk psychology is usually dismissed as being explanatorily weak, historically stagnating, and conceptually isolated (Churchland 1979, 1981). It usually is argued that folk psychological explanations are inexact and will be replaced in the future by a more mature and exact neuroscience, although in everyday life folk psychology can be helpful (Churchland 1981).

It is beyond the scope of this chapter to consider all of the pros and cons of folk psychology in any detail (see Clark 1989; Bogdan 1991; Greenwood 1991; Heil 1992; Christensen and Turner 1993); most of the arguments, especially those against folk psychology, have very deep philosophical roots, some of which might benefit from a good watering. However, a few words can be said about the nature of the arguments that are used either to refute the utility of folk psychological explanations or to claim that, while they may be of some limited use now, they will be replaced when we know all that there is to know about neuroscience. Such arguments suggest an extreme, almost religious-like faith, in the ability of science to handle difficult problems such as animal minds, and in this and other areas such faith may be wishful thinking (Heil 1992; Moussa and Shannon 1992). Indeed, arguments against folk psychology that appeal to neuroscience have their own weaknesses (Cling 1990; Gilman 1990; Saidel 1992). While it will be useful to learn more and more about nervous systems in analyses of different types of animal cognition (e.g., Howlett 1993), the hope that this knowledge will clear up all of the messy issues in cognitive ethology seems a bit lofty (Akins 1990; see also Brunjes 1992 for some worries about commonly used methods in the study of neurobiology and behavior). While it may happen that someday neuroscientists will be able to map an animal's beliefs in its nervous system, it will probably have to be in a very simple nervous system. Thus, it might be possible that this individual's beliefs are nothing like our beliefs, or even similar to those of animals to whom we might feel comfortable attributing beliefs.

One major problem with the arguments put forth by those who appeal to the future of neuroscience is that appeals to the future require us to wait and keep waiting for events that might never occur. Here, too, personal opinions concerning just what science can do enter (not surprisingly) into how folk psychology is viewed. It is important to ask a few questions here. For example, how patient should we be? Should we dispense with what we now know about the behavior of nonhumans, explanations of which rely on the careful use of folk psychology, until skeptics are satisfied that they are right and proponents of folk psychology are wrong? How will we know when we have a mature neuroscience? Will it be the time when neuroscience answers the questions that some want answers to in a way with which they feel comfortable? Why cannot skeptics be asked to wait for a mature cognitive ethology? When these questions are answered, we will be able to assess the utility of folk psychological explanations. Indeed, one thing that is convenient about future talk is that the future can always be put off until we like what it brings. We will not know what the future will bring until we get there (Akins 1990). Of course, appealing to the future of cognitive ethology is as nebulous as appealing to the future of neuroscience.

In summary, it is important to continually assess the relationships among (1) how much we know or think we know about certain aspects of an individual's behavior, (2) how much explanatory power there is in the sentences and the data that we use to demonstrate our ability to use this knowledge to make predictions about behavior, and (3) how much tolerance we are asking for in using folk psychological explanations. Social play behavior and vigilance against intruders (potential predators) are two areas in which folk psychological explanations, along with empirical data, provide valuable insights into animal cognition. These areas of research will be discussed in the next section.

SOCIAL PLAY AND ANTIPREDATORY VIGILANCE: WHAT MIGHT INDIVIDUALS KNOW ABOUT THEMSELVES AND OTHERS?

Space does not allow me to cover the plethora of areas of research (e.g., food caching, individual recognition and discrimination, assessments of dominance, habitat selection, mate choice, teaching, imitation, communication, tool use, injury feigning, observational learning) in which cognitive ethological approaches have been or could be useful in gaining an understanding of the behavior of nonhumans.[4] Here I will discuss the communication of play intention and antipredatory vigilance, because empirical research in both of these areas has benefited or will benefit from a cognitive approach. Furthermore, in both areas (and others) folk psychological explanations have been useful for informing and motivating further research and have also turned out to be very good predictors of behavior.

The Communication of Play Intention

Social play is a behavior that lends itself nicely to cognitive studies and poses a great challenge to slayers, skeptics, and proponents alike (de Waal 1991; but see Rosenberg 1990 and Allen and Bekoff 1994; numerous references about play can be found in Bekoff and Byers 1981; Fagen, 1981; Bekoff 1989; Mitchell 1990; Bekoff and Allen 1992). Play may provide more promising evidence of animal minds than many other areas. Furthermore, understanding activities such as play is important for developing new research dealing with comparative approaches to cognition (Caudill 1992, p. 5). It would have been unfortunate if people had decided that, just because play was difficult to study, it was impossible to study.

When animals play, they typically use action patterns that are also used in other contexts such as predatory behavior, antipredatory behavior, and mating. Thus, it has been argued that social play behavior cannot be studied without using a cognitive vocabulary (Jamieson and Bekoff 1993). For example, if you were merely told that Jethro and Henrietta were performing a series of movements and these movements were described with respect to anatomy, you would not know that they were playing or that they were engaging in an activity that they probably enjoyed; for that matter, you could not know what they were doing for play is typically composed of motor patterns that are also used in a variety of other contexts (for a discussion see Golani 1992; Bekoff 1992b).

Because play is typically composed of motor patterns that are also used in a variety of other contexts, an individual needs to be able to communicate to potential play partners that he is not trying to dominate them, eat them, or mate with them. Rather, he is trying to play with them. Behavioral observations of many animals who engage in social play suggest that they desire to do so and believe that their thoughts of the future—how the individuals to whom their intentions are directed will be likely to behave—will be realized if they clearly communicate their desires to play using signals that in some cases seem to have evolved specifically to communicate play intention. According to this view, play is seen as a cooperative enterprise.

In most species in which play has been described, play-soliciting signals appear to foster some sort of cooperation between players so that each responds to the other in a way consistent with play and different from the responses the same actions would elicit in other contexts (Bekoff 1975, 1978); play-soliciting signals aid the interpretation of other signals by the receiver (Hailman 1977, p. 266). For example, in coyotes the response to a threat gesture made *after* a play signal given immediately preceding the threat or in the beginning of an interaction is different from the response to a threat gesture made in the absence of any preceding play signal (Bekoff 1975). The play signal somehow alters the meaning of a threat signal by establishing (or maintaining) a "play mood." Unfortunately, there have been no other similar quantitative studies to the best of my knowledge, but observations of play in diverse species support the idea that play signals can, and do, establish play moods and alter the significance of behavior patterns that are borrowed from other contexts and used in social play.

Let us consider in more detail the question of whether signals that appear to be used to communicate play intention (play-soliciting signals) to other individuals (Symons 1974; Bekoff 1975, 1977, 1978; 1995a; Bekoff and Byers 1981; Fagen 1981) can foster the cooperation among participants that is necessary for play to occur. It is assumed that such play-soliciting signals transmit messages such as "What follows is play," "This is still play," or "Let's play again; wasn't it fun?" (The latter two messages may be sent after a very short break or after rough play has occurred.) Supporting evidence concerning the importance of play signals for allowing cooperative social play comes from studies in which it has been shown that play-soliciting signals show little variability in form or temporal characteristics and that they are used almost solely in the context of play. For example, one action that is commonly observed in the context of social play among canids is the "bow," during which an individual crouches (as if bowing) on her forelimbs while keeping her hindlimbs relatively straight; tail wagging and barking may accompany the bow. In various canids, the bow is a highly stereotyped movement that seems to function to stimulate recipients to engage (or to continue to engage) in social play (Bekoff 1977). Furthermore, the first bows that very young canids have been observed to perform are highly stereotyped, and learning seems to be relatively unimportant in their development. These features of bows can be related to the fact that, when engaging in social play, canids typically use action patterns that are also used in other contexts, such as predatory behavior, agonistic encounters, or mating, where misinterpretation of play intention could be injurious.

Available data strongly suggest that play-soliciting actions seem to be used to communicate to others that actions such as biting, biting and shaking of the head from side to side, and mounting are to be taken as play and not as aggression, predation, or reproduction (for details see Bekoff and Byers 1981 and Fagen 1981). On this view, bows are performed when the signaler wants to communicate a specific message about her desires or beliefs. How intentional explanations of different orders (Dennett 1983) might be related to the communication of social play is shown as follows:

Order of Explanation	General Explanation	Explanation with Respect to Play Behavior
zero-order	J performs behavior	J performs bow
first-order	J *believes* p J *wants* p	J *wants* H to play with him
second-order	J *wants* H to *believe* that x	J *wants* H to *believe* that H should play with him
third-order	J *wants* H to *believe* that J *wants* x	J *wants* H to *believe* that J *wants* H to play

While we cannot be sure that two dogs, for example, are engaging in first- or second-order intentional behavior, some data suggest this possibility. For example, suppose we wanted to know why Henrietta permitted Jethro to nip at her ears. One explanation may be that Henrietta believes Jethro is playing. This gives rise to further questions, such as whether Jethro believes that Henrietta believes that Jethro is playing.

Providing answers to questions such as these is one of the challenges of research in cognitive ethology.

Some other characteristics of play bows and some of the properties of social play support a cognitive explanation of play and can be used to stimulate future research. For example, play bows themselves occur throughout play sequences, but usually at the beginning or toward the middle of playful encounters. In a detailed analysis of the form and duration of play bows (Bekoff 1977), it has been shown that duration is more variable than form and that play bows are always less variable when performed at the beginning, rather than in the middle, of ongoing play sequences. Recall, too, that the first play bows very young canids have been observed to perform are highly stereotyped and that learning seems to be relatively unimportant in their development. One can ask why bows performed during play sequences are more variable than bows performed at the beginning of play sequences. Right now I can only offer some possibilities that need to be pursued empirically. Thus, bows performed during play bouts may be more variable (1) because of fatigue, (2) because of the fact that animals are performing them from a wide variety of preceding postures, and/or (3) because there is less of a need to communicate that this is still play than there was when trying to initiate a new interaction.

Analyses of play sequences may also inform future studies of social play. For example, in intraspecific comparisons it has been found that sequences of social play are usually more variable than sequences of nonplay behavior (Bekoff and Byers 1981). Is it possible that animals "read" differences in behavioral sequences that are performed during play and in other contexts? Might increased (or consistent variations in) variability in sequences also (along with play signals) convey the message "This is play" and enable individuals to predict what is likely to occur or to understand what has already occurred?

Future Research

A cognitive perspective will be very useful in future analyses of social play. Some of my own thoughts of the future direction of empirical research center on learning more about what a bowing (or soliciting) dog, for example, expects to happen after (or even as) she performs what is called a play-soliciting signal. Comparative observations strongly suggest that she expects that play will ensue if she performs a bow; she acts as if she wants play to occur. On what sorts of grounds is this claim based? Specifically, it looks as if the dog is frustrated or surprised when her bow is not reciprocated in a way that is consistent with her belief about what is most likely to occur—namely, social play. Dogs and other canids are extremely persistent in their attempts to get others to play with them; their persistence suggests a strong desire to engage in some sort of activity. Frustration may be inferred from the common observation that canids and other mammals often engage in some sort of self-play, such as tail chasing, after a bow or other play-soliciting signal is ignored, or they rapidly run over to another potential individual and try to get that individual to play; play is redirected to the signaler herself or to other individuals.

Surprise is more difficult to deal with, but often my students and I have agreed that a dog or coyote looked surprised when, on very rare occasion, a bow resulted in the recipient's attacking the signaler. The soliciting animal's eyes opened widely, her tail dropped, and she rapidly turned away from the noncooperating animal to whom she had directed a play-soliciting signal, as if what had happened was totally unexpected and perhaps confusing. (See also Tinklepaugh's [1928] observation of surprise in monkeys when an expected and favored piece of food was replaced with lettuce.) After moving away, the surprised animal often looked at the other individual, cocked her head to one side, squinted, furrowed her brow, and seemed to be saying, "Are you kidding? I want to play; this is not what I wanted to happen." The concept of surprise and the having of beliefs may be closely tied together. For example, if Jethro believes that social play will occur after performing a bow (p), then he will be surprised to discover that social play does not occur after performing a bow (not p, -p). If he is surprised to discover that -p, then he comes to believe that his original belief was false. This involves his having the second-order belief that his first-order belief was false, which involves having the concept of belief.

With respect to the solicitor's beliefs about the future, detailed analyses of movie film also show that on some occasions a soliciting animal begins to perform another behavior *before* the other animal commits himself. The solicitor behaves as if she expects that something specific will happen and commits herself to this course of action. The major question, then, is how to operationalize these questions: What would be convincing data? How do we know when we have an instance of a given behavior(s)? Thus, we need to consider questions such as these: What is frustrated? What is the goal? What is the belief about? How could we study these questions? There is simply no substitute for detailed descriptions of subtle behavior patterns that might indicate surprise—facial expressions, eye movements, and body postures.

In summary, studies of social play are challenging and fascinating; I have been doing research on social play in canids for over 20 years, and there are many questions to which I do not have satisfactory answers. The cognitive approach has helped me to come to terms with old data and has also raised new questions that need to be studied empirically.

Antipredator Vigilance

Most animals are both predators and prey (Lima 1990). Thus, there is some conflict between avoiding being eaten and eating. Scanning for predators is called vigilance behavior, and in studies of vigilance it is generally assumed, for simplicity's sake, that individuals compromise their ability to detect predators when feeding with their heads down and compromise their food intake when scanning for predators with their heads up (see Lima 1990, figure 1, p. 247). Thus, it has been argued that there are good reasons for individuals to live—or at least to forage for food—in groups if doing so increases the probability of detecting a predator or reduces the time spent scanning for predators, thus permitting more time to be spent doing other things. Not surprisingly, there has been a lot of interest in antipredatory vigilance among those interested in the evolution of social behavior, and many different aspects of this behavior pattern have been analyzed, mainly in birds and in a few mammals (Pulliam 1973; Bertram 1978; Lazarus 1979, 1990; Elgar 1989; Rasa 1989; Dehn 1990; Lima 1990; Lima and Dill 1990; Quenette 1990).

A very popular question in the comparative study of vigilance is How does the behavior of individuals vary in groups of different sizes? Generally, it has been found that there is a negative relationship between group size and rates of scanning by individuals and a positive relationship between group size and the probability of predator detection. This is because in large groups there are more eyes and perhaps other sense organs that can be used to scan for predators. In his comprehensive review, Elgar (1989) notes that, although the negative relationship between group size and individual scanning rate is quite robust and is approaching the status of dogma (Lima 1990), few studies have actually controlled for confounding variables, such as variation in the density and type of food resources, group composition, ambient temperature and time of day, proximity to a safe place and to the observer, visibility within the habitat, and group composition (see also Lima 1990 and Lima and Dill 1990).

There are also problems associated with the researcher's ability to really know whether an individual is actually scanning; behavioral data can be equivocal, and attention must also be given to anatomical and physiological constraints. (The same can be said for the relationship between predator detection and escape: in the absence of any discernible response, it is impossible to know whether an individual has detected a predator, and it is possible that a prey may be aware of a predator(s) before he decides to flee; see Ydenberg and Dill 1986.) With respect to whether an individual is really being vigilant, Lazarus (1990, p. 65) notes that "researchers have simply assumed that the behaviour in question is vigilant, and have then sought its function." It is important to stress that such adaptive and evolutionary tales are not necessarily any more plausible than explanations of nonhuman behavior that invoke notions such as intentionality. In both instances convincing data may still be lacking, and a lot of faith is placed in folk explanations.

In the future, experimental cognitive studies will help to answer many questions that have either been ignored or have arisen in previous studies of antipredator vigilance. Of course, these studies must adhere to the strictest guidelines with respect to ethical considerations (Bekoff and

Jamieson 1991; Bekoff et al. 1992). Perhaps in some instances it will be the case that the coordination of vigilance among group members is not cost effective (Ward 1985), but there are not enough data now to make any sweeping generalizations. In his review Lima (1990) notes that there seem to have been no studies that have directly examined the question of whether foragers pay any attention to the behavior of other group members. He concludes that very little is known about the perceptions of the animals being studied and that many models of vigilance reflect mainly the perceptions of the modelers themselves (p. 262).

I will assume here that the negative relationship between group size and individual scanning rate is a genuine one and ask a number of cognitive questions that bear on this general finding. Furthermore, although cooperation in vigilance is not to be expected, I will argue that, although individuals do not sign binding contracts (Lima 1990) and although cheating could occur, the evidence at hand does not refute the possibility of cooperation among at least some group members (see also Lima 1990, p. 262). Although Dehn (1990) does not suggest any explicit reasons for individuals to cooperate in collective group vigilance, he notes that even if they live in large groups (> 10 individuals), individuals might benefit in terms of lifetime fitness if they are somewhat vigilant.

A cognitive analysis of vigilance in which we are concerned with what an individual might know about itself and others would involve asking at least the following questions, all of which are interconnected and all of which lend themselves to empirical study. One major question is Why does the relationship between group size and scanning rates fail where it is to be expected to hold? Another question to which I will also return is this: Is there some association between the degree of coordination or possibly cooperation among group members and the geometry of the group? To the best of my knowledge, these questions have not been pursued rigorously. For some of the questions I am asking and for some of the analyses I am suggesting, it easier to assume that there is some stability in the composition of the groups, although some models would allow for individuals to learn about general behavior patterns of other individuals regardless of who they are. I will discuss this in more detail later. Some of the questions that I pose here are not directly related to a cognitive inquiry, but all can inform and motivate such an approach.
1. What is a group to a nonhuman? To a human? What does it mean to say that an individual is a member of a group, and is our conception of group the same as that of animals? Questions that inform the conception of group membership include these: What types of behavioral criteria can be used to assess if an individual thinks he is a member of a group? Is there a critical distance between individuals below which we can say with some degree of certainty that they are members of the same group? Do individuals have to spend a certain amount of time together within a certain distance to justify calling them a group? With respect to studies

of vigilance, Elgar, Burren, and Posen (1984) found that a house sparrow who was in visual contact with other house sparrows but separated by 1.2 meters scanned as if she was alone. I am presently pursuing the use of mirrors to help to answer this question.

Other questions also arise. For example, we also need to ask How do we measure group size, and how might nonhumans measure group size? This question deserves special consideration on its own because, even if we can come up with a working definition of group, we also need to be able to present measures of instantaneous and long-term effective group size. In studies of vigilance (and other activities), variations in group size are often used to explain variation in other patterns of behavior, such as individual scanning rates, so precise measurements of group size are essential.

2. Does the size of a group or the geometric distribution or orientation of individuals influence individual vigilance? I have already mentioned the often-found relationship between group size and scanning rates. However, it is important to keep in mind that there are confounding variables, such as the geometric relationships among group members (or neighboring birds (figure 7.2) and how individuals are oriented in space, that might influence scanning rates of individuals. Answers to the question How does the geometric distribution of individuals influence individual vigilance? will likely have something to say about animal cognitive abilities. Thus, while it is known that the location of an individual in her

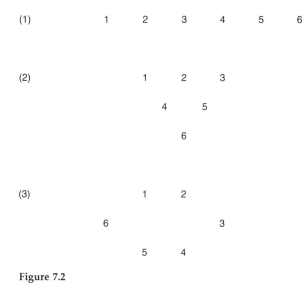

Some Possible Geometric Distributions of Six Individuals

When individuals are organized differently in space—for example, in a straight line rather than in a circle—it may be more difficult for them to see one another. Thus, spatial distribution might influence individual scanning rates based on what an individual can and cannot see. The orientation of individuals also needs to be considered.

(1)   1   2   3   4   5   6

(2)   1   2   3
              4   5
              6

(3)   1   2
         6   3
           5   4

Figure 7.2

Cognitive Ethology and Nonhuman Animal Behavior

group (center or periphery) can influence her pattern of vigilance, it remains to be studied how the geometry of the whole group influences the ease with which an individual is able to assess what others are doing by seeing or hearing them (and to relate their behavior to her own). For example, it seems that it would be easier to see what others were doing if individuals were organized in a circle rather than in a straight line, but this is not known. Since this chapter was completed in February 1993, data have been collected that show that flock geometry does influence scanning and other behavior patterns (Bekoff 1995b). Determining how each variable singly and in combination with others influences scanning is important so that we can determine the precise role of group size itself in influencing individual patterns of vigilance (Elgar 1989).

Questions such as How does a bird or other nonhuman assess group geometry? also need to be considered. While it is known that in some species group structure changes in response to the presence of a predator (Lima and Dill 1990, p. 627), it is not known if and how an individual actually assesses the geometry of the group of which she is a member.

3. Do changes in group size or geometry influence patterns of social interactions? It is possible that, as group size and geometry change, either singly or together, there is also a change in how individuals interact. If this is the case, then it might be possible for an individual to gain information about these variables from changes in encounter patterns without having to read them directly (e.g., Gordon, Paul, and Thorpe 1992; see also Deneubourg and Goss 1989 and Warburton and Lazarus 1991). To the best of my knowledge, there are no data for birds or mammals that can be used to answer these questions with any degree of certainty. Of course, the problems in studying these questions are enormous, but trying to get answers to them should be an exciting venture.

Some other interesting questions that may be informed by a cognitive approach include these: Do individuals change their relative positions in a group to make it more likely for them to feed more efficiently and/or detect potential predators more easily? Is this a cooperative endeavor? Does one's position in a group influence whether she can assess changes in group size or geometry? Here I am asking if and how the location of an individual in a group makes it easier or more difficult for her to know how many other individuals are there and how they are distributed in space. It might be very useful for an individual to be able to see what others are doing because, while scanning, an individual might also pick up and store information about what individuals in a particular part of the group are most likely to be doing, or she might generalize from her own previous experience in that part of the group what others are most likely to be doing when they are in that position. If we can get answers to these sorts of questions, we might be able to assess if it possible that the inverse relationship between group size and individual scanning rate levels off or fails because individuals are unable to monitor the behavior of too many other animals who might also be hard to see. Elgar, Burren, and Posen (1984) and Metcalfe (1984a, b) present data suggesting that in some birds there seems to be visual inspection among individuals in a flock.

The results of cognitive studies of vigilance would not only be useful for furthering our knowledge about antipredatory scanning, but would also inform and motivate other studies (e.g., assessments of dominance) that are concerned with the question of how individuals assess what they know and what others know based either on the result of direct interactions with them or on observations of how others interact with individuals with whom they themselves have not had direct encounters (observational learning). In large groups it would probably be impossible to know about every possible paired interaction, nor might it be possible or desirable for an individual to interact with every other individual. In these instances, having the ability to read interaction patterns among others and then to use this information in one's own encounters would be extremely useful. How individuals glean information from their nonsocial environments is also important to consider (e.g., the location of a potential predator or safety and how this information influences whether and how rapidly assessments of group size and group geometry and changes in group size and geometry are made). We will also learn more about the accuracy of folk psychological explanations for many of the behavior patterns that are of great interest to us.

CONCLUSIONS

There are many reasons why people are interested in the study of non-human minds and cognition. While each does not necessarily warrant a cognitive approach, taken together they justify the current interest in cognitive ethology. These include the following (in no order of importance):

1. Many models in ethology and behavioral ecology presuppose cognition (see Ristau 1991a, Yoerg 1991, and Griffin 1992 for examples). It would be useful to have informed ideas about the types of knowledge that nonhumans have about their social and nonsocial environments and how they use this information.

2. It may be more economical or parsimonious to assume that not everything that an individual needs to be able to do in all situations in which he finds himself is preprogrammed. While general rules of thumb may be laid down genetically during evolution, specific rules of conduct that account for all possible contingencies are too numerous to be hard wired (Griffin 1984). Behavioristic learning schemes can account for some flexibility in organisms, but learning at high degrees of abstraction from sensory stimulation seems less amenable to behavioristic analysis (Allen and

Hauser 1991). Cognitive models of learning provide explanatory schemes for such cases.

3. The assumption of animal minds leads to more rigorous empirical analyses of behavioral plasticity and flexibility in the many and diverse situations that many nonhumans regularly encounter. Yoerg (1991) argues that considerations of cognitive function can lead to original ideas about behavioral adaptation.

4. By providing different perspectives of behavior, cognitive ethology can raise new questions that may be approached from different levels of analysis by people coming from different disciplines. For example, neurobiological studies would be important for informing further studies in animal cognition and might also be useful for explaining data that are already available.

5. Animal welfare issues are tightly connected to views on the cognitive abilities of nonhumans.[5]

Of course, more comparative data dealing with animal cognition are needed, especially those that could be analyzed using rigorous methods that have been applied to other types of comparative studies (e.g., Gittleman and Luh 1994); detailed field data would be particularly welcomed, at least enough information to reliably inform more controlled studies of animal cognition. While some are of the opinion that advanced cognition is confined to the laboratory (e.g., Premack 1988, pp. 171–172), those who have studied animals in the wild disagree (e.g., de Waal 1991, p. 311; McGrew 1992, pp. 83ff).[6] More concentration is also needed on individual differences in cognitive abilities; sweeping generalizations concerning the "typical" behavior of species are often misleading because of great intraspecific variation in social behavior and social organization (Lott 1991; White 1992) and in the performance of behavior patterns (e.g., tool use) that are often cited in generalizations about cognition (Gibbons 1991; McGrew 1992).

Interdisciplinary efforts, despite possible pitfalls (Heil 1992, p. 235), are essential in our quest for knowledge about animal minds. In these joint efforts, open minds and pluralism would also be useful at this stage of the game (Roitblat and Weisman 1986). Philosophers need to be clear when they tell us what they think about animal minds, and those who carefully study the behavior of nonhumans need to tell philosophers what we know, what we are able to do, and how we go about doing our research. Although providing alternatives might not be a requirement in thought experiments that conclude that animals do not have beliefs for one reason or another, it would be useful for students of behavior to be presented with some viable alternatives that could be used in their empirical investigations. If it is because philosophers do not have the experience with empirical work that they make realistic suggestions for experimental design, then it would be useful for philosophers to watch ethologists at work (Dennett 1987, 1988). This experience might allow philosophers to gain a better understanding of what ethology is all about. Even then, ethologists might be ill advised to look to philosophers for a crisp and empirically rigorous definition of intentionality (for example), even if some philosophers promised to provide one (C. Allen, this volume).

Obviously, I do not think that cognitive ethologists should hang up their field glasses and have nothing to do with talk about nonhuman intentional behavior. Rather, cognitive ethologists should put their noses to the grindstone and welcome the fact that they are dealing with difficult and important questions. I expect that in the future cognitive ethologists will be pursuing the answers to the challenging questions that confront them rather than looking for other work.

NOTES

I thank Jean-Arcady Meyer and Herbert Roitblat for allowing me to partake in this conference and for their help in defraying some of the costs associated with traveling to France. The University of Colorado also provided financial aid for the preparation of my oral presentation and this chapter. A large number of people have helped me along the way, and to them I extend many thanks. They include Dale Jamieson, Susan Townsend, Carol Powley, Lori Gruen, Ruth Millikan, Robert Eaton, Mark Anderson, Anderson Brown, John A Fisher, Bernard Rollin, Jack Hailman, Kim Sterelney, Deborah Gordon, Gordon Burghardt, Donald Griffin, and especially Colin Allen. To those I have inadvertently overlooked, I extend my deepest apologies. John Heil, Andrew Whiten, and James R. Anderson graciously provided unpublished manuscripts. The comments of Herb Roitblat, Colin Allen, Susan Townsend, and John Lazarus on an ancestral version of this chapter were especially helpful. None of these scholars necessarily agrees with what I have written.

1. See, for example, Griffin 1976, 1981, 1984, 1991, 1992; Dennett 1983, 1987; Millikan 1984; Roitblat, Bever, and Terrace 1984; Wyers 1985; Mitchell and Thompson 1986; Byrne and Whiten 1988; Cheney and Seyfarth 1990, 1992; Allen and Hauser 1991; Bekoff and Jamieson 1990a, b, 1991; Hauser and Nelson 1991; Ristau 1991a, b; Yoerg 1991; Bekoff and Allen 1992; Beer 1992; Real 1992; Roitblat and von Fersen 1992; Jamieson and Bekoff 1993.

2. Kennedy's claims about anthropomorphism are wide-ranging, but simple-minded and unargued. For more detailed and scholarly discussions of anthropomorphism as they are related to studies of animal behavior, see Fisher 1990, 1991.

3. Sometimes it is difficult to differentiate between skeptics and moderate proponents, who argue that, if there is to be a science of cognitive ethology, we must develop empirical methods for applying cognitive terms and making talk about animal minds respectable (e.g., Kummer, Dasser, and Hoyningen-Huene 1990). Jamieson and Bekoff's (1993) differentiation between weak cognitive ethology—where a cognitive vocabulary can be used to explain, but not to describe, behavior—and strong cognitive ethology—where cognitive and affective vocabularies can be used to describe and to explain behavior—may be relevant here.

4. For numerous and diverse examples, see Chance and Larsen 1976; Griffin 1976, 1981, 1984, 1992; Dennett 1983, 1987; Roitblat, Bever, and Terrace 1984; Byers and Bekoff 1986; Mitchell and Thompson 1986; Schusterman, Thomas, and Wood 1986; Byrne and Whiten 1988; Bateson 1990; Blaustein and Porter 1990; Cheney and Seyfarth 1990, 1992; Pepperberg 1990; Philips and Austad 1990; Rosenzweig 1990; Smith 1990; Allen and Hauser 1991; Bekoff and Jamieson 1991; Hauser and Nelson 1991; Ristau 1991a; Yoerg 1991; Bekoff and Allen

1992; Beer 1992; Caro and Hauser 1992; Fiorito and Scotto 1992; McGrew 1992; Whiten and Ham 1992; Roitblat and von Fersen 1992.

5. For discussion see Rachels 1990; Bekoff and Jamieson 1991; Harrison 1991; Bekoff et al. 1992; Griffin 1992; G. W. Levvis 1992; M. A. Levvis 1992; Lynch 1992; Bekoff 1994.

Byrne (1991, p. 47) has gone so far as to claim that "if explorations of the minds of chimpanzees and other animals do nothing more than inform the debate about the ethics of animal use in research, the work will have been well worthwhile." Griffin (1992, p. 251) notes that "no one seriously advocates harming animals just for the sake of doing so, although cruelty is unfortunately prevalent in some circles." Unfortunately, Griffin does not tell us where. Despite a very large data base demonstrating highly developed cognitive skills in many animals, there are those who ignore research on animal cognition, misinterpret data from studies on humans, and base their conclusions on the moral status of animals on an intuitionistic comparison of animal and human behavior (e.g., Carruthers 1989; Leahy 1991; but see Clark 1991; Jamieson and Bekoff 1992; Singer 1992). Thus, Carruthers (1989, p. 265), who compares the behavior of animals with the behavior of humans who are driving while distracted and humans who suffer from blindsight, writes, "I shall assume that no one would seriously maintain that dogs, cats, sheep, cattle, pigs, or chickens consciously think things to themselves. . . . The experiences of all these creatures [are of] the nonconscious variety" (p. 265). Furthermore, "Similarly then in the case of brutes: since their experiences, including their pains, are nonconscious ones, their pains are of no immediate moral concern. Indeed since all the mental states of brutes are nonconscious, their injuries are lacking even in indirect moral concern. Since the disappointments caused to the dog through possession of a broken leg are themselves nonconscious in their turn, they, too, are not appropriate objects of our sympathy. Hence, neither the pain of the broken leg itself, nor its further effects upon the life of the dog, have any rational claim upon our sympathy" (p. 268). And finally, "It also follows that there is no moral criticism to be leveled at the majority of people who are indifferent to the pains of factory-farmed animals, which they know to exist but do not themselves observe" (p. 269). For discussion of this minority opinion, see Johnson (1991), Bekoff and Jamieson (1991), and Jamieson and Bekoff (1992). Recently, Carruthers (1992, p. xi) has come to regard "the present popular concern with animal rights in our culture as a reflection of moral decadence" that distracts "attention from the needs of those who certainly do have moral standing—namely, human beings" (p. 168).

Another issue that bears on studies of both animal cognition and animal welfare concerns the naming of animals, for this practice is often taken to be nonscientific. Historically, it is interesting to note that Jane Goodall's first scientific paper dealing with her research on the behavior of chimpanzees was returned by the *Annals of the New York Academy of Sciences* because she named, rather than numbered, the chimpanzees she watched. This journal also wanted her to refer to the chimpanzees using "it" or "which" rather than "he" or "she" (Montgomery 1991, pp. 104–105). Goodall refused to make the requested changes, but her paper was published anyway. As has been pointed out elsewhere (Bekoff 1993b), the words "it" and "which" are typically used for inanimate objects (*Random House Dictionary* 1978). Given that the goal of many studies of animal cognition is to come to terms with animals' subjective experiences—the animals' points of view—making animals subjects rather than objects seems a move in the right direction.

Finally, the results of comparative approaches to cognition will raise numerous and complex ethical concerns about the moral status of androids, for example (e.g., Caudill 1992, chapter 13). These thorny issues cannot be dismissed, but rather should be accepted as challenges for future consideration. Undoubtedly, many of these ethical concerns will be informed by the ways in which nonhumans are viewed.

6. One area in which information from the wild would be very useful concerns the question of whether animals can count (Boysen and Capaldi 1993). While I have no hard data concerning this ability in the free-living coyotes I have studied, when pups were moved

from one den to another, I never saw a mother either forget a pup or go back to a den to retrieve a pup who was not there, even when she had help from another coyote in moving the infants. McGrew (1992, p. 223) also points out that we need to learn about accounting abilities in other animals to see if accounting informs decisions about reciprocity.

REFERENCES

Akins, K. 1990. Science and our inner lives: Birds of prey, bats, and the common (featherless) bi-ped. In M. Bekoff and D. Jamieson, eds. *Interpretation and Explanation in the Study of Animal Behavior, Vol. I: Interpretation, Intentionality, and Communication.* Boulder, Colorado: Westview Press.

Alcock, J. 1992. Review of D. R. Griffin 1992. *Natural History* September, 62–65.

Allen, C. 1992a. Mental content. *British Journal of the Philosophy of Science* 43: 537–553.

Allen, C. 1992b. Mental content and evolutionary explanation. *Biology and Philosophy* 7: 1–12.

Allen, C., and Bekoff, M. 1994. Intentionality, social play, and definition. *Biology and Philosophy* 9: 63–74.

Allen, C., and Hauser, M. D. 1991. Concept attribution in nonhuman animals: Theoretical and methodological problems in ascribing complex mental processes. *Philosophy of Science* 58: 221–240.

Archer, J. 1992. *Ethology and Human Development.* London: Barnes and Noble.

Bateson, P. P. G. 1990. Choice, preference, and selection. In M. Bekoff and D. Jamieson, eds. *Interpretation and Explanation in the Study of Animal Behavior, Vol. I: Interpretation, Intentionality, and Communication.* Boulder, Colorado: Westview Press.

Beck, B. 1982. Chimpocentrism: Bias in cognitive ethology. *Journal of Human Evolution* 11: 3–17.

Beer, C. 1992. Conceptual issues in cognitive ethology. *Advances in the Study of Behavior* 21: 69–109.

Bekoff, M. 1975. The communication of play intention: Are play signals functional? *Semiotica* 15: 231–239.

Bekoff, M. 1977. Social communication in canids: Evidence for the evolution of a stereotyped mammalian display. *Science* 197: 1097–1099.

Bekoff, M. 1978. Social play: Structure, function, and the evolution of a cooperative social behavior. In G Burghardt and M. Bekoff, eds. *The Development of Behavior: Comparative and Evolutionary Aspects.* New York: Garland.

Bekoff, M. 1989. Behavioral development of terrestrial carnivores. In J. L. Gittleman, ed. *Carnivore Behavior, Ecology, and Evolution.* Ithaca, New York: Cornell University Press.

Bekoff, M. 1992a. Scientific ideology, animal consciousness, and animal protection: A principled plea for unabashed common sense. *New Ideas in Psychology* 10: 79–94.

Bekoff, M. 1992b. Description and explanation: A plea for plurality. *Behavioral and Brain Sciences* 15: 269–270.

Bekoff, M. 1993a. Review of Griffin 1992. *Ethology* 95: 166–170.

Bekoff, M. 1993b. Experimentally induced infanticide: The removal of females and its ramifications. *Auk,* 110: 404–406.

Bekoff, M. 1994. Cognitive ethology and the treatment of nonhuman animals: How matters of mind inform matters of welfare. *Animal Welfare* 3: 75–96.

Bekoff, M. 1995a. Play signals as punctuation: The structure of social play in canids. *Behaviour*, in press.

Bekoff, M. 1995b. Vigilance, flock size, and flock geometry: Information gathering by western evening grosbeaks (Aves, Fringillidae). *Ethology* 99: 150–161.

Bekoff, M., and Allen, C. 1992. Intentional icons: Towards an evolutionary cognitive ethology. *Ethology* 91: 1–16.

Bekoff, M., and Allen, C. 1996. Cognitive ethology: Slayers, skeptics, and proponents. In R. W. Mitchell, N. Thompson, and L. Miles, eds. *Anthropomorphism, Anecdote, and Animals: The Emperor's New Clothes?* Albany, SUNY Press.

Bekoff, M., and Byers, J. A. 1981. A critical reanalysis of the ontogeny of mammalian social and locomotor play: An ethological hornet's nest. In K. Immelmann, G. W. Barlow, L. Petrinovich, and M. Main, eds. *Behavioral Development: The Bielefeld Interdisciplinary Project.* New York: Cambridge University Press.

Bekoff, M., Gruen, J., Townsend, S. E., and Rollin, B. E. 1992. Animals in science: Some areas revisited. *Animal Behaviour* 44: 473–484.

Bekoff, M., and Jamieson, D., eds. 1990a. *Interpretation and Explanation in the Study of Animal Behavior, Vol. 1: Interpretation, Intentionality, and Communication.* Boulder, Colorado: Westview Press.

Bekoff, M., and Jamieson, D., eds. 1990b. *Interpretation and Explanation in the Study of Animal Behavior, Vol. 2: Explanation, Evolution, and Adaptation.* Boulder, Colorado: Westview Press.

Bekoff, M., and Jamieson, D. 1991. Reflective ethology, applied philosophy, and the moral status of animals. *Perspectives in Ethology* 9: 1–47.

Bekoff, M., Townsend, S. E., and Jamieson, D. 1994. Beyond monkey minds: Towards a richer cognitive ethology. *Behavioral and Brain Sciences,* 17: 571–572.

Bennett, J. 1991. How to read minds in behaviour: A suggestion from a philosopher. In A. Whiten, ed. *Natural Theories of Mind: Evolution, Development and Simulation of Everyday Mindreading.* Cambridge, Massachusetts: Basil.

Bertram, B. C. R. 1978. Living in groups. In J. R. Krebs and N. B. Davies, eds. *Behavioural Ecology: An Evolutionary Approach.* Sunderland, Massachusetts: Sinauer.

Blaustein, A. R., and Porter, R. H. 1990. The ubiquitous concept of recognition with special reference to kin. In M. Bekoff and D. Jamieson, eds. *Interpretation and Explanation in the Study of Animal Behavior, Vol. I: Interpretation, Intentionality, and Communication.* Boulder, Colorado: Westview Press.

Bogdan, R. J., ed. 1991. *Mind and Common Sense: Philosophical Essays on Commonsense Psychology.* New York: Cambridge University Press.

Boysen, S. T., and Capaldi, E. J., eds. 1993. *The Development of Numerical Competence: Animal and Human Models.* Hillsdale, New Jersey: Erlbaum.

Brunjes, P. C. 1992. Lessons from lesions: The effects of olfactory bulbectomy. *Chemical Senses* 17: 729–763.

Burghardt, G. M. 1991. Cognitive ethology and critical anthropomorphism: A snake with two heads and hognose snakes that play dead. In C. Ristau, ed. *Cognitive Ethology: The Minds of Other Animals.* Hillsdale, New Jersey: Erlbaum.

Byers, J. A., and Bekoff, M. 1986. What does "kin recognition" mean? *Ethology* 72: 342–345.

Byrne, R. W. 1991. Review of Cheney and Seyfarth 1990. *The Sciences* July: 142–147.

Byrne, R. W., and Whiten, A., eds. 1988. *Machiavellian Intelligence: Social Expertise and the Evolution of Intellect in Monkeys, Apes, and Humans.* New York: Oxford University Press.

Caro, T. M., and Hauser, M. D. 1992. Is there teaching in nonhuman animals? *Quarterly Review of Biology* 67: 151–174.

Carruthers, P. 1989. Brute experience. *Journal of Philosophy* 86: 258–269.

Carruthers, P. 1992. *The Animals Issue: Moral Theory in Practice.* New York: Cambridge University Press.

Caudill, M. 1992. *In Our Own Image: Building an Artifiical Person.* New York: Oxford University Press.

Chance, M. R. A., and Larsen, R. R., eds. 1976. *The Social Structure of Attention.* New York: Wiley.

Cheney, D. L., and Seyfarth, R. M. 1990. *How Monkeys See the World: Inside the Mind of Another Species.* Chicago: University of Chicago Press.

Cheney, D. L., and Seyfarth, R. M. 1992. Précis of *How Monkeys See the World: Inside the Mind of Another Species. Behavioral and Brain Sciences* 15: 135–182.

Christensen, S. M., and Turner D. R., eds. 1993. *Folk Psychology and the Philosophy of Mind.* Hillsdale, New Jersey: Erlbaum.

Churchland, P. M. 1979. *Scientific Realism and the Plasticity of Mind.* New York: Cambridge University Press.

Churchland, P. M. 1981. Eliminative materialism and the propositional attitudes. *Journal of Philosophy* 78: 67–89.

Clark, A. 1989. *Microcognition: Philosophy, Cognitive Science, and Parallel Distributed Processing.* Cambridge, Massachusetts: The MIT Press.

Clark, S. R. L. 1991. Not so dumb friends. *The Times Literary Supplement, London* 13 December: 5–6.

Cling, A. D. 1990. Disappearance and knowledge. *Philosophy of Science* 57: 226–247.

Cling, A. D. 1991. The empirical virtues of beliefs. *Philosophical Psychology* 4: 303–323.

Colgan, P. 1989. *Animal Motivation.* New York: Chapman and Hall.

Cronin, H. Review of Griffin. 1992. *New York Times Book Review* November 1: 14.

Dehn, M. M. 1990. Vigilance for predators: Detection and dilution effects. *Behavioral Ecology and Sociobiology* 26: 337–342.

Dennett, D. C. 1983. Intentional systems in cognitive ethology: The "Panglossian paradigm" defended. *Behavioral and Brain Sciences* 6: 343–345.

Dennett, D. C. 1987. Reflections: Interpreting monkeys, theorists, and genes. In *The Intentional Stance.* Cambridge, Massachusetts: The MIT Press.

Dennett, D. C. 1988. Out of the armchair and into the field. *Poetics Today* 9: 205–221.

Dennett, D. C. 1991. *Consciousness Explained.* Boston: Little, Brown and Company.

Deneubourg, J. L., and Goss, C. 1989. Collective patterns and decision-making. *Ethology, Ecology, & Evolution* 1: 295–311.

de Waal, F. B. M. 1991. Complementary methods and convergent evidence in the study of primate social cognition. *Behaviour* 118: 299–320.

Elgar, M. A. 1989. Predator vigilance and group size in mammals and birds: A critical review of the empirical evidence. *Biological Reviews* 64: 13–33.

Elgar, M. A., Burren, P. J., and Posen, M. 1984. Vigilance and perception of flock size in foraging house sparrows, *Passer domesticus Behaviour* 90: 215–223.

Fagen, R. 1981. *Animal Play Behavior*. New York: Oxford University Press.

Fiorito, G., and Scotto, P. 1992. Observational learning in *Octopus vulgaris*. *Science* 256: 545–546.

Fisher, J. A. 1990. The myth of anthropomorphism. In M. Bekoff and D. Jamieson, eds. *Interpretation and Explanation in the Study of Animal Behavior, Vol. I: Interpretation, Intentionality, and Communication*. Boulder, Colorado: Westview Press.

Fisher, J. A. 1991. Disambiguating anthropomorphism. *Perspectives in Ethology* 9: 49–85.

Gibbons, A. 1991. Chimps: More diverse than a barrel of monkeys. *Science* 255: 287–288.

Gilman, D. 1990. The neurobiology of observation. *Philosophy of Science* 58: 496–502.

Gittleman, J. L., and Luh, H.-K. 1994. Phylogeny, evolutionary models, and comparative methods: A simulation study. In P. Eggleton and D. Vane-Wright, eds. *Phylogenetics and Ecology*. London: Academic Press.

Golani, I. 1992. A mobility gradient in the organization of vertebrate movement. *Behavioral and Brain Sciences* 15: 249–308.

Gordon, D. M., Paul, R. E., and Thorpe, K. 1993. What is the function of encounter patterns in ant colonies? *Animal Behaviour* 45: 1083–1100.

Greenwood, J. D., ed. 1991. *The Future of Folk Psychology: Intentionality and Cognitive Science*. New York: Cambridge University Press.

Griffin, D. R. 1976. *The Question of Animal Awareness: Evolutionary Continuity Mental Experience*. New York: The Rockefeller University Press.

Griffin, D. R. 1978. Prospects for a cognitive ethology. *Behavioral and Brain Sciences* 4: 527–538.

Griffin, D. R. 1981. *The Question of Animal Awareness: Evolutionary Continuity Mental Experience*. Second edition. New York: The Rockefeller University Press.

Griffin, D. R. 1984. *Animal Thinking*. Cambridge, Massachusetts: Harvard University Press.

Griffin, D. R. 1991. Progress toward a cognitive ethology. In C. Ristau, ed. *Cognitive Ethology: The Minds of Other Animals*. Hillsdale, New Jersey: Erlbaum.

Griffin, D. R. 1992. *Animal Minds*. Chicago: University of Chicago Press.

Gustafson, D. 1986. Review of D. R. Griffin 1984. *Environmental Ethics* 8: 179–182.

Hailman, J. P. 1977. *Optical Signals: Animal Communication and Light*. Bloomington, Indiana: Indiana University Press.

Harman, G. 1965. The inference to the best explanation. *Philosophical Review* 74: 88–95.

Harrison, P. 1991. Do animals feel pain? *Philosophy* 66: 25–40.

Hauser, M. D., and Nelson, M. 1991. 'Intentional' signaling in animal communication. *Trends in Ecology and Evolution* 6: 186–189.

Heil, J. 1992. *The Nature of True Minds*. New York: Cambridge University Press.

Heyes, C. 1987a. Cognisance of consciousness in the study of animal knowledge. In W. Callebaut and R. Pinxten, eds. *Evolutionary Epistemology*. Boston: D. Reidel.

Heyes, C. 1987b. Contrasting approaches to the legitimation of intentional language within comparative psychology. *Behaviorism* 15: 41–50.

Howlett, R. 1993. Beauty on the brain. *Nature* 361: 398–399.

Jamieson, D., and Bekoff, M. 1992a. Some problems and prospects for cognitive ethology. *Between the Species* 8: 80–82.

Jamieson, D., and Bekoff, M. 1992b. Carruthers on nonconscious experience. *Analysis* 52: 23–28.

Jamieson, D., and Bekoff, M. 1993. On aims and methods of cognitive ethology. *Philosophy of Science Association* 2: 110–124.

Johnson, E. 1991. Carruthers on consciousness and moral status. *Between the Species* 7: 190–193.

Kennedy, J. S. 1992. *The New Anthropomorphism.* New York: Cambridge University Press.

Kummer, H., Dasser, Z., and Hoyningen-Huene, P. 1990. Exploring primate social cognition: Some critical remarks. *Behaviour* 112: 85–98.

Lazarus, J. 1979. The early warning function of flocking in birds: An experimental study with captive quela. *Animal Behaviour* 27: 855–865.

Lazarus, J. 1990. Looking for trouble. *New Scientist* 125: 62–65.

Leahy, M. P. T. 1991. *Against Liberation: Putting Animals in Perspective.* New York: Routledge.

Levvis, G. W. 1992. Why we would not understand a talking lion. *Between the Species* 8: 156–162.

Levvis, M. A. 1992. The value of judgments regarding the value of animals. *Between the Species* 8: 150–155.

Lima, S. L. 1990. The influence of models on the interpretation of vigilance. In M. Bekoff and D. Jamieson, eds. *Interpretation and Explanation in the Study of Animal Behavior, Vol. II: Explanation, Evolution, and Adaptation.* Boulder, Colorado: Westview Press.

Lima, S. L., and Dill, L. M. 1990. Behavioral decisions made under the risk of predation: A review and prospectus. *Canadian Journal of Zoology* 68: 619–640.

Lindzen, R. S. 1990. Some coolness concerning global warming. *Bulletin of the American Meteorological Society* 71: 288–299.

Lott, D. F. 1991. *Intraspecific Variation in the Social Systems of Wild Vertebrates.* New York: Cambridge University Press.

Lynch, J. J. 1992. Toward an Interspecific Psychology. Ph.D. Dissertation. California: The Claremont Graduate School.

Mason, W. A. 1976. Review of Griffin 1976. *Science* 194: 930–931.

Mason, W. A. 1979. Environmental models and mental modes: Representational processes in the great apes. In D. A. Hamburg and E. R. McCown, eds. *The Great Apes.* Menlo Park, California: The Benjamin/Cummins Publishing Company.

Mason, W. A. 1986. Behavior implies cognition. In W. Bechtel, ed. *Science and Philosophy: Integrating Scientific Disciplines.* Boston: Martinus Nijhoff Publishers.

McFarland, D. 1989. *Problems of Animal Behaviour.* New York: Wiley.

McGrew, W. C. 1992. *Chimpanzee Material Culture: Implications for Human Evolution.* New York: Cambridge University Press.

Metcalfe, N. B. 1984a. The effects of habitat on the vigilance of shorebirds: Is visibility important? *Animal Behaviour* 32: 981–985.

Metcalfe, N. B. 1984b. The effects of mixed-species flocking on the vigilance of shorebirds: Who do they trust? *Animal Behaviour* 32: 986–993.

Michel, G. F. 1991. Human psychology and the minds of other animals. In C. Ristau, ed. *Cognitive Ethology: The Minds of Other Animals.* Hillsdale, New Jersey: Erlbaum.

Millikan, R. G. 1984. *Language, Thought, and Other Biological Categories: New Foundations for Realism.* Cambridge, Massachusetts: The MIT Press.

Mitchell, R. W. 1990. A theory of play. In M. Bekoff and D. Jamieson, eds. *Interpretation and Explanation in the Study of Animal Behavior, Vol. I: Interpretation, Intentionality, and Communication.* Boulder, Colorado: Westview Press.

Mitchell, R. W., and Thompson, N. S., eds. 1986. *Deception: Perspectives on Human and Nonhuman Deceit.* Albany, New York: SUNY Press.

Montgomery, S. 1991. *Walking with the Great Apes: Jane Goodall, Dian Fossey, and Birutè Galdikas.* New York: SUNY Press.

Moussa, M., and Shannon, T. A. 1992. The search for the new pineal gland: Brain life and personhood. *Hastings Center Report* 22: 30–37.

Pepperberg, I. M. 1990. Some cognitive capacities of an African grey parrot *(Psittacus erithacus). Advances in the Study of Behavior* 19: 357–409.

Philips, M., and Austad, S. N. 1990. Animal communication and social evolution. In M. Bekoff and D. Jamieson, eds. *Interpretation and Explanation in the Study of Animal Behavior, Vol. I: Interpretation, Intentionality, and Communication.* Boulder, Colorado: Westview Press.

Premack, D. 1988. "Does the chimpanzee have a theory of mind?" revisited. In R. Byrne and A. Whiten, eds. *Machiavellian Intelligence: Social Expertise and the Evolution of Intellect in Monkeys, Apes, and Humans.* New York: Oxford University Press.

Pulliam, H. R. 1973. On the advantages of flocking. *Journal of Theoretical Biology* 38: 419–422.

Purton, A. C. 1978. Ethological categories of behavior and some consequences of their conflation. *Animal Behaviour* 26: 653–670.

Quenette, P.-Y. 1990. Functions of vigilance behaviour in mammals: A review. *Acta Oecologica* 11: 801–818.

Rachels, J. 1990. *Created From Animals: The Moral Implications of Darwinism.* New York: Oxford University Press.

Random House Dictionary. 1978. New York: Ballantine Books.

Rasa, O. E. A. 1989. The costs and effectiveness of vigilance behaviour in the dwarf mongoose: Implications for fitness and optimal group size. *Ethology, Ecology & Evolution* 1: 265–282.

Real, L. A. 1992. Information processing and the evolutionary ecology of cognitive architecture. *American Naturalist* 140:S108–S145.

Ristau, C. ed. 1991a. *Cognitive Ethology: The Minds of Other Animals.* Hillsdale, New Jersey: Erlbaum.

Ristau, C. 1991b. Aspects of the cognitive ethology of an injury-feigning bird, the piping plover. In C. Ristau, ed. *Cognitive Ethology: The Minds of Other Animals.* Hillsdale, New Jersey: Erlbaum.

Roitblat, H. L., Bever, T. G., and Terrace, H. S., eds., 1984. *Animal Cognition.* Hillsdale, New Jersey: Erlbaum.

Roitblat, H. L., and von Fersen, L. 1992. Comparative cognition: Representations and processes in learning and memory. *Annual Review of Psychology* 43: 671–710.

Roitblat, H. L., and Weisman, R. G. 1986. Tactics of comparative cognition. In M. Rilling, D. Kendrick, and M. R. Denny, eds. *Theories of Animal Memory.* Hillsdale, New Jersey: Erlbaum.

Rollin, B. E. 1989. *The Unheeded Cry: Animal Consciousness, Animal Pain and Science*. New York: Oxford University Press.

Rollin, B. E. 1990. How the animals lost their minds: Animal mentation and scientific ideology. In M. Bekoff and D. Jamieson, eds. *Interpretation and Explanation in the Study of Animal Behavior, Vol. I: Interpretation, Intentionality, and Communication*. Boulder, Colorado: Westview Press.

Rosenberg, A. 1990. Is there an evolutionary biology of play? In M. Bekoff and D. Jamieson, eds. *Interpretation and Explanation in the Study of Animal Behavior, Vol. I: Interpretation, Intentionality, and Communication*. Boulder, Colorado: Westview Press.

Rosenzweig, M. L. 1990. Do animals choose habitats? In M. Bekoff and D. Jamieson, eds. *Interpretation and Explanation in the Study of Animal Behavior, Vol. I: Interpretation, Intentionality, and Communication*. Boulder, Colorado: Westview Press.

Saidel, E. 1992. What price neurophilosophy? *Philosophy of Science Association* 1: 461–468.

Schusterman, R. J., Thomas, J. A., and Wood, F. G., eds. 1986. *Dolphin Cognition and Behavior: A Comparative Approach*. Hillsdale, New Jersey: Erlbaum.

Singer, P. 1992. Bandit and friends. *New York Review of Books* 9 April: 9–13.

Smith, W. J. 1990. Communication and expectations: A social process and the cognitive operations it depends upon and influences. In M. Bekoff and D. Jamieson, eds. *Interpretation and Explanation in the Study of Animal Behavior, Vol. I: Interpretation, Intentionality, and Communication*. Boulder, Colorado: Westview Press.

Snowdon, C. T. 1991. Review of Ristau 1991a. *Science* 251: 813–814.

Sober, E. 1983. Mentalism and behaviorism in comparative psychology. In D. W. Rajecki, ed. *Comparing Behavior: Studying Man Studying Animals*. Hillsdale, New Jersey: Erlbaum.

Stich, S. 1979. Do animals have beliefs? *Australasian Journal of Philosophy* 57: 15–28.

Stich, S. 1983. *From Folk Psychology to Cognitive Science*. Cambridge, Massachusetts: The MIT Press.

Symons, D. 1974. Aggressive play and communication in rhesus monkeys *(Macaca mulatta)*. *American Zoologist* 14: 317–322. Press.

Tinklepaugh, O. L. 1928. An experimental study of representative factors in monkeys. *Journal of Comparative Psychology* 8: 197–236.

Warburton, K., and Lazarus, J. 1991. Tendency-distance models of social cohesion in animal groups. *Journal of Theoretical Biology* 150: 473–488.

Ward, P. I. 1985. Why birds in flocks do not coordinate their vigilance periods. *Journal of Theoretical Biology* 114: 383–385.

White, F. J. 1992. Pygmy chimpanzee social organization: Variation with party size and between study sites. *American Journal of Primatology* 26: 203–214.

Whiten, A. 1992. Review of Griffin 1992. *Nature* 360: 118–119.

Whiten, A. 1993. Evolving a theory of mind: The nature of non-verbal mentalism in other primates. In S. Barton-Cohen, H. Tager-Flusberg, and D. J. Cohen, eds. *Understanding Other Minds: Perspectives from Autism*. New York: Oxford University Press.

Whiten, A., and Ham, R. 1992. On the nature and evolution of imitation in the animal kingdom: Reappraisal of a century of research. *Advances in the Study of Behavior* 21: 239–283.

Williams, G. C. 1992. *Natural Selection: Domains, Levels, and Challenges*. New York: Oxford University Press.

Wyers, E. J. 1985. Cognitive behavior and sticklebacks. *Behaviour* 95: 1–10.

Ydenberg, R. C., and Dill, L. M. 1986. The economics of escaping from predators. *Advances in the Study of Behavior* 16: 229–249.

Yoerg, S. I. 1991. Ecological frames of mind: The role of cognition in behavioral ecology. *Quarterly Review of Biology* 66: 287–301.

Yoerg, S. I., and Kamil, A. C. 1991. Integrating cognitive ethology with cognitive psychology. In C. A. Ristau, ed. *Cognitive Ethology: The Minds of Other Animals.* Hillsdale, New Jersey: Erlbaum.

Zabel, C. J., Glickman, S. E., Frank, L. G., Woodmansee, K. B., and Keppel, G. 1992. Coalition formation in a colony of prepubertal hyenas. In A. H. Harcourt and F. B. de Waal, eds. *Coalitions and Alliances in Humans and Other Animals.* New York: Oxford University Press.

Zuckerman, L. 1991. Review of Cheney and Seyfarth 1990. *New York Review of Books* May 30: 43–49.

8 Perceptual Control Theory

W. Thomas Bourbon

Life is control—an uninterrupted process of specifying, creating, and maintaining—a process in which all that is not essential is free to change, preventing change in what is essential. Surroundings change, genotypes change, phenotypes change, and self-replicating molecules survive. Environmental conditions change, behavioral actions change, and selected results of actions remain as intended by the actors. Control by living systems is universal, but it goes unnoticed or unexplained by most behavioral and cognitive theorists. Many who do discuss control assume that the behavior of organisms is the object of control originating in the environment or in plans, commands, or programs from the brain-mind. Few theorists recognize that behavior is the means by which organisms routinely achieve and maintain control; among them are perceptual control theorists, who model organisms as systems that specify and control many of their own perceptions and incidentally, but importantly, control parts of the environment.

Here I describe core concepts of perceptual control theory (PCT) and review a series of computer simulations in which the PCT model "behaves," at the same speed as people or faster, under a variety of modeled environmental conditions, duplicating many features of behavior. Like the conference which resulted in this book, my chapter is intended for students, not for experts. Students can decide for themselves whether other models in behavioral and cognitive science behave in simulation, on line, and produce the range of results described here. I cite publications that describe the simulations in more detail, and in the appendix I tell where readers, students and experts alike, may inquire concerning computer programs for the simulations.

BEHAVIORAL CONTROLS OF PERCEPTION

Control occurs when an organism creates or maintains selected states of certain environmental variables, defending those states against the effects of disturbances independent of the organism's actions. I should say that, as observers, we see living systems control the states of environmental variables, but a controlling organism knows only its own sensory signals or perceptions. Organisms (people included) do not objectively know or control a world beyond perception.

Perceptual control theorists understand that organisms control (many, not all of) their own perceptions, not their observed actions. At gymnastics competitions, judges see and evaluate outward appearances of gymnasts' actions, but gymnasts do not directly know those appearances; they control their own perceptions (including those of effort, touch, movement, pain, sound, and sight) that no judge can experience or evaluate.

At another level of observation, a scientist sees bacteria in a petri dish trace dissimilar trajectories when they are selectively attracted and repelled by various substances, moving up concentration gradients toward attractants and down gradients from repellents. But, as I will demonstrate later, it is likely that bacteria are not attracted or repelled and that they do not sense gradients. Instead, they increase the magnitudes of some internal signals and decrease others; they control the magnitudes of signals equivalent to perceptions.

With bacteria as with gymnasts, scientific observers often notice and try to explain outwardly visible phenomena that do not exist in the experience of those who are observed. An unfortunate consequence of this unavoidable difference in perceptual worlds is that many theorists explain things organisms do not do. In contrast, in perceptual control theory many of the outward appearances of behavior are recognized to be incidental side effects of what an organism is doing. If that idea is right, the implications for the behavioral and cognitive sciences are great. For instance, the PCT simulations in this chapter will show that human movement, and control behavior in general, need not depend on prior plans, commands, or solutions of problems in inverse kinematics; that coordinated, patterned interactions can occur when independent systems (organisms, artificial systems, body parts) control their own sensations of local variables, with no system "in charge" or aware of the full consequences; and that bacteria and humans can quickly and reliably arrive at a specific place, even when the immediate consequences of their attempts to change direction are random.

DEMONSTRATIONS OF PERCEPTUAL CONTROL THEORY

In the following series of demonstrations, the PCT model simulates (1) a person who performs a sensorimotor tracking task, (2) "gradient following" by an intestinal bacterium and by a person, (3) the movements of multiple individuals in a gathering and the spatial patterns they create by their eventual positions, and (4) a person who visually fixates a moving target and continuously touches it with a finger. The organization and functioning of the PCT model are very simple. During each time period represented in a simulation, a modeled system "senses" momentary values of local variables, compares the resulting sensory signals to a specified reference value, calculates any discrepancy between specified and sensed values, calculates a conversion from the perceptual discrepancy to a change in behavioral output, and calculates the values of all variables affected by the model's behavior change. These processes occur continuously and concurrently; this is not a model of serial processing.

Tracking: A Basic Example of Control

In the first demonstration, a person uses a control device to keep a cursor aligned with an independent moving target and a PCT model duplicates the results of the person's performance. For anyone tempted to dismiss tracking as overly simple or not representative of the complexity and abstraction of "true" cognitive tasks, it is no accident that a common phrase in English, "on track," applies to phenomena as diverse as keeping trains on railroad tracks and the progress of conversations, wars, peace negotiations, vacations, and love affairs.

Tracking by One System

The Tracker's Perspective   The experimental conditions for tracking are illustrated in the center and right-hand portions of figure 8.1. A person observes three marks on a computer screen and uses a control handle (h) to affect the position of one of the marks. At the same time, two sources independent of the person's actions affect the positions of the three marks.

The causal relationships among environmental variables are illustrated in the lower left-hand portion of figure 8.1. The left and right marks, designated left and right target (tl and tr), move up and down in unison, their momentary positions determined by a triangular function (t) generated by the computer program. The handle does not affect the position of the target, which is an uncontrolled variable (vu) from the perspective of the person.

In figure 8.1, light from the screen that reaches and affects the person's eye is designated as an input quantity (gi). On the screen, the position of the middle mark (cursor, cur) is affected by a series of random numbers (disturbance, d) generated by the computer. Through a game port, every $1/30$ of a second the computer samples the position of the handle, with a resolution of 200 discrete positions, and converts the sampled position into one of 200 ordered integers. The momentary position of the cursor is determined by the algebraic sum of d and the position of h, so ($cur = h + d$). If the person does not move the handle, the cursor moves up and down across most of the height of the screen, its position determined by the monetary value of d; if the person moves the handle, the position of cur is determined jointly by d and h. If the person attempts to keep cur

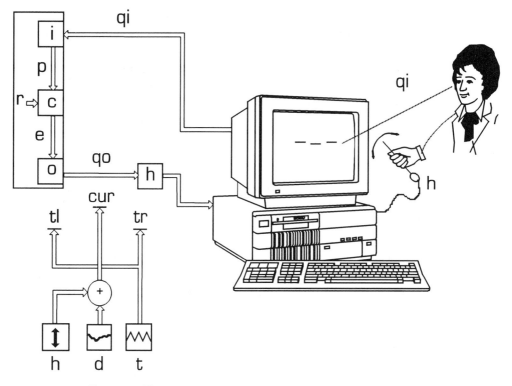

Figure 8.1 The generic model of a perceptual control system and the arrangement in which a person, represented by the PCT model, performs pursuit tracking, using a control handle (*h*) to keep a cursor (*cur*) aligned with two target marks (*tl, tr*) that follow a programmed function (*t*), while the position of *cur* is also affected by an unpredictable random disturbance (*d*). All functions, signals, and connections in the model are identified in the text.

in some relationship to the target, the intended relationship becomes a controlled variable *(vc)* from the perspective of the person.

In passing notice that, when a person controls the relationship of cursor to target, there are no independent and dependent variables (IVs and DVs) in the traditional sense of those terms. The position of the target is always independent of the person's actions, but the cursor-target relationship is not; it is always a joint function of target position and cursor position, and the latter is always a function of the random disturbance and the person's actions as they affect the handle position. The absence of genuine IVs and DVs from control relationships is significant for cognitive science, where modelers often use traditional associative learning paradigms, with their assumed IVs and DVs (in the guise of stimulus and response or input and output) as sources of empirical data. If creatures do not work that way, then cognitive models that do are probably inappropriate representations of living systems.

If the person controls the relationship of cursor to target, there are accompanying changes in many variables the person does not care about, or know about, such as the specific way the person grips the handle, the relationship between the person's elbow and waist, friction-generated heat in the shaft of the control handle, or consumption of electrical power by the computer. For the person, each of the infinite number of affected, potentially observable, but uncontrolled variables is an incidental variable *(vi)*; understandably observers, both casual and scientific, often mistakenly believe observed changes in those incidental variables are what the person's behavior is "about," that they are what the person is "doing."

In the present setup, the person selects an intended spatial relationship between cursor and target or adopts one suggested by the experimenter. The person must continuously perceive the present relationship on the screen and compare the perception against the intended one as he or she remembers or imagines it. If the perceived relationship matches the intended one, the person does not move the handle; if not, the person moves the handle to eliminate the discrepancy. It is crucial for the reader to remember that the person intends a perceived relationship, not the actions affecting that perception, and the intention is in the person, not outside; even if the experimenter provides an external indicator of "degree of relationship," the person must intend to see the indicator at some particular position or value rather than any other.

A person can easily perform this task, as is shown at the bottom of figure 8.2, which presents the positions of target, handle, and cursor, all as functions of time, during a 60-second run by a relatively inexperienced person. The person kept the cursor close to the target (the mean distance between cursor and target rounds to zero units of screen resolution, *S. D.* < 2, for $n = 1800$ data pairs, or 30/sec for 60 seconds). The target followed an irregular triangular path. At each change of direction, the target's rate of movement was randomly selected from one of three possible values. To produce the intended perceptual result, the person moved the handle on an irregular path different from those of the cursor and target. Herein lies another easily missed fundamental of control: to produce intended perceptions in a setting where sources other than the person affect the intended result, the person must use unintended actions of just the right magnitude and direction to eliminate influences by the independent sources. In most settings no person, or plausible model of a person, can create advance plans and commands for those actions. Even plans and commands followed by negative-feedback servomechanisms are overcome by modestly variable environments where a person or a PCT model will succeed.

A PCT Model of the Tracker   Several researchers have used PCT to model tracking by single participants in tasks like the one described here—for example, Bourbon and Powers (1993); Bourbon et al. (1990); Marken (1980); Pavloski (1989); Pavloski, Barron, and Hogue (1990); and Powers (1978,

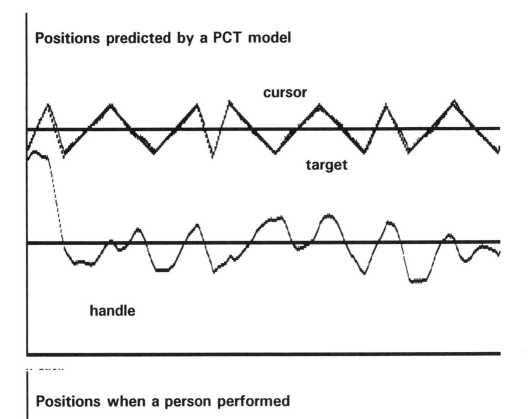

Positions predicted by a PCT model

cursor

target

handle

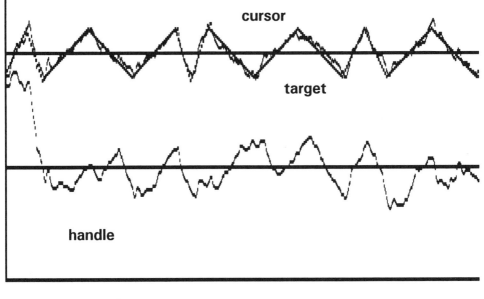

Positions when a person performed

cursor

target

handle

0   **Time (sec)**   60

Figure 8.2 Positions of the cursor and the target on the computer screen (up = top of screen) and positions of the control handle (up = away from person) as functions of time. The PCT model predicted the results (top portion) several minutes before the person (bottom portion) performed the task. (After Bourbon and Powers 1993.)

1989). The PCT model of the person in the present task is illustrated in the upper left-hand portion of figure 8.1.

If a model of a person is to produce perceptual control, it must include a feature to represent the person's intended perceptions. In the PCT model, intention is represented by a reference signal *(r)* specifying a particular magnitude of perceptual signal *(p)*. The perceptual signal comes from an input function *(i)* that transforms an input quantity *(qi)* from environmental units into signals; in the present case, there is a one-to-one correspondence between *p* and the distance between cursor and target on the screen at each sampling interval (every 30th of a second). To represent the person's comparison between perception and intention and determine if there is any momentary discrepancy (error signal, *e*), the model must compare *p* with *r*. It does that through simple subtraction $(e = r - p)$. If error is nonzero (if cursor and target are not in the intended relationship), the model must "move the handle" in simulation. But how much should it move for a given magnitude of error?

The output function *(o)* converts the error signal into simulated units of output quantity *(qo)*—in the present case, handle movement in the environment. In the simple form used here, at *o* the error signal *(e)* is multiplied by an integration factor *(k)* representing the velocity with which the person moves the control handle during 1 second for a perceived unit of error $(k = \Delta qo/\text{sec}/\text{unit of error})$. The multiplication determines the change (Δ) in *qo* during each modeled time interval $(\Delta qo = [k \cdot e] \cdot dt)$, where *dt* is the sampling interval (here, $^1/_{30}$ sec) during a behavioral task or a simulation. The magnitude of *k* was estimated using earlier data from the person whose results are shown in figure 8.1. The procedure for estimating *k* is described in detail by Bourbon and Powers (1993).

When all of the necessary steps are written as program steps in Turbo Pascal, the simplest possible PCT model is:

$$vc := qo + d; \tag{1}$$

$$qo := qo + (k \cdot error) \cdot dt; \tag{2}$$

where the symbols have meanings described earlier. (In Turbo Pascal, the symbol ":=" stands for the operation of replacement, not for the algebraic symbol "equals.")

Whether for a model or a living system, when *vc* is not controlled, *d* is unopposed and produces a change (Δ) of a certain magnitude in *vc* $(\Delta vc_{\text{uncontrolled}})$. Control is said to be "good," or "tight," if $\Delta vc_{\text{controlled}} <<<< \Delta vc_{\text{uncontrolled}}$ and $qo \cong -d$. In words, control is good when an organism's actions have effects nearly equal in magnitude and opposite in sign to *d*'s effects on *vc*; consequently, *vc* changes much less than if the effects of *d* are unopposed. Good control is ubiquitous in nature.

The program steps I have just described are used, either exactly as shown or with only slight modifications, in all demonstrations I report here. In the present example of tracking, the person is modeled with a reference signal *(r)* to perceive the cursor aligned with the target *(r = [cur − t = 0])*. The computational steps for the model become:

$$cur := h + d; \tag{3}$$

$$h_{next} := h_{former} + (k \cdot error) \cdot dt; \tag{4}$$

where error $= r − p = (0 − (c − t))$.

During the simulation, all variables were set to initial values, and then the model was iterated 1,799 times, once for every $^1/_{30}$ second during the modeled 60-second run. On each iteration, the new (independent) values of *t* and *d* were inserted into the program steps, error was calculated, any change (including 0) in the "position" of *h* was calculated, and the new position of *cur* was determined. Both the modeled positions of handle and cursor and the positions of the target changed on the screen in "real time" (at the same speed as with which the action was performed by the person). A record of those positions is shown at the top of figure 8.2 and is very similar to the record of the positions produced by the person: the correlation between 1800 pairs of predicted and actual positions of the handle exceeded +.99. This is a common outcome for PCT modeling of tracking tasks; in studies cited a few paragraphs earlier, correlations between many thousands of predicted and actual positions of handles and cursors were greater than +.97, often above +.99.

The performances of the person and the PCT model would not always agree as closely as that. For example, predictions by the present model would eventually fail were the person to abandon control of the perceived relationship between cursor and target, controlling instead so as to perceive the handle moving to match an imagined pattern of movements or to make the handle move back and forth to match perceived up and down movements of the target. In either case, a PCT model with a reference signal calling for a specific cursor-target distance would not duplicate the person's performance, but I showed elsewhere (Bourbon 1993, 1994) that the model could easily "recover," given nothing more than a new reference signal for the appropriate perception.

Tracking by Interacting Systems

At the conference represented in this book, I demonstrated interactive tasks with pairs comprising two people, two hands of one person, two PCT models, or a PCT model and a person, performing together, creating results that one system acting alone could not create. There is not enough space here for me to include results of interactive tracking and modeling using PCT, but interactions among various combinations of human hands and PCT models have been described and modeled by Bourbon (1989, 1990); Marken (1986, 1991); and several of my thesis students including Chong (1988); Gann (1992); Lazare (1992); and Duggins-Schwartz (1993). In those studies, when two PCT models each controlled their own perceptual signals, their actions duplicated many features of interactions between people (social interactions) and between the hands (hence, the cerebral hemispheres) of a single person. No central plans, commands, or monitoring were necessary for two PCT models to duplicate the results of human interactions or for a PCT model to interact, on line, with a person.

Bacterial Locomotion: Precise Control via Random Consequences

Among the enduring questions about the design of computer models, and of artificial systems such as robots, are those concerning how much prior knowledge to build into the system. How intelligent or informed should we make the learning process? How much prior knowledge, or knowledge of remote variables, should we build into a system that must navigate in unpredictable real or simulated environments? To what degree is central planning of movements necessary?

A novel perspective of such questions appears when we model bacteria as systems that control their perceptual signals. Daniel Koshland (1977, 1980) described how *Escherichia coli,* the human intestinal bacterium, senses "attractants" and "repellents" and moves relative to them. *E. coli* moves straight ahead, its flagella twisted into a spiral by its "motor," or it "tumbles," flagella spread, and points in a new, randomly different direction in which it then moves straight ahead. (Koshland verified that the change in direction during tumbles is genuinely random in three-dimensional space.)

E. coli has a brief memory and discriminates the time rate of change in signals from each of its sensors. The activity of each of over 20 types of sensors correlates with the local concentration of a specific substance. Using their observations of the behavior of *E. coli* as their sole criterion, people have classified some of the substances as "attractants," others as "repellents." But, from the perspective of *E. coli,* if the rate of change in a certain sensor signal is positive, the next tumble is postponed (not eliminated) and the bacterium continues straight ahead; if the integral is negative or zero, *E. coli* tumbles, its direction changes randomly, and then it moves straight ahead and the observer calls the substance an attractant. For "repellents," the relation between increasing and decreasing signals, on the one hand, and tumbling or delaying a tumble, on the other, is the reverse of that for "attractants." By this seemingly crude method, *E. coli* reliably moves up and down concentration gradients, even with no knowledge of directions, concentrations, or gradients.

To simulate the behavior of a bacterium in the presence of an "attractant," Marken (1985) and Marken and Powers (1989) modeled *E. coli* as a control system with a reference signal to sense positive rates of change in perceptual signals for the attractant. (Both articles are reprinted in Marken 1992.) The model they used differed from the one described in my example on tracking only in that the reference signal was for the perceived rate of change in a signal and the modeled actions did not involve a handle. Figure 8.3 shows results from four runs of the model for *E. coli*. In each case, the model began at a different, randomly determined, location relative to the attractant. Moving straight ahead or tumbling randomly, the modeled bacterium quickly reached and stayed near the attractant.

In their chemotactic behavior, *E. coli* and the PCT model control rates of change in perceptual signals, not relationships like those in tracking tasks. Neither the bacterium nor the model uses a "map" of its environment, knowledge of environmental relationships, or plans for its actions or for trajectories. *E. coli* cannot control trajectories or positions on a map,

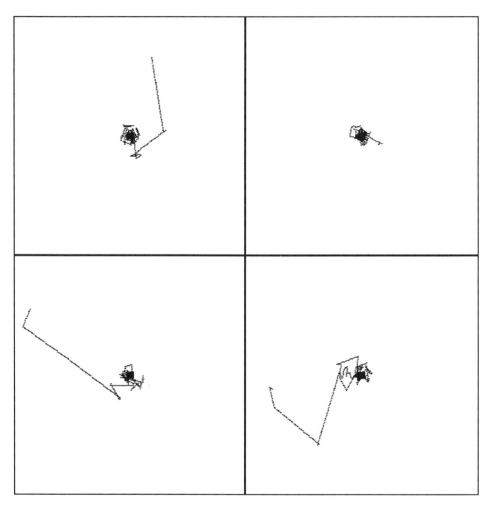

Figure 8.3 Four simulations, each completed in a few seconds using the model of behavior from perceptual control theory, of chemotaxis ("moving up a gradient") by the bacterium *Escherichia coli*. Small dots = successive positions of *E. coli*; large square = location of "attractant." On each run, *E. coli* began at a randomly determined position pointing in a randomly determined direction relative to the attractant, then moved to the attractant. (After Marken and Powers 1989.)

for it cannot sense them; it lives in a world of briefly remembered one-dimensional signals.

In *E. coli*, each sensor detects the magnitude of a local concentration. In the PCT model for *E. coli*, the magnitude of the sensor signal is compared against an internal standard. Any discrepancy between a standard and a sensor signal produces an error signal that leads to tumbling. (In a more complex version of the model with several sensors, error signals from all comparisons sum to produce a net error signal that determines whether the bacterium tumbles or moves straight ahead.)

The randomness inherent in tumbling did not impede control; for a perceptual control system like *E. coli* or a PCT model of the bacterium, random results of actions are as good as any others. To determine whether people can also achieve precise control through random results of their actions or whether the phenomenon is confined to "simpler" creatures, Marken (1985) and Marken and Powers (1989) conducted studies in which a dot moved across the computer screen, continuing in the same direction until a person tapped a key on the keyboard, at which time the program selected a direction for the dot at random. On each run, the dot began at a randomly different position. Every person who performed the demonstration selected a target position on the screen and used key taps that produced random changes as the only means to "guide" the dot. In every case, the dot reached the target with about 70 percent of the efficiency of a system moving it there directly. When controlled by people, the dots followed trajectories indistinguishable from those traced by the PCT model of *E. coli*. People, like *E. coli* and the PCT model, used random consequences of actions to produce precise and reliable control of the results they intended.

A word of warning to readers intent on developing a comparative cognitive science. When Marken and Powers submitted their report of these results to journals on animal behavior, editors and reviewers alike told them the work was unacceptable: bacteria and people are not animals. Also, several reviewers insisted the changes in direction could not have been random; they were simply denying the facts.

Perceptual control theorists suspect that control through random consequences ("the *E. coli* method") plays a significant role in many aspects of behavior. They are especially interested in the degree to which the *E. coli* method might drive the process of reorganization, the learning that occurs when a living system encounters circumstances in which its prior set of reference signals and control loops no longer effects control.

Gatherings and Crowds: Control Systems in Parallel

In the previous examples, living systems were modeled by single control loops. But we know that even the allegedly simplest organisms (like *E. coli*, for example) comprise many control loops working in parallel.

Parallel control plays a large role in the behavior of single organisms, but it might also give rise to many observed features of interactions among control systems—to social aspects of control.

The following demonstrations illustrate PCT models in parallel. Multiple independent control loops in each of several independent simulated agents (they could be persons, cellular robots, or social animals) act in concert, with no central plan or hierarchy of goals. When they interact in a common space, the agents create trajectories and collective "social" patterns that no one of them intends or senses. The social phenomena illustrated here were originally reported in studies by the sociologist Clark McPhail and several colleagues of people in gatherings of many kinds—including situations in which it is popular to say that people are "out of control." Their empirical work is reported in sources such as McPhail and Wohlstein (1986), McPhail and Tucker (1990), and McPhail (1991), and their data refute the idea that people in gatherings lose control. The computer program used here was written by Bill Powers for an article by McPhail, Powers, and Tucker (1992).

Two runs of the first demonstration are shown in figure 8.4. One simulated character (D) had a reference to perceive being at a specific destination; a second (P) "intended" to perceive being near D. Characters D and P each had references to perceive being no nearer than a certain distance to any other character. (In the setup procedure for the program, the user assigns reference signals and gain factors (integration factors) for each control loop in each simulated active person.) During each run, D and P began at the same locations, but simulated stationary people occupied randomly different locations, so the paths followed by D and P were necessarily different on each run, illustrating one of the defining features of control: unvarying ends created by variable means in a variable world. Control was achieved with no central, hierarchical commands and with no formal decision rule. In each model, each of six possible control loops sensed the local state of its variable and calculated any difference between its reference signal and what it sensed, and the difference became an error signal. Error signals from all of the control loops in a simulated actor were summed to become the reference signal for movement.

Exactly the same principles are illustrated in figure 8.5, which shows the results of two runs during which D had a reference to perceive being at a destination and each of four Ps "intended" to perceive being a certain distance from D. The various trajectories and the arc that forms around D at the destination are characteristic of many instances of social interaction and organization: they occur with no plan or intention, and there is no need for the actors to be aware their actions produce those externally observable consequences. (The image of the run at the top of figure 8.6 was captured before one P reached a stable location near D. The "loop" traced by that P near the destination is clearly visible. Shortly after this

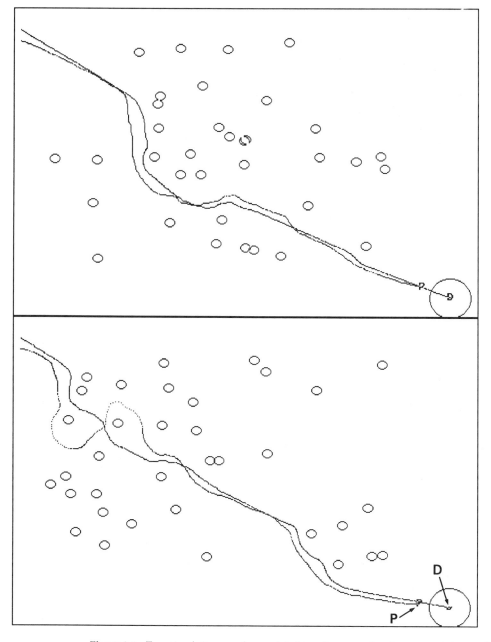

Figure 8.4 Two simulations, each completed in a few seconds, of movements by two PCT models of persons. The small dots represent successive positions of persons as they move from the far left of the screen. Person D "intends" to perceive being at a destination; person P intends to perceive being near D. P and D each intend to perceive being no nearer than a certain distance to any other person, including 35 randomly placed stationary people (O). (After McPhail, Powers, and Tucker 1992.)

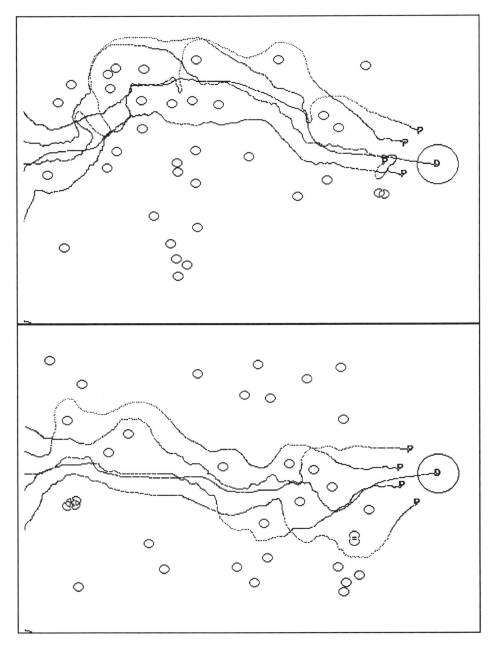

Figure 8.5 Two simulations, each completed in a few seconds, of movements by five PCT models of persons. The small dots represent successive positions of persons as they move from the far left of the screen. Person D intends to perceive being at a destination; the other four Ps intend to perceive being near D. Ps and D each intend to perceive being no nearer than a certain distance to any other person, including 35 stationary people (O). (After McPhail, Powers, and Tucker 1992.)

image was "grabbed," the simulation continued; the character moved to the top of the arc, and the other Ps "shuffled" sideways until each sensed all of its perceptions at their reference states.)

The phenomenon of social coordination among independent agents, illustrated in these demonstrations, should be of interest to students of the social behavior of animals. For example, these results suggest an answer to the question of whether animals in social groups such as flocks, schools, or swarms must know they are part of such a structure or whether their actions might simply become coordinated with those of their immediate neighbors when each of them controls its own perceptions. Also, it seems that principles of perceptual control like those shown here would be applicable in the creation of coordinated independent robots. Ideally, no single robot should know the "mission" of all of the group, but the robots must nonetheless scout out target locations or conditions (the *E. coli* method at work in D agents?), communicate with one another and move toward or away from locations or conditions (the *E. coli* method at work in D agents?), and at times link up to create self-assembling structures (the *E. coli* method at work in P agents?). And there is still the question of whether people in crowds lose their minds, becoming victims who fall under the control of emotional "viruses," as many social psychologists say.

Pointing: Control Systems in Parallel and in a Hierarchy

The idea of hierarchy is out of fashion in many circles. Some of its critics react against the idea that a privileged "top" can "command" lower levels. If that is their objection, it is shared by PCT theorists, who recognize that plans and commands from "higher" centers probably play no role in the production of coordinated human movements. Command-driven systems of any kind are poor analogies for adaptive living systems. But human nervous systems reveal both hierarchical and parallel structure, and when that structure is incorporated in a PCT model, the result is a singularly clear demonstration that what is traditionally called "the problem of motor control" might be more effectively modeled as perceptual control.

Many people who try to explain movement—for example, moving an arm to point at a moving object—assume that the mind-brain first computes the inverse kinematics of the movement. That is, it calculates the pure geometry of all successive positions the arm will occupy during the movement. Only then, it is assumed, can the mind-brain prepare and issue a pattern of "commands" to the muscles and thereby produce the dynamics of movement, which are independent of the kinematics. Bizzi, Mussa-Ivaldi, and Giszter (1991) take that position. Others, such as Kugler and Turvey (1987), do not discuss inverse kinematics, arguing that the language of nonlinear dynamical self-organizing systems offers an appropriate path toward understanding movement. To my knowledge, no proponent of either of these views has demonstrated a functional model that "behaves" as the PCT model does in the present demonstrations; their explanations of human movement are descriptive models (often impressive mathematical descriptions) rather than functional ones.

The computer program for this demonstration is from a paper by Powers and Williams (in press). The model includes multiple PCT systems in parallel and in a hierarchy, but there are no central plans or commands for movements; instead there are top-level reference signals for certain visual perceptions. Furthermore, the kinematics and dynamics of movement appear in the descriptions of the model's behavior; they are not incorporated within the model as causes for its behavior, as they are not needed in that role.

A group of hierarchical-parallel systems controls the perceptual signals, hence the behavior, of the stick figure shown in figure 8.6. The triangular target can move in x, y, and z. The figure has a high-level reference signal to perceive the target located at the center of the x and y coordinates of its visual field. If the target is not there, the resulting error signals act as reference signals for two lower-level control systems that move the character's head in x and y until it sees the target at the specified place. (The character has simple depth perception, produced by retinal disparity.)

The character also has a high-level reference signal that specifies seeing the end of its finger touching the target. If the perceived relationship between the finger and the target does not match the specified one, the ensuing visual error signals in x, y, and z serve as reference signals for independent lower-level kinesthetic control systems that move the figure's arm in x and y at the shoulder and in z at the elbow. For the arm and the head, independent systems control each degree of freedom (axis of movement); no "master system" oversees the operations of these independent control loops. The model includes stretch and tendon reflexes, spring constants for the muscles, masses, variable torque as a function of the length of a muscle, and other details of the physiology, anatomy, and physics of movement. Gravity can be turned on or off or adjusted, and the model can run with a simplified arm that has no mass. The model behaves at or near the same speed as a person, depending on the personal computer and on the program options in effect.

Figure 8.6 shows positions of the fingertip when the character, with all aspects of modeled physical realism at their maxima, pointed at a moving target. In the top panel the target moved left to right; in the bottom panel it moved up and down. In each case, the path traced by the finger reveals improvements in pointing when the "person" learned to compensate for errors in reaching that occur due to the distance between the eyes and the attachment of the arm at the shoulder. The simple learning algorithm

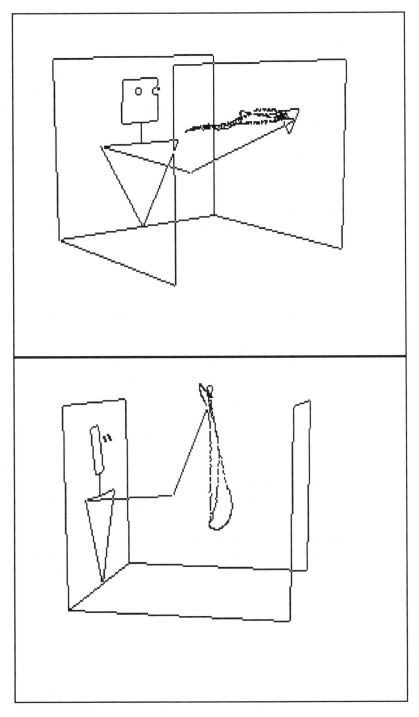

Figure 8.6 Traces of positions of the fingertip of the stick character when it "intended" to perceive its finger touching a target that moved repeatedly from left to right (top) and up and down (bottom). Accuracy of pointing improved when the character "learned" to compensate for initial errors caused by the discrepancy between positions of the eyes and the shoulder; the traces are "loopy" at the start and quickly become straight. During these two runs, all modeled physical properties of the arm were active, as was simulated gravity. No prior plans or solutions of inverse kinematics were used. The simulations occurred slightly faster than a person could complete them. (After Powers and Williams, in press.)

produced corrections in the reference signals for where the character should see its hand move.

The behavior in these demonstrations occurs as the unintended means by which the model controls its simulated perceptual signals, not as a result of prior plans or commands. The success of the hierarchical PCT model used in this demonstration should signal the demise of most plan-driven and command-driven models of movement.

PCT and the History of Cognitive Science

On their first encounter with PCT, many people believe it derives from contemporary cognitive science, but PCT predates the "cognitive revolution," cognitive science, and many associated concepts and applications, such as artificial intelligence, parallel distributed processing, neural networks, chaos, bottom-up processing, nonlinear dynamics, strange attractors, reactive or adaptive systems, situated agents, and whatever else has come along since I began the final draft of this chapter. In the late 1950s William T. Powers and a few colleagues developed PCT, known then as feedback theory and later as control systems theory (CST). Their first publications were in 1960 (Powers, Clark, and McFarland 1960a, b, and they were reprinted along with a number of other early papers in Powers 1990; some of the earliest, previously unpublished, manuscripts on PCT are available in Powers 1992). After that early collaboration, Powers (1973a, 1973b, 1978) worked alone to refine control system theory. Only in the 1980s did a number of other people begin to participate in developing the PCT model.

Work on PCT occurred outside of any major school or movement in behavioral and cognitive science. By choice, perceptual control theorists did not identify with or borrow ideas from those research communities. An advantage of the relative isolation of PCT theorists is that they offer independent, often novel perspectives of topics that interest people in the mainstream of cognitive science. Some examples have been included in this chapter. Of course, isolation has its disadvantages, one of which is that people who work in other traditions often assume they already understand and can explain the phenomena addressed in PCT. That belief is often mistaken.

SUMMARY AND CONCLUSIONS

What has been demonstrated here? Precise, reliable control, in spite of unpredictably changed or disturbed circumstances, with no plans, no commands, no inverse kinematics, no language of nonlinear dynamics. Control of sensed local variables. Parallel, hierarchical control, with error from higher systems serving as reference signals for lower systems. Precise control achieved through random consequences of actions. Learning that alters reference signals for perceptions rather than altering commands for actions. And all of this has been demonstrated by a model that controls its perceptions, not its actions. I know of no other model in behavioral or cognitive science that behaves in simulation under conditions as diverse as those illustrated here.

S → R?

Some readers have challenged my last statement, citing work like that of Randall Beer (1990) and Rodney Brooks (1989), whose models also behave without plans or representations. Beer and Brooks both describe their models and robots as reflexive S → R systems in which specific stimuli elicit specific behaviors. Nothing could be further from a closed-loop perceptual control system. Most models that use a sequential chain of cause and effect, whether it is called S → R, I → PROCESSING → O, or some variation on that time-worn theme, cannot produce unvarying results in variable environments. That failure is especially common in systems that control their actions rather than their perceptions. If reflexive S → R systems cannot succeed in disturbed settings, how can models like those of Beer and Brooks work as well as they do?

Beer and Brooks acknowledge that their goals are to explain and model the production of specific actions as seen by an observer—the sorts of things that are usually in the category of unintended variables (*vi*) as far as the behaving system is concerned. Each "reflex" they describe is in fact a specific stimulus-response association that operates around a threshold value for a perceptual signal. In such a system, thresholds are functionally equivalent to reference signals provided by, but not always acknowledged or explained by, the modeler. In perceptual control theory, reference signals are made explicit and are central to the operation of the model.

Also, in the hierarchical PCT model, lower-level control loops are general-purpose devices that affect perceptual signals for all higher levels in the system; there are no special loops analogous to the single-purpose reflexes in the models of Beer and Brooks. Adding a new "behavior" to one of their reflexive systems requires building a new S → R circuit that must be carefully integrated into the existing architecture, a task that proves more daunting as the complexity of their systems grows. In a perceptual control system model, all that may be needed is a new reference signal for an existing control loop.

The best comparison of PCT and S → R or I → O models will occur when both models are implemented in the same artificial device (cellular or distributed robots would be good choices), which must behave in unpredictably variable environments. No perceptual control theorist has been in a position to conduct that test, but comparisons have been run in computer simulations by Bourbon and Powers (1993) and by Marken (1993). The results of those simulations challenge the validity of any theory that portrays behavior as part of a linear process of S → R or of I → PROCESSING → O.

Intentions

Folk psychology recognizes that people often know what they intend to experience, but they do not know all of the actions needed to create those experiences, and they do not anticipate all consequences of their actions. In contrast, in cognitive science and neuroscience, some writers say people never know what they are doing—that people who claim such knowledge are deluded or lying. Perceptual control theorists doubt that millennia of human history were acted and written (entirely) by charlatans and deluded fools. The notion that people are necessarily ignorant or deceptive about their own motives and actions starts to take hold when scientists ask people what they are doing, believing the actions they (the scientists) see are what people are doing. Often what people describe in response to that question does not match what the scientists have observed. However, as observers uninformed about control, many scientists have merely noticed the unintended side effects of the actors' successful purposive behavior.

Living systems use necessarily variable actions, the details of which need not be objects of their awareness, to create intended perceptions that only they experience. Living systems intentionally "do" many of their own perceptions. Any general theory of behavior and comparative cognition must explain that simple, universal fact.

APPENDIX

These addresses will allow readers to obtain more information about PCT and to inquire about executable copies of PCT demonstrations. Tom Bourbon: Department of Neurosurgery, University of Texas Medical School - Houston, 6431 Fannin, Suite 7.148, Houston, TX 77030 USA (e-mail: TBOURBON@HEART.MED.UTH.TMC.EDU) Rick Marken: 10459 Holman Avenue, Los Angeles, CA 90024 USA (e-mail: MARKEN@AERO.-ORG [The Aerospace Corporation]). Clark McPhail: Department of Sociology, University of Illinois, Urbana-Champaign, IL 61801 USA (e-mail: CMCPHAIL@VMD.CSO.UIUC.EDU). Bill Powers: 73 Ridge Place CR510, Durango, CO 81301 USA (e-mail: POWERS_W%FLC@VAXF.COLORA-DO.EDU). Greg Williams: 460 Black Lick Road, Gravel Switch, KY 40328 USA (e-mail: 4972767@MCIMAIL.COM).

Information about computer programs for PCT demonstrations may be requested from the following sources: tracking tasks, Tom Bourbon; bacterial movement, Rick Marken or Bill Powers; crowds or gatherings, Clark McPhail or Bill Powers; arm movement, Bill Powers or Greg Williams. Powers also created two disks, DEMO1 and DEMO2, as tutorials on the fundamentals of control and of PCT. At the discretion of the authors, certain programs are available to individuals or to institutions. There may be a fee for the expenses of distribution.

The computer network addresses for PCT are, on Bitnet, CSG-L@UIUC-VMD.BITNET, and on Internet, CSG-L@VMD.CSO.UIUC.EDU.

REFERENCES

Beer, R. D. (1990). *Intelligence as Adaptive Behavior: An Experiment in Computational Neuroethology.* New York: Academic Press.

Bizzi, E., Mussa-Ivaldi, F. A., and Giszter, S. (1991). Computations underlying the execution of movement: A biological perspective. *Science,* 253, 287–291.

Bourbon, W. T. (1989). A control-theory analysis of interference during social tracking. In W. A. Hershberger (Ed.). *Volitional Action: Conation and Control.* Amsterdam: North-Holland, pp. 235–251.

Bourbon, W. T. (1990). Invitation to the dance: Explaining the variance when control systems interact. *American Behavioral Scientist,* 34, 95–105.

Bourbon, W. T. (1994). Program-level control of a sequence of perceived relationships: Perceptual control theory in the cognitive domain. In M. A. Rodrigues and M. H. Lee (Eds.), *Proceedings of the 1st European Workshop on Perceptual Control Theory, Gregynog, The University of Wales.*

Bourbon, W. T., and Powers, W. T. (1993). Models and their worlds. *Closed Loop: Threads from CSGnet,* 3(1), 47–72. (Available from CSG Book Publishing, 460 Black Lick Road, Gravel Switch, KY 40238.)

Bourbon, W. T., Copeland, K. E., Dyer, V. R., Harman, W. K., and Mosely, B. L. (1990). On the accuracy and reliability of predictions by control-system theory. *Perceptual and Motor Skills,* 71, 1331–1338.

Brooks, R. A. (1989). A robot that walks: Emergent behaviors from a carefully evolved network. *Neural Computation,* 1, 253–262.

Chong, E. (1988). *Cooperation interpreted in terms of control system theory.* Unpublished Master's thesis, Stephen F. Austin State University, Nacogdoches, TX.

Duggins-Schwartz, M. (1993). *Computer helper interacting with a human: When is helping helping?* Unpublished Master's thesis, Stephen F. Austin State University, Nacogdoches, TX.

Gann, C. P. III (1992). *Nonverbal communication in a cooperative task modeled by perceptual control theory.* Unpublished Master's thesis, Stephen F. Austin State University, Nacogdoches, TX.

Koshland, D. E. (1977). A response regulator model in a simple sensory system. *Science* 196, 1055–1063.

Koshland, D. E. (1980). *Behavioral Chemotaxis as a Model Behavioral System.* New York: Raven Press.

Kugler, P. N., and Turvey, M. T. (1987). *Information, Natural Law, and the Self-Assembly of Rhythmic Movement.* Hillsdale, NJ: Erlbaum.

Lazare, M. A. (1992). *A perceptual control theory analysis of cooperation and social interaction.* Unpublished Master's thesis, Stephen F. Austin State University, Nacogdoches, TX.

Marken, R. S. (1980). The cause of control movements in a tracking task. *Perceptual and Motor Skills,* 51, 755.

Marken, R. S. (1985). Selection of consequences: Adaptive behavior from random reinforcement. *Psychological Reports*, 56, 379–383.

Marken, R. S. (1986). Perceptual organization of behavior: A hierarchical control model of coordinated action. *Journal of Experimental Psychology: Human Perception and Performance*, 12, 267–276.

Marken, R. S. (1991). Degrees of freedom in behavior. *Psychological Science*, 2, 92–100.

Marken, R. S. (Ed.) (1992). *Mind Readings: Experimental Studies of Purpose*. Gravel Switch, KY: Control Systems Group.

Marken, R. S. (1993). The blind men and the elephant. *Closed Loop: Threads from CSGnet*, 3(1), 37–46. (Available from CSG Book Publishing, 460 Black Lick Road, Gravel Switch, KY 40238.)

Marken, R. S., and Powers, W. T. (1989). Random-walk chemotaxis: Trial-and-error as a control process. *Behavioral Neuroscience*, 103, 1348–1355.

McPhail, C. (1991). *The Myth of the Madding Crowd*. New York: Aldine de Gruyter.

McPhail, C., and Tucker, C. W. (1990). Purposive collective action. *American Behavioral Scientist*, 34, 81–94.

McPhail, C., and Wohlstein, R. T. (1986). Collective locomotion as collective behavior. *American Sociological Review*, 51, 447–463.

McPhail, C., Powers, W. T., and Tucker, C. T. (1992). Simulating individual and collective action in temporary gatherings. *Social Science Computer Review*, 10, 1–28.

Pavloski, R. P. (1989). The physiological stress of thwarted intentions. In W. A. Hershberger (Ed.). *Volitional Action: Conation and Control*. Amsterdam: North-Holland, pp. 215–232.

Pavloski, R. P., Barron, G. T., and Hogue, M. A. (1990). Reorganization: Learning and attention in a hierarchy of control systems. *American Behavioral Scientist*, 34, 32–54.

Powers, W. T. (1973a). *Behavior: The Control of Perception*. Chicago: Aldine.

Powers, W. T. (1973b). Feedback: Beyond behaviorism. *Science*, 179, 351–356.

Powers, W. T. (1978). Qualitative analysis of purposive systems: Some spadework at the foundations of scientific psychology. *Psychological Review*, 85, 417–435.

Powers, W. T. (1989). Quantitative measurement of volition: A pilot study. In W. A. Hershberger (Ed.). *Volitional Action: Conation and Control*. Amsterdam: North-Holland, pp. 315–332.

Powers, W. T. (1990). *Living Control Systems: Selected Papers of William T. Powers*. Gravel Switch, KY: Control Systems Group.

Powers, W. T. (1992). *Living Control Systems II: Selected Papers of William T. Powers*. Gravel Switch, KY: Control Systems Group.

Powers, W. T., and Williams, G. (in press). A control-system model of pointing behavior. *International Journal of Human-Computer Studies*.

Powers, W. T., Clark, R. K., and McFarland, R. I. (1960a). A general feedback theory of human behavior: Part I. *Perceptual and Motor Skills*, 11, 71–78.

Powers, W. T., Clark, R. K., and McFarland, R. I. (1960b). A general feedback theory of human behavior: Part II. *Perceptual and Motor Skills*, 11, 309–323.

III Representation

9 Natural and Relational Concepts in Animals

Roger K. R. Thompson

NATURAL AND RELATIONAL CONCEPTS IN ANIMALS

Fairy Tale or Reality?

There is a scene from the animated film version (Disney 1939) of *The Ugly Duckling* (Andersen 1984) in which the young bird has just been rejected by those he had thought until then were his siblings and mother. As described by Thompson and Contie (1994), the Ugly Duckling looks longingly towards this small, self-contained group as they waddle away in disdain. Then, moving toward the lake edge, he catches sight of his distorted features reflected by the shimmering surface of the water. The Ugly Duckling turns toward the viewer and points with a look of abject despair at himself.

Can one doubt the conceptual basis of the Ugly Duckling's behavior? First, until they rejected him, the Ugly Duckling had acted as if he believed that he and his presumed mother and siblings belonged to the same natural category of ducks. Second, the Ugly Duckling's categorical behavior, conjoined with his self-labeling of his reflected image, further suggests that his categorical judgments are made on the basis of abstract relational identity. Finally, one's suspicion that the Ugly Duckling has a self-concept is confirmed by his negative emotional evaluation of himself.

But is the conceptual understanding expressed by the Ugly Duckling anything more than a fairy tale? Does the behavior of real nonhuman animals provide the same evidence of conceptual knowledge, including that of the self? Those areas in animal cognition which speak directly to this issue are discussed in this chapter. The first and major part of the chapter focuses on whether and how animals perceptually organize natural objects into categories, including that of the self. The remainder of the chapter looks at the evidence of abstract relational concepts in animals.

Conceptual Properties of Natural Concepts

What do different approaches to the study of natural concepts in animals have in common? First and foremost, conceptually mediated animal behavior involves the adoption of a response strategy organized at some level by the perception and representation of *similarity* (Murphy and Medin 1985; Medin 1989). When animals learn to discriminate between classes of what humans perceive as open-ended natural categories (e.g., trees, tree leaves, people, and fish), their behavior is labeled as conceptual if it cannot be easily attributed to either rote learning or generalization along a single physical stimulus dimension like wavelength (e.g., Hernstein 1990). The assumption is that animals detect and use similar invariant *within-class* feature sets shared by members of the natural category under study. Animals may also learn a rule-based concept based on a nonphysical or abstract relationship between items that transcends any particular set of exemplars. In same/different discrimination tasks, for example, the interest is in whether animals can match one of several alternatives to a previously displayed sample item using conceptual identity—i.e., match like with like—rather than absolute stimulus values—i.e., match red with red—(e.g., Premack 1983a).

The *behavioral evidence* that an animal perceives, or has learned, a natural object concept is the same as that used in studies of abstract relational concepts. In both cases, it is an animal's ability to transfer its performance spontaneously to novel exemplars of the category or relationship in question (e.g., see Thomas and Kerr 1976). In some studies, analyses of error patterns rather than correct responses on transfer tests are used to infer the nature and boundaries of an animal's conceptual codes (e.g., Zentall, Jackson-Smith, and Jagielo 1990). For example, an animal that responds to novel pictures with people in them, but rejects novel pictures of both monkeys and other mammals, might be thought of as having learned a person concept. However, another animal that responds to novel pictures with either persons or monkeys in them, but rejects all other mammals, might be thought of as having learned a primate concept rather than a person concept (cf. Schrier and Brady 1987).

Conceptually mediated behavior is often assumed to be *functional*. Categorization, it is argued, economically reduces the amount of invariant sensory-perceptual information an organism needs to attend to and remember in a complex world (Cook, Wright, and Kendrick 1990; Hernstein 1990; Wasserman 1993). Similarly, animals whose response rules are based on relational concepts can generate functional response classes to specific cases, situations, and domains with which they have had no prior experience or reinforcement history (Premack 1978; Wright et al. 1988). Despite the nod to functional concerns, many if not all investigators of both natural object and relational concepts in animals adopt what has been labeled a proto-evolutionary approach (Timberlake 1993). Different species are used primarily to clarify our own conceptual understanding and organization of psychological phenomena (e.g., Hernstein 1990) rather than to make explicit ecological and phylogenetic comparisons (cf. Pietrewicz and Kamil 1977; Real et al. 1984).

Despite the similarities in research on natural object and relational concepts in animals, integrative studies are rare (but see, for example, Platt, Thompson, and Boatright 1991; Sands, Lincoln, and Wright 1982; Cheney and Seyfarth 1990a). Studies of conceptual categorization primarily address questions of complex stimulus perception, discrimination, and representation. They are seldom concerned with the nature of the response rule by which an animal identifies an object as belonging or not belonging to a category. Discussions of self-concepts in animals may be couched in terms of self-awareness and consciousness (Griffin 1981; Ristau 1991) rather than complex stimulus control or action systems. Students of relational concepts like those of sameness and difference usually ignore the question of whether animals' stimulus equivalence judgments are constrained across categorical classes.

NATURAL CATEGORICAL CONCEPTS

Contemporary interest in the study of natural categorical concepts in nonhumans increased significantly in the 1970s when researchers demonstrated that pigeons *(Columba livia)* could be trained to discriminate pictures of open-ended natural object classes such as tree leaves, trees, bodies of water, pigeons, people, and even fish (e.g., Cerella 1979; Hernstein 1984; Hernstein and de Villiers 1980; Hernstein, Loveland, and Cable 1976). Although pigeons were often used as subjects (Hernstein and Loveland 1964; Siegel and Honig 1970; Lander and Poole 1971), other species also served. Categorization of natural classes has been studied in chickens (Ryan 1982; Ryan and Lea 1990), budgerigars (Trillmich 1976), blue jays (Pietrewicz and Kamil 1977), an African Grey parrot (Pepperberg 1983), old- and new-world monkeys (e.g., Roberts and Mazmanian 1988; D'Amato and van Sant 1988; Schrier, Angarella, and Povar 1984), and apes (e.g., Hayes and Hayes 1953; Gardener and Gardener, 1985).

Experimental Methodologies

Operant and Instrumental Discrimination Tasks
An operant go/no-go discrimination task is commonly used in studies of natural categories (e.g., see review in Herrnstein 1984). The typical procedure with pictorial stimuli is as follows: Subjects are intermittently rewarded on a variable interval (VI) reinforcement schedule for touching a key when a photographic slide containing, say, a tree is presented (i.e., a positive display) and for not responding when slides containing no tree are presented (i.e., a negative display). Dependent measures are based on response rates to the two displays. For example, a discrimination ratio may be calculated as the proportion of total responses (i.e., key touches) emitted in the presence of positive displays. Hence, a discrimination ratio of 1.0 would imply perfect categorical discrimination, and a ratio of 0.5

would indicate no discrimination. Following acquisition of the initial training discrimination task to a preordained criterion level, transfer tests with both novel positive and negative stimuli are run.

Other instrumental methods used to study natural object categorization include discrete trial simultaneous and successive forced-choice procedures (e.g., Bhatt et al. 1988; D'Amato and van Sant 1988). Dependent measures in these tasks may include latency to first response, percentage of correct trial-1 choices, overall percentage of correct responses, and rate of operant responding (e.g., Bhatt et al. 1988; Cook, Wright, and Kendrick 1990).

Sensory Reinforcement

In sensory reinforcement procedures an animal is allowed to choose freely whether or not it will observe a stimulus and for how long (e.g., Fujita and Matsuzawa 1986). Sensory reinforcement procedures are also useful for mapping out natural categories in the sense that they reveal how animals spontaneously partition objects in their world. Sensory reinforcement procedures also have the advantage that no long-term discrimination training is necessary. They also eliminate the problem of performance differences between species that are attributable to motivational rather than perceptual factors. Examples of how these different methods are used are discussed throughout the remainder of this chapter.

In most studies, animals are trained with only one category (e.g., person) as the positive stimulus set; the content of the negative stimulus set is usually defined simply by positive class exclusion (i.e., nonperson). However, other methods may require animals to concurrently classify stimuli from multiple different categories. For example, Wasserman and his colleagues use a forced-choice procedure in which pigeons peck one of four keys depending upon which of four categories the discriminative stimulus belongs to (cf. Bhatt et al. 1988; Gardener and Gardener 1985; Wasserman, Keidinger, and Bhatt 1988).

As noted above, categorization is inferred from the evidence that animals transfer their discriminative performances to novel exemplars. This measure rules out *rote memorization* of the original training list of items, which is not a trivial concern. There is good evidence that both pigeons and monkeys have good long-term memory for large photographic slide sets of individual natural objects (Jitsumori, Wright, and Cook 1988; Ringo and Doty 1985; Vaughan and Green 1984). Transfer of performance to novel exemplars, however, does not in itself unequivocally demonstrate that an animal's categorical discriminations are conceptual in nature.

Discriminative responding in the face of stimulus variability is itself not a sufficient criterion for conceptual categorization. In human eyes, within-category stimuli may resemble one another more than other stimuli. Nevertheless, it does not necessarily follow that an animal's acquisition and subsequent transfer of the requisite discrimination result from its detecting features common to the category defined by the experimenters. Performance can be controlled by extraneous factors (Ryan and Lea 1990) such as categorically irrelevant background cues (Green 1983) and even perceptual artifacts like overall luminosity of photographic slides (Lea and Ryan 1983; Lubow 1974). The effects of these extraneous factors can be controlled by using matched pairs of slides that are created by photographing the same scene twice, once with the category member in it and again with it absent (e.g., D'Amato and van Sant 1988; Edwards and Honig 1987; Siegel and Honig 1970).

In one such study, Edwards and Honig (1987) trained pigeons to discriminate between slides of scenes containing humans from those that did not. Interestingly, those birds trained with positive and negative slides containing matching backgrounds acquired the discrimination task more slowly than those birds trained with slides in which the backgrounds did not match. This finding suggests that the pigeons were predisposed to attend to many potential discriminative cues that were available in the complex visual displays and had difficulty in attending to only the relevant conceptual human-feature within the visual field.

Even when background and context are controlled, there is still no guarantee that the animal's correct performance is controlled by the same category as that perceived and conceived of by the human investigators. A study of the person concept in new-world monkeys by D'Amato and van Sant (1988) is an instructive case in point.

A Person Concept in Monkeys?

D'Amato and van Sant (1988) used a go/no-go discrimination task to measure the ability of Capuchin monkeys *(Cebus apella)* to learn a "person" concept (cf. Schrier et al. 1984; Schrier and Brady 1987). Seven monkeys were trained to discriminate photographic slides containing a person from those that did not. Some subjects were rewarded for responding to "person" slides, others for responding to "nonperson" slides. After the animals had reached the training performance criterion, they were given transfer tests with stimuli consisting of both familiar and novel person/nonperson slides. Statistically significant transfer (i.e., 75 percent or better correct) was obtained with both unmatched (experiment 1) and matched (experiment 2) novel person/nonperson slides including, in experiment 4, those used previously by Schrier and Brady (1987). The results of the latter transfer test are shown in figure 9.1. Transfer to novel person slides also did not depend on human skin color in the training slides (experiment 3). Taken together, all the results suggested that discrimination of person from nonperson slides was not controlled by an obvious single stimulus feature.

D'Amato and van Sant's (1988) results seemed to provide strong evidence that their monkeys had learned a concept-mediated person vs.

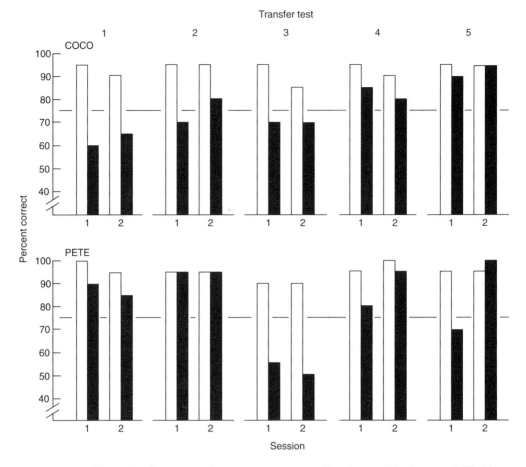

Figure 9.1 Percentage of correct responses on old and new slides (open and filled bars, respectively) during the first two sessions of the four transfer tests of experiment 4. The solid line indicates the .05 level of significance. (From D'Amato and van Sant 1988, in *Journal of Experimental Psychology: Animal Behavior Processes*, copyright © 1988 by the American Psychological Association.)

nonperson discrimination. The investigators themselves, however, questioned this conclusion after they analyzed identification errors made on specific slides by their subjects. They found that a significant proportion of misidentified nonperson slides contained a red patch. Furthermore, those nonperson slides in which the red patch was a feature of an animal or flower were more likely to elicit errors than those in which it was associated with inanimate objects. D'Amato and van Sant (1988) concluded, "Apparently, the conjoint features of red patch/animal comprised an irresistible instance of the 'category' that controlled the monkeys' classificatory behavior" (p. 54).

The revised conclusion was that the monkeys had not necessarily learned a person concept. Perhaps they had, but the data did not rule out other possibilities. Despite the attempts to control irrelevant cues via matched slides, some control was exerted by a categorically irrelevant red hue. Also, to the extent that the monkeys had identified salient features associated with humans, they were not categorically specific. Could it be that the animals' discriminations were controlled by featural relationships shared by a more basic categorical distinction that humans might label "animal versus nonanimal" or even "animate versus inanimate"? It is difficult to tell, given the lack of controls for the categorical content of slides in the negative nonperson stimulus set. In fairness, however, one should note that this methodological failing is endemic to studies of natural object categorization (cf. Astley and Wasserman 1992). Its importance, however, was clearly demonstrated in a study, described later, of categorical learning at different hierarchical levels in pigeons, monkeys, and humans by Roberts and Mazmanian (1988).

Hierarchical Categorical Levels

Basic Categories

Humans organize categories at different levels. For example, as noted above, one could sort the slides used by D'Amato and van Sant (1988) not only into person vs. nonperson categories, but also into animal vs. nonanimal and even animate vs. inanimate categories. The slides containing humans could themselves be further subcategorized along the lines of gender, race, and age. Studies of natural object categorization by humans reveal that a single subcategory or level is spontaneously preferred over others (Rosch et al. 1976). The preferred, or *basic*, level is an intermediate level rather than the most concrete or most abstract level (Berlin, Breedlove, and Raven 1973; Rosch et al. 1976). Hence, dog is at a basic categorical level, not collie or animal. Collie is at a concrete subordinate level nested under the basic level of dog; both collie and dog are further taxonomically nested under the superordinate level of animal.

Is there a parallel hierarchical structure in the natural object categories of animals and, if so, then what is its basic level? The issue of concept learning at different levels was explicitly addressed by Roberts and Mazmanian (1988), who were interested in whether humans, squirrel monkeys *(Saimiri scurieus)*, and Silver King pigeons *(Columba livia)* could learn natural object categorical discriminations that differed at the taxonomic levels of animal species, class, and kingdom.

Species Differences in Taxonomic Abstraction

Roberts and Mazmanian (1988) trained all three species using a two-alternative forced-choice discrimination learning procedure on three types of problems. At the most concrete level, they were rewarded for choosing photographic slides (i.e., multiple exemplars) of a single bird species, the common kingfisher *(Alcedo atthis)*, which were simultaneously paired with slides of other bird species; choices of the latter species were not rewarded.

In the second intermediate-level problem, the same subjects were rewarded for choosing pictures of bird species paired with pictures of animals that were not birds. In the most abstract-level problem, responses to animal pictures paired with nonanimal pictures were rewarded. Roberts and Mazmanian (1988) hypothesized that, if animals learned only those categories consisting of exemplars that "looked alike" (Premack 1983a), then their pigeon and squirrel monkey subjects would learn the most concrete kingfisher vs. other bird discrimination more readily than the other two more abstract problem types.

The human subjects rapidly learned all three discriminations as measured by above-chance correct-choice performance levels with novel stimuli presented during probe trials in test sessions. Also as predicted, the pigeons and monkeys performed well on the "kingfisher vs. other bird species" problem (experiment 1), but they needed extended training with more examples (experiment 3) before they learned the most abstract level "animal vs. nonanimal" discrimination. Neither pigeon nor monkey, however, chose at a level better than chance with novel pictures in the intermediate-level "bird vs. other animal" problem (experiments 1, 2, and 3). The results from the first two experiments are summarized in figure 9.2.

The pigeons and monkeys had difficulty discriminating between different classes of animals in general, but they could discriminate between animals and nonanimals. These results support D'Amato and van Sant's (1988) suggestion that their Cebus monkeys had learned an "animal vs. nonanimal" categorical discrimination rather than the "person vs. nonperson" distinction the experimenters had made. Roberts and Mazmanian's (1988) results are also interesting because they indicate that it was easiest for the squirrel monkeys and pigeons to discriminate between the two categories (i.e., kingfisher vs. other bird species) with exemplars that presumably were physically the most similar. One might conclude that the basic category level for these animals was species, which is a subordinate-level category for humans. The supposedly intermediate basic-level for humans (i.e., bird vs. other animal) was extraordinarily difficult for the nonhuman subjects to discriminate, and they failed to master it as measured by transfer to novel pictures. Discrimination of the superordinate category (i.e., animal vs. nonanimal), whose members were presumably most dissimilar in human eyes, was acquired only with difficulty by the animals after they had experienced many different exemplars. As Roberts and Mazmanian (1988) pointed out, "This pattern of results is just the opposite of that predicted by the basic category model" (p. 257; cf. Rosch et al. 1976).

Species as a Basic Category
The hypothesis that "species" is a categorical basic level for animals is also supported by other studies with birds and nonhuman primates (e.g.,

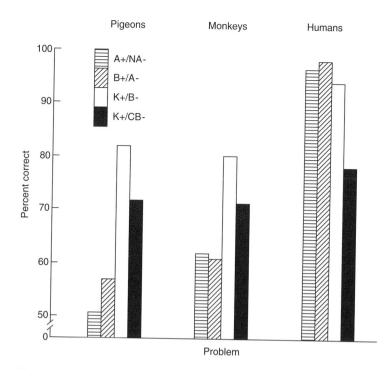

Figure 9.2 Mean percentage of correct responses on probe tests with 16 novel pairs of pictures. The first three bars in each set represent data from experiment 1; the fourth bar in each set represents data from experiment 2. A = animals; NA = nonanimals; B = birds; CB = colorful birds; K = kingfisher; + = reinforced; − = nonreinforced. (From Roberts and Mazmanian, in *Journal of Experimental Psychology: Animal Behavior Processes,* copyright © 1988 by the American Psychological Association.)

Edwards and Honig 1987; Jitsumori and Matsuzawa 1991; Schrier and Brady 1987; Schrier, Angarella, and Povar 1984; Swartz 1983; Yoshikubo 1985). Yoshikubo (1985), for example, reported that rhesus monkeys (*Macaca mulatta*) discriminated not only between new pictures with rhesus monkeys and those without, but also between new pictures of rhesus monkeys and other Japanese macaques (*M. fuscata fuscata*). However, comparisons between macaques as a class and other monkey genera (analogous to Roberts and Mazmanian's "bird vs. other animal"), were not made.

Schrier and Brady (1987) trained rhesus monkeys (*Macaca mulatta*) to categorically discriminate between positive slides with humans and negative ones without humans. Subsequently, in a second experiment, the same animals were presented with pictures of monkeys or apes (M&A). The M&A probes were chosen randomly on 50 percent of the trials when they were paired with negative slides without humans. However, M&A probes were chosen on only 25 percent of those trials in which they were paired with positive slides of humans. The same animals responded at

Natural and Relational Concepts in Animals

chance levels to positive human slides only when they were paired with negative probe slides consisting of upright humans placed against inverted backgrounds.

Did the discrimination procedures themselves influence, if not determine, the basic level category adopted by nonhuman subjects in these studies? Apparently not, because results from other tasks that employ measures of visual fixation or orientation confirm the saliency of species as a basic level for at least nonhuman primates. Sackett (1970) reported that infant monkeys oriented to and approached live adult conspecifics for longer durations than those of other species. In a habituation/dishabituation task, Swartz (1983) found that infant pigtail macaque monkeys *(Macaca nemestrina)* looked longer at monkey slides if they were of a different species than the one in the initial habituation slide. These studies indicate that macaque monkeys spontaneously discriminate pictures of different species.

Similar results are obtained in sensory reinforcement tasks in which animals learn a simple operant for the opportunity to look at pictorial stimuli. Humphrey (1974) found that, given a choice, rhesus monkeys preferred to look at their own species over other mammals. Similarly, Demaria and Thierry (1988) and Swartz and Rosenblum (1980) reported that adult female stumptailed *(Macaca arctoides)* and bonnet macaques *(Macaca radiata)*, respectively, looked longer at pictures or videotapes of their own species than at others. Candland and Judge (1991) also found that Japanese macaques *(M. fuscata)* and baboons *(Papio hamadyas)*, given the opportunity to select from among different visual classes of primate species, preferred to look at slides of conspecifics.

Categorization: A Reproductive Isolating Mechanism?

Many macaques are sympatric (i.e., geographically overlapping) species (Fooden 1980). The above results showing preferences for conspecifics are not surprising, therefore, given the functional significance of species recognition and preference as a reproductive isolating mechanism discouraging hybridization. This hypothesis was further supported by Fujita (1987), who used a sensory reinforcement procedure (Fujita and Matsuzawa 1986) to compare the characteristics of species discriminations among five species of macaque monkeys. Sixteen monkeys of five macaque species *(Macaca fuscata fuscata, M. mulatta, M. radiata, M. nemestrina, and M. arctoides)* were trained to press a lever to produce slides, each of which showed one of seven macaque species. A slide remained continuously visible as long as the lever was pressed, and the same slide was presented each time the interval between lever presses was 10 seconds or less. A new slide was presented if more than 10 seconds had passed since the last lever press.

With the exception of stumptailed macaques *(M. arctoides)* and two infant Japanese monkeys *(M. fuscata)*, monkeys looked at pictures of their conspecifics the longest. Fujita (1987) also plotted two-dimensional distributions of response duration and inter-response interval for slides of different species. The data for pictures of conspecifics were distributed at different locations than those of other species. Results of a multidimensional scaling procedure and cluster analysis of species distance matrixes provided Fujita (1987) with estimations of the perceived categorical distances among close species. All species except stumptailed macaques (*M. arctoides*) located themselves distantly from all other species. Stumptailed macaque subjects, however, recognized as distant species those with which they are sympatric. The results, therefore, were consistent with the reproductive isolation hypothesis. Interestingly, Fujita (1987) also reported that multidimensional scaling and cluster analyses of the sum of all data from all five subject species revealed that their categorical distances between species correlated with phylogenetic distances between species (Cronin, Cann, and Sarich 1980; Delson 1980). The resulting clusters were similar to Fooden's (1980) morphological classification of macaque groups.

The Perception of Categorical Coherence

Fujita's (1987) results provide good evidence that macaque monkeys spontaneously detect the perceptual similarities and differences between natural categories at the species level. Other studies further demonstrate that animals spontaneously perceive the perceptual coherence within natural categories at other levels as well.

Fujita and Matsuzawa (1986) developed the sensory reinforcement procedure used by Fujita (1987) to demonstrate that "human" was a natural (i.e., spontaneous) category for an adult chimpanzee. The experimentally sophisticated subject, Ai (e.g., Matsuzawa 1985a), was trained to press a button to produce, in random order, commercially produced slides that either did or did not contain one or more humans. Otherwise the procedures and analyses were very similar to those used by Fujita (1987). The results revealed two different clusters in the two-dimensional space as summarized in figure 9.3. The chimpanzee spontaneously categorized the slides into one of two groups that can be labeled "human" and "no human." The latter group also included "ambiguous" slides in which humans occupied less than 1.5 cm of the projection screen; "light" slide mounts with no film; and "nothing" control slides with black paper on the film.

A multidimensional scaling procedure was also used by Sands and associates (1982) to identify the object categories perceived by rhesus monkeys in a task involving same/different judgments. The monkeys were trained to move a lever in one direction if the content of two successively presented slides was physically identical and to move the lever in the opposite direction when they differed. The slides consisted of six different exemplars from each of five categories, which included monkey

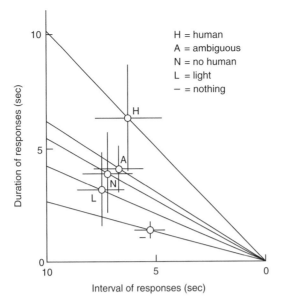

Figure 9.3 The centers of distribution for the slides of each group (i.e., group mean of slide durations and intervals). Standard deviations of the durations and intervals of the groups are shown in the horizontal and vertical lines. (From Fujita and Matsuzawa 1986, in *Primates.*)

faces, human faces, flowers, fruit, and trees. As shown in figure 9.4, an analysis of confusion errors revealed that monkey and human faces fell in the same region of multidimensional space. That is, a monkey was more likely to incorrectly label two physically different slides as being identical if the negative stimulus came from the same category of face rather than, say, flower, fruit, or tree. Likewise, more errors were likely when the initial and comparison stimuli were both fruits than if the negative comparison stimulus was from a different category.

Findings similar to those of Sands, Lincoln, and Wright were reported by Astley and Wassermann (1992), who trained pigeons with 12 exemplars of one category as positive stimuli to which key pecking was intermittently reinforced on a fixed-interval schedule. These stimuli were intermixed with 48 different negative stimuli, 12 each from four categories, including that from which the 12 positive pictures were drawn. Although the pigeons were never reinforced in the presence of any negative stimulus, their response rates were higher when a negative stimulus belonged to the same category as the positive stimuli.

The results from experiments like those above (i.e., Astley and Wassermann 1992; Fujita and Matsuzawa 1986; Sands, Lincoln, and Wright 1982) support the view that animals in categorical discrimination tasks detect the perceptual coherence within natural categories rather than arbitrary relationships established during training. Additional evidence for this

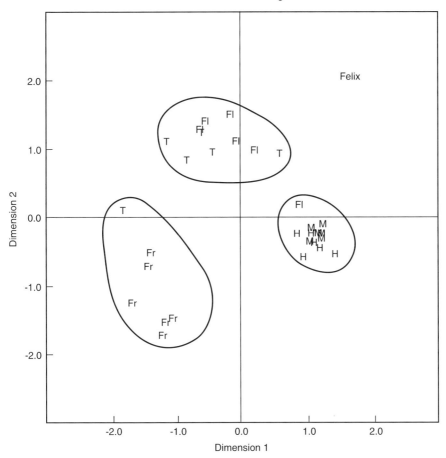

Figure 9.4 Alscal two-dimensional scaling of Felix's confusion matrix in experiment 1. The different types of pictures are represented by the following one- or two-letter symbols: H = humans, M = monkeys, T = trees, Fr = fruit, Fl = flowers. Circled items indicate clusters with diameters of 2.5 or less. (From Sands et al. 1982, in *Journal of Experimental Psychology: General,* © 1982 by the American Psychological Association.)

conclusion includes the finding that pigeons rewarded for classifying pictures that correspond to human categorical labels (e.g., cats and flowers) learn faster than those rewarded for classifying the same pictures into random assortments of so-called pseudocategories (Astley and Wasserman 1992; Edwards and Honig 1987; Herrnstein and de Villiers 1980; Wassermann, Kiedinger, and Bhatt 1988).

Stimulus Typicality

Even if animals are sensitive to the categorical coherence of the same natural categories as are humans, it is not always clear that their concept of the "ideal" exemplar is the same. Some researchers (e.g., Herrnstein 1979; Herrnstein and de Villiers 1980; Roberts and Masmanian 1988) report that animal pictures rated by humans as ideal (i.e., typical) did not match up with pictures that were highly discriminable by their animal subjects.

The relationship between typicality rankings by humans and transfer performances with novel exemplars by pigeons on a categorization task was further studied by Cook, Wright, and Kendrick (1990). Line drawings of birds and mammals were rated by humans on the basis of their proto-typicality. Pigeons were then trained to discriminate the two classes with examples drawn from only a part of the resulting typicality gradient. Hence, some pigeons were trained only with "good" representatives, while others were trained with "poor" exemplars. Subsequently, all birds were given transfer tests with novel exemplars drawn from the "interme-diate" as well as "good" and "poor" portions of the typicality gradient. Cook and his colleagues (1990) reasoned that, if their birds were insensitive to the same categorical structure as the human typicality rankers, transfer would be influenced by position of the test stimulus on the typicality gradient.

Birds trained with "good" exemplars transferred better to "intermedi-ate" test stimuli than to "poor" ones. Interestingly, birds trained with "poor" exemplars also showed better transfer to "intermediate" than to "good" test stimuli. Despite their mutual sensitivity to the categorical coherence of birds, the results suggest that human rankers and pigeon subjects represented the common category differently. Whatever features are typical of a "good" bird for humans were not salient for the pigeons. The pigeons' choices were determined by the specific range of exemplars experienced during training and not by the particular features of a prototype.

Is Categorization Conceptual?

Despite the evidence cited that animals can learn multiple opened-ended categories, one is left with the question of whether it is *conceptually* medi-ated by the perception and representation of shared relationships or, at the very least, shared multiple features. Attempts to identify the critical features controlling this behavior, even in instances in which it corre-sponds with human categorical verbal labels, have lagged far behind demonstrations of the phenomenon. Ironically, failures to unequivocally identify defining categorical features support the assumption that the inherent variability in open-ended categories precludes their being identi-fied by any single feature.

Identification of Categorical Features
Schrier and Brady (1987), in their study of the "person concept," presented their monkeys with probes consisting of human silhouettes, inverted hu-mans, and humans with scrambled body parts. The monkeys selected the latter two, but not the silhouette, probe types when they were paired with negative slides that did not contain a person. None of the three

probe types, however, was chosen when paired with positive pictures consisting of upright humans (cf. Cerella 1979). Adverse effects of inverted pictures on multiple-class categorization by pigeons were also reported by Wasserman, Kiedinger, and Bhatt (1988, experiment 3), who suggested that their birds were matching patterns.

Schrier and Brady (1987) concluded that their monkeys' categorization of person slides was based neither on a sole global property, like outline, nor on a single isolated feature, like eyes or limbs. D'Amato and van Sant (1988) suggested that the monkeys in their study of the "person concept" might have detected a limited number of features which, alone or in combination, identified positive slides. This assumption is similar to the classical view of concept learning, that all members within a category share a finite set of necessary and sufficient features (Smith and Medin 1981). Roberts and Mazmanian's (1988) results, however, indicated that the features that permitted their pigeons and monkeys to discriminate kingfishers from other birds, and animals from nonanimals, did not permit them to discriminate birds from other animals. What those features might be, Roberts and Mazmanian (1988) could not say: "Differences between pictures in terms of space occupied by the animal, amount of the animals shown, colorfulness or compactness of the animals, or the presence of limbs did not distinguish pictures of high and low discriminability" (p. 259).

In contrast to Roberts and Masmanian (1988), Cook, Wright, and Kendrick (1990) reported that their pigeons learned a "bird vs. mammal" categorical discrimination in which responses to monochrome line drawings of birds were rewarded. These investigators used a "binary search algorithm," which entailed systematically dividing the effective stimulus into smaller units (e.g., figure/ground), to investigate the discriminative roles of various cues in discriminative performance. Like Schrier and Brady (1987), they found that simple global factors like overall shape did not play a major role in controlling the categorical behavior of their birds. Transfer tests were also conducted with chimera probes composed of one part bird and one part mammal. A chimera probe might consist of a bird's head appended to a mammal's body, or vice versa. Control within-category chimera probes consisted of heads and bodies from different birds and mammals respectively combined. Results of the tests with chimera probes, shown in figure 9.5, suggested that the pigeons' discrimination of the positive bird category from the negative mammal category was primarily controlled by features associated with the body rather than the head.

Theories of Representation
Attempts to understand how categorical information is represented have been hampered by the lack of progress in identifying the controlling features in categorization (Herrnstein 1984; Lea 1984). The open-ended

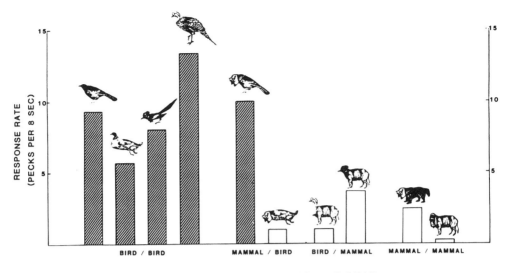

Figure 9.5 Results of chimera probe test. An example of each chimera is presented over its data point. The composition of the four probe types is designated so that the first part refers to the category type of the head, whereas the second part refers to the category type of the body. Hatched bars represent probe types apparently perceived by the pigeons as birds. The open bars represent probe types apparently perceived as mammals. (From Cook et al. 1990, in *Quantitative Analyses of Behavior, vol. VIII*, copyright Erlbaum Associates.)

nature of natural categories has led most investigators to reject the *classical view* that categories have a set of necessary and sufficient absolute defining properties. Instead they favor either an interpretation borrowed from human cognition that categorization is based on either probabilistic feature analysis or, alternatively, on the retention of multiple specific exemplars (Medin 1989; Smith and Medin 1981).

Probabilistic feature analysis models recognize that natural categories are polymorphic in nature (Ryle 1949). A number of different features may be associated with a particular category, but an exemplar need possess only some limited subset (e.g., "m out of n") to be identified as a member of the category. Particular features are more likely to be identified with certain natural categories than others, so an added assumption in one model is that animals vary the "attentional" weight given to different features. One such model is the *variably weighted linear feature model* (Lea and Ryan 1983, 1990). Tests of the linear feature model of polymorphous concept discrimination apply multiple regression models to determine the proportion of variance in performances that is attributable to different features (e.g., Lea and Ryan 1983).

According to the *exemplar model*, animals "represent perceptual categories with an undetermined number of stored exemplars and respond to novel stimuli according to their similarity to previously experienced ones" (Cook, Wright, and Kendrick 1990, p. 210). Novel exemplars supposedly are compared with stored sets of positive and negative instances. If the novel picture matches an item within the remembered set of positive exemplars, it is treated as a category member. If the picture is not within the remembered set, but its choice is rewarded, then it too is included in the exemplar set in memory for future comparisons (Roberts and Mazmanian 1988).

Neither approach is universally supported either theoretically or empirically. Critics of the exemplar model argue that it fails to specify the dimensions along which the similarities and differences of exemplars are evaluated. Recent developments have included attempts to incorporate principles of generalization and discrimination into exemplar models of categorization (e.g., see Astley and Wasserman 1992; Medin and Shaeffer 1978; Pierce 1988). Tests of linear feature models are usually conducted using artificial rather than natural stimuli (Cerella 1990), and they often lead to conflicting results (cf. Lea and Ryan 1990; Huber and Lenz 1993).

As Huber and Lenz (1993) have stated, "the type of category learning process employed by a subject may well be determined by the structure of the stimulus set" (p. 15). If so, then the question of how animals represent categorical information will not be resolved until investigators adopt new computer imaging technologies that can manipulate pictorial representations in ways previously not possible with simple slide projection systems (e.g., see Rilling, De Marse, and La Claire 1993). It is hoped that these methodological advances will also foster a more systematic approach to operational definitions and theoretical uses of the terms "feature" and "stimulus" (Fetterman, Stubbs, and MacEwen 1992; Steele 1990).

Within-Class Discriminations

The notion that different objects have common class attributes that permit them to be distinguished from others is at the core of conceptual categorization. Natural object categorization is not conceptual if animals fail to discriminate between individual members within a category. In such cases, transfer to novel exemplars following training is attributable to their perceiving the different exemplars as being the same thing rather than as different instances of the same category. Curiously, despite reservations as to the conceptual basis of natural categorization by animals (e.g., Cabe 1980; Herrnstein and de Villiers 1980; Premack 1983a, b), few investigators have addressed the issue experimentally.

One notable exception is a study by Wasserman, Kiedinger, and Bhatt (1988, experiment 1), who claimed to have demonstrated that discriminably different stimuli from the same class occasioned the same response from pigeons. However, their procedures and results and the language of their text suggest that they had provided a clearer example of subcategorization than of conceptual categorization as defined above (cf. Roberts and Mazmanian 1988).

As in another study (Bhatt et al. 1988), birds were rewarded for pecking one of four keys depending upon the nature of the categorical picture presented (e.g., cat, flower, car, and chair). Responses to one of two keys were reinforced in the presence of, say, cat pictures used during training. Responses to the second key were rewarded in the presence of flower pictures that were also used during training. Responses to a third and fourth key, respectively, were rewarded in the presence of cat and flower pictures used in post-training categorization tests. Hence, a bird's choice of key provided measures not only of between-class categorization (i.e., cat vs. flower), but also of discrimination between the "training and testing" subcategories nested within each object category.

The results (Wasserman et al. 1988, experiment 1) revealed that the pigeons perceived pictures within both the same category (cat vs. flower) and subcategory (training vs. testing stimulus) to be more similar than those of different categories and subcategories. As shown in the top of figure 9.6, the percentage of correct responses increased over days to an overall mean discriminative performance level of 72 percent (chance was 25 percent). There were no performance differences between the categories that included chairs and cars in addition to the natural cat and flower categories. The pigeons had learned to categorize the pictures not only on the basis of natural class, but also on the basis of whether they were training or testing stimuli (i.e., subcategories). Interestingly, however, as is shown in the bottom half of figure 9.6, an increase in conceptual errors over days was associated with the overall increase in percentage of correct categorical responses. A conceptual error consisted of incorrectly identifying a categorical level stimulus as a subcategorical training or test stimulus, respectively.

If they were uncertain of a picture's status, then the pigeons used by Wasserman, Kiedinger, and Bhatt (1988) were less likely to "mislabel" the natural category to which it belonged than they were its subcategory. The ability of these birds to distinguish the subcategories nested within the object categories is further evidence of a hierarchical as opposed to a global categorical organization (Mandler and Bauer 1988). The systematic increase in the number of conceptual errors further suggests that perhaps the basis for the subcategories represented by "training and test stimuli" was their relative familiarity/novelty, which decreased over days. One cannot conclude, however, that cats and flowers are basic categories for pigeons, as they supposedly are for humans (Rosch and Mervis 1975; Rosch et al. 1976). In contrast to the animals used by Roberts and Mazmanian (1988), these pigeons were never exposed to cats vs. other animals or to flowers vs. other plants (cf. Astley and Wasserman, 1992). More important to the present discussion as to the conceptual basis of natural

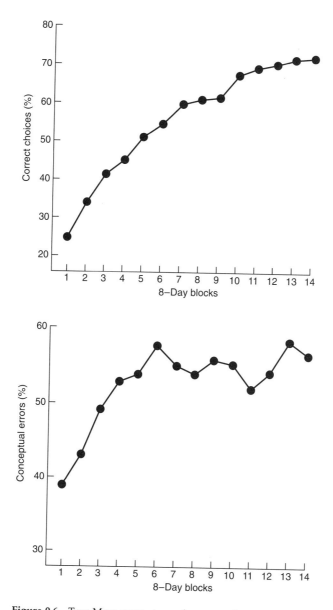

Figure 9.6 Top: Mean percentage of correct subcategorization responses in experiment 1 (14 eight-day blocks). Bottom: Mean percentage of conceptual errors in experiment 1 (14 eight-day blocks). (From Wasserman et al. 1988, in *Journal of Experimental Psychology: Animal Behavior Processes*, © 1988 by the American Psychological Association.)

categorization is the fact that there was no attempt to determine whether the pigeons could discriminate, say, one cat from another or even from other felids (cf. Roberts and Mazmanian 1988).

NATURAL CONCEPTS OF MOTION AND NUMBER

Concepts of Natural Movement

Studies of natural categories employ static visual representations of animate objects that are typically dynamic in nature. Labels in ethograms (i.e., descriptive inventories of a species' behavior), for example, provide good evidence that humans parse the flow of biological motion into diverse but categorically coherent events and actions. With respect to locomotion, for example, we speak of crawling, walking, running, leaping, jumping, dancing, flying, swimming, and so on. The study of biological motion as a natural category, however, has been practically ignored by researchers.

Motion as a Natural Category
One study indicates that pigeons can discriminate videotaped scenes on the basis of natural movement alone (Dittrich and Lea 1993). The investigators first trained pigeons to discriminate between 40 dynamic and static videotaped scenes of different pigeons in the same setting. Responses by pigeons in the motion group were rewarded whenever they viewed scenes of other pigeons walking, turning, and flying short distances. The negative set of still scenes consisted of static (i.e., frozen frames) taken from the moving set and shown for the same 6-second duration. Birds in the static group were rewarded for responding in the presence of the still scenes rather than the motion scenes. A third group was trained on a pseudocategory discrimination in which the 40 still and dynamic scenes were assigned to two 20-item sets, one of which was rewarded.

Subsequently, transfer tests were conducted using novel scenes of pigeons from different viewing points and distances against different backgrounds. Tests were also conducted with novel scenes consisting of seven different motions against varied backgrounds performed by novel animals, plants, automobiles, and geometrical shapes (e.g., humans walking). Those birds for whom motion was positive learned to respond differentially in the presence of motion and transferred their performances to the novel scenes. However, the birds from whom static scenes were positive responded in the presence of both motion and static scenes. Learning of the discrimination by the latter group was demonstrated only under modified conditions of reinforcement as described by Dittrich and Lea (1993). The results of further tests (Dittrich and Lea 1993, experiment

2) revealed that differential responding to the videotaped scenes was unaffected by changes in the color and brightness of the stimuli and by slight blurring of the images.

The pigeons' successful discrimination between videotapes of complex natural scenes on the basis of motion alone was interpreted by Dittrich and Lea (1993) as evidence of a concept of motion. They argued against the possibility of control by a single common feature on account of what they saw as evidence of the categorical nature of the movement stimuli, concluding that "movements of different kinds led to different degrees of generalization" (Dittrich and Lea 1993, p. 128). However, as in studies of static natural categories, the nature of these presumed common categorical movement features remain unknown. A technique involving point-light animation, however, promises to be a productive way of identifying these dynamic features.

Biological Motion

Adults and infants correctly identify the activity (e.g., walking, running, dancing) and gender of a moving human or animal when all they can see is a small number of light points strategically placed on the otherwise invisible major limb joints (Johansson 1973; Fox and McDaniel 1982). This spontaneous and immediate phenomenon was labeled by Johansson (1973) as, "the perception of biological motion."

Blake (1993) reported that cats could discriminate biological from nonbiological motion using information from only a few points of computer-generated light (Cutting 1978). In this study, 14 dots were presented against a dark background on each of a pair of video monitors (see figure 9.7). One light-point display depicted a sequence of an otherwise invisible walking or running cat. The other displayed one of several "foil" sequences, including Brownian motion, random dot motion, positionally scrambled motion, and phase-scrambled motion. In the latter phase-scrambled foil condition, for example, the dot motions were in the same spatial positions as for the respective walking and running cats, but their individual starting phases were scrambled.

The cat subjects were rewarded in this two-alternative forced-choice situation for depressing with their noses the response key in line with the monitor depicting biological motion. Initially, the rewarded display was left unchanged while the foil condition was altered. The cats' performances remained above the level of chance despite these changes, although the discrimination of the phase-scrambled vs. the biological motion condition proved to be difficult, perhaps because to human eyes it resembled a limping cat. The results indicated that the cats must have responded to the global organization of the biological motion sequence, because the requisite discriminations could not be made using individual motion patterns or local grouping of moving points. The detection of

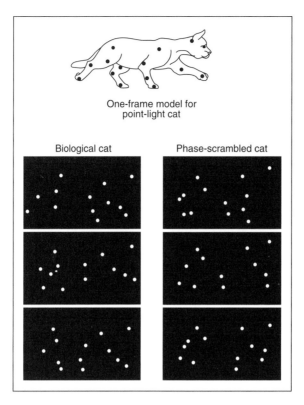

One-frame model for
point-light cat

Biological cat   Phase-scrambled cat

Figure 9.7 Generation of light-point animation sequences used for assessing cats' detection of biological motion. (From Blake 1993, in *Psychological Science,* © 1993, American Psychological Society.)

biological motion can be considered relational, and hence conceptual, to the extent that it depends on the perceptual connection of joints "in an oriented hierarchy involving the nested movement of body parts (e.g., the paw moves in the context of the leg)" (Blake 1993, p. 56).

Categorical perception of biological motion by the cats was suggested, although not unequivocally demonstrated, by Blake's report (1993) that they maintained the discrimination when exposed to the "running cat" display and also when the direction in which the "walking biological motion" display proceeded was reversed from left to right to right to left. Turning the biological display upside down or displaying a light-point cat "speeding," however, reduced discriminative performances to chance levels, as had been independently reported for human subjects (Sumi 1984). Although no data were presented, Blake (1993) also reported that the biological motion discrimination by the cats transferred successfully to a pair of light-point sequences depicting a walking human vs. a positionally scrambled foil. In the latter foil, the starting positions of the same dot motions as those in the walking human display were spatially randomized.

Conceptual Use of Number

Many of the natural object categories that animals discriminate often occur in aggregations. One speaks, for example, of a pigeon flock, a school of fish, a bunch of bananas, a bed of flowers, and a grove of trees. These groups or collections can be discriminated in terms of not only relative size and volume, but also relative and absolute numbers, which can vary over both time and space. For example, one may decide to buy the *larger* bunch of bananas because it appears to have *more* than the other. *Counting* the bananas, one finds that, in fact, the larger bunch contains *eight* as opposed to the other bunch's *four*. However, over the week the *larger* bunch becomes noticeably *smaller*; there are *fewer* bananas because *two* are eaten each day.

The initial judgments (i.e., larger/smaller) are based on *size* or *volume*; the others are based on judgments of *relative numerosity* (more/fewer) and *counted numbers*. Simultaneous and successive judgments like these are conceptual to the extent that they can be applied to any categorical collection, regardless of its constituent members. The potential functional utility of these conceptual abilities in, for example, foraging situations (e.g., Honig and Stewart 1989; Thomas 1992) has prompted interest in the ability of other species to make similar judgments of relative numerosity and to count (e.g., Boysen and Capaldi 1993; Davis and Memmott 1982; Davis and Perusse 1988).

Relative Numerosity Discriminations

Nonhuman species can respond to relative numerosity even when differences between arrays in terms of size, area, brightness, and placement of items are controlled (e.g., Perusse and Rumbaugh 1990; Thomas and Chase 1980). Honig and Stewart (1989, experiments 4 and 5), for example, used arrays of different-colored bird and flower sketches to test the ability of pigeons to discriminate the relative numerosity of categorical stimuli. Each array contained a constant number of total stimuli to control for size differences that were correlated with absolute numbers of stimuli. The pigeons were trained first to peck at positive slides in which all 16 items within an array were from the same category, flowers or birds. After the pigeons learned the initial discrimination, they were tested with arrays comprised of items of several different proportions (e.g., .75, .50, .25, and .00 of positive items). Transfer data from new arrays of novel flowers and a novel unicorn category were also obtained (Honig and Stewart 1989, experiment 5). As shown in figure 9.8, orderly discrimination gradients were associated with changes in the proportions of positive categorical items. Honig and Stewart (1989) interpreted these results as evidence that pigeons could judge the relative numerosity of different categories.

Although animals can discriminate relative numerosity, it is not clear that they always do it categorically in terms of what humans label as

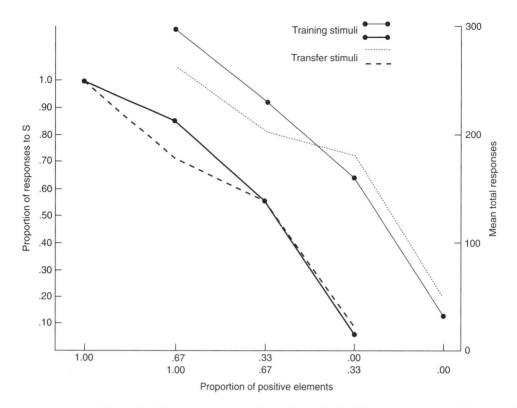

Figure 9.8 Mean numerosity gradients obtained with different proportions of flowers and unicorns in the discrimination test of experiment 5. The relative gradients are at the left; the gradients based on total responses are at the right. (From Honig and Stewart 1989, in *Animal Learning and Behavior*, © 1989, Psychonomic Society.)

"more" or "less." The relative proportion measures used in studies of relative numerosity are in principle continuous, much like wavelength. If relative numerosity is perceived categorically like color, then one might anticipate generalization curves that reveal two discrete response areas with a distinctive boundary (cf. Harnad 1987). The orderly generalization gradients generated by Honig and Stewart's (1989) pigeons suggest that their relative numerosity discriminations were not categorical.

Animals may find themselves in situations in which salient categorical stimuli are encountered successively over time rather than simultaneously in a spatially distributed array. For example, a foraging animal may come across differing numbers of food items at different sites. How might the animal perceive these differences? One possibility is that it discriminates relative numbers, but another possibility is that it discriminates the relative differences temporally (cf. Lydersen and Crossman 1974; Rilling 1967). The two approaches are not necessarily mutually exclusive, as Fetterman (1993) found in a study of relative numerosity discrimination in pigeons.

Fetterman (1993) trained pigeons to choose between two colored (red or green) side keys on the basis of the number of key pecks required preceding their choice. The initial number of key pecks required was either small or large (e.g., fixed ratio 10 vs. fixed ratio 30). Different values of the small and large fixed ratio requirements were used such that the ratio between the two response values differed both absolutely and relatively. On probe trials, ratios intermediate to those used in the training conditions were presented. The time it took each pigeon to emit the response ratios was recorded in addition to the probability of correct postratio response choice. With the exception of one bird, psychophysical analyses revealed similarly shaped correct-response probability curves regardless of changes in the relative differences between the two response runs (e.g., 2:1 to 4:1).

Monkeys (Washburn and Rumbaugh 1991) and rats (Davis and Albert, 1986) can discriminate number even when temporal cues are controlled. Washburn, Hopkins, and Rumbaugh (1989) used computer-generated Arabic numerals to represent different numbers of reward pellets. When pairs of numbers (0–5) were displayed on a video monitor, the rhesus monkey subjects could manipulate a joystick so as to bring a cursor into contact with one of the numbers. The animals were rewarded with the number of pellets corresponding to the selected number (cf. Mitchell et al. 1985). The animals learned to select the larger numeral even when the rate of delivery of the pellets was arrhythmic (Washburn and Rumbaugh 1991, experiment 3). The same two subjects were also presented with arrays of five different numerals (1–9) simultaneously; as before, the rate of delivery of the reward pellets was arrhythmic. Both animals significantly chose the largest numeral available in each array, indicating that they could make ordinal judgments.

Counting

Washburn and Rumbaugh (1991) did not argue that their monkeys were counting. As they said, "To make ordinal judgments does not compel the conclusion that the quantities are enumerated" (p. 193). Thomas and his colleagues similarly adopted a conservative "noncounting" interpretation of their squirrel monkeys' conceptual ability to discriminate the smaller of two numbers up to seven vs. eight (Thomas 1992; Thomas and Lorden 1993), regardless of whether the stimuli were discrete dots (Thomas, Fowlkes, and Vickery 1980) or connected sides of randomly constructed polygons (Terrell and Thomas 1990). If the monkeys could not count, then the mechanism by which they estimated up to seven and eight numbers in an array remains unclear. Thomas (1992) argued that the animals form a numeric prototype against which arrays are compared, but he was silent as to what such a prototype might look like. An alternative explanation is that the monkeys were subitizing (Mandler and Shebo 1982)—that is, apprehending the numbers via direct perception.

Thomas's reluctance to attribute a counting ability to his animals was because of the lack of evidence for at least the first three of the five principles of counting proposed by Gelman and Gallistel (1978). The three principles regarded by Thomas to be critical in evaluating whether animals count were (1) there must be a one-to-one correspondence between symbolic number labels and objects being counted; (2) the number labels must be applied in a consistent order (the stable order principle); and (3) the last label used must indicate the number of objects being counted (the cardinality principle). The two remaining principles are (4) any set of things can be counted (the abstraction principle) and (5) items within a set can be counted in any order (the order-irrelevance principle).

An African Grey parrot *(Psittacus erithacus)* (Pepperberg 1987a, 1990) and a chimpanzee *(Pan troglodytes)* (Matsuzawa 1985b; Matsuzawa et al. 1986) used vocal and computer-generated numeric labels, respectively, to distinguish cardinal sets of items. The parrot, Alex, unlike the chimpanzee, Ai, was reported to immediately transfer this ability to novel collections of familiar categorical objects. The parrot also proved capable of responding correctly at above chance levels when queried as to the number of items in only one of two categorical subsets within the same array. Faced with a six-item array consisting of two corks and four pennies, the parrot correctly responded "Two" when asked for the number of corks.

When all three of Thomas's essential principles from Gelman and Gallistel (1978) are stringently applied, there is little evidence of counting in nonhuman animals other than chimpanzees (Boysen and Bernston 1989a; Rumbaugh et al. 1989). Sheba, a female chimpanzee, has demonstrated that she can count from one to nine, use number symbols both productively and reflexively, and derive the sum of two quantities represented symbolically (Boysen and Bernston 1989b). However, these skills emerged only after what Boysen (1993) called a heroic training effort. Sheba was one of three chimpanzees who were first trained on four tasks, which included discriminating the one-to-one correspondence of arrays, matching object arrays first with marked placards and then with the appropriate Arabic numeral. The chimpanzees then performed a number comprehension task in which they picked the correct array corresponding to a displayed Arabic number. The evidence of summation came from Sheba's spontaneous ability to choose the correct number corresponding to the sum of food items (zero to four) found at two of three sites. The experimenters then baited the sites with Arabic numbers rather than food items and, as previously, Sheba chose the Arabic number corresponding to the sum of the combined two numbers. As shown in table 9.1, Sheba's performances in both cases were above chance levels and transferred to novel tests with both food items and Arabic numbers.

A CONCEPT OF ONESELF

Given all the evidence that animals perceive the natural world categorically, one might wonder whether that ability extends reflexively to themselves. Are animals aware of themselves as entities distinct from other

Table 9.1 *Symbolic counting task.* (From Boysen and Bernston 1989, in *Journal of Comparative Psychology* © 1989 American Psychological Association.)

Stimuli	No. of sessions	No. of trials	No. of correct trials	Probability		$X^2 (1)$
				Correct	Chance	
1–4	3	21	16	.76	.25	28.94*
Blind	4	20	17	.85	.25	35.27*

*$p < .001$

individuals and classes? That is, do animals have a self-concept? Can an animal, in Gallup's (1982, 1987) words, become the object of its own attention? Most of the research on this topic uses a methodology in which investigators look for evidence of self-recognition by animals when they are confronted with their reflection in a mirror. For a recent review of this topic, see Parker, Mitchell, and Boccia (1994).

Self-Recognition Studies

Animals act as if they are faced with another conspecific when they initially see their reflection in a mirror (Gallup 1968, 1975). Monkeys, for example, may even reach behind or go behind the mirror as if to locate the novel animal. Over time, however, social responses elicited by the mirror-image gradually decline, and eventually most animals ignore the reflected image of themselves. Temporarily removing the mirror and even changing its location may produce a temporary reappearance of the social displays (Gallup and Suarez 1991). Although they show a similar decline in social behaviors, chimpanzees often show an increase in what appears to be mirror-guided self-directed behaviors. They also experiment with unusual facial gestures and/or postures, using the mirror to investigate parts of their bodies that are not easily observed directly. The overall pattern of behavior suggests that they recognize it is their self-image, not that of another animal, which is reflected in a mirror.

In an attempt to validate the above impression of self-recognition, Gallup (1970) developed what has become known as the "mark test." Following ten days of mirror exposure Gallup (1970) anesthesistized his chimpanzees, and while they were unconscious he applied a red, odorless dye to their eyebrow ridges and the top half of the opposite ears. After the animals had recovered from the anesthesia, they were observed for 30 minutes in the absence of the mirror to establish a baseline of the number of times they spontaneously touched the marked portions of their heads and faces. Following the baseline period, the animals were exposed to a mirror. When they saw their reflections, all the chimpanzees repeatedly attempted to touch the marked areas, which were otherwise invisible. After touching the marked areas, they often looked at and smelled their fingers as if trying to identify what it was on their faces and ears. There was also a significant increase in the total time they spent looking at their reflections in the mirror associated with the mark test period. In contrast, chimpanzees treated the same way, but without prior experience with mirrors, showed no mark-directed responses during either the baseline period or the subsequent mirror test. Instead these control animals responded to their reflections as if they were seeing another chimpanzee. For a review of the research methodologies and logic, see Gallup (1994).

Most, but not all, socially adept chimpanzees at the age of five years or older "pass" the mark test (cf. Calhoun and Thompson 1988; Gallup et al. 1971; Lin, Bard, and Anderson 1992; Povinelli 1994; Swartz and Evans 1991, 1994), and language-trained chimpanzees, like normal humans, may even label their reflections as being themselves. Among the great apes, orangutans (Lethmate and Drucker 1973; Miles 1994) and gorillas (e.g., Ledbetter and Basen 1982; Patterson 1984; Patterson and Cohn 1994) show evidence that they can recognize themselves in a mirror.

No monkey has ever unequivocally passed the mark test of self-recognition (e.g., Anderson 1983; Gallup, Wallnau, and Suarez 1980). Nevertheless, Epstein, Lanza, and Skinner (1981) claimed to have used operant conditioning to demonstrate spontaneous mirror-mediated mark-directed behavior in pigeons that was functionally equivalent to that shown by chimpanzees. Epstein, Lanza, and Skinner (1981) reported that three pigeons spontaneously pecked at dots on their bodies that were invisible by means other than reflection in a mirror. These birds were first trained to peck visible blue stick-on dots placed on their bodies. Next they were rewarded for turning around and pecking one of several possible locations behind them where a dot had been flashed briefly while they faced a mirror. These dots were assumed to be visible only in the mirror as they were flashed. Presumably during training the birds learned to use their reflections in the mirror to find which location to approach and peck after the dots, and hence their reflections, had vanished. After a bird acquired the two operants, a cloth bib was placed on it, which prevented the bird from seeing directly any dots placed on its body. When the mirror was available, Epstein, Lanza, and Skinner (1981) reported that the birds pecked at the otherwise invisible body dots, but that they never did so when the mirror was not present.

Epstein, Lanza, and Skinner (1981) interpreted their results as evidence that one need not appeal to a "self-concept" to explain mirror-directed responding in animals or humans; they thought the behavior was best interpreted as an operant emerging from a history of conditioning. The argument has been challenged as suspect on a number of grounds. Gallup (1994), for example, reemphasized that none of the pigeons used by Epstein, Lanza, and Skinner (1981) ever showed any collateral instances of self-directed behavior; therefore, they had missed the point of the mark test—namely, that "the mark test is not so much a measure of self-recognition as it is a means of validating impressions which emerge as a result of seeing animals engage in a variety of what would appear to be mirror-mediated patterns of self-directed behavior" (Gallup 1994, p. 36).

Attempts to replicate the work of Epstein, Lanza, and Skinner (1981) have been unsuccessful. Thompson and Contie (1994), for example, reported that six pigeons in repeated tests used mirror-images to identify where dots had been flashed and, in the mirror's absence, they pecked visible dots placed on their bodies. However, none of these pigeons, contrary to those of Epstein, Lanza, and Skinner (1981), used the mirror to locate body dots whose positions were otherwise hidden by a bib. Follow-up tests by Thompson and Contie (1994) revealed that the mirror did, in fact, exert varying levels of discriminative stimulus control over their birds' behavior. In some cases, for example, the dot reflections were conditioned discriminative stimuli for locating flashed dots via peripheral vision before they had disappeared completely. In other cases, the birds learned the one-to-one spatial correspondence between dot reflections and holes in the walls. But there was no evidence that operant conditioning was a sufficient condition for the spontaneous emergence of "self-recognition."

On the one hand, monkeys and even elephants can be trained to use mirror cues to identify and locate otherwise invisible objects (e.g., Anderson 1986; Itakura 1987a, b; Povinelli 1989). On the other hand, monkeys and elephants are no different from pigeons in their failure to spontaneously display mirror-guided, self-directed behaviors and to pass the mark test of self-recognition (e.g., Anderson 1984; Povinelli 1989). Even after extensive shaping and training, monkeys fail to provide convincing evidence that they can use a mirror to inspect their bodies. Boccia (1994), for example, reported only a single case of a mark-directed response in a pigtail macaque (*M. nemestrina*) with a history of exposure to mirrors. Thompson and Boatright-Horowitz (1994) addressed the question of whether previous failures by monkeys to pass the mark test was related to eye contact avoidance. They managed to train a pigtail macaque to make eye contact with its own reflection, but reported no incidence of self-directed behavior prior to the mark test. In this test the monkey was reported to brush the mark on its face with its hand only once. Gallup (1994) has further claimed that a videotape of this single case shows that the monkey's brushing the mark was immediately followed by its making a social "jawthrust" response to its reflection.

Self-Concept or Mirror-Concept?

How might one account for the apparent discrepancy between mirror-mediated self-recognition by monkeys as opposed to mirror-mediated object recognition and location? The puzzle is this: Why can monkeys use mirrors as tools to obtain information about the environment, but not about themselves? For some, the puzzle is resolved by appealing to the absence of a self-concept or self-awareness that is present in most great apes and humans (Gallup 1982, 1987). Although self-recognition in a mirror has been interpreted as evidence for, if not the cause of, a "self-concept" in apes, there has been relatively little progress in relating the phenomenon with mirrors to other possible behavioral measures of the concept (cf. Anderson 1994). Gallup's (1982, 1987) definition of self-awareness in terms of an animal becoming the object of its own attention can be criticized as being no more than a restatement of self-recognition. What is needed are independent measures of a self-concept, including, perhaps, the demonstration of self-conscious emotional states, as has been reported for children (Lewis 1992; Lewis et al. 1989). Thus far, most attempts by advocates of a "theory of mind" (Astington and Gopnick 1991; Premack 1988; Premack and Woodruff 1978; Woodruff and Premack 1979; but cf. Hobson 1990, 1991) have been to correlate self-deception to others of like mind. Results thus far indicate that species differences in attributional tasks mirror those in self-recognition studies; chimpanzees can attribute intentions or states of knowledge to another animal, but monkeys cannot (e.g., Cheney and Seyfarth 1990b; Povinelli, Nelson, and Boysen 1990; Povinelli, Parks, and Novak 1991; Woodruff and Premack 1979).

An alternative approach to conducting self-recognition and mirror-usage studies is to focus on the requisite perceptual and cognitive processes needed to use mirrors primarily as perceptual tools rather than as a means of self-recognition per se (e.g., Platt, Thompson, and Boatright 1991; Mitchell 1993; Thompson and Contie 1994). The issue, then, is not whether or not animals have a self-concept, but rather whether they have even a mirror-concept (Thompson and Contie 1994). In other words, one can ask if there is any compelling evidence that animals understand the *reflective* properties (Loveland 1986) of mirrors at all. The performances of monkeys on mirror-guided reaching tasks, for example, may be functionally no different from demonstrations that macaque monkeys can capture static or moving video targets with a cursor by manipulating a joystick (Washburn, Hopkins, and Rumbaugh 1989).

Both the mirror- and video-guided tasks require an animal to learn the conditional spatial/temporal matching relations between hand movements and images, but neither necessarily demands a symmetrical equivalence judgment based on physical identity (Thompson and Contie 1994; Washburn et al. 1989). Success on mirror-guided reaching tasks need not necessarily depend upon the perception and use of physical identity relations, but it is difficult to see how an animal could learn to use mirrors for self-recognition without using response rules based on broadly construed concepts of stimulus equivalence and identity (e.g., Premack 1983a, b).

SECONDARILY EQUIVALENT NONPERCEPTUAL CATEGORIES

The open-ended natural objects discussed thus far, including that of one-self, can in principle be classified on the basis of perceptually similar features alone. Lea (1984), however, argued that categorization cannot be unequivocally viewed as conceptual unless there is some evidence that the "glue" holding categorical equivalent (i.e., the same) items together includes relationships that are not based solely on perceptual similarity. Otherwise, Lea (1984) argued, the idea of a "concept" has no utility and classification of open-ended categories could be accounted for in terms of perceptual discrimination and generalization processes. In the real world, categories are informative: "If you know that a pomelo is a *fruit*, you can infer that is *edible, grows on trees,* and so forth" (Tversky and Hemenway 1991, p. 439).

The so-called pseudocategories described earlier might be thought of as categorical sets consisting of members related secondarily by means of their common reinforcement history rather than by means of any systematic perceptual similarity. Wasserman, DeVolder, and Coppage (1992) trained pigeons to make a common response to two sets of stimuli that belonged to the perceptually dissimilar categories of chairs and cars. Then a novel response was associated with just one of the categorical sets (e.g., cars only). When tested, the pigeons tended to make the new response rather than the old to the second category (e.g., chairs) even though they had not been previously rewarded for doing so. Wasserman, DeVolder, and Coppage (1992) concluded that the prior association with a common response produced a category of functionally equivalent but physically different items.

Secondary categorical relationships are not precluded by exposure to perceptually similar items, but their formation may be more difficult to establish than when animals are exposed to perceptually different items. Vaughan (1988), for example, found that pigeons formed secondarily mediated categorical links between perceptually similar tree stimuli. The birds were reinforced for responding to one set of tree slides, but not another. After they had acquired the initial discrimination, Vaughan (1988) subjected his birds to a series of discrimination reversals in which the previously positive set of tree slides became negative, and vice versa. Eventually (after dozens of reversals) the pigeons appropriately reversed their response patterns to all slides within each set after the first few trials, thereby indicating that they finally discriminated each tree slide as belonging to a common set. The formation of such links, however, occurred only after many reversals, supporting the notion that perceptual similarity may overshadow and hinder the formation of secondary categorical associations when standard training procedures are used (cf. Bhatt and Wasserman 1989).

Physically Nonequivalent Natural Categories

Social Relationships

Social relationships between animals provide good evidence that natural categories can be based on mediating associations other than perceptual similarity (e.g., Cheney and Seyfarth 1990a). Social responses associated with one individual or a group subset might generalize to other individuals not because the latter physically resemble the former, but because they have a history of similar functional associations. Dasser (1988a, b), for example, reported that two adult female Java monkeys *(Macaca fascicularis)* in discrimination and match-to-sample tasks correctly discriminated mother-offspring pairs and subsequently sibling pairs within their social group. There was no evidence that the basis for identifying pairs of animals within this social category was based on physical resemblance. However, the years spent together in the same group by the subjects and both positive and negative stimulus animals would have provided ample opportunity for the formation of social categories mediated by common functional associations such as temporal/spatial proximity and interactive outcomes.

Functionally Equivalent Vocal Categories

Vervet monkeys functionally categorize two acoustically different calls, labeled "wrrs" and "chutters," at the approach of a neighboring group (Cheney and Seyfarth 1988). In a field experiment the investigators used a modified habituation/dishabituation procedure (cf. Eimas et al. 1971) in which they first exposed their animals to an individual's chutter call. The next day they repeatedly (eight times with a 30-minute inter-trial interval) played the same individual's wrr call. The monkeys habituated to the vocalization as measured by gazes toward the speaker emitting the call. About 30 minutes after the eighth trial, the animals heard the chutter call from the same individual and showed less interest in it than they had on day 1. A similar but diminished result was obtained when the wrr and chutter calls came from different individuals.

The lack of appropriate controls precludes the formation of strong conclusions, but the results suggest that perhaps the vervet monkeys categorized the two calls on the basis of their common referent in much the same way that a prior association with a common response produced a category of functionally equivalent but physically different items for the pigeons of Wasserman, DeVolder, and Coppage (1992). No decrease in the vervet monkeys' responsiveness was reported by Cheney and Seyfarth for two additional conditions in which the monkeys were exposed to two alarm calls that differed acoustically and had different referents. First the animals heard an individual's eagle alarm call, and then they repeatedly heard the same individual's acoustically distinct leopard alarm call. After the eighth habituation trial, the monkeys heard the eagle alarm call once more. In this case, responsiveness to the first and last eagle calls did not differ significantly, presumably because they, unlike the wrr and chutter calls, were associated with different referents and hence in different categories.

RELATIONAL CONCEPTS

The vervet monkeys' responses to repeated playback of their wrr and chutter calls can be seen as evidence of categorization via secondary generalization mediated by a common response or referent (Hull 1943). Seyfarth and Cheney (1988), however, assumed that the monkeys compare two stimuli on the basis of some abstract relationship (cf. Premack 1983a). They concluded, "Results provide clear evidence that vervet monkeys use meaning to *make judgments about the relation* between two vocalizations" (p. 74, emphasis added). They went on to add, "Such *judgments* require that an animal both *recognize* the relationship between a call and its referent and *compare* two referents" (p. 74, emphases added). The difference between the two explanations bears not so much on the content of the category, but rather on the nature of the conceptual rules mediating the animals' responses.

Absolute and Relative Class Concepts

According to the definitions introduced by Thomas (1980), Seyfarth and Cheney (1988) claimed that the vervet monkeys possess a relative class concept. By explicitly comparing stimuli, the monkeys are assumed to have adopted a generalized response rule based on relational similarity and not on inherent stimulus features. The alternative interpretation, in Thomas's (1980) terms, is that the vervet monkeys had acquired an absolute class concept.

The vocalizations in Seyfarth and Cheney's (1988) habituation experiments were presented successively, which is also the case in the standard discrimination procedures used to study natural object concepts. When stimuli are presented successively, it is not necessary to compare them in order to confirm that they are different exemplars of the same category (Premack 1983a; Steirn and Thomas 1990; Thomas 1980). In such cases, the animal can affirm or reject a stimulus as a category member on the basis of absolute discriminative features alone. If the wrr and chutter vocalizations successively evoked a representation of the same concrete referent, then a vervet monkey need simply decide if it had or had not previously occurred. The processes need be no more complex than those involved in associative conditioning.

A Concept of Identity

The relative class concept of relational identity, or sameness and difference, has been studied extensively in animals (e.g., D'Amato and Colombo 1989; Premack 1978, 1983a; Wright et al. 1984; Zentall, Edwards, and Hogan 1984). The procedures include oddity discriminations (e.g., Thomas and Boyd 1973), spontaneous sorting (Matsuzawa 1990; McClure and Culbertson 1977), and analogical reasoning (Gillan, Premack, and Woodruff 1981). Paired comparison same/different (S/D) or matching-to-sample (MTS) tasks, however, are most likely to be used.

Paired Comparison S/D Tasks

In the standard paired comparison S/D task with visual stimuli, a trial begins with the simultaneous presentation of a pair of slides on adjacent screens placed side by side or one above the other. If the pictures are identical (i.e., a same trial), then the animal is rewarded for one response to a manipulandum like a lever or response key. If the two pictures are not identical (i.e., a different trial), then another response is rewarded. The task can be turned into a memory test by successively presenting stimuli, visual or otherwise, and removing the first before the second is presented sometime later (e.g., Sands, Lincoln, and Wright 1982). The procedure can be further modified for tests of serial list memory by presenting a single probe after a sequence of stimuli. The animal's task is to judge if the probe had or had not appeared in the first list (e.g., Thompson and Herman 1977).

Matching-to-Sample Tasks

In the standard MTS task, the subject first observes a single stimulus, the sample, which is followed by two comparison stimuli. The subject is rewarded for responding to the comparison stimulus that is identical to (i.e., matching) the sample (e.g., Carter and Werner 1978; Nissen, Blum, and Blum 1948). Typically, the sample remains present when the comparison stimuli are produced. In some cases, the subject may be rewarded for responding to the comparison stimulus that is not identical (i.e., nonmatching) to the sample (e.g., Irle and Markowitsch 1987). As with S/D tasks, MTS procedures become memory tests when the sample is removed before the comparison stimuli are presented sometime later (e.g., D'Amato 1973).

Criteria for Conceptual Matching

As in studies of natural object concepts, transfer of performance on paired comparison S/D and MTS tasks to novel stimuli is taken as evidence of a relational identity concept (i.e., "respond same," "match like with like") as opposed to control by absolute stimulus features (i.e., "respond red again," "match red with red") (e.g., Premack 1983a). Alex, an African Grey parrot *(Psittacus erithacus),* when asked verbally, "What's same?" or "What's different?" when presented with pairs of familiar and unfamiliar objects, can label the actual attribute (e.g., color, shape, or matter) from among several (Pepperberg 1987b). By all accounts, however, it is difficult for many species, like pigeons, to demonstrate a conceptual understanding of identity or nonidentity. Generalized matching to novel stimuli often depends upon investigators' using a large number of training exemplars regardless of the sensory modality being tested (e.g., Wright et al. 1988; Wright, Shyan, and Jitsumori 1990).

Problems in Interpreting Performance

Generalized matching to novel stimuli is a necessary, but not sufficient, criterion for concluding that an animal has a matching concept. Matching with novel stimuli may be mediated by factors other than reflexive identity (i.e., A *is* A) (see Dube, McIlvane, and Green 1992; Kastak and Schusterman 1992). One of these factors is the exclusion effect, which can occur when the comparison stimuli consist of a positive matching stimulus paired with a familiar negative nonmatching stimulus. In such cases, the animal can respond correctly not by matching, but by excluding the familiar choices stimulus because it has previously been associated with another sample (Schusterman et. al. 1993). Pairing novel matching stimuli with only novel nonmatching stimuli would seem to be the obvious solution, but even this procedure has its problems.

Abruptly introducing all novel stimuli to an animal that has experienced only familiar ones during training can disrupt performance and thereby mask any evidence of conceptual learning. Repeatedly presenting and rewarding responses to the same configuration of novel stimuli over trials, however, leaves open the possibility of discriminative learning based on absolute cues only. Using novel stimuli on each and every trial can lead to accurate performances mediated by an absolute class concept rather than the relational one of reflexive identity. With trial-unique stimuli an animal can respond correctly simply by affirming it has seen one of the choice stimuli previously as sample rather than discriminating between the stimuli presented at the relational class level of abstract identity.

Evidence of an Identity Concept

Given the many problems of interpretation, results from MTS studies are often difficult to evaluate with respect to the investigators' claims that their animals do or do not have a matching concept. Ideally, the best evidence of a relational matching concept based on reflexive identity would come from a study with the following characteristics. First, the animals should learn to match with a small number—ideally two—training stimuli that appear as both the matching and nonmatching alternative over trials. Once criterion is reached, transfer tests should be run with novel stimuli that differ both physically and conceptually from the training stimuli. Responses should be nondifferentially rewarded or tested under extinction, and performances on the first presentation of the transfer stimuli should be compared with those over several trials in which both alternatives serve as sample.

Oden, Thompson, and Premack (1988) conducted a study with the above characteristics that provided clear evidence of a relational identity matching concept in chimpanzees *(Pan troglodytes)*. Four infant animals were first trained to match using a metal lock and cup alternatively as matching and nonmatching alternatives. First, the animals were rewarded for placing the matching alternative into a pan where they had put the sample object. After each animal reached criterion, it was given a series of transfer tests with novel three-dimensional objects, cloth swatches and food items. No differential feedback was provided on the transfer tests. The overall correct MTS performance on trial 1 was 77 percent (p < .05, binomial test), and two animals were always correct. There was no evidence of a practice effect on performance in the transfer tests and, as is shown in figure 9.9, performance levels in the transfer tests with novel objects and fabrics did not differ significantly from those obtained in the

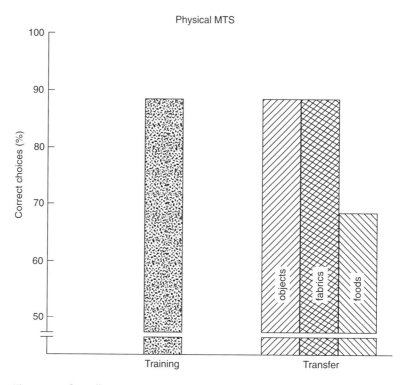

Figure 9.9 Overall mean percentage of correct matching choices by four infant chimpanzees. See text for details. (Derived from Oden et al. 1988 in *Journal of Experimental Psychology: Animal Behavior Processes*.)

last two training sessions. The decline in performance with the food items was attributable to preferences for specific items. Nevertheless, even in this case two of the animals responded at levels above chance with food items.

Not All Identity Judgments Are the Same

Abstract Relational Judgments

The identity concept demonstrated by the infant chimpanzees (Oden, Thompson, and Premack 1988) was based on physical resemblance and did not transfer to the more abstract level of same/different judgments about relationships (Oden, Thompson, and Premack 1990). In this regard, these animals were no different from other chimpanzees who have not been exposed to "language training" with concrete tokens as described by Premack (1976) and by Premack and Premack (1972) (but cf. Smith et al. 1975). The latter ability is revealed if an animal can match a pair of identical objects with a different pair of identical objects rather than a pair of nonidentical objects. Likewise, a nonidentical pair should be matched with a different nonidentical pair rather than an identical pair. If one represents individual objects with letters, then the task is to match AA with BB (and not CD) and to match EF with GH and not JJ.

To perform the relational task correctly, an animal must ultimately compare abstract identity and nonidentity relations and judge whether they are the same or different independently of the objects used to exemplify them. This process is fundamentally more complex than either physical matching or paired comparison S/D tasks (Premack 1983a, b; Thompson and Oden 1993). In the latter sort of task, for example, the correct response can be identified from the outcome (identity or nonidentity) of only a single comparison between two physical stimuli. To match relations, however, one must first carry out three such comparisons, one each for the sample pairs and the two comparison pairs. Next, representations of the outcomes from the three within-pair comparisons must themselves be compared. Then, and only then, can the correct response choice be identified from this final outcome (i.e., same or different). This latter comparison of relational representations is not required in other conceptual tasks, including conditional discriminations with identity and nonidentity pairs (Burdyn and Thomas 1984). Thompson and Oden (1993) have argued that the ability to encode the outcomes of these latter comparisons presupposes a capacity for propositional representations.

Implicit if Not Explicit Recognition of Abstract Concepts

As noted above, the four infant chimpanzees who a had physical matching concept failed to match relations despite heroic training efforts, including the use of trial-unique stimulus pairs (Oden, Thompson, and Premack

1990, experiment 3). The chimpanzees' conceptual understanding of identity and nonidentity based on physical resemblance did not extend to abstract relations. This did not mean, however, that they were perceptually insensitive to abstract same/different relations. Oden, Thompson, and Premack 1990, experiment 2) demonstrated that the same chimpanzees spontaneously perceived abstract same/different relations.

On the initial familiarization trial, the chimpanzees were allowed over five minutes to handle a single object pair mounted on a masonite base. The paired objects were either identical (AA) or nonidentical (CD). On the second test trial, the animals were presented with a new object pair (e.g., BB or EF), which was either the same relation experienced on trial 1 or the alternative relation. As shown in figure 9.10, handling times on trial 2 were affected by the relation experienced on trial 1. If the within-pair relation on trial 2 was the same as that experienced on trial 1 then handling time was less than if differed. Whatever the reason for the infant chimpanzees' failure to match relations, it did not result from their inability to detect such relations.

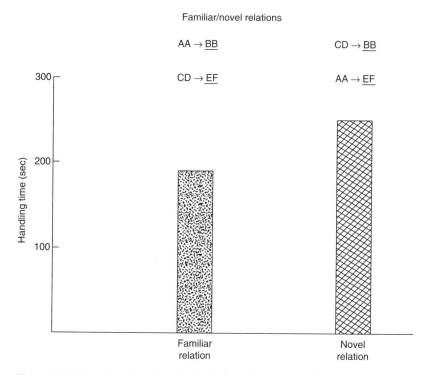

Figure 9.10 Mean handling time by four infant chimpanzees of object pairs on trial 2 of a familiarization/novelty test for the perception of abstract relations. The first and second letter pairs above each bar represent the object pair relation (i.e., identity or nonidentity) experienced on trial 1 and trial 2, respectively. (Derived from Oden et al. 1990, experiment 2, in *Child Development*.)

Human infants fail to match abstract same/different relations before the age of about five years, but like the infant chimpanzees they can perceive abstract relations in preference-for-novelty tests as young at about 29 weeks of age (Tyrrell, Stauffer, and Snowman 1991). Adult rhesus monkeys *(M. mulatta)*, when tested with the same preference-for-novelty procedures as those used with children, showed a preference for novel objects as measured by differential looking times. The monkeys preferred to gaze at the novel object pair. In contrast to human and chimpanzee infants, however, they showed no preference for novel abstract same/different relations (Thompson, Arlinsky, and Christie 1992).

One could argue that the difference in performance between the two relational tasks—familiarization/novelty tasks matching tasks—reflects the difference between recognition and discrimination, with the term "conceptual" reserved for the latter ability only. The object pairs were presented successively in the familiarization/novelty procedure; therefore, the children and animals did not have to directly compare them. The task might be conceived of as an instance of Thomas's (1980) absolute class rather than relative class discrimination. That is, the chimpanzees and children had only to confirm whether a relationship had occurred previously. But if performance on the familiarization/novelty procedure represents an absolute class concept, then it is a special one based on relational and not physical features. Also, as in the case of other concepual tasks—for example, mirror-mediated self-recognition tasks—there appears to be a fundamental distinction between humans and chimpanzees on the one hand and other nonhuman primates on the other hand.

CONCLUSION

If by now readers have concluded that the story of the Ugly Duckling is a fairy tale, then I hope they will recognize that there is more than a grain of truth in it. Admittedly, with the possible exception of chimpanzees, no one species—certainly not ducks or swans—exhibits the full range of conceptual knowledge displayed by the Ugly Duckling. There is increasing evidence, however, that animals categorize their world and do so on the basis of perceptual, if not abstract, relational similarity. On the one hand, investigators have developed standard procedures that permit them to map the nature and range of these concepts. On the other hand, they are sadly lacking in theory. Our understanding of the actual information controlling conceptual behavior in animals lags far behind our ability to document categorical classes. Theories of how concepts are perceived and possibly represented are largely *post hoc* theories and seldom predictive. Finally, there have been few advances in our understanding of evolutionary species differences and similarities from either an adaptational or a phylogenetic perspective. In short, there is much to attract new investigators to this area of comparative cognition.

ACKNOWLEDGMENTS

My thanks to the members of the Department of Ethologie at the Université de Rennes 1 for their kind hospitality and support during the preparation of this chapter.

REFERENCES

Andersen, H. C. (1984). *Hans Andersen's Fairy Tales.* Oxford: Oxford University Press.

Anderson, J. R. (1993). To see ourselves as others see us. *New Ideas in Psychology,* 11, 339–343.

Anderson, J. R. (1983). Responses to mirror-image stimulation, and assessment of self recognition in mirror- and peer-reared stumptail macaques. *Quarterly Journal of Experimental Psychology,* 35, 201–222.

Anderson, J. R. (1984). Monkeys with mirrors: Some questions for primate psychology. *International Journal of Primatology,* 5, 81–98.

Anderson, J. R. (1986). Mirror-mediated finding of hidden food by monkeys (*Macaca tonkeana* and *Macaca fascicularis*). *Journal of Comparative Psychology,* 100, 237–242.

Astington, J. W., and Gopnick, A. (1991). Theoretical explanations of children's understanding of the mind. *British Journal of Developmental Psychology,* 9, 7–31.

Astley, S. L., and Wasserman, E. A. (1992). Categorical discrimination and generalization in pigeons: All negative stimuli are not created equal. *Journal of Experimental Psychology: Animal Behavior Processes,* 18, 193–207.

Berlin, B., Breedlove, D. E., and Raven, P. H. (1973). General principles of classification and nomenclature in folk biology. *American Anthropologist,* 75, 214–242.

Bhatt, R. S., and Wasserman, E. A. (1989). Secondary generalization and categorization in pigeons. *Journal of the Experimental Analysis of Behavior,* 52, 213–224.

Bhatt, R. S., Wasserman, E. A., Reynolds, W. F., and Knauss, K. S. (1988). Conceptual behavior in pigeons: Categorization of both familiar and novel examples from four classes of natural and artificial stimuli. *Journal of Experimental Psychology: Animal Behavior Processes,* 14, 219–234.

Blake, R. (1993). Cats perceive biological motion. *Psychological Science,* 4, 54–57.

Boccia, M. L. (1994) Mirror behavior in macaques. In S. T. Parker, R. W. Mitchell, and M. L. Boccia (Eds.). *Self Awareness in Animals and Humans: Developmental Perspectives.* New York: Cambridge University Press. Pp. 350–360.

Boysen, S. T. (1993). Counting in chimpanzees: Nonhuman principles and emergent properties of number. In S. T. Boysen and E. J. Capaldi (Eds.). *The Development of Numerical Competency: Animal and Human Models.* Hillsdale, NJ: Erlbaum Associates. Pp. 39–59.

Boysen, S. T., and Bernston, G. G. (1989a). Numerical competence in a chimpanzee *(Pan troglodytes). Journal of Comparative Psychology,* 103, 23–31.

Boysen, S. T., and Bernston, G. G. (1989b). The development of numerical skills in chimpanzees *(Pan troglodytes).* In S. T. Parker and K. R. Gibson (Eds.). *"Language" and Intelligence in Nonhuman Primates.* New York: Cambridge University Press. Pp. 435–450.

Boysen, S. T., and Capaldi, E. J. (Eds.) (1993). *The Development of Numerical Competency: Animal and Human Models.* Hillsdale, NJ: Erlbaum Associates.

Burdyn, L. E., and Thomas, R. K. (1984). Conditional discrimination with conceptual simultaneous and successive cues in the squirrel monkey *(Saimiri sciureus)*. *Journal of Comparative Psychology,* 98, 405–413.

Cabe, P. A. (1980). Picture perception in nonhuman subjects. In M. A. Hagen (Ed.). *The Perception of Pictures, vol. 2.* New York: Academic Press. Pp. 305–343.

Calhoun, S., and Thompson, R. L. (1988). Long-term retention of self-recognition by chimpanzees. *American Journal of Primatology,* 15, 361–365.

Candland, D. K., and Judge, P. G. (1991). Visual (social perceptual) categories of *Macaca fuscata* and *Papio hamdryas.* In A. Ehara et al. (Eds.). *Primatology Today.* Amsterdam, The Netherlands: Elsevier Science Publishers B. V. (Biomedical Division). Pp. 289–292.

Carter, D. E., and Werner, T. J. (1978). Complex learning and information processing by pigeons: A critical analysis. *Journal of the Experimental Analysis of Behavior,* 29, 565–601.

Cerella, J. (1979). Visual classes and natural categories in the pigeon. *Journal of Experimental Psychology: Human Perception and Performance,* 5, 68–77.

Cerella, J. (1990). Shape constancy in the pigeon: The perspective transformations decomposed. In M. L. Commons, R. J. Herrnstein, M. Kosslyn, and D. B. Mumford (Eds.). *Quantitative Analyses of Behavior, vol. VIII.* Hillsdale, NJ: Erlbaum Associates. Pp. 145–163.

Cheney, D. L., and Seyfarth, R. M. (1988). Assessment of meaning and the detection of unreliable signals by vervet monkeys. *Animal Behavior,* 36, 477–486.

Cheney, D. L., and Seyfarth, R. M. (1990a). The representation of social relations by monkeys. *Cognition,* 37, 167–196.

Cheney, D., and Seyfarth, R. (1990b). Attending to behavior versus attending to knowledge: Examining monkeys' attribution of mental states. *Animal Behaviour,* 40, 742–753.

Cook, R. G., Wright, A. A., and Kendrick, D. F. (1990). Visual categorization by pigeons. In M. L. Commons, R. J. Herrnstein, S. M. Kosslyn, and D. B. Mumford (Eds.). *Quantitative analyses of behavior, vol. VIII.* Hillsdale, NJ: Erlbaum Associates. Pp. 187–214.

Cronin, J. E., Cann, R., and Sarich, V. M. (1980). Molecular evolution and systematics of the genus *Macaca.* In D. G. Linburg (Ed.). *The Macaques: Studies in Ecology, Behavior, and Evolution.* New York: Van Nostrand Reinhold. Pp. 31–51.

Cutting, J. (1978). A program to generate synthetic walkers as dynamic point-light displays. *Behavioral Research Methods and Instrumentation,* 10, 91–94.

D'Amato, M. R. (1973). Delayed matching and short-term memory in monkeys. In G. H. Bower (Ed.). *The Psychology of Learning and Motivation: Advances in Research and Theory, vol. 7.* New York: Academic Press. Pp. 227–269.

D'Amato, M. R., and Colombo, M. (1989). On the limit of the matching concept in monkeys *(Cebus apella). Journal of the Experimental Analysis of Behavior,* 52, 225–236.

D'Amato, M. R., and van Sant, P. (1988). The person concept in monkeys *(Cebus apella). Journal of Experimental Psychology: Animal Behavior Processes,* 14, 43–55.

Dasser, V. (1988a). A social concept in Java monkeys. *Animal Behavior,* 36, 225–230.

Dasser, V. (1988b). Mapping social concepts in monkeys. In R. W. Byrne and A. Whiten (Eds.). *Machiavellian Intelligence.* Oxford: Oxford University Press. Pp. 85–93.

Davis, H., and Albert, M. (1986). Numerical discrimination by rats using sequential auditory stimuli. *Animal Learning and Behavior,* 14, 57–59.

Davis, H., and Memmott, J. (1982). Counting behavior in animals: A critical evaluation. *Psychological Bulletin,* 92, 547–571.

Davis, H., and Perusse, R. (1988). Numerical competence in animals: Definitional issues, current evidence, and a new research agenda. *Behavioral and Brain Sciences*, 11, 561–615.

Delson, E. (1980). Fossil macaques, phyletic relationships, and a scenario of deployment. In D. G. Linburg (Ed.). *The Macaques: Studies in Ecology, Behavior, and Evolution*. New York: Van Nostrand Reinhold. Pp. 10–30.

Demaria, C., and Thierry, B. (1988). Responses to animal stimulus photographs in stumptailed macaques *(Macaca arctoides)*. *Primates*, 29, 237–244.

Dittrich, W. H., and Lea, S. E. G. (1993). Motion as a natural category for pigeons: Generalization and a feature-positive effect. *Journal of the Experimental Analysis of Behavior*, 59, 115–129.

Disney, W. (Producer) (1939). *The Ugly Duckling*. [Short film].

Dube, W. V., McIlvane, W. J., and Green, G. (1992). An analysis of generalized identity matching-to-sample test procedures. *The Psychological Record*, 42, 17–28.

Edwards, C. A., and Honig, W. K. (1987). Memorization and "feature selection" in the acquisition of natural concepts in pigeons. *Learning and Motivation*, 18, 235–260.

Eimas, P. D., Siqueland, P., Jusczyk, P., and Vigorito, J. (1971). Speech perception in infants. *Science*, 171, 303–306.

Epstein, R., Lanza, R. P., and Skinner, B. F. (1981). "Self-awareness" in the pigeon. *Science*, 212, 695–696.

Fetterman, J. G. (1993). Numerosity discrimination: Both time and number matter. *Journal of Experimental Psychology: Animal Behavior Processes*, 19, 149–164.

Fetterman, J. G., Stubbs, D. A., and MacEwen, D. (1992). The perception of the extended stimulus. In W. K. Honig and J. G. Fetterman (Eds.). *Cognitive Aspects of Stimulus Control*. Hillsdale, NJ: Erlbaum Associates. Pp. 1–20.

Fooden, J. (1980). Classification and distribution of living macaques (Macaca Lacepede, 1799). In D. G. Lindburg (Ed.). *The Macaques: Studies in Ecology, Behavior, and Evolution*. New York: Van Nostrand Reinhold Co. Pp. 1–9.

Fox, R., and McDaniel, C. (1982). The perception of biological motion by human infants. *Science*, 218, 486–487.

Fujita, K. (1987). Species recognition by five macaque monkeys. *Primates*, 28, 353–366.

Fujita, K., and Matsuzawa, T. (1986). A new procedure to study the perceptual world of animals with sensory reinforcement: Recognition of humans by a chimpanzee. *Primates*, 27, 283–291.

Gallup, G. G., Jr. (1968). Mirror image stimulation. *Psychological Bulletin*, 70, 782–793.

Gallup, G. G., Jr. (1970). Chimpanzees: Self-recognition. *Science*, 167, 86–87.

Gallup, G. G., Jr. (1975). Towards an operational definition of self-awareness. In R. H. Tuttle (Ed.). *Socioecology and Psychology of Primates*. The Hague, The Netherlands: Mouton. Pp. 309–342.

Gallup, G. G., Jr. (1982). Self-awareness and the emergence of mind in primates. *American Journal of Primatology*, 2, 237–248.

Gallup, G. G., Jr. (1987). Self-awareness. In G. Mitchell and J. Erwin (Eds.). *Comparative Primate Biology, vol. 2, part B: Behavior, Cognition, and Motivation*. New York: Alan R. Liss. Pp. 3–16.

Gallup, G. G., Jr. (1994). Self-recognition: Research strategies and experimental design. In

S. T. Parker, R. W. Mitchell, and M. L. Boccia (Eds.). *Self-Awareness in Animals and Humans: Developmental Perspectives.* New York: Cambridge University Press. Pp. 35–50.

Gallup, G. G., Jr., McClure, M. K., Hill, S. D., and Bundy, R. A. (1971). Capacity for self-recognition in differentially reared chimpanzees. *The Psychological Record,* 21, 69–74.

Gallup, G. G., Jr., and Suarez, S. D. (1991). Social responding to mirrors in rhesus monkeys *(Macaca mulatta):* Effects of temporary mirror removal. *Journal of Comparative Psychology,* 105, 376–379.

Gallup, G. G., Jr., Wallnau, L. B., and Suarez, S. D. (1980). Failure to find self recognition in mother-infant and infant-infant rhesus monkey pairs. *Folia Primatologica,* 33, 210–219.

Gardener, R. A., and Gardener, B. T. (1985). A vocabulary test for chimpanzees *(Pan troglodytes). Journal of Comparative Psychology,* 98, 381–404.

Gelman, R., and Gallistel, C. R. (1978). *The Child's Understanding of Number.* Cambridge, MA: Harvard University Press.

Gillan, D. J., Premack, D., and Woodruff, G. (1981). Reasoning in the chimpanzee: I. Analogical reasoning. *Journal of Experimental Psychology: Animal Behavior Processes,* 7, 1–17.

Green, S. L. (1983). Feature memorization in pigeon concept performance. In M. L. Commons, R. J. Herrnstein, and A. R. Wagner (Eds.). *Quantitative Analyses of Behavior, vol. IV.* Cambridge, MA: Ballinger. Pp. 209–229.

Griffin, D. R. (1981). *The Question of Animal Awareness,* 2nd ed. New York: Rockefeller University Press.

Harnad, S. (1987). Introduction: Psychophysical and cognitive aspects of categorical perception: A critical overview. In S. Harnad (Ed.). *Categorical Perception: The Groundwork of Cognition.* New York: Cambridge University Press. Pp. 1–25.

Hayes, K. J., and Hayes, C. (1953). Picture perception in a home-raised chimpanzee. *Journal of Comparative and Physiological Psychology,* 46, 470–474.

Herrnstein, R. J. (1979). Acquisition, generalization, and discrimination reversal of a natural concept. *Journal of Experimental Psychology: Animal Behavior Processes,* 5, 116–129.

Herrnstein, R. J. (1984). Objects, categories, and discriminative stimuli. In H. L. Roitblat, T. G. Bever, and H. S. Terrace (Eds.). *Animal Cognition.* Hillsdale, NJ: Erlbaum. Pp. 233–261.

Herrnstein, R. J. (1990). Levels of stimulus control: A functionalist approach. *Cognition,* 37, 133–166.

Herrnstein, R. J., and de Villiers, P. A. (1980). Fish as a natural category for people and pigeons. In G. H. Bower (Ed.). *The Psychology of Learning and Motivation, vol. 14.* New York: Academic Press. Pp. 59–95.

Herrnstein, R. J., and Loveland, D. H. (1964). Complex visual concept in the pigeon. *Science,* 16, 549–551.

Herrnstein, R. J., Loveland, D. H., and Cable, C. (1976). Natural concepts in pigeons. *Journal of Experimental Psychology: Animal Behavior Processes,* 2, 285–302.

Hobson, R. P. (1990). Concerning knowledge of mental states. *British Journal of Medical Psychology,* 63, 199–213.

Hobson, R. P. (1991). Against the theory of "Theory of Mind." *British Journal of Developmental Psychology,* 9, 33–51.

Honig, W. K., and Stewart, K. E. (1989). Discrimination of relative numerosity by pigeons. *Animal Learning and Behavior,* 17, 134–146.

Huber, L., and Lenz, R. (1993). A test of the linear feature model of polymorphous concept discrimination with pigeons. *The Quarterly Journal of Experimental Psychology,* 46B, 1–18.

Hull, C. L. (1943). *Principles of Behavior: An Introduction to Behavior Theory.* New York: Appleton-Century-Crofts.

Humphrey, N. K. (1974). "Interest" and "pleasure": Two determinants of a monkey's visual preferences. *Perception,* 1, 395–416.

Irle, E., and Markowitsch, H. J. (1987). Conceptualization without specific training in squirrel monkeys *(Saimiri sciureus):* A test using the non-match-to-sample procedure. *Journal of Comparative Psychology,* 101, 305–311.

Itakura, S. (1987a). Mirror guided behavior in Japanese monkeys *(Macaca fuscata fuscata). Primates,* 28, 149–161.

Itakura, S. (1987b). Use of a mirror to direct responses in Japanese monkeys *(Macaca fuscata fuscata). Primates,* 28, 343–352.

Jitsumori, M., and Matsuzawa, T. (1991). Picture perception in monkeys and pigeons: Transfer of rightside-up versus upside-down discriminations of photographic objects across conceptual categories. *Primates,* 32, 473–482.

Jitsumori, M., Wright, A. A., and Cook, R. G. (1988). Long-term proactive interference and novelty enhancement effects in monkey list memory. *Journal of Experimental Psychology: Animal Behavior Processes,* 14, 146–154.

Johansson, G. (1973). Visual perception of biological motion and a model for its analysis. *Perception and Psychophysics,* 14, 201–211.

Kastak, D. A., and Schusterman, R. J. (1992). Comparative cognition in marine mammals: A clarification on match-to-sample tests. *Marine Mammal Science,* 8, 414–417.

Lander, J., and Poole, D. G. (1971). The pigeon's concept of pigeon. *Psychonomic Science,* 25, 157–158.

Lea, S. E. G. (1984). In what sense do pigeons learn concepts? In H. L. Roitblat, T. G. Bever, and H. S. Terrace (Eds.). *Animal Cognition.* Hillsdale, NJ: Erlbaum. Pp. 263–276.

Lea, S. E. G., and Ryan, C. M. E. (1983). Featural analysis of pigeons' acquisition of discrimination between letters. In M. L. Commons, R. J. Herrnstein, and A. R. Wagner (Eds.). *Quantitative Analyses of Behavior, vol. IV.* Cambridge, MA: Ballinger. Pp. 239–253.

Lea, S. E. G., and Ryan, C. M. E. (1990). Unnatural concepts and the theory of concept discrimination in birds. In M. L. Commons, R. J. Herrnstein, S. M. Kosslyn, and D. B. Mumford (Eds.). *Quantitative Analyses of Behavior, vol. VIII.* Hillsdale, NJ: Erlbaum Associates. Pp. 187–214.

Ledbetter, D. H., and Basen, J. A. (1982). Failure to demonstrate self-recognition in gorillas. *American Journal of Primatology,* 2, 307–310.

Lethmate, J., and Drucker, G. (1973). Untersuchungen zum Selbsterkennen im spiegel bei Orang-utans und eingen anderen Affenarten [Studies on self-recognition in a mirror by orangutans and some other primate species]. *Zeitschrift fur Tierpsychologie,* 33, 248–269.

Lewis, M. (1992). *Shame, the Exposed Self.* New York: Free Press.

Lewis, M., Sullivan, M. W., Stanger, C., and Weiss, M. (1989). Self-development and self-conscious emotions. *Child Development,* 60, 146–156.

Lin, A. C., Bard, K. A., and Anderson, J. R. (1992). Development of self-recognition in chimpanzees *(Pan troglodytes). Journal of Comparative Psychology,* 106, 120–127.

Loveland, K. A. (1986). Discovering the affordances of a reflecting surface. *Developmental Review*, 6, 1–24.

Lubow, R. E. (1974). High-order concept formation in the pigeon. *Journal of the Experimental Analysis of Behavior*, 21, 475–483.

Lydersen, T., and Crossman, E. K. (1974). Fixed-ratio discrimination: Effects of response produced blackouts. *Journal of the Experimental Analysis of Behavior*, 22, 547–551.

Mandler, G., and Shebo, B. J. (1982). Subitizing: An analysis of its component processes. *Journal of Experimental Psychology: General*, 111, 1–22.

Mandler, J. M., and Bauer, P. J. (1988). The cradle of categorization: Is the basic level basic? *Cognitive Development*, 3, 247–264.

Matsuzawa, T. (1985a). Color naming and classification in a chimpanzee *(Pan troglodytes)*. *Journal of Human Evolution*, 14, 283–291.

Matsuzawa, T. (1985b). Use of numbers by a chimpanzee. *Nature*, 315, 57–59.

Matsuzawa, T. (1990). Spontaneous sorting in human and chimpanzee. In S. T. Parker and K. R. Gibson (Eds.). *"Language" and Intelligence in Nonhuman Primates*. New York: Cambridge University Press. Pp. 451–468.

Matsuzawa, T., Asano, T., Kubota, K., and Murofushi, K. (1986). Acquisition and generalization of numerical labeling by a chimpanzee. In D. M. Taub and F. A. King (Eds.). *Current Perspectives in Primate Social Dynamics*. New York: Van Nostrand Rheinhold. Pp. 416–430.

McClure, M. K., and Culbertson, G. (1977). Chimpanzees' spontaneous temporal sorting of stimuli on the basis of physical identity. *Primates*, 18, 709–711.

Medin, D. L. (1989). Concepts and conceptual structure. *American Psychologist*, 44, 1469–1481.

Medin, D. L., and Shaeffer, M. M. (1978). Context theory of classification learning. *Psychological Review*, 85, 207–238.

Miles, H. L. (1994). Me Chantek: The development of self-awareness in a signing orangutan. In S. T. Parker, R. W. Mitchell, and M. L. Boccia (Eds.). *Self-Awareness in Animals and Humans: Developmental Perspectives*. New York: Cambridge University Press. Pp. 254–272.

Mitchell, R. W. (1993). Mental models of mirror self-recognition: Two theories. *New Ideas in Psychology*, 11, 295–325.

Mitchell, R. W., Yao, P., Sherman, P. T., and O'Regan, M. (1985). Discriminative responding of a dolphin *(Tursiops truncatus)* to differentially rewarded stimuli. *Journal of Comparative Psychology*, 99, 218–225.

Murphy, G. L., and Medin, D. L. (1985). The role of theories in conceptual coherence. *Psychological Review*, 92, 289–316.

Nissen, H. W., Blum, J. S., and Blum, R. A. (1948). Analysis of matching behavior in chimpanzee. *Journal of Comparative and Physiological Psychology*, 41, 62–74.

Oden, D. L., Thompson, R. K. R., and Premack, D. (1988). Spontaneous transfer of matching by infant chimpanzees *(Pan troglodytes)*. *Journal of Experimental Psychology: Animal Behavior Processes*, 1, 326–334.

Oden, D. L., Thompson, R. K. R., and Premack, D. (1990). Infant chimpanzees spontaneously perceive both concrete and abstract same/different relations. *Child Development*, 61, 621–631.

Parker, S. T., Mitchell, R. W., and Boccia, M. L. (Eds.). (1994). *Self-Awareness in Animals and Humans*. New York: Cambridge University Press.

Patterson, F. (1984). Self-recognition by Gorilla gorilla gorilla. *Journal of the Gorilla Foundation,* 7, 2–3.

Patterson, F. G. P., and Cohn, R. H. (1994). Self-recognition and self-awareness in lowland gorillas. In S. T. Parker, R. W. Mitchell, and M. L. Boccia (Eds.). *Self Awareness in Animals and Humans.* New York: Cambridge University Press. Pp. 273–290.

Pepperberg, I. M. (1983). Cognition in the African Grey parrot: Preliminary evidence for auditory/vocal comprehension of the class concept. *Animal Learning and Behavior,* 11, 179–185.

Pepperberg, I. M. (1987a). Evidence for conceptual quantitative abilities in the African Grey parrot: Labeling of cardinal sets. *Ethology,* 75, 37–61.

Pepperberg, I. M. (1987b). Acquisition of the same/different concept by an African Grey parrot *(Psittacus erithacus):* Learning with respect to categories of color, shape and material. *Animal Learning and Behavior,* 15, 423–432.

Pepperberg, I. M. (1990). Conceptual abilities of some nonprimate species, with an emphasis on an African Grey parrot. In S. T. Parker and K. R. Gibson (Eds.). *"Language" and Intelligence in Nonhuman Primates.* New York: Cambridge University Press. Pp. 469–507.

Perusse, R., and Rumbaugh, D. M. (1990). Summation in chimpanzees *(Pan troglodytes):* Effects of amounts, number of wells and finer ratios. *International Journal of Primatology,* 11, 425–437.

Pierce, J. M. (1988). Stimulus generalization and the acquisition of categories by pigeons. In L. Weiskrantz (Ed.). *Thought without Language.* Oxford, England: Clarendon Press. Pp. 132–154.

Pietrewicz, A. T., and Kamil, A. C. (1977). Visual detection of cryptic prey by blue jays. *Science,* 195, 580–582.

Platt, M. M., Thompson, R. L., and Boatright, S. L. (1991). Monkeys and mirrors: Questions of methodology. In L. M. Fedigan and P. J. Asquith (Eds.). *The Monkeys of Arashiyama: Thirty-five years of Research in Japan and the West.* Albany, NY: State University of New York Press. Pp. 274–290.

Povinelli, D. J. (1989). Failure to find self-recognition in Asian elephants *(Elephas maximus)* in contrast to their use of mirror cues to discover hidden food. *Journal of Comparative Psychology,* 103, 122–131.

Povinelli, D. J. (1994). How to create self-recognizing gorillas (but don't try it on macaques). In S. T. Parker, R. W. Mitchell, and M. L. Boccia (Eds.). *Self-Awareness in Animals and Humans.* New York: Cambridge University Press. Pp. 291–300.

Povinelli, D. J., Nelson, K. E., and Boysen, S. T. (1990). Inferences about guessing and knowing by chimpanzees *(Pan troglodytes). Journal of Comparative Psychology,* 104, 203–210.

Povinelli, D. J., Parks, K. A., and Novak, M. A. (1991). Do rhesus monkeys *(Macaca mulatta)* attribute knowledge and ignorance to others? *Journal of Comparative Psychology,* 105, 318–325.

Premack, A. J., and Premack, D. (1972). Teaching language to an ape. *Scientific American,* 227, 92–99.

Premack, D. (1976). *Intelligence in Ape and Man.* Hillsdale, NJ: Erlbaum Associates.

Premack, D. (1978). On the abstractness of human concepts: Why it would be difficult to talk to a pigeon. In S. Hulse, H. Fowler, and W. K. Honig (Eds.). *Cognitive Processes in Animal Behavior.* Hillsdale, NJ: Erlbaum Associates. Pp. 423–451.

Premack, D. (1983a). Animal cognition. *Annual Review of Psychology,* 34, 351–362.

Premack, D. (1983b). The codes of man and beast. *The Behavioral and Brain Sciences,* 6, 125–137.

Premack, D. (1988). "Does the chimpanzee have a theory of mind" revisited. In R. Byrne and A. Whiten (Eds.). *Machiavellian Intelligence.* New York: Oxford University Press. Pp. 160–179.

Premack, D., and Woodruff, G. (1978). Does the chimpanzee have a theory of mind? *The Behavioral and Brain Sciences,* 4, 515–526.

Real, P. G., Iannazzi, R., Kamil, A. C., and Heinrich, B. (1984). Discrimination and generalization of leaf damage by blue jays *(Cyanocitta cristata). Animal Learning and Behavior,* 12, 202–208.

Rilling, M. (1967). Number of responses as a stimulus in fixed interval and fixed ratio schedules. *Journal of Comparative and Physiological Psychology,* 63, 60–65.

Rilling, M., De Marse, T., and La Claire, L. (1993). Contour deletion as a method for identifying the weights of features underlying object recognition. *The Quarterly Journal of Experimental Psychology,* 46B, 43–61.

Ringo, J. R., and Doty, R. W. (1985). A macaque remembers pictures briefly viewed six months earlier. *Behavioral Brain Research,* 18, 289–294.

Ristau, C. A. (Ed.) 1991. *Cognitive Ethology: The Minds of Other Animals: Essays in Honor of Donald R. Griffin.* Hillsdale, NJ: Erlbaum.

Roberts, W. A., and Mazmanian, D. S. (1988). Concept learning at different levels of abstraction by pigeons, monkeys and people. *Journal of Experimental Psychology: Animal Behavior Processes,* 14, 247–260.

Rosch, E., and Mervis, C. B. (1975). Family resemblances: Studies in the internal structure of categories. *Cognitive Psychology,* 7, 573–605.

Rosch, E., Mervis, C. B., Gray, W., Johnson, D., and Boyes-Braem, P. (1976). Basic objects in natural categories. *Cognitive Psychology,* 7, 573–605.

Rumbaugh, D. M., Hopkins, W. D., Washburn, D. A., and Savage-Rumbaugh, E. S. (1989). Lana chimpanzee learns to count by "Numath": A summary of a videotaped experimental report. *Psychological Record,* 39, 459–470.

Ryan, C. M. E. (1982). Concept formation and individual recognition in the domestic chicken *(Gallus gallus). Behavior Analysis Letters,* 2, 213–220.

Ryan, C. M. E., and Lea, S. E. G. (1990). Pattern recognition, updating, and filial imprinting in the domestic chick *(Gallus gallus).* In M. L. Commons, R. J. Herrnstein, S. M. Kosslyn, and D. B. Mumford (Eds.). *Quantitative Analyses of Behavior, vol. 8.* Hillsdale, NJ: Erlbaum Associates. Pp. 89–110.

Ryle, G. (1949). *The Concept of Mind.* London: Hutchinson.

Sackett, G. P. (1970). Unlearned responses, differential rearing experiences, and the development of social attachments by rhesus monkeys. In L. A. Rosenblum (Ed.). *Primate Behavior: Developments in Field and Laboratory Research, vol. 1.* New York: Academic Press. Pp. 111–140.

Sands, S. F., Lincoln, C. E., and Wright, A. A. (1982). Pictorial similarity judgments and the organization of visual memory in the rhesus monkey. *Journal of Experimental Psychology: General,* 3, 369–389.

Schrier, A. M., Angarella, R., and Povar, M. L. (1984). Studies of concept formation by stumptailed monkeys: Concepts of humans, monkeys, and letter A. *Journal of Experimental Psychology: Animal Behavior Processes,* 10, 564–584.

Schrier, A. M., and Brady, P. M. (1987). Categorization of natural stimuli by monkeys *(Macaca mulatta):* Effects of stimulus set size and modification of exemplars. *Journal of Experimental Psychology: Animal Behavior Processes,* 13, 136–143.

Schusterman, R. J., Gisiner, R., Grimm, B. G., and Hanggi, E. B. (1993). Behavioral control by exclusion and attempts at establishing semanticity in marine mammals using matching-to-sample paradigms. In H. S. Roitblat, L. M. Herman, and P. Nachtigall (Eds.). *Language and Communication: Comparative Perspectives*. Hillsdale, NJ: Erlbaum Associates. Pp. 249–274.

Seyfarth, R. M., and Cheney, D. L. (1988). Do monkeys understand their relations? In R. W. Byrne and A. Whiten (Eds.). *Machiavellian Intelligence*. Oxford: Oxford University Press. Pp. 69–84.

Siegel, R. K., and Honig, W. K. (1970). Pigeon concept formation: Successive and simultaneous acquisition. *Journal of the Experimental Analysis of Behavior*, 13, 385–390.

Smith, E. E., and Medin, D. L. (1981). *Categories and Concepts*. Cambridge, MA: Harvard University Press.

Smith, H. J., King, J. E., Witt, E. D., and Rickel, J. E. (1975). Sameness-difference matching from sample by chimpanzees. *Bulletin of the Psychonomic Society*, 6, 469–471.

Steele, K. M. (1990). Configural processes in pigeon perception. In M. L. Commons, R. J. Herrnstein, S. M. Kosslyn, and D. B. Mumford (Eds.). *Quantitative Analyses of Behavior, vol. VIII*. Hillsdale, NJ: Erlbaum. Pp. 111–125.

Steirn, J. N., and Thomas, R. K. (1990). Comparative assessments of intelligence: Performances of *Homo sapiens* on hierarchies of oddity and sameness-difference tasks. *Journal of Comparative Psychology*, 104, 326–333.

Sumi, S. (1984). Upside down presentation of the Johansson moving light spot pattern. *Perception*, 13, 283–286.

Swartz, K. S. (1983). Species discrimination in infant pigtail macaques with pictorial stimuli. *Developmental Psychobiology*, 16, 219–231.

Swartz, K. S., and Evans, S. (1991). Not all chimpanzees *(Pan troglodytes)* show self-recognition. *Primates*, 32, 483–496.

Swartz, K. S., and Evans, S. (1994). Social and cognitive factors in chimpanzees and gorilla mirror behavior and self-recognition. In S. T. Parker, R. W. Mitchell, and M. L. Boccia (Eds.). *Self-Awareness in Animals and Humans: Developmental Perspectives*. New York: Cambridge University Press. Pp. 190–206.

Swartz, K. S., and Rosenblum, L. A. (1980). Operant responding by bonnet macaques for color videotaped recordings of social stimuli. *Animal Learning and Behavior*, 8, 311–321.

Terrell, D. F., and Thomas, R. K. (1990). Number-related discrimination and summation by squirrel monkeys (*Saimiri sciureus sciureus* and *S. bolivensus boliviensus*) on the basis of the number of sides of polygons. *Journal of Comparative Psychology*, 104, 238–247.

Thomas, R. K. (1980). Evolution of intelligence: An approach to its assessment. *Brain, Behavior, and Evolution*, 17, 454–472.

Thomas, R. K. (1992). Conceptual use of number: Ecological perspectives and psychological processes. In T. Nishida, W. C. McGrew, P. Marler, M. Pickford, and F. B. M. de Waal, (Eds.). *Topics in Primatology, vol. 1: Human Origins*. Tokyo: Tokyo University Press. Pp. 305–314.

Thomas, R. K., and Boyd, M. G. (1973). A comparison of *Cebus albifrons* and *Samiri sciureus* on oddity performance. *Animal Learning and Behavior*, 1, 151–153.

Thomas, R. K., and Chase, L. (1980). Relative numerosity judgments by squirrel monkeys. *Bulletin of the Psychonomic Society*, 16, 79–82.

Thomas, R. K., Fowlkes, D., and Vickery, J. D. (1980). Conceptual numerousness judgments by squirrel monkeys. *American Journal of Psychology*, 93, 247–257.

Thomas, R. K., and Frost, T. (1983). Oddity and dimension-abstracted oddity (DAO) in squirrel monkeys. *American Journal of Psychology*, 96, 51–64.

Thomas, R. K., and Kerr, R. S. (1976). Conceptual conditional discrimination in *Saimiri sciureus*. *Animal Learning and Behavior*, 4, 333–336.

Thomas, R. K., and Lorden, R. B. (1993). Numerical competence in animals: A conservative view. In S. T. Boysen and E. J. Capaldi (Eds.). *The Development of Numerical Competency: Animal and Human models*. Hillsdale, NJ: Erlbaum Associates.

Thompson, R. K. R., and Contie, C. L. (1994). Further reflections on mirror-usage by pigeons: Lessons from Winnie-the-Pooh and Pinocchio too. In S. T. Parker, R. W. Mitchell, and M. L. Boccia (Eds.). *Self-Awareness in Animals and Humans: Developmental Perspectives*. New York: Cambridge University Press. Pp. 392–409.

Thompson, R. K. R., and Herman, L. M. (1977). Memory for lists of sounds by the bottle nosed dolphin: Convergence of memory processes with humans? *Science*, 202, 991–994.

Thompson, R. K. R., and Oden, D. L. (1993). "Language training" and its role in the expression of tacit propositional knowledge in chimpanzees *(Pan troglodytes)*. In H. S. Roitblat, L. M. Herman, and P. Nachtigall (Eds.). *Language and Communication: Comparative Perspectives*. Hillsdale, NJ: Erlbaum Associates. Pp. 365–384.

Thompson, R. K. R., Arlinsky, M., and Christie, A. (1992). Spontaneous perception of concrete but not abstract same/different relations by rhesus monkeys *(Macaca mulatta)*. Paper presented at the VI biennial meeting of the International Society for Comparative Psychology. Brussels, July.

Thompson, R. L., and Boatright-Horowitz, S. (1994). The question of mirror-mediated self recognition in apes and monkeys: Some new results and reservations. In S. T. Parker, R. W. Mitchell, and M. L. Boccia (Eds.). *Self-Awareness in Animals and Humans: Developmental Perspectives*. New York: Cambridge University Press. Pp. 330–349.

Timberlake, W. (1993). Animal behavior: A continuing synthesis. *Annual Review of Psychology*, 44, 675–708.

Trillmich, F. (1976). Learning experiments on individual recognition in budgerigars. *Zeitschrift fur Tierpsychologie*, 41, 372–395.

Tversky, B., and Hemenway, K. (1991). Parts and the basic level in natural categories and artificial stimuli: Comments on Murphy (1991). *Memory and Cognition*, 19, 439–442.

Tyrrell, D. J., Stauffer, L. B., and Snowman, L. G. (1991). Perception of abstract identity/difference relationships by infants. *Infant Behavior and Development*, 14, 125–129.

Vaughan, W. Jr. (1988). Formation of equivalence sets in pigeons. *Journal of Experimental Psychology: Animal Behavior Processes*. 14, 36–42.

Vaughan, W. Jr., and Green, S. L. (1984). Pigeon visual memory capacity. *Journal of Experimental Psychology: Animal Behavior Processes*, 10, 256–271.

Washburn, D. A., Hopkins, W. D., and Rumbaugh, D. M. (1989). Video-task assessment of learning and memory in macaques *(Macaca mulatta):* Effects of stimulus movement on performance. *Journal of Experimental Psychology: Animal Behavior Processes*, 15, 393–400.

Washburn, D. A., and Rumbaugh, D. M. (1991). Ordinal judgments of numerical symbols by macaques *(Macaca mulatta)*. *Psychological Science*, 2, 190–193.

Wasserman, E. A. (1993). Comparative cognition: Beginning the second century of the study of animal intelligence. *Psychological Bulletin*, 113, 211–228.

Wasserman, E. A., DeVolder, C. L., and Coppage, D. J. (1992). Nonsimilarity-based conceptualization by pigeons via secondary or mediated generalization. *Psychological Science*, 3, 374–379.

Wasserman, E. A., Kiedinger, R. E., and Bhatt, R. S. (1988). Conceptual behavior in pigeons: Categories, subcategories, and pseudocategories. *Journal of Experimental Psychology: Animal Behavior Processes*, 14, 235–246.

Woodruff, G., and Premack, D. (1979). Intentional communication in the chimpanzee: The development of deception. *Cognition*, 7, 333–362.

Wright, A. A., Cook, R. G., Rivera, J. J., Sands, S. F., and Delius, J. D. (1988). Concept learning by pigeons: Matching-to-sample with trial-unique video picture stimuli. *Animal Learning and Behavior*, 18, 287–294.

Wright, A. A., Santiago, H. C., Urcuioli, P. J., and Sands, S. F. (1984). Monkey and pigeon acquisition of same/different concept using pictorial stimuli. In M. L. Commons and R. J. Herrnstein (Eds.). *Quantitative Analyses of Behavior, vol. 4*. Cambridge, MA: Ballinger. Pp. 295–317.

Wright, A. A., Shyan, M. R., and Jitsumori, M. (1990). Auditory same/different concept learning by monkeys. *Animal Learning and Behavior*, 18, 287–294.

Yoshikubo, S. (1985). Species discrimination and concept formation by rhesus monkeys *(Macaca mulatta)*. *Primates*, 26, 285–299.

Zentall, T. R., Edwards, C. A., and Hogan, D. E. (1984). Pigeons' use of identity. In M. L. Commons, R. J. Herrnstein, and A. R. Wagner (Eds.). *Quantitative Analyses of Behavior Discrimination Processes, vol. 4*. Cambridge, MA: Ballinger. Pp. 273–293.

Zentall, T. R., Jackson-Smith, P., and Jagielo, J. A. (1990). Categorical color and shape coding by pigeons. In M. L. Commons, R. J. Herrnstein, S. M. Kosslyn, and D. B. Mumford (Eds.). *Quantitative Analyses of Behavior*, vol. VIII. Hillsdale, NJ: Erlbaum Associates. Pp. 3–21.

10 The Integration of Content with Context: Spatiotemporal Encoding and Episodic Memories in People and Animals

Julie J. Neiworth

A question often asked of researchers of animats and animals is whether their subjects are "cognitive" beings. Superficially, the answer must be Yes, because most species and many programmed devices are able to adapt in the face of events that occur throughout their lives. Experiences modify the nervous systems and/or computer programs and, as a result, the organism/machine learns and remembers. But this conclusion generates a host of other questions about memory as it is naturally used by animals and as it is planned for use by robots: Where is memory stored? Is there a single kind of memory, or are there many different systems of memories? What combination of subsystems seems most efficient for thinking about certain problems? What physical structures and psychological processes are involved in remembering and thinking? At the heart of these questions is a controversy about whether memories seem to be stored diffusely in a distributed network or separately in subsystems that can be distinguished from each other physically and functionally. In addition, there is the problem of determining the basic elements of the world that are attended to, encoded, and remembered by the memory system(s). We must determine the subsystems or the distributed processing descriptions that accurately reflect an animal's thinking and, of equal importance, the elements of the world about which animals think in order to discover the true architecture of memory.

CONTEXT AND CONTENT MEMORY

While most researchers currently agree that memory is not a unitary faculty, but rather is made up of a set of subsystems (Gazzaniga 1988; Kosslyn 1988; Squire 1989), the list of possible subsystems has grown quite long. The various types of memories in humans include short-term and long-term memories (Atkinson and Shiffrin 1968) and working and reference memories (Honig 1978; Roitblat 1982), and these classifications have spawned other descriptions such as procedural and declarative memories (Squire 1989), episodic and semantic memories (Tulving 1983), and implicit and explicit memories (Warrington and Weiskrantz 1974;

Jacoby and Whiterspoon 1982; Schacter 1987). Declarative memory is accessible to conscious awareness and includes the facts, episodes, and routes of everyday life. Often episodic memory (i.e., memory of specific time, places, and events) and semantic memory (i.e., memory of facts and general information) are considered part of declarative memory. In contrast, procedural memory includes learning skills, games, and physical abilities not necessarily accessible to conscious awareness and thus also termed implicit. The data that support the existence of each of these types of memory are not in dispute. How these types of memory fit together into a coherent model and how each evolved to exist in the human system are subjects of speculation by many researchers in the fields of cognitive science and cognitive neuroscience. A review of the literature of amnesic patients delineates the differences between these types of memory. Once defined, the memories are woven into a coherent model and investigated in animals.

Amnesia is colloquially regarded as a failure to remember events shortly after they occur, but in fact amnesic patients rarely show a complete failure of memory. The initial studies of amnesic patients by Milner, Corkin, and Teuber (1968) showed that H. M., an amnesic patient, retained information for a short period without rehearsal, but quickly forgot if new information was presented to him. It was as though the patient's short-term memory was intact, but he was unable to place anything in a longer-term memory store. The dissociation between short-term and long-term memory accounted for the data in 1968, but it does not well explain the deficits and skills amnesics have demonstrated lately. Cohen and Squire (1980) reported that amnesic patients learned to read mirror images of words at the same rate as do normal subjects. They could not, however, report having done the task before. From this finding, Cohen and Squire introduced the idea of procedural and declarative memories in the long-term store. They thought amnesics were using procedural or skill-based memories, but could not add conscious verbal rules or experiences (in other words, declarative memories) to their long-term memories.

Another perplexing finding was that amnesic patients benefited from previous exposures to words when accomplishing a word completion task. In the task, both amnesic patients and normal subjects were more likely to complete a word starting with "abs" with "absent" if they had previously seen the word "absent" in a list (Warrington and Weiskrantz 1974; Squire 1989). The difference was that amnesic patients, unlike normal subjects, could not recall "absent" when asked, and they did not complete the word correctly if asked to try to recall a studied word to finish the beginning of "abs." Schacter (1987) regarded this as evidence of an implicit-explicit memory division in long-term memory that made amnesics capable of using implicit memory, but not explicit memory to solve the problem. Cermack et al. (1985) and Squire (1989) argued that the word completion ability revealed a sparing of semantic memories in the long-term memories of amnesics, because they could retrieve meaningful information that they had processed as long as they were not asked to recall the episode within which it was processed.

The distinctions between the memories termed declarative vs. procedural, explicit vs. implicit, and semantic vs. episodic seem to be directly related to fact learning and skill learning or to verbalized and nonverbalized memory. In this sense, procedural, implicit, and episodic memories are based on nonverbal skill-based memory, and thus they should be present in other lower organisms. In fact, Squire suggested that nondeclarative memory (consisting of procedural and implicit memories) is likely to be phylogenetically older memory than is declarative memory. Procedural and implicit memories seem to be intact in amnesic patients. Episodic memories seem to be lacking in amnesic patients, along with the conscious recollection of rules, verbal information, and facts newly learned. Data from amnesic patients imply that there is a clear distinction between access to and use of memories retrieved by an appropriate probe or cue, a kind of memory amnesics have, and a purposeful, systematic search of memories and conscious recollection of events that have occurred, which is suspiciously lacking in them.

Several distinctions have also been made between the types of encoding (or initial processing) of information to be remembered in normal humans. It seems that information about the spatial location, temporal order, and frequency or number of occurrences of an event may be encoded automatically and without any effort or plan of thinking by humans, while information about the content of an event must be encoded effortfully in order to be accurately remembered later (Hasher and Zacks 1979). A coherent model of memories that incorporates all the memories so far identified must relate these encoding differences to the creation of different types of memories.

Figure 10.1 illustrates how different types of information are encoded differently and, because of this, might enter memory subsystems more or less prominently. The basic elements of the world that are processed are space, time, and frequency information. This information is encoded automatically, effortlessly, and without awareness. It activates processes throughout the memory subsystems, because this information is necessary for the accurate construction of all types of memories. In contrast to the information stored by means of this effortless processing, the details and meaning of an event, or the *content* of an event, are encoded effortfully. The combination of spatiotemporal and frequency information, together with some details about the event, make up the *context* in which the event occurs. Once encoded and stored, information can be retrieved from any of the memory subsystems if probes or cues appropriate to that system are provided. In addition, information can be retrieved by means of a purposeful and systematic search of memories if the content was integrated with the context of the event.

There is an important relationship between the automatic, effortless encoding of spatiotemporal information, the effortful processing of

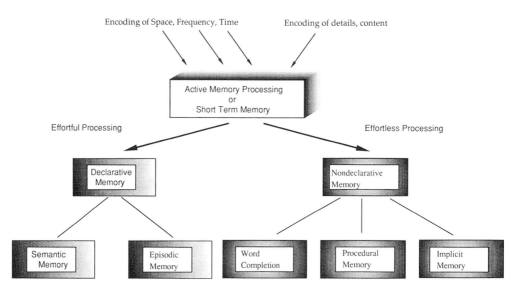

Figure 10.1 An organization of memory systems into categories. Declarative, procedural, and implicit are types of long-term memories. Episodic and semantic memories are subsumed under the heading "declarative memory." Nondeclarative memories are phylogenetically older and include procedural and implicit memories.

content, and specific memory stores. Specifically, the encoding of the context (i.e., space, time, and frequency) with content is necessary for conscious recollection later. This means that effortful content encoding must accompany effortless spatiotemporal encoding for conscious recollections (in the form of episodic and semantic memories) to form.

One means of testing this model is to determine if it can account for amnesic patients' memories that are spared and those that are lost. Another test is to determine if the model can be fitted into what is known about brain structures, connections, and functions. A discovery central to this fit is the brain structure that provides the connection between effortful and effortless processing so that episodes and consciously processed memories are saved. The hippocampus is hypothesized here as the structure that connects the processing of these types of information. Research with animals can shed light on the validity of the model, the evolution of these memory subsystems, and the activation changes that caused humans to become qualitatively different from animals in their conscious thinking.

TESTING THE MODEL NEUROLOGICALLY, BIOLOGICALLY, AND EMPIRICALLY

Reintegrating the Amnesic's Memory

With regard to the model in figure 10.1, the processing power lost to amnesics is the effortful encoding of context with content. Without this, spatiotemporal and frequency information is encoded automatically, but is not associated with the content of an event. If amnesics cannot encode the context of to-be-remembered events, they should show a lack of episodic memories, but should have procedural memories in the form of skill learning and semantic memories in the form of implicit reactions if the right probe or cue to retrieve an exact memory is offered. Still, with no context encoded, events would not be related along spatial and temporal dimensions, and so there would be no conscious recollection of engaging in the task before and no conscious ability to scan a memory for a particular item.

A diverse set of memories were reviewed of amnesic patients who forgot easily, but remembered rules of games; who claimed not to have played games or not to have seen objects or events, but profited from exposure as demonstrated by better memory or performance; and who showed priming effects of language as long as the actual words were not requested for recall. These diverse findings have been reconciled into a single connection between the context of an event (i.e., the space, time, and frequency information, along with what happened) and the meaning of the event. When the connection is severed, the disturbance is dramatic but understandable within the model proposed.

Reintegrating the Mind with the Brain

Many biological models of memory assume that memories are created by changes in neuronal connections because of chemical changes at the synapse (Hawkins and Kandel 1984), neural growth (Stevens 1979), or changes in the dendritic receptors (Shephard 1988). Connectionist models of memory follow this globalist view and assume that memory is realized by changes in weights ascribed to certain neural connections. The location of the neurons and even the number used is often less important in these models than is the assumption that they are interconnected and that input to one affects in subtle ways the processing rates of all. Alternatively, there remain brain diagrams of memory that localize functions within particular brain structures. Evidence from clinical patients and from animals with particular types of brain damage support the notion that certain cognitive and perceptual functions are located in particular brain sites and are not distributed holistically by the mass action of the brain.

A reconciliation of these ideas has been attempted in recent brain-mind models (Kosslyn and Anderson 1992). It is clear that the process of perceiving, attending to, and thinking about stimuli is accomplished by many different underlying processes located in various areas of the brain, with each of them conferring a particular ability to the process. For example, recent studies of attention show that lesions in different attention-related cortical areas produce different attentional deficits (Mesulam 1981; Posner et al. 1987). The same research shows that attending invokes activity in many brain areas; thus, the process of attention seems distributed in a network, but with particular functions carried out in particular brain areas.

The brain model in figure 10.2 is a diagram of localized brain-mind functions similar to that recently suggested by Edelman (1989, 1992), but modified to fit the memory processing model.[1] In it, information is put in the system in a distributed fashion. Space, time, number, and identification of object are processed through sensory primary cortical areas and higher cortical pathways, and the pattern is passed directly to neocortical areas. From this processing, memories of what, where, and when are each created. It is possible to retrieve memories of previously experienced events, but the retrieval of those memories is contingent upon the proper sensory input to the system to reactivate the appropriate pattern in the pathways to the neocortical regions. Thus, some cognitive processing (i.e., thinking and remembering) can occur in a sentient being who can automatically and effortlessly process the basic elements of

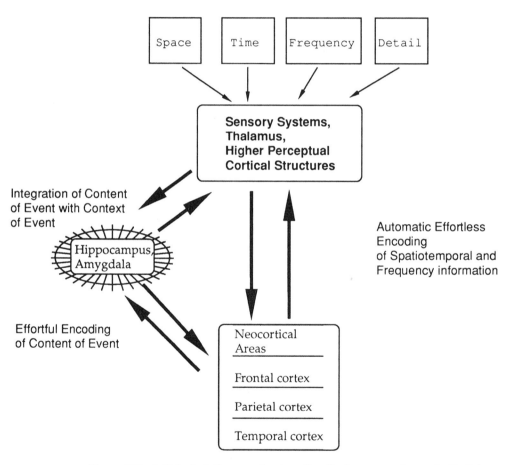

Figure 10.2 A biological diagram of automatic, effortless processing and effortful processing. New memories are formed when information is passed to the neocortical areas (including the frontal, parietal and temporal cortices).

space, time, and number and can process sensory details about an object for identification.

The information processed by the sensory and higher perceptual cortical areas is also passed through the hippocampus and then to the neocortical areas. It is because of activity in this pathway that the knowledge of what, when, and where gets integrated and forms a memory of context. Damage to the hippocampus does not block memory formation entirely, but it does block the host's ability to integrate the basic types of information or to form complex associations of this information. The hippocampus has been implicated as a structure critical for short-term memory processing, long-term memory storage, and even learning associations. It is extraordinary in that it receives inputs from almost all regions of the cerebral cortex through the entorhinal cortex. The hippocampus is also remarkable because it perpetuates activity within itself through a sequence of three successive synapses and via neurons capable of sustaining activity. This activity has been called long-term potentiation (LTP), or, more recently, long-term enhancement (LTE). The hippocampus also receives connections indirectly from the midbrain and other limbic structures, so it seems intricately involved with hedonic events (e.g., pain and pleasure) and with stimulus associations. The hippocampus then provides the extra activity, or the glue, that binds various types of information that are being processed together. It does this by providing a reentrant path and more excitation that might be considered "effortful" processing.

The Role of the Hippocampus

It is suggested here that the circuitry provided by the hippocampus is necessary for the creation of contextual information in memories. Without it in this model, memories are formed with no relational sense of when the events remembered occurred and in what context they occurred. The famous amnesic patient H. M. had both hippocampi removed as well as much of his temporal lobes, and subsequently he was unable to consciously recall new experiences. Memories spared in H. M. and in amnesic patients with hippocampal damage included memories built before the removal of the hippocampi, motor skill learning, perceptual skill learning, word priming, and classical conditioning. In brief, destruction of the hippocampus leads to an inability to consciously recall a previous event, but information about a previous event can be remembered through performance, action, or resensing it (Zola-Morgan and Squire 1991).

Many animals with hippocampal damage show a deficit in remembering context-dependent spatial and time-related information such as which object was presented moments ago, where they have been, and where they need to go next (Mishkin 1982; Morris 1983; Kesner 1990). The blocking of LTP in the hippocampi of rats disrupted the acquisition of spatial water maze traversing (Morris, Hagan, and Rawlins 1986) and debilitated their performance in a radial arm maze (Danysz, Wroblewski, and Costa 1988). Unfortunately, most studies of animals with hippocampal blockage or damage focus on the animals' inability to process spatial information and to navigate spatially rather than on how the damage might lead to a loss in contextual time- and space-related information. The hippocampus has been regarded as the localized structure for holding a cognitive map of space (O'Keefe and Nadel 1978). But how does this processing contribute to the construction of memories?

Traditional theories of spatial processing postulate a reference memory of the environment that may be as fixed as the sun's position, along with an ability to dead reckon or navigate to a fixed point (Gallistel 1989; Wehner and Menzel 1990). Described in this way, navigating through space does not seem to require the building of memories in many of the subsystems described; it may require only some specialized (procedural) learning abilities and a means of adding sensory information during the spatial learning experience. But it is also clear that for many species studied, including various birds (Balda and Kamil 1988; Sherry and Vaccarino 1989; Shettleworth 1990), rats (Nadel 1991), hamsters (Tomlinson and Johnston 1991), monkeys, and people (Squire 1987; Pick 1991), spatial memory involves much more than holding a map of fixed landmarks and keeping track of a number of steps in a particular direction. In addition to these abilities, a rat running a maze in search of food maintains a working or on-line memory of where it has been most recently, and this memory might include relations between locations, sensory information, and time. The variety of abilities involved in this type of spatial memory must involve an integration of space, time, and egocentric information and a changing sensory view.

The author has in fact conducted a preliminary study of spatial and temporal processing in rats that were temporarily incapacitated by AP-5 (2-amino-5-phosphonovaleric acid), a substance that blocks a particular type of enhanced activity, LTP, in the hippocampus.[2] The rats (n = 24) were first trained to traverse a 12-arm open maze to forage for fruit-flavored cereal. After they had demonstrated an ability to forage through the maze without repeating visits to the 12 arms, cannulae were surgically implanted in the hippocampi of half of the subject population. After the subjects recovered from surgery, they were placed back on the maze and their memories of visiting arms on the maze were tested. On each trial, they were allowed to visit just a few of the arms on the maze (3, 6, or 9 arms). Then they were removed from the maze for a period of time (1 minute, 10 minutes, or 60 minutes), after which they were placed back on the maze and allowed entry to all 12 arms. If they could remember the arms they had previously visited and could sustain that memory across the delay period, then they would accurately select arms they had not previously visited. To the extent that they forgot where they had gone before the delay, they would begin searching anew and make many errors by revisiting arms they had already visited that day. The surgically altered animals were injected with AP-5 five minutes before they were placed on the maze for the first time (i.e., to visit only a few arms). The purpose of the study was to examine what characteristics of spatial and temporal processing were disturbed by eliminating the enhanced activity provided by the hippocampus.

What was not surprising in this study was that blocking LTP in the hippocampus produced a spatial deficit in rats traversing a radial maze (see figure 10.3). What was intriguing about the results was that spatiotemporal processing by the hippocampus, not necessarily spatial processing and navigation, was the deficit indicated. Figure 10.3 shows the performance of the AP-5–injected rats as compared to their control cohorts. Both sets of subjects could forage efficiently if only a few arms had been visited before and if the delay between the first visit and the second was short. Clearly, then, animals with blocked hippocampal enhancement can still retrieve a reference map of the space, they can traverse the maze well, and they can remember for a brief time a few spatial locations visited. What they cannot do is remember where they have visited for a long period of time (i.e., for more than 1 minute), and they have great difficulty remembering many places they have previously visited. Normal subjects forget spots visited as the number of them gets longer and as the time between visits is extended. But animals without fully functioning hippocampi seem unable to sustain any memory of where they have been for any length of time beyond a minute after the visit. The context of their previous visit slips away from them and they are left making many errors and re-searching the entire maze.

What memory processing can rats accomplish without enhanced activity in the hippocampus? They can retrieve a memory of the space and of what to do in it (i.e,. forage for fruit-flavored cereal); therefore, they seem to have implicit and procedural memory. However, they show great difficulty in sustaining memories in the short term of where they have been that day. This may be a result of an inability to construct an episodic memory. Finally, they show an uncanny ability to perform well when they have previously visited large numbers of arms (see figure 10.3). This is supported by their return to accurate performance when they have visited the most arms; logically this result appears to indicate a switch in their remembering from where they have been (retrospective) to where they need to go (prospective). In this study, the animals with ill-functioning hippocampi switched to this kind of forward thinking much sooner than did the control animals with the same level of experience on the maze. This new strategy shows that the rats rely on the rules of the game (i.e., visit each arm only once for efficient food gathering) rather than on episodic memory, or memory of which arms they have visited during

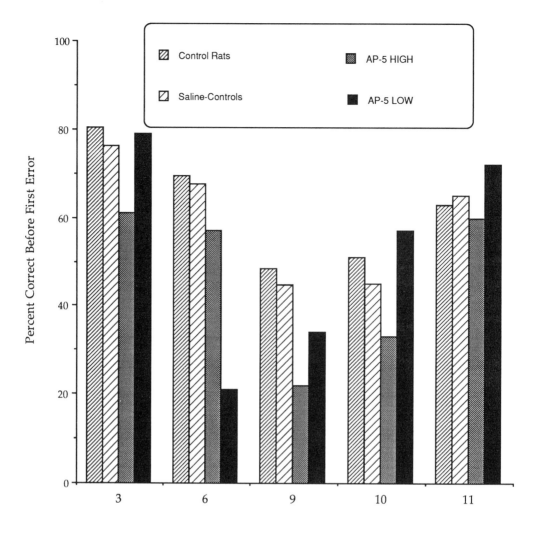

ARMS VISITED BEFORE TEST

Figure 10.3 Mean percentage of correct scores for the surgical groups and the control animals by delay condition and by number of arms previously visited.

that particular trial. The animals actually seemed sensitive to their inabilities and switched to a strategy that proved more profitable and relied less on memory for many visits within the episode.

There is other evidence from electrophysiological study that specific contextual functions are located in the hippocampus. There are place cells in the hippocampus that fire selectively in response to spatial orientation, but contemporary work shows that the place cells' firing is not singularly spatial and is uncomfortably complicated; hippocampal cells have been found to fire in response to different phases of experiments (Wible et al.

1986; Rolls et al. 1985) and to different features of experiments, including visual and time-related features (Watanabe and Niki 1985) as well as space-related features. Olton, Wible, and Shapiro (1986), and Kesner (1990) converged on a description of integrated processing of space and time in the hippocampus.

In the same way that a cognitive map establishes the topological interrelations among different places, a temporal map may establish the chronological interrelation among different events. Both types of maps require the interrelation of components within the map, a process that must involve memory in order to establish the correct contextual framework. The hippocampus may be the brain structure that allows each of the various components of a place and an event to be linked together and compared with other places and events. (Olton, Wible, and Shapiro 1986, p. 854).

The hippocampal formation is directly involved in coding all new spatial-temporal incoming information that is likely to be relevant in trial unique situations but that could also be of importance for all trials within a learning task (data-based memory), but is not involved in coding information based on expected nonvarying information in the form of maps, rules, strategies, and procedures (Kesner, pp. 192–193).

Thus, the hippocampus allows for chronological and topographic information to be integrated. By means of this integration, the hippocampus provides the context for the event, but it is not necessarily the seat of spatial processing or of temporal processing per se. The speculation here is that the automatic encoding of spatiotemporal and frequency information can occur without intact hippocampi, but that automatic processing will engender a limited recall of the experiences. The data collected thus far are too impoverished to support this second speculation.

FUTURE TESTS OF THE SPATIOTEMPORAL PUZZLE

The brain-memory models offered here are only loosely supported by the data presented from clinical and animal work. Certain themes emerge from this work that require further exploration. Additionally, the study of imagery might provide a profitable venue for exploring spatiotemporal encoding and specific memories in animals and humans. A list of potential research projects is provided with the following goals in mind: to construct a veridical architecture of memory, to direct the physical implementation of memory processing in devices, to form a deeper understanding of memory systems in animals, and to generate a scheme for the evolution of the various memory subsystems that have been identified.

1. *Extend the research on animals' spatial processing to test for contextual savings and for space, time, and number processing.* To determine the specific role of the hippocampus and its activity on memory processing, systematic research is needed to isolate the encoding of space, time, and number and to isolate the use of contextual information to remember various

tasks. There is an intriguing dissociation suggested here between the automatic encoding of spatiotemporal and frequency information and the building of episodic memories. This relationship remains unexplored.

2. *Examine the abilities of specific human populations to form episodic memories and to use space, time, and number information.* While the elderly and the young have shown automaticity in encoding space, time, and frequency information, it is unclear whether amnesics show a sustained ability to do this. In addition, a result of Alzheimer's disease is great degradation of functioning in the entorhinal cortex and the hippocampus. Is the memory deficit of Alzheimer's patients one of episodes specifically? Can they encode space, time, and frequency automatically and incidentally, but not effortfully? Research on these issues would test the model proposed and would help us to determine what kinds of mental strategies remain in the elderly Alzheimer's patient, the amnesic, and possibly species with impoverished hippocampal connections.

3. *Employ other research methodologies, including imagery, to investigate the relationship between spatiotemporal processing and memories formed.* The construction, maintenance, and transformation of an image requires the use of spatial and time-related memory processes. (Try rotating a red cube that is imaged to introspect about this.) The question raised about imagery is: What mental processes used in perception and in retrieving and thinking about any memory subserve the process of imaging? There has been a systematic examination of imagery abilities in clinical populations with certain brain deficits (Farah 1988), and there are well-developed localized diagrams of the mental processes subserving imagery (Kosslyn 1980, 1988) that have been related to certain gross brain deficits (Farah 1984). Still, a clear fit between the memory subsystems described before and imagery is not evident. In the current model, imaging could be subserved by the automatic encoding of space, time, and frequency and thus could be acquired and constructed without the use of the hippocampal reentrant pathways. Alternatively, imaging is a conscious process that seems effortful and somewhat context-dependent, and so it might rely to some extent on hippocampal integration.

Because the process of imaging involves spatial and temporal processing in memory but does not necessarily involve remembering episodes, investigations of imagery abilities in the populations identified above (amnesics, Alzheimer's disease patients, and certain animals) might help to delineate the relationships between spatiotemporal processing and episodic memories. A successful method for studying imagery in pigeons has already been established (Neiworth 1992; Neiworth and Rilling 1987), and this species is particularly interesting in that pigeons rely heavily on spatiotemporal processing for flight, foraging, and, most likely, for imaging and anticipating moving stimuli in laboratory experiments. Other species of foragers who rely primarily on visual information would be good candidates for this type of investigation.

Neuroscientists interested in memory often focus on cellular and chemical analyses to explain how synapses change as a result of memory. Psychologists often build models based on human behavior with little regard for brain structures, but with some regard for the computations that might support learning and memory. In this chapter I have attempted to establish middle ground by examining memory subsystems and relating them to each other to explain the contribution of a particular process, spatiotemporal processing, to remembering. The contribution is distributed in the sense that spatiotemporal processing occurs within many memory subsystems, and it is localized because a certain combination of processing events produces effortful contextual processing.

NOTES

1. Edelman suggests that there are differences in types of consciousness in his model, with the primary consciousness shared by many species accomplished by information passing through the hippocampus to the neocortical regions, and higher-order consciousness emerging from connections with language areas of the brain.

2. This research was conducted with Thane Fremouw, an undergraduate at Carleton who is now a graduate student in neuroscience at the University of Utah.

REFERENCES

Atkinson, R. C., and Shiffrin, R. M. (1968). Human memory: A proposed system and its control processes. In K. W. Spence and J. T. Spence (Eds.). *The Psychology of Learning and Motivation: Advances in Research and Theory, Vol. 2.* New York: Academic Press.

Balda, R. P., and Kamil, A. C. (1988). The spatial memory of Clark's nutcrackers *(Nucifraga columbiana)* in an analogue of the radial arm maze. *Animal Learning and Behavior,* 16 (2), 116–122.

Cermack, L. S., Talbot, N., Chandler, K., and Wolbarst, L. R. (1985). The perceptual priming phenomenon in amnesia. *Neuropsychologia,* 23, 615–622.

Cohen, N. J., and Squire, L. R. (1980). Preserved learning and retention of pattern-analyzing skill in amnesia: Dissociation of knowing how and knowing that. *Science,* 210 (1), 207–210.

Cook, R. B., Brown, M. F., and Riley, D. A. (1985). Flexible memory processing by rats: Use of prospective and retrospective information in the radial maze. *Journal of Experimental Psychology: Animal Behavior Processes,* 11, 453–469.

Danysz, W., Wroblewski, J. T., and Costa, E. (1988). Learning impairment in rats by N-methyl-D-aspartate antagonists. *Neuropharmacology,* 27, 653–656.

Edelman, G. M. (1989). *The Remembered Present.* New York: Basic Books.

Edelman, G. M. (1992). *Bright Air, Brilliant Fire: On the Matter of the Mind.* New York: Basic Books.

Farah, M. J. (1984). The neurological basis of mental imagery: A componential analysis. *Cognition,* 18, 245–272.

Farah, M. J. (1988). Is visual imagery really visual? Overlooked evidence from neuropsychology. *Psychological Review,* 95, 307–317.

Freyd, J. J., and Finke, R. A. (1984). Representational momentum. *Journal of Experimental Psychology: Learning, Memory, and Cognition*, 10, 126–132.

Gallistel, C. R. (1989). Animal cognition: The representation of space, time and number. *Annual Review of Psychology*, 40, 155–189.

Gazzaniga, M. S. (1988). *Perspectives in Memory Research*. Cambridge, MA: The MIT Press.

Hasher, L., and Zacks, R. T. (1979). Automatic and effortful processes in memory. *Journal of Experimental Psychology: General*, 108, 356–388.

Hawkins, R. D., and Kandel, E. R. (1984). Is there a cell-biological alphabet for simple forms of learning? *Psychological Review*, 97, 375–391.

Honig, W. K. (1978). Studies of working memory in the pigeon. In S. H. Hulse, H. Fowler, and W. K. Honig (Eds.). *Cognitive Processes in Animal Behavior*. Hillsdale, NJ: Lawrence Erlbaum Associates.

Jacoby, L. L., and Whiterspoon, D. (1982). Remembering without awareness. *Canadian Journal of Psychology*, 36, 300–324.

Kesner, R. P. (1990). Learning and memory in rats with an emphasis on the role of the hippocampal formation. In R. P. Kesner and D. S. Olton (Eds.). *Neurobiology of Comparative Cognition*. Hillsdale, NJ: Lawrence Erlbaum Associates.

Kosslyn, S. M. (1980). *Image and Mind*. Cambridge, MA: Harvard University Press.

Kosslyn, S. M. (1988). Imagery in learning. In M. S. Gazzaniga (Ed.). *Perspectives in Memory Research*. Cambridge, MA: The MIT Press.

Kosslyn, S. M., and Anderson, R. A. (1992). *Frontiers in Cognitive Neuroscience*. Cambridge, MA: The MIT Press.

Lynch, G., Muller, D., Seubert, P., and Larson, J. (1988). Long-term potentiation: Persisting problems and recent results. *Brain Research Bulletin*, 21, 363–372.

Mesulam, M. M. (1981). A cortical network for directed attention and unilateral neglect. *Annals of Neurology*, 10, 309–325.

Milner, B., Corkin, S., and Teuber, H. L. (1968). Further analysis of the hippocampal amnesic syndrome: 14 year follow-up study of H. M. *Neuropsychologia*, 6, 215–234.

Miserendino, M. J. D., Sananes, C. B., Melia, D. R., and Davis, M. (1990). Blocking of acquisition but not expression of conditional fear-potentiated startle by NMDA antagonists in the amygdala. *Nature*, 345, 716–718.

Mishkin, M. (1982). A memory system in the monkey. *Philosophical Transactions of the Royal Society of London*, 298, 85–95.

Morris, R. G. M. (1983). An attempt to dissociate "spatial-mapping" and "working-memory" theories of hippocampal function. In W. Seifert (Ed.). *Neurobiology of the Hippocampus*. New York: Academic Press.

Morris, R. G. M. (1989). Synaptic plasticity and learning: Selective impairment of learning in rats and blockade of long-term potentiation *in vivo* by the N-methyl-D-aspartate receptor antagonist APS. *The Journal of Neuroscience*, 9 (9), 3040–3057.

Morris, R. G. M., Hagan, J. J., and Rawlins, J. N. P. (1986). Allocentric spatial learning by hippocampectomised rats: A further test of the "spatial mapping" and "working memory" theories of hippocampal function. *The Quarterly Journal of Experimental Psychology*, 38B, 365–395.

Nadel, L. (1991). Varieties of spatial cognition: Psychobiological considerations. *Annals New York Academy of Sciences*, 609, 613–636.

Neiworth, J. J. (1992). Cognitive aspects of movement estimations: A test of imagery in animals. In W. K. Honig and J. G. Fetterman (Eds.). *Cognitive Aspects of Stimulus Control.* Hillsdale, NJ: Lawrence Erlbaum Associates.

Neiworth, J. J., and Rilling, M. E. (1987). A method for studying imagery in animals. *Journal of Experimental Psychology: Animal Behavior Processes,* 13 (3), 203–214.

O'Keefe, J., and Nadel, L. (1978). *The Hippocampus as a Cognitive Map.* Oxford: Oxford University Press.

Olton, D. S. (1979). Mazes, maps, and memory. *American Psychologist,* 34, 583–596.

Olton, D. S., Wible, C. G., and Shapiro, M. L. (1986). Mnemonic theories of hippocampal function. *Behavioral Neuroscience,* 100 (6), 852–855.

Pick, H. (1991). Spatial cognition in children. Presentation at Carleton College, Northfield, MN, March.

Pontecorvo, M. J., Clissold, D. B., White, M. F., and Ferkany, J. W. (1991). N-methyl-D-aspartate antagonists and working memory performance: Comparison with the effects of scopolamine, propranolol, diazepam, and phenylisopropyladenosine. *Behavioral Neuroscience,* 105 (4), 521–535.

Posner, M. I., Inhoff, A. W., Friedrich, F. J., and Cohen, A. (1987). Isolating attentional systems: A cognitive-anatomical analysis. *Psychobiology,* 15, 107–112.

Roitblat, H. L. (1982). The meaning of representation in animal memory. *Behavioral and Brain Sciences,* 5, 353–406.

Rolls, E. T., Myashita, Y., Cahusac, P., and Kesner, R. O. (1985). The responses of single neurons in the primate hippocampus related to the performance of memory tasks. *Society for Neuroscience Abstracts,* 11, 525.

Schacter, D. L. (1987). Implicit memory: History and current status. *Journal of Experimental Psychology: Learning, Memory, and Cognition,* 13, 501–518.

Shephard, G. M. (1988). A basic circuit of cortical organization. In M. S. Gazzaniga (Ed). *Perspectives in Memory Research.* Cambridge, MA: The MIT Press.

Sherry, D. F., and Vaccarino, A. L. (1989). Hippocampus and memory for food caches in blackcapped chickadees. *Behavioral Neuroscience,* 103 (2), 308–318.

Shettleworth, S. J. (1990). Spatial memory in food-storing birds. Royal Society Discussion Meeting on Behavioral and Neural Aspects of Learning and Memory, London, February 1–2.

Squire, L. R. (1987). *Memory and Brain.* New York: Oxford University Press.

Squire, L. R. (1989). Mechanisms of memory. In K. L. Kelner and D. E. Koshland (Eds.). *Molecules to Models: Advances in Neuroscience.* Washington, DC: American Association for the Advancement of Science.

Stevens, C. F. (1979). The neuron. *Scientific American,* 241, 55–65.

Tomlinson, W. T., and Johnston, T. D. (1991). Hamsters remember spatial information derived from olfactory cues. *Animal Learning and Behavior,* 19 (2), 185–190.

Tulving, E. (1983). *Elements of Episodic Memory.* New York: Oxford University Press.

Warrington, E. K., and Weiskrantz, L. (1974). The effect of prior learning on subsequent retention in amnesic patients. *Neuropsychologia,* 12, 419–428.

Watanabe, T., and Niki, H. (1985). Hippocampal unit activity and delayed response in the monkey. *Experimental Brain Research,* 325, 241–254.

Wehner, R., and Menzel, R. (1990). Do insects have cognitive maps? *Annual Review of Neuroscience*, 403–414.

Wible, C. G., Shapiro, M., Findling, R. L., Lang, E. J., Crane, S., and Olton, D. S. (1986). Mnemonic correlates of unit activity in the hippocampus. *Experimental Brain Research*, 399, 97–110.

Winocur, G. (1991). Functional dissociation of the hippocampus and prefrontal cortex in learning and memory. *Psychobiology*, 19 (1), 11–20.

Zola-Morgan, S., and Squire, L. R. (1991). The neuropsychology of memory: Parallel findings in humans and nonhuman primates. *Annals New York Academy of Sciences*, 609, 434–456.

11 Spatial Information Processing in Animals

Catherine Thinus-Blanc

Even if the existence of highly adaptable robots moving around with ease within complex environments is still something we only imagine, the potential benefits of such robots warrant any efforts likely to contribute to progress in this domain. From this perspective, the study of animal spatial processing appears to be especially relevant for several reasons. First, this approach allows us to have an insight into "pure" spatial mechanisms without the interference of highly symbolic tools mediated by the use of language in human beings.

Second, a wide variety of means of orienting is found in animals. Indeed, the fact that they are able to cope with spatial problems without the mediation of highly symbolic processes does not mean that the mechanisms that they implement are rudimentary and primitive. That may be the case, but not always. Some species display extremely sophisticated means of orienting. Many examples are provided by migrations in birds and fishes and by pigeon homing behavior. In spite of the imaginative research strategies of ethologists, experimental psychologists, and neuro-ethologists, the spatial orientation of many animal species is still an enigma. With regard to this difficulty, it should be kept in mind that, unlike human beings, animals need to know their environments or to implement simple, efficient strategies if they are unable to acquire spatial knowledge in order to survive. Consequently, it is not surprising that evolution has shaped complex species-specific means for orienting.

Finally, of course, the study of the brain bases of animal spatial processing may be of interest for roboticians since it provides information about the basic elements—namely, the various brain structures—that cooperate to achieve a complex behavior and about their functional relationships. Spatial information processing can be studied at various levels. Many mechanisms are amalgamated under the heading "spatial behavior," which usually refers to the retrieval and use of environmental knowledge when it is necessary to reach a goal, for instance. But spatial information processing when an animal is first confronted with an unfamiliar situation and is exploring it, also constitutes an actual spatial activity that determines the behaviors that follow. In this chapter, some data demonstrating the spatial function of exploration are presented. Then I shall propose a simple psychological model aiming to account for the conversion of initial information into maps and for their main functional properties.

EXPLORATORY ACTIVITY AND THE ACQUISITION OF SPATIAL KNOWLEDGE

Exploration and Problem Solving

When confronted with a novel situation, most mammal species display exploratory activity. This reaction can take several forms, depending both on the nature of the new event and on the species under study. In rodents, exploratory reactions are obvious. For instance, rats exposed to novel objects in a laboratory environment display a feverish activity, sniffing the objects and the floor, walking around, scanning the surroundings, rearing, etc. Exploratory activity habituates—that is, it decreases to an asymptotic level—with continued exposure to the environment. The motivation (mere unselective curiosity or search for a precise object?) that triggers investigatory reactions has been the subject of debate (Fowler 1970; Marler and Hamilton 1966), but the overall interpretation of the result of this activity is that it corresponds to the processing, integration, and storage of some characteristics of the initially unfamiliar situation. A large number of experimental data (some of them presented below) support the idea that, among these characteristics, spatial features of the environment are spontaneously encoded by the animals.

The beneficial effect of exploratory experience has been demonstrated in problem-solving tasks. An early study by Maier (1932), who was also a pioneer of cognitive psychology, is of particular interest. Rats were allowed to explore a "three-table" apparatus, which consisted of three platforms and interconnecting runways (figure 11.1). This exploration, however, was not free, but unidirectional and fragmented; one day the rats ran X-Y several times, finding food at Y; the following day, they ran Y-Z, the food being at Z; and the third day they ran Z-X, with food at X. During the test, the rats were shown the food on one of the platforms—X, for example—and for a few seconds they were allowed to eat a small part of it. They were then released from Y. The aim of the exercise was for the rats to return directly to the table where they had just been fed by running a segment (Y-X) of the apparatus they had not explored before. A screen with a door before each table prevented the animals from seeing from one table to another. Unlike a control group that had been allowed to freely explore each leg of the apparatus, those rats submitted to a unidirectional and fragmented exploration failed to choose the shorter path during the first test trial, running along the longer one in the direction they were familiar with.

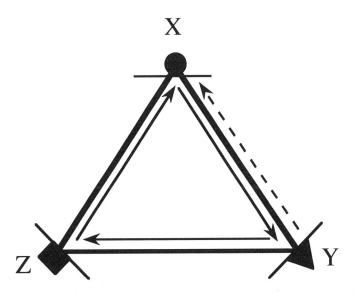

Figure 11.1 Top view of the Maier three-table maze (1932). A screen with a door is placed before each platform in order to prevent the rats from seeing the other platforms, and eventually the reward, from each of them. The inner arrows (continuous line) indicate the direction of exploratory displacements. The outer arrow (broken line) represents the shortcut leading from Y to the goal, X.

In a follow-up experiment, the segments X-Z and Z-Y could be explored in both directions, and in a second pretest phase the rats ran X-Y-Z for food. Consequently, only the third leg was run unidirectionnally (X-Y). During the tests, the rats were fed at X and placed at Y (figure 11.2). Therefore, the optimal choice corresponded to the path Y-X which had not been explored in that direction before. Unlike in the previous experiment, a large number of rats immediately chose the shorter path.

This elegant experiment is a demonstration of the functional role of exploratory activity in the setup of spatial relationships; it also illustrates some respective properties of "routes" versus maps as they have been defined by O'Keefe and Nadel (1978). In the case where rats are denied bidirectional exploration (figure 11.1), they learn a route—that is, a succession of places. The behavior is dependent on the sequence in which information has been collected. In contrast, rats provided with bidirectional exploration (figure 11.2) appear to set up spatial relationships between places regardless of the temporal features of the acquisition phase. Even when bidirectional exploration did not take place on the segment of the maze concerned by the test, the spatial representation of the whole situation would have allowed for the inference of the direction of the goal—that is, the shorter path hitherto not experienced in that direction.

In a modified version of Maier's three-table task with a different runway configuration (figure 11.3), Ellen, Soteres, and Wages (1984) showed that a "piecemeal" exploration of the apparatus can lead to successful performances depending on the segments that have been separately explored.

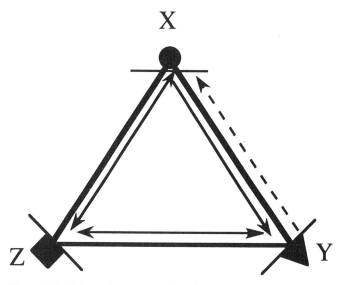

Figure 11.2 Schematic representation of the exploratory activity allowed in Maier's second experiment. The inner arrows (continuous line) indicate the direction of exploratory displacements. The outer arrow (broken line) represents the shortcut leading from Y to the goal, X.

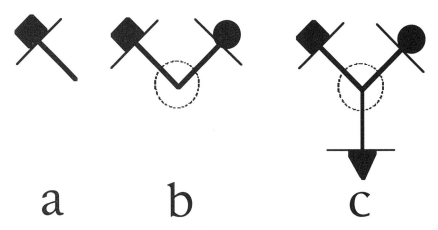

a   b   c

Figure 11.3 A version of the Maier three-table maze and the various segmentations of the maze used for exploration. The configuration represented in figure 11.3c is used for the tests. (Adapted from Ellen, Soteres, and Wages 1984.)

For instance, no rat that explored one table and runway per day (figure 11.3a) was able to perform the task (i.e., to reach the platform where they have been shown the food a few seconds before), whereas 60 percent of the rats that explored two tables and their interconnecting runways (figure 11.3b) succeeded. All rats that explored the entire apparatus (figure 11.3c) on each exploratory day were able to perform the task. It is to be underlined that the amount of exploration was the same for all groups. In another experiment, Ellen and associates (1982) demonstrated that exploration of either the tables only or the runways only led to unsuccessful performance. From both these experiments, it appears that there are connections of the segments of the apparatus which, although the segments have been investigated separately, lead to spatial problem-solving success rather than mere exploratory activity. Animals need to have been allowed the *continuous* exploration of basic elements of the apparatus—i.e., two tables and the runway linking them. As a matter of fact, the three basic elements (the runways) have one part in common corresponding to their junction. This place appears to be of particular importance with regard to the understanding of the whole situation.

Indeed, results obtained by Poucet, Bolson, and Herrmann (1990) in a modified version of the maze supports this interpretation. Interconnecting systems with longer runways could be added to the initial apparatus consisting of the three tables and direct runways (figures 11.4). The primary aim of this experiment was to test the deficits of brain-damaged

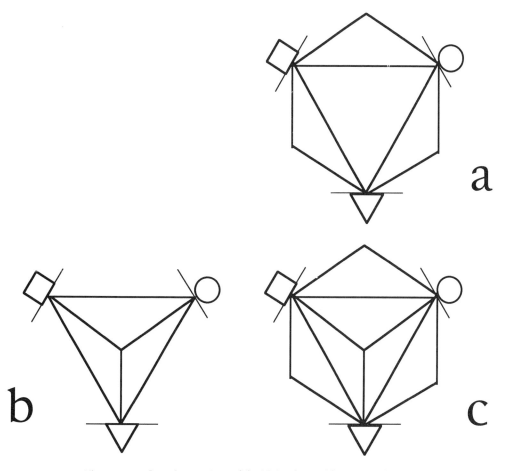

Figure 11.4 Complex versions of the Maier three-table maze with various interconnecting runways. (Adapted from Poucet et al. 1990.)

Spatial Information Processing in Animals

animals. But the observation of intact rats' strategies is of particular interest in term of their adaptation to the increased complexity of the situation. The groups submitted to conditions a and b (figure 11.4) consistently chose the most direct route between tables. In the more complex situation c, however, normal rats demonstrated a strong preference for the inner route leading to the central choice point, rather than the direct route. The main difference between condition b (which also provided an inner runway pattern) and condition c is that the latter situation provided a much more complex runway pattern as compared with the former condition in terms of the number of possible routes.

When the rats became more familiar with the problem, their preferences switched from the inner route to the direct route. Together with the experiments described above about the effects of a "piecemeal" exploratory experience, these data demonstrate that some places and their interrelations are of particular importance with regard to spatial organization. One of these places in the Y-shape three-table apparatus (figure 11.3c) is the central choice point. A feature of this place is that the panoramic view involving the three possible goals and the visual background can be perceived from the same location and that, at the same time, this location is the connecting point for the three subspaces (i.e., for one table and its associated arm). This central choice point where the three pathways converge may have served as a reference for the organization of the whole situation (this issue will be further developed later).

Exploration and the Encoding of Spatial Features: The Dishabituation Experiments

Other arguments supporting the spatial function of exploration are provided by "dishabituation" studies. The procedure is based on the decrease in exploratory activity over time (habituation) and its reactivation following a change (dishabituation). Animals are first allowed to explore an open field containing one or several objects. The number as well as the duration of contacts with these objects is recorded. Although this measure of exploratory activity is not exhaustive, it is a valid index of object investigation that can be easily contrasted with more diffuse locomotor activity (Buhot, Soffié, and Poucet 1989). After habituation, the spatial arrangement of the object set is modified. The novelty is exclusively spatial, since the objects themselves are not changed. Usually, a renewal of exploration is then observed. This renewal may sometimes be as intense as if the whole situation had been changed. The intensity of the renewed exploration has been found to depend largely on the spatial parameters that are affected by the change.

Such data have been found not only in tests performed on primates (Menzel and Menzel 1979; Joubert and Vauclair 1986), but also in tests performed on several species of rodents, including rats (Poucet 1989;

Sutherland 1957), gerbils (Cheal 1978; Thinus-Blanc and Ingle 1985), and hamsters (Poucet et al. 1986; Thinus-Blanc et al. 1987). In the latter experiments it has been shown, for example, that hamsters are more likely to encode geometrical relationships (i.e., the shape defined by the object set) than absolute distances between the objects. For instance, moving away the four objects that defined a square did not induce any renewal of exploration, whereas moving away only one of the objects (and consequently modifying the shape of the arrangement) induced a strong and selective reexploration of the displaced object (figure 11.5). In a recent study we have shown that an animal's behavior in response to a spatial change would depend, to some extent, on the animal's starting its exploration from a particular place that could be used as a point of reference associated with a specific perspective of the arrangement of the objects (Thinus-Blanc, Durup, and Poucet 1992). These data suggest that knowledge of the geometrical relationships between objects could take the form of stored images or local views of an array of landmarks as seen from a particular location.

The use of the term "local view" does not mean that all of the spatial information is visual. However, even in rodents, whose vision is relatively poor in comparison with that of other mammals such as felidae and primates, casual observations and experimental data reveal that rats are highly sensitive to the visual features of their environment. For instance, in an elegant experiment, Save et al. (in press) examined the respective

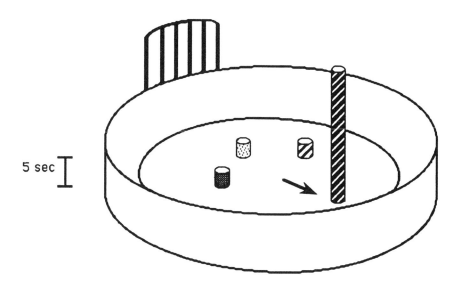

Figure 11.5 Example of a deformation of the initial square arrangement that induces a selective reexploration of the displaced object. The "height" of the objects represents the difference of exploratory activity between the test session and the last session of habituation. (Adapted from Thinus-Blanc 1988.)

role of vision and kinesthetic information using the dishabituation paradigm. Rats were allowed to separately and successively explore the two halves of a circular open field containing objects. The partition separating the two halves was either opaque or transparent. In addition, locomotor access to the other half could be allowed or not by means of two openings at the extremity of the partition (see figure 11.6). Therefore, four experimental conditions were defined: transparent and opened partition (group V+/L+), transparent and closed partition (group V+/L−), opaque and opened partition (group V−/L+), and opaque and closed partition (group V−/L−).

Once exploration was complete, the rats were exposed during the test session to the whole field without the partition. For four control groups submitted to the same situations as those presented above, the partition remained closed during the test session. The degree to which a unitary spatial organization had been built up was examined by measuring reaction to novelty (contacts with the objects). Whatever their locomotor experience (continuous or discontinuous) of the two halves of the apparatus, rats that had had a visual discontinuous experience (i.e., with the opaque partition) displayed a renewal of exploratory activity. Conversely, rats that had explored with the transparent partition did not significantly react to its removal (figure 11.7). This lack of reactivity strongly suggests that

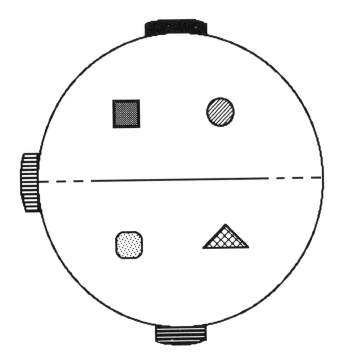

Figure 11.6 Top view of the open field containing four objects and an opaque or transparent partition that could be opened at each of its extremities. (Reproduced from Save et al., in press.)

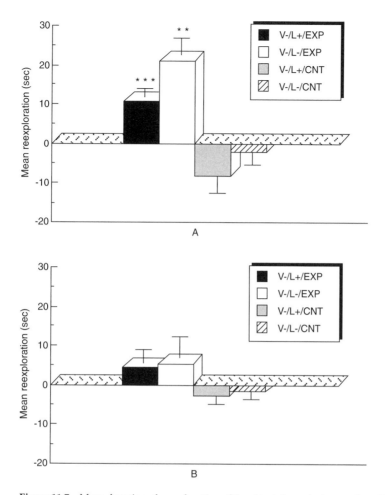

Figure 11.7 Mean duration of reexploration of the objects from the last session of habituation to the test session for the groups with the opaque barrier (A) and the transparent barrier (B) (see text for details). (Reproduced from Save et al., in press.)

spatial relationships between the four objects had already been established by the rats on the basis of visual information, since removing the partition did not induce an updating of the spatial relationships already set up. When local views of the whole object arrangement had not been available, then the setup of spatial relationships between the objects could not have been fully completed, and the rats reexplored after the removal of the partition.

Such data demonstrate the methodological interest of exploratory activity and habituation in the study of spatial memory. The rats' renewal of investigative activity after habituation implies that a change bearing exclusively upon the spatial features of the situation has been detected. The rats could detect such a change only by referring to the initial situation, no longer present as a whole, of which the subject has stored a memory or representation which needs to be compared to the present situation; novelty does not exist per se, but only by reference to familiarity. However, the demonstration of the spatial function of exploratory activity does not account for the mechanisms whereby information gathered during exploration is transformed into spatial representations. The next section deals with this issue.

FROM PERCEPTION TO REPRESENTATION

Local Views and Path Integration

Information collected during exploration, as during any perceptual activity, is initially organized along a body-centered (or egocentered) referent entailing the position of the sensory receptors, the direction of the displacement, gravitational forces, and so on. This implies that, while moving around, the animal perceives visual (and nonvisual) scenes that directly depend on its position at a given moment. For instance, the visual image or local view of three objects A, B, and C (figure 11.8) is not the same when the objects are as perceived from P1 as from P2. The spatial relationship between the objects and the subject is different (A is on the left and C on the right from P1, and on the opposite sides from P2). In addition, the aspect of the objects themselves may change according to the perspective from which they are perceived. However, they are the very same objects in the very same arrangement even though they may not immediately be perceived as such.

In contrast, by their very nature, spatial representations such as cognitive maps must be independent of the subject's position at a given time. This property allows a subject to reach a place charted on the map independent of the starting location. The information is said to be "allocentered"—that is, organized on the basis of "absolute" coordinates such as the cardinal points, for instance, which do not vary with the subject's changes of position. The nature of a place and its relationships with other places are not different according to whether they are approached from the north or the south. They are independent of their appearance. This implies that a subject must process information about the places so as to extract what remains invariant in spite of the variability of the subject's percept.

Attempting to account for the spatial function of exploratory activity is a tough problem since it is necessary to define the processing allowing the transformation of information from an egocentered to an allocentered frame of reference. While an animal or any organism is moving around, two classes of information are provided by this activity. The first category, already discussed, concerns the environmental features such as the various local views corresponding to the same objects perceived on different

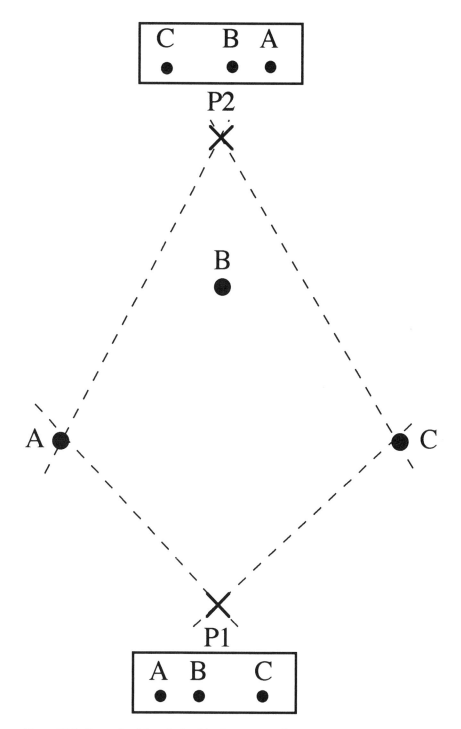

Figure 11.8 Example of the relationships between an observer and the three objects A, B, and C according to the perspective from which they are perceived.

perspectives. Gibson (1979) emphasized the importance of the variability of the percepts in the following rather paradoxical terms:

If change means to become different but not to be converted in something else, the assertion ("the more it changes, the more it is the same thing") is true and the saying emphasizes the fact that whatever is invariant is more evident with change than it would be without change. One arrangement does not become a wholly different arrangement by a displacement of viewpoint. There is no jump from one to another, only a variation of structure that serves to reveal the nonvariation of structure. (Gibson 1979, p. 73)

In this regard, the spatial function of exploration is unequivocal, since it provides the subject with a multiplicity of viewpoints from which the invariant features can be extracted. However, this statement has no explicative value without referring to another class of information, at least as important as the first, that relates to the displacement itself. Indeed, the notion that perceptual changes must be matched with information about the movements that generate these changes is at the very core of the function of exploration as "spatial builder." Exploratory activity can be considered from two tightly interconnected aspects, one concerning the perception of the external physical environment (perception of local views, for instance), the other related to self-generated internal feedbacks (information provided by muscle and tendon receptors, by the vestibular system, and by the perception of the optical flow). The self-generated internal feedbacks matched with the perceptual changes resulting from the displacement assure the subject of the stability of the external world by indicating that the subject itself is moving within an invariable environment. Without indication about the subject's movement itself, the variability of the percepts related to various perspectives of the same objects would be interpreted as actual (and not perceptual) changes of the world.

Spatial encoding on the basis of self-generated internal feedbacks or "path integration" (also called in some cases "dead reckoning") has been extensively studied in many species. Dead reckoning or path integration plays a predominant role as a route-based navigation system (Gallistel 1990). Whenever a subject moves from one place to another, it generates different signals that are correlated with the angular and linear components of the pattern of displacements. If the knowledge constituted on the basis of these signals is updated—i.e., if these signals about the path that is travelled are "integrated" in a continuous manner—the subject can know its location with respect to its point of departure. Dead reckoning may occur on the basis of purely internal cues, such as vestibular signals (Potegal 1982, 1987). Many species, however, assess the angular components of their progress with the help of an external referent such as the sun. In natural conditions, dead reckoning allows foragers to return safely to their home, the central point from which most of their displacements are usually radiating and to which they are converging.

Path integration has been studied extensively in hymenopterous insects, which use the sun as a directional referent (Wehner and Wehner 1990). In nocturnal mammals, such as the gerbil (Mittelstaedt and Mittelstaedt 1980), dead reckoning relies entirely on self-generated internal cues. But the most extensive studies of path integration have been conducted in the hamster by Etienne and her collaborators in situations in which there is both an outward and a return journey. The choice of the hamster was justified by the fact that, when this animal encounters food in sufficient amounts, it fills up its cheek pouches and is strongly motivated to return directly to its nest whether or not the outward journey has been circuitous. In the studies of Etienne and co-workers, each subject's nest-box was permanently connected to an arena located in a cue-controlled environment. A heap of hazelnuts was placed at the center of the arena. The animal coming from its nest filled its cheek pouches with hazelnuts and then had to return to its nest under several conditions. In the absence of visual cues (when tested under infrared light), hamsters are capable of orienting by means of route-based information. However, in the case of conflict between route-based and location-based information, the latter prevailed. For instance, in an experiment by Teroni, Portenier, and Etienne (1987), the visual cue was displaced by 90 degrees after each animal had arrived at the central food source. Therefore, the route-based information was in conflict with the location-based (visual) information. The hamsters relied on the displaced visual cue and searched for their nest at the location indicated by that cue in spite of conflicting route-based information.

The moment when the visual cues are available is also an important factor; for instance, a light spot exerts its influence mainly during the phase of food collection, just before the subjects start to return to their nest. However, its effect remains noticeable even when it is presented only briefly at the beginning of the hoarding excursion (Etienne et al. 1990). In addition, active or passive rotations in the dark while the animal is at the food source are compensated for within certain limits (Etienne, Maurer, and Saucy 1988).

The general aim of these studies was to define the conditions in which an accurate return journey toward the home can be made on the basis of an initial outward trip to the food source. With regard to the function of exploration, these results demonstrate at a general level the importance of internal information to spatial knowledge, since the latter is efficient even if the displacement cannot be perceptually inscribed at any moment within an allothetic frame of reference. However, this knowledge remains extremely limited. It is subject to cumulative errors, since no updating is possible in the absence of external information. It is only when both internal and external information is available that true spatial representations can be constituted.

Abstract Processing of Places

On the basis of the data described above, it is possible to sketch a schematized map-building process. In this regard, I shall not enter into the old debate started by Tolman (1948) related to the existence and nature of maps in animals. The importance of maps has been exaggerated in the interpretation of many data (Thinus-Blanc 1988). The fact remains, however, that in some cases efficient displacements performed by animals in natural or experimental conditions cannot be accounted for without recourse to an overall representation of the environment (see Poucet 1993 for a critical review of this issue) endowed with specific properties. O'Keefe and Nadel, in their seminal book *The Hippocampus as a Cognitive Map* (1978), have described the properties of maps vs. other kinds of simpler representations, such as S-R associations that are involved in the use of "routes."

Very complex displacements can be performed on the basis of learned sequences of reorientations. In our everyday life, the changes of direction we take in the iterated journey from home to office are not the objects of conscious decisions. Some automatisms are implemented that result in "turn left at the red traffic light, turn right at the church," for example. Similarly, in animals, various maze studies (see Blancheteau 1969, Munn 1950 for reviews) have demonstrated that in many cases rats' displacements rely on S-R associations. However, such behaviors are much more temporal than spatial. A segment of any route forms part of a sequence, and before and after it there are other segments. If one link of the chain comes to be missing or modified (an obstacle through a familiar pathway), it is likely that the subject will be lost unless the knowledge of the relative positions of the places allows the behavior to be released from the temporal constraints.

In contrast, the most important functional feature of maps is their flexibility of use. For instance, shortcuts, detours, or reaching a goal from unfamiliar directions of approach imply that places have their own status regardless of their appearance, the perspective from which they are perceived, and the temporal features of the displacements that usually take place in the environment. These features provide the maps with plasticity. Until now, it appears impossible to account for the "innovative" behaviors seen above without recourse to the notion of a map whose intimate mechanisms are far from being fully discovered. For these reasons, in the present discussion I shall merely define maplike representations as a set of places connected with each other by angle and distance relationships.

A prerequisite for the constitution of maps is that the local views that correspond to a concrete spatial description are first processed in a way leading to the extraction of places independent of the vantage point from which they are perceived. This abstract description corresponds to the extraction of spatial invariants whose characteristic is to remain stable in spite of the variations of the percepts. An abstract description has the property of removing the constraint of directionality related to particular viewpoints. On that account, a main correlative feature of the maps is that they lose serial and temporal relationships to the benefit of spatial coherence. Places exist independently of the temporal course of actions. Hence, any place can virtually be related to any other one (even if they are not adjacent), and spatial inferences—i.e., computations of pathways never experienced before—can be made provided that the basic structure has been acquired.

By considering the importance of exploration and, more generally, of locomotor activity in spatial knowledge (discussed earlier), one can propose a schematized scenario of the abstract processing of places on the basis of what is actually perceived—that is, local views—matched with the proprioceptive information correlated with locomotor activity. A place can be characterized by the fact that the various local views provided by a 360-degree rotation onsite are recognized as having in common the point from which they are perceived (Poucet 1993). This can be visualized by means of a bundle of diverging vectors (figure 11.9a). In this case, the various overlapping local views, on the one hand, and proprioceptive and vestibular information, on the other hand, generated by the rotation onsite must be matched and integrated. Then the place where the rotation has taken place is the common denominator of visual (and nonvisual) scenes, which may be extremely different according to the subject's position. For instance, it is likely that the local view that is perceived when the subject is turned toward the north does not share any common feature with the local view available when the subject is looking to the south. However, both local views can be perceived from the same place, whose existence is independent from a particular position of the subject.

Similarly, if the subject is moving around a set of objects that characterize a place, the varying overlapping local views that the subject perceives must be combined with the proprioceptive and vestibular information generated by the subject's translation (figure 11.9b). In that case, the object arrangement that is perceived may be very different from P1 and P2, for instance, but these diversified local views "describe" the same invariant arrangement. It is legitimate to term the result of such a processing "abstract" since the knowledge of a place, although derived from a concrete description, is independent of it.

With regard to the further organization of so-defined places, only an abstract label is necessary and should be stored (for instance "goal," "home," "cluster of trees," etc.). However, these places need to be visually identified when the subject is moving around and has to find his or her way. Therefore, it is necessary for a minimal sample of local views to be stored in long-term memory. Their number is dependent on the complexity of the situation and the variability of its aspects when it is viewed from various perspectives.

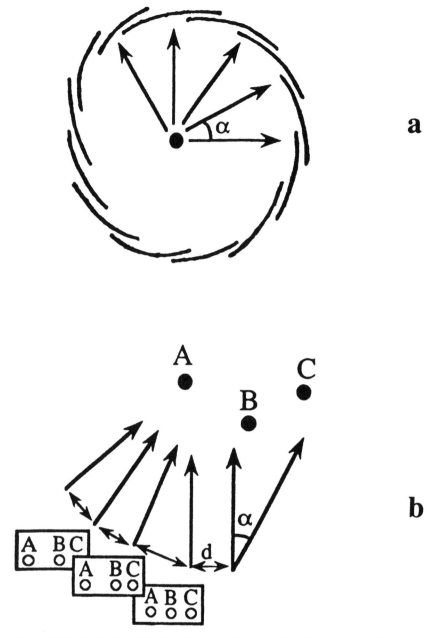

Figure 11.9 Illustration of the definition of a place based on the overlapping local views provided by (*a*) a rotation onsite and (*b*) a translation around the set of objects.

The Abstract Processing of Places at the Brain Level

Interestingly enough, the "place cells" in the rat hippocampus, which were first discovered and so christened by O'Keefe and Dostrovski (1971), appear to correlate with the abstract processing of places as sketched in figure 11.9a. Single-unit recordings have revealed that a number of pyramidal complex spike cells in the CA1 and CA3 areas of the hippocampus fire in relation to the rat's location within the environment (McNaughton, Barnes, and O'Keefe 1983; Muller and Kubie 1987; O'Keefe and Conway 1978; O'Keefe and Speakman 1987; Olton, Branch, and Best 1978). The firing fields of these "place cells" (i.e., the region of the apparatus where there is firing) is independent of a particular orientation of the subject, but relies on the environmental configuration of cues. If the latter is rotated, the firing field is also rotated to the same degree. Although place cell activity depends on the configuration of visual (and nonvisual) cues, these cells, as underlined by Muller and colleagues (1991), are not sensory because they do not depend on information coming in at a given moment and for a given position of the subject, but represent an encoding of the animal's absolute location within the environment regardless of the scene that is currently being considered (O'Keefe and Nadel 1978).

The question that arises, then, is this: What is the process leading to this location-specific firing? Sharp has recently (1991) provided a simple model that satisfactorily accounts for this processing and fits with the sketch of abstract processing of places that I propose. The basic framework of her model is a neural network with the characteristics of a competitive learning, pattern classification device (e.g., Rumelhart and Zipser 1986; Von der Marlsburg 1973). It is made up of three layers of neuron-like elements. Each element of one layer can be connected to each element of the next lower layer by Hebb-like synapses. The first layer is an input layer of neocortical cells corresponding, in the model, to polysensory association cortex. The second layer is the entorhinal cortex, which receives massive inputs from polysensory association areas such as the temporal cortex (e.g., Van Hoesen and Pandya 1975, in monkeys). The entorhinal cortex is also the main source of neocortical input to the hippocampus, which corresponds to the third layer in the model. These last two layers are divided into "winner-take-all" clusters. This design implies that only one cell in each cluster fires—the cell that receives the largest input from the first layer and, consequently, has the strongest connections with currently active cells. The firing established in the input layers projects to the second layer (the entorhinal cortex), which itself projects to the third (the hippocampus layer) according to the above principle. The displacements of a fictive rat equipped with the above described brain properties are simulated under the same conditions used by Muller, Kubie, Bostock, and associates (1991) during actual place cell recording. Samples of the firing are taken at the frequency of the theta rhythm at which pyramidal cells fire.

Sharp's model depends on the following principles. While an animal is moving around within a given environment, various local views are available from each of its locations. Local views available from contiguous locations or from different directions within the same location are very similar, since they share many elements in common. Consequently, they will be placed in the same class. A crucial factor that determines the grouping of two patterns or local views is the number of intermediate local views between them. The local views experienced when the animal is facing opposite directions (for instance the north and the south) in a given location are very different. However, if intermediate local views between these opposite views are available, then it is probable that they will be placed in the same category (i.e., that the same place cell will fire regardless of the view that is currently faced). If no intermediate views are provided, the views available from each opposite direction are more likely to be placed in different categories (see figure 11.10).

The function of Sharp's pattern-classification device is to classify and store local views on the basis of their similarities. According to its competitive learning features, in the model one given cell (a place cell) fires in one precise region of space (a place field) where similar local views are available. Even if local views perceived from opposite directions but from the same location are not similar, the continuity ensured by a succession

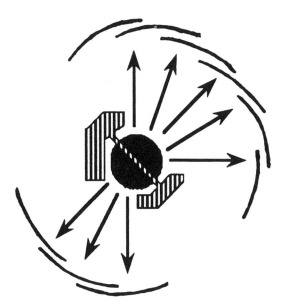

Figure 11.10 Example of a case where a complete rotation onsite does not provide a continuous perception of the overlapping local views. The striped blocks represent visual occluders. This configuration may encourage the formation of two categories of places.

of overlapping intermediate local views makes possible their classification into the same category. According to the principles of Hebb-like synapses, all connections that were activated when the place cell fired are strengthened. Therefore, they are more likely to fire during subsequent presentations of one of the local views belonging to the same class—that is, those available from one location. The simulation of the displacement of a fictive rat within a cylinder, according to the principles enunciated above, leads to firing-rate maps that are strikingly similar to those found in actual recording experiments using the same apparatus (Muller, Kubie, and Ranck 1987). In addition, the properties of the firing fields share the same properties seen in the actual experiments.

Sharp's model leads to interesting predictions. For instance, she assumes that the likelihood that two locations (or views within locations) with some sensory overlap are represented by the same place cell should be very dependent on the amount of exposure to the intermediate scenes between them. The data obtained by Save et al. (in press), which was presented in the first section, lends some experimental support to this hypothesis at the psychological level. These researchers suggest that the critical factor for setting up objective spatial relationships is not the possibility of traveling along direct trajectories between two subspaces, but rather the number and continuity of available local views from locations within each hemifield. It may be expected that the firing fields of place cells recorded in each of the four situations they describe (with transparent-closed, transparent-open, opaque-closed, opaque-open barriers) and after changes from a situation to any other one should display a variability depending on the situation currently experienced.

This model represents a plausible explanation of the constitution of place cell firing fields, but it could also incorporate other categories of cells found in the hippocampal formation. For instance, when recording from the CA1 field of the hippocampus, Wiener, Paul, and Eichenbaum (1989) found that the firing rate of some pyramidal cells varied systematically in relation to the speed, direction, and turning angle of the rat moving through the place field. On the other hand, Quirk, Muller, and Kubie (1990) have shown that the firing field of place cells is not disrupted by turning the light off when the rat is already in the recording chamber. If the rat is put in the recording chamber in the dark, there is a strong modification of the patterns of the firing fields. The authors propose that in the dark rats may keep track of their position using vestibular and proprioceptive information, although it is unlikely that this information can be sufficiently accurate to maintain constant field location over the long recording duration because of the cumulative error of this system due to the lack of external feedback. Altogether, these data suggest that proprioceptive information contributes to the hippocampal cell activity. These findings could be incorporated into Sharp's model, which does not take into account kinesthetic information and its matching with the visual results of the subject's displacements.

Finally, it should be underlined that the model proposed by Sharp accounts only for the encoding of the subject's location with regard to the perceived environmental configuration. In that case, the notion of "place" refers to a momentary entity since the rat, which is moving around in its environment, is the only "object" that transiently labels this particular part of space. This projective view of space, although important in navigation within small-scale situations all of whose parts can be perceived, cannot be considered the basis of spatial orientation within large-scale environments whose parts are too remote to be perceived from the starting place where the choice of a direction is made. Spatial representations consist of the knowledge of interrelationships between places, and they are useful, for instance, in reaching a goal that is hidden and/or far away. There are not yet electrophysiological data supporting, at the brain level, the notion of a representation of distant parts of space. Indeed, place cell activity must be considered an electrophysiological correlate of spatial encoding, but—and this remark does not weaken the interest of these findings—in no case should it be taken as accounting for the whole process of mapping.

To summarize, the first stage of map building is the establishment of representations of abstractly defined places. The second step, developed in the next section, is the establishment of representations for the relations among these places.

THE FUNCTIONAL RELATIONSHIPS BETWEEN ABSTRACTLY DEFINED PLACES

The second step of map building corresponds to the setting up of spatial relationships between abstractly defined places. These relationships can be defined in terms of angles and distances. I believe, however, that the metric features of animal spatial representations are of ancillary interest with regard to their functional role. In other words, what spatial "operations" are made possible by the use of a map even if angles and distances are approximately encoded?

The representation of several places linked by angle and distance relations constitutes a network which, depending on the number of places that are charted, may quickly reach a high level of complexity. In order to simplify, it is possible to consider only one "mesh" (Chapuis 1988) made up of three places defining a triangle. All the other spatial arrangements can be defined as combinations of triangles. In addition to their geometric relations, which are specific to a given triangular configuration, these places are interrelated by functional properties. For instance, two places belonging to the triangle can be linked by at least two paths, one being shorter than the other (cf. Maier's experiment with the "three-table" test, described earlier).

The simpler definition of the spatial functional properties had been provided by Piaget (1937) in his formalization of the development of children's spatial knowledge. The displacements of any moving element between the three apexes of a triangle have several properties that constitute the *"groupe logique des déplacements."* This group can be summarized as follows (figure 11.11): (1) the routes are transitive: AB and BC can be combined into one journey AC belonging to the same spatial structure, which does not run through B and conversely (shortcuts and detours);

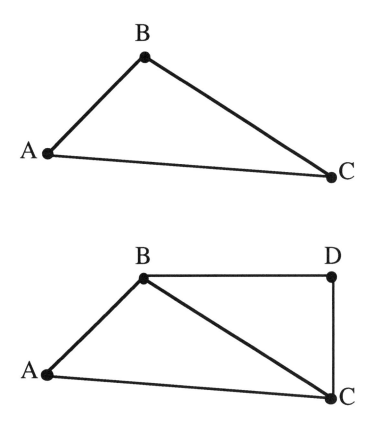

Transitivity: AB+BC=AC
Reversibility: AB implies BA
Annulation: AB+BA=0
Associativity: AB+BD=AC+CD

Figure 11.11 Illustration of Piaget's "Groupe logique des déplacements."

(2) the routes are reversible: any route AB has its reverse BA, and (3) the combination of AB and BA results in no route; (4) the routes are associative: in the sequence ABCD, AB + BD = AC + CD. This means that the location D can be reached by different pathways. This illustrates the property of the "equivalence of the pathways."

The two important complex spatial computations, the determination of shortcuts and detours, are contained in these few words, which summarize in functional terms what is necessary to successfully travel in space and to adapt to unexpected modifications of the familiar pathways. The triangular arrangement and the functional properties that link the three places constitute a *prototype*—that is, an abstract schema that can be applied to any triangular configuration and combination of configurations. The advantage of such a prototype is that it minimizes the information to be stored, since inferences can be made on the basis of partial information. The following study, conducted by Chapuis and Varlet (1987), illustrates the kind of inferential process that can be computed on the basis of a partial knowledge of the situation.

The experiment was conducted outdoors in a meadow. The animals (Alsatian dogs) were first taken on a leash along the path ADB (figure 11.12). They were shown pieces of meat at points A and B, but were not allowed to eat them. The task consisted of finding the food hidden at A and B when released from D. The three points A, B, and D were far enough apart to prevent the animals from seeing the reward. In addition, the field was covered with thornbushes. Control trials were conducted at the end of the experiment without food to ascertain that the animals were not guided by olfactive cues, and the experiment was also carried out in different parts of the meadow. In 96 percent of the trials, the animals went directly from A to B rather than returning to the starting point and taking the familiar pathway. The segment AB was not known by the subjects, which had never had the opportunity to experience it. Thus, the animals were able to work out an unfamiliar shortcut on the basis of a partial knowledge of the situation.

The experiments by Maier (1932) are another example of the property of the equivalence of the pathways provided that the subjects have been allowed a minimal free exploration. Other data have shown detour abilities in many species, such as rats (Tolman and Honzik 1930), cats (Poucet et al. 1986), dogs (Chapuis et al. 1988), and primates (Köhler 1937).

Altogether, these findings illustrate a distinctive property of maps—namely, the reorganization of spatial information independent of the sequence during which it has been acquired. Maps are endowed with plasticity. Once spatial relationships are established between places—i.e., once they are charted on a survey map—there is more than one pathway (that usually taken, for instance) that can link them. The orientation process relies not on rigid routes, but on the precise localization of the places. It follows, therefore, that if the possibility of a shorter path is offered,

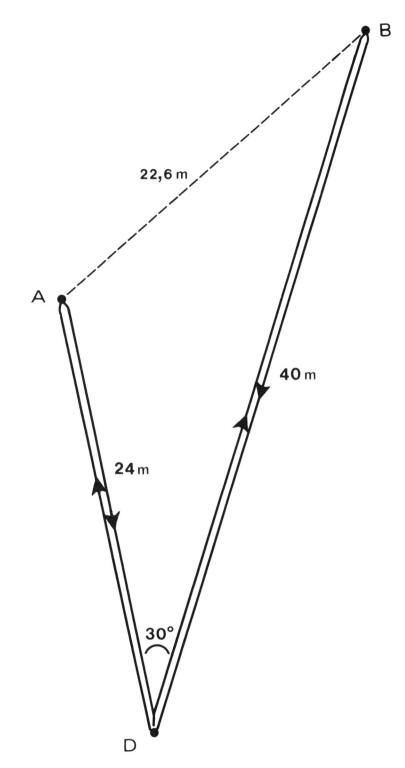

Figure 11.12 Schemas of the situation used with dogs. D = starting point. A and B = food points. D-A, A-D, D-B, B-D vectors (solid) = exploratory runs (dogs on leash); A-B segment (dotted) = optimally oriented task run. (Reproduced from Chapuis and Varlet 1987.)

Spatial Information Processing in Animals

pointing in the direction of the goal, it is chosen without hesitation. Similarly, if a detour is necessary, the subject is able to situate himself or herself while deviating from the straight route to the goal.

According to the concept of map building that is presented above, the successful performance of the dogs can be accounted for in the following terms. During the initial phase of exploration, the places D, A, and B are abstractly processed. Some local views allowing their identification are stored. While the dogs have been running in both directions the paths DA and DB, two corresponding subspaces having the place D in common have been constituted. D is important, since it constitutes the link between the two subspaces DA and DB and the reference from which the relative lengths of the two paths can be evaluated. It is also from D that the evaluation of the angle alpha can be made which, combined with the evaluations of the two paths, may contribute to the construction of a precise map of the situation.

The schemas represented in figure 11.13 summarize the whole process. When an animal is at D, the identification of this place on the basis of the available local views activates both the subspaces that have been experienced, DA and DB. Let us assume that the dog has stored the prototype of the triangular arrangement and the functional rules (which constitute the *"groupe logique des déplacements"*) that link three places (figure 11.11). Since the situation is made up of three points, one of which is common to both subspaces, the prototype DAB is activated, which corresponds with the simultaneous representation on the map of the three places. The functional rules allow us to infer that the shortcut AB is possible, and a more or less precise metric evaluation provides rough information about the angle to be made from A in order to reach B. The activation of the prototype triggers, in turn, the activation of both places A and B and related local views (the black rectangles at the bottom of figure 11.13). The triangular arrangement can be evoked without metric information, but it may reveal less adapted to a precise computation of the optimal path.

I give much more weight to functional links in the representations than to metric links. When metric features are encoded, they are likely to be relative (distances) and approximate (angles). This assertion is supported by the charting of the paths taken by the dogs, which reveals the relative imprecision of the encoding. Only 41 percent of them point directly to the goal. In the other cases, either the shortcuts intersect DB before B (42 percent) or the angle of the shortcut with regard to DA is overestimated (17 percent). Interestingly enough, there are only a few errors of this kind, which would lead the subject into an unfamiliar region. The consequence is that, in spite of its errors, the animal is seldom out of the area defined by the three points A, D, and B but joins the final part of familiar path DB before getting to B. It is only when the metrical information is precise and absolute that it allows a perfectly accurate computation of the direction to be taken. However, even with approximate metrical information

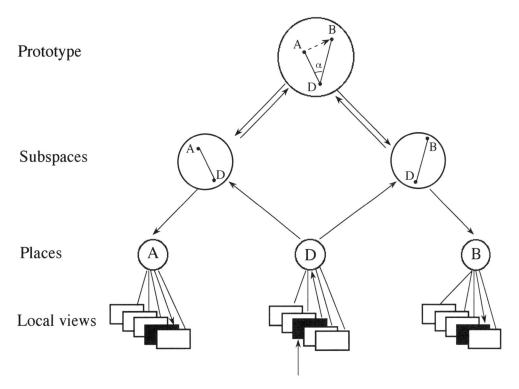

Prototype

Subspaces

Places

Local views

Figure 11.13 Schematic representation of map use in inferential processes. The black rectangles represent the local views that have been stored during the abstract processing of the three places D, B, and A. These places have been related to each other during the initial phase of exploration so as to constitute subspaces. One incoming local view available from D activates (ascending arrows from D) the triangular prototype, which indicates that a shortcut links the two other places to be reached, A and B, and, in turn, co-activates (descending arrows from the upper level) the local views associated with A and B.

inferences can be made, whereas, without functional rules, metrical information would not be of any help in making a shortcut.

CONCLUSION

It is highly probable that the psychological model that is proposed in this chapter represents an oversimplified sketch of the map-building process that actually takes place. However, it is not more implausible than the widespread view of maps conceived as accurate cartographic copies of the reality, endowed with quasi-magical properties that allow the animal to reach any place from any other one. Indeed, other attempts to account for spatial knowledge in a more realistic way have recently been made by several authors (for instance, Collett, Cartwright, and Smith 1986; Poucet 1993). Among other advantages, such models have, above all, the merit of helping us think about animal spatial cognition in more ''parsimonious'' terms concerning the level of representation than what has been done according to the classical theoretical framework. It follows, therefore, that new experiments can be devised to test the hypotheses and predictions generated by the models.

In addition to this heuristic interest, accounting for animal spatial processing in simple terms has the advantage of coming closer to the present concern of roboticians. I argue that, if it were technologically possible (and it might be in the future) to equip a robot with a device releasing it from constraints related to the direction of approach (abstract processing of places) and allowing it to perform operations based on the triangular arrangement evoked above (prototype), this robot would be spatially adaptable and efficient. Indeed, the abstract processing of places relies not on symbolic processes but, as proposed by Sharp (1991), on the continuity of the perception, which may lead to the perception of very different local views during a rotation onsite or during the translation around a set of objects. One could imagine a robot equipped with a continuous comparison system (similar to a short-term memory device) that would allow it to constantly search for the elements common to two successive (and consequently, adjacent) local views. The fact that the abstract processing of places appears to have electrophysiological correlates encourages us to implement biologically derived models in artificial neural networks. Unfortunately, only the activity of isolated place cells has been recorded so far, and the connections between various place cells whose firing fields correspond to several places are still unknown. Several models have been proposed that incorporate the activity of single cells into wider functional scenarios (for instance, see Muller, Kubie, and Saypoff 1991; Muller et al. 1991; Rolls 1991). However, the question of the relations among place cells and, correlatively, among places is not considered in these models.

Even though the study of the cortical bases of animal spatial behavior is less advanced than that of the behavior itself, both are now indissociable and benefit from their reciprocal contributions. They also benefit from studies of artificial intelligence, connectionist theories, and robotics. In return, for the reasons discussed in the introduction to this chapter, the study of animal spatial behavior and of its cortical bases allows us to speculate about possible applications in the domain of robotics, especially concerning the design of robot navigation systems. Such speculations may appear to be fancy. But would it not have seemed fancy, 20 years ago or so, to consider that ethology, experimental psychology, and cognitive neurosciences could contribute to the advancement of robotics?

REFERENCES

Blancheteau, M. (1969). L'orientation spatiale chez l'animal, ses indices et ses repères. Paris: *Monographies Françaises de Psychologie*, 15, CNRS.

Buhot, M.-C., Soffié, M., and Poucet, B. (1989). Scopolamine affects the cognitive processes involved in selective object exploration more than locomotor activity. *Psychobiology*, 17, 409–417.

Chapuis, N. (1988). Les opérations structurantes dans la connaissance de l'espace chez les Mammifères: Détour, raccourci et retour. Thèse de Doctorat d'Etat ès-Sciences, Université d'Aix-Marseille II.

Chapuis, N., Thinus-Blanc, C., and Poucet, B. (1983). Dissociation of mechanisms involved in dogs' oriented displacements. *Quarterly Journal of Experimental Psychology*, 35B, 213–219.

Chapuis, N., and Varlet, C. (1987). Shortcuts by dogs in natural surroundings. *Quarterly Journal of Experimental Psychology*, 39B, 49–64.

Cheal, M.-L. (1978). Stimulus-elicited investigation in the Mongolian gerbil *(Meriones unguiculatus)*. *The Journal of Biological Psychology*, 20, 26–32.

Collett, T. S., Cartwright, B. A., and Smith, B. A. (1986). Landmark learning and visuospatial memories in gerbils. *Journal of Comparative Physiology*, 158, 835–851.

Ellen, P., Parko, E. M., Wages, C., Doherty, D., and Herrmann, T. (1982). Spatial problem solving by rats: Exploration and cognitive maps. *Learning and Motivation*, 13, 81–94.

Ellen, P., Soteres, B. J., and Wages, C. (1984). Problem solving in the rat: Piecemeal acquisition of cognitive maps. *Animal Learning and Behavior*, 12, 232–237.

Etienne, A. E., Maurer, R., and Saucy, F. (1988). Limitations in the assessment of path dependent information. *Behaviour*, 106, 81–111.

Etienne, A. S., Teroni, E., Hurni, C., and Portenier, V. (1990). The effect of a single light cue on homing behaviour of the golden hamster. *Animal Behaviour*, 39, 17–41.

Fowler, H. (1970). *Curiosity and Exploratory Behavior.* New York: Macmillan.

Gallistel, C. R. (1990). *The Organization of Learning.* Cambridge, MA: Bradford Books/The MIT Press.

Gibson, J. J. (1979). *The Ecological Approach to Visual Perception.* Boston, MA: Houghton-Mifflin.

Joubert, A., and Vauclair, J. (1986). Reaction to novel objects in a troop of Guinea baboons: Approach and manipulation. *Behaviour*, 96, 92–104.

Köhler, W. (1927). *L'intelligence des Singes Supérieurs.* Paris: Librairie Félix Alcan.

Maier, N. R. F. (1932). A study of orientation in the rat. *Journal of Comparative Psychology*, 14, 387–399.

Marler, P., and Hamilton, W. J. (1966). *Mechanisms of Animal Behavior.* New York: Wiley.

McNaughton, B. L., Barnes, C. A., and O'Keefe, J. (1983). The contributions for position, direction, and velocity to single-unit activity in the hippocampus of freely-moving cats. *Experimental Brain Research*, 52, 41–49.

Menzel, E. W., and Menzel, C. R. (1979). Cognitive developmental and social aspects of responsiveness to novel objects in a family group of marmosets *(Saguinus fuscicollis)*. *Behaviour*, 70, 251–278.

Mittelstaedt, M. L., and Mittelstaedt, H. (1980). Homing by path integration in a mammal. *Naturwissenschaft*, 67, 566.

Muller, R., Kubie, J., and Ranck, J. (1987). Spatial firing patterns for hippocampal complex-spike cells in a fixed environment. *Journal of Neuroscience*, 7, 1935–1950.

Muller, R., Kubie J., and Saypoff, R. (1991). The hippocampus as a cognitive graph (abridged version). *Hippocampus*, 1, 243–246.

Muller, R. U., and Kubie, J. L. (1987). The effects of changes in the environment on the spatial firing of hippocampal complex-spike cells. *Journal of Neuroscience*, 7, 1951–1968.

Muller, R. U., Kubie, J. L., Bostock, E. M., Taube, J. S., and Quirk, G. J. (1991). Spatial firing correlates of neurons in the hippocampal formation of freely moving rats. In J. Paillard (Ed.). *Brain and Space*. Oxford: Oxford University Press. Pp. 296–333.

Munn, N. L. (1950). *Handbook of Psychological Research on the Rat*. Boston: Houghton-Mifflin.

O'Keefe, J., and Conway, D. H. (1978). Hippocampal place units in freely moving rat: Why they fire where they fire. *Experimental Brain Research*, 31, 573–590.

O'Keefe, J., and Dostrovsky, J. (1971). The hippocampus as a spatial map: Preliminary evidence from unit activity in the freely-moving rat. *Brain Research*, 34, 171–175.

O'Keefe, J., and Nadel, L. (1978). *The Hippocampus as a Cognitive Map*. London: Oxford University Press.

O'Keefe, J., and Speakman, A. (1987). Single unit activity in the rat hippocampus during a spatial memory task. *Experimental Brain Research*, 68, 1–27.

Olton, D. S., Branch, M., and Best, P. (1978). Spatial correlates of hippocampal unit activity. *Experimental Neurology*, 58, 387–409.

Piaget, J. (1937). *La Construction du Réel Chez L'enfant*. Neuchâtel: Delachaux and Niestlé.

Potegal, M. (1982). Vestibular and neostriatal contributions to spatial orientation. In M. Potegal (Ed.). *Spatial Abilities: Development and Physiological Foundations*. New York: Academic Press.

Potegal, M. (1987). The vestibular navigation hypothesis: A progress report. In P. Ellen and C. Thinus-Blanc (Eds.). *Cognitive Processes and Spatial Orientation in Animal and Man, Vol. 2*. Dordrecht, Neth.: Martinus-Nijhoff, Publ. Pp. 28–34.

Poucet, B. (1989). Object exploration, habituation and response to a spatial change following septal or medial frontal cortical damage. *Behavioral Neuroscience*, 103, 1009–1016.

Poucet, B. (1993). Spatial cognitive maps in animals: New hypotheses on their structure and neural mechanisms. *Psychological Review*, 100, 163–182.

Poucet, B., Bolson, B., and Herrmann, T. (1990). Spatial behaviour of normal and septal rats on alternate route maze problems. *The Quarterly Journal of Experimental Psychology*, 42B, 369–384.

Poucet, B., Chapuis, N., Durup, M., and Thinus-Blanc, C. (1986). Exploratory behavior as an index of spatial knowledge in hamsters. *Animal Learning and Behavior*, 14, 93–100.

Poucet, B., Thinus-Blanc, C., and Chapuis, N. (1983). Route-planning in cats related to the visibility of the goal. *Animal Behaviour*, 31, 594–599.

Quirk, G. J., Muller, R. U., and Kubie, J. L. (1990). The firing of hippocampal place-cells in the dark depends on the rat's recent experience. *Journal of Neuroscience*, 2008–2017.

Rolls, E. T. (1991) Functions of the primate hippocampus in spatial processing and memory. In J. Paillard (Ed.). *Brain and Space*. Oxford: Oxford University Press. Pp. 353–378.

Rumelhart, D. E., and Zipser, D. (1986). Feature discovery by competitive learning. In D. E. Rumelhart, J. M. McClelland, and the PDP Research Group (Eds.). *Parallel Distributed Processing: Explorations in the Microstructure of Cognition, Vol. 1*. Cambridge, MA.: The MIT Press. Pp. 151–193.

Save, E., Granon, S., Buhot, M.-C., and Thinus-Blanc, C. (in press). Effects of limitations on the use of some visual and kinesthetic information in spatial mapping. *The Quarterly Journal of Experimental Psychology*, Section B.

Sharp, P. E. (1991). Computer simulation of hippocampal place cells. *Psychobiology*, 19, 103–115.

Sutherland, N. S. (1957). Spontaneous alternation and stimulus avoidance. *Journal of Comparative and Physiological Psychology,* 50, 358–362.

Teroni, E., Portenier, V., and Etienne, A. S. (1987). Spatial orientation of the golden hamster in conditions of conflicting location-based and route-based information. *Behavioral Ecology and Sociobiology,* 20, 389–397.

Thinus-Blanc, C. (1988). Animal spatial cognition. In L. Weiskrantz (Ed.). *Thought without Language.* Oxford University Press. Pp. 371–395.

Thinus-Blanc, C., Bouzouba, L., Chaix, K., Chapuis, N., Durup, M., and Poucet, B. (1987). A study of spatial parameters encoded during exploration in hamsters. *Journal of Experimental Psychology: Animal Behavior Processes,* 13, 418–427.

Thinus-Blanc, C., Durup, M., and Poucet, B. (1992). The spatial parameters encoded by hamsters during exploration: A further study. *Behavioural Processes,* 26, 43–57.

Thinus-Blanc, C., and Ingle, D. (1985). Spatial behaviour in gerbils. *Journal of Comparative Psychology,* 99, 311–315.

Tolman, E. C. (1948) Cognitive maps in rats and men. *Psychological Bulletin,* 55, 189–208.

Tolman, E. C., and Honzik, C. H. (1930). Degrees of hunger, reward and non-reward on maze learning in rats. *University of California Publications in Psychology,* 4, 241–256.

Van Hoesen, G. W., and Pandya, D. N. (1975). Some connections of the entorhinal area (area 28) and perirhinal area (area 35) cortices in the monkey: I. Temporal lobe afferents. *Brain Research,* 95, 1–24.

Von der Malsburg, C. (1973). Self-organizing of orientation sensitive cells in the striate cortex. *Kybernetik,* 14, 85–100.

Wehner, R., and Wehner, S. (1990). Insect navigation: Use of maps or Ariadne thread? *Ethology, Ecology and Evolution,* 2, 27–48.

Wiener, S. I., Paul, C. A., and Eichenbaum, H. (1989). Spatial and behavioral correlates of hippocampal neural activity. *The Journal of Neuroscience,* 9, 2737–2763.

12 Complex Adaptive Systems as Intuitive Statisticians: Causality, Contingency, and Prediction

Patricia W. Cheng and Keith J. Holyoak

INTRODUCTION

Any complex adaptive system—whether a human, some other type of animal, or an intelligent machine—that operates in a realistic environment must be able to induce causal connections among events. Causal knowledge is required to predict future states of the environment and consequences of the system's own actions. In addition, causal knowledge can potentially be used to generate and evaluate explanations of why significant events occur (or fail or occur). Part of this knowledge is based on statistical regularity among events.

At least for the past quarter century, many psychologists have seriously considered the possibility that untutored humans as well as other animals are capable of acquiring and using statistical knowledge about the structure of the environment. Peterson and Beach (1967) called people "intuitive statisticians," and Kelley (1967) proposed that people are "intuitive scientists." In the context of experimental paradigms investigating classical conditioning, other theorists have suggested that lower animals operate as intuitive statisticians (e.g., Gallistel 1990; Miller and Schachtman 1985). Although there has in fact been broad agreement that various forms of causal induction depend on the implicit computation of statistical information, the question of precisely what is computed has yet to be resolved. In the field of animal conditioning, as well as in human categorization and causal induction, various theorists have proposed that animals perform some implicit computation of statistical contingency, the difference between the proportion of events for which an effect occurs when a factor is present and that proportion when it is absent.

In all these fields, the contingency approach has been contrasted with the associationist approach exemplified by the connectionist learning rule incorporated in the Rescorla and Wagner (R-W) model of conditioning (Rescorla and Wagner 1972). The R-W model is directly related to a number of issues that lie at the very core of cognitive science. The R-W model was originally proposed as a model of classical conditioning in animals; however, a number of researchers have extended the model to account for apparently higher-order learning in humans, such as categorization and causal induction. The R-W learning rule is equivalent to the least mean squares (LMS) learning rule that is commonly used to adjust the weights on links in connectionist networks (Widrow and Hoff 1960; see also Sutton and Barto 1981). Gluck and Bower (1988), for example, have applied an adaptive connectionist network using the LMS rule to model data on human categorization (also Estes et al. 1989). Similarly, Shanks (1991) applied a connectionist implementation of the R-W model to attempt to account for the effects of cue competition in a task involving classification of diseases on the basis of symptoms (see also Chapman and Robbins 1990; Wasserman 1990). Because of its apparent simplicity and evident generality, the R-W model remains highly influential as an approach to inductive learning in adaptive systems.

Some theorists have argued that the R-W model can account for phenomena involving cue competition and other cue interactions that cannot be explained by contingency. We shall argue, however, that these advantages claimed for the R-W model over contingency theory disappear when the concept of contingency is suitably generalized along lines suggested by a number of philosophers and psychologists. In fact, the R-W model can itself be analyzed as a mechanism that computes contingency under a certain restricted condition that we will discuss later. For such cases, the R-W model is successful in predicting cue competition, although even here its successes are qualified for domains in which the adaptive system operates on representations coded in terms of the probabilities of events, for which the additivity assumption underlying the model is inappropriate. Outside of cases that satisfy the restricted condition, the R-W model does not compute contingency, and in such situations the model appears to be empirically inadequate. In contrast, a generalized contingency theory can explain a number of the phenomena that contradict predictions of the R-W model.

In this chapter we present a contingency analysis of the successes and failures of the R-W model. Our theoretical analysis may provide a framework for understanding the weakness of an important associationist model. We hope that it will guide future research concerning how statistical regularity is computed by adaptive systems to infer the causal structure of their environments in the course of learning, on the basis of which predictions are made.

WHAT IS COMPUTED IN ASSESSING REGULARITY?

The Probabilistic Contrast Model

It has long been argued that contingency is a component of the normative criterion for inferring a causal link between a factor and an effect (e.g., Kelley 1967; Rescorla 1968; Salmon 1980). Cheng and Novick (1990) proposed an extended version of contingency theory, which they termed the *probabilistic contrast model* (PCM), as a descriptive account of the use of statistical regularity in human causal induction. The model, which applies to events describable by discrete variables, assumes that one of the initial criteria for identifying potential causes is perceived temporal priority (i.e., causes must be perceived to precede their effects). The model assumes that potential causes are then evaluated by contrasts computed over a focal set. (We shall use the terms *contrast* and *contingency* interchangably.) The focal set for a contrast is a contextually determined set of events that the reasoner selects to use as input to the computation of that contrast. It is often not the universal set of events, contrary to what has been assumed by previous contingency theories in psychology. Consider the set of events selected for inferring what causes a forest fire. Reasoner will normally restrict their focal set to terrestrial events, in which oxygen is always present, and will not consider events that occur in oxygen-free outer space.

Using the events in the focal set, a *main effect* contrast specifying a potential cause i is defined as

$$\Delta p_i = p_i - p_{\bar{i}}, \tag{1}$$

where p_i is the proportion of events for which the effect occurs when factor i is present, and $p_{\bar{i}}$ is the proportion of events for which the effect occurs when factor i is absent. (The proportions are estimates of the corresponding conditional probabilities.) If Δp_i is noticeably different from 0, i is perceived as a cause. Note that, if a factor i is constantly present within the focal set, the second term in the contrast, $p_{\bar{i}}$, cannot be calculated. Thus in our forest fire example it will be impossible to compute a contrast for oxygen, since this factor is never absent within the focal set of terrestrial events; as a result, oxygen will not be considered a cause of the fire (even though people would agree, if probed, that the presence of oxygen was in fact necessary for the fire to have occurred).

Contrasts can be either positive, in which case the cause is *excitatory*, or they can be negative, in which case the cause is *inhibitory*. For example, smoking presumably has a positive contrast with respect to lung cancer, and hence can be viewed an an excitatory cause of the disease; whereas exercise has a negative contrast with respect to heart disease, and hence can be viewed as an inhibitory cause of the disease. Confidence in the assessment of a contrast is presumed to increase monotonically with the number of cases observed.

Cheng and Novick (1995) show that, for situations in which alternative causes occur and act independently of i, a positive main effect contrast for i gives an estimate of the causal power of i, as represented by the probability with which i produces the effect. This estimate is unbiased when alternative causes are absent within the focal set and/or the alternative factors present do not produce the effect. To the extent that these conditions are violated, the contrast for i tends to be an underestimate of the power of i. In the extreme case in which some alternative cause is always present within the focal set and it always produces the effect, the contrast for i, which is zero, is uninterpretable.

The above derivation also shows that, for situations in which alternative causes do not occur independently of i, the main effect contrast for i is confounded by the influence of these causes and is not interpretable as an estimate of the power of i. To eliminate this confounding, it is therefore important to compute what we will call *conditional contrast*, the contrast for the candidate factor that is conditional on holding constant the status of one (or more) other factors. A number of philosophers have proposed conditional contrasts as a criterion for inferring causality (see Cartwright 1983, 1989; Reichenbach 1956; Salmon 1980; Suppes 1970).

Main effect contrasts assess the causal status of each factor considered individually. However, it is also possible for combinations of factors to influence the effect in ways that could not be predicted by the independent influences of the individual factors. Such situations involve interactions between factors, which can be assessed by means of a generalization of main effect contrasts (Cheng and Novick 1995). For example, a two-way interaction contrast specifying the conjunction of potential causal factors i and j is defined as

$$\Delta p_{ij} = (p_{ij} - p_{\bar{i}j}) - (p_{i\bar{j}} - \bar{p}_{\bar{i}\bar{j}}) + (p_{\bar{i}j} \cdot p_{i\bar{j}}) - (p_{ij} \cdot p_{\bar{i}\bar{j}}) \qquad (2)$$

where p, as before, denotes the observed proportion of cases in which the effect occurs when a potential contributing factor is either present or absent, as denoted by its subscripts. If Δp_{ij} is noticeably greater than zero, then i and j combine to produce the effect.[1] A two-way interaction contrast is thus based on a difference of differences—here, the contrast for i when j is present minus the contrast for i when j is absent—with the nonadditivity of probabilities taken into account by the product terms in equation 2. Suppose, for example, that there are two drugs, A and B, which are safe when taken individually but usually fatal when taken together. The contrast for drug A with respect to death will therefore be high when B is also present, but zero when B is absent. Both product terms will also be zero. Accordingly, the interaction contrast (the difference between the above two contrasts corrected by the product terms) will be high.

Notice that each of the two constituent contrasts in an interaction contrast is a conditional contrast. Also notice that conditional contrasts can be described in terms of variations of the focal set. We could say that, in the focal set of events in which drug B is administered, the contrast for drug A is high whereas, in the focal set of events in which drug B is not administered, the contrast for drug A is zero. Furthermore, both of these conditional contrasts will differ from the unconditional contrast for A. This unconditional contrast is equivalent to the main effect contrast for drug A over the focal set of all events involving the presence or absence of drug B.

Cheng and Novick (1990, 1991, 1992) have provided support for contrasts computed over an accurately identified focal set as a descriptive model of human causal inference. The model successfully predicts simple and conjunctive causal attributions and explains a number of empirical phenomena involving human causal attributions that had previously been considered biases. To illustrate the role of focal sets, consider the psychological distinction between causes and enabling conditions. In our example about what causes a forest fire, people might consider a lightning strike as the cause, but they will view the presence of oxygen as merely an enabling condition. Although oxygen is necessary for the fire, it is constant in the relevant focal set so that a contrast cannot be computed. Notice that, in a different context, which evokes a focal set within which the presence of oxygen may vary (for example, a special laboratory intended to be oxygen-free), oxygen will be considered the cause of a fire that breaks out when oxygen leaks into that environment. The assessment of causation thus depends on pragmatic contextual influences. In terms of PCM, a potential causal factor that covaries with the effect (i.e., has a noticeable contrast with respect to the effect) within the contextually determined focal set (e.g., lightning with respect to forest fires in the context of a forest) will be viewed as a cause, whereas a factor that is constant within that focal set (e.g., oxygen in a forest), but is known to covary with the effect in some other focal set (e.g., oxygen covaries with fire in special environments in which the occurrence of oxygen varies), is viewed as an enabling condition. As will be elaborated later, an enabling condition can be distinguished from an alternative cause that happens to be constantly present in the current focal set. We will return to the challenge that the distinction between causes and enabling conditions poses for R-W.

The most central claim of contingency theory, which is reflected in PCM, is that causal attributions depend not only on the probability of the effect given the presence of a cue, but also on the probability of the effect given the absence of the cue. In other words, a cue is viewed as causal only if its presence makes a difference to the probability of the effect. However, theorists have often resisted the notion that humans and other animals implicitly tally information about what happens in the absence of a potential cause. In particular, associationist models of animal conditioning have eschewed any direct representation of cause-absent information. One apparent reason for the reluctance to posit representations of cause-absent information is that any event could potentially be defined in terms of an indefinitely large number of absent factors. It would indeed be bizarre to suppose, for example, that your understanding of this passage might be caused by the (presumed) absence of ravens in the room in which you now sit. The generalized contingency model addresses

Complex Adaptive Systems as Intuitive Statisticians

this problem by restricting the initial tabulation of cause-absent information to those factors that are plausible causes according to prior knowledge or according to observed pairing with the effect. The challenge for associationist models has been to account for apparent influences of contingency on learning without introducing representations of the absence of potential causal factors. As we will see, the empirical successes and failures of the R-W model can be differentiated by when it succeeds or fails to implicitly tally cause-absent information.

The Rescorla-Wagner Model

The most influential associationist theory of conditioning over the past two decades has been the R-W model. Interestingly, Rescorla (1968) was a harbinger of the importance of contingency in classical conditioning, which he demonstrated with elegant experiments showing that conditioning depends on events that occur in the absence as well as the presence of a cue. Nonetheless, he then went on to develop an associationist model that avoided postulation of representations of the absences of cues. The R-W model represents the learning of an association between cue i (e.g., a tone that is present in the current event) and outcome j (e.g., shock) by a change in the strength of a link between two elemental units, one representing cue i, and the other representing outcome j. (Cue i and outcome j are traditionally termed the *conditioned stimulus* and the *unconditioned stimulus*, respectively.) For any cue i that is present during the event, strength is revised according to the rule

$$\Delta V_{ij} = \alpha_i \beta_j \left(\lambda_j - \sum_{k=1}^{n} V_{kj} \right),$$
(3)

where ΔV_{ij} is the change in associative strength between cue unit i and outcome unit j as a result of the current event, α_i and β_j are rate parameters that depend on the salience of i and j, respectively, and λ_j is the desired output corresponding to the actual outcome. Typically, if the outcome is present, λ_j is defined as 1; if the outcome is absent, this value is defined as 0.

$$\sum_{k=1}^{n} V_{kj},$$

defined as the sum of the current strengths of links to unit j from all units representing the n cues present in that event, is the actual output of the network predicting the outcome. If cue i is not present during the event, the associative strength of its cue unit remains unchanged. (The absence of a cue is not represented by any unit.) Learning continues until there is no discrepancy between the desired and actual outputs (averaged over a number of trials). In addition to the particular stimuli present (e.g., a tone), the cues are assumed to include one that represents a context present in every event (e.g., the conditioning cage). In causal terms, each cue i is a potential cause, and j is the effect. The strengths that are updated according to equation 3 are equivalent to weights on the links in a two-layered connectionist network, with the predicting cues represented on the input layer and the predicted outcome on the output layer.

A major attraction of R-W is its ability to explain the effects of interaction between cues. For example, it predicts the phenomenon of *blocking* (e.g., Kamin 1969; Rescorla 1981). Let P be a previously trained predictive cue (i.e., the presence of P has been paired with the outcome, and the absence of P has been paired with the absence of the outcome). Consider the situation in which a novel cue, R, in combination with P, is paired with the outcome. It has been shown that, despite the positive unconditional contrast for R, the learning of this cue is blocked if it is presented only in combination with P. According to R-W, learning occurs only when there is some discrepancy between the predicted and actual outcomes. Because a predictive cue fully predicts the outcome as a consequence of prior pairings, no conditioning would accrue to R.

Rescorla (1968) demonstrated that no conditioning accrues at asymptote to a cue if the effect occurs equally often in its absence as in its presence. The R-W model explains this effect of contingency by the reduction of learning to the varying cue as a result of the strength that accrues to the constant context cue. More generally, the greater the strength of the context cue, the more it reduces the strength of the varying cue.

A second effect of cue interaction explained by R-W concerns the phenomenon of *conditioned inhibition*. It has been shown that a novel cue, I, acquires inhibitory associative strength when it—in combination with a predictive cue, P—is paired with the absence of the outcome. In comparison, a novel cue that by itself is paired with the absence of the outcome acquires zero strength. According to R-W, the combination of P and I is initially expected to produce the outcome (due to the summing of the positive strength of P and the zero strength of I). A discrepancy between the predicted and actual outcomes therefore arises when the combination is paired with the absence of the outcome. This discrepancy leads to a reduction in the strength of I, which therefore becomes negative. (Although the strength of P will also be reduced on such trials, P will regain its strength on other trials in which the outcome continues to be predicted by the occurrence of P in the absence of I.) At asymptote the negative strength of I offsets the positive strength of P, leading to a net expectation of 0 on trials on which the combination of P and I is presented.

Limitations of the R-W Model

Despite its notable successes, the R-W model has several well-known limitations (see Gallistel 1990; Holland et al. 1986; Miller and Matzel 1988). First, whereas the model predicts that the strength of a conditioned inhibitor should be revised upward toward zero when it is presented alone without reinforcement, in fact such a procedure fails to extinguish the conditioned inhibitor (Zimmer-Hart and Rescorla 1974). Second, the R-W model is unable to account for apparent changes in the associative strength of a cue that occur over a period in which that cue has not been presented (because the model updates only the strengths of cues that are present on a trial). For example, even though presentation of an inhibitor without reinforcement does not reduce its inhibitory power, extinction of the excitatory cue with which the inhibitor had been paired during acquisition can effectively weaken the inhibitor (Kaplan and Hearst 1985; Kasprow, Schachtman, and Miller 1987; Miller and Schachtman 1985). It is as if, when the animal learns that the excitor no longer signals danger, it also loses confidence that the previously paired inhibitor signals safety, even though the inhibitor has not been presented during the extinction phase. Similarly, a cue that was initially "overshadowed" by a more potent excitor will later gain excitatory potential during its absence if the overshadowing cue is extinguished (Kaufman and Bolles 1981; Matzel, Schachtman, and Miller 1985; see also Miller and Matzel 1987). These "indirect" effects on conditioning cannot be explained by R-W, according to which the associative strength of a cue that is absent should not be updated (see equation 3).

Third, the R-W model does not explain the learned irrelevance of a cue that has been randomly paired with an unconditioned stimulus (i.e., the effect) before the effect is made contingent on the cue. Contradicting R-W, the conditioning of such a cue relative to a novel cue is severely retarded. These types of cues are predicted by the model to be equivalent, because they both should begin the conditioning phase with zero associative strength. Fourth, the R-W model predicts that the learning of the novel cue in the blocking paradigm described above will be completely blocked at asymptote. Available empirical results regarding causal induction by humans show, however, that blocking is only partial (e.g., Chapman and Robbins 1990; Shanks 1991; Shanks and Dickinson 1987; Waldmann and Holyoak 1992).

INTERPRETING CONDITIONING PHENOMENA IN TERMS OF CONTINGENCIES

Associative learning models are often contrasted with models based on statistical contingency. Shanks and others (e.g., Chapman and Robbins 1990; but see Chapman 1991) have examined the special case in which the contingency of each of the multiple potentially causal factors that are present is calculated unconditionally over what might be termed the "universal focal set"[2] of all events in the experiment. However, when multiple candidate causal factors are present, contingency for a factor should be computed over subsets of the universal set of events that are conditional on the constant presence or absence of other factors. We shall now argue that contingency theory, as elaborated with the notion of focal sets in PCM, can account not only for phenomena that have been viewed as major successes for the R-W model, but also for phenomena that contradict the R-W model. Moreover, it provides a framework for understanding when and why the R-W model fails.

Learned Irrelevance

According to PCM, conditioning cue i requires creating a difference between p_i and $p_{\bar{i}}$. The rate at which this difference is created by any single event will be slower for a cue that has been randomly paired with an outcome than for a novel cue, because the cue that had been randomly paired, unlike the novel cue, begins conditioning with large denominators in the two proportions. The impact of any single event in the conditioning phase, therefore, is smaller for the old cue than for the novel cue. Suppose that a cue was present on 100 trials and absent on another 100 trials, and the outcome occurred on 40 trials of each type. The resulting contrast would be zero. Now suppose that, in a subsequent conditioning phase, the outcome always occurs on 5 trials in which this preexposed cue is present, and it never occurs on 5 trials on which this cue is absent. These 10 trials, together with the 200 initial trials, will lead to a contrast of $5/105$ (i.e., $45/105 - 40/105$). In comparison, for a novel cue, the same 10 trials in the conditioning phase will lead to a contrast of 1 (i.e., $5/5 - 0/5$). The result, then, will be a marked attenuation of the rate of conditioning for the preexposed cue relative to a novel cue.

Conditional Contingencies and the Interpretation of Cue Interaction

When multiple potential causal factors are present, philosophers and computer scientists have proposed that assessment of causal relations should not be based on contingencies computed over the universal set of events (Cartwright 1983, 1989; Pearl 1988; Reichenbach 1956; Salmon 1980, 1984; Simpson 1951; Suppes 1970, 1984), because in these situations unconditional contingencies do not reflect what people intuitively judge to be normative causal inferences. In particular, people distinguish between a genuine cause and a spurious cause—a factor that is contingently related to the effect, but is not a cause of it. Unconditional contingencies do not reflect this difference.

These theorists have proposed that, normatively, if a factor is known to be a cause of an effect, then determining the causal status of another factor requires that the contingency of the latter be calculated separately conditional on the presence and on the absence of that cause (a test of "conditional independence").[3] Testing for conditional independence is analogous to comparing experimental conditions to control conditions in standard experimental design, where extraneous variables are kept constant across conditions. Although this criterion has not been uncontested among philosophers (e.g., Cartwright 1989; Salmon 1984), the prevalent adoption of the analogous principle of experimental design gives an indication of its normative appeal. One important difference between conditional contrasts and comparisons involving experimental design is that conditional contrasts includes observational situations, which generally provide less firm support for causal inferences. In terms of PCM, the adoption of the criterion of conditional contrasts involves computing contrasts for a potential causal factor separately for focal sets that are restricted to events of which the known cause is (a) present, and (b) absent rather than computing them over the universal set of events.

We shall next consider the interpretation of tests of conditional independence, describe a process model for assessing conditional independence, and illustrate the explanation of cue interaction effects according to conditional contingencies in terms of this process model. Let us first consider the interpretation of some possible outcomes of the test of conditional independence for a target factor that has a positive unconditional contingency with the effect (i.e., a possible excitatory cause). For example, suppose we are assessing possible causes of cancer and that smoking cigarettes is an established cause. Now we observe that coffee drinking is also statistically relevant to cancer in that the probability of cancer is higher for people who drink over five cups per day than for those who drink less coffee. However, let us further suppose that people who drink large quantities of coffee also tend to smoke. To tease the influence of coffee drinking apart from that of smoking, it is desirable to calculate the conditional contingency between coffee drinking and cancer separately for cases involving the presence vs. the absence of smoking. The following are four possible outcomes that will be relevant in interpreting blocking and similar cue interaction effects:

Case 1: If both conditional contingencies for the target factor are positive, then the target factor will be interpreted as a genuine cause. For example, if coffee drinking increases the risk of cancer both for smokers and for nonsmokers, then coffee drinking will be interpreted as a genuine cause (unless it turned out to be confounded with some other cause of cancer, such as eating fatty foods).

Case 2: If contingencies for the target factor conditional on both the presence and the absence of the established cause are zero, then that factor will be interpreted as a spurious cause. It is said to be "screened off" (i.e., normatively blocked) from the effect by the conditionalizing cause. For our example, the statistical link between coffee drinking and cancer would be attributed entirely to the confounding between coffee drinking and smoking.

Case 3: If the effect always occurs in the presence of the established cause, regardless of whether the target factor occurs (therefore, the contingency conditional on the presence of the established cause is zero), but the contingency conditional on the absence of the causal factor is positive, then the target factor will be interpreted as a genuine cause. This situation would arise if smoking always caused cancer, so that coffee drinking did not increase the risk of cancer for smokers, but did increase the risk for nonsmokers. In this situation coffee drinking would be interpreted as a genuine cause of cancer. As noted earlier, the zero contingency for a candidate factor (coffee drinking) in the presence of an alternative factor that always produces the effect (smoking) does not give an interpretable estimate of the causal power of the candidate factor. In other words, it would likely be attributed to a ceiling effect (i.e., smoking by itself generates the maximal cancer risk, so that the detrimental impact of coffee drinking is masked for smokers).

Case 4: If the contingency of the target factor conditional on the presence of the established cause is positive, but the effect never occurs in the absence of the established cause (therefore, the contingency conditional on the absence of the established cause is zero), then the two factors will be interpreted as interacting to produce the effect (see equation 2). Such an interaction would exist if coffee drinking in combination with smoking increased the risk of cancer for smokers, but had no effect on the probability of cancer for nonsmokers.

One problem that complicates the test of conditional independence is that the information required for computing the two conditional contingencies is not always available. Recall that in the blocking paradigm a novel cue R is paired with the outcome only when a predictive cue P is also present. Table 12.1 gives a schematic representation of the typical probability of the outcomes for the two cues. The $\overline{P}$ and R cell receives no information, and the outcome always occurs when P is present. Because P is known to have a positive contingency with respect to the outcome, the status of R should be based on conditional contrasts. When the focal set is restricted to events in which P is present (the top row), R has a zero contrast. When the focal set is restricted to events in which P is absent (the bottom row), however, the contrast for R cannot be computed. Because this cue is never presented in the absence of P in this paradigm, $p_{R \cap \overline{P}}$ is undefined due to division by zero. As Waldmann and Holyoak (1992) noted, because the level of the effect produced by P is already at ceiling, it is

Table 12.1 Probability of the outcomes for cues P and R in the blocking paradigm

	R	$\overline{R}$
P	+	+
$\overline{R}$		0

+ = a positive probability of the outcome
0 = zero probability of the outcome

Complex Adaptive Systems as Intuitive Statisticians

impossible to determine whether the redundant cue R is a spurious cause (case 2 above) or a genuine cause (case 3). Given that relevant information is missing from the blocking design, subjects who adopt the criterion of conditional independence will be uncertain about the predictive status of the redundant cue, as opposed to being certain that this cue is not predictive, as implied by the R-W learning rule.[4]

It is important to note that there is an asymmetry between the informativeness of tests conditional on the absence vs. the presence of other causes: the tests most likely to clearly rule out a target factor as an independent excitatory cause are those based on the absence of conditionalizing cues. In particular, finding a zero contingency conditional on the absence of other causes clearly rules out a factor as an independent excitatory cause (i.e., it is either spurious, as in case 2, or a component of an interaction contrast, as in case 4), whereas finding a zero contingency conditional on the presence of a known cause is inconclusive (the target might be spurious, as in case 2, but it might instead be genuine, as in case 3). (This interpretation excludes consideration of inhibitory causes, to which we shall return.) Similarly, finding a positive contingency conditional on the absence of other causes constitutes evidence that the cue is an independent excitatory cause (for which case 1 or case 3 might obtain), but a positive contingency conditional on the presence of a known cause could indicate either a genuine independent excitatory cause (as in case 1) or a component of an interactive excitatory cause (as in case 4). Moreover, as noted earlier, the main effect contrast for a candidate factor conditional on the absence of alternative factors gives a better estimate of the causal power of that factor than its contrast conditional on the presence of alternative factors. The fact that tests conditional on the absence rather than the presence of other causes are more informative is reflected in experimental design: if only one type of conditionalizing test can be performed, scientists generally favor designs in which a target factor is manipulated while ensuring that other known causes are absent rather than present. We therefore assume that people will prefer to conditionalize each target factor on the simultaneous absence of all established or likely causes, because this is the test that will be maximally informative.

The above analyses of the informativeness of conditional contingency tests apply in the case of possible excitatory causes, but not in that of possible inhibitory causes. A test of a target factor in the absence of all established causes cannot demonstrate that the factor is an inhibitor because, unless some excitatory cause is operating, the impact of an inhibitor will be obscured by a cellar effect. That is, if the outcome is not being produced by some excitatory cause, an inhibitor cannot achieve a nonzero contingency. We assume that, as a general principle based on a preference for cognitive simplicity, a factor will not be deemed causal unless positive evidence of a causal interpretation is obtained. Accordingly, the default interpretation of a zero contingency is that the factor is noncausal (rather than inhibitory). This assumption is supported by the fact that simply presenting a cue alone without reinforcement, while another cue presented alone is reinforced, generally does not yield strong conditioned inhibition (Baker 1977). The former cue has a negative unconditional contingency, but its contingency conditional on the presence of the latter cue cannot be computed due to the lack of information on the frequency of the effect when both cues are present. Thus for a candidate inhibitory factor the most informative tests will involve computation of its contingency conditional on the presence of a single excitor, coupled with the absence of all other known causal factors. If there is more than one known excitor, it will be desirable to perform separate tests for the candidate factor conditional on the presence of each excitor in turn. If the candidate yields a negative contingency conditional on the presence of an excitor, it will be interpreted either as a main effect inhibitory cause or as a component of an inhibitory interaction.

Conditioned Inhibition and "Indirect" Extinction of Associative Strength

PCM can account both for the acquisition of conditioned inhibition and for the failure to extinguish a conditioned inhibitor by presenting it alone without the outcome. Table 12.2 schematically represents the typical probability of the outcomes for the two cues in the learning phase of the conditioned inhibition paradigm. When P is presented alone, the outcome occurs, but when P and I are presented in combination, the outcome does not occur. No information is received about the $\bar{P}$ and I cell (the empty one in the table) during the learning phases. Notice that the set of events so far shows a negative conditional contrast for I conditional on the presence of P (i.e., $p_{I|P} < p_{\bar{I}|P}$). Therefore, PCM predicts that I will become inhibitory. Now consider an extinction phase in which I is presented alone without the outcome. The $\bar{P}$ and I cell will be filled in with the information that the probability of the outcome in the presence of I alone is zero. This information will have no impact on the crucial conditional contingency—that of I in the presence of P—and hence will not yield extinction (Zimmer-Hart and Rescorla 1972).

Table 12.2 Probability of the outcomes in the learning phase of the conditioned inhibition paradigm

	I	$\bar{I}$
P	0	+
$\bar{P}$		0

+ = a positive probability of the outcome
0 = zero probability of the outcome

In addition to correctly predicting that inhibition cannot be extinguished directly by presenting the inhibitory cue without reinforcement, PCM can account for results demonstrating that conditioned inhibition can be extinguished indirectly, by extinguishing the excitatory strength of the cue with which the inhibitor had been paired (Kaplan and Hearst 1985; Kasprow, Schachtman, and Miller 1987; Miller and Schachtman 1985). As we explained, this counterintuitive finding contradicts the R-W model. In this indirect extinction procedure, P rather than I is presented alone without the outcome. Reducing the frequency of the outcome in the P and $\bar{\text{I}}$ cell reduces the magnitude of the negative contrast for I conditional on the presence of P, and hence diminishes the perceived inhibitory impact of I (e.g., Miller and Schachtman 1985).

A Process Model for Assessing Conditional Dependence and Independence

We have so far been describing contingency theory at the computational level of analysis. Here we will describe an algorithmic instantiation of the theory. This process model is based on PCM, with extensions to specify which conditional contingencies are computed. Contingency analysis can of course be evaluated independently of this particular instantiation, but this model will serve to provide a detailed illustration of how contingency theory might account for cue interactions.

A plausible psychological model of causal inference based on contingency analysis must specify mechanisms that would allow people to decide (a) what cues should be used to conditionalize others, (b) what conditional tests to perform once a set of conditionalizing cues has been selected, and (c) how to integrate the resulting contingency information to make causal assessments of the cues. In situations in which there is no guidance from prior knowledge, every cue is potentially causal. Given n binary cues, exhaustively conditionalizing the contingencies for each target cue on every combination of the presence and absence of the other cues requires computing $2^{n-1} \cdot n$ contingencies. Given processing limitations, it is crucial to specify how people select which contingencies to compute. It is also likely that many of the cue combinations that would be relevant to a contingency analysis will never actually occur. Accordingly, it is necessary to specify which contingencies will be computed in the face of missing information.

Let us first consider the selection of conditionalizing cues. The ideal set of conditionalizing cues will include all those and only those that are actually causal. Given the limitations of knowledge, the best people can do is to select as conditionalizing cues those they currently believe to be plausible causes. In cases in which prior knowledge is relevant, such knowledge will be used to establish certain cues as likely causes, and the contingencies for other cues will then be conditionalized on the (perhaps tentatively) established causes. If such prior knowledge is lacking, people may nonetheless use some heuristic criterion to select an initial set of conditionalizing cues. A simple heuristic that might be employed is to include any cue that is noticeably associated with the effect. That is, people may follow the tacit rule: If the effect is likely to occur when the cue occurs, tentatively assume that the cue may be causal. Contingencies are not computed in this initial phase of selecting conditionalizing cues; rather, people simply identify a pool of cues that have been paired with the effect, which will be treated as an initial set of plausible causes. There is some evidence of such an initial phase of cue selection based on positive associations. For example, Rescorla (1972) found that a cue that was randomly paired with the outcome (i.e., one that was associated with the outcome but noncontingent with it) appeared to initially acquire associative strength, which eventually disappeared after several sessions of training. The association heuristic suggested here implies that this phase implicitly ignores the possibility of cues' being interactive or inhibitory causes. The sole presence of an inhibitory cause, for example, will be perceived as a lack of association.

Contingency assessment will occur in the subsequent phase, in which people will compute the conditional contingencies of all cues based on the set of conditionalizing cues identified in the initial phase. In Cheng and Novick's (1990) terminology, the set of conditionalizing cues defines the focal sets for contingency computations. The initial set of conditionalizing cues can be dynamically updated if contingency assessments indicate that cues that at first appeared to be plausible causes are in fact spurious or that cues initially viewed as causally irrelevant are in fact causal. That is, after conditional contrasts are calculated based on the initial set of conditionalizing cues, these contrasts will be used to update that set of cues. Cues in the set that have zero or low contrasts may be dropped, and other cues outside the set that have noticeable positive or negative contrasts may be added. Changes in the set of conditionalizing cues will in turn change the relevant conditional contingencies for all cues, which may alter subsequent causal assessments. The entire assessment process will thus be iterative. If the values of the cues stabilize as the process iterates, the process will return these values and stop. Otherwise, the process will stop after an externally determined number of iterations.

In assessing conditional contingencies, heuristics will be required to determine which tests (of those possible given the cue combinations that are actually presented) should in fact be performed. We assume, based on the arguments presented earlier, that people will prefer to conditionalize the contingency for each target factor on the simultaneous absence of all conditionalizing cues. If this is not possible, then they will try to select a focal set in which as many conditionalizing cues are absent as possible, while the rest of the conditionalizing cues are constantly present.

In general, application of the contingency analysis will necessarily be constrained by the information actually provided by observation.

In addition to specifying what cues are selected to form the conditionalizing set and which conditional contingencies are computed, a process model must specify a response mechanism that translates the calculated contingencies into causal judgments. If all conditionalizing cues can be kept either absent or present and there are no ceiling effects for excitatory cues, the confidence associated with the contrast values based on these focal sets will be relatively high. But if the experimental design omits cases that would be relevant in assessing the conditional dependence or independence of a target factor such that there are ceiling effects or some of the conditionalizing cues cannot be kept constant, the confidence associated with the contrast values based on these focal sets will be relatively low. In such experiments, if subjects are not given the choice of withholding judgment, they may base their causal assessments on a mixture of the best available focal sets—for example, the unconditional as well as the conditional contingencies for cues. Mean ratings over subjects may therefore reflect some mixture of the evidence provided by conditional and unconditional contingencies.

When subjects do not all use one and the same focal set to compute contingencies, the mean causal judgment about a cue (averaged across subjects in an experimental condition) should reflect some mixture of assessments based on the multiple focal sets used. These may include the universal focal set of all events in the experiment (i.e., unconditional contingencies) and various more restricted focal sets (i.e., conditional contingencies). The response mechanism must then account for how multiple contingencies are integrated. The clearest situation is that in which the relevant unconditional and conditional contingencies for a factor are all computable and equal to zero, in which case subjects should be certain that the factor is noncausal. Beyond this limiting case, we make no claim about the exact quantitative mapping between contingency values and subjects' responses. Our assumption is that subjects' causal estimates will increase monotonically with a nonnegatively weighted function of the contingency values of their focal sets. Individual subjects may compute and integrate multiple contingencies for a cue (e.g., by simple averaging). Alternatively, each subject may use only one focal set, but different subjects may use different focal sets, in which case the mean ratings may mask distributions that are in fact multimodal. We will refer to the assumption that causal ratings may be based on multiple contingencies (calculated either by individual subjects or by different subjects) as the "mixture-of-focal-sets" hypothesis. As we will see, this hypothesis helps to explain circumstances in which partial rather than complete blocking is observed.

Computing contingency conditional on the presence of an alternative cause raises the problem of how an alternative cause that happens to be constantly present in the current focal set can be distinguished from an enabling condition. To distinguish between them, Cheng and Novick (1992) refined their definition of an enabling condition as follows. Let i be a factor that is constantly present in the current focal set. Factor i is an enabling condition for a cause j in that focal set if i covaries with the effect in another focal set and j no longer covaries with the effect in a focal set in which i is constantly absent. In contrast, i is an alternative to cause j if i covaries with the effect in another focal set and there exists a focal set in which i is constantly absent, but j continues to covary with the effect in that set.

To summarize, our proposed process model assumes that subjects will (a) identify as initial conditionalizing cues those that are noticeably associated with the effect; (b) compute contingencies for each target factor conditional on the absence of as many conditionalizing cues as possible, dynamically revising the set of conditionalizing cues in the process; and then (c) use the computed conditional contingencies and/or unconditional contingencies to produce causal assessments for the cues.

Interpreting Blocking, Partial Blocking, and Other Cue Interaction Effects

We will now consider how generalized contingency theory, in particular as implemented in the process model we have described, can account for blocking, partial blocking, overshadowing, retroactive extinction of overshadowing, and other cue-interaction effects.

Blocking and Partial Blocking

In the standard blocking design illustrated in table 12.1, the unconditional contingency is higher for the predictive cue P than for the redundant cue R (because the outcome sometimes occurs in the absence of R, but never in the absence of P), although the contingency is positive for both. Thus even subjects who compute contingency over the universal focal set would be expected to show at least partial blocking (i.e., the higher response strength for P than R, both strengths being positive). It is possible, however, to design an experiment in which unconditional contingency is held constant for two cues, and yet their causal statuses differ. Such designs have been used in classical conditioning experiments, as well as in experiments on causality judgments by humans (Chapman and Robbins 1990, experiment 1; Shanks 1991, experiment 2). The design used by Shanks is schematized in table 12.3. After being presented with a series of "case histories" (patterns of patients' symptoms associated with various fictitious diseases), subjects were asked to rate how strongly they associated each symptom with each disease using a 0–100 rating scale. In what Shanks termed the "contingent" set, the compound cue AB signaled the presence of disease 1 (15 trials), but symptom C by itself did so as well

Table 12.3 Conditions, trial types, number of trials, and percentage of correct diagnoses for experiment 2 of Shanks (1991). (Adapted from Shanks 1991.)

Condition	Trial type	Trials	% correct
"Contingent"	C → D1	15	100
	AB → D1	15	100
	B → 0	15	94
"Noncontingent"	DE → D2	15	100
	E → D2	15	100
	F → 0	15	94

(15 trials). However, cue B by itself signaled the absence of the disease (15 trials), as did the absence of A, B, and C (45 trials). In the "noncontingent"[5] set, compound cue DE signaled the presence of disease 2 (15 trials), as did the presence of cue E alone (15 trials). In contrast, cue F alone signaled the absence of the disease (15 trials), as did the joint absence of D, E, and F (45 trials).

The critical comparison is between the association rating given to symptom A for disease 1 and the association rating given to symptom D for disease 2. Although the contingency computed over the entire set of events presented for both relations is .8 (see figure 12.1), the R-W model predicts that, because D is paired with a better predictor, E, subjects should rate D as less associated than the corresponding symptom A, which is paired only with a nonpredictor, B. This difference was observed. In other words, the rating given to a cue was reduced if a competing cue was a better predictor of the relevant disease, even through unconditional contingency was equated. But although subjects gave higher mean ratings to A than to D (59 vs. 34, respectively), even cue D received modestly positive ratings, whereas the R-W model predicts that at asymptote the strength of the association between D and disease 2 should be 0 (see Melz et al. 1993). Shanks's experiment is representative of several other cases in which human subjects show only partial blocking rather than complete blocking as the R-W model would predict (e.g., Chapman and Robbins 1990; Shanks and Dickinson 1987; Waldmann and Holyoak 1992).

A contingency analysis of this and another cue competition experiment by Shanks is provided by Melz and co-workers (1993). Figure 12.1 illustrates the computation of contingencies for the cues crucial for comparison, A in the "contingent" set and D in the "noncontingent" set. As shown in the figure, the unconditional contingency (i.e., the contingency computed over the universal set of all events) is .8 for critical cue A with respect to disease 1, as is that for cue D with respect to disease 2. To test conditional independence of these cues with respect to the particular disease, we apply the process model described above. With respect to disease 1 (see the left half of figure 12.1), only cues A, B, and C will be identified as initial conditionalizing cues, because these are the only cues that are ever accompanied by disease 1. Cue B has a contingency of 0 in

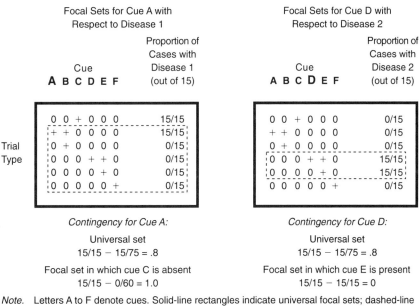

Focal Sets for Cue A with Respect to Disease 1

Focal Sets for Cue D with Respect to Disease 2

	Cue A B C D E F	Proportion of Cases with Disease 1 (out of 15)		Cue A B C D E F	Proportion of Cases with Disease 2 (out of 15)
Trial Type	0 0 + 0 0 0	15/15		0 0 + 0 0 0	0/15
	+ + 0 0 0 0	15/15		+ + 0 0 0 0	0/15
	0 + 0 0 0 0	0/15		0 + 0 0 0 0	0/15
	0 0 0 + + 0	0/15		0 0 0 + + 0	15/15
	0 0 0 0 + 0	0/15		0 0 0 0 + 0	15/15
	0 0 0 0 0 +	0/15		0 0 0 0 0 +	0/15

Contingency for Cue A:

Universal set

15/15 − 15/75 = .8

Focal set in which cue C is absent

15/15 − 0/60 = 1.0

Contingency for Cue D:

Universal set

15/15 − 15/75 = .8

Focal set in which cue E is present

15/15 − 15/15 = 0

Note. Letters A to F denote cues. Solid-line rectangles indicate universal focal sets; dashed-line rectangles indicate conditional focal sets. Large bold letters denote the crucial cues for comparison.

Figure 12.1 Potential focal sets in Shanks's (1991) experiment 2. (From Melz et al. 1993.) *Note:* Letters A to F denote cues. Solid-line rectangles indicate universal focal sets; dashed-line rectangles indicate conditional focal sets. Large bold letters denote the crucial cues for comparison.

the focal set, from which both A and C are absent (rows 3–6). Cue C has a conditional contingency of 1.0 in the focal set, from which cues A and B are both absent (rows 1 and 4–6). Each of the remaining cues (D, E, and F) has a conditional contingency of 0 in the focal set, from which all conditionalizing cues (A, B and C) are absent (rows 4–6).

The contingency for cue A conditional on the absence of both B and C cannot be computed, because A does not occur in the absence of B. However, A has a contingency of 1.0 in the focal set, in which B is present and C is absent (rows 2–3). From the first iteration of conditional contingency assessment, it follows that B will be assessed as noncausal and be dropped from the set of conditionalizing cues, so that only A and C will remain as conditionalizing cues. The relevant contingency for A then becomes that which is conditional on the absence of C (rows 2–6, enclosed by a dashed rectangle in the illustration) and has a value of 1.0. This is equal to the value of the relevant conditional contingency obtained for A in the previous iteration. As is the case for A, none of the values of the relevant conditional contingencies for any of the other cues change as a result of dropping B from the conditionalizing set.

For disease 2 (see the right half of figure 12.1), cues D and E will be selected as conditionalizing cues. Because D never occurs in the absence

Complex Adaptive Systems as Intuitive Statisticians

of E, its contingency can be calculated conditional only on the presence of E. For this focal set (enclosed by the dashed rectangle in the illustration), the conditional contingency for D with respect to disease 2 is 0. The difference between the computed contingency for cue A with respect to disease 1 (1.0) and that for cue D with respect to disease 2 (0) provides an explanation for cue competition—the lower ratings given to D than to A. In addition, cue E has a contingency of 1.0 conditional on the absence of D (rows 1–3 and 5–6 in the right half of figure 12.1). All other cues have a contingency of 0 with respect to disease 2 in the absence of cues D and E.

Now consider how partial blocking might arise. As we mentioned, the R-W model predicts that associative learning of a novel cue in the blocking paradigm will be completely blocked at asymptote; yet all available empirical results regarding humans show that blocking is not complete. The above contingency of 0 for cue D was conditional on the presence of cue E. However, in the presence of E the effect always occurs. Since it was not possible to conditionalize the contingency for D on the absence of E, subjects should be uncertain of the interpretation of the contingency value of 0. Accordingly, at least some subjects may assess the unconditional contingency for D (i.e., over the universal set of events), which is 0.8. Assuming that subjects' causal ratings reflect a mixture (either within individual subjects or across subjects) of these two contingencies, D will receive a relatively low but positive mean rating. That is, it will be partially blocked. Moreover, the prediction of cue competition remains, since the contingency for A (1.0) is still higher than the mixture of the contingencies for D (0.8 and 0). In sum, for situations in which there is no focal set that allows an unambiguous interpretation, if there is a mixture of focal sets either within subjects or across subjects, contingency theory predicts partial blocking in addition to cue competition.

Overshadowing and Retroactive Reduction of Overshadowing

A similar contingency interpretation can be provided for experiments that have demonstrated that a salient predictive cue acquires greater strength than a less salient cue that is perfectly correlated with it (i.e., the salient cue overshadows the less salient cue) and that extinguishing the salient competing predictor can increase the excitatory power of the previously overshadowed cue (Kaufman and Bolles 1981; Matzel, Schachtman, and Miller 1985).[6]

When two cues are perfectly correlated with each other, the association of the salient cue with the outcome is likely to be noticed earlier than the association of the less salient cue. Accordingly, the former cue will be selected earlier than the latter as a conditionalizing cue. It follows that the subject will initially attempt to conditionalize the contingency of the nonsalient or "pallid" cue on the state of the salient cue, but not vice versa. But due to the absence of information in this design regarding the occurrence of the outcome in the presence of one cue and the absence of the other cue, neither of the relevant contingencies for the pallid cue (i.e., those conditional on the presence and on the absence of the salient cue) can be computed. Accordingly, the subject will be uncertain about the causal status of the pallid cue during this phase. Meanwhile, given the positive unconditional contingency of the salient cue with respect to the outcome, this cue will be judged causal. Hence, it will be confirmed as a conditionalizing cue for computing the contingency of the pallid cue, whereas the pallid cue may never acquire that status with respect to the salient cue. In the phase that ensues in a retroactive paradigm, however, the salient cue is presented alone (and it is not followed by the outcome). Information then becomes available for computing the contingency of the pallid cue conditional on the presence of the salient cue. The resulting positive value of this conditional contingency predicts the increased causal strength of the pallid cue.[7]

Direction of Causality

The above analyses of Shanks's results assume that subjects based their inferences on calculations that were in turn based on probabilities of diseases conditional on the various symptoms. This seems likely for at least some subjects in view of the instructions and the learning procedure. The instructions did not make it clear, for example, whether a disease name referred to the cause of the associated symptoms or was simply a label for them. However, if the causal direction is made salient to subjects, then the predictions of the R-W versus contingency approaches are very different indeed. The R-W model, although often interpreted as an account of causal induction, does not in fact draw any distinction between a context in which cues are interpreted as possible causes of an effect (the typical situation involving *predictive* learning) and a context in which cues are interpreted as possible effects of a common cause (*diagnostic* learning). Diagnostic tasks require reasoning in a backward causal direction (e.g., from symptoms, which are effects, to underlying diseases, which are interpreted as causes of the symptoms).

Waldmann and Holyoak (1992) have shown that the degree of cue competition is radically different depending on whether people interpret the cues as the causes of an effect to be predicted or as the effects of a cause to be diagnosed. In their experiment 3, Waldmann and Holyoak exposed subjects to a series of trials in which states of previously unfamiliar cues (buttons connected to an alarm system) were paired with states of the alarm system. Each button had two settings, on and off, as did the alarm system. Subjects in a predictive condition were told that pressing one or more buttons would cause the alarm to go on. In this condition the states of the buttons were thus characterized as possible causes, and the states of the alarm system were characterized as possible effects. In contrast, subjects in a diagnostic condition were told that one or more of the buttons signaled whether the alarm system was on. Notice that the direction of causality was reversed in this cover story relative to that in the cover story for the predictive condition. As in the predictive condition, however, subjects saw only the state of the buttons. They had to respond by predicting the state of the alarm, and then they received feedback as to the actual state of the alarm. The cues presented and the responses required were thus equated across the conditions.

The experimental design in both conditions included two phases corresponding to a standard blocking paradigm. Phase 1 established a certain button (P) as a perfect predictor of the state of the alarm. A second button (C) was constantly set to the value off, and a third button (U) varied in a fashion that was uncorrelated with the state of the alarm. Phase 2 maintained these same contingencies, but also added a fourth button (R) that was always on when P was on and off when P was off. Thus, if subjects learned to predict the state of the alarm from the states of the buttons according to the R-W rule, in both conditions learning should have have been blocked in phase 2 for button R by the associative strength that would already have accrued to button P in phase 1.

After each phase of the design, subjects in both conditions rated the degree to which the state of each button was predictive of the state of the alarm using a scale from 0 to 10, where 10 indicated that the cue was a perfect predictor and 0 indicated that the cue was not a predictor. As would be expected on the basis of both contingency theory and the R-W model, the ratings obtained after phase 1 (panel A of figure 12.2) indicated that in both the predictive and diagnostic conditions button P was established as a strong predictor of the state of the alarm, whereas both cues C and R were rated as very weak predictors.

The most important findings involve the predictiveness ratings obtained after phase 2 of the experiment (panel B of figure 12.2). According to the R-W model, the associative strength acquired for the redundant button R should have approached 0 in both the predictive and diagnostic conditions (as should also have happened for the noncontingent buttons C and U). That is, associative learning for cue R should have been entirely blocked by the prior strength of cue P. However, a very different prediction follows from causal contingencies. If people tend to compute contingencies from causes to effects rather than from effects to causes—even when the causal direction is opposite to the order of cue-outcome presentation—then contingency theory predicts that no blocking will be observed in the diagnostic condition. In the diagnostic context the redundant cue, button R, is not an alternative possible cause, the contingency of which should be conditionalized on the status of the established predictor, button P; rather, the state of R is simply a second possible effect of the same cause. If alternative effects, unlike alternative causes, are given separate contingency analyses, then no cue competition should be observed. And indeed, Waldmann and Holyoak found that, while button P was rated

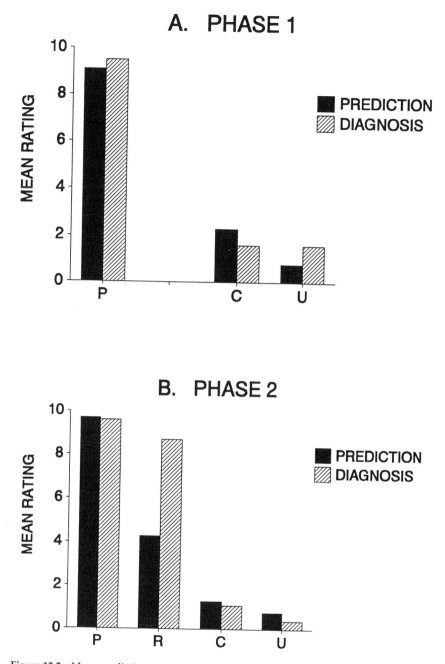

Figure 12.2 Mean predictiveness ratings for predictive and diagnostic conditions obtained in phase 1 (panel A) and phase 2 (panel B) of Waldmann and Holyoak's experiment 3 for the initial predictive cue (P), the redundant predictive cue (R), the constant uncorrelated cue (C), and the varying uncorrelated cue (U). (From Waldmann and Holyoak 1992.)

higher than button R in the predictive condition (9.7 and 4.3, respectively), in the diagnostic condition buttons P and R were given high and statistically equal ratings (9.6 and 8.7, respectively). This interaction between causal direction and the difference in the mean ratings for buttons P and R was highly significant. In addition, the results indicated that, even in the predictive condition, blocking for button R was only partial: the rating for cue R was significantly higher than the ratings for the noncontingent cues C and U. The latter finding is consistent with other evidence that blocking is only partial in human causal induction, as we discussed earlier.

In sum, evidence from studies of human causal induction using paradigms formally similar to blocking studies in animal conditioning has revealed phenomena that are inconsistent with the predictions of the R-W model, but interpretable in terms of a contingency theory such as PCM.

UNDERSTANDING FAILURES OF THE R-W MODEL FROM A CONTINGENCY PERSPECTIVE

Our analysis indicates that contingency theory, as generalized by PCM to apply to various focal sets, including ones for computing conditional contrasts, can account for a wide range of phenomena that are obtained in studies of animal conditioning and human causal induction—not only those that are explained by the R-W model, but also those that are problematic for that model. In addition, our process model makes a number of predictions that have yet to be tested. For example, this model predicts when the causal status of a cue can be uncertain and when the distribution of judgments regarding a cue can be multimodal.

One of the primary attractions of the R-W model is the apparent simplicity and generality of its learning algorithm. However, the simplicity of the model can be questioned (Gallistel 1990); and whether or not it is simple, its wide range of empirical shortcomings indicates that it is simplistic. It may be instructive to consider when and why the R-W model fails to account for phenomena concerning conditioning and causal induction.

First, the R-W model does not represent cause-absent information—in particular, the proportion of trials on which the outcome occurs in the absence of a cue. To understand why the lack of representation of the cause-absent proportion is a weakness, let us first consider the reason for the model's successes. On the basis of interaction among cues that are defined solely in terms of their presence, the model is able to account for a number of apparent effects of cause-absent information: it accounts for the role of contingency (Rescorla 1968), the acquisition of conditioned inhibition (e.g., Chapman and Robbins 1990), blocking (e.g., Rescorla 1981), and other cue interaction effects (e.g., Wagner et al. 1968). In each of these cases, two or more cues that had an identical cause-present proportion, but a different conditional or unconditional cause-absent proportion, have been observed to elicit different behavior, as predicted by the model.

Two properties of the model allow it to arrive at these predictions. First, the model indirectly tallies the cause-absent proportion with respect to a target cue in terms of the cause-present proportion of one or more other cues that are present when the target cue is absent; these surrogate cues therefore acquire weights that reflect the cause-absent proportion of the target cue. In some applications of the model, the surrogate cue is one that represents the context, which is constantly present (and hence is present on occasions when the target cue is absent). Second, on trials when the two cues are both present, the strength of the target cue is adjusted toward the difference between the cause-present proportion of the target cue and the cause-present proportion of the surrogate cues (i.e., the cause-absent proportion of the target cue), potentially yielding contingency as the asymptotic output. In sum, R-W relies on the pairing of cues to transmit the indirectly tallied cause-absent proportion.

Cheng and Novick (1995) present a derivation of when the R-W model does and does not compute conditional contingencies at asymptote. Their analysis shows that it does so for a type of design with multiple cues in which every combination of cues except the one with a single cue can be characterized as a proper superset of all sets with fewer cues (i.e., the cue combinations are nested). In such designs, the strengths of the cues in each combination sum to the relative frequency of the outcome for that combination, implying that, for any combination with multiple cues, the strength of the cue in it that does not belong to the next smaller combination is equal to the contingency of that cue conditional on the presence of the cues in the smaller combination (i.e., the rest of the cues in the larger combination).

Cheng and Novick (1995) also present a derivation of the conditions under which conditional contingencies estimate the causal power of a cue. Their analysis of the R-W model and of conditional contingencies shows that in some nested designs the conditional contingencies computed by the R-W model give an estimate of causal power, whereas in others the conditional contingencies computed by this model do not give such an estimate. Those situations in which the R-W model estimates causal power include those represented by Kamin's (1969) blocking design, unconditional contingency (Rescorla 1968), and the acquisition of conditioned inhibition. In these situations, the R-W model is successful in predicting the observed results (see Cheng and Novick 1995, however, for an explanation of the partial success of the R-W model in predicting the amount of blocking). Those designs in which the R-W model does not estimate causal power include the extinction of conditioned inhibition, retroactive unblocking, and the retroactive reduction of overshadowing (see Miller and Matzel 1988). In these situations, the R-W model fails to predict the observed results.

A second problem with the R-W model is that the causal or conditioning strength of a cue with respect to an effect is represented by a single parameter—the associative strength of the link between the cue and the outcome. The model therefore loses information about sample size, leading to its failure to account for learned irrelevance and, more generally, people's sensitivity to reliability as a function of sample size (Koslowski et al. 1989; Nisbett et al. 1983). Moreover, the R-W model does not offer any way to represent the difference between lack of certainty about a causal association and high certainty that such an association has some medium strength. In contrast, the outcome of a contingency analysis can include not only a definite evaluation of the causal status of a cue, but also uncertainty about its status. Uncertainty naturally falls out of PCM when a relevant contingency is not computable, as in the case of the redundant cue in the blocking paradigm.

For the same reason, the R-W model cannot account for causal assessments that result from comparing the distinct causal status that a cue has in different focal sets. In particular, the R-W model cannot represent the distinction between a cause and an enabling condition or that between an enabling condition and a causally irrelevant cue. This deficit arises because the status of an enabling condition results from the cue's being causal in one focal set and having a noncomputable contingency in another focal set.

This last point brings up the related problem of the need to specify (potentially multiple) focal sets. Our explanations of enabling conditions and of partial blocking provide examples of the use of such an assumption. One might ask, Will the R-W model be able to explain these phenomena if it is amended with the assumption of computation over multiple focal sets? With respect to blocking (see table 12.1), R-W predicts that a redundant cue, R, should have zero associative strength regardless of which focal set is adopted. For none of the focal sets that arise in a contingency analysis is there ever a discrepancy between the expected outcomes based on R-W and the target outcomes for any trial on which R is present. (See the appendix for derivations of the asymptotic weights of the cues assuming various focal sets.) Considering either the focal set in which the predictive cue is always present (i.e., the top row in Table 12.1) or the universal focal set (i.e., the entire table), the outcome is completely predicted by P. Considering the focal set in which the predictive cue is always absent (i.e., the bottom row), R is never present. Therefore, the strength of R is never revised from zero. In sum, even when amended with the concept of a focal set, the R-W model, unlike our process model, cannot predict the partial blocking of R. Nor can it predict a possible multimodal distribution of judgments regarding R. With respect to the status of an enabling condition, because the R-W model does yield a definite value of strength for a constant cue, it cannot yield the uncertainty that leads to the reliance on the status of the cue in another focal set. Even if the model is applied to a focal set in which the cue is constant and another in which it varies, the result will be two strengths for that cue. It is not clear how this result (i.e., an enabling condition represented by two strengths) can be distinguished from that involving a cause that has different strengths in different focal sets.

Finally, the R-W model does not provide any way to distinguish the case in which cues are possible causes (predictive learning) from that in which cues are possible effects (diagnostic learning). That is, cues and outcomes are defined with respect to their roles as stimuli presented vs. responses made rather than with respect to their conceptual roles as causes or effects. However, a cause can be either a stimulus or a response (as can an effect). As a result, the R-W model is unable to explain interactions between perceived causal direction and cue competition (Waldmann and Holyoak 1992).

It is not obvious to us that any of the above shortcomings of the R-W model can be readily amended. Contingency theory provides a basis for formulating alternative models of how natural adaptive systems operate as intuitive statisticians.

APPENDIX: ASYMPTOTIC WEIGHTS OF A NETWORK WITH A BLOCKING DESIGN OBTAINED BY APPLYING THE R-W MODEL TO VARIOUS FOCAL SETS

We show that amending the R-W model with the same assumptions regarding focal sets as those made by contingency theory does not change its prediction of complete blocking.

Deriving Asymptotic Weights

Because our derivation is based on asymptotic weights, we first describe a method for deriving such weights. To obtain the asymptotic weights of a network according to the R-W model, we note the equivalence between the R-W learning rule and the least-mean-squares (LMS) rule of Widrow and Hoff (1960) (cf. Sutton and Barto 1981). The Rescorla-Wagner/Widrow-Hoff rule implements an iterative algorithm for computing the solution to a set of linear equations defined by the set of stimulus-response patterns presented to the network. A pattern is a configuration of stimuli and responses deterministically describing a set of trials. If the input stimulus patterns are linearly independent, then the updating rule will discover a unique solution. Even if the stimulus patterns are not linearly independent, the network will still converge provided that the learning rate is sufficiently small and that the various stimulus patterns occur with sufficient frequency in the input sequence. The network will converge so as to minimize the sum of the squared errors over the stimulus patterns. That is, the equation

$$ \mathbf{E} = \sum_p \pi_p \iota_p \left(\lambda_p - \sum_i V_{pij} \right)^2 \tag{4} $$

will be minimized, where p is the index for a particular stimulus-response pattern, π_p is the frequency of pattern p, ι_p *is the learning rate associated with pattern p* (β_j and γ_j, respectively, for the presence and the absence of outcome j), λ_p is the desired output for the outcome of the pattern (usually either 0 or 1), and

$$\sum_i V_{pij}$$

is the actual output for the pattern, which is equal to the sum of the weights V_i associated with every present cue i for the pattern. If the reinforcement learning rate β_j is equal to the nonreinforcement learning rate γ_j, the ι_p term may be omitted from the equation. We assume that the learning rates β_j and γ_j are equal in the rest of this chapter. Thus the asymptotic weights of a network according to the R-W model can be calculated analytically by minimizing the sum of the squared errors given by equation 4. This minimum value may be obtained by setting the partial derivatives with respect to each weight to 0 and solving the resulting set of equations.

A Predictive Cue and a Redundant Cue

First, consider the network corresponding to the design summarized by table 12.1. There are three patterns of trials: When P and R are both present, the outcome always occurs; when P is present and R is absent, the outcome also always occurs; but when P and R are both absent, the outcome never occurs. Because the π_p and ι_p terms do not affect our result, for simplicity of exposition we assume that the three patterns occur with equal frequency and that the learning rates for the various patterns are equal, so that we omit π_p and ι_p from equation 4. Applying the equation to all events in the table (the universal focal set),

$$E = [1 - (V_P + V_R)]^2 + (1 - V_P)^2.$$

We see that E will have its lowest value when $V_P + V_R = 1$ and $V_P = 1$. Therefore, the asymptotic solution for this network is $V_P = 1$ and $V_R = 0$. That is, the redundant cue R is completely blocked. Note that the pattern involving the joint absence of P and R does not lead to any error terms, because no cue is present. Therefore, applying the R-W model to the focal set consisting of trials in which P is always present yields the same asymptotic solution for V_P and V_R.

Adding a Constant Context Cue

Applications of the R-W model often assume that there is a constantly present context cue, K. The error for the universal set is then

$$E = [1 - (V_P + V_R + V_K)]^2 + [1 - (V_P + V_K)]^2 + (0 - V_K)^2.$$

We see that $\mathbf{E}$ will have its lowest value when $V_K = 0$, $V_P = 1$, and $V_R = 0$. That is, R is completely blocked. If we adopt the focal set consisting of trials on which P is constantly present, we drop the third error term above, obtaining

$$\mathbf{E} = [1 - (V_P + V_R - V_K)]^2 + [1 - (V_P + V_K)]^2.$$

By inspection, $\mathbf{E}$ will be at a minimum when

$$V_P + V_R + V_K = 1 \tag{5}$$

$$V_{P+} V_K = 1. \tag{6}$$

There is no unique solution of V_P and V_K in this case. But subtracting equation 6 from equation 5 yields the solution $V_R = 0$. Thus R is completely blocked in this as well as in all of the above networks.

NOTES

Preparation of this paper was supported by NSF Grant DBS 9121298 to Cheng and by a UCLA Academic Senate Research Grant to Holyoak. We thank Michael Waldmann and Eric Melz for their extensive contributions to the research reviewed as well as for their helpful discussions of the chapter. Herbert Roitblat provided valuable comments on an earlier draft. Requests for reprints may be sent to Patricia Cheng at the Department of Psychology, Franz Hall, University of California, Los Angeles, California 90095-1563.

1. This definition of a two-way interaction contrast differs from the one proposed by Cheng and Novick (1990), which does not contain the product terms and is therefore less normative.

2. What is referred to here as the "universal set" is actually the pragmatically restricted set of events that occur in the conditioning experiment (i.e., a small subset of the "truly" universal set of all events known to the subject). This contextual delimitation of the largest relevant focal set implies that even the cases in the "cause-and-effect-both-absent" cell are restricted to a small finite number.

3. When there are multiple known causes, assessing the status of a potential causal factor normatively requires computing its contingencies while exhaustively conditionalizing on every combination of the presence and absence of the other cues. We do not mean to imply that a test of conditional independence is the only process for differentiating between genuine and spurious causes (Lien and Cheng 1992).

4. The prediction of uncertainty does not generalize to situations in which the representation of the target phenomenon does not have a maximum value, as does the probability of a phenomenon.

5. Because the critical cues in Shanks's "noncontingent conditions" were contingently related to the respective diseases by the conventional definition, the labels for his stimulus sets in experiments 1 and 2—"contingent condition" and "noncontingent condition"— do not conform to conventional usage.

6. It should be noted, however, that analogous conditioning experiments with animals that attempted to find indirect effects of increasing (rather than decreasing) the excitation of a previously paired cue have failed to obtain such effects (see Miller and Matzel 1988). However, "retroactive blocking"—reduction in the causal value of one cue as a result of increasing the apparent predictiveness of another cue with which it had been previously paired—has been observed in studies of causal induction by humans (Chapman 1991; Shanks 1985). These effects, however, have been relatively small in magnitude.

Complex Adaptive Systems as Intuitive Statisticians

7. Consideration of the unconditional contingency for the pallid cue yields the same prediction. As the salient cue becomes extinguished, it no longer maintains its conditionalizing status. The positive unconditional contingency of the pallid cue then becomes interpretable as evidence that the latter is in fact causal.

REFERENCES

Alloy, L. B., and Tabachnik, N. (1984). Assessment of covariation by humans and animals: The joint influence of prior expectations and current situational information. *Psychological Review, 91,* 112–149.

Baker, A. G. (1977). Conditioned inhibition arising from a between-session negative correlation. *Journal of Experimental Psychology: Animal Behavior Processes, 3,* 144–155.

Cartwright, N. (1983). *How the Laws of Physics Lie.* Oxford: Clarendon Press.

Cartwright, N. (1989). *Nature's Capacities and Their Measurement.* Oxford: Clarendon Press.

Chapman, G. B. (1991). Trial order affects cue interaction in contingency judgment. *Journal of Experimental Psychology: Learning, Memory, and Cognition, 17,* 837–854.

Chapman, G. B., and Robbins, S. I. (1990). Cue interaction in human contingency judgment. *Memory & Cognition, 18,* 537–545.

Cheng, P. W., and Novick, L. R. (1990). A probabilistic contrast model of causal induction. *Journal of Personality and Social Psychology, 58,* 545–567.

Cheng, P. W., and Novick, L. R. (1991). Causes versus enabling conditions. *Cognition, 40.*

Cheng, P. W., and Novick, L. R. (1992). Covariation in natural causal induction. *Psychological Review, 99,* 365–382.

Cheng, P. W., and Novick, L. R. (1995). From covariation to causation: A causal power theory. Unpublished manuscript, Department of Psychology, University of California, Los Angeles.

Estes, W. K., Campbell, J. A., Hatsopoulos, N., and Hurwitz, J. B. (1989). Base-rate effects in category learning: A comparison of parallel network and memory storage-retrieval models. *Journal of Experimental Psychology: Learning, Memory, and Cognition, 15,* 556–571.

Gallistel, C. R. (1990). The organization of learning. Cambridge, MA: The MIT Press.

Gluck, M. A., and Bower, G. H. (1988). From conditioning to category learning: An adaptive network model. *Journal of Experimental Psychology: General, 117,* 227–247.

Holland, J. H., Holyoak, K. J., Nisbett, R. E., and Thagard, P. (1986). *Induction: Processes of Inference, Learning, and Discovery.* Cambridge, MA: The MIT Press.

Kamin, L. J. (1969). Predictability, surprise, attention, and conditioning. In B. A. Campbell and R. M. Church (Eds.), *Punishment and Aversive Behavior.* New York: Appleton-Century-Crofts. Pp. 276–296.

Kaplan, P. S., and Hearst, E. (1985). Excitation, inhibition, and context: Studies of extinction and reinstatement. In P. D. Balsam and A. Tomie (Eds.), *Context and Learning.* Hillsdale, NJ: Erlbaum. Pp. 195–224.

Kasprow, W. J., Schachtman, T. R., and Miller, R. R. (1987). The comparator hypothesis of conditioned response generation: Manifest conditioned excitation and inhibition as a function of relative excitatory strengths of CS and conditioning context at the time of testing. *Journal of Experimental Psychology: Animal Behavior Processes, 13,* 395–406.

Kaufman, M. A. and Bolles, R. C. (1981). A nonassociative aspect of overshadowing. *Bulletin of the Psychonomic Society, 18,* 318–320.

Kelley, H. H. (1967). Attribution theory in social psychology. In D. Levine (Ed.), *Nebraska Symposium on Motivation, 15* Lincoln: University of Nebraska Press. Pp. 192–238.

Koslowski, B., Okagaki, L., Lorenz, C., and Umbach, D. (1989). When is covariation not enough: The role of causal mechanism, sampling method, and sample size in causal reasoning. *Child Development,* 60, 1316–1327.

Lien, Y., and Cheng, P. W. (1992). How do people judge whether a regularity is causal? Paper presented at the 33rd Annual Meeting of the Psychonomic Society, St. Louis.

Matzel, L. D., Schachtman, T. R., and Miller, R. R. (1985). Recovery of an overshadowed association achieved by extinction of the overshadowing stimulus. *Learning and Motivation,* 16, 398–412.

Melz, E. R., Cheng, P. W., Holyoak, K. J., and Waldmann, M. R. (1993). Cue competition in human categorization: Contingency or the Rescorla-Wagner rule? Comments on Shanks (1991). *Journal of Experimental Psychology: Learning, Memory, and Cognition,* 19, 1398–1410.

Miller, R. R., and Matzel, L. D. (1988). The comparator hypothesis: A response rule for the expression of associations. In G. H. Bower (Ed.), *The Psychology of Learning and Motivation, Vol. 22.* San Diego, CA: Academic Press. Pp. 51–92.

Miller, R. R., and Schachtman, T. R. (1985). Conditioning context as an associative baseline: Implications for response generation and the nature of conditioned inhibition. In R. R. Miller and N. E. Spear (Eds.), *Information Processing in Animals: Conditioned Inhibition.* Hillsdale, NJ: Erlbaum. Pp. 51–88.

Nisbett, R. E., Krantz, D. H., Jepson, D., and Kunda, Z. (1983). The use of statistical heuristics in everyday inductive reasoning. *Psychological Review,* 90, 339–363.

Pearl, J. (1988). *Probabilistic Reasoning in Intelligent Systems.* San Mateo, CA: Morgan Kaufmann.

Peterson, C. R., and Beach, L. R. (1967). Man as an intuitive statistician. *Psychological Bulletin,* 68, 29–46.

Reichenbach, H. (1956). *The Direction of Time.* Berkeley and Los Angeles: University of California Press.

Rescorla, R. A. (1968). Probability of shock in the presence and absence of CS in fear conditioning. *Journal of Comparative and Physiological Psychology,* 66, 1–5.

Rescorla, R. A. (1972). Informational variables in Pavlovian conditioning. In G. H. Bower and J. T. Spence (Eds.), *The Psychology of Learning and Motivation, Vol. 6.* New York: Academic Press. Pp. 1–46.

Rescorla, R. A. (1981). Within-signal learning in autoshaping. *Animal Learning and Behavior,* 9, 245–252.

Rescorla, R. A., and Wagner, A. R. (1972). A theory of Pavlovian conditioning: Variations in the effectiveness of reinforcement and nonreinforcement. In A. H. Black and W. F. Prokasy (Eds.), *Classical Conditioning II: Current Theory and Research.* New York: Appleton-Century-Crofts. Pp. 64–99.

Salmon, W. C. (1980). Probabilistic causality. *Pacific Philosophical Quarterly,* 61, 50–74.

Salmon, W. C. (1984). *Scientific Explanation and the Causal Structure of the World.* Princeton, NJ: Princeton University Press.

Shanks, D. (1985). Forward and backward blocking in human contingency judgment. *Quarterly Journal of Experimental Psychology,* 37B, 1–21.

Shanks, D. R. (1991). Categorization by a connectionist network. *Journal of Experimental Psychology: Learning, Memory, and Cognition,* 17, 433–443.

Shanks, D. R., and Dickinson, A. (1987). Associative accounts of causality judgment. In G. H. Bower (Ed.), *The Psychology of Learning and Motivation, Vol. 21.* San Diego, CA: Academic Press. Pp. 229–261.

Simpson, E. H. (1951). The interpretation of interaction in contingency tables. *Journal of the Royal Statistical Society,* Series B (Methodological), 13, 238–241.

Suppes, P. (1970). *A Probabilistic Theory of Causality.* Amsterdam: North Holland.

Suppes, P. (1984). *Probabilistic Metaphysics.* Oxford: Basil Blackwell.

Sutton, R. S., and Barto, A. G. (1981). Toward a modern theory of adaptive networks: Expectation and prediction. *Psychological Review,* 88, 135–170.

Wagner, A. R., Logan, F. A., Haberlandt, K., and Price, T. (1968). Stimulus selection in animal discrimination learning. *Journal of Experimental Psychology,* 76, 171–180.

Waldmann, M. R., and Holyoak, K. J. (1992). Predictive and diagnostic learning within causal models: Asymmetries in cue competition. *Journal of Experimental Psychology: General,* 121, 222–236.

Wasserman, E. A. (1990). Attribution of causality to common and distinctive elements of compound stimuli. *Psychological Science,* 1, 298–302.

Widrow, B., and Hoff, M. E. (1960). Adaptive switching circuits. *Institute of Radio Engineers, Western Electronic Show and Convention,* Part 4, 96–104.

Zimmer-Hart, C. L., and Rescorla, R. A. (1974). Extinction of Pavlovian conditioned inhibition. *Journal of Comparative and Physiological Psychology,* 86, 837–845.

IV Memory and Attention

13 A Model of the Brain and the Memory System

J. Delacour

INTRODUCTION

A prerequisite for a description of the memory system is a scientific model of the whole brain, and this is the first and perhaps the main difficulty: presently, only metaphors and block diagrams of the brain are available. They reflect either philosophical views or prevailing technology (Daugman 1990), such as the computer brain. The inadequacy of this metaphor is now well established (Churchland, Koch, and Sejnowski 1990; Rumelhart and McClelland 1987; Wilkes 1990).

This lack of scientific models is mainly due to the computational difficulty of simulating large-scale neural networks and the technical difficulty of obtaining synthetic views of the real brain. These obstacles will certainly be overcome but, in the meantime, only prescientific representations are possible. I have adopted an empirical and eclectic course: the framework of my model is based on the functional anatomy of the brain as outlined by clinical and experimental neuropsychology. This model involves viewing the brain as consisting of three systems.

The first system is made of the neurons that code, or represent, sensory information or motor programs with the highest precision. Let us call this system R for representation. Its delimitation is rather simple: R comprises the primary sensory and motor structures as well as the sets of neurons that code high-level sensory and motor information—the association cortex and, on the efferent side, the premotor cortex, the supplementary motor area, the striatum, and the cerebellum. In humans, the cortical areas involved in the precise coding of linguistic activity should also be included in R. This system is distributed among modules—for instance, the visual or the motor structures, as well as some parts of the language neural bases (Ojemann 1991). The concept of module that I use here is in great part inspired by Fodor (1983). It is a device with the following properties: it is domain-specific, mandatory (automatic obligatory processing), inaccessible to consciousness, fast, and informationally encapsulated (impenetrable from outside the module), and it exhibits specific breakdown patterns, as in apraxia and agnosia. At least some modules

have a topographic organization. Even at the highest level, R is characterized by a modular organization; for instance, 32 distinct cortical areas
associated with visual processing have been described in the primate
brain (Van Essen, Anderson, and Felleman 1992).

The second system is made up of neurons whose activity has no precise
relationship with sensory inputs or motor outputs. On the other hand, the
activity of these neurons is highly correlated with arousal or motivational
states. Let us call this system A for activation of the type meant in cerebral
neurobiology (Steriade 1991).[1] The main anatomical structures that make
up A are the reticular formation, the raphe and the locus ceruleus, some
thalamic and hypothalamic nuclei, the nucleus basalis of the telencephalon, and the limbic system—the hippocampus, amygdala, septal nuclei,
etc. (Kandel, Schwartz, and Jessel 1991; Steriade 1991). Experimental and
clinical data clearly show that some of these structures are directly involved in the control of arousal and/or motivation; their central projections modulate the spontaneous and evoked activity of the neurons of R.
Their lesion disturbs the sleep-wakefulness cycle, food intake, or sexual
activity. The role of other A structures is more complex, but their lesion
has a remarkable effect: the global amnesic syndromes. In contrast to the
organization of R, that of A is neither modular nor topographic; it is
integrative. Information is not analyzed by separate, "encapsulated," specialized modules; typically A neurons receive convergent afferents from
heterogeneous sources and project onto different targets through highly
divergent efferents. Moreover, the different subsystems of A are densely
interconnected (see a typical example of this kind of organization in a
recent description of the networks of cholinergic neurons of the A system
in Woolf 1991).

The third system certainly is the most difficult to define and to delimit.
Nevertheless, it is an essential component of any description of the brain:
some neural entity should account for the goal-directed character of behavior. The best illustration of its functions is the human "voluntary act":
it involves a representation of a goal and of the appropriate strategies,
the evaluation of results, and the correction of errors. Time is an important
dimension of this component, especially the representation and organization of the future. Let us call this entity S for supervision. The delimitation
of S is much more difficult than that of R or A. S is perhaps only a dynamic
reality, a certain mode of cooperative activity of the whole brain. However,
the effects of lesions of the prefrontal cortex in man reflect mostly a
deficit in the S functions (Luria 1973; Shallice 1988; Stuss 1991). Data from
neuroimaging in normal man (Frith et al. 1991; Ingvar 1985; Pardo, Fox,
and Raichle 1991) and from neurophysiology and experimental neuropsychology in monkeys (Goldman-Rakic 1987) also suggest that the frontal
cortex could at least be a part of S.

After this preliminary sketch, a word of caution. The framework of our
model is anatomy, which remains the basis of all the macrodescriptions

of the brain. However, this representation has some drawbacks. The anatomical structure is a gross division of the brain, in most cases consisting of different populations of neurons in terms of neurotransmitters, patterns of connections, intrinsic membrane properties etc. More fine grain divisions, such as the cortical column, should also be considered as frameworks of cellular and molecular data. Moreover, the anatomical representation a priori favors localizationist and static conceptions. R, A, and S are characterized not only by anatomical delimitations; they have dynamic aspects that transcend anatomical limits—for instance, different patterns of physiological activity that set into play different structures. Moreover, it is conceivable that the same structure, at different stages of the same task, belongs to different systems.

The three systems interact and are, more or less, set into play by any kind of behavior. Some states of A are a necessary condition for S functions: for instance, a certain arousal state is a necessary condition for the voluntary act. Reciprocally, S allocates resources of attention, which supposes a control upon A. Likewise, the arousal/motivation level (A) influences sensory receptions and motor activity (R). Reciprocally, some sensory stimuli, due to their novelty or their biological value, have an arousal/motivational effect. S depends on the sensory/motor capacities of R, but reciprocally S controls the functioning of R modules by focusing attention on some targets, by correcting the motor output, and so forth.

AN OUTLINE OF THE MEMORY SYSTEM

In spite of its imperfections, the above model of the brain allows one to clearly pose an important question: Does a separate anatomically delimited memory system exist? In its naive form—the "center of memory"—the "localizationist" thesis is rejected by most scientists, but it is still predominant in more sophisticated forms (Mishkin and Appenzeller 1987; Squire and Zola-Morgan 1991). According to its recent developments, there are several anatomically distinct memory systems. Clinical and experimental evidence seems to be compelling: brain lesions in specific locations produce memory deficits, while sparing other components of cognition; moreover, even in global amnesic syndromes only some forms of memory are impaired. However, it should be noted that the main arguments in favor of one or several separate memory systems are the effects of lesions—that is, a priori localizationist data. Moreover, if global amnesic syndromes are not associated with gross disturbances of behavior, memory disturbances may be associated with less detectable changes in other cognitive capacities, such as a deficit in some forms of awareness. This is well established at least for Korsakoff patients, whose attentional capacity is impaired (McEntee and Mair 1984).

Holistic views are the opposite of the localizationist concept: the memory system is the whole brain, which has a diffuse, fully distributed organization. This is hardly tenable: neural bases of memory, as those of any other function, have a significant degree of local organization as shown by clinical and experimental data. Our thesis is intermediate: as shown by experimental data, plastic neurons—that is, neurons whose properties are modified by experience—are found in all three systems, R, A, and S. Thus, at cellular and molecular levels, the memory system is distributed. However, at network or circuit level, the memory system has a significant degree of local specialization. There is no contradiction between the distributed character of the memory system at cellular and molecular levels and a local organization at more global levels. Different subsystems, having different locations in a system, may be made up of identical elements and connections, with the same laws of activation and weight modification.

So, at an elementary level, the system is distributed. However, due to different patterns or densities of connections, the emergent properties of the different subsystems may largely differ, which will give a local organization of the system at a global level. Thus, at brain level the memory system is an interaction between R, A, and S in which the three subsystems have different, though complementary, roles reflecting their respective functions in the overall organization of the brain (table 13.1). Thus, R is especially involved in the encoding and storage of fine-grain representation of sensory data and motor programs. A plays a role in learning and memory through the control of the excitability and activity coherence of large populations of neurons, especially at cortical levels. The role of S depends on the action in progress and plans for the future; thus, S intervenes in learning and memory through focal attention, cognitive strategies, spatiotemporal context representation, and so on.

Depending on the task, learning and memory set into play different types of interaction between R, A, and S as defined by the pattern of activity of each system and the special involvement of some subsystems. For instance, the global amnesic syndromes suggest that certain types of memory (explicit and declarative) depend on certain forms of awareness—that is, certain interactions of A and S where thalamic nuclei and the hippocampus play an important role. On the other hand, other forms of memory (implicit or procedural) are essentially based on a relatively autonomous functioning of some R modules. The relative importance of R, A, and S and their types of interaction also depend on the stage of the task. For instance, the role of A may be much more important at the initial and intermediate stages than when the task is perfectly mastered.

This conception of the memory system has at least two advantages. First, it accounts economically for the neural bases of the great diversity of learning and memory phenomena without creating ad hoc separate memory systems. Second, it accounts for the interaction of learning and memory with the other components of behavior—perception, arousal/motivation state, and goal-directed activity—and, in parallel, for the integration of the memory system into the whole brain. Memory is an aspect

modality or its verbal/nonverbal character; on the contrary, type I–type II opposition is not relevant. Conversely, for the role of A—at least that of the subsystems involved in the global amnesic syndromes—dimension 2 is irrelevant, whereas dimension 3 is critical: deficits in amnesic patients do not depend on the nature of information, but on the process; only type I memory is impaired.

The Role of R

A typical example of the role of R is given by the inferotemporal cortex (IFT) in the monkey. This area is a visual association cortex. Its neurons respond only to visual stimuli, especially to complex visual objects such as a hand or a primate face. Lesion or stimulation of the IFT produces deficits only in visual learning and memory tasks; tasks based on other sensory modality are spared (Gross 1992). On the other hand, the type I–type II dimension is not critical. Lesion of the IFT impairs trial-unique delayed match-to-sample tasks (generally considered as measuring type I memory), as well as pattern or object discriminations based on the repeated association of a cue and a reward (generally considered as measuring type II memory).

Similar data show that in monkeys lesions in the unimodal association cortex produce memory deficits that are specific for a particular sensory modality (Pribram 1984): gustative (anterior temporal), auditory (middle temporal), or somesthesic (parieto-occipital). Limited cortical lesions in man produce rather specialized deficits in face recognition or in the recall of the meaning of some classes of words (Ojemann 1991).

The Role of A

The best illustration of the role of the A system is the temporal lobe amnesic syndrome. As already noted, the memory deficit in patients with this syndrome depends not on the nature of the material, but on the type of process: only type I memory is impaired (Squire and Zola-Morgan 1991).

Experimental reproduction of this syndrome remains controversial due to the difficulty of devising animal models of type I memory. Even in monkeys, these models are not entirely convincing: the most popular test, based on recognition of visual objects (Mishkin and Delacour 1975), may set into play implicit—that is, type II—forms of memory; it is the same for other tasks sensitive to temporal lobe lesions in monkeys (Squire 1992). In rats the problems is even more difficult. However, based on reviews of the literature (Chozik 1983; Delacour 1994; Eichenbaum, Otto, and Cohen 1992; Gray and McNaughton 1983; Jarrard 1980; O'Keefe and Nadel 1978; Schmajuk 1984; Squire 1992), encouraging similarities appear between experimental and clinical data.

Tests that are sensitive to hippocampal lesions[3] (selective or associated with lesions of other structures) in rats or monkeys have at least one of the following three properties:

1. The relevant information is not repeated, or its meaning changes from trial to trial. This is typically the case for the object recognition task used by the Mishkin group in monkeys (Mishkin and Delacour 1975) and for the working memory tasks (Olton 1983) in rats.

2. The relevant information is ambiguous, somewhat contradictory. For example, the relationships between discriminative stimuli, responses, and reinforcers on a given trial may be the opposite of what they were during the previous trial. In other words, these tasks require relational processing and representational flexibility (Eichenbaum, Otto, and Cohen 1992).

The latter is the case for working memory tests such as delayed match-to-sample or delayed alternation tests, in which only two discriminative stimuli are used throughout the experiment: from trial to trial, the choice of the same stimulus is sometimes "correct," sometimes "incorrect." It is also the case for some reference or procedural memory tasks that are sensitive to hippocampal lesions. Reference memory (a case of type II memory) is an abstract, context-free knowledge of general rules and properties that is progressively acquired through the repetition and consistency of facts. Likewise, in animals this form of memory is involved in tasks in which the relevant information is constant from trial to trial and requires no updating or modification across trials. The learning of a maze in which the pattern of blind alleys is the same all through the experiment sets into play reference memory. Some typical reference memory tasks are not disturbed by hippocampal lesions. Interestingly enough, those that are disturbed by the lesion involve some change, some ambiguity in the experimental conditions. A typical example is the "spatial reversal," which is very sensitive to hippocampal lesions. In a T maze, one of the two arms, say the left, is first the correct one; when a learning criterion is reached, the rule is changed to its opposite, and the "correct" arm is now the right. When criterion is again reached, the discrimination is again "reversed," and the left arm once more becomes the correct one, etc. The introduction of cues that make the information less ambiguous and less conflicting may decrease the effects of hippocampal lesions; this was observed in an experiment in which the initial discrimination and the "reversed" one were acquired in a different context (Winocur 1982). Another test of spatial learning set[4] is also impaired by hippocampal lesions (M'Harzi et al. 1987).

In other tests sensitive to hippocampal lesions, animals have to adapt to a temporal interval. In a DRL schedule of reinforcement, a given behavior—for example, bar pressing—is reinforced only if its successive occurrences are separated by a given interval, say 20 seconds. If the end of that interval is not signaled, hippocampal lesions produce significant deficits; the introduction of a cue suppresses the deficit (Gray and Mc-Naughton 1983).

3. The difficulty of the task also determines the effects of hippocampal lesions. For example, there is no effect on the acquisition or retention of a one-blind linear maze, but the acquisition and retention of a five-blind maze are severely impaired (M'Harzi et al. 1988).

Conversely, in tasks that are not impaired by hippocampal lesions, the relevant information is repeated: it is present in each trial in a stable, nonambiguous form. This is the case for simple procedures of classical conditioning, as well as for those of operant conditioning based on a continuous reinforcement schedule, "standard" simultaneous discriminations, and so forth. These tasks are considered instances of type II learning and memory tests. Moreover, hippocampal lesions appear not to be modality-specific, though their effects on olfaction deserve more attention.

The comparison of experimental and clinical data is difficult, since in patients lesions are usually not limited to one anatomical structure; moreover, they are very frequently unilateral and produced by slow degenerative processes. On the other hand, typical experimental lesions are made bilaterally during a one-stage operation and tend to be limited to a given anatomical structure.

Nevertheless, there are at least significant similarities between the global amnesic syndromes (temporal as well as diencephalic) and the effects of hippocampal lesions in animals,[5] as follows:

1. The deficits in hippocampal animals in tasks in which the relevant information is not repeated may be an acceptable equivalent of the special vulnerability of episodic,[6] contextual memory in patients.

2. The impairment of these animals in tasks in which the relevant information is incomplete, ambiguous, or conflicting appears to reproduce the susceptibility seen in patients to different types of interference (Kinsbourne 1987; Knight and Wooles 1981; Winocur 1982). In some amnesic people, as in hippocampal rats, the introduction of cues that eliminate the ambiguities attenuates the deficits. Moreover, patients are more impaired in performing free recall than in performing recognition tests (Hirst 1982; Hirst et al. 1986): in the former, the information to be retrieved is absent during the retention test; it is present in the latter, which increases the number of retrieval cues and thus decreases the possibility of interference.

3. The deficit does not depend on the nature of the learned information.

4. Simple forms of classical conditioning and other type II tasks are not impaired.

A likely interpretation of these similarities is that in animals lesions in the hippocampal formation produce deficits in tasks that, due to their

A Model of the Brain and the Memory System

demand for relational processing and representational flexibility (Eichenbaum, Otto, and Cohen 1992), require consciousness in humans or, in neurobiological terms, some level of cerebral activation. As stressed above, temporal lobe lesions in humans especially impair conscious, explicit forms of memory. (On the relationships between memory and consciousness in the scope of amnesic syndromes, see Tulving 1987.)

This interpretation of the hippocampal role in terms of activation is fully compatible with the anatomophysiological properties of the hippocampal formation, and it is even strongly suggested by them (Delacour 1988, 1994). However, it is in disagreement with a very popular, though highly controversial, theory according to which the function of the hippocampus would be specifically to build a representation of the spatial environment (O'Keefe and Nadel 1978). A detailed discussion of this theory is not possible (see Delacour 1994). Briefly, it raises the following serious objections:

1. It is hardly compatible with the basic anatomophysiological properties of the hippocampus.

2. The existence of hippocampal "place units" is still not sufficiently established.

3. In animals, lesions of the hippocampus have no effect on some "spatial" tests, while disturbing nonspatial ones.

4. In humans, in whom pure spatial and nonspatial tests are possible, the theory is directly invalidated: people with temporal lobe lesions have no specific deficits in space representation; this kind of deficit is produced by right posterior parietal lesions.

The fact that the hippocampus is critically involved in the temporal lobe syndrome does not mean that it is the "center of memory." Several other structures of the temporal lobe are also involved (Squire and Zola-Morgan 1991). Moreover, this set of structures does not itself store the engrams: these, insofar as they require precise coding, are stored in the modules of R, especially the association cortex, that are put into play by the task. The role of temporal lobe structures is to facilitate the long-term storage and retrieval of type I memories through their interaction with the neocortex (Squire and Zola-Morgan 1991).

Moreover, due to the integrative organization of A, other structures of that system are involved in learning and memory through a role in cerebral activation. The main example is the Korsakoff syndrome produced by diencephalic lesions. Due to the lack of precision in its anatomopathology and the frequent association of memory deficits with other cognitive dysfunctions, this syndrome had much less influence on the neurology of memory than the temporal lobe syndrome. However, a significant number of clinical cases have shown that lesions limited to the thalamus produce amnesia comparable to that observed in temporal lobe patients. These data are confirmed by the effects of experimental thalamic lesions in rats and monkeys (Delacour 1994). Moreover, recent progress in the study of thalamocortical interactions (McCormick 1992; Steriade 1991) clearly show how some thalamic nuclei may play a key role in learning and memory through the control of cortical activation. It is more and more obvious that the importance of the thalamic part of the A system in type I memory is comparable to that of the temporal lobe structures.

Clinical and experimental data suggest that the Meynert nucleus, another important component of the A system, is also involved in learning and memory. However, the role of system A is not uniform. In spite of its integrative character, its different subsystems may have different functions due to their high-level properties—for instance, the pattern and the more or less direct character of their connections with the neocortex—or to some elementary properties—for instance, the postsynaptic effects of the neurotransmitters they release.

From anatomophysiological and behavioral data, it appears that system A may be divided into two subsystems. One (A1) is in charge of the basic regulation of the sleep-wakefulness cycle. Its lesions produce long-lasting coma or the loss of some sleep stages. The reticular formation and other structures of the brain stem as well as some parts of the hypothalamus are the main components of A1. Normal functioning of A1 is a necessary condition for any conscious cognitive activity. A second subsystem (A2), which comprises the hippocampal formation, some thalamic nuclei, and the Meynert nucleus, has no primary role in sleep and wakefulness. On the other hand, it plays a critical role in the long-term storage and retrieval of type I memories through interactions with the R modules.

The Role of S

The role of S in learning and memory is more difficult to determine due to the complexity of its functions and the lack of precise data on its neural implementation. However, if we assume that the prefrontal cortex is at least a part of the anatomical basis of S, clinical and experimental data fit the model rather well.

In agreement with the notion that all three systems—R, A, and S—are involved in learning and memory but play different roles, frontal lesions in humans produce memory deficits, but these deficits differ from those produced by lesions of R or A. Frontal lobe patients have impairments of source memory (Janowsky et al. 1989), metamemory (Janowsky, Shimamura, and Squire 1989), and memory of the temporal order (Shimamura, Janowsky, and Squire 1990). Experimental findings are also suggestive: one of the most robust results of experimental neurology is the deficit produced in working memory tests by lesions of the frontal cortex in monkeys.

Though still fragmentary, these data are remarkably concordant with the role of S in total behavior. As the pilot of goal-directed behavior, S should have privileged access to contextual forms of memory such as source memory and working memory; its relationship with working memory is especially important insofar as this form of memory underlies cognitive activities in progress (Baddeley 1983). Representation of the time order of events, as well as evaluation and organization of learning and memory by cognitive strategies (metamemory), are also S functions.

From the above data, S as well as A appear to be especially involved in type I forms of memory, irrespective of the nature of the information; however, from the global amnesic syndromes it appears that the role of A is critical only in long-term type I memory, whereas S is also involved in short-term (working) forms of memory. Moreover, through its metamemory capacities S probably influences type II as well as type I forms of memory.

THE COOPERATION OF R, A, AND S IN LEARNING AND MEMORY

In the normal brain, all three systems cooperate in learning and memory. This has already been strongly suggested by the synthetic views from brain imaging[7]; progress of this technique will allow for direct observation of the dynamics of the interactions between all three systems, their evolution, and their specificities according to the stage and the nature of the task, etc. From the combined results of different approaches, the cooperation of R, A, and S has been well established in the case of spatial working memory tasks—delayed response (DR) and delayed alternation (DA) tests—in monkeys.

The data—in great part those of the Goldman-Rakic group (Goldman-Rakic 1987; Diamond and Goldman-Rakic 1989)—may be summarized as follows. DR and DA tests put into play:

1. A certain level of attention that depends on an interaction between the prefrontal cortex and subsystems of A (monoaminergic structures of the brain stem, the hippocampus, and the mediodorsal thalamus).

2. The use by the prefrontal cortex of the visuospatial information coded by the posterior parietal cortex, a part of system R.

3. The programming of the correct motor responses and the inhibition of incorrect ones through the interaction of the frontal cortex and motor structures of R (the striatum, motor and premotor cortex, etc).

4. The representation of the temporal order of past events, such as the last baited foodwell or the last reinforced response. This temporal representation depends particularly on the frontal cortex, but the problem of proactive interference it poses may require frontal hippocampal interaction.

Though less precise, other data also strongly suggest that interactions between R, A, and S are critical in some forms of memory: some features of the Korsakoff syndrome are "frontal," such as the lack of metamemory (Janowsky et al. 1989; Janowsky, Shimamura, and Squire 1989b). This could be explained by the fact that diencephalic lesions, especially those of the mediodorsal nucleus of the thalamus, which are the main causes of that syndrome, may induce anterograde and retrograde degeneration in the frontal cortex. Memory deficits associated with normal aging and dementia suggest that cholinergic projections from the Meynert nucleus to the frontal cortex may play a crucial role in working memory. Insofar as these projections facilitate responses of the sensory cortex to natural stimuli, they may also be involved in type II forms of memory (such as priming and classical conditioning) that are impaired in dementia.

LEVELS OF ORGANIZATION

As already stressed, a complete description of the memory system should consider all the organization levels of the nervous system. Such a description is beyond the scope of this chapter (see Delacour 1994). We shall consider only some general points.

A level of organization is not an ontological category, only an epistemological one: it reflects only a state of science; it is a view of a system made possible by some techniques and formalisms. New levels—microscopic, mesoscopic, or macroscopic—made accessible by technical progress will appear in the future. There is no fixed, definitive list of levels, nor is there a definitively critical or "best" one; rather, more simply, in a given nervous system for a given task and in a given state of the technology, data from one level may provide more information, may allow us to make more precise predictions. Therefore, it is not justified to privilege one level of organization at the expense of all the others: none of the levels appears to be able to "swallow up" or to "reduce" the others; they have bidirectional "causal" relationships and exert mutual constraints. For instance, changes in some membrane ionic conductances in a few neurons or even in a single one may cause an increase in the synchrony of discharges of a network; conversely, an increase in the synchrony of that network may render some of its intrinsic connections more efficient by fulfilling the condition of a Hebb's synapse.

This epistemological view has precise consequences with regard to representation of the memory system. For instance, from this view pure reductionist conceptions have only a limited value. A statement such as "The neural basis of so-and-so learning task is so-and-so neuropeptide or so-and-so subclass of neurotransmitter receptor" makes hardly any sense. Such elementary realities as a molecule may play a role in a learning task (or any other behavior) only within the framework of cells, networks, and circuits of neurons.

More generally speaking, the notion of a mechanism of learning and memory should be questioned: it implies that the different levels of organization are ontological categories and that events located at a given level (the lowest in most cases) exert a unilateral causal action on events located at other levels. It seems preferable to replace this notion with that of a neurobiological correlate or equivalent. The most informative equivalents of a learning phenomenon—that is, the neurobiological events that best map or predict the behavioral data—may be found at a certain level of organization, but this level is privileged only in a given state of the technology, in a given organism, and for a given task.

During the last two decades, major advances in analytic techniques that have given us access to more and more elementary levels of organization have allowed for the accumulation of a huge amount of "elementary" data and favored reductionist views. But the development of new techniques will give us more global views of the memory system. We have already stressed the importance of brain imaging. Likewise, multiunit recording techniques have opened a new window on the neural bases of learning and memory, that of intermediate levels of organization—small networks such as the cortical column. Recent data from Singer's group (Engel et al. 1992) suggest that synchronous oscillations in neuron activity within and between cortical columns may play a role in visual perception.

THE MEMORY SYSTEM AND BASIC ISSUES IN COGNITIVE NEUROSCIENCE: FACTS AND SPECULATIONS

The study of the memory system leads to the central problems of the cognitive neurosciences: the concepts of representation and consciousness. Instead of a priori rejecting these concepts, which reflect an undeniable experience in humans, the neuroscientist should try to find their neurobiological translation. In order to facilitate this translation, let us first try some objective analogs of representation and consciousness as intermediate steps between the mental experience and the nervous system.

Perhaps the simplest analog of a representation is a state M of a system that maps another reality, O; thus, objective equivalents of representation may be maps in the common acceptation or states of hidden units connecting the input layer to the output in a network, and so on. Note that a full analogy requires that the system be able to produce the mapping state "spontaneously," in the absence of O, just as mental representations may occur in the absence of their referents (memories or expectancies). Representations have another property: they are not isolated, independent events; they all have in common the property of appearing only in a certain global state, called consciousness. Within that state, their succession is smooth and melodic, forming a continuous stream: they interact according to some laws; they are referred to a stable world and to a self perceived as identical through different states, and so on.

Perhaps the simplest analog of consciousness is a space that may be occupied by different objects, which allows but also constrains their relationships and is centered on a stable origin (the self). Let us call it internal space (IS). It is a necessary condition for any particular representation. Depending on the type of action in progress, on the target of attention, it will be occupied by different representations—for example, a map of the perceptual world or a piece of a semantic network. The IS is structured, constrained by species-specific and individual genetic factors. Its structure may be modified through learning; however, there is no separate memory space: all particular representation, perceptual or semantic, learned or innate, is incorporated into a unique IS; but time is one of the dimensions of this space; this is a condition for an explicit recall of past events as such, as well as the representation of possible outcomes and plans.

Another means of scientifically validating the notion of representation and consciousness is based on animal behavior. Numerous data strongly suggest that animal behavior is controlled by representations (Ristau 1991; Roitblat 1982). For instance, the most economical explanation of long-range exploratory behaviors is that they are guided by maps of the environment. In some cases, the principles of these maps have been identified. Moreover, in species like bees these maps appear to be used in social communication. The behavior of monkeys could also be controlled by representations of external objects (predators for instance) and social relationships, and these representations could be the basis of social communications (Cheney and Seyfarth 1990).

What is the evolutionary value of representations? Cognitive activity in a given organism depends on the world delimited, structured, and shaped by its sensorimotor and computational capacities and, in social species, by the structure of the social group. It is in that framework that information is perceived, stored, and recalled. By allowing the organism to take into account data not directly observable because of their distance in time and space or actively masked by competitors, representations based on a "model of the world" or a "theory of the mind" (Cheney and Seyfarth 1990) of the members of the group would confer an important biological advantage.

Now what about internal space, consciousness, reference to a self in animals? This remains an open question. Self-awareness is perhaps limited to some apes (Gallup 1991), but more elementary forms of the IS may exist in any species in which activation systems of the brain are well developed (see the discussion below of the role of activation systems in the generation of the IS). More generally, there is a growing body of evidence in favor of a continuity between animal and human cognition, which makes at least conceivable the neurobiological translation of mentalistic notions.

A representation may be a state M of the nervous system that controls behavior through the mapping of either (1) a reality O outside the nervous system (some state of the environment or of the organism) or (2) another state of the nervous system. At least case 1 corresponds to a well-established property of R modules—for instance, visual or somatic systems. However, in the framework of classical neurophysiology, where the reflex is the dominant model, M is tightly and rigidly dependent on O. In modern views, relations between M and O are much more flexible. Due to the self-organization capacities of the nervous system, M may appear and evolve "spontaneously" in the absence of O while retaining its functional value, its capacity to map some Os just as "mental" representations.

The notion of map is used by the neurobiology of sensory receptions, the neurobiology of attention (Crick and Koch 1990), and the field of modeling in cognitive neuroscience (Kohonen 1990; Miikkulainen 1992; Schmajuk and Thieme 1992). It is well supported by the data of cerebral neurophysiology. Some sensory systems have an undeniable topographic organization. Moreover temporary maps or neuronal assemblies could be generated internally by the divergent projections of activation systems to the cortex or by corticocortical connections, creating a co-activation space. Only purely theoretical for a long time, the notion of neural assembly recently received experimental support from the results of Singer's group: the synthesis of visual information—shape, color, movement, and location—necessary for the representation of stable objects distinct from the background could be based on the correlation between the activity of distant neurons—or, in other words, on a "synchronization" space more flexible and more powerful than the co-activation space of the first models (Engel et al. 1992).

Might these limited, temporary neural spaces belong to a larger and more stable "internal space"? What about consciousness? It is now widely accepted that the issue of consciousness is a real scientific problem and that the time has come for scientists to tackle it (Dennett 1991; Eccles 1992; Edelman 1989; Gray 1992; Libet 1989). A neurobiology of consciousness might have firm grounds in the neurobiology of attention (Crick and Koch 1990; Posner and Petersen 1990) and sleep-wakefulness regulation (Steriade 1991). Consciousness is a certain mode of system A functioning.

A positive contribution may also come from the neurobiology of memory. The most suggestive data are from the global amnesic syndromes. In spite of the diversity of interpretations, it clearly appears that the kind of memory impaired in these syndromes (type I memory) is representational, conscious; it is this characteristic that make it explicit, relational. Type I memory puts into play a "memory space" (Eichenbaum, Otto, and Cohen 1992) where what is learned or recalled consciously is represented as a node in a network of concepts or images that maps a certain reality. For instance, learning and recalling a fact such as the name of the capital of a country or the number of its population puts into play a network of semantic relationships connecting many other geographical, economical, and political facts. An event, such as the meeting of a friend in a certain place two months ago, is perceived and recalled within the framework of the "real" world, a spatiotemporal framework where objects obey some static and dynamic laws, as well as within a set of social relationships, and so on.

Let us try to use the concept of IS in a neurobiological context. Insofar as fine-grain representations are involved, part of the neural implementation of the IS is made up of the modules of the R system of our model. However, under the influence of A supramodular relationships are acquired or actualized—for instance, those necessary to the representation of a polymodal object or a complex scene. Consequently, a particular content or node of the IS may be reached in numerous ways, some of them produced by the "spontaneous," self-organizing activity of the nervous system. This property makes possible the flexible, relational, comparative character of conscious cognitive activity such as type I memory.

The IS is functional, and it has some significant role in behavior only in a certain level or pattern of activity of A.[8] This reflects the fact that some forms of cognitive activity, such as type I memory, are possible only in some states of cerebral activation equivalent to what is called consciousness in humans. In the absence of such activation, networks or maps of the IS are only virtual. This is the case in slow-wave sleep. The case in paradoxical sleep is different: cerebral activation in paradoxical sleep and in wakefulness is in great part identical (Llinas and Paré 1991; Steriade 1991). During dreams some parts of the IS may be actualized, but without the constraints of sensory experience, which explains the mixture of realism and irrealism, of coherence and incoherence, of oniric representations.

However, system A, in spite of its integrative organization, is not perfectly homogeneous. As already stressed, two subsystems may be distinguished from anatomophysiological and behavioral data,[9] and correlatively system A is involved in cognition at two levels. A1 (described earlier) provides the basic regulation of sleep-wakefulness. A certain mode of activity of A1 is the necessary condition for the actualization of IS and, consequently, for any form of conscious cognitive activity. A2 has no primary role either in sleep-wakefulness or in basic conscious cognitive activities, such as perception; it is critically involved in the long-term acquisition and retrieval of learned information represented in the IS. In other words, a certain mode of activity of A2 is a necessary condition for the formation and the long-term storage and retrieval of contents of type I memory. This functional difference between A1 and A2 explains why in global amnestic syndromes (which are produced by lesions of A2) basic cognitive activities are spared. Such activities include perception, short-term memory, and the fundamental structure of the IS—reference to a permanent self and world and to the basic perceptual or symbolic categories, whether of genetic origin or acquired in the most remote past.[10] This fundamental structure is altered in dementia.

What gives to A2 structures a special mnesic role? In the case of the hippocampal formation, this role is generally ascribed to a low-level property, the form of synaptic plasticity called LTP. However, LTP is not a special property of the hippocampus: it also occurs in R and S; therefore, network properties should be considered—for instance, the density and distribution of the reciprocal connections between A2 and the cortex.

In our interactive model, S is also involved in the generation of the IS. As for the other functions of S, data are less precise than for R and A. However, some clinical and experimental data on the frontal lobe give a coherent picture. S has no primary role in the regulation of sleep-wakefulness; its integrity is not necessary for basic forms of consciousness, but it is critical for other forms associated with focal attention, self-awareness, time representation, and metacognition (Stuss 1991). In terms of the IS, S could be especially involved in the reference to a self, the time dimension, and the generation and use of supramodular representations necessary for the organization of action.

FINAL REMARKS AND SUMMARY

The respective roles of R and A have been well distinguished by dimensions 2 and 3 of learning and memory phenomena: type of information and type of process. Dimension 1, the duration of retention, is less discriminative, though the distinction between short- and long-term memory has some neuropsychological grounds. It is generally accepted that in temporal lobe patients it is only the long-term type I memory that is impaired; reciprocally, short-term memory would be selectively impaired in other patients (Shallice 1988). The role of S seems not to be critically dependent on any of the three dimensions; however, as S is the pilot of the action in progress, it may be especially involved in forms of short-term (working) memory.

Most facts and speculations in this chapter concern type I memory, for the problem of its neural implementation is especially difficult. On the other hand, as type II tests are relatively easy to devise in animals, precise data have been obtained on the neural bases of forms of this type of memory: habituation, sensitization, and classical conditioning. Obviously type II memory is as important as type I, even in humans. Moreover, both types are closely associated and interact in most tasks. It is conceivable that forms of type II memory modulate type I: habituation, sensitization, or conditioning phenomena, putting into play only a few R modules, could facilitate or block conscious learning or retrieval. This modulation would be unconscious; it could explain phenomena such as the repression of memories. Conversely, conscious regulation controls both types of memory through the training of attention, acquisition of cognitive strategies, and progress in the evaluation of memory demands and capacities. This metamemory probably depends on A-S interaction insofar as it requires an integrative, supramodular organization.

In conclusion, the main feature of our model is that the memory system has no strict anatomical location; it is the interaction of the three components of the brain—R, which codes information with the highest precision; A, which controls the excitability and activity coherence of large populations of neurons; and S, which is the pilot of goal-oriented behavior.

Depending on the type and stage of learning and memory, different subsystems of R, A, and S, as well as different interaction modes, are put into play.

This model is at least compatible with most experimental and clinical data, and it is supported by many of them. It has the advantage of economically accounting for the diversity of learning and memory phenomena, their integration into total behavior, and their intricate relationships with other aspects of cognitive activity: perception, attention, and meta-memory.

In this integrative perspective, it finally appears that any description of the memory system should be placed in the framework of evolutionary biology. Since learning and memory phenomena depend on the world structured by sensory and motor repertoires as well as the computational capacities of the organism shaped by evolution, data from neuroecoethology are necessary for a comprehensive view of the memory system.

NOTES

1. "Attention," one of the psychological avatars of the notion of activation, obtained neurobiological status in the last decade (Posner and Petersen 1990).

2. Brief trains of high-frequency stimulation to monosynaptic excitatory pathways cause a sustained increase in the efficiency of synaptic transmission. This facilitation (LTP) can last for hours, days, and even weeks. In the past ten years, LTP in the hippocampus has become the dominant model of activity-dependent synaptic plasticity in the mammalian brain.

3. Experimental reproduction of temporal lobe syndrome has been almost exclusively focused on the hippocampus since lesions of this structure seem to be the critical factor of the syndrome.

4. Discrimination reversal is a special case of learning set phenomena. These are defined as follows: If organisms are trained on a series of similar problems, they may become more proficient at solving each new problem. Learning set tasks put into play reference or procedural memory, but with some changes in the experimental conditions for each new problem.

5. In some tests, thalamic lesions in humans and in animals have effects comparable to those of hippocampal ones (Delacour 1994); however, data are still fragmentary.

6. Episodic memory is the memory of unique events experienced in a particular time and place (see Tulving 1987).

7. Techniques such as positron emission tomography and nuclear magnetic resonance imaging allow the structure and activity of the human brain to be visualized. As a result, one can examine the brain when people are thinking, learning, perceiving, and initiating voluntary actions without using invasive procedures (Martin, Brust, and Hilal 1991).

8. The notion of "internal space" is related to that of "behavioral and central nervous state" as illustrated by the neurobiology of sleep-wakefulness (Hobson, Lydic, and Baghdoyan 1986).

9. This distinction is not radical. The differences between subsystems of A are quantitative. For example, according to the density of its connections, the extent of the projection area

of these connections, their degree of convergence, and the postsynaptic effects of the neuro-transmitter they release, the action of a subsystem of A may be more or less lasting, diffuse, etc., accordingly, it will affect only the perception or short-term memory or transition to long-term memory, etc.

10. In global amnesic syndromes, retrograde amnesia is limited to a few years; older memories are spared. Different explanations of this fact are possible. Their examination is beyond the scope of this chapter.

REFERENCES

Baddeley, A. D. (1983). Working memory. *Phil. Trans. R. Soc. Lond.*, B 302, 311–324.

Bliss, T. V. P., and Collingridge, G. L. (1993). A synaptic model of memory: Long-term potentiation in the hippocampus. *Nature*, 361, 31–39.

Cheney, D. L., and Seyfarth, R. M. (1990). *How Monkeys See the World.* Chicago: University of Chicago Press.

Chozik, B. S. (1983). The behavioral effects of lesions of the hippocampus: A review. *Intern. J. Neurosci.*, 22, 63–80.

Churchland, P. S., Koch, C., and Sejnowski, T. J. (1990). What is computational neuroscience? In E. L. Schwartz (ed). *Computational Neuroscience*. Cambridge, Mass.: The MIT Press. Pp. 46–55.

Crick, F., and Koch, C. (1990). Toward a neurobiological theory of consciousness. *Semin. Neurosci.*, 2, 263–275.

Daugman, J. G. (1990). Brain metaphor and brain theory. In E. L. Schwartz (ed). *Computational Neuroscience*. Cambridge, Mass.: The MIT Press. Pp. 9–18.

Delacour, J. (1988). A view on the memory system of the mammalian brain. In J. Delacour and J. C. Levy (eds). *Systems with Learning and Memory Abilities*. Amsterdam: Elsevier. Pp. 83–104.

Delacour, J. (1994). The memory system of the brain. In J. Delacour (ed). *The Memory System of the brain*. Singapore: World Scientific Publishing. Pp. 1–65.

Delacour, J., Houcine, O., and Costa, J. C. (1990). Evidence for a cholinergic mechanism of ''learned'' changes in the responses of the barrel field neurons of the awake and undrugged rat. *Neuroscience*, 34, 1–8.

Delacour, J., Houcine, O., and Talbi, B. (1987). ''Learned'' changes in the responses of the rat barrel field neurons. *Neuroscience*, 23, 63–71.

Dennett, D. C. (1991). *Consciousness Explained*. Boston: Little, Brown.

Diamond, A., and Goldman-Rakic, P. S. (1989). Comparison of human infants and rhesus monkeys on Piaget's AB task: Evidence for dependence on dorsolateral prefrontal cortex. *Exp. Brain Res.*, 74, 24–40.

Eccles, J. C. (1992). Evolution of consciousness. *Proc. Natl. Acad. Sci.*, USA, 89, 7320–7324.

Edelman, G. M. (1989). *The Remembered Present: A Biological Theory of Consciousness*. New York: Basic Books.

Eichenbaum, H., Otto, T., and Cohen, N. J. (1992). The hippocampus: What does it do? *Behav. Neur. Biol.*, 57, 2–36.

Engel, A. K., Konig, P., Kreiter, A. K., Schillen, T. B., and Singer, W. (1992). Temporal coding in the visual cortex: New vistas on integration in the nervous system. *Trends Neurosci.,* 15, 218–226.

Fodor, J. D. (1983). *The Modularity of the Mind.* Cambridge, Mass.: The MIT Press.

Frith, C. D., Friston, K., Liddle, P. F., and Frackowiak, R. S. J. (1991). Willed action and the prefrontal cortex in man: A study with PET. *Proc. Roy. Soc. London,* B 244, 241–246.

Gallup, G. (1991). Toward a comparative psychology of self-awareness: Species limitations and cognitive consequences. In J. Strauss and G. R. Goethals (eds). *The Self: Interdisciplinary Approaches.* New York: Springer. Pp. 121–135.

Goldman-Rakic, P. S. (1987). Circuitry of primate prefrontal cortex and regulation of behavior by representational memory. In *Handbook of Physiology, vol. 5: The Nervous System.* Bethesda, Md.: American Physiological Society. Pp. 373–417.

Gray, J. (1992). Consciousness on the scientific agenda. *Nature,* 358, 277.

Gray, J., and McNaughton, N. (1983). Comparison between the behavioral effects of septal and hippocampal lesions: A review. *Neurosci. Biobehav. Rev.,* 7, 119–188.

Gross, C. G. (1992). Representation of visual stimuli in inferior temporal cortex. *Phil. Trans. Roy. Soc. London,* B 335, 3–10.

Hirst W. (1982). The amnestic syndrome. *Psychol. Bull.,* 91, 435–460.

Hirst, W., Johnson, M. K., Kim, J. K., Phelps, E. A., Risse, G., and Volpe, B. T. (1986). Recognition and recall in amnesics. *J. Exp. Psychol.: Learning, Memory, and Cognition,* 12, 445–451.

Hobson, J. A., Lydic, R., and Baghdoyan, H. A. (1986). Evolving concepts of sleep cycle generation: From brain centers to neuronal populations. *Behav. Brain Sci.,* 9, 371–448.

Ingvar, D. H. (1985). Memory of the future: An essay on the temporal organization of conscious awareness. *Human Neurobiol.,* 4, 127–136.

Janowsky, J. S., Shimamura, A. P., Kritchevsky, M., and Squire, L. R. (1989). Cognitive impairment following frontal lobe damage and its relevance to human amnesia. *Behav. Neurosci.,* 103, 548–560.

Janowsky, J. S., Shimamura, A. P., and Squire, L. R. (1989a). Source memory impairment in patients with frontal lobe lesions. *Neuropsychologia,* 27, 1043–1046.

Janowsky, J. S., Shimamura, A. P., and Squire, L. R. (1989b). Memory and metamemory: Comparisons between patients with frontal lobe lesions and amnesic patients. *Psychobiol.,* 17, 3–11.

Jarrard, L. E. (1980). Selective hippocampal lesions and behavior. *Physiol. Psychol.,* 8, 198–206.

Kandel, E. R., Schwartz, J. H., and Jessel, T. M. (1991). *Principles of Neural Science, part VIII.* Amsterdam: Elsevier. Pp. 733–819.

Kinsbourne, M. (1987). Brain mechanisms and memory. *Hum. Neurobiol.,* 6, 81–92.

Knight, R. G., and Wooles, I. M. (1981). Experimental investigation of chronic organic amnesia: A review. *Psychol. Bull.,* 88, 753–771.

Kohonen, T. (1990). The self-organizing map. *Proc. IEEE,* 78, 1464–1480.

Lee, S. M., and Ebner, F. F. (1992). Induction of high-frequency activity in the somatosensory thalamus of rats: In vivo results in long-term potentiation of responses in SI cortex. *Exp. Brain Res.,* 90, 253–261.

Libet, B. (1989). Conscious subjective experience vs. unconscious mental functions: A theory of the cerebral processes involved. In R. M. Cotterill (ed). *Models of Brain Function.* Cambridge: Cambridge University Press. Pp. 35–49.

Lin, Y., and Phillis, J. W. (1991). Muscarinic agonist-mediated induction of long-term potentiation in rat cerebral cortex. *Brain Res.,* 551, 342–345.

Llinas, R., and Paré, D. (1991). Of dreaming and wakefulness. *Neuroscience,* 44, 521–535.

Luria, A. R. (1973). *The Working Brain: An Introduction to Neuropsychology.* New-York: Basic Books.

Martin, J. H., Brust, J. C. M., and Hilal, S. (1991). Imaging the living brain. In E. R. Kandel, J. H. Schwartz, and T. M. Jessel (eds). *Principles of Neural Science.* Amsterdam: Elsevier. Pp. 309–324.

McCormick, D. A. (1992). Neurotransmitter actions in the thalamus and the cerebral cortex and their role in neuromodulation of thalamo-cortical activity. *Progr. Neurobiol.,* 39, 337–388.

McEntee, W. J., and Mair, R. G. (1984). Some behavioral consequences of neurochemical deficits in Korsakoff psychosis. In L. R. Squire and N. Butters (eds). *Neuropsychology of Memory.* New York: Guilford Press. Pp. 224–235.

Merzenich, M. M., Recanzone, G. H., Jenkins, W. M., and Grajski, K. A. (1990). Adaptive mechanisms in cortical networks underlying cortical contributions to learning and non declarative memory. *Cold Spring Harb. Symp. Quant. Biol.,* 55, 873–887.

M'Harzi, M., Palacios, A., Monmaur, P., Willig, F., Houcine, O., and Delacour, J. (1987). Effects of selective lesions of fimbria-fornix on learning set in the rat. *Physiol. Behav.,* 40, 181–188.

M'Harzi, M., Willig, F., Costa, J. C., and Delacour, J. (1988). D-amphetamine enhances memory performance in rats with damage to the fimbria. *Physiol. Behav.,* 42, 575–579.

Miikkulainen, R. (1992). Trace feature map: A model of episodic associative memory. *Biol. Cybern.,* 66, 273–282.

Mishkin, M., and Appenzeller, T. (1987). The anatomy of memory. *Scient. Amer.,* 255, 80–89.

Mishkin, M., and Delacour, J. (1975). An analysis of short-term visual memory in the monkey. *J. Exp. Psychol.: Anim. Behav. Proc.,* 1, 326–334.

Ojemann, G. A. (1991). Cortical organization of language. *J. Neurosci.,* 11, 2281–2287.

O'Keefe, J., and Nadel, L. (1978). *The Hippocampus as a Cognitive Map.* Oxford: Clarendon Press.

Olton, D. S. (1983). Memory function and the hippocampus. In W. Seifert (ed). *Neurobiology of the Hippocampus.* New York: Academic Press. Pp. 335–373.

Pardo, J. V., Fox, P. T., and Raichle, M. E. (1991). Localization of a human system for sustained attention by positron emission tomography. *Nature,* 349, 61–64.

Posner, M. I., and Petersen, S. E. (1990). The attention system of the human brain. *Ann. Rev. Neurosci.,* 13, 25–42.

Pribram, K. H. (1984). The organization of memory in a nonhuman primate model system. In Squire, L. R., and Butters, N. (eds). *Neuropsychology of Memory.* New York: The Guilford Press. Pp. 340–363.

Ristau, C. A. (1991). *Cognitive Ethology.* Hillsdale, N. J.: Erlbaum.

Roitblat, H. L. (1982). The meaning of representation in animal memory. *Behavior. Brain Sci.,* 5, 353–406.

Rumelhart, D. E., and McClelland, J. L. (1987). *Parallel Distributed Processing.* Cambridge, Mass.: The MIT Press.

Schmajuk, N. A. (1984). Psychological theories of hippocampal function. *Physiol. Psychol.,* 12, 166–183.

Schmajuk, N. A., and Thieme, A. D. (1992). Purposive behavior and cognitive mapping. *Biol. Cybern.* 67, 165–174.

Shallice, T. (1988). *From Neuropsychology to Mental Structure.* Cambridge: Cambridge Univ. Press.

Shimamura, A. P., Janowsky, J. S., and Squire, L. R. (1990). Memory for the temporal order of events in patients with frontal lobe lesions and amnesic patients. *Neuropsychologia,* 28, 803–813.

Squire, L. R. (1992). Memory and the hippocampus: A synthesis from findings with rats, monkeys, and humans. *Psychol. Rev.,* 99, 195–231.

Squire, L. R., and Zola-Morgan, S. (1991). The medial temporal lobe memory system. *Science,* 253, 1380–1386.

Steriade, M. (1991). Alterness, quiet sleep, dreaming. In A. Peters (ed). *Cerebral Cortex,* Vol. 9. New York: Plenum Press. Pp. 279–356.

Stuss, D. T. (1991). Self, awareness, and the frontal lobes: A neuropsychological perspective. In J. Strauss and G. R. Goethals (eds). *The Self: Interdisciplinary Approaches.* Berlin: Springer. Pp. 254–278.

Tsumoto, T. (1994). Long-term potentiation and depression in visual cortex: Functional significance and molecular basis. In J. Delacour (ed). *The Memory System of the Brain.* Singapore: World Scientific Publish. Pp. 493–523.

Tulving, E. (1987). Multiple memory systems and consciousness. *Human Neurobiol.,* 6, 67–80.

Van Essen, D. C., Anderson, C. H., and Felleman, D. J. (1992). Information processing in the primate visual system: An integrated systems perspective. *Science,* 255, 419–423.

Wilkes, K. V. (1990). Modelling the Mind. In K. A. Mohyeldin Said, W. H. Newton-Smith, R. Viale, and K. V. Wilkes (eds). *Modelling the Mind.* Oxford: Clarendon Press. Pp. 63–82.

Winocur G. (1982). The amnestic syndrome: A deficit in cue utilization. In L. S. Cermak (ed). *Human Memory and Amnesia.* Hillsdale: Erlbaum. Pp. 139–166.

Woolf, N. J. (1991). Cholinergic systems in mammalian brain and spinal cord. *Progr. Neurobiol.,* 37, 475–524.

14 Factors in Visual Attention Eliciting Manual Pointing in Human Infancy

George Butterworth

INTRODUCTION

Developmental psychology contributes to comparative cognitive science through the study of age-graded changes and developmental continuities in cognitive processes. A unique contribution concerns the origins of human cognitive processes in human infants, where it is possible to observe the precursors of thought and language in systems of perception and action. Of course, the developmental method is itself situated in a broader, comparative context whereby processes of cognition can be better understood both in nature and in machines (Baldwin 1902; Roitblat and Von Fersen 1992). Although the evidence from developmental cognitive psychology is not yet widely used to inform work in artificial intelligence (AI), some of the implications of recent theoretical advances are beginning to find application (see, for example, Agre and Chapman 1990 for an account of "situated" planning in AI).

This chapter is concerned with the spatial signaling function of gaze and the associated postures of the human head and hand that serve as the foundation for human referential communication. Joint visual attention, or deictic gaze as it is also called, may be defined simply as looking where someone else is looking. Deictic gaze is thought to pave the way in human development for deictic gestures, such as manual pointing, which draw attention to a particular object by locating it for another person. For humans, joint visual attention and pointing offer one of the bases in shared experience for the acquisition of language (Bruner 1983).

A series of studies carried out in our laboratories with human infants will be reviewed. We were concerned with three interrelated questions: (1) How does a baby know where someone else is looking? (2) How does a baby know where someone else is pointing? and (3) How does the production of pointing relate to prehension and to social communication? (For reviews of the implications of this research program, for theories of childhood egocentrism, for theories of the origins of thought and language, and for the phylogeny of visual attention and theories of mind, see Butterworth 1987; Butterworth and Grover 1988; Butterworth 1991a).

COMPREHENSION OF GAZE

There is little doubt that adults very closely monitor the focus of an infant's attention and adjust their own gaze to maintain shared experience. A mother vocalizes at suitable moments when she can see that her baby is attending to a particular object or event, and by establishing joint visual attention she creates a suitable tutorial environment. Schaffer (1984) reviewed a number of studies that show that the majority of episodes of joint attention arise as a result of the mother's monitoring the infant's line of gaze. Perhaps because young babies have traditionally been considered totally egocentric, it has been assumed that they must be incapable of following the gaze of an adult, since this implies taking into account another person's point of view. Furthermore, babies under 8 or 9 months of age are notoriously distractible, and this may also have seemed to preclude their sharing attention with adults.

It was therefore an important discovery when Scaife and Bruner (1975) showed that infants as young as two months would readjust their gaze contingent on a change in the focus of attention of an adult. It suggests that the capacity for joint attention is a reciprocal phenomenon; the baby may be aware of a spatial objective of the mother's change of gaze. Butterworth and Cochran (1980) and Butterworth and Jarrett (1991) performed an extensive series of studies in an attempt to establish the mechanisms serving joint visual attention.

The studies were carried out under strictly controlled conditions in an undistracting environment, with identical targets placed at various positions relative to a mother and infant. These conditions allowed relatively unambiguous conclusions to be drawn concerning how the baby was able to single out the referent of the mother's gaze, since distractions and other possible artifacts were eliminated. In these experiments the mother was instructed to interact naturally with the infant and then, on a signal, to turn, in silence and without pointing manually, to inspect a designated member of a set of targets placed at various positions relative to the mother and baby around the room. Babies between the ages of 6 and 18 months were studied; each interaction was videotaped and subsequently scored by two independent observers who noted the direction and accuracy of the infant's response relative to the mother's line of gaze.

Evidence was obtained for three successive mechanisms of joint visual attention in babies in the age range between 6 and 18 months. At 6 months, a baby looks to the correct side of the room, as if to see what the mother is looking at, but they cannot tell on the basis of the mother's action alone which of the two identical targets on the same side of the room the mother is attending to, even with angular separations as large as 60 degrees between the targets. Although the babies are accurate in locating the object referred to by their mother's change of gaze when the correct target is first along their path of scanning from the mother to the target, they are at chance level when the correct target is second along the scan path. Furthermore, an infant localizes only the targets within his own visual field and hardly ever locates targets at which the mother looks in the region behind the baby, out of view.

If the mother looks at a target behind the baby, the infant either fixates a target in front of him and within his visual field or does not respond. This phenomenon is not caused by any inability of babies to turn behind them; indeed, they would often turn behind them on first being seated in the laboratory or in response to some inadvertent noise. The most likely explanation is that there is a basic inability to attribute the mother's signal to the space outside the immediate visual field. This basic finding of failure to search "behind" (first reported in Butterworth and Cochran 1980) has subsequently been replicated on several occasions in our own laboratories. It is noteworthy that a similar inability to search at locations out of view of the infant has recently been demonstrated in a manual search task involving rotation of the infant relative to objects that were first hidden in the field of view (Landau and Spelke 1988).

On the other hand, so long as all the possible locations are within his field of view, an infant is capable of correctly locating targets presented one at a time at visual angles that introduce separations between the mother and the referent of her gaze of up to 135 degrees. This demonstrates that babies are perfectly capable of noting even very small changes in their mothers' head orientation. Thus, failure to search behind cannot be attributed to failure to perceive the change of head orientation.

Within the field of view, accurate localization of the referent among the youngest babies seems to depend not only on the adult's signal, but also on the intrinsic differentiating properties of the object being attended by the mother. Grover (1988), for example, showed that adding movement to both targets elevated the probability of a response among 9-month-old babies and also raised the level of accuracy of the response. This earliest mechanism of joint visual attention we have called ecological, since we believe that it is the differentiated structure of the natural environment that completes for the infant the communicative function of the adult's signal. What initially attracts the mother's attention and leads her to turn is also likely, in the natural environment, to capture the attention of the infant. The ecological mechanism enables a "meeting of minds" focused on the self-same object. It is as if the change in the mother's gaze signals to the infant the direction in which to look and the object encountered completes the communicative link.

By 12 months the infant is beginning to localize each target correctly whether it is first or second along the scan path when the target is stationary in the visual field. The only information allowing this is the angular displacement of the mother's head and eye movement. It is interesting to note that the infant fixates intently on the mother while she is turning;

then, when the mother is still, the infant makes a rapid eye and head movement in the direction of the target. The mean latency of response after the end of the mother's head movement is about 1 second (Butterworth and Cochran 1980). This brief interval may be sufficient for the baby to register information about the angular orientation of the mother's head. We call this new ability the geometric mechanism, since it seems to involve extrapolation of an invisible line between the mother and the referent of her gaze as plotted from the infant's position. That is, the mother's change of gaze now signals to the infant both the direction of the object and the location in which to look.

Despite this newfound geometric ability, however, babies at 12 months still fail to search for targets located behind them. We have carried out control studies in which the visual field was emptied completely of targets, yet babies of 1 year did not turn behind them at their mothers' signal. Instead they turned to scan to about 40 degrees of visual angle and then gave up the search when they failed to encounter a target. It seems that, if the geometric mechanism is available, it must still be restricted to the infant's perceived space.

By 18 months babies are as accurate when the correct target is second along their scan path from the mother as when it is the first target they encounter, and this suggests that a geometric mechanism may be available that allows discrimination between targets separated by at least 60 degrees of visual angle. Furthermore, although the babies still do not search behind them when there are targets in their field of view, they will do so if the visual field is empty of targets. We have found that head and eye movements to targets behind the baby will elicit turning to the correct target so long as there is nothing in front of the 18-month-old infant in the field of view. Thus infants seem to be able to access the invisible portion of space at 18 months (but not at 12 months) so long as there is no competition from locations within the visual field. This finding leads us to postulate the development of a third spatial mechanism for controlling joint visual attention, a "representational" mechanism that is based on an understanding of being contained within space.

In summary, with regard to the comprehension of gaze we have evidence that in the first 18 months of life three successive mechanisms are involved in "looking where someone else is looking." The earliest, the ecological mechanism, depends on the completion of joint attention by the intrinsic, attention-capturing properties of objects in the environment, as well as on the change in the mother's direction of gaze. We also have evidence of the beginning, at around 12 months, of a new mechanism, a geometric process whereby the infant from his own position extrapolates from the orientation of the mother's head or gaze the intersection of a line with a relatively precise zone of visual space. Finally, at sometime between 12 and 18 months, there is an extension of joint reference to a represented space that contains the infant and other objects outside his immediate visual field (see Butterworth and Jarrett 1991).

The Relation Between Comprehension of Gaze and Comprehension of Manual Pointing

In our more recent unpublished studies we have attempted to establish how an infant's comprehension of gaze may be related to comprehension of manual pointing. Manual pointing, defined as the use of an outstretched arm and index finger to denote an object in visual space, is species-specific to humans, and it is thought to be intimately linked to language acquisition. It is the specialized referential function that is of interest here, since it is a particularly human type of social cognition. Could the comprehension of pointing be related to the comprehension of looking?

It is generally agreed that comprehension of manual pointing occurs toward the end of the first year, somewhat in advance of production of the gesture (Schaffer 1984). Looking where others point is observed in most babies by about 12 months (Guillaume 1926/1962; Leung and Rheingold 1981; Schaffer 1984), whereas pointing for others is observed in most babies at about 14 months (Schaffer 1984). Piaget (1945/1952) thought that comprehension of manual pointing arises simultaneously with comprehension of other complex signs, between 10 and 12 months.

Grover (1988) has obtained extensive data on the infant's comprehension of pointing, which can be readily summarized. She compared the accuracy of responses of babies when their mothers merely looked at the correct target to those when the mothers looked and pointed to the target. She found that an infant at 12 months fails to locate a target behind him whether his mother looks or looks and points. He can correctly locate his mother's referent target within his own visual field whether the target is first or second on his scan path. Thus, the addition of pointing by the mother does not make the space outside the field of view more accessible to the infant. The main effect of adding manual pointing is to significantly increase the probability that the infant will respond. Adding manual pointing to simple change of gaze has a compelling effect on the infant's attention, but results in greater accuracy only after 12 months, once the baby comprehends the meaning of the sign. Cognitive development may be one of the rate-limiting factors in the comprehension of manual pointing, since from approximately 12 months an infant may be able to locate the referent of an adult's pointing hand "geometrically." That is, the infant may extrapolate a "trajectory" from the adult's hand to the target to single out an object of mutual interest at a relatively precisely specified location.

We recently showed that a baby is very much more accurate in locating the target when the adult looks and points at it than when the signal involves only a reorientation of the adult's head and eyes (Butterworth 1991b). Targets separated by as little as 25 degrees of visual angle at approximately 4 meters from an adult and baby can be localized by the infant when the adult looks and points. Our results are consistent with previous research in suggesting that pointing becomes effective as a signal redirecting the infant's attention toward the end of the first year of life, since we obtained no evidence that pointing assists younger babies.

In summary, a long apprenticeship in the comprehension of gaze is not sufficient for the comprehension of manual pointing. Cognitive developmental changes—in particular the acquisition of a geometric/mechanism for localizing the referent of manual pointing, which becomes available to babies at approximately 10 to 12 months of age—is involved. The geometric process allows the infant to determine not only the correct direction in visual space in which to look (also common to the ecological mechanism), but also the precise location within the visual hemifield to look at. The evidence is consistent with the hypothesis that an infant may extrapolate a straight line along the arm of an adult to intersect with a potential object of joint attention in visual space.

Relation of Pointing to Prehension and to Social Communication

Theorists do not agree on the ontogenetic origins of pointing. The use of an outstretched arm and index finger to denote an object in visual space may reflect hominid evolutionary adaptations of the index finger and thumb and be species-specific to man (Hilton 1986). Preyer (1896) considered pointing a movement that originally expressed a wish to seize. Vygotsky (1926/1962) similarly argued that pointing develops out of a mother's interpretation of her infant's failed attempts at prehension. Shinn (1900/ 1984) suggested that manual pointing may develop out of conjoint visual-tactual inspection of objects. The infant of 8 or 9 months will touch an object with the tip of his index finger while engaged in close visual exploration. Shinn suggested that pointing may begin soon after by the application of this intersensorimotor coordination to an extended space. All these hypotheses suppose that pointing, which occurs at the average age of about 14 months, develops out of prehension.

An alternative contemporary point of view consistent with the species typicality and universality of the pointing gesture is that it serves a specialized communication function. Fogel and Hannan (1985) showed that index finger extensions occur reliably in face-to-face interaction in infants as young as 2 months. The index finger does not single out a particular object; it is not correlated with the direction of the infant's gaze or with arm extension. However, the "point" is reliably preceded or succeeded by vocalization or mouth movement. By 6 months the hand may spontaneously adopt the pointing posture when an object attracts the infant's attention in a social context, but again the arm is not extended. Extension of the arm and index finger in a communicative gesture is observed at the beginning of the second year of life. Thus, according to Fogel and Hannan (1985), the specialized function of the index finger in relation to shared attention may be innate, while the progression to instrumental use of the gesture may be explained by successive acquisition of arm control, fine manipulative skills, and cognitive integration of the communicative roles of infant and adult.

Part of our research program has been concerned with disambiguating the two major classes of theory concerning the development of pointing: namely, that it derives from prehension or that it serves a species-typical communication function from the outset. This program of studies has also led us to consider the relationship between focal and ambient attention processes and pointing. We carried out a pilot study, using a radio-controlled toy truck that was very successful in eliciting pointing in babies as young as 8 months and 3 weeks (Butterworth and Adamson-Macedo 1987). We also carried out a number of preliminary data analyses which showed that, although the incidence of index finger pointing increased with age from 8 months to 21 months, the rate of pointing was similar in all age groups. Babies generally point with the ipsilateral hand; that is, when a toy truck was on a baby's right side she pointed with her right hand, and when the toy truck was on her left side she pointed with her left hand. Checking with the social partner and vocalization are closely associated with the pointing gesture and constitute evidence for the social-communicative purpose of the act (Franco and Butterworth 1991).

In another series of studies, we gave the baby the opportunity to reach or point for objects at different distances and showed that babies at the outset of their pointing careers do not confuse pointing with reaching (Franco and Butterworth 1991). Furthermore, cognitive asymmetry between the participants is not necessary. Once pointing begins, a baby will point at an object for another baby, which shows that pointing by the baby does not depend upon contingent behavior from an adult, as Vygotsky had supposed (Franco, Perrucchini, and Butterworth 1992). Thus from its inception pointing occurs when a social recipient for the communicative gesture is available. The most plausible interpretation of our data, when it is taken in this wider context, is that pointing is not socially transmitted, nor is it derived from prehension. Our findings support the view that pointing is a species-specific form of reference that is basic to human nonverbal communication.

CONCLUSION

Our program of research has demonstrated that even very young babies may enter into a communication network with others through comprehension of an adult's direction of gaze; communication is not solely dependent upon the greater cognitive sophistication of the adult. The direction of an adult's gaze has a signal function for an infant from early in infancy. At 6 months the signal value of the mother's head and eye movement will indicate the general direction (left or right) in which the baby is to look. Communication occurs because the easily distractible baby will attend to the same attention-compelling features of objects in the environment as the mother. Such agreement on the objects of shared experience might be reasonably considered a protocommunicative behavior. When seen in a social context, the earliest ecological mechanism allows communication in relation to publicly shared objects through their common effects on the intrinsic attention mechanisms of mother and baby. This basic intermental process depends on the fact that attentional mechanisms in infants and adults operate in much the same way.

During an infant's first year, joint visual attention remains limited to locations within the infant's own visual space. The infant behaves as if her own field of vision is shared with the adult, and this gives us an insight into the nature of infant intersubjectivity. During the first year, the infant is limited by the boundaries of her immediate visual field, but this nevertheless allows communication. Even though the cognitive development of each of the participants in the interaction is at a very different level, the process of immediate perception provides a basis for agreement on the objects of their joint experience.

With cognitive development, a more precise geometric localization of the referent of the mother's gaze is superimposed on this basic mechanism. This seems to be one of the cognitive changes necessary for comprehension of manual pointing. The geometric mechanism lessens the ambiguity of reference, since now targets that are identical in all respects except position can be singled out by the infant. Once this geometric mechanism is available, communication does not require differential, intrinsic properties of the object to be singled out; the infant will choose the correct object in relation to the angular displacement of the mother's head and arm. This change enables the comprehension of manual pointing, itself an important species-typical, social means of redirecting attention and entering into language.

The production of manual pointing operates in an interpersonal context from its inception. It comprises a specialized posture of the index finger, vocalization, social referencing, and attentional processes involved in object identification. It does not develop out of prehension, but makes use of the specialized evolutionary adaptations of the hand for referential communication.

Finally, our research shows the importance of constituent subsystems for understanding the earliest origins of language. We are currently investigating the role of focal and peripheral vision in the production of pointing (Butterworth, Franco, and Graupner n.d.). Our results have not yet been fully analyzed, but we can say that although pointing generally terminates in focal attention, it does not depend solely on focal or peripheral vision. Infants point because they are attracted by interesting events that first occur either focally or peripherally, which they wish to share with others. This line of research promises to reunite the characteristics of the ecology with the processes of attention and communication in a comprehensive theory of the origins, development, and functions of pointing in infancy.

ACKNOWLEDGMENT

The research summarized here was supported by a series of grants from the Economic and Social Research Council of Great Britain.

REFERENCES

Agre, P. E., and Chapman, D. (1990). What are plans for? *Robotics and Autonomous Systems,* 6, 17–34.

Baldwin, J. M. (1902). *Development and Evolution.* New York: Putnam's.

Bruner, J. S. (1983). *Child's Talk.* Oxford: University Press.

Butterworth G. E. (1987). Some benefits of egocentrism. In J. S. Bruner and H. Haste. *Making Sense: The Child's Construction of the World.* London: Methuen. Pp. 62–80.

Butterworth, G. E. (1991a). The ontogeny and phylogeny of joint visual attention. In A. Whiten (Ed.). *Natural Theories of Mind.* Oxford: Blackwell. Pp. 223–232.

Butterworth, G. E. (1991b). Evidence for the geometric comprehension of manual pointing. Paper presented at the Society for Research in Child Development meeting, Seattle, Washington, April.

Butterworth, G. E., and Adamson-Macedo, E. (1987). The origins of pointing: A pilot study. Paper presented at the Annual Conference of the Developmental Psychology Section, British Psychological Society, York, England, September.

Butterworth, G. E., and Cochran, E. (1980). Towards a mechanism of joint visual attention in human infancy. *International Journal of Behavioural Development,* 3, 253–272.

Butterworth, G. E., Franco, F., and Graupner, L. n.d. Dynamic aspects of visual event perception and the origins of pointing in human infants. Research currently being carried out under a grant from the Economic and Social Research Council of Great Britain.

Butterworth, G. E., and Grover, L. (1988). The origins of referential communication in human infancy. In L. Weiskrantz (Ed.). *Thought Without Language.* Oxford: Oxford University Press. Pp. 5–25.

Butterworth, G. E., and Jarrett, N. L. M. (1991). What minds have in common is space. Spatial mechanisms serving joint visual attention in infancy. *British Journal of Developmental Psychology,* 9, 55–72.

Fogel, A., and Hannan, T. E. (1985). Manual actions of nine to fifteen week old human infants during face to face interactions with their mothers. *Child Development,* 56, 1271–1279.

Franco, F., and Butterworth, G. E. (1991). Infant pointing, prelinguistic reference and co-reference. Paper presented at the Society for Research in Child Development meeting, Seattle, Washington, April.

Franco, F., Perrucchini, P., and Butterworth, G. E. (1992). Referential communication between babies. Paper presented at the 5th European Conference on Developmental Psychology, Seville, Spain, Sept.

Grover, L. (1988). Comprehension of the manual pointing gesture in human infants. Unpublished Ph.D. thesis, University of Southampton, England.

Guillaume, P. (1926/1962). *Imitation in Children.* Chicago: Chicago University Press.

Hilton, C. E. (1986). Hands across the old world: The changing hand morphology of the hominids. Unpublished paper, Department of Anthropology, University of New Mexico.

Landau, B., and Spelke, E. (1988). Geometric complexity and object search in infancy. *Developmental Psychology,* 4, 512–521.

Leung, E. H. L., and Rheingold, H. (1981). Development of pointing as a social gesture. *Developmental Psychology,* 17, 215–220.

Piaget, J. (1945/1952). *The Origins of Intelligence in the Child.* New York: Basic Books.

Preyer, W. (1896). *The Senses and the Will.* New York: Appleton.

Roitblat, H., and Von Fersen, L. (1992). Comparative cognition: Representations and processes in learning and memory. *Annual Review of Psychology,* 43, 671–710.

Scaife, M., and Bruner, J. S. (1975). The capacity for joint visual attention in the infant. *Nature,* 253, 265–266.

Schaffer, R. (1984). *The child's entry into a social world.* New York: Academic Press.

Shinn, M., reported in Schaffer, R. (1900/1984). *The Child's Entry into a Social World.* New York: Academic Press.

Vygotsky, L. (1926/1962). *Thought and Language.* Cambridge: Cambridge University Press.

V Communication

15 Language and Animal Communication: Parallels and Contrasts

Christopher S. Evans and Peter Marler

There is an ancient perception that humans are unique organisms. At least until 1859, this must have seemed self-evident. But with the triumph of Darwinian theory, the case for some sort of massive evolutionary discontinuity separating us from other animals has become progressively more tenuous. The recent evidence from molecular biology that we share over 98 percent of our genome with chimpanzees (Sibley and Ahlquist 1984, 1987; Sibley, Comstock, and Ahlquist 1990) is one of many arguments for continuity.

Attempts to identify uniquely human behavioral traits have been concerned with a series of issues, including the incidence of tool use, killing of members of one's own species (Lorenz 1966), and language (e.g., Descartes 1662; Chomsky 1972). Since both tool use (e.g., Beck 1980; Goodall 1986; Thompson this volume) and killing conspecifics (e.g., Hrdy 1977; Hausfater and Hrdy 1984) have been documented in a number of nonhuman animals, language has become the major focus (Lieberman 1984; Premack 1986; Bickerton 1990; Corballis 1991; Locke 1993).

Language is dependent upon such a complex package of cognitive and anatomical features that at first it seems to be the exception to the otherwise clear pattern of continuity apparent between humans and other vertebrates, particularly the higher primates. It is, however, possible to isolate the different functional attributes of language (e.g., Hockett 1960) and then to search for these traits in the cognitive and communicative abilities of other animals. This approach takes advantage of one of the most important legacies of the early ethologists, who demonstrated that comparative studies allow us to discriminate between attributes that are phylogenetically ancient and those that have evolved much more recently (e.g., Lorenz 1958; Tinbergen 1959, 1960).

Any program of experiments designed to identify potential precursors for language in the behavior of animals is immediately faced with a considerable hurdle, which is the lack of a common communicative system between us and our subjects. There have been two principal approaches to this problem. Beginning in the 1960s, a series of projects have documented the behavior of chimpanzees (see reviews by Gardner and Gard-

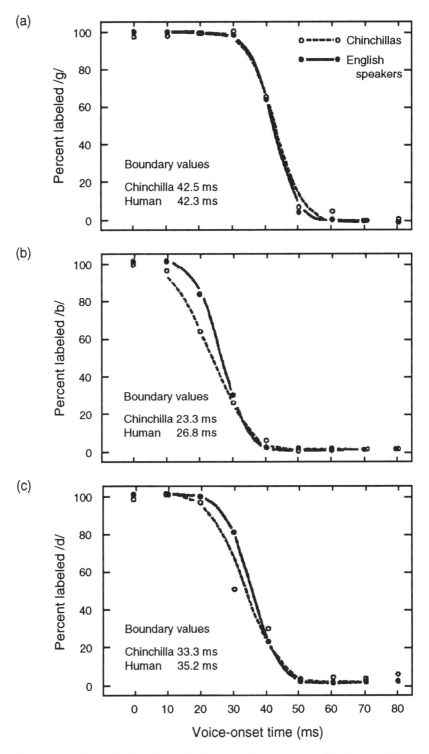

Figure 15.1 Categorization of sounds from speech continua by chinchillas and humans. (*a*) /g-k/, (*b*) /b-p/, (*c*) /d-t/. (Redrawn from Kuhl and Miller 1978, with permission.)

Evans and Marler

speech processing are not so narrowly tuned that other auditory signals are excluded. In addition, a wide range of animals, including Japanese macaques (May, Moody, and Stebbins 1989; but see Hopp et al. 1992), pygmy marmoset monkeys (Pola and Snowdon 1975), swamp sparrows (Nelson and Marler 1989), and mice (Ehret and Haack 1981) have all been shown to perceive variation in their own species-typical sounds categorically. Although this is not invariably true (e.g., Gerhardt 1978; Weary 1989), abundant evidence now exists to demonstrate that categorical perception is not unique to the processing of speech sounds by humans. Rather, it rests upon basic information-processing capabilities that are shared by many vertebrates.

This conclusion has clear implications for models of the evolution of speech. One current view is that speech recognition is dependent upon a tacit understanding of the articulatory maneuvers involved in speech production (e.g., Liberman et al. 1967; Liberman and Mattingly 1985, 1989). This logically requires that perceptual processes evolved either synchronous with, or slightly later than, speech itself. However, the comparative data suggest that events proceeded in the reverse order. That is, speech may have evolved to produce signals that were maximally discriminable given the preexisting biases of our ancestors' auditory systems (e.g., Kuhl 1986). There is a clear parallel between this argument and the recent finding that the perceptual properties of receivers have selected for particular features during the evolution of animal signals (e.g., Ryan 1991; Ryan and Keddy-Hector 1992).

ANIMAL SIGNALS AND THE PROBLEM OF MEANING

Further parallels between the communicative behavior of humans and that of other animals are revealed by attempts to understand the type of information encoded in animal signals (see reviews by Marler 1985; Gouzoules, Gouzoules, and Marler, 1985; Cheney and Seyfarth 1990; Marler, Evans and Hauser 1992; Macedonia and Evans 1993).

Animal Signals as Displays of Emotion

It has long been believed that only humans have the ability to label objects. The biblical account is that God created all of the animals and brought them each in turn to Adam so that he could invent names for them. In some versions of the legend, this act established Adam's intellectual superiority over the rest of creation, including even the angels (Ginzberg 1909). The ability to assign arbitrary acoustic labels to categories of visual stimuli is hence viewed as uniquely human and even assumes supracorporeal significance.

Conventional models of animal communication are entirely consistent with this view. They suggest that signals principally reflect the motivational state of the signaler, and perhaps its subsequent behavior (Rowell and Hinde 1962; Bastian 1965; Lancaster 1965; Premack 1975; Luria 1982). This position implies a particular model of the relationship between eliciting conditions, signal morphology, and receiver response (Figure 15.2a). The traditional model suggests that variation in the sender's internal state is matched by continuous gradation in signal structure. Calls of this type are produced in a wide variety of circumstances and are interpretable only with the aid of contextual information. For example, we might produce anguished yells after hitting a thumb with a hammer or on learning that a manuscript has been rejected. A listener without access to contextual cues (e.g., the rejection letter or the half-driven nail) and our nonvocal behavior would be hard pressed to tell the difference. This model undoubtedly fits many animal signals, but not all.

The system represented in figure 15.2b is very different. Calls are evoked by identifiable external events that form qualitatively distinct and nonoverlapping stimulus classes. Variation in call structure is discrete rather than graded, so that intermediate vocalizations do not occur. There is also a reliable relationship between call type and eliciting stimulus. In this example, calls of type A, which are whistles, are always evoked by hawks, and calls of type B, which are grunts, are always evoked by

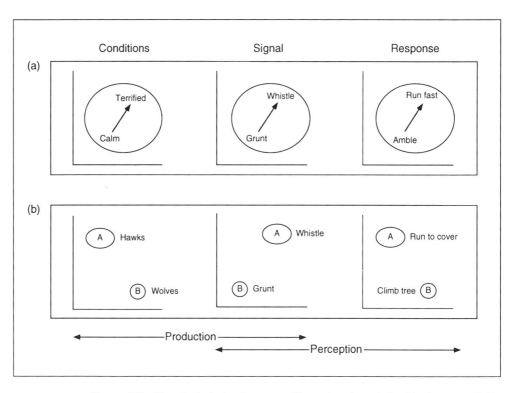

Figure 15.2 Hypothetical signal systems illustrating the relationship between eliciting conditions, signal morphology, and receiver response. (*a*) Traditional model; (*b*) functional reference.

wolves. These calls consequently provide enough information about the circumstances of production for conspecifics to respond appropriately, even when no contextual information is available. We refer to signal systems with all of these properties (production specificity, discrete structure, and context independence) as functionally referential (Marler, Evans, and Hauser 1992; Macedonia and Evans 1993). Notice that classifying signals in this way requires data both from studies of production (i.e., the relationship between call morphology and eliciting stimulus) and from studies of perception (i.e., the relationship between signal type and response elicited).

The term "functionally referential" was coined to acknowledge both the power of philosophical arguments on the problem of meaning (e.g., Grice 1957; Quine 1973; Dretske 1988) and the constraints inherent in the study of alien communication systems, including those of nonhuman animals. It is, for example, particularly difficult to determine whether signals should be thought of as denotative (i.e., as labels for stimulus categories) or as imperative (i.e., as instructions describing appropriate responses) (e.g., Marler 1961, 1992; Cheney and Seyfarth 1990, 1992; Baron-Cohen 1992).

By classifying some signal systems as functionally referential, we do not intend to imply that they provide information only about the eliciting event. Abundant and compelling evidence indicates that information is also encoded about species, individual identity (e.g., Cheney and Seyfarth 1988), affective state (Jürgens 1979; Seyfarth, Cheney, and Marler, 1980b), and, at least probabalistically, about the subsequent behavior of the signaler (Smith 1977, 1981, 1991; Evans, Evans, and Marler, 1993).

Evidence of Functional Reference

Until quite recently, there was little reason to think that any system of animal signals might reasonably be regarded as functionally referential. The first evidence to the contrary came from field observations and experiments with vervet monkeys conducted in Amboseli national park in Kenya. Vervets live in social groups and have a large vocal repertoire that includes a variety of calls used in social interactions and several types of alarm calls. Vervet predators fall into three principal classes: large mammalian carnivores, the most dangerous of which is the leopard; raptors, particularly the martial eagle; and snakes, particularly the python. Struhsaker (1967) discovered that vervet alarm calls fall into at least three acoustically distinct classes, each of which corresponded quite closely to a single type of predator. Further, each of these call types appeared to elicit a different, and apparently adaptive, response. Vervets on the ground that heard a call elicited by an approaching leopard ran into the topmost branches of the tree canopy, where their greater agility made them difficult to catch. In contrast, calls evoked by eagles caused vervets to run out of the tree canopy, where they were vulnerable, or to run into bushes if they were in the open. When conspecifics called in response to pythons, other monkeys stood bipedally and peered into the grass around them.

The reactions of other vervets to the alarm calls of a group member were thus well matched to the hunting tactics of each of the three types of predators. However, these observational data could not exclude the possibility that the apparent responses to calls might, in fact, have been mediated principally by other cues, such as those provided by the caller's nonvocal behavior (e.g., Smith 1981, 1991).

Seyfarth, Cheney, and Marler (1980a, b) addressed this problem by conducting a series of field experiments in which tape-recorded vervet alarm calls were played back through a loudspeaker, in the absence both of the caller and of the predator to which it was responding. Under these conditions, the only information available to the monkeys was that contained in the acoustic structure of the sounds; other cues that would normally be available to aid interpretation, such as the nonvocal behavior of the signaler, perhaps including its gaze fixed upon the predator, were excluded. The results demonstrated that sufficient information was encoded in the calls for members of the group to select appropriate responses, even when contextual information was absent. Leopard alarms caused vervets to run into trees, while eagle alarms caused them to run into cover and to look upward. Snake alarms caused them to stand bipedally and look down.

These findings are consistent with the conclusion that vervet monkey alarm calls are functionally referential. That is, the calls seem to encode information about external events, in this case about the three major classes of predators. Companions are able to decode this information and put it to effective use in taking precautions against attack.

A similar system has recently been described in ring-tailed lemurs (Macedonia 1990; Pereira and Macedonia 1991) based on studies of individually marked captive animals in a seminatural setting. Like vervets, lemurs give different types of alarm calls in response to aerial and terrestrial predators. Playback experiments have demonstrated that the calls evoke qualitatively different and adaptive responses.

Experimental Analyses of an Avian Call System

Functional reference has also been investigated in birds, focusing especially on chickens. Perhaps surprisingly, the humble and much-maligned chicken has a large vocal repertoire (Konishi 1963; Collias 1987). Like vervets and lemurs, chickens give qualitatively different vocalizations in response to aerial and terrestrial predators. In fact, this trait seems to be widespread in gallinaceous birds (e.g., Goodwin 1953; Stokes 1961, 1967; Hale, Schleidt, and Schein 1969; Williams 1969; Maier 1982). We have worked with domesticated golden Sebrights, because they are better suited to handling and laboratory testing than jungle fowl, but they have not been subjected to artificial selection for rapid growth or egg production. Extensive comparisons of the vocalizations of jungle fowl and Sebrights suggest that both the total size of the vocal repertoire and call morphology are very similar.

As in the earlier work with vervets (Struhsaker 1967), the first step was to study the way in which chicken alarm calls are used during natural encounters with potential predators. A library of recordings was obtained from individually identified birds living in large outdoor enclosures (Gyger, Marler, and Pickert 1987). Each male was fitted with a wireless microphone that broadcast on a unique frequency, so it was straightforward to identify callers and to correlate their behavior with external events. Under these conditions, terrestrial alarm calls were produced in response to predators moving on the ground, such as dogs, while aerial alarm calls were elicited almost exclusively by objects moving overhead, such as red-tailed hawks and turkey vultures (Gyger, Marler, and Pickert 1987).

The two types of alarm calls have very different acoustic characteristics. Aerial alarm calls are made up of two components: an introductory pulse and a second unit, which may be either quite broadband (i.e., scream-like; figure 15.3a) or quite tonal (i.e., whistle-like; figure 15.3c). In contrast,

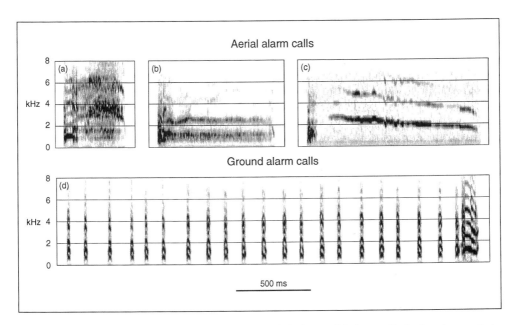

Figure 15.3 Acoustic characteristics of chicken aerial alarm calls (*a–c*) and ground alarm calls (*d*). The calls in panels *a* through *c* were produced by three different males in response to a computer-generated "hawk" stimulus. Note the individual variation in call structure. Panel *d* is part of a long bout of ground alarm calling.

Pre-stimulus

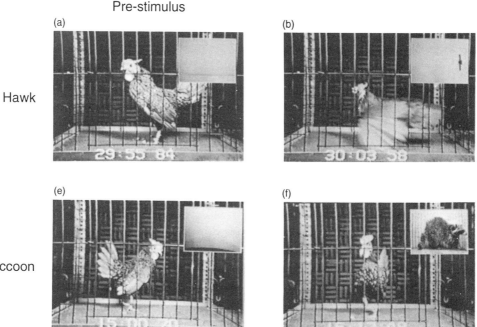

Figure 15.4 Photographs from test session videotapes depicting the aerial and terrestrial predator stimuli employed and the responses evoked by them. Frames *a* and *e* are prestimulus, while frame *b* through *d* and *f* through *h* illustrate the antipredator behavior elicited. The predator image seen by the males is represented in the small "window" in the upper right-hand corner of each frame. The "hawk" stimulus was presented overhead and was visible for 5 seconds, while the raccoon stimulus was presented at ground level and was visible for 60 seconds. The elapsed time covered by frames *b* through *d* is 1.3 seconds, while that covered by frames *f* through *h* is 44 seconds. (Redrawn from Evans, Evans, and Marler 1993.)

ground alarm calls are short, broadband pulses, which are typically produced in bouts (figure 15.3d).

The next phase of this research was conducted in the laboratory. An immediate advantage conferred by this move was that we were no longer dependent upon the chance appearance of potential predators. In addition, we were able for the first time to study a putatively referential call system under controlled conditions. Our experiments capitalized upon the recent discovery that chickens respond appropriately to videorecorded and computer-generated images of predators. The use of video image sequences provides great flexibility in defining stimulus characteristics, and this has facilitated analyses of the relationship between predator morphology and call type. To record aerial alarm calls, we placed males in a sound-attenuating chamber, with a large video monitor mounted on a frame above them so that the face was horizontal (see figure 1 in Evans and Marler 1992). Computer-generated animations simulating the flight of a soaring raptor were then displayed on the screen overhead (figure 15.4b–d).

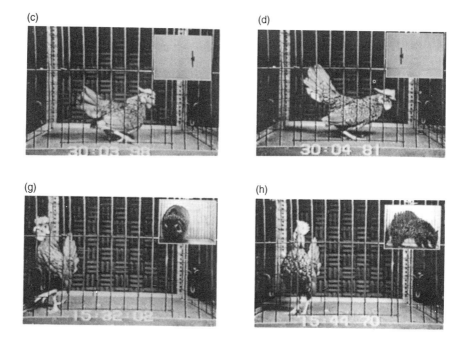

We selected a raccoon as a representative terrestrial predator. Raccoons are common in Dutchess County, N.Y., where these experiments began, and are known predators of our outdoor chicken colonies. An adult male raccoon was videotaped in a glass-fronted cage, which was constructed so that the front face matched the screen dimensions of the video monitor used for stimulus presentations, producing a life-sized image. We then edited the raw footage to create a 60-second stimulus sequence that contained almost continuous movement (figure 15.4 f–h). To elicit ground alarm calls, we displayed this video sequence on a large video monitor mounted at ground level adjacent to the subject's cage and behind a baffle, so that only the screen was visible.

The video images of aerial and terrestrial predators both elicited unambiguous changes in behavior of the type normally associated with the appearance of a real predator (Evans, Evans and Marler 1993). As in other experiments (Evans and Marler 1992; Evans, Macedonia, and Marler 1993), animated sequences of raptor-shaped stimuli were sufficient to elicit the full gamut of responses to flying raptors (figure 15.4 a–d). Males rolled their heads to fixate upward with one eye, crouched down, sleeked their feathers, and produced aerial alarm calls. Males often also "froze," remaining immobile for several seconds after the hawk image disappeared. In contrast, males responded to the videotaped raccoon sequence by assuming a very erect posture, fixating on the monitor, moving rapidly to the other end of the cage, and producing ground alarm calls while pivoting to and fro (figure 15.4 e–h). Only aerial alarm calls were evoked by the hawk animations, while only ground alarm calls were produced in response to the raccoon videotape. With these representative stimuli, there were no exceptions to this pattern of usage (Evans, Evans, and Marler 1993).

If chicken alarms are functionally referential, then we would expect playback of tape-recorded calls to elicit adaptively different responses even when other information, such as that provided by the nonvocal behavior of the calling male (crouching to a hawk or moving away from a raccoon) was absent. To test this prediction, we selected six exemplars of each call type, systematically sampling the natural variation in call duration and in spectral characteristics. Each aerial alarm call was matched to a bout of ground alarm calls so that the total duration of all of the ground alarm call pulses equaled that of the aerial alarm call with which they were paired.

We then randomly assigned a pair of these stimuli to each of 32 females. We also played back a control sound, which was constructed by editing out a section of background noise from the recording with the lowest signal-to-noise ratio (i.e., the loudest background). The noise sample was then iterated to create a pulse equal in total duration to the average of the 12 alarm call stimuli. This design allowed us to compare the responses evoked by the two types of alarm calls and also to assess the difference between the effects of call playback and those attributable to the background sounds with which calls are inevitably associated (e.g., nonspecific orienting responses).

Playbacks were conducted in a sound-attenuating chamber. Each hen was confined in the test cage, which was provided with food and with a small area of cover occupying one-fourth of the total floor area. The test session videorecordings were then analyzed frame by frame by raters who were "blind" (i.e., unaware of the stimulus that the hen had received in a given trial).

All three types of acoustic stimuli evoked obvious startle-like responses, interrupting activities such as feeding or preening and causing the birds to look in the direction of the loudspeaker. Following playback of aerial alarm calls, almost half of the hens ran toward or into the covered area of the cage. In contrast, neither ground alarm calls nor the background noise control had an appreciable effect on their use of cover (Evans, Evans, and Marler 1993).

The most revealing result concerns the way in which the birds monitored their surroundings after each type of playback. For this purpose, we assumed that chicken heads, like aircraft, can move in all three axes. All head movements in the two minutes following the stimuli were noted and coded by axis (pitch, yaw, and roll) and by direction and amplitude. From this detailed record, we were then able to reconstruct scanning movements and to compare the effects of the three types of sounds. We concentrated especially on horizontal scanning, which involves side-to-side head movements, and on looking upward, which, because chickens have laterally placed eyes, involves a stereotyped head-rolling movement.

Formal analyses were based on unambiguous movements with an amplitude greater than approximately 45 degrees. Horizontal scanning (figure 15.5a) was significantly increased by both ground alarm calls and aerial alarm calls relative to the background noise control. In contrast, the probability of hens looking up (figure 15.5b) was almost three times greater following aerial alarm call playback than after playback of either background noise or ground alarm calls, the responses to which did not differ on this measure (Evans, Evans, and Marler 1993).

There were also reliable changes in posture associated with alarm call playbacks. Aerial alarm calls caused hens to crouch down, with head and tail lowered, while ground alarm calls caused them to adopt an unusually erect, alert posture. These responses were so characteristic that raters familiar with chicken behavior could identify the type of alarm call presented from tracings of body position alone with an accuracy of 78 to 95 percent. The performance of the raters was, in every case, significantly better than chance.

These data, together with those on scanning and the use of cover, demonstrate that chicken alarm calls meet both production and perception criteria for functional reference. Videotaped and computer-generated images simulating terrestrial and aerial predators evoked structurally distinct alarm calls specific to stimulus type. "Hawk" animations elicited only aerial alarm calls, while video footage of a raccoon elicited only ground alarm calls. This pattern of call usage is consistent with that observed under natural conditions (Gyger, Marler, and Pickert 1987). Subsequent playback presentations of each call type were sufficient to evoke responses that were qualitatively distinct and, in each case, appropriate to the visual stimulus that originally elicited the call. The chicken alarm call system thus appears to share with the call systems of vervets and lemurs the property of encoding information about predator type.

Further Studies of Alarm Call Usage

Chicken alarm calls seem to allow receivers to predict something about external events, but refining our estimate of what this might be required a more comprehensive characterization of call usage (i.e., the relationship between the characteristics of a visual stimulus and the type of call produced). One logical possibility was that call type might simply encode the location of danger. By this account, aerial alarm calls would mean "something overhead," and ground alarm calls would mean "something on the ground." Alternatively, the alarm calls might be thought of as taxonomic labels for predator type, so that the same call would always be evoked by a hawk, regardless of its position. The data reviewed so far are consistent with both models.

To differentiate between these hypotheses it was necessary to manipulate the position of predator images, assessing the relative importance of morphology and spatial location by showing chickens a raccoon overhead

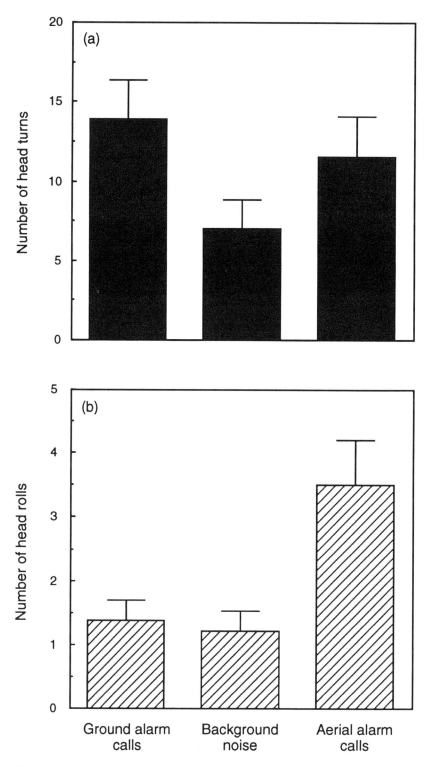

Figure 15.5 Visual monitoring by hens following playbacks. (*a*) Scanning in the horizontal plane (i.e., moving the head in an arc from side to side). Mean (+ SE) number of head turns. (*b*) Looking upward (i.e., rolling the head to fixate laterally with one eye). Mean (+ SE) number of head rolls. (Redrawn from Evans, Evans, and Marler 1993.)

and a soaring hawk at ground level. We encountered an obstacle, however, because our videorecordings contained not only predator images, but also the backgrounds against which they had been filmed. The image of the raccoon overhead would thus have been accompanied by the cage in which he was confined and the substrate on which he was walking, in contrast with the background of blue sky visible on all of the raptor footage. Such stimuli would not have permitted an unconfounded test of the role of position, because we would have been simultaneously manipulating both predator type and background cues.

We addressed this problem by using digitized image sequences. We began by videotaping the raccoon in a glass-fronted cage. Sequences containing movement were then identified and edited together, creating the illusion of continuous circling movements. Each frame in this sequence was then digitized and manipulated using a microcomputer. We used a "paint" program to erase everything in the image other than the raccoon, leaving the predator isolated on a homogenous white background (figure 15.6a). The resulting edited images were then compiled into an animation using a "page-flipping" algorithm. Our aerial predator sequence was of

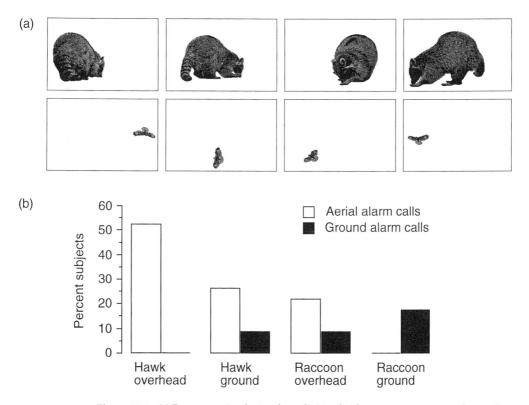

Figure 15.6 (*a*) Representative frames from digitized video sequences presented to explore the relative importance of spatial location and morphology in determining alarm call usage. (*b*) Alarm calls elicited by each of the predator type and position combinations.

a soaring rough-legged hawk that had been videorecorded under natural conditions. This footage was manipulated in exactly the same way as the raccoon footage (figure 15.6a). The isolated hawk and raccoon stimuli were each presented both at ground level and overhead. Prior to stimulus presentations, each of the video monitors displayed a uniform white field. We then gradually superimposed a randomly chosen predator image on one of them.

Figure 15.6b depicts the type of call elicited by each of the four predator type and position combinations. The results replicate our original demonstration that cocks produce only aerial alarm calls in response to a raptor presented above and only ground alarm calls when shown a terrestrial predator in the normal position. The hawk at ground level and raccoon overhead both evoked a mixed response, but each of these stimuli was significantly less effective than the hawk overhead. It was particularly striking that the overhead raccoon failed to evoke the sort of nonvocal responses typically associated with aerial predators, such as crouching and prolonged immobility. Evidently, placing a terrestrial predator overhead is not sufficient to evoke the full aerial predator response. On the other hand, spatial location clearly plays a role, because the number of calls elicited by both types of predators was reduced when they were in inappropriate positions.

One initially surprising result was the reduced effectiveness of the digitized raccoon when it was presented at ground level. Only about a quarter of the birds tested produced alarm calls. This is unlikely to be an artifact of digitization, as the hawk was also digitized and response levels were much greater. One likely possibility is that cues provided by the substrate and background are important for recognition of ground predators. The original raccoon footage included the floor of the cage and the wire side walls, which made it much easier to assess depth (figure 15.4 f–h). In addition, the moving raccoon obscured the parts of the cage behind him, thereby providing an interposition cue. Such background information would not be expected to play an important role in recognition of aerial predators, which, as seen from below, are essentially two-dimensional silhouettes against a featureless background.

Criteria for Production of Aerial Alarm Calls
It has proved more straightforward to produce aerial predator stimuli that elicit robust and reliable responses. There is no hint here of the complexities of figure-ground relationship that we may need to resolve to understand ground alarm calling. Chicken aerial alarm calling does present something of a puzzle, however, as becomes evident from data on call specificity under natural conditions (figure 15.7). The pie diagrams in figure 15.7 represent the proportion of vervet "eagle" alarms and chicken aerial alarm calls elicited by various environmental events. Fully 49 percent of vervet calls were associated with martial eagles, while only

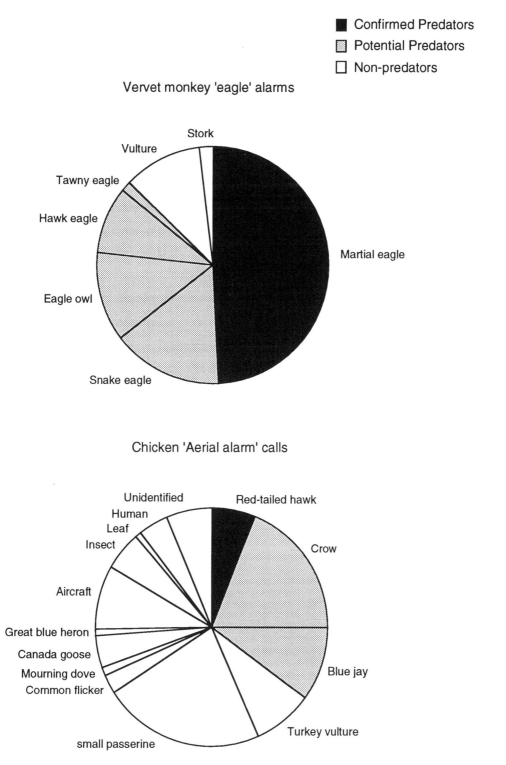

Figure 15.7 Specificity of vervet monkey "eagle" alarms and chicken aerial alarm calls recorded under natural conditions. Vervet data are from Cheney and Seyfarth (1980); chicken data are from Gyger et al, (1987.)

6 percent of chicken alarm calls were elicited by red-tailed hawks or kestrels, which were the two most likely predators in our study area. If potential predators are included, then a similar contrast is evident; 88 percent of vervet calls were given to martial eagles, snake eagles, eagle owls, hawk eagles, and tawny eagles combined. If crows, which may take chicks and eggs, together with blue jays, which are likely egg predators, are added, then chicken aerial alarm calls were still associated with predators only 35 percent of the time. It is also striking that adult chickens gave aerial alarm calls to such innocuous objects as falling leaves and insects. While vervet monkey infants sometimes made what might be called "mistakes" of this type, adults clearly did not (Seyfarth and Cheney 1980).

It seems then that analogous vervet and chicken calls are appropriately named. Vervet eagle calls are highly specific, while chicken aerial alarm calls are less so. Field observations suggest that chicken aerial alarm calls are associated with a broad range of stimuli that have the common characteristic of being airborne. This contrast is all the more striking when we consider the cues that vervets seem to be using to recognize aerial predators. As in other work on visual categories (e.g., Herrnstein, Loveland, and Cable 1976; Herrnstein 1984, 1991) and concept formation (e.g., Lea 1984; Pepperberg 1987a, b), the analysis of errors is revealing. Most vervet eagle alarms were given in response to martial eagles, and the other species that elicited alarms shared not only the general silhouette, but also aspects of the ventral markings of martial eagles (Seyfarth and Cheney 1980). Observational studies of natural interactions between vervets and their avian predators thus suggest that relatively subtle visual features are important.

To obtain comparable data on the perceptual basis of aerial alarm call production in chickens, we have conducted a series of experiments using computer-generated animations. This approach has allowed us to perform a series of "titrations," manipulating the apparent size, speed, and shape of synthetic raptor images while controlling other parameters, such as the total duration of stimulus presentations. We began with apparent size (i.e., the angle subtended at the chicken's eye by the body of a raptor-shaped silhouette). A series of stimuli was created, ranging in apparent size from 1 to 8 degrees. Each silhouette in the series had twice the length and wingspan of the one before. Apparent speed was held constant. Almost no alarm calls were elicited by the two smallest shapes, subtending 1 and 2 degrees. There was then a qualitative increase in alarm calling as apparent size was increased to 4 and 8 degrees (Evans, Macedonia, and Marler 1993; figure 15.8). Analyses of the males' nonvocal responses revealed that they visually fixated all of the hawk stimuli, so we are confident that the low level of alarm calling to smaller images was not simply an artifact of reduced visibility.

There was a similar increase in the probability of calling when apparent speed, in lengths per second, was varied, this time holding size constant

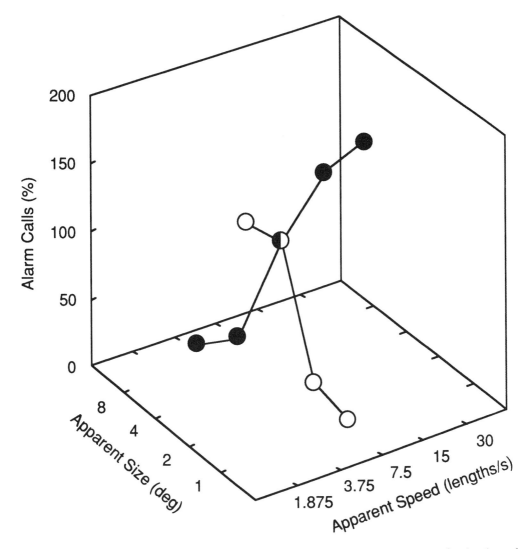

Figure 15.8 Number of aerial alarm calls elicited by computer-generated animations of hawk silhouettes varying in apparent size (angle subtended at the subject's eye) and apparent speed. Alarm calling has been expressed as a percentage of the response evoked by a standard stimulus subtending 4 degrees and moving at 7.5 lengths per second. (Redrawn from Evans, Macedonia, and Marler 1993.)

at 4 degrees (Evans, Macedonia, and Marler 1993; figure 15.8). The range of speeds chosen extended from that characteristic of an almost-stationary hawk soaring slowly on a thermal at one end to that of a stooping falcon at the other end (Meinertzhagen 1955). Slow-moving hawk shapes evoked very few calls, while large numbers of calls were given to stimuli moving at 7.5 lengths per second or faster.

To test the importance of shape cues, we borrowed an idea from classical ethology (Tinbergen 1948, 1951) and began with a simple disc, which has the unique property of being the same size in all dimensions. We then used a "morphing" algorithm to gradually transform the disc into the silhouette of a red-tailed hawk. By sampling at points along this continuum, we created a series of stimuli that became progressively more like an aerial predator, while holding total area constant (figure 15.9). Each of these shapes was animated, so that they all flew across the screen of the video monitor at the same speed. Since actual speed (in meters per second) was held constant, transforming the disc shape into a raptor silhouette produced a gradual increase in apparent speed (in lengths per second) as body length was reduced. To assess whether this change affected chicken aerial alarm calling, we added a "fast disc" control stimulus. This disc moved at the same apparent speed as the most realistic hawk silhouette (10.14 lengths per second) and provided a direct comparison with the disc at one pole of the shape continuum, which moved at 7.5 lengths per second.

Although some alarm calls were elicited by the disc, chickens were significantly more likely to call in response to the more realistic raptor-shaped stimuli (figure 15.9). We are confident that this increase in alarm calling is attributable to variation in shape, because there was no difference between the number of calls elicited by the disc and the number evoked by the fast disc control. In addition, the males gave significantly more calls to the red-tailed hawk silhouette than to either the disc (moving at the same actual speed) or the fast disc (moving at the same apparent speed).

In summary, male chickens gave aerial alarm calls to objects that were overhead, large (apparent size greater than 4 degrees), fast-moving (apparent speed greater than 7.5 lengths per second), and approximately bird-shaped. There is no reason to think that this is an exhaustive list. Our current estimate of the information content of aerial alarm calls is thus "large, fast-moving, bird-shaped aerial object."

The Response Urgency Model

An alternative interpretation parallels that suggested for ground squirrel alarm calls (Owings and Hennessy 1984). Chicken predators differ not only in morphology, but also in their hunting tactics, and hence in the nature of the threat that they present. A stooping hawk represents an immediate danger, with at most a few seconds available for escape, while the relatively slow approach of a terrestrial predator, such as a fox or a raccoon, usually allows a more deliberate response. Alarm calls might thus provide information not about predator characteristics, but rather about urgency (i.e., about the probability of attack or the time available for escape). For example, the aerial alarm call might instead by thought of as a "high-urgency" call and the ground alarm call as a "low-urgency" call. Two lines of evidence militate against this account.

We might logically suppose that chickens perceive large (and hence apparently low-altitude) raptor silhouettes as the most threatening, and

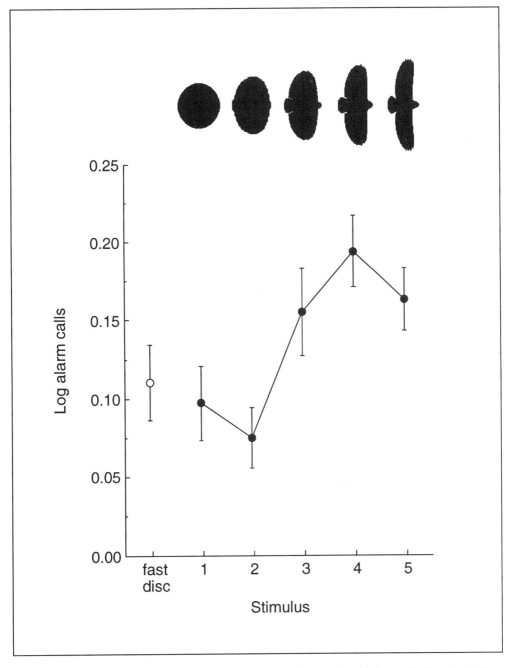

Figure 15.9 Effect of stimulus shape on production of aerial alarm calls. The stimuli shown at the top all moved at the same speed and were equal in area. Significantly more alarm calls were evoked by the more realistic raptor-shaped images.

hence as requiring the most urgent response. In the apparent size experiment, such stimuli reliably evoked aerial alarm calls. However, smaller silhouettes, although clearly fixated and sufficient to elicit crouching and other antipredator behavior, elicited very few calls. Without exception, the calls produced were aerial alarms (Evans, Macedonia, and Marler 1993). A switch to ground alarms would have been predicted if transitions between call types simply reflected the level of response urgency.

A second line of evidence is provided by the responses of males to the videorecorded raccoon. The raccoon video image was presented at an apparent distance of approximately 0.3 metres. A life-size ground predator appearing suddenly at this distance presumably simulates a high probability of attack. These conditions closely resemble those under which ground squirrels switch from "chatter" calls, normally associated with terrestrial predators, to the "whistles" normally evoked by raptors (Owings and Hennessy 1984). Nevertheless, chickens invariably responded with ground alarm calls rather than with aerial alarm calls, as might be predicted by an "urgency" model. Experiments with ring-tailed lemurs have similarly revealed that alarm call type is dependent upon predator class rather than apparent probability of attack (Pereira and Macedonia 1991).

The balance of the evidence thus favors a model of signaling principally about predator characteristics rather than about response urgency. This is not to suggest that the alarm calls do not encode information about the immediacy of the threat presented by a predator, in addition to that about morphology, but rather that differences in response urgency are not sufficient to explain the observed patterns of call usage.

Comparative Studies of Alarm Call Specificity
It is perhaps not surprising that chicken aerial alarm calls are less highly specific than the eagle alarms of vervet monkeys. If only for reasons of phylogenetic chauvinism, we might expect primates to have a more sophisticated predator recognition system than birds. But this is not invariably so. Field studies of antipredator behavior in southern lapwings (Walters 1990) demonstrate that their alarm calling, like that of vervets, is apparently dependent on subtle cues. For example, lapwings call to several species of large hawks, but ignore one which, although similar in appearance to the others, eats only fish and consequently does not present a danger to them. Walters suggests that this very discriminating antipredator behavior is a consequence of habitat characteristics. Lapwings inhabit open grasslands, such as the Venezuelan llanos. Potential predators are visible much of the time, and a predator recognition strategy that produced high false alarm rates would be costly because of frequent and unnecessary interruptions in behavior.

In contrast, domesticated chickens are thought to have been derived from red jungle fowl, which live in forests and dense brush where visibility is limited (Collias and Collias 1967). They may consequently be using a simple "rule of thumb" for responding to aerial objects not because of any fundamental limitation in their ability to discriminate visual stimuli, but rather because this allows rapid responses, although at the cost of a higher false alarm rate (Evans, Macedonia, and Marler 1993). By this account, alarm call specificity is in part the product of selection for different balances between type I and type II error rates. To borrow from classical signal detection theory (e.g., Swets 1961), lapwings seem to have a rather conservative response criterion, while that of jungle fowl is more liberal. Systematic comparative work, ideally on closely related species with very different habitats, will be necessary to test this hypothesis.

Unanswered Questions About Referential Signal Systems

One of the many challenges for the future is a laboratory analysis of the development of functionally referential call systems, including descriptions of ontogenetic change in both call morphology and call usage. For example, infant vervet monkeys have a clear predisposition to give eagle alarms to aerial objects, but the range of effective stimuli is much more broadly defined than in adulthood. Calls are initially evoked by obviously inappropriate events, such as falling leaves. Over the first year of life, however, there is a dramatic increase in call specificity, so that eagle alarms eventually are produced only in response to martial eagles and a few very similar species (Seyfarth and Cheney 1980). Under field conditions, it has proved impossible to disentangle the relative importance of maturational change, experience with the behavior of adults faced with predators, and experience with predators themselves.

We shall also have to determine the meaning of more fine-grained variation in signal structure. Analyses of referential signal systems conducted to date have been principally concerned with call type. Very little is currently known about the perceptual significance of within-category variation in call morphology (e.g., figure 15.3 a–c), although efforts have been made to ensure that it is adequately represented in the set of exemplars chosen for playback experiments (e.g., Seyfarth, Cheney, and Marler 1980b; Gouzoules, Gouzoules, and Marler 1984; Evans, Evans, and Marler 1993). Theoretical models have been developed of the ways in which affective state and stimulus characteristics might interact to determine signal structure (Marler, Evans, and Hauser 1992). Empirical studies will be required to test these ideas, beginning perhaps with food-elicited calls, since motivational state and food characteristics can both be readily manipulated (e.g., Elowson, Tannenbaum, and Snowdon 1991; Evans and Marler 1994).

Finally, it will be important to systematically assess the role of contextual factors (Smith 1965, 1977, 1991; Leger 1993). Playback experiments, by design, eliminate information that might normally be gleaned from the nonvocal behavior of callers. If companions are nevertheless able to select appropriate responses, then it follows that cues provided by the nonvocal behavior of the signaler are not essential. This does not, however, imply that such cues are not salient to conspecifics or that they do not mediate the response to vocalizations when they are available. We anticipate that contextual information often plays an important role, perhaps especially in species that have stable social groups (Marler, Evans, and Hauser 1992; Evans, Evans and Marler 1993).

SOCIAL CONTEXT AND ANIMAL SIGNAL PRODUCTION

Classical treatments of animal signaling behavior tend to assume that call production is essentially reflexive (e.g., Lyons 1972). That is, that when a stimulus sufficient to elicit antipredator behavior is presented (e.g., a hawk simulation), then alarm calls will necessarily be produced. Bickerton (1990, p. 143) has suggested that the capacity to control the production of vocal signals independent of the other reactions to a stimulus was an essential event in the evolution of language.

The Audience Effect and Alarm Calling

There are, however, now several descriptions of such flexibility in the signaling behavior of nonhuman animals. The probability of alarm calling by vervet monkeys (Cheney and Seyfarth 1985), ground squirrels (Sherman 1977), and downy woodpeckers (Sullivan 1985) is known to change dependent on social circumstances. Work by Gyger, Karakashian, and Marler (1986) provided the first experimental demonstration of sensitivity to social context in the alarm-calling behavior of chickens. They used a technique like that described in the classic work of Lorenz and Tinbergen, eliciting alarm calls by presenting small raptor-shaped models overhead. Subject males were confined in a wire cage on the floor, and audience birds could be introduced into a second adjacent cage. Males were presented with a hawk stimulus in the presence of either a female chicken, a female bobwhite quail, or an empty cage. They gave significantly more alarm calls with the hen present than with either the bobwhite quail or the empty cage. It is important to note that, even when males did not produce alarm calls, they still engaged in the other components of response to an avian predator, including crouching down, fixating upon the stimulus, and remaining immobile. So call production was not inextricably linked to other antipredator behavior. Rather, it could be decoupled from nonvocal responses and was sensitive to the presence of a potential receiver (Gyger, Karakashian, and Marler 1986; Karakashian, Gyger, and Marler 1988). We refer to this selective potentiation of calling as an audience effect.

Audience Characteristics and Alarm Calling
What constitutes an adequate audience for production of alarm calls? We have sought answers to this question in a series of studies that exploit the finding that, in addition to recognizing video images of predators,

male chickens respond socially to videorecorded hens. In an initial experiment, we compared the effectiveness of videorecorded and live companions by replacing the audience cage with a large video monitor and a loudspeaker (Evans and Marler 1991). Males were then tested for aerial alarm calling with both live and videotaped audiences of female chickens, bobwhite quail, and an empty cage.

The results obtained with live audiences replicated those of earlier experiments (Gyger, Karakashian, and Marler 1986; Karakashian, Gyger, and Marler 1988): significantly more alarm calls were elicited with a female chicken adjacent than with either a bobwhite quail or an empty cage (figure 15.10a). Exactly the same pattern of statistically significant comparisons was obtained with the videotaped audiences (figure 15.10b). The female chicken videotape was a significantly more effective audience than either the bobwhite quail videotape or the empty cage. Pairwise comparisons of the number of alarm calls elicited by hawk models with the live and videotaped audiences of each type revealed no significant differences. Most remarkably, a videotape of a hen, with sound, was as effective as a live female.

Comparisons of the responses of males to videorecorded chicken and bobwhite quail images also illustrate one advantage of the increased level of stimulus control that can be achieved with videotape playbacks. During videotaping, female chickens had tended to move and vocalize more than bobwhite quail. In assembling the audience videotapes, we deliberately eliminated this contrast by including substantially more vocal and locomotor activity in the edited bobwhite video sequences than in the chicken ones. Cocks nevertheless produced a larger number of alarm calls with a videorecorded chicken audience (figure 15.10b). This comparison demonstrates that the apparent species-specificity of audience effects cannot be explained solely on the basis of gross differences in overall levels of activity.

It was not, however, clear which attributes of the videorecorded audiences males were responding to. One reasonable hypothesis was that they were simply attending to the soundtrack. Hundreds of conventional playback experiments have demonstrated that acoustic signals alone are often sufficient to elicit a full response (e.g., Becker 1982). For example, a loudspeaker placed in a sparrow's territory broadcasting species-typical song will evoke much of the aggressive behavior normally directed at an intruding male.

To resolve this issue, we conducted a second experiment, which was designed to assess the relative importance of the visual and acoustic components of a videorecorded sequence. We presented a hawk model to males with one of four types of audiences: a hen image with contact calls, the same video sequence with a silent soundtrack, contact calls played back while an empty cage was displayed on the screen, and a silent empty cage. There was again a reliable audience effect when both

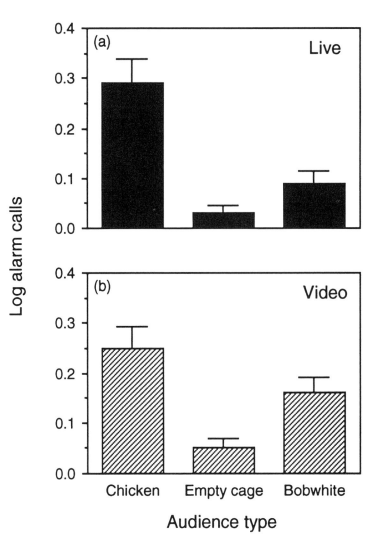

Figure 15.10 A comparison of the rates of male alarm calling (expressed as mean log call rate + SE) in the presence of live (*a*) or videotaped (*b*) audiences. Audiences consisted of a female chicken, a bobwhite quail, and an empty cage. (Redrawn from Evans and Marler 1991.)

the image and sound were presented (figure 15.11). Males gave significantly fewer alarm calls when either the sound or the visual image was removed, although both of these audience stimuli remained significantly more effective than the silent empty cage. There was no significant difference in the number of alarm calls elicited in the image-only and sound-only conditions.

These two experiments show that a videotaped image of a conspecific with sound can be as effective as a live hen in potentiating production of aerial alarm calls (Evans and Marler 1991). Further, both visual and

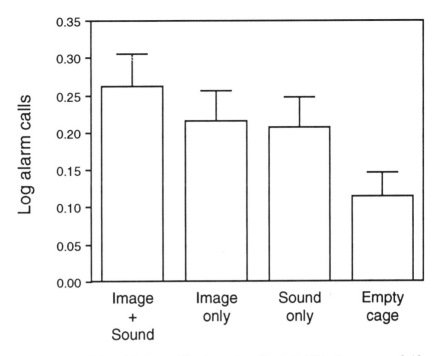

Figure 15.11 Male aerial alarm calling (mean log call rate + SE) in the presence of video-taped audiences consisting of chicken images and contact calls (image + sound), chicken images with a silent soundtrack (image only), an empty cage image with chicken sounds (sound only), and a silent empty cage (empty cage). (Redrawn from Evans and Marler 1991.)

acoustic stimulation is necessary to elicit the full audience effect, although either component alone can significantly increase call production. Visual and acoustic cues seem to be of comparable importance. Future studies will take advantage of the great flexibility conferred by digital image processing techniques, like those employed in our studies of predator recognition, to more fully describe the visual characteristics necessary for an audience effect.

Audience Effects and Food Calling

The sensitivity of male chickens to social context is not restricted to alarm calling. When cocks find something edible, they often produce a distinctive "food call," which consists of a string of repeated high-pitched pulses (Collias 1987). One correlate of this behavior is that they will allow hens, which are often attracted by the calling, to approach and take the food either directly from their beaks or from the ground in front of them (Marler, Dufty, and Pickert 1986a, b).

The effects of an audience on food calling are more complex than those on alarm calling. While production of aerial alarm calls is potentiated by the presence of other chickens whether they are cocks, hens, or chicks

(Karakashian, Gyger, and Marler 1988), the probability of food calling is sensitive to audience gender. Males call quite readily when they are alone, particularly if the food item presented is highly preferred (Marler, Dufty, and Pickert 1986a). The call rate increases in the presence of a hen, especially if she is unfamiliar (Marler, Dufty, and Pickert 1986b). In contrast, when another male is present, calling is abolished. Production of food calls is thus dependent upon both food characteristics and the nature of potential receivers; males are capable of increasing their call rate under some social conditions and of reducing it in others.

In our recent studies of food call audience effects, we have employed simple operant techniques to obtain control over both the motivational state of males and stimulus characteristics (Evans and Marler 1994). We first trained cocks to keypeck for food reinforcement, and then conducted experiments in which social context was manipulated. During some tests the males were alone, while during others there was a hen in the adjacent cage. Each test began with a two-minute "baseline" period during which no food was available. The response key was then lit, and males could obtain food on a fixed-ratio schedule (i.e., every 16 pecks produced a delivery of small food pellets). Under these conditions, the full complement of food-related behavior occurred; males called and also engaged in the stereotyped "tidbitting" display in which the food item is repeatedly picked up and dropped in front of the hen (Evans and Marler 1994).

Figure 15.12 depicts the distribution of food calling over time. Food calling increased dramatically (in fact, ten-fold) when food first became available (figure 15.12a). This was true both when a hen was present and when males were alone. There was also clear evidence of an audience effect. Males produced significantly more food calls when there was a hen in the adjacent cage. No such change in the probability of food calling was observed during control trials when food was unavailable (figure 15.12b). Under these conditions, the vocal behavior of males was unaffected by the presence of a hen (Evans and Marler 1994).

The Food Call Audience Effect and Social Facilitation
Just as with alarm calling, the effects of social context were specific to vocal behavior. Figure 15.13a displays the number of food calls produced by males in association with each food delivery. Call rates dropped somewhat over the course of the test session, but at each reinforcement males called significantly more when they had a female audience than when they were alone. In contrast, there was no effect of social context on the rate at which the cocks worked to obtain food (figure 15.13b). Males pecked slightly more slowly with successive reinforcements, but this behavior was entirely unaffected by the presence of a hen.

This finding suggests that increases in food calling with a female audience were not simply a consequence of a generalized increase in arousal (Dewsbury 1992), since such a change would be expected also to affect the rate of male feeding behavior. The food call audience effect can thus

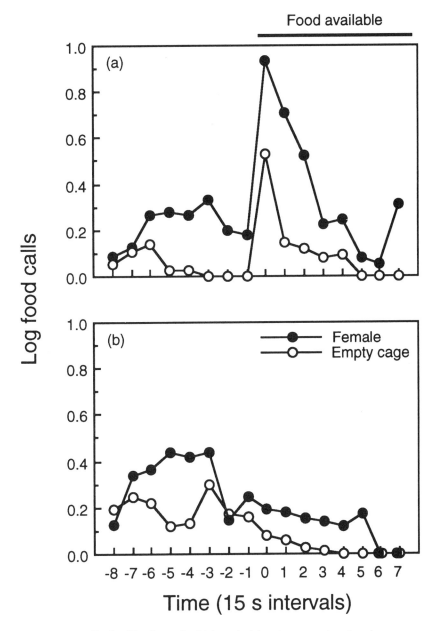

Figure 15.12 Food calling by male chickens in laboratory experiments using an operant paradigm to control access to food. (*a*) Food trials. Note the pronounced increase in call production synchronous with the onset of food availability (interval 0). Males emitted food calls at a higher rate when a hen was present than when they were alone. (*b*) No-food control trials. There was no effect of social context when food was unavailable. (Redrawn from Evans and Marler 1994.)

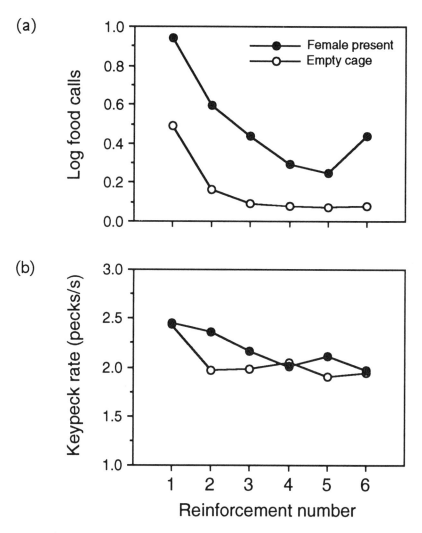

Figure 15.13 Comparison of the effects of social context on (*a*) food calling and (*b*) operant performance. There was a clear audience effect on food calling in association with each of the six food deliveries (*a*). In contrast, the presence of a hen had no detectable influence on the rate at which males pecked a key to obtain food (*b*). Redrawn from Evans and Marler 1994.)

be distinguished from classical social facilitation (Zajonc 1965), which is characterized by improved performance of a well-learned motor skill in the presence of an observer. The presence of an appropriate receiver appears to act specifically to potentiate call production, and this effect is independent of other nonsignaling behavior.

SOME UNIQUE PROPERTIES OF LANGUAGE

The work that we have reviewed demonstrates that nonhuman animals have cognitive abilities analogous to those that in humans give rise to phenomena such as categorical perception, labeling of objects, and a sensitivity to social context. The alarm calls of vervet monkeys, ring-tailed lemurs, and chickens function like words in the sense that they are arbitrary acoustic labels that are reliably associated with defined categories of visual stimuli. We might thus begin to make the case that some of the differences between animal systems and language are quantitative rather than qualitative, although the difference between a "vocabulary" of a few calls and one of some tens of thousands of words, as in human adults, is a prodigious one.

Further parallels between animal communication and language are suggested by studies of song learning in birds, which reveal the existence of a sensitive period early in life and the importance of auditory feedback (e.g., Marler 1970a, b, 1991). Song learning thus provides an example of traditional transmission (Hockett 1960) in nonhuman animals. The vocal learning process also gives rise to geographical variation in structure analogous to linguistic dialects (Marler and Tamura 1962). In addition, production of learned song, like speech, is controlled by anatomically distinct regions on one side of the brain (Nottebohm 1971, 1991).

Research with primates has provided evidence of a speech-like degree of lateralization in the perceptual processing of vocal signals. Japanese macaques have an enhanced ability to discriminate species-typical calls when they are presented to the right ear (and hence to the left hemisphere) (Petersen et al. 1978; Petersen et al. 1984). This improved performance was apparently specific to recognition of meaningful variation in call structure, since it did not occur either when other species were tested with Japanese macaque calls or when the discrimination involved an auditory dimension that would normally be irrelevant. The ability of female mice to recognize the ultrasonic distress calls produced by their pups is similarly dependent upon left hemispheric processing (Ehret 1987b). As in macaques, perceptual lateralization was apparent only when the sounds presented had communicative significance (Ehret 1987b). Recent experiments with zebra finches demonstrate that hemispheric differences in auditory processing also occur in birds (Cynx, Williams, and Nottebohm 1992). The history of comparative studies on the lateralization of perceptual processing hence parallels that of research on categorical perception. In both cases, a phenomenon once regarded as a unique adaptation for speech processing has been shown instead to be shared with a number of other vertebrates.

Nonhuman animals also engage in precisely timed vocal interactions, of which duets are the most striking example (see reviews by Farabaugh 1982; Haimoff 1984). In some species, there is evidence of "turn-taking" reminiscent of that which occurs during conversations, suggesting that there are rules determining when call production is appropriate (e.g., Snowdon and Cleveland 1984; Chaiken 1990). Recent experiments using interactive playbacks have demonstrated that both birds (Dabelsteen and

Pedersen 1990; Evans 1991; McGregor et al. 1992) and frogs (Schwartz 1991; Schwartz and Rand 1991) are sensitive to the timing relationship between their signals and those that are broadcast to them.

Although these parallels between the functional properties of animal communication and those of human language are extensive, there are no animal signal systems that have all of the characteristics that we have described. For example, although vocal learning has been demonstrated in many passerine birds, it does not occur in the chicken (Konishi 1963), which is the only avian species currently known to have functionally referential alarm calls. There is similarly no compelling evidence of vocal learning in nonhuman primates (Snowdon 1990; Owren et al. 1992). Other comparisons between language and the signaling behavior of nonhuman animals reveal a number of attributes that are entirely unique. We will not attempt to provide an exhaustive list of these features (see reviews by Aitchison 1983; Crystal 1987; Bickerton 1990), but will instead focus on a few properties that seem to be of fundamental importance.

The apparent analogy between referential signals and words is not as straightforward as it at first appears. The animal call systems that have so far been studied appear to provide information about phenomena such as the approach of potential predators or the discovery of food. Linguistic labels refer not to environmental events directly, but rather to mental representations of those events. We consequently have words (e.g., "altruist" or "hypocrite") that may map onto identifiable external stimuli, but the characteristics defining such a category can be described only in terms of behavioral conventions; that is, they have no reliable physical correlates. We also have words for entirely hypothetical constructs (unicorns are a classic example), and we can coin neologisms whenever there is a need to do so. The difference between nouns and calls is thus not merely one of vocabulary size. We are able to describe abstract concepts, while the natural signals of animals seem to be limited to describing a small array of functionally significant events, together with the subsequent behavior of the sender.

In addition, only about half of the words used in either spoken English or prose are lexical items that correspond to concepts or categories. The balance are grammatical items (e.g., *of, that, which, if, and*), which lack referents entirely. We can find no analogues for these words in the communicative behavior of animals. Grammatical items have a multiplicity of functions, allowing us to encode information about relative properties such as size, position, and number and to indicate tense.

Perhaps the most dramatic contrast between animal communication and language is provided by syntax. Many animal signals superficially resemble sentences in that they have a hierarchical structure (i.e., "phonological syntax"; Marler 1977). For example, the songs and calls of birds are made up of discrete elements that may be combined into longer utterances according to organizational rules, some of which have now been formally described (e.g., Hailman and Ficken 1986; Hailman, Ficken, and Ficken 1987; Lemon, Dobson, and Clifton 1993). The product of this process is a set of characteristic sequences. There is, however, little evidence for the property of "lexical syntax" (Marler 1977)—that is, for variation in the order of elements that causes changes in meaning—except in the trivial sense that artificially altered sequences are not recognized (e.g., Ficken and Ficken 1973; Boughey and Thompson 1976; Ewert 1980).

In contrast, assessment of the meaning of speech is critically dependent upon syntactic structure. The sentence "Chimpanzees have a greater cognitive capacity than chickens" is a very different assertion from that obtained by shuffling the elements to produce "Chickens have a greater cognitive capacity than chimpanzees." Nor is meaning dependent simply upon temporal order. Formal analyses of syntactic structure stress that the construction of grammatical sentences is dependent upon a complex rule-governed process that may be modeled as a hierarchical series of nested levels (e.g., Crystal 1987).

The rule-based nature of syntax gives rise to the property of "productivity" (Hockett 1960), the ability to generate an essentially infinite variety of meaningful new utterances using a relatively small set of basic components. Despite the extraordinary flexibility conferred by productivity, studies of referential signal systems provide no evidence of the evolution of such an ability in nonhuman animals. Alarm calls are often single utterances, so that analyses for the presence of syntactic structure are not possible. When trains of calls are produced, they tend simply to be repetitions of a single element or of morphologically similar elements (e.g., Cheney and Seyfarth 1990; Evans, Evans, and Marler 1993). While such repetition is probably salient to companions and may connote variation in perceived threat, such as that posed by the continued presence of a predator, there is no qualitative change in meaning. As a number of recent reviews have pointed out (Bickerton 1990; Snowdon 1990; Corballis 1991), productivity seems to be a genuinely unique feature of language.

A related point is that very few animal signals have the property of "temporal displacement"—that is, the ability to describe events that have occurred in the past or that might occur in the future. The dance of honeybees (von Frisch 1967) is a conspicuous exception, as workers are invariably providing information about a food source that they have visited sometime earlier. Even here, the time window does not exceed a few hours (Lindauer 1957; von Frisch 1967).

The vocal signals upon which we have concentrated seem entirely limited to communication about the present. Vervet alarms might reasonably be glossed "Leopard!", but not "Remember that old leopard we saw last week?" or "Do you imagine that we might meet a leopard tomorrow?". Note, however, that the frequently observed phenomenon of animals producing alarm signals for extended periods after a predator has

Descartes, R. (1662). *Trait de l'homme*. E. S. Haldane and G. R. T. Ross (Trans.). Cambridge: Cambridge University Press.

Dewsbury, D. A. (1992). Surplusage, audience effects and George John Romanes. *Behavioral and Brain Sciences,* 15, 152.

Dooling, R. J., Soli, S. D., Kline, R. M., Park, T. J., Hue, C., and Bunnell, T. (1987). Perception of synthetic speech sounds by the budgerigar *(Melopsittacus undulatus)*. *Bulletin of the Psychonomic Society*, 25, 139–142.

Dretske, F. (1988). *Explaining Behavior*. Cambridge, MA: The MIT Press.

Ehret, G. (1987a). Categorical perception of sound signals: Facts and hypotheses from animal studies. In S. Harnad (Ed.). *Categorical Perception: The Groundwork of Cognition*. Cambridge: Cambridge University Press. Pp. 301–331.

Ehret, G. (1987b). Left hemisphere advantage in the mouse brain for recognizing ultrasonic communication calls. *Nature,* 325, 249–251.

Ehret, G., and Haack, B. (1981). Categorical perception of mouse pup ultrasound by lactating females. *Naturwissenschaften,* 68, 208.

Elowson, A. M., Tannenbaum, P. L., and Snowdon, C. T. (1991). Food-associated calls correlate with food preference in cotton-top tamarins. *Animal Behaviour,* 42, 931–937.

Evans, C. S. (1991). Of ducklings and Turing machines: Interactive playbacks enhance subsequent responsiveness to conspecific calls. *Ethology,* 89, 125–134.

Evans, C. S., Evans, L., and Marler, P. (1993). On the meaning of alarm calls: Functional reference in an avian vocal system. *Animal Behaviour,,* 46, 23–38.

Evans, C. S., Macedonia, J. M., and Marler, P. (1993). Effects of apparent size and speed on the response of chickens *(Gallus gallus)* to computer-generated simulations of aerial predators. *Animal Behaviour,* 46, 1–11.

Evans, C. S., and Marler, P. (1991). On the use of video images as social stimuli in birds: Audience effects on alarm calling. *Animal Behaviour,* 41, 17–26.

Evans, C. S., and Marler, P. (1992). Female appearance as a factor in the responsiveness of male chickens during anti-predator behaviour and courtship. *Animal Behaviour,* 43, 137–145.

Evans, C. S., and Marler, P. (1994). Food-calling and audience effects in male chickens *(Gallus gallus):* Their relationships to food availability, courtship and social facilitation. *Animal Behaviour,* 47, 1159–1170.

Ewert, D. N. (1980). Recognition of conspecific song by the rufous-sided towhee. *Animal Behaviour,* 28, 379–386.

Farabaugh, S. M. (1982). The ecological and social significance of duetting. In D. E. Kroodsma and E. H. Miller (Eds.). *Acoustic Communication in Birds, Vol 2*. New York: Academic Press. Pp. 85–124.

Ficken, M. S., and Ficken, R. W. (1973). Effect of number, kind and order of song elements on playback responses of the golden-winged warbler. *Behaviour,* 46, 114–127.

Gardner, R. A., and Gardner, B. T. (1978). Comparative psychology and language acquisition. *Annals of the New York Academy of Sciences,* 309, 37–76.

Gerhardt, H. C. (1978). Discrimination of intermediate sounds in a synthetic call continuum by female green tree frogs. *Science,* 199, 1089–1091.

Ginzberg, L. (1909). *The Legends of the Jews, Vol. 1*. H. Szold (Trans.). Philadelphia: Jewish Publication Society of America.

Goodall, J. (1986). *The Chimpanzees of Gombe: Patterns of Behavior.* Cambridge, MA: Harvard University Press.

Goodwin, D. (1953). Observations on voice and behaviour of the red-legged partridge, *Alectoris rufa. Ibis,* 95, 581–614.

Gouzoules, S., Gouzoules, H., and Marler, P. (1984). Rhesus monkey *(Macaca mulatta)* screams: Representational signalling in the recruitment of agonistic aid. *Animal Behaviour,* 32, 182–193.

Gouzoules, H., Gouzoules, S., and Marler, P. (1985). External reference in mammalian vocal communication. In G. Ziven (Ed.). *The Development of Expressive Behavior: Biology-Environment Interactions.* New York: Academic Press. Pp. 77–101.

Grice, H. P. (1957). Meaning. *Philosophical Review,* 66, 377–378.

Gyger, M., Karakashian, S., and Marler, P. (1986). Avian alarm calling: Is there an audience effect? *Animal Behaviour,* 34, 1570–1572.

Gyger, M., Marler, P., and Pickert, R. (1987). Semantics of an avian alarm call system: The male domestic fowl, *Gallus domesticus. Behaviour,* 102, 15–40.

Hailman, J. P., and Ficken, M. S. (1986). Combinatorial animal communication with computable syntax: Chick-a-dee calling qualifies as "language" by structural linguistics. *Animal Behaviour,* 34, 1899–1901.

Hailman, J. P., Ficken, M. S., and Ficken, R. W. (1987). Constraints on the structure of combinatorial "chick-a-dee" calls. *Ethology,* 75, 62–80.

Haimoff, E. H. (1984). Acoustic and organizational features of gibbon songs. In D. J. Chivers, H. Preuschoft, W. Y. Brockelman, and N. Creel (Eds.). *The Lesser Apes. Evolutionary and Behavioural Biology.* Edinburgh: Edinburgh University Press. Pp. 333–353.

Hale, B., Schleidt, W. M., and Schein, M. W. (1969). The behavior of turkeys, In E. S. E. Hafez (Ed.). *The Behavior of Domestic Animals.* Baltimore: Williams and Wilkins. Pp. 554–592.

Hausfater, G., and Hrdy, S. B. (Eds.). (1984). *Infanticide: Comparative and Evolutionary Perspectives.* Hawthorne, NY: Aldire Press.

Herman, L. M. (1980). Cognitive characteristics of dolphins. In L. M. Herman (Ed.). *Cetacean Behavior: Mechanisms and Functions.* Malabar, FL: Robert E. Krieger Publishing Company. Pp. 363–429.

Herman, L. M., and Forestell, P. H. (1985). Reporting presence or absence of named objects by a language-trained dolphin. *Neuroscience and Biobehavioral Reviews,* 9, 667–681.

Herrnstein, R. J. (1984). Objects, categories and discriminative stimuli. In H. L. Roitblat, T. G. Bever, and H. S. Terrace (Eds.). *Animal Cognition.* Hillsdale, NJ: Lawrence Erlbaum Assoc. Pp. 233–261.

Herrnstein, R. J. (1991). Levels of categorization. In G. M. Edelman, W. E. Gall, and W. M. Cowan (Eds.). *Signal and Sense.* New Jersey: Wiley-Liss. Pp. 385–413.

Herrnstein, R. J., Loveland, D. H., and Cable, C. (1976). Natural concepts in pigeons. *Journal of Experimental Psychology (Animal Behavior),* 2, 285–311.

Hersek, M. J., and Owings, D. H. (1993). Tail flagging by adult California ground squirrels: A tonic signal that serves different functions in males and females. *Animal Behaviour,* 46, 129–138.

Hockett, C. F. (1960). Logical considerations in the study of animal communication. In W. E. Lanyon and W. N. Tavolga (Eds.). *Animal Sounds and Communication.* Washington, DC: American Institute of Biological Sciences. Pp. 392–430.

Hopp, S. L., Sinnott, J. M., Owren, M. J., and Petersen, M. R. (1992). Differential sensitivity of Japanese macaques *(Macaca fuscata)* and humans *(Homo sapiens)* to peak position along a synthetic coo call continuum. *Journal of Comparative Psychology,* 106, 128–136.

Hrdy, S. B. (1977). Infanticide as a primate reproductive strategy. *American Scientist,* 65, 40–49.

Jürgens, U. (1979). Vocalization as an emotional indicator: A neuroethological study in the squirrel monkey. *Behaviour,* 69, 88–117.

Karakashian, S. J., Gyger, M., and Marler, P. (1988). Audience effects on alarm calling in chickens *(Gallus gallus). Journal of Comparative Psychology,* 102, 129–135.

Kluender, K. R., Diehl, R. L., and Killeen, P. R. (1987). Japanese quail can learn phonetic categories. *Science,* 237, 1195–1197.

Konishi, M. (1963). The role of auditory feedback in the vocal behavior of the domestic fowl. *Zietschrift für Tierpsychologie,* 20, 349–367.

Kuhl, P. K. (1981). Discrimination of speech by nonhuman animals: Basic auditory sensitivities conducive to the perception of speech-sound categories. *Journal of the Acoustical Society of America,* 70, 340–349.

Kuhl, P. K. (1986). Theoretical contributions of tests on animals to the special-mechanisms debate in speech. *Experimental Biology,* 45, 233–265.

Kuhl, P. K. (1987). The special-mechanisms debate in speech research: Categorization tests on animals and infants. In S. Harnad (Ed.). *Categorical Perception: The Groundwork of Cognition.* Cambridge: Cambridge University Press. Pp. 355–386.

Kuhl, P. K. (1989). On babies, birds, modules and mechanisms: A comparative approach to the acquisition of vocal communication. In R. J. Dooling and S. H. Hulse (Eds.). *The Comparative Psychology of Audition: Perceiving Complex Sounds.* Hillsdale, NJ: Lawrence Erlbaum Assoc. Pp. 379–419.

Kuhl, P. K., and Miller, J. D. (1975). Speech perception by the chinchilla: Voiced-voiceless distinction in alveolar plosive consonants. *Science,* 190, 69–72.

Kuhl, P. K., and Miller, J. D. (1978). Speech perception by the chinchilla: Identification functions for synthetic VOT stimuli. *Journal of the Acoustical Society of America,* 63, 905–917.

Kuhl, P. K., and Padden, D. M. (1982). Enhanced discriminability at the phonetic boundaries for the voicing feature in macaques. *Perception and Psychophysics,* 32, 542–550.

Kuhl, P. K., and Padden, D. M. (1983). Enhanced discriminability at the phonetic boundaries for the place feature in macaques. *Journal of the Acoustical Society of America,* 73, 1003–1010.

Lancaster, J. (1965). *Primate Behavior and the Emergence of Human Culture.* New York: Holt, Rinehart and Winston.

Lea, S. E. G. (1984). In what sense do pigeons learn concepts? In H. L. Roitblat, T. G. Bever, and H. S. Terrace (Eds.). *Animal Cognition.* Hillsdale, NJ: Lawrence Erlbaum Assoc. Pp. 263–276.

Leger, D. W. (1993). Contextual sources of information and responses to animal communication signals. *Psychological Bulletin,* 113, 295–304.

Lemon, R. E., Dobson, C. W., and Clifton, P. G. (1993). Songs of american redstarts *(Setophaga ruticilla):* Sequencing rules and their relationships to repertoire size. *Ethology,* 93, 198–210.

Liberman, A. M., Cooper, F. S., Shankweiler, D. P., and Studdert-Kennedy, M. (1967). Perception of the speech code. *Psychological Review,* 74, 431–461.

Liberman, A. M., and Mattingly, I. G. (1985). The motor theory of speech perception revised. *Cognition,* 21, 1–36.

Liberman, A. M., and Mattingly, I. G. (1989). A specialization for speech perception. *Science*, 243, 489–494.

Lieberman, P. (1984). *The Biology and Evolution of Language*. Cambridge, MA: Harvard University Press.

Lindauer, M. (1957). Sonnenoreientierung der Bienen unter der Äquatorsonne und zur Nachtzeit. *Naturwissenschaften*, 44, 1–6.

Locke, J. L. (1993). *The Child's Path to Spoken Language*. Cambridge, MA: Harvard University Press.

Lorenz, K. Z. (1958). The evolution of behavior. *Scientific American*, 199, 67–78.

Lorenz, K. Z. (1966). *On Aggression*. New York: Bantam.

Luria, A. (1982). *Language and Cognition*. Cambridge, MA: Harvard University Press.

Lyons, J. (1972). Human language. In E. A. Hinde (Ed.). *Non-verbal Communication*. Cambridge: Cambridge University Press. Pp. 49–85.

Macedonia, J. M. (1990). What is communicated in the antipredator calls of lemurs: Evidence from antipredator call playbacks to ringtailed and ruffed lemurs. *Ethology*, 86, 177–190.

Macedonia, J. M., and Evans, C. S. (1993). Variation among mammalian alarm call systems and the problem of meaning in animal signals. *Ethology*, 93, 177–197.

Maier, V. (1982). Acoustic communication in the Guinea fowl *(Numida meleagris)*: Structure and use of vocalizations, and the principle of message coding. *Zietschrift für Tierpsychologie*, 59, 29–83.

Marler, P. (1961). The logical analysis of animal communication. *Journal of Theoretical Biology*, 1, 295–317.

Marler, P. (1970a). Birdsong and human speech: Could there be parallels? *American Scientist*, 58, 669–674.

Marler, P. (1970b). A comparative approach to vocal learning: Song development in white-crowned sparrows. *Journal of Comparative and Physiological Psychology*, 71, 1–25.

Marler, P. (1977). The structure of animal communication sounds. In T. H. Bullock (Ed.). *Recognition of Complex Acoustic Signals*. Berlin: Dahlem Konferenzen. Pp. 17–35.

Marler, P. (1985). Representational vocal signals of primates. *Fortschritte der Zoologie*, 31, 211–221.

Marler, P. (1991). Song-learning behavior: The interface with neuroethology. *Trends in Neurosciences*, 14, 199–206.

Marler, P. (1992). Functions of arousal and emotion in primate communication: A semiotic approach. In T. Nishida, W. C. McGrew, P. Marler, M. Pickford, and F. B. de Waal (Eds.). *Topics in Primatology, Vol. 1: Human Origins*. Tokyo: University of Tokyo Press. Pp. 225–233.

Marler, P., Dufty, A., and Pickert, R. (1986a). Vocal communication in the domestic chicken, I: Does a sender communicate information about the quality of a food referent to a receiver? *Animal Behaviour*, 34, 188–193.

Marler, P., Dufty, A., and Pickert, R. (1986b). Vocal communication in the domestic chicken, II: Is a sender sensitive to the presence and nature of a receiver? *Animal Behaviour*, 34, 194–198.

Marler, P., Evans, C. S., and Hauser, M. D. (1992). Animal signals: Motivational, referential, or both? In H. Papousek, U. Jürgens, and M. Papousek (Eds.). *Nonverbal Vocal Communication: Comparative and Developmental Approaches*. Cambridge: Cambridge University Press. Pp. 66–86.

Marler, P., and Tamura, M. (1962). Song "dialects" in three populations of white-crowned sparrows. *Condor*, 64, 368–377.

Mattingly, I. G. (1972). Speech cues and sign stimuli: An ethological view of speech perception and the origin of language. *American Scientist*, 60, 327–337.

May, B., Moody, D. B., and Stebbins, W. C. (1989). Categorical perception of conspecific communication sounds by Japanese macaques, *Macaca fuscata. Journal of the Acoustical Society of America*, 85, 837–847.

McGregor, P. K., Dabelsteen, T., Shepherd, M., and Pedersen, S. B. (1992). The signal value of matched singing in great tits: Evidence from interactive playback experiments. *Animal Behaviour*, 43, 987–998.

Meinertzhagen, R. (1955). The speed and altitude of bird flight. *Ibis*, 97, 81–117.

Miller, J. D., Wier, C. C., Pastore, R. E., Kelly, W. J., and Dooling, R. J. (1976). Discrimination and labeling of noise-buzz sequences with varying noise-lead times: An example of categorical perception. *Journal of the Acoustical Society of America*, 60, 410–417.

Nelson, D. A., and Marler, P. (1989). Categorical perception of a natural stimulus continuum: Birdsong. *Science*, 244, 976–978.

Nottebohm, F. (1971). Neural lateralization of vocal control in a passerine bird, I: Song. *Journal of Experimental Zoology*, 177, 229–262.

Nottebohm, F. (1991). Reassessing the mechanisms and origins of vocal learning in birds. *Trends in Neurosciences*, 14, 206–211.

Owings, D. H., and Hennessy, D. F. (1984). The importance of variation in sciurid visual and vocal communication. In J. O. Murie and G. R. Michener (Eds.). *Biology of Ground Dwelling Squirrels: Annual Cycles, Behavioral Ecology and Sociality*. Lincoln, NB: University of Nebraska Press. Pp. 169–200.

Owings, D. H., Hennessy, D. F., Leger, D. W., and Gladney, A. B. (1986). Different functions of "alarm" calling for different time scales: A preliminary report on ground squirrels. *Behaviour*, 99, 101–116.

Owren, M. J., Dieter, M. A., Seyfarth, R. M. and Cheney, D. L. (1992). Food calls produced by adult female rhesus *(Macaca mulatta)* and Japanese *(M. fuscata)* macaques, their normally-raised offspring, and offspring cross-fostered between species. *Behaviour*, 120, 218–231.

Pepperberg, I. M. (1987a). Acquisition of the same/different concept by an African grey parrot *(Psittacus erithacus):* Learning with respect to categories of color shape and material. *Animal Learning and Behavior*, 15, 423–432.

Pepperberg, I. M. (1987b). Evidence for conceptual quantitative abilities in the African grey parrot: Labeling of cardinal sets. *Ethology*, 75, 37–61.

Pereira, M. E., and Macedonia, J. M. (1991). Ringtailed lemur anti-predator calls denote predator class, not response urgency. *Animal Behaviour*, 41, 543–544.

Petersen, M. R., Beecher, M. D., Zoloth, S. R., Green, S., Marler, P., Moody, D. B, and Stebbins, W. C. (1984). Neural lateralization of species-specific vocalizations by Japanese macaques: Communicative significance is more important than acoustic structure. *Behavioral Neuroscience*, 98, 779–790.

Petersen, M. R., Beecher, M. D., Zoloth, S. R., Moody, D. B., and Stebbins, W. C. (1978). Neural lateralization of species-specific vocalizations by Japanese macaques. *Science*, 202, 324–327.

Pisoni, D. B. (1977). Identification and discrimination of the relative onset time of two component tones: Implications for voicing perception in stops. *Journal of the Acoustical Society of America*, 61, 1352–1361.

Pola, Y. V., and Snowdon, C. T. (1975). The vocalizations of pygmy marmosets *(Cebuella pygmaea)*. *Animal Behaviour*, 23, 826–842.

Premack, D. (1975). On the origins of language. In M. S. Gazzaniga and C. B. Blakemore (Eds.). *Handbook of Psychobiology*. New York: Academic Press. Pp. 591–605.

Premack, D. (1986). *Gavagai! Or the Future History of the Animal Language Controversy*. Cambridge, MA: The MIT Press.

Quine, W. V. (1973). On the reasons for the indeterminacy of translation. *Journal of Philosophy*, 12, 178–183.

Rowell, T. E., and Hinde, R. A. (1962). Vocal communication by the rhesus monkey *(Macaca mulatta)*. *Proceedings of the Zoological Society of London*, 138, 279–294.

Ryan, M. J. (1991). Sexual selection and communication in frogs. *Trends in Ecology and Evolution*, 6, 351–355.

Ryan, M. J., and Keddy-Hector, A. (1992). Directional patterns of female mate choice and the role of sensory biases. *American Naturalist*, 139, S4–S35.

Savage-Rumbaugh, E. S. (1986). *Ape Language from Conditioned Response to Symbol*. New York: Columbia University Press.

Savage-Rumbaugh, E. S., and Rumbaugh, D. M. (1978). Symbolization, language and chimpanzees: A theoretical reevaluation based on initial language acquisition processes in four young *Pan troglodytes*. *Brain and Language*, 6, 265–300.

Schusterman, R. J. (1988). Artificial language comprehension in dolphins and sea lions: The essential cognitive skills. *The Psychological Record*, 38, 311–348.

Schusterman, R. J. (1989). Please parse the sentence: Animal cognition in the procrustean bed of linguistics. *The Psychological Record*, 39, 3–18.

Schwartz, J. J. (1991). Why stop calling? A study of unison bout singing in a neotropical treefrog. *Animal Behaviour*, 42, 565–577.

Schwartz, J. J., and Rand, A. S. (1991). The consequences for communication of call overlap in the Tungara frog, a neotropical anuran with a frequency-modulated call. *Ethology*, 89, 73–83.

Seyfarth, R. M., and Cheney, D. L. (1980). The ontogeny of vervet monkey alarm calling: A preliminary report. *Zietschrift für Tierpsychologie*, 54, 37–56.

Seyfarth, R. M., Cheney, D. L., and Marler, P. (1980a). Monkey responses to three different alarm calls: Evidence for predator classification and semantic communication. *Science*, 210, 801–803.

Seyfarth, R. M., Cheney, D. L., and Marler, P. (1980b). Vervet monkey alarm calls: Semantic communication in a free-ranging primate. *Animal Behaviour*, 28, 1070–1094.

Sherman, P. W. (1977). Nepotism and the evolution of alarm calls. *Science*, 197, 1246–1253.

Sibley, C. G., and Ahlquist, J. E. (1984). The phylogeny of the hominoid primates, as indicated by DNA-DNA hybridization. *Journal of Molecular Evolution*, 20, 2–15.

Sibley, C. G., and Ahlquist, J. E. (1987). DNA hybridization evidence of hominoid phylogeny: Results from an expanded data set. *Journal of Molecular Evolution*, 26, 99–121.

Sibley, C. G., Comstock, J. A., and Ahlquist, J. E. (1990). DNA hybridization evidence of hominoid phylogeny: A reanalysis of the data. *Journal of Molecular Evolution*, 30, 202–236.

Smith, W. J. (1965). Message, meaning and context in ethology. *American Naturalist*, 99, 405–409.

Smith, W. J. (1977). *The Behavior of Communicating*. Cambridge, MA: Harvard University Press.

Smith, W. J. (1981). Referents of animal communication. *Animal Behaviour*, 29, 1273–1274.

Smith, W. J. (1991). Animal communication and the study of cognition. In C. A. Ristau (Ed.). *Cognitive Ethology: The Minds of Other Animals*. Hillsdale, NJ: Lawrence Erlbaum Assoc. Pp. 209–230.

Snowdon, C. T. (1987). A naturalistic view of categorical perception. In S. Harnad (Ed.). *Categorical Perception: The Groundwork of Cognition*. Cambridge: Cambridge University Press. Pp. 332–354.

Snowdon, C. T. (1990). Language capacities of nonhuman animals. *Yearbook of Physical Anthropology*, 33, 215–243.

Snowdon, C. T., and Cleveland, J. (1984). "Conversations" among pygmy marmosets. *American Journal of Primatology*, 7, 15–20.

Stokes, A. W. (1961). Voice and social behavior of the chukar partridge. *Condor*, 63, 111–127.

Stokes, A. W. (1967). Behavior of the bobwhite, *Colinus virginianus*. *Auk*, 84, 1–33.

Struhsaker, T. T. (1967). Auditory communication among vervet monkeys *(Cercopithecus aethiops)*. In S. A. Altmann (Ed.). *Social Communication Among Primates*. Chicago: University of Chicago Press. Pp. 281–324.

Sullivan, K. (1985). Selective alarm calling by downy woodpeckers in mixed-species flocks. *Auk*, 102, 184–187.

Swets, J. A. (1961). Is there a sensory threshold? *Science*, 134, 168–177.

Tinbergen, N. (1948). Social releasers and the experimental method required for their study. *Wilson Bulletin*, 60, 6–51.

Tinbergen, N. (1951). *The Study of Instinct*. Oxford: Clarendon Press.

Tinbergen, N. (1959). The evolution of behavior in gulls. *Scientific American*, 203, 118–129.

Tinbergen, N. (1960). Comparative studies of the behaviour of gulls *(Laridae):* A progress report. *Behaviour*, 15, 1–70.

von Frisch, K. (1967). *The Dance Language and Orientation of Bees*. Cambridge, MA: Harvard University Press.

Wallman, J. (1992). *Aping Language*. Cambridge: Cambridge University Press.

Walters, J. R. (1990). Anti-predator behavior of lapwings: Field evidence of discriminative abilities. *Wilson Bulletin*, 102, 49–70.

Weary, D. M. (1989). Categorical perception of bird song: How do great tits *(Parus major)* perceive temporal variation in their song? *Journal of Comparative Psychology*, 103, 320–325.

Williams, H. W. (1969). Vocal behavior of the adult California quail. *Auk*, 86, 631–659.

Zajonc, R. B. (1965). Social facilitation. *Science*, 149, 269–274.

16 Toward the Acquisition of Language and the Evolution of Communication: A Synthetic Approach

Michael G. Dyer

INTRODUCTION

Our long-term goal is to obtain insights into the nature of human and animal communication systems. Our approach is synthetic (versus analytic). Rather than attempting to analyze how human natural language and animal communication systems actually function in society or nature (as do linguists, neuropsychologists, ethologists, etc.), we have taken a simulation modeling approach in which we construct (through a combination of engineering, adaptive learning, and evolution) computational systems capable of exhibiting different aspects of human natural language and animal communicative behavior.

We are attempting to develop sophisticated software tools for modeling the development, interactional dynamics, and evolution of populations of situated, communicating, intelligent agents. By "situated" we mean that each agent must be capable of sensing and acting within a simulated environment. Such agents must also be able to evolve and/or learn how to communicate with one another in order to survive in an environment containing other cooperating and competing reproductive groups.

Note, however, that it has taken Nature billions of years to evolve both human and animal-level forms of language and communication and that Nature has had the advantage of being able to "model" all agents in parallel and in real time. Therefore, we cannot expect (even using a supercomputer) to start with simple neural networks and magically evolve (or train) them into ones capable of human-level language learning or performance.

Since the range of language behaviors (and their underlying cognitive/neural processes) is so broad (from animal to human), we must take a multilevel research approach. That is, problems must be broken down into manageable subproblems and the issue of complexity addressed through designing computational models at different levels of abstraction. These levels range from the artificial intelligence (AI) approach (based on logic and recursive symbol structures) to connectionist networks and neuroevolutionary models (based on spread of activation and the manipulation of entire populations of artificial genomes, with each genome specifying a neural architecture). Modeling at each level turns out to have its own advantages and disadvantages (Dyer 1991), so another long-term goal becomes that of ultimately embedding the most abstract (symbolic) models, capable of the most complex language behavior, within the lower (neural) levels.

Since the Artificial Intelligence Laboratory was founded at UCLA in 1984, my students and I have explored numerous dimensions of natural language processing (NLP), including:

Cognitive/symbolic: how language relates to abstract symbolic thought, the organization/dynamics of memory, processes of learning, planning, reasoning, logic, emotion, and creativity

Neural/developmental: how language is acquired via processes of self-organization in connectionist and artificial neural networks (ANNs) and realized via parallel spreading activation

Perceptual/motor: how language is "grounded" in the physical world via association with perceptual/motor experiences

Social/evolutionary: how connectionist/neural networks capable of supporting simple features of communication might come about through evolutionary processes—i.e., via cooperation and competition among multiple populations of animals undergoing selectional pressures and the processes of mutation and recombination.

In this chapter, we first very briefly describe some of the research our lab has accomplished at each of these levels. Then we focus on two projects—one involving the role of perception in language acquisition and the other involving the evolution of animal-like communication. We report on the resulting systems, DETE and BioLand, that have been developed. Finally, we draw some conclusions concerning how this kind of synthetic research might ultimately be useful in comparative cognitive science.

Symbolic Level

In symbolic-level NLP systems, knowledge is represented in terms of symbolic structures—for example, frames (Minsky 1985), scripts (Schank and Abelson 1977), goals/plans (Dyer 1983a), and beliefs (Alvarado, Dyer, and Flowers 1990a, b). At this level, all cognitive processes are implemented in terms of symbol manipulation—that is, via list-based processing (e.g., LISP programming language), rules, or logic (e.g., Prolog programming language). Using these knowledge representation and symbolic manipulation technologies, we have designed NLP systems that exhibit a wide range of high-level cognitive phenomena, including story comprehension and analysis of themes in stories (Dyer 1983a), moral/ethical reasoning (Reeves 1991), comprehension of emotions and their relation to other cognitive processes (Dyer 1983b, 1987), automatic word/phrase learning from context (Zernik and Dyer 1987), acquisition of world knowledge via goal/plan analysis and generalization of multiple events in episodic memory (Pazzani 1990; Pazzani and Dyer 1989), modeling continuous stream of thought (Mueller 1989; Mueller and Dyer 1985), analysis of argumentation and beliefs for editorial comprehension (Alvarado 1990; Alvarado, Dyer, and Flowers 1990a, b), and modeling creativity in the domain of story invention (Turner 1992).

For instance, the OpEd system (Alvarado 1990; Alvarado, Dyer, and Flowers 1990a, b) takes fragments of editorial text as input and constructs an argument graph of attack/support belief structures in the domain of economic protectionism. OpEd can answer questions about who believes what (and why) by searching this argument graph. Knowledge structures called argument units (AUs) are accessed and applied during editorial comprehension. For example, one AU represents the following:

AU-1: Belief B2, held by y, attacks belief B1, held by x,
      where B1 $=$ [plan P ought to be executed to achieve goal G1],
            B2 $=$ [as a side-effect of executing P, P will cause the
                    failure of a more important goal G2].

AUs are used by OpEd both to represent arguments and to link up components of editorial text into coherent argument structures.

A major advantage of the symbolic approach is that it allows one to construct and experiment with models that produce high-level cognitive phenomena. Major disadvantages are (a) all the prerequisite representational constructs and processing capabilities must be engineered by hand; (b) because symbols are all-or-none constructs, the resulting systems tend to be fragile, and (c) symbolic systems, being so abstract, have few points of contact with their underlying neural substrates; thus, it is extremely difficult to address issues involving how such knowledge and cognitive skills might have evolved (or might be acquired through learning or development). One way to address these shortcomings is to design connectionist networks capable of natural language processing.

Connectionist Level

The design of connectionist networks has been inspired by known properties of processing in neural systems. This is in contrast to symbolic systems, which rely on an underlying von Neumann computer architecture (with its separate registers, memory addressing scheme, and sequential instruction fetch-execute cycle). Although the von Neumann architecture supports the construction of complex recursive data structures (i.e., via pointers), it violates numerous neural processing constraints. For example, one neural constraint is that new neural connections (and neurons) cannot "grow" within the time frame of language comprehension tasks. In symbolic models, new connections among symbols can be created "on the fly" simply by creating new symbols or by linking up existing knowledge structures via pointers. In symbolic models, complex knowledge structures can be passed around from module to module simply by passing a parameter to a subroutine. In contrast, the processing units of connectionist systems are restricted to passing a single scalar value (termed activation) over weighted links. A major connectionist NLP research goal is to figure out how high-level symbolic communication and thought can be modeled in terms of networks of such simple, brain-like processing units. These connectionist networks usually come in two varieties: localist and distributed.

Localist Connectionist (LC) Networks

In localist connectionist (LC) networks, each individual processing unit represents a high-level predicate, relation, or argument—for example, SELLS, OWNS. A high-level inference can then be modeled by setting up connections that pass activation among multiple processing units (Feldman and Ballard 1982; Shastri and Ajjanagadde 1993). An example of a high-level inference is [if John sells Mary a TV, then Mary owns it]:

[*AGENT* = JOHN; *ACT* = SELLS; *OBJECT* = TV; *TO* = MARY]
→ [*AGENT* = MARY; *ACT* = OWNS; *OBJECT* = TV].

Here, each role value is represented by a single connectionist unit, and a connection between processing units causes activation to flow—for example, from SELLS to OWNS.

LC networks have several advantages over symbolic models. The use of parallel, spreading activation allows multiple inference paths to be explored simultaneously. Differing activation levels and weighted links can represent differing amounts of evidence for (or commitment to) a given object, class, or proposition. For instance, a strongly weighted connection from DOG to MAMMAL can represent the inference that being a dog implies being a mammal. In contrast, a weakly weighted link from MAMMAL to DOG represents the fact that being a mammal supplies only weak evidence that the object in question will turn out to be a dog.

In connectionist NLP research, a fundamental problem is to represent abstract concepts and to propagate information for the inferencing required in language comprehension. For example, if we read "Fred sold a book to Betty. She took it home." we must infer that Betty now owns the book (and that is why she can take it home). The SELLS → OWNS inference above, however, is applicable only to John's selling a TV to Mary. To make an inference general, we need to be able to (a) represent variables, (b) dynamically assign bindings to them, and (c) propagate them from one knowledge structure to another. For example:

[*AGENT* = X; *ACT* = SELLS; *OBJECT* = Z; *TO* = Y]
→ [*AGENT* = Y; *ACT* = OWNS; *OBJECT* = Z].

For this more general commonsense reasoning rule to work for the Fred-sell-Betty-book instance above, the variables must be represented and bound (e.g., Y = Mary).

To partially solve this binding problem (without violating connectionist constraints), we have developed networks in which activation is used in two distinct ways. *Evidential* activation is used to increase/decrease the network's commitment to a given interpretation of the input, while *signature* activation is used to uniquely represent each binding that is being propagated during inferencing. The ROBIN system (Lange and Dyer 1989) propagates these two forms of activation along distinct pathways in order to perform plan/goal analysis for dynamic word disambiguation and reinterpretation. For instance, given the input "John put the pot in the dishwater," the word "pot" is at first interpreted by ROBIN as a cooking pot. However, if subsequent input is "because he saw the police coming," then "pot" is reinterpreted as marijuana. Performing this disambiguation actually requires goal/plan and physical object analysis—that is, a determination that John's goal to avoid arrest involves using a plan of hiding the marijuana in an opaque container (which, in this case, happens to be a dishwasher). This goal/plan analysis is realized strictly through spread of activation over connectionist processing units.

LC networks have the advantage of being able to represent symbolic knowledge and inferences in a manner that very closely corresponds to that of symbolic systems. This correspondence makes LC networks easier to design and interpret. Although these networks are less fragile than symbolic systems, the structure of these networks must be engineered by hand. One way around this problem is to design distributed connectionist (DC) networks.

Distributed Connectionist (DC) Networks

In DC networks, a predicate or role is represented as a pattern of activation over an entire ensemble of processing units. There are a variety of adaptive learning techniques for DC networks in which the connection weights are adjusted automatically as the result of presenting examples (input/output pairs) to the network. The best-known method is that of backpropagation learning (Rumelhart and McClelland 1986), in which the output of a DC network is compared against the desired output and an error signal is generated. This error signal is propagated backward through the network during learning, causing the connection weights to be adjusted (up or down) according to their effect in reducing the overall error.

In our lab we have developed a variety of novel DC architectures, binding propagation schemes, and learning techniques in order to model acquisition of language and inferential world knowledge (Dyer 1990). For example, the DISPAR system (Miikkulainen and Dyer 1991) makes use of multiple DC subnetworks. These networks have a recurrent layer (Elman 1990; Pollack 1990), which allows them to learn and generate word sequences. DISPAR acquires both word meanings and script-based knowledge from a training corpus of script-based stories. DISPAR is trained to perform the task of generating complete paraphrases for novel stories—that is, paraphrases in which unstated information must be inferred and then made explicit on output. After training on, say, restaurant stories, DISPAR will infer (when reading a novel restaurant story) that the diner ate the food (i.e., that was ordered), even if the eating event itself is not explicitly mentioned in the input text.

In symbolic systems, such word analysis and script-based knowledge (and its application to the input text) must be encoded by hand. In contrast, DISPAR forms word representations automatically from examples. DISPAR starts out with a lexicon of words whose distributed representations (encoded over an ensemble of processing units) are set at random. Over time, as the weights in each subnetwork are modified, the word representations in the lexicon are also modified automatically. Thus, DISPAR learns the meanings of words at the same time that it is learning those tasks involved in paraphrase generation (i.e., sentence/event/script analysis and generation). In addition, DISPAR's learning technique results in words with similar meanings acquiring similar distributed representations. This similarity of representation allows the network to generalize to cases not encountered before. For example, even if the network has never read the fragment "ate meat with a spoon," it will handle it much like the familiar text "ate meat with a fork" because the representation formed for "spoon" was similar to that formed for "fork" (as the result of both utensils being used in similar ways in the training data).

While DC networks are robust (in the face of noise and simulated lesioning) and can learn their mapping tasks, the current models (e.g., Elman 1990), are architecturally very simple, and, as a result, require many thousands of iterations to learn multiple sequences. One way of overcoming this problem is to model neurons in more detail, especially in terms of their temporal dynamics.

Neural Dynamics Level

The neural dynamics level is concerned with more realistic neural models in which more of the spatial, temporal, and intercellular aspects of real neural networks are taken into account. This level of modeling is important when considering how language is grounded in the spatiotemporal dynamics of real-world perceptual/motor experiences. For instance, consider the word "passing." The meaning of this word is acquired by children through observing numerous objects (of different colors, sizes, shapes, etc.) moving past one another (at different speeds and in different directions). What remains invariant over many passing experiences is the relative speed/direction of one object in relation to the other object; namely, the passing object comes from behind, moves more quickly in the same direction, and finally overtakes the slower object. All of these experiences have strong spatiotemporal aspects that must be associated in memory as some kind of generalized image sequence "trace" of what is invariant across all visual contexts involving the acts of passing. This generalized visual memory trace must be associated with a generalized verbal memory trace—that is, all linguistic encounters of the word "passing" as it appears in sequence with other words. The resulting association (encoded in the connection patterns of the neurons) can then serve as a meaning for the word—one that is grounded in experience.

DETE (Dyer and Nenov 1993; Nenov 1991; Nenov and Dyer 1994) is a system that learns the meanings of words and phrases (e.g., "red ball passing green square") by associating in memory a sequence of simplified phonemes with visual sequences of moving objects on an artificial retina of neural processing units. DETE employs novel neurons, neural architectures, and learning to perform its tasks. DETE is discussed in more detail later.

Evolutionary Level

The encoding and acquisition of language in neural networks is too complex a task to perform without the modeler's supplying a good deal of structure to the underlying neural architecture. In Nature, this underlying neural structure comes about as the result of evolution (Belew and Booker 1991; Goldberg 1989; Goldberg and Holland 1988; Holland 1992). Consequently, one can design neural structures either by hand, via learning, or through evolutionary processes, which involves specifying entire environments and letting selectional pressures (along with mutation and recombination) act upon populations of networks (Belew, McInerney, and Schraudolph 1992). We are exploring this evolutionary approach in an attempt to arrive at connectionist networks capable of supporting animal-like communicative behavior. BioLand (Werner and Dyer 1993, 1994) is a modeling environment for experiments in the evolution of communication in populations of simple creatures (called biots) where each biot's behavior is controlled by its connectionist network architecture (that is specified by that biot's individual genome). BioLand is discussed in more detail later.

PERCEPTUALLY GROUNDED LANGUAGE ACQUISITION IN DETE

DETE (Dyer and Nenov 1993; Nenov 1991; Nenov and Dyer 1994) is a system that learns a simple subset of natural language by associating phoneme sequences with perceptual/motor sequences. DETE takes three modalities of concurrent input: visual, verbal, and motor. Visual input consists of moving (or stationary) 2-D shapes presented to DETE's single retina. Verbal input contains a stream of simplified phonemes representing utterances describing the visual input. Motor input causes DETE to shift/zoom its visual focus of attention or to touch/push objects with a single simulated effector. After learning, the system can verbally describe those (possibly novel) image sequences it observes. Also, given a (possibly novel) verbal sequence, DETE can generate visual representations for what is being described verbally. By "novel" we mean sequences consisting of words/images already learned by DETE, but presented in particular combinations not encountered during training.

Blobs World Task/Domain

DETE learns language in the context of Blobs World which consists of 2-D moving shapes presented to DETE's retina. The 2-D shapes presented to DETE are called blobs because they are monocolored and lack any kind of structural complexity (i.e., contain no subparts). Examples of blobs are noisy rectangular, triangular, and circular objects. Blobs appear on a simulated visual screen (VS) that is 64×64 pixels. Blobs can vary in color, size, location, speed, and direction of motion. They can be stationary or in motion, and their dynamic behavior can include acceleration, change in direction (e.g., bouncing), and change in size over time. For example, after learning DETE is able to take as input a verbal sequence representing the phrase "ball grows" and, as a result, generate a sequence of neural activity that represents an image sequence of a circular object increasing in size.

The idea behind Blobs World is to restrict the complexity of visual processing required while at the same time making available to DETE an environment that is still quite rich in potential potential/motor interactions. For example, visual scenes/events in Blobs World are describable by the following words or phrases:

	Sample words
Size related:	grows, shrinks, big, small, tiny, huge, bigger than, smaller than, . . .
Location related:	above, below, under, over, near, far, close, left of, right of, north, south, east, diagonally, vertically, horizontally, up, down, center, periphery, . . .
Shape/object related:	ball, circle, round, circular, square, triangle, triangular, wall, object, thing, . . .
Color related:	white, black, red, green, blue, yellow, . . .

Motion related:	fast, slow, quickly, accelerates, decelerates, speeds up, slows down, hits, bounces, contacts, passes, stationary, moves, toward, away from, grows, shrinks, . . .
Time related:	will bounce, will hit, will move, is bouncing, is hitting, is moving, bounced, did hit, moved, was moving, . . .

Given the spatiotemporal dynamics of Blobs World, events that are quite complex can be presented visually to DETE, along with their corresponding verbal representations. For example, after learning individual words/phrases, DETE is able to comprehend the meaning of the following novel word sequence:

small red ball moves diagonally up, will hit wall, bounce . . . move down

DETE also contains attentional and motor subsystems. The attentional subsystem learns to focus/zoom its retina ("eye") on the visual field. The motor subsystem learns to move a single effector ("finger"). As a result, Blobs World tasks can include learning eye/finger motor commands:

Attention-related commands:	look, up, look down, look at big green triangle in center, . . .
Motor-related commands:	touch small red square under large triangular object, push little square northeast, . . .

DETE can also be trained to learn the meaning of question words. To do so, DETE is given a sequence that begins with a question word and that ends with the answer. Later, when given the question, DETE uses its sequence-completion capabilities to generate the answer.

The Blobs World task/domain is not restricted to any particular natural language. The words mentioned above could just as well have been, for instance, in Spanish or Japanese. For each natural language, the preferred order of words must therefore be learned. For example, in English adjectives tend to precede nouns, while in Spanish they tend to follow nouns and must also agree in number and gender. Also, each language tends to "carve up" or categorize reality in different ways. For example, English distinguishes between "shade" and "shadow" (based on what is movable/stationary and what casts shade on what), while Spanish has only one word ("sombra") for both situations. Spanish, however, distinguishes the inside of a corner ("rincon") from the outside of a corner ("esquina"), while English uses the single word "corner." Clearly, the perceptual reality available to both English and Spanish speakers is essentially the same, but each language organizes verbal access to knowledge of that reality in different ways. For instance, a firefighting event is quite complex, consisting of spraying water on a fire, wearing protective clothing, arriving at the fire in a fire engine, and so on. English speakers refer to those who put out fires as "firefighters." How does Spanish access the same role? The term Spanish uses is "bombero" (i.e., pumping person), which, while different, also makes sense, since pumping the water is part of the overall event.

Every child is faced with the same language acquisition task—namely, given a sequence of (initially nonsensical-sounding) utterances and a perceptual/motor event, the child must place the utterances in proper correspondence with the relevant features of the event being described. During earlier stages of language learning, the child must associate basic words (e.g., *eat, touch, mama, cry, footsie, diaper, sad,* etc.) with corresponding objects/actions/states being perceived in the world. Only after language has been "grounded" in the perceptual/motor world can the developing child learn more abstract concepts (e.g., *irresponsibility, fairness,* etc.).

DETE Architecture

The DETE system is a procedural/neural hybrid. The procedural modules deal with transforming initial visual input (which is a sequence of array values) into internal neural representations that are then processed by memory subsystems, which are implemented as neural networks.

Sensorimotor Subsystems

Each procedural module extracts specific features from the input image sequence and produces as its output a localized, contiguous set of active neurons on a corresponding *feature plane* (FP). Each feature plane consists of a 2-D array of neurons in which each region in a given FP represents a particular range of values over a given feature space. For example, different regions on the size feature plane (ZFP) represent different sizes. Some FPs are topographic; for example, neural activity in the upper right-hand corner of the location feature plane (LFP) represents the existence of a blob in the upper right-hand corner of the visual screen (VS). DETE contains five sensory feature planes:

1. Location Feature Plane (LFP)

2. Color Feature Plane (CFP)

3. Size Feature Plane (ZFP)

4. Shape Feature Plane (SFP)

5. Motion Feature Plane (MFP)

In addition, DETE represents the location/diameter of its eye and the position/motion of its finger as neural activity in regions of its eye location diameter FPs and its finger position/motion FPs.

DETE represents visual events as sequences of changing neural activity on these feature planes. For example, a circle moving in an upward direction on the visual screen (VS) is represented as a changing sequence of neural activity over the location FP. This neural activity itself moves upward over time. On the motion FP, increased speed is represented as increased distance from its center (see figure 16.1).

Topographic feature planes have the advantage that spatial relationships are represented in a fashion that is closely analogous to the input (e.g., objects near one another in the VS will be near each other on the location FP). In addition, sequencing over distinct feature planes allows DETE to learn/represent a combinatorial number of events. For instance, DETE learns color, shape, and size words (and word order preference) in independent trials; once these have been learned, DETE can immediately handle all (size, color, and shape) sequences it has not yet encountered.

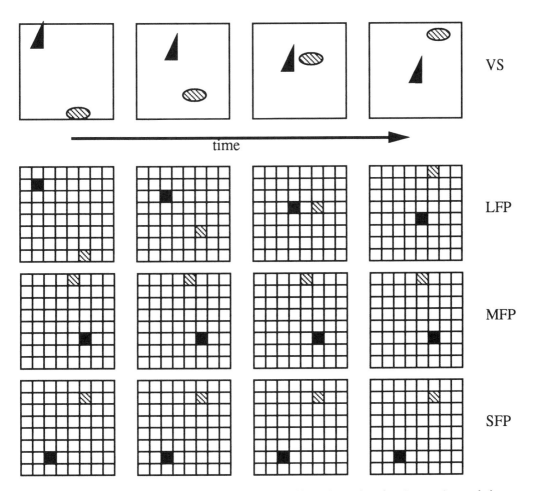

Figure 16.1 Sequences of neural activity (through time) on location, motion, and shape feature planes. The texture of active neuronal regions (black vs. striped) is used to iconically represent the distinct phases of each object in the VS feature plane. For example, all "black" neural activities are locked in phase across all FPs and represent properties of the triangle, while "stripped" neural activity is in phase with the oval.

Attentional and Binding Subsystems

While separate feature maps provide a combinatorial capability, the problem of "crosstalk" (i.e., confusion of feature association) can arise when more than one object is being represented at the same time. For example, if there is a large red circle in the middle of the VS and a small green square in the lower left-hand corner, then there will be neural activity in the following feature planes:

Feature planes	Active regions
Color FP	red; green
Size FP	small; large
Location FP	lower left-hand corner; center
Shape FP	circular; square-like

Given these regions of activity, how does DETE determine which regions should be associated or "bound" to one another? This binding problem is solved in DETE by having active neurons in each FP oscillate with a characteristic phase (van Essen and Maunsell 1983). All neurons oscillating in phase across all feature planes are then considered to be bound together and thus represent the same object. The memory subsystems (that form memory traces of associated verbal/visual sequences) are designed to be sensitive to such phases. That is, DETE learns to associate verbal sequences with only those visual features that are in phase. DETE's neurons can oscillate in any one of five distinct phases, so DETE can represent (without crosstalk) up to five distinct objects concurrently on each feature plane.

To determine which phase to assign to each visual input, DETE makes use of an attentional subsystem (implemented procedurally). This subsystem is controlled by DETE's simulated eye and is designed so that the phase of whatever object is on the center of DETE's retina becomes the focus-of-attention phase. For instance, if there are two objects on the VS (e.g., a green circle and a red triangle) and the eye is focused on the triangle and DETE receives a verbal input "red triangle," then this input will be associated with the triangle (vs. the circle) because the triangle's phase is the same as the current focus-of-attention phase.

Figure 16.1 shows two different objects moving at different (constant) speeds on the visual screen (VS), along with their corresponding neural representations, as sequences of activity on a subset of the feature planes (FPs). Because object location is constantly changing on the VS in figure 16.1, so too is the location of active neurons on the location FP. In contrast, since speed, direction, and shape are constant, neural activity on the motion FP and the shape FP remain constant over time. The triangle is moving slowly; therefore, its activity region is closer to the center of the motion FP (where stationary objects are represented). The oval is moving rapidly, so its activity region is toward the periphery of the motion FP.

The direction of motion is represented by where on the periphery the activity is located.

DETE Verbal Representation

Verbal input to DETE is a sequence of "gra-phonemes," which encode aspects of both orthographic and phonemic information. Each gra-phoneme is represented as a binary pattern over a bank of 64 verbal units. Each bit location (loc) in the verbal bank represents a sound frequency range of 40 Hz, extending from 270 Hz (loc 1) to 2790 Hz (loc 64). This scheme allows DETE to encode simplified information concerning acoustic formants. DETE currently uses 26 gra-phonemes; each one is placed into a simple, one-to-one correspondence with a letter of English. This current scheme (of 26 gra-phonemes) is limited in numerous ways:

Non-English sounds: sounds unique to other languages are not currently used (e.g., the "rr" sound of Spanish).

Duration: In real speech, the durations of phonemes (e.g., vowels and consonants) vary widely. In the current representation, however, each gra-phoneme has a constant duration.

Formants: Currently, the formant frequencies are stationary. In actual speech their onset and termination frequencies vary markedly.

Segmentation: In spoken language, people usually do not make significant pauses between words. However, in DETE there is a pause (using wide 64 bits patterns consisting of zeros) between the end of one word and the onset of the next. This makes it easier for DETE to learn to recognize word boundaries.

In spite of these limitations, the current representational scheme still allows DETE to process some of the internal structure of words, such as inflections of verbs and prefixes/suffixes of adjectives and adverbs. This gra-phoneme representation provides DETE with a simulated sequence of at least partially realistic acoustical information whose temporal duration is then placed in correspondence with the temporal duration of visual image sequences.

DETE Neurons and Katamic Memory

To perform its tasks, DETE must be able to represent, learn, store, and manipulate sequences, including recalling/recognizing/completing sequences from fragmentary inputs. DETE makes use of a novel sequential associative memory architecture dubbed katamic memory. (The term *katamic* is simply an identifying label. It has no particular meaning). DETE's neural modules consist of over 50 interconnected katamic memories. Each modality (visual/verbal/motor) has katamic modules with slightly different internal connectivity and parameter settings. Katamic memory is made up of three novel neural processing units: predictron, recognitron, and bi-stable switch.

Predictron: Each predictron's task is to predict the next input given its memory of past inputs and information concerning inputs from neighboring predictrons. Each predictron's "soma" has a pipeline of dendritic compartments (DCs) as its input. A single bit of information (0 or 1) is shifted in time from one DC to the next until it arrives at the soma. Thus, information from more distant DCs takes longer to reach the soma. To handle patterns that are n bits wide, n predictrons are laid down in parallel, with the DCs of each predictron also receiving inputs from the DCs/somas of neighboring predictrons (figure 16.2).

Memories in DETE are stored in the predictron's dendritic compartments. The DC of each predictron holds both short-term memory (stm) and long-term memory (ltm) state variables, each with a real number range of between 0 and 1. *Ltm variables* hold positive (and negative) correlations concerning the spatial and temporal distance between active (i.e., 1) bits in all input sequences. *Spatial distance* involves how far apart the 1 bits are within a given (n-bit–wide) pattern. *Temporal distance* involves how far apart the 1 bits are within the DCs of the same predictron.

The *stm variable* is used to store spatiotemporal correlations among the 1 bits of only the most recently seen patterns in a given sequence. The stm in each DC is reset to its initial value at the beginning of every new sequence presented to the network. The stm value in each DC is shifted, in a pipeline fashion, from DC to DC toward the soma. This shifting is done with a speed of one DC per B cycle (basic neural processing cycle of the model). At the same time, as it is shifted each particular stm value decays by a constant amount. This pipeline shifting (of stms in the DCs of a given predictron) creates a temporal delay line, thus encoding the temporal dynamics of a sequence of patterns 1 bit wide. Sequences of patterns n bits wide can be processed with a bank of n predictrons.

The soma of the predictron has an activation value that is computed at each time cycle as the dot product of two vectors: (1) the shifted stms and (2) the ltm values in the dendritic branch. Comparison against the shifted stms creates a "look one-step ahead" mechanism and is used for generating a prediction. If the somatic activation is larger than the soma's threshold value, then the predictron fires (generating a 1-bit), otherwise it is silent (0-bit). Thus, each predictron generates an output (0 or 1) that is a prediction of the next output based on the spatiotemporal history of its own past input sequences and those of its neighbors (since each DC is receiving inputs from its neighboring predictrons's DCs).

Recognitron: The recognitron's function is to recognize its input sequence. The dendritic compartment (DC) of each recognitron receives two inputs: (1) *external,* a bit from the input pattern, and (2) *internal,* a bit generated by a corresponding predictron (figure 16.2). Each DC evaluates to 0 when both inputs are the same (i.e., the predictron's output is

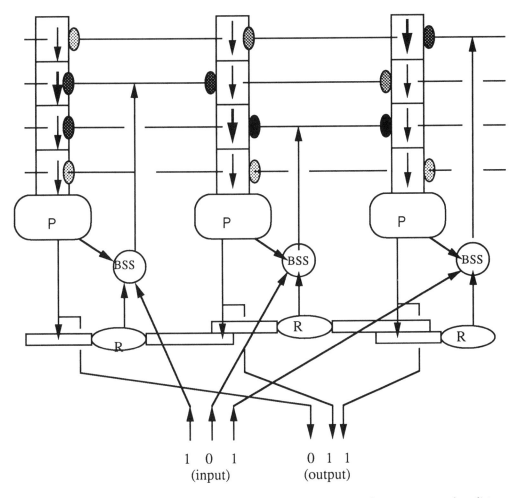

1 0 1   0 1 1
(input)   (output)

Figure 16.2 Small segment of katamic memory, showing the arrangement of predictrons (Ps), recognitrons (Rs), bi-stable switches (BSSs), predictron dendritic compartments (DCs; large squares), and recognitron DCs (thin rectangles). The flow of *stm* memories (e.g., representing the diffusion of proteins/ions toward soma) is indicated by the arrows within the predictron DCs. Ltm state variables are also associated with each predictron DC, but are not shown here. The shading of the vertical ovals indicates the strength of input to a DC from neighboring DCs.

recognized) and to 1 when the two inputs do not match (i.e., the predictron's output is not recognized).

Bi-Stable Switch: There is one bi-stable switch (BSS) per predictron (figure 16.2). The function of the BSSs is to support the completion of fragmentary sequences. That is, after a particular sequence has been learned the BSSs turn off the external input and allow the outputs of the predictrons to be used as inputs at the next B cycle. Figure 16.2 shows a simplified katamic memory fragment containing just three predictrons (P), with only 4 DCs for each. In DETE, verbal input is 64 bits wide and thus is processed by a bank of 64 predictrons. Visual input is processed by having 256 (16 × 16) predictrons for each visual feature plane.

Each recognitron (R) in figure 16.2 is shown sampling both its corresponding predictron's output and the output of just one neighboring predictron. One pattern (here, 3 bits wide) is shown entering and being fed to each BSS, which determines whether input to the corresponding predictron DCs should come from the predictron itself (for pattern completion tasks) or from external input. Each input bit is fed (via BSSs) to DCs at different heights (i.e., the distance of a DC from its soma). Information in a given DC is fed to corresponding DCs of neighboring predictrons (the lateral lines in figure 16.2). Katamic memory connectivity is usually set up so that each DC receives stronger input (i.e., the vertical ovals in figure 16.2) from neighboring DCs (i.e., at the same height), with connection strength from more distant neighbors being weaker. During learning, ltm values are updated so that subsequent predictions become more accurate. The design of recognitrons/BSSs allows katamic memory performance and learning to be interleaved on a bit-by-bit basis. Due to space limitations, the details of katamic memory processing and learning (which involves a nine-step algorithm with sixteen equations) cannot be described here; for details see Nenov (1991) and Nenov and Dyer (1994).

In summary, each predictron generates a 0 or 1 at each basic time step (B cycle) based on the spatiotemporal relation of that output to all other past bits in the sequence, which are distributed both spatially (across all predictrons) and temporally (across the DCs of a given predictron). The network's ability to determine when to accept external input (vs. performing internal pattern sequence completion) is controlled by the recognitrons and BBSs. The network can be set so that a recognitron accepts a predictron's output based on the correctness of its neighboring predictron's predictions. Thus, katamic memory acts as a robust spatiotemporal sequence associator in which the prediction of each next pattern is based on traces (i.e., generalized correlations) of all past histories of all previous patterns distributed across both space (pattern width) and time (pattern sequences).

Katamic Memory Properties

Experiments with a range of parameter settings and sequences (of varying widths and lengths) indicate that katamic memory has very useful properties:

Rapid learning: On average, only four to six exposures to a pattern sequence are sufficient for learning a given sequence. This is a major improvement over recurrent PDP networks based on backpropagation learning (e.g., Elman 1990). Such networks typically require hundreds/thousands of training epochs to achieve reliable performance.

Flexible and scalable memory capacity: Multiple sequences of different lengths can be stored. Wider patterns can be handled by adding predictrons, and sequences of greater length can be more rapidly stored and discriminated by increasing the number of dendritic compartments in each predictron.

Sequence completion/recall: A short cue is sufficient to discriminate and retrieve a previously recorded sequence.

Fault and noise tolerance: Missing bits (up to 30 percent of 1 bits) can be tolerated, and the memory's ability to interpolate/extrapolate from existing data degrades gracefully with noise.

Robust performance: The model operates within a wide range of values for its memory parameters.

Integrated processing: The katamic memory is capable of concurrent learning, recognition, and recall of sequences. Its built-in pattern recognition mechanism allows it to automatically switch from a learning mode to a performance mode on a pattern-by-pattern basis.

Major Neural Memory Groups in DETE

DETE contains about fifty katamic memory modules. Katamic memory modules receive inputs from verbal/visual/motor inputs and function to store and associate sequences across these modalities. Major neural memory groups include the following:

Feature memories: Associated with each feature plane (FP) is a katamic memory module called a feature memory (FM) consisting of a 2-D plane of predictrons. For instance, for each position in the shape feature plane (SFP) there is a corresponding predictron in the corresponding shape feature memory. The task of each visual feature memory is to encode memory traces of all sequences of activities coming in from the corresponding visual FP.

Verbal memory: The task of this katamic module is to encode memory traces of input sequences of gra-phonemes.

Morphological/syntactic procedural memory (MSPM): This group of modules is used to detect and store correlations among gra-phonemes and word transitions. It is the MSPM that allows DETE to learn simple word preferences, such that in English color words (e.g., "red") come before a shape words (e.g., "triangle").

Temporal memory: In addition to explicit representations of time (e.g., minutes, hours, days, years), people also appear to have an implicit (or experiential) sense of the "flow" of time. DETE contains only implicit representations of time. The "flow" of time in DETE has its direct analog in the flow (i.e., shifting and decay of) stm in each predictron.

DETE's implicit representation of time must be extended, however, in order to learn language descriptions concerning events that have occurred in the recent past or that will occur in the immediate future. This is accomplished by making multiple copies of DETE's verbal memory and visual/motor feature memories. Eight copies are made for each modality. They are labeled temporal planes (i.e., TP-0 to TP-7). To represent the flow of these longer durations of time (dubbed "moments"), the output of each lower-numbered TP is shifted, in a pipeline fashion, to the next higher TP. The detailed connectivity and dynamics of how this is accomplished are described by Nenov (1991).

To learn descriptions about the recent past, DETE is shown a visual event of one moment in duration (e.g., a ball hitting a wall) with no verbal input. Then, at a later moment, DETE receives the verbal input "ball hit wall." As a result, DETE lays down memory traces across several TPs. In the future-tense case, DETE first receives verbal input (e.g., "ball will hit wall") at the first moment, and then at a later moment sees the ball actually hit the wall. This distinct TP configuration represents DETE's experience of a future-tense sentence. The particular configuration of activation (across the TPs) forms DETE's representation of the entire visual/verbal association, with the verbal input displaced in time from the visual.

DETE Learning/Performance

First, DETE was taught the names of blobs by being given scenes of blobs with a single shape, but with varying colors, sizes, locations, and motions. As a result, DETE extracted what was invariant (i.e., shape) and formed the strongest associations between a word (e.g., "circle") and the appropriate activity on the shape feature map (i.e., in the region of round objects). Using this same approach, DETE next learned the meanings of words for color, size, and location (e.g., above, below, left, right, in center, near, far), and words for motion in a straight line and at constant speed (e.g., still, slow, fast, north, east, northeast, etc.). Subsequently, DETE was taught single words for events. Such words include moves (changes of location), accelerates (change of motion speed), turns (change of motion direction), bounces (change of direction of motion while in contact with another blob), shrinks (change of size relative to previous size), and transforms (change of shape relative to previous shape).

For example, to learn the word "moves," DETE was presented with multiple pairs containing the gra-phoneme sequence for "moves" and a sequence of visual frames showing a moving blob with constant shape, color, and size and moving in a given direction with a fixed speed. The training set included blobs of different shapes, each moving at a different speed and in a different direction. As a result, only movement was invariant. In a similar manner, DETE learned "bounces" by watching different blobs bouncing off the walls of the visual screen (with different speeds and at different locations, etc.). Generalization ability was tested by presenting a novel sequence (but with familiar words) as input. Once DETE has learned word sequences involving separate feature planes, it can handle novel combinations of word sequences automatically (because each feature plane processes the input independently).

DETE was taught to answer questions by being trained on [question-word, . . . answer-word] sequences in particular visual contexts, such as the following:

Visual input	*Verbal input*
large green triangle	"what__size . . . large"
small red ball	"what__color . . . red"
large blue triangle	"what__shape . . . triangle"
stationary circle, moving square	"what__moves . . . "square""

DETE was then able to generate the correct verbal answer when given a question-word and a visual scene as input.

DETE is also able to learn motor sequences. For example, in one experiment DETE was given 100 separate visual scenes, each containing two stationary blobs of different shapes and different sizes. In each case, one blob was larger than the other. DETE was trained by being given the word "what__is__bigger" as input, while at the same time directing DETE's eye to the correct blob and then presenting the correct verbal answer. If DETE's attention was initially on the smaller blob, then its eye was shifted (by the teacher) to the other blob. However, if its eye was already on the bigger blob, then its eye was allowed to remain there. DETE was then tested by presenting novel images of two blobs of different sizes, paired with "what__is__bigger" and seeing which blob DETE selected through its eye movement and verbal response. DETE's successful performance indicated that it had learned also to redirect its eye to the appropriate object.

DETE has also been taught temporal relations, such as past (e.g., "bounced") and future (e.g., "will bounce"), as described earlier.

DETE Implementation Status

DETE currently runs on a massively parallel (16K processor) CM-2 in *Lisp with a Sun 4/830 as a front end. It uses over 1 million virtual processors (vps) and 7/8 of available heap (16K processors × .5 Mbits stack per processor). Each of the five visual feature memories is mapped onto a 3-D data structure with dimensions of 16 × 16 predictrons (i.e., the size of each feature plane) × 64 (the number of DCs per predictron), for a total of 5 × 256 × 64 = 81,920 vps. For each feature memory there are 16 × 16 = 256 recognitrons. Each memory contains both a short-term and long-term component, which doubles the number of vps (2 × 81,920 = 163,840 vps). Each memory is furthermore copied into the eight temporal memory planes (8 × 163,840 = 1,310,720 vps). The verbal memory is mapped to a 2-D data structure with dimensions of 64 predictrons × 256 DCs per predictron.

The DETE system takes approximately 1 hour of CM-2 time to learn the meanings of three separate words. This is due to the need for varying features in the input; the system extracts what is invariant. To learn more complex sentences can take up to 8 hours. For a single katamic memory, it takes approximately 5 minutes on the CM-2 to learn three separate, arbitrary sequences, each 64 patterns in length, where each pattern is 512 bits (predictrons) wide. Katamic memory has been tested on various configurations up to 1024 predictrons, each with 1024 dendritic compartments, along with 1024 recognitrons, with 8 DCs per recognitron and 1024 BBSs total (one per predictron).

EVOLVING POPULATIONS OF NEURAL NETWORKS IN BIOLAND

BioLand (Werner and Dyer 1994) is a 2-D artificial environment designed for studying the evolution of communication in cooperating/competing populations of simple creatures (termed *biots*) whose behavior is controlled by a small neural network (20 to 50 neurons) in which a biot's neural network is specified by its genome. Several species of biots can coexist, along with simple physical objects, such as plants, trees, and holes (which serve as food, landmarks, and/or safety zones for nesting and/or predator escape). Individual biots, biot species, and physical objects produce distinct smell gradients that spread out and diffuse over distance with time. Biots also produce sound gradients. Some sounds are involuntary—for example, are the result of movement. Sounds can also be produced voluntarily—that is, under biot neuromotor control. Each biot can generate a variety of distinct sounds (termed "frequencies"). Louder sounds propagate farther than do softer sounds. Similar, overlapping sounds cause an increase in intensity, leading to complex gradients. Different frequencies allow biots to employ and discriminate different sounds and sound combinations.

Biot Neural Structure and Morphology

Each species of biot possesses sensory, internal, and motor neurons, with particular operations/behaviors assigned to each sensorimotor neuron (depending on the species). For example, if a mating motor neuron passes threshold and the biot is close to a receptive female biot (i.e., her metabolism is above a given level and she also fires her mating motor neuron), then mating will occur, producing offspring. Biots can also grasp/release objects, eat food, and turn/move about in a smooth manner and at varying speeds. Biots have a simple metabolism, which affects their behavior (e.g., biots with low metabolism move more slowly and cannot produce offspring). A very low metabolism results in biot death.

Each biot has sensory neurons for each type of smell and sound. These neurons are bilateral (i.e., on each side of its body). Different sensory neurons are sensitive to distinct smell/sound gradients, along with gradient intensity. Some smells represent the internal state of a biot, and sounds generated by biots should be able to evolve to indicate internal states (e.g., age, sickness, gender, species/family membership, emotional state, mating receptivity, metabolism, etc.) and thus supply useful information to other biots. For instance, in an earlier model (Werner and Dyer 1991), female neural networks evolved that generated simple "sounds" with directional information. This information was used by (co-evolved) male neural networks to help them locate females for mating.

Activation of nonsensory neurons is a sigmoidal function of their inputs from other neurons. More complex *axoaxonal* connections allow neurons to gate connections between other neurons. Several of the output neurons, including the mating and eating motor neurons, have fixed thresholds. The remaining motor neurons allow graded responses. Thus, biots may produce several actions concurrently; for example, a biot may grasp and eat food while turning or moving. Figure 16.3 shows a portion of a sample evolved neural network.

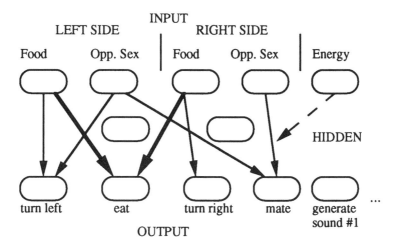

Figure 16.3 Simplified neural network fragment. The connection strengths are indicated by the thickness of the arrows. A single axoaxonal connection is indicated as a dashed arrow. Additional input/output neurons and connections to internal neurons are not shown.

Biot Genome and Function

Each biot's genome consists of several lists of genetic information. The first list consists of triples. Each triple encodes a standard single connection between two neurons. Each triple specifies a source neuron, a target neuron, and the strength of the connection between them. For example, the triple [5, 3, 0.4] within the genome encodes a connection from neuron N5 to neuron N3, with a connection weight of 0.4. A second list contains four-tuples, with each encoding axoaxonal connections. Each four-tuple specifies the gating neuron, the source and target neurons being gated, and the strength of the gating synapse. Additional lists are being designed so that each neuron may exhibit learning, with the particular type of learning under genetic control.

For any maximum genome length, there is a tradeoff between the number of neurons and the number of connections among neurons. PDP networks (Rumelhart and McClelland 1986) have full connectivity between neurons in the input, hidden, and output layers. In contrast, sparse connectivity allows for many more neurons to be employed. Braitenberg (1987) has shown that sparse connectivity augmented with axoaxonal connections can produce complex behavior. Sparse connectivity also greatly reduces the parameter search space, since each connection represents a parameter that must be adjusted. Rather than starting with full connectivity and then searching such a high-dimensional parameter space, we have chosen to start with smaller genomes and allow selectional pressures to increase genome length over time.

Biots can evolve in complexity by increasing the number of connections between neurons (i.e., within the space allocated for encoding the genome). New connections can arise in biot offspring through mutation or recombination or both. For example, suppose a given species of biot can have at most n neurons, and a segment of a male biot's genome contains the triple [5, XX, XX], where XX means that the value of these bits is uninterpretable—for instance, outside the range of n neurons or, for weights, outside the range of weight values. If crossover occurs right after the 5 and at the same site in the female's genome there is a triple [XX, 7, .25], then one crossover result will be [5, 7, .25], thus creating a new connection in the offspring, from neuron N5 to N7, with a connection weight of .25.

Current BioLand Environment

The current environment contains three biot species of neural network controlled biots dubbed "prairie dogs," "hawks," and "snakes." Nonbiots include plants, trees, and holes. Prairie dogs increase their metabolism by eating plants, with new plants constantly added to provide energy. Hawks and snakes are predators that eat prairie dogs. Trees and holes

volved in human language acquisition: (1) a more realistic neural architecture capable of learning, associating, generalizing, recognizing, and retrieving multiple input sequences and (2) a task domain for attempting to ground language in the world so that the acquisition of language semantics (at least in early childhood) comes about through an interaction between perceptual/motor experiences and the utterances that refer to such experiences. To our knowledge, DETE is the only neural architecture that learns word sequences via association with visual sequences involving multiple moving objects.

At some point in our evolutionary past, humans must have evolved a neural architecture capable of forming such utterance-to-visual-sequence associations. This capability ultimately allowed any individual X to inform Y of the behavior of Z. Such ability (to describe action sequences) would have been very useful in many tasks requiring cooperation, such as group hunting, maintaining social cohesion (e.g., X tells leader Y that Z has done some act, perhaps one that breaks a taboo), planning for warfare, spreading innovative behaviors, and so on.

In spite of its complexity, DETE is still extremely primitive when compared to human capabilities. For example, DETE suffers from the following limitations:

• Lack of verbal-to-verbal association. After initial symbol grounding, children learn the meaning of many words through verbal-to-verbal association. For example, one can tell a five-year-old, "A stack is one block on top of another, with a pyramid at the very top." DETE lacks this word-defining capability.

• No sense of self vs. others. DETE has no explicit representation of either itself or the teacher in the environment. As a result, it cannot learn indexicals, such as "me" vs. "you."

• Lack of goals and plans. DETE has no desires of its own (e.g., "I want the ball"), nor does it have planning mechanisms to achieve those goals. Consequently, DETE is incapable of learning the meanings of goal/plan-based sentences of the sort that are processed by symbolic NLP systems, such as PAM (Wilensky 1983) or BORIS (Dyer 1983a).

• Inability to handle model-level vision. Currently, DETE can see only "blobs"—that is, homogeneous objects. In contrast, most objects and agents in the world are structured; for example, images of people consist of arms, legs, torsos, etc. Consequently, DETE is currently incapable of learning the meaning of words involving composite motions (e.g., "He bent his arm").

• Inability to represent abstract concepts and generate high-level inferences. At this point, DETE cannot represent abstract concepts or relationships, such as buying and ownership.

Augmenting DETE with such capabilities will require fundamental research on how to embed high-level, symbolic cognitive skills within neural architectures, along with research concerning how to represent model-level visual dynamics (i.e. the motions of composite objects) in neural architectures.

BioLand and the Evolution of Animal Communication

Ethological studies indicate that animals possess a wide variety of signaling systems. For example, domesticated chickens signal the quality of available food (Marler et al., 1986), while real prairie dogs produce signals that distinguish not only different species of predators, but also different individual predators within a given species (Slobodchikoff, Fischer, and Shapiro 1986, Slobodchikoff et al. 1991). Our early success in evolving mate-finding signals (Werner and Dyer 1991) and later, other types of behaviors, such as predation and prey avoidance (Werner and Dyer 1993, 1994), has led us to believe that BioLand is a good initial environment for experimentation in the evolution of animal communication. For instance, our current hypothesis (ongoing research) is that differential safety zones (along with other parameters, such as the relative speed/sensing ranges of predators vs. prey) will lead to the evolution of differential prey-warning signals among our biot prey populations. If this turns out to be the case, then we should be able to say something about the complexity and evolutionary history of the biot neural architectures that exhibit this behavior and about the interactional dynamics and selectional pressures that lead to it. This computational ethology approach should someday allow actual ethologists to test their models on synthetic biots as a point of comparison with real animal population data.

A current major limitation of Bioland is that learning has not yet been incorporated into the model. An ability to learn, however, is probably essential for more rapidly evolving biots capable of modifying their behavior as the result of signals from other biots. Consider child-parent communication. Young biots should signal their parents when they are hungry. Parents should then respond by finding food and bringing it back to their young. Parents could coordinate food-gathering and nest-guarding tasks via communication. One parent could signal that it has brought back some food and will guard the nest, thus freeing the other to go eat.

Very Long-Term Goals

A long-term goal of BioLand research is to evolve biots that can learn from experience and communicate their knowledge to others; for example, that a particular plant is good/bad to eat. Other biots would then seek out (or avoid) that plant. Some biot might even discover a novel solution to a task and then tell others. An example of this might be a prey biot's accidentally killing a predator by dropping a rock on it. Communication of this type of useful information is the beginning of a primitive form of culture.

Another very long-term goal is to create a population of biots with DETE-style retinas and katamic memory architectures. Such "DETE biots" would then have the capability of communicating descriptions of the visual statics/dynamics of the environment to other biots, which could then learn from them. A population of such DETE biots could then evolve in a "V-BioLand" that would support visual processing (in contrast to the simple scent/sound gradients supported in the current BioLand environment). Of course, the genome (and the genome-mapping function) would have to be much more complex. At this time, the DETE model (with its katamic neurons, multiple modules, and learning behavior) is too computationally intensive. We have just enough computer power for a single DETE model, which takes up all the processing power of our 16K CM-2, let alone a population of thousands of DETEs. However, such an environment should become more feasible as increasingly powerful, massively parallel computers are developed.

CONCLUSIONS

There are currently enormous gaps in our theoretical understanding of the neurodevelopment and neuroevolution of both animal and human cognitive systems. To fill in these theoretical gaps will require continuing exploration of computational models operating at different levels of abstraction. Symbolic, connectionist, perceptually grounded, and evolutionary computer modeling technologies each have capabilities and limitations that the others lack. They also supply distinct modeling opportunities due to their different levels of abstraction. Our multilevel, simulation-based research approach allows us to begin to address issues in human language and animal communication that range from high-level, individual phenomena (e.g., argument comprehension of editorial text) to low-level, group phenomena (e.g., evolving alarm signals among prey). Interacting agents with complex sensing and neural architectures must be situated in perceptually rich, dynamic environments in order to address the neural, developmental, social, and evolutionary dimensions of animal communication and human language. The DETE and BioLand systems presented here represent some initial steps in exploring how both human language and animal communication might be acquired/evolved in such environments.

ACKNOWLEDGMENTS

This research was supported in part by NSF grant IRI-910730 and a W. M. Keck interdisciplinary grant for cognitive science research. The CM-2 Connection Machine on which the models are implemented was acquired through NSF equipment centers grant #BBS-87-14206 and has been maintained through both NSF grant #DIR-90-24251 and the

W. M. Keck Foundation grant. A special thanks to my students Valeriy Nenov and Greg Werner for their central roles in the design and development of the DETE and BioLand models, respectively.

REFERENCES

Alvarado, S. J. (1990). *Understanding Editorial Text: A Computer Model of Argument Comprehension.* Boston, MA: Kluwer Academic Publishers.

Alvarado, S., Dyer, M. G., and Flowers, M. (1990a). Argument Comprehension and Retrieval for Editorial Text. *Knowledge-Based Systems,* Vol. 3, No. 3, 139–162.

Alvarado, S., Dyer, M. G., and Flowers, M. (1990b). Argument Representation for Editorial Text. *Knowledge-Based Systems,* Vol. 3, No. 2, 87–107.

Belew, R. K., and Booker, L. B. eds. (1991). *Proceedings of the Fourth International Conference on Genetic Algorithms.* San Mateo, CA: Morgan Kaufmann.

Belew, R. K., McInerney, J., and Schraudolph, N. N. (1992). Evolving Networks: Using the Genetic Algorithm with Connectionist Learning. In Langton, C. G., Taylor, C., Farmer, J. D., and S. Rasmussen, eds. *Artificial Life II.* Reading, MA: Addison-Wesley.

Braitenberg, V. (1987). *Vehicles: Experiments in Synthetic Psychology.* Cambridge, MA: The MIT Press.

Cheney, D. L., and Seyfarth, R. M. (1991). Truth and Deception in Animal Communication. In C. A. Ristau (ed.). *Cognitive Ethology: The Minds of Other Animals.* Hillsdale, NJ: Lawrence Erlbaum Assoc.

Dyer, M. G. (1983a). *In-Depth Understanding: A Computer Model of Integrated Processing for Narrative Comprehension.* Cambridge, MA: The MIT Press.

Dyer, M. G. (1983b). The Role of Affect in Narratives. *Cognitive Science,* Vol. 7, No. 3, 211–242.

Dyer, M. G. (1987). Emotions and Their Computations: Three Computer Models. *Cognition and Emotion,* Vol. 1, No. 3, 323–347.

Dyer, M. G. (1990). Distributed Symbol Formation and Processing in Connectionist Networks. *Journal of Experimental and Theoretical Artificial Intelligence,* Vol. 2, 215–239.

Dyer, M. G. (1991). Symbolic Neuroengineering for Natural Language Processing: A Multi-Level Research Approach. In J. Barnden and J. Pollack (eds.). *High-Level Connectionist Models.* Norwood, NY: Ablex Publishers. Pp. 36–86.

Dyer, M. G., and Nenov, V. I. (1993). Language Learning via Perceptual/Motor Experiences. *Proceedings of the Fifteenth Annual Conference of the Cognitive Science Society.* Hillsdale, NJ: Lawrence Erlbaum Assoc.

Elman, J. L. (1990). Finding Structure in Time. *Cognitive Science,* Vol. 14, 179–211.

Feldman, J., and Ballard, D. (1982). Connectionist Models and Their Properties. *Cognitive Science,* Vol. 6, 205–254.

Goldberg, D. E. (1989). *Genetic Algorithms in Search, Optimization, and Machine Learning.* Reading, MA: Addison-Wesley.

Goldberg, D. E, and Holland, J. H., eds. (1988). *Machine Learning,* Vol. 3, Nos. 2–3, Special Issue on Genetic Algorithms. Boston, MA: Kluwer Academic Publishers.

Holland, J. H. (1992). *Adaptation in Natural and Artificial Systems.* Cambridge, MA: The MIT Press.

Lange, T. E., and Dyer, M. G. (1989). High-Level Inferencing in a Connectionist Network. *Connection Science*, Vol. 1, No. 2, 181–217.

Marler, P., Dufty, A., and Pickert, R. (1986). Vocal Communication in the Domestic Chicken: I. Does a Sender Communicate Information About the Quality of a Food Referent to a Receiver? *Animal Behavior*, Vol. 43, 188–193.

Miikkulainen, R. P. (1990). DISCERN: A Distributed Artificial Neural Network Model of Script Processing and Memory. Computer Science Ph.D. dissertation, UCLA.

Miikkulainen, R., and Dyer, M. G. (1991). Natural Language Processing with Modular PDP Networks and Distributed Lexicon. *Cognitive Science*, Vol. 15, No. 3, 343–399.

Minsky, M. (1985). *The Society of Mind*. New York: Simon and Schuster.

Mueller, E. T. (1989). *Daydreaming in Humans and Machines: A Computer Model of the Stream of Thought*. Norwood, NJ: Ablex.

Mueller, E., and Dyer, M. G. (1985). Daydreaming in Humans and Computers. *Proceedings of International Joint Conference on Artificial Intelligence*. Los Altos, CA: Morgan Kaufmann. Pp. 278–280.

Nenov, V. I. (1991). Perceptually Grounded Language Acquisition: A Neural/Procedural Hybrid Model. Computer Science Dept. Ph.D. dissertation, UCLA.

Nenov, V. I., and Dyer, M. G. (1994). Language Learning via Perceptual/Motor Association: A Massively Parallel Model. In H. Kitano and J. A. Hendler (eds.). *Massively Parallel Artificial Intelligence*. Cambridge, MA: AAAI/The MIT Press. Pp. 203–245.

Pazzani, M. J. (1990). *Creating a Memory of Causal Relationships: An Integration of Empirical and Explanation-Based Learning Method*. Hillsdale, NJ: Lawrence Erlbaum Associates.

Pazzani, M. J., and Dyer, M. G. (1989). Memory Organization and Explanation-Based Learning. *International Journal of Expert Systems: Research and Applications*, Vol. 2, No. 3, 331–358.

Pinker, S., and Bloom, P. (1990). Natural Language and Natural Selection. *Behavioral and Brain Sciences*, Vol. 13, No. 4, 707–784.

Pollack, J. B. (1990). Recursive Distributed Representations. *Artificial Intelligence*, Vol. 46, 77–105.

Reeves, J. F. (1991). Computational Morality: A Process Model of Belief Conflict and Resolution for Story Understanding. Computer Science Dept. Ph.D. dissertation, UCLA.

Rumelhart, D. E., and McClelland, J. L., eds. (1986). *Parallel Distributed Processing*, Vols. 1 and 2. Cambridge, MA: Bradford/The MIT Press.

Schank, R. C., and Abelson, R. (1977). *Scripts, Plans, Goals and Understanding*. Hillsdale, NJ: Lawrence Erlbaum Assoc.

Shastri, L., and Ajjanagadde, V. (1993). From Simple Associations to Systematic Reasoning: A Connectionist Representation of Rules, Variables and Dynamic Bindings Using Temporal Synchrony. *Behavioral and Brain Sciences*, Vol. 16, No. 3, 417–494.

Slobodchikoff, C., Fischer, C., and Shapiro, J. (1986). Predator-Specific Alarm Calls of Prairie Dogs. *American Zoology*, Vol. 26, 557.

Slobodchikoff, C., Kiriazis, J., Fischer, C., and Creef, E. (1991). Semantic Information Distinguishing Individual Predators in the Alarm Calls of Gunnison's Prairie Dogs. *Animal Behavior*, Vol. 42, 713–719.

Turner, S. R. (1992). MINSTREL: A Computer Model of Creativity and Storytelling. Computer Science Dept. Ph.D. dissertation, University of California, Los Angeles.

van Essen, D. C., and Maunsell, J. H. R. (1983). Hierarchical Organization and Functional Systems in the Visual Cortex. *Trends in Neuroscience,* Vol. 4, 370–375.

Werner, G. M., and Dyer, M. G. (1991). Evolution of Communication in Artificial Organisms. In J. D. Farmer, C. Langton, S. Rasmussen, and C. Taylor (eds.). *Artificial Life II.* Reading, MA: Addison-Wesley. Pp. 659–687.

Werner, G. M., and Dyer, M. G. (1993). Evolution of Herding Behavior in Artificial Animals. In J. A. Meyer, H. L. Roitblat, and S. W. Wilson (eds.). *From Animals to Animats 2: Proceedings of the Second Interational Conference on Simulation of Adaptive Behavior.* Cambridge, MA: Bradford Books/The MIT Press. Pp. 393–399.

Werner, G. M., and Dyer, M. G. (1994). BioLand: A Massively Parallel Simulation Environment for Evolving Distributed Forms of Intelligent Behavior. In H. Kitano and Hendler, J. (eds.). *Massively Parallel Artificial Intelligence.* Cambridge, MA: AAAI/The MIT Press. Pp. 317–349.

Wilensky, R. (1983). Planning and Understanding. Reading, MA: Addison-Wesley.

Zernik, U., and Dyer, M. G. (1987). The Self-Extending Phrasal Lexicon. *Computational Linguistics,* Vol. 13, Nos. 3–4, 308–327.

VI Motivation and Emotion

17 Opportunity versus Goals in Robots, Animals, and People

David McFarland

In the next millennium humans will be living with robots, and robots will be living with us. What will these robots be like? The evolution of these robots will converge with that of animals. But this does not mean that the robots will be modeled on animals or humans. They will be designed in terms of what is best for their own ecological circumstances. The robots will be bought and sold and will therefore have to compete in the marketplace against other robots and against humans willing to carry out the same tasks. This ecological competition will lead to the evolution of certain attributes (McFarland 1991a), among which will be robustness, speed of reaction, self-sufficiency, and autonomy.

Self-sufficiency and autonomy are not the same thing (McFarland 1993). To be self-sufficient, a robot must not incur any debts of vital resources that it cannot repay through its own behavior. Such debts may include energy debts (i.e., the robot must not get itself into a position where it cannot regain energy balance by foraging, recharging, or whatever), and task debts that relate to those features of robot behavior that are designed to please the customer (McFarland and Bösser 1993). For example, suppose we design a robot to fly in after a nuclear catastrophe and measure the radiation at various locations. It will be no good for the robot to come back and report that it was so busy refueling that it had no time to gather any data. Self-sufficiency is largely a matter of behavioral stability, a concept that can be mathematically defined (McFarland 1993; McFarland and Bösser 1993). To maintain stability, the resilience of the various activities must be suitably tuned.

In animal behavior studies, resilience is a measure of the cost to the animal of abstaining from each activity in its natural repertoire (McFarland and Houston 1981). If an animal did no feeding, for example, the cost would be high, but if it abstained from grooming the cost would probably be relatively low. An animal that had equal motivation to feed and groom would incur less cost (in terms of fitness decrement) if it devoted its available time to feeding. If it used up much of its time feeding, there would be less time for grooming. In terms of the time budget, feeding would have high resilience, while grooming would have low resilience to being pushed out by other activities. Thus behavioral resilience is a measure of the extent to which an activity can be squashed in terms of time by other activities. It reflects the importance of an activity in a long-term sense. When given mathematical expression, behavioral resilience can be shown to be important in the optimal allocation of behavior. It is also closely related to the economic demand functions that are a common feature of animal behavior (McFarland and Houston 1981).

The self-sufficient robot must also have the appropriate motivation for debt recovery. That is, it must have the motivation to regain lost energy, to avoid temperature extremes, to avoid predators and traps, and to carry out its tasks. For example, our flying robot must want to find high-radiation spots. It must want to map them. It must want to remain viable, etc. These various aspects of motivation have to be satisfied simultaneously, but the robot can do only one thing at a time, so it needs some kind of action selection mechanism (discussed later).

The self-sufficient robot must have some degree of autonomy, because it must have the freedom to engage in that behavior that is in its own vital interests. Autonomy implies freedom from control. If A controls B, then A can make B behave in the way that A wants. To do this, A must have sufficient knowledge of B. If B is autonomous, then B must be self-controlling. That is, B must want B to behave in a certain way, and B must have sufficient knowledge of B to be able to do this. In other words, an autonomous agent must have some degree of motivation and cognition organized in such a way that an outside agent cannot obtain sufficient knowledge to control the autonomous agent (McFarland 1993).

Once an autonomous agent comes under the control of another agent, its autonomy is lost. Our autonomous flying robot must be able to make its own decisions about what to do next, and it must be able to resist interference from outside agents such as humans and other robots.

Of course, we humans would hope to be able to influence the behavior of such robots, much as we hope to influence the behavior of a sheep dog or guide dog. Nevertheless, the dog and the robot remain autonomous, capable of overriding our aspirations at any moment. The autonomous robot will have simultaneous motivational pressures, but will be able to carry out only one activity at a time. We are now back with the problem of activity selection.

ACTIVITY SELECTION

The most important feature of the activity selection system of a self-sufficient autonomous robot is that it should be sensitive to opportunity profiles. An opportunity profile is a function of time that indicates what benefit the agent will derive if it performs a particular action at a particular time. The magnitude of an opportunity is determined partly by environmental circumstances and partly by motivational state. For example, for an agent that is hungry for fuel, there will be a high opportunity value when stimuli indicating high fuel availability are present in the environment. For an agent that is less hungry in the same environment, the opportunity will be less, because foraging for fuel will be less beneficial. Similarly, at a given hunger level an agent that senses high fuel availability will have a higher opportunity than one that senses low availability, because foraging when high availability is signaled is likely to be more beneficial.

The units of benefit will vary from agent to agent. If the agent is an animal, then the benefit will be related to fitness. We must be careful here to distinguish between the real benefit as determined by environmental circumstances and the notional benefit as perceived by the agent. In animal behavior studies the former is sometimes called cost (the negative of the benefit), and the latter is sometimes called utility (McFarland and Houston 1981). In robotics the former is a measure of marketability, and the latter may be called value (McFarland and Bösser 1993). Thus the value of an opportunity to a robot is the benefit in terms of future change of state that the robot would gain if it engaged in the appropriate behavior. There are various ways (both implicit and explicit) in which the robot may measure the value (McFarland 1992), but the details need not concern us here.

Obviously, a robot that is able to exploit opportunities will have higher marketability than one that allows opportunities to pass it by. The former will appear to be more efficient than the latter. Pushed to its logical conclusion, this line of thinking results in the idea of optimal activity selection based upon trade-off among the alternative courses of action at any one time. Thus we arrive at a principle similar to the trade-off principle of animal behavior (Stephens and Krebs 1986; McFarland 1989a, b, c). The trade-off principle implies that optimal activity selection can be achieved only if the activity selection mechanism involves a "level playing field" in which all players (i.e., all candidates for behavioral expression) have equal status. This means that all variables in the trade-off have equal status, there being no bias in favor of any particular activity (including the ongoing activity) (McFarland and Sibly 1975).

In animal behavior studies (e.g., Alexander 1982; Stephens and Krebs 1986; Lendrem 1986; Sibly and Calow 1986) we have growing evidence of refined trade-offs, but we know little about the mechanisms by which these are achieved. What we can say is that, if a proposed mechanism violates basic principles of animal design, such as those maintaining behavioral stability and activity trade-off, then such a mechanism is unlikely to be a good model of the mechanisms found in nature. The same argument applies to self-sufficient autonomous robots. That is, the activity selection mechanisms should not incorporate mechanisms that violate such principles, because such robots will be poorly designed compared with robots that conform. The argument is worth making, because many current proposals in robotics incorporate some version of goal-directed behavior that does violate these principles.

ACTION THEORY

Apparently purposive behavior can be achieved by a variety of mechanisms, ranging from simple goal-achieving behavior to complex intentional behavior. I review some of these below. The most popular theory, and the one with which I wish to take issue, is action theory. Action theory has its origins in attempts to provide a psychological role for the will. Thus Ach (1910, p. 256) defined action as an object-oriented act of will. The action is related to an anticipated result (the goal) and to an intention (will) to reach the goal. For the early German psychologists (Wundt 1907; Ach 1910; Lewin 1935) and for Tolman (1932), the concept of goal-oriented action (Handlung) was a fundamental one. In the more behavioristic American psychology, the concept can be traced from Watson (1913) to the cybernetic view of Miller, Galanter, and Pribram (1960; see Silver 1985).

Historically, the cybernetic approach began with Rosenblueth, Wiener, and Bigelow (1943), who defined purposeful behavior in terms of negative feedback systems. The behavior of such a system is controlled by the difference between the present state of the system and the "intended" state, or goal. Miller, Gallanter, and Pribram (1960) developed this idea and proposed that action can be understood in terms of Test-Operate-Test-Exit (TOTE) units. According to this model, the actions that an animal performs are continually guided by the outcomes of various tests. The "image" of a goal supplies the criteria that must be met before the test is passed. Comparison of test outcomes continues until the incongruity between test outcome and criterion is zero. TOTE units can be arranged hierarchically into larger TOTE units. Miller, Gallanter, and Pribram (1960) suggested that "the compound of TOTE units unravels itself simply enough into a coordinated sequence of tests and actions, although the underlying structure that organizes and co-ordinates the behavior is itself hierarchical, not sequential" (p. 34).

We can illustrate this approach by referring to the problem of using a map. The conventional approach is to suppose that a person selects a goal, such as Madison Square Garden, in Manhattan and then uses a map, together with information about his current position on the map, to select a route to the goal. The map is then used to guide the person along the route. There are various possible versions of this approach, but all require that a (mental) representation of the goal be compared with information about the current position and that the outcome of this comparison be the main variable controlling the behavior, so that a feedback loop is created.

It is not difficult to imagine devising a TOTE system to solve the Manhattan map problem. Starting from the Guggenheim Museum, the task is to drive to Madison Square Garden. The subject pinpoints her current position on the map (either a real map or a cognitive map). If she does not think she is at Madison Square Garden (the goal), then she checks her position on the road. If this does not correspond to her position on the map, then she corrects her position on the map. The subject then tests her direction of movement. If this is not toward the goal, then she corrects her direction of movement. Then she tests her vehicle (e.g., makes a turn) until the vehicle is moving in the right direction. The loop is now closed, and it is time for the subject to test her current position on the map again. This is not a perfect illustration, but it is the kind of thing that Miller, Gallanter, and Pribram (1960) envisaged.

The TOTE model is concerned with the guidance and monitoring of ongoing behavior, and it has much in common with the action theory. There are, however, many forms of action theory (Brand 1970; 1984), and it is not possible to give a single, generally agreed-upon, precise definition of an action. Probably the most widely held view among philosophers is the causal theory, which maintains that the difference between a movement pattern and an action is that the latter is accompanied by a particular kind of mental event, which plays a causal role, whereas the latter is not so accompanied. For example, in putting his hands forward to break a fall, John may follow the same pattern of movement as when he puts his hands forward to perform a somersault. The latter is an action, because some mental event (the nature of which depends upon the variety of action theory) played a causal role in the behavior. The former is not an action, because this (special) kind of mental event is lacking (note that there must have been some kind of neural event that caused the hands to move).

In ordinary language, we might say that the former was a reflex, while the latter was deliberate. This type of theory was held by Hobbes, Locke, and Hume, and it has recently been advocated by Davidson (1963, 1978), Goldman (1970, 1976), Sellars (1966, 1973), and Searle (1979, 1981), among others. Basically, all are goal-directed theories, because they envisage a mental state of affairs that is related to the goal (i.e., some form of knowing about the likely consequences) that is instrumental in guiding the behavior.

Among psychologists there is also a variety of approaches to action theory. For some (e.g., von Cranach 1982), goal-directed action refers to a person's goal-directed, planned, intended, and conscious behavior. For others, actions need not be intentional, but must involve some sort of mental representation that guides the behavior, including schemata (Bartlett 1932; Neisser 1976), frames (Minsky 1975), or scripts (Schank and Abelson 1977). Thorndyke (1984) discusses the essential similarities underlying these terms. Current thinking among psychologists (e.g., Frese and Sabini 1985) seems to take it for granted that actions are largely the result of cognition and involve some kind of mental representation of the goal to be achieved. A similar view is developing in artificial intelligence (e.g., Roitblat 1991). Indeed, any means-end approach is a type of action theory.

There are alternatives to action theory, some of which have long pedigrees (e.g., Ashby 1960). Why, then, is action theory so popular?

APPARENTLY PURPOSIVE BEHAVIOR

Part of the answer is that people, including scientists, tend to find sense in actions, messages, and scientific theories that they can easily assume to be purposeful or meaningful. Indeed, there is now considerable evidence that people readily attribute to other people, animals, and even machines mental processes that they imagine to be responsible for much of their own behavior (Weizenbaum 1983; Suchman 1987; Morris 1987). It has been suggested that this tendency is part and parcel of our primate heritage. The political lives of primates are complex and require continual assessment of the "intentions" of other members of the group (de Waal 1982). Thus people are predisposed to attribute intention and purpose to other people and to (some) animals.

I have argued elsewhere (McFarland 1989b) that humans have a "teleological imperative" as a result of which we attribute purpose where there is no purpose and seek for meaning where there is no meaning. I am not alone in holding this view. According to Dasser, Ulbaek, and Premack (1989), ascribing intentions plays the same role in our interpretation of our social environment as ascribing causes does in our understanding of the physical environment. They present experimental evidence that young children have such a percept of intention. Children were shown videotapes depicting two moving balls interacting. A large and a small ball appear on the screen, for instance, and the small ball falls over a cliff and moves frantically. The large ball descends the cliff and carries up the small one. In another scene, the small ball approaches and touches the large ball. The small ball is pushed away by the large ball, and then it jumps upon the large ball and is again pushed away. The large ball then hits the small ball, which rapidly quits the scene. The children differentiated between scenes such as these and control scenes where the same movements were desynchronized. Their comments indicated that they interpreted the behavior of the balls in intentional terms.

The problem is that, despite our predeliction for folk psychology (Kummer, Dasser, and Hoyningen-Huene 1990), apparently purposive behavior can be achieved by a variety of mechanisms. These fall into three main classes, which I now review.

Goal-Achieving Behavior

A goal-achieving system is one that can recognize a goal once it is arrived at (or at least change its behavior when it reaches the goal), but the process of arriving at the goal is largely determined by the environmental circumstances. What happens at each point in the causal chain depends partly on what has just happened and partly on the environmental circumstances. A similar principle can be seen in immunological and other biochemical systems, in which there is some form of template recognition. In such systems the significant events occur when one molecule recognizes another (a kind of lock-and-key mechanism) within a suitable environment or medium. These systems are goal-achieving by virtue of the fact that matters are so arranged that the necessary environmental features are generally present at the appropriate stage in the causal chain.

Bertrand Russell (1921) put forward a goal-achieving type of theory as a general theory of purposive behavior: "A hungry animal is restless until it finds food: then it becomes quiescent. The thing which will bring a restless condition to an end is said to be what is desired (its purpose)" (p. 32). The implication here is that the animal is in an environment in which the restless behavior is appropriate. When it encounters and recognizes the relevant (food) stimuli, the animal changes its behavior. This simple goal-achieving view of animal behavior does not, in fact, accord with modern knowledge of foraging behavior.

Goal-achieving behavior in humans is probably more commonplace than we tend to imagine. Consider the collector of matchboxes or any other artifact with a long and varied history. The collector does not deliberately set out to search for matchboxes, but relies upon serendipity—the habit of making happy and unexpected discoveries by accident. The main characteristic of goal-achieving behavior is preprogrammed recognition. The goal is achieved by being in the right place at the right time and recognizing this state of affairs.

Goal-Seeking Behavior

A goal-seeking system is one that is designed to seek a goal without the goal's being explicitly represented within the system. Many physical systems are goal-seeking in this sense. For example, a marble rolling around a bowl will always come to rest in the same place. It may take various different routes, depending upon the starting conditions. The marble appears to be goal-seeking, because the forces acting on it are so arranged that the marble is "pulled" toward the goal. In some goal-seeking systems that are designed to maintain a particular level or direction, a dynamic equilibrium is maintained by self-balancing forces. Such systems may be based on osmosis, gyroscopic forces, etc. The goal-seeking system achieves its effects by virtue of the forces acting on and within the system. There is no internal representation of the goal-to-be-achieved, nor does the system depend for its working on being in a particular environment, as does a goal-achieving system. In many respects a goal-achieving system is like a physical system that obeys some extremal principle.

Historically, the first extremal principle is Fermat's Principle of Least Time, which states that a ray of light moving through a medium (whose

Opportunity vs. Goals in Robots, Animals, and People

refractive index may vary from point to point) will follow, of all possible paths, that path for which the transit time is a minimum. In the seventeenth century the Dutch scientist Willebrod Snell discovered an algebraic law linking incident and outgoing angles. As the French scientist Pierre Fermat soon pointed out, in traveling from A to B, light does not necessarily travel the path of minimum distance, but rather that of shortest time (for an illuminating discussion see Schoemaker 1990).

The mechanical analogue of Fermat's principle is Maupertuis's (1744) Principle of Least Action. Both these principles were generalized by Hamilton in the nineteenth century and incorporated into Hamilton's principle, one of the major unifying concepts of theoretical physics (Rosen 1967). The behavior of any physical system can be accounted for both in terms of certain rules, such as Newton's laws, and in terms of Hamilton's principle. Thus the behavior of a stone thrown into the air is determined by Newtonian forces, but at the same time it conforms with Hamilton's principle in minimizing the "action" (a function of the potential and kinetic energy).

Extremal principles may be regarded as teleological statements (Nagel 1961), but the systems whose behavior they describe would not normally be regarded as goal-directed. Many physical systems come to a natural equilibrium, at a minimal energy configuration, simply as a result of the resolution of counteracting forces. To regard such minimal states as goals would be to trivialize the usefulness of the concept (see also Woodfield 1976, pp. 67–68). A ball that comes to rest after rolling down a hill would not normally be said to have reached its goal or to have rolled down the hill in order to achieve a certain state. It is, nevertheless, goal-seeking in the sense described above. The behavior of the ball conforms to an extremal principle that is analogous to the principles used, for example, to account for the optimality principles that are employed in the explanation of animal behavior (McFarland 1995). In other words, there is an analogy between the extremal principles of physics and the optimality principles of biology (Rosen 1967).

A stone thrown through the air obeys a "least action" law, minimizing a particular function of kinetic and potential energy. The stone behaves as if seeking an optimal trajectory, although its behavior is in fact determined by forces acting in accordance with Newton's laws of motion. Similarly, an animal may behave as if seeking an optimal trajectory through a state space (Sibly and McFarland 1976; McFarland and Houston 1981), although its behavior is in fact determined by motivational forces and decision rules.

Optimality principles say little about the mechanisms involved. Optimality principles are, in effect, functional explanations that describe how an animal ought to behave in order to attain some objective. For a causal explanation, the equivalent of physical forces must be established. These will presumably take the form of a set of rules of thumb governing behavior or of some equivalent mechanism. Examples of rules of thumb in animals can be found in Stephens and Krebs (1986). The behavior of some well-designed animals may be goal-seeking by virtue of the way in which the causal mechanisms are put together. In accounting for the behavior of such animals, there is no need for such concepts as purpose or intention.

Goal-Directed Behavior

Goal-directed behavior involves an explicit representation of the goal to be achieved, which is instrumental in directing the behavior. Since the goal of behavior is achieved at the end of the relevant behavior sequence, it is obvious that the goal itself cannot direct the behavior. By "goal-directed behavior" we mean that a representation of the goal directs the behavior. If there is no (explicit) representation of the goal, then the behavior cannot be goal-directed.

I am reserving the term "goal-directed" to indicate behavior (of a human, animal, or machine) that is directed by reference to an internal representation of the goal to be achieved. By "directed" I mean that the behavior is actively controlled by reference to the (internally represented) goal. If the behavior is subject to outside disturbances, these will usually be corrected for. Thus by "directed" we mean that the behavior is guided or steered toward the goal, despite disturbances.

A goal representation is a physically (or physiologically) identifiable (in principle) representation that is "explicit" in the sense of Dennett (1983). In this category are included the "set point" of simple servomechanisms, the "Sollwert" and "search image" of classical ethologists, and any form of explicit mental representation that functions as a source of comparison in a goal-directed system.

Although it can always be said of a goal-seeking system that the goal must be somehow represented since there must be features of the system that are responsible for the goal-seeking behavior, such representation is merely implicit or tacit (Dennett 1983). This tacit form of representation is purely a way of naming the parameters of the system (which we normally think of as "distributed" throughout the system), which may be said to "represent" the goal by virtue of their role in the design of the system. Note that this is true of any system that does what it does by virtue of its design—a goal-achieving system, for example. It is not equivalent to the type of goal representation that involves an explicit representation that is capable of directing behavior.

In the paradigm case of goal-directed behavior, the difference between the "desired" state of affairs and the actual state of affairs (as monitored in the negative feedback pathway) provides the (error) signal that actuates the behavior control mechanism. The behavior may also be affected by disturbances, including influences from other systems. The exact nature

Opportunity vs. Goals in Robots, Animals, and People

of the input to the behavior control mechanism will vary from system to system. In some (called proportional control systems) the actuating signal is proportional to the error. In more sophisticated systems the control may be very complex.

An essential feature of a goal-directed system is that some of the consequences of the behavior are monitored and this information made available to the control mechanism. Few or many features of the behavior consequences may be monitored, and the information gained may influence the control system in various ways. If for some reason it is not possible to monitor the behavior consequences, then it is not possible to attain goal-directed behavior.

A simple example of a goal-directed system is provided by the thermostatic theory of temperature regulation in animals. True thermal homeostasis is found in birds and mammals, which are able to maintain a constant body temperature despite fluctuations in environmental temperature. They are called endotherms, because their high metabolic rate provides an internal source of heat and their insulated body surface prevents uncontrolled dissipation of this heat. (Animals that gain heat primarily from external sources like sunlight are called ectotherms.) Endotherms maintain a body temperature that is usually higher than that of their surroundings. The brain receives information about the temperature of the body and is able to exercise control over mechanisms of warming (such as shivering) and cooling (such as panting). According to the thermostatic theory, when the brain temperature gets too high (compared with some reference temperature), the cooling mechanisms are activated, and when it gets too low, heat losses are reduced and warming mechanisms may be activated. The principle of operation is the same as that of a thermostatically controlled domestic heater.

The essential features of the thermostatic theory are as follows: (1) There is an internally represented reference temperature (often called the set point) with respect to which the body temperature is judged to be too low or too high. (2) There is a mechanism (called a comparator) for comparing the set temperature with the body temperature. (3) The output of the comparator actuates the heating and cooling mechanisms. (4) The resulting body temperature is measured by appropriate sense organs (which we will call thermometers), and the comparison between set and body temperature is made on the basis of this information. The overall principle of operation is called negative feedback, since the comparator essentially subtracts the measured body temperature from the set temperature, and the difference (called the error) provides the actuating signal.

Intentional behavior is a form of goal-directed behavior, because it involves some kind of (mental) representation of the goal to be achieved. This definition of intentional behavior is somewhat narrower than that usually employed by philosophers (e.g., Dennett 1987), but it conforms more to the commonsense meaning of intention. The notion of representation is important in this view of intentional behavior, because it plays a vital role in guiding the behavior. In short, the intention (i.e., representation of the goal to be achieved) is a cause of behavior (see also Noble 1989). Gallistel (1985) insists that "the representation whose use leads us to call the resulting behavior intentional must have three distinct components: a component representing the act, a component representing a consequence, and a component representing the fact that this act has a consequence" (p. 56). Gallistel follows Irwin (1971) in believing that the act-outcome representation is a *sine qua non* of intentional behavior. There is some difficulty of terminology here, because to me the act-outcome representation (where it exists) is an aspect of a planning mechanism (McFarland and Bösser 1993).

PROBLEMS WITH ACTION THEORY

Action theory is a body of theory that sets out to account for purposeful behavior by providing a model that is essentially a goal-directed model. To recapitulate, a system can be goal-achieving or goal-seeking without being goal-directed. A goal-achieving system is one that can recognize the goal once it is arrived at (or at least change its behavior when it reaches the goal), but the process of arriving at the goal is largely determined by the environmental circumstances. A goal-seeking system is one that is designed to seek the goal without the goal's being explicitly represented within the system. A goal-seeking system can be based upon a dynamic equilibrium of various forces operating within the system. A goal-directed system involves an explicit representation of the goal to be achieved, which is instrumental in directing the behavior.

Doubts about goal-directed types of theory arise on various grounds. Perhaps the most straightforward are those that arise from consideration of animal behavior. Discussions of goal-directed behavior in animals often involve a simplistic account of what is really a complex matter. For example, Woodfield (1976) uses the following example: "A man is standing on a river bank watching a rat swim across to the far side. The rat is steadily swimming towards that part of the bank which is nearest the food. The man frames the judgement that the rat is swimming across the river in order to get the food. For the man, this teleological judgement is a hypothesis. . . . The man is not judging that the rat will get the food, or even that it will reach the river bank. Another rat may reach the food first or the swimming rat may drown." So if any prediction is entailed by the teleological description, it is one of the following nature: "The rat will get the food provided that no obstacles prevent it" (Woodfield 1976, p. 92).

The teleological judgment made by Woodfield's observer is, in effect, a hypothesis that the behavior of the rat is goal-directed. The goal of the rat is to get the food, and a representation of this goal is instrumental in guiding the rat's behavior. We may postulate, however, that the rat may decide, having experienced the strength of the current, that the food is not worth the effort. This possibility introduces an entirely new element into the discussion.

The simple teleological hypothesis implies that the rat aims to get the food at all costs and will fail only on account of insurmountable obstacles. This scenario has the advantage that the issue is compartmentalized. The food-seeking behavior of the rat can be considered in isolation from the rest of the animal's behavioral repertoire. In real life this will never be the case, and a more realistic hypothesis is called for.

The more naturalistic hypothesis supposes that the rat will get the food provided that it is able to and provided that the rat continues to judge that the project is worthwhile. Here we have a new ingredient in the form of a different kind of goal. To be worthwhile an activity must be accountable in terms of some economic goal involving time and energy expenditure. Woodfield (1976) implies that the rat takes the shortest or quickest route towards the food. But this is not a necessary condition for attaining the food. If the rat's goal is simply to attain the food, then it can take any route. If its goal is to attain the food by the most direct route, then there are really two types of goals: (1) attaining the food and (2) satisfying some economic criterion. In considering animal behavior, the economic considerations should be taken seriously, because in real life no activity is undertaken in isolation from other possible activities. To assume that an animal's goal is simply to attain food is unrealistic.

Even the guided missile, a favorite example of goal-directed behavior, is not immune from economic considerations. Guided missiles working on negative-feedback principles are capable of goal-directed behavior (as will be discussed later). The design of the missile is, however, subject to strict performance criteria. For most missiles these criteria are designed to ensure that the target is reached as quickly as possible. The missile is thus goal-directed in the sense of two goals: (1) to reach the target and (2) to minimize the flight time and fuel expenditure. The reason that missiles are designed this way is that the designers have to worry about not only one missile, but the whole missile program. This program is in competition with other government programs for the limited resources of money, manpower, and materials.

Just as the individual missile is tailored to fit into the missile program as a whole, so the individual item of goal-seeking behavior is designed by natural selection to fit into an animal's overall behavior program. The time and energy involved in the rat's foraging behavior and the other activities that it may otherwise engage in will have a profound influence upon its behavior (e.g., see Stephens and Krebs 1986).

In the case of animal behavior, the argument may be summarized as follows: Natural selection has designed animals not to pursue a single goal at a time, but to pursue a course of action that is optimal in relation to a large number of internal and external factors. The result of this design is a continual trade-off among the costs and benefits of various possible activities. The result is that behavior is directed not by any goal-representation, but in a holistic manner that takes into account all (relevant) aspects of the animal's internal state and of the (perceived) external situation (McFarland 1989a). This is essentially an argument from design. The assertion that behavior is not controlled by goal representations implies that behavior is not goal-directed. There are various reasons for this assertion (see McFarland 1989b), but the most important one is that the notion of goal-directedness is incompatible with the trade-off principle.

The problem becomes apparent when we consider what is to make an agent stop a particular task and start another. One scenario with which the goal-directed approach has no difficulty is that the agent changes to a new task if another goal suddenly becomes more important than the goal it is currently pursuing. In the normal course of events, however, we have to ask whether the well-designed agent should (1) finish one task before starting another (this is difficult to engineer, because it requires a lock-out mechanism that may prevent the agent from responding to emergencies); (2) change to a new task when the importance of the current task drops (as a consequence of the agent's behavior) below the level of an alternative goal (this means that tasks will rarely be completed); or (3) change to a new task when the balance of considerations, including the cost of changing to another task, favors the change.

A sophisticated version of this arrangement employs a complex set of trade-off rules. Their implementation makes the goal representation redundant; it has no role to play, since the behavior is governed entirely by trade-off mechanisms in which all variables have equal status. Goal-directed behavior is defined (earlier in this chapter) in a way that requires the goal representation (a variable with special status) to be instrumental in guiding the behavior. If the behavior is determined entirely by trade-off considerations and the goal representation has no role to play, then it is not guiding the behavior, and the behavior cannot be goal-directed.

At this point, I should perhaps summarize the basic argument (spelled out in full in McFarland and Bösser 1993). Animals are rational beings. This means that the individual is designed to behave in such a way that some entity is maximized (subject to certain constraints). We may call this entity utility. Now, there must be some mathematical function with respect to which the utilities of particular states and activities are judged (i.e., the dynamic equivalent of utility functions). We call this mathematical function the *value function* (this is the same as the goal function of McFarland and Houston 1981). It describes the notional costs and benefits attributable to all possible states and activities of the animal (the actual costs and benefits are described by the cost function). The value function specifies the motivational design of the individual (individuals have different value functions). Specifying the value function tells us nothing about the

Opportunity vs. Goals in Robots, Animals, and People

mechanisms by which animal behavior is controlled, but it does tell us the design criteria. If certain proposed mechanisms violate the design criteria, then those mechanisms cannot be responsible for the control of behavior. An important aspect of the design criteria is the trade-off principle (described earlier), which is the essence of good design.

If it is correct that goal-directed behavior, a mechanism proposed for the control of behavior, violates the trade-off principle, then goal-directed behavior (as defined in this chapter) cannot be a viable model for the control of behavior. Since action theory is a goal-directed theory, we must question whether action theory is a good model for the control of apparently purposeful behavior.

It might be helpful to elucidate these arguments by discussing a specific example. Allen (1984) used the example of turning on a light to illustrate the problem of the relationship between actions and intended effects:

There are few physical activities that are a necessary part of performing the action of turning on a light. Depending on the context, vastly different patterns of behaviour can be classified as the same action. For example, turning on a light usually involves flipping a light switch, but in some circumstances it may involve tightening the light bulb (in the basement) or hitting the wall (in an old house). Although we have knowledge about how the action can be performed, this does not define what the action is. The key defining characteristic of turning on the light seems to be that the agent is performing some activity which will cause the light, which was off when the action started, to become on when the action ends. An important side effect of this definition is that we could recognise an observed pattern of activity as "turning on the light" even if we had never seen or thought about that pattern previously. (p. 126)

The first point to make here is that what Allen calls an action I call a task (see McFarland and Bösser 1993). The task is to move from one state (light off) to another (light on). The task is a property of the situation that can be recognized by an outside observer and by the agent, but this does not mean that the task is involved in the control of the behavior in a teleological manner.

The second point to make is that implicit in Allen's formulation is the notion that the agent has in mind an intended effect (or goal) that is instrumental in guiding the behavior (in other words, the behavior is goal-directed). In ordinary (folk psychology) terms, the agent wants the light to be on, forms the intention (a representation of the goal to be achieved) to put the light on, and seeks a way to achieve that end. Allen identifies the indeterminate relationship of intended effect to behavior as a problem for planning or plan recognition.

I depart from Allen (and from any other goal-directed formulation) in one important respect. For Allen the problem is a closed one, whereas for us it is an open one. Allen's problem is closed because it begins with one state-of-affairs (light off) and ends with another (light on). For us it is open because the two states (light off and light on) are simply states in a series of possible states of the world that an observer (including the agent) can identify as a task. In other words, in Allen's system knowledge of the task is instrumental in guiding the behavior, whereas we maintain that this goal-directed aspect is not necessary.

An anthropomorphic scenario may help to provide an intuitive understanding of our position. In this scenario the agent enters the room and recognizes that things would be better if the light were on. In other words, the state "light on" is a desirable state of affairs (but so are many other states). In ordinary terms, the agent wants the light to be on (up to this point we agree with Allen). Having entered the room, the agent reviews the behavioral options. Let us say that these are (a) turn on light, (b) pick up book, and (c) exit room. The consequences of each are then evaluated, and the option with the most beneficial consequences is then chosen. Let us suppose that this is option (a). The agent then starts to walk toward the light switch, but at the same time is reevaluating the options, which now include (d) avoid chair in middle of room. This type of reevaluation is a frequent (unconscious) occurrence, and the agent simply chooses the most beneficial option each time. This may or may not result in the agent's turning on the light. If the agent does turn on the light, we may say that a task has been accomplished, but at no point does the goal (accomplishing the task) control the behavior of the agent. (for a similar scenario see McFarland 1989a, p. 287).

INTENTIONAL BEHAVIOR

Human behavior can be said to be intentional when it involves some representation of a goal that is instrumental in guiding behavior. Thus, if a man has a mental picture of the desirable arrangement of items on his desk, and if this mental representation guides his behavior in placing books on the desk, then he can be said to place them intentionally. If, however, he places items on the desk haphazardly or on the basis of simple habit rules, then his arrangement of the items may not be intentional. For his behavior to be intentional, the mental representation of the book arrangement does not have to be a conscious one. Although consciousness and intentionality are sometimes linked, it is better to treat them separately (Dennett 1978).

According to this type of definition, intentional behavior is a form of goal-directed behavior. It is close to our everyday notion of intentional behavior, but once we start to define our terms rigorously we find that we deviate from the everyday view. Matters are complicated by the fact that the term "intention" is used differently in different disciplines (see Allen this volume).

Ethologists have long recognized intentional movements in animals as indications of what animals were about to do. Both human observers and members of an animal's own species can often predict the future behavior of the animal from its intentional movements, and it may seem silly to assume that the animal cannot anticipate the next steps in its own behavior (Griffin 1976/1981). It is more likely, however, that intentional movements are merely the initial stages of behavior patterns that are terminated prematurely, either because the animal is in a motivational conflict or because its attention is diverted to other possible aspects of behavior. Indeed, it is difficult to imagine how such incipient behavioral fragments could be avoided in an animal with a complex repertoire of activities (McFarland 1985).

Another aspect of animal behavior that has the appearance of intentionality is the injury-feigning distraction display of certain birds. When an incubating bird like a sandpiper *(Ereunetes mauri)* is disturbed by a ground predator, it may leave its nest and act as though injured, trailing an apparently broken wing and luring the predator away from the nest. When the predator has been led a safe distance from the nest, the bird suddenly regains its normal behavior and flies away (e.g., Skutch 1976). While most ethologists are content to account for this type of behavior in terms of ritualized display, some (e.g., Griffin 1981, p. 135) wish to keep open the possibility that the bird is behaving intentionally. Many ethologists see little difference between the deception practiced by injury-feigning birds and that evident in primate behavior (e.g., Kummer, Dasser, and Hoyningen-Huene 1990; McFarland 1989b), but others are less skeptical (Mitchel and Thompson 1986).

In philosophy the term "intention" is often used to signify "aboutness." An intentional statement is a statement that is about something. The philosopher's concept of intentionality is clearly explained by Dennett and Haugeland (1987). According to Dennett (1978):

An intentional system is a system whose behavior can be (at least sometimes) explained and predicted by relying on ascriptions to the system of beliefs and desires (and other intentionally characterized features)—what I will call intentions here, meaning to include hopes, fears, intentions, perceptions, expectations, etc. There may, in every case be other ways of predicting and explaining the behavior of an intentional system—for instance, mechanistic or physical ways—but the intentional stance may be the handiest or most effective or in any case a successful stance to adopt, which suffices for the object to be an intentional system. (p. 271)

Dennett (1978) notes that in considering the behavior of a complex system we can take a number of different stances that are not necessarily contradictory. One might be a design stance, which takes a functional viewpoint; another a physical stance, which bases predictions on the physical state of the system; and another the intentional stance, which Dennett is adopting in the above quotation. This assumes that the system under investigation is an intentional system possessing certain information and beliefs and directed by certain goals. In adopting this stance, Dennett is attempting not to refute behavioral or physiological explanations, but to offer a higher level of explanation for the behavior of systems so complex that they become unmanageable.

As suggested earlier, it may well be that humans are prone to adopt an intentional stance while assessing the behavior of others. It may be that this trait is so ingrained that we think of our own behavior in this way and explain our own behavior to others in intentional terms (see McFarland 1989a for a discussion). If we think that our own behavior is really governed by such goal-directed mechanisms, then we may be deceiving ourselves.

REFERENCES

Ach, N. (1910). *Ueber den Willensakt und das Temperament: Eine experimentelle Untersuchung.* Leipzig: Quelle und Meyer.

Allen, J. (1984). Towards a general theory of action and time. *Artificial Intelligence,* 23, 123–154.

Alexander, R. M. (1982). *Optima for Animals* London: Edward Arnold.

Ashby, W. R. (1960). *Design for a Brain.* London: Chapman and Hall.

Bartlett, F. C. (1932). *Remembering.* Cambridge: Cambridge University Press.

Brand, M. (1970). *The Nature of Human Action.* Scott, Foresman.

Brand, M. (1984). *Intending and Acting.* Cambridge, Mass.: The MIT Press.

Dasser, V., Ulbaek, I., and Premack, D. (1989). The perception of intention. *Science,* 243, 365–367.

Davidson, D. (1963). Actions, reasons and causes. *Journal of Philosophy,* 60, 685–700.

Davidson, D. (1978). Intention. In Y. Yoval (ed.). *Philosophy of History and Action.* Dordrecht, Holland: D. Reidel.

Dennett, D. C. (1978). *Brainstorms.* Cambridge, Mass: Bradford Books/The MIT Press.

Dennett, D. C. (1983). Intentional systems in cognitive ethology: The "Panglossian paradigm" defended. *Behavioral and Brain Sciences,* 6, 343–390.

Dennett, D. C. (1984). *Elbow Room.* Oxford: Oxford University Press.

Dennet, D. C. (1987). *The Intentional Stance.* Cambridge, Mass.: The MIT Press/A Bradford book.

Dennett, D. C., and Haugeland, J. (1987). Intentionality. In R. Gregory (ed.). *The Oxford Companion to the Mind.* Oxford: Oxford University Press.

Frese, M., and Sabini, J., eds. (1985). *Goal Directed Behavior.* Hillsdale, N.J.: Lawrence Erlbaum.

Gallistel, C. R. (1985). Motivation, intention and emotion: Goal directed behavior from a cognitive-neuroethological perspective. In M. Frese and J. Sabini (eds.). *Goal Directed Behavior.* Hillsdale, New Jersey: Lawrence Erlbaum Associates.

Goldman, A. (1970). *A Theory of Human Action.* Englewood Cliffs, N.J.: Prentice-Hall.

Goldman, A. (1976). The volitional theory revisited. In M. Brand and W. Watson (eds.). *Action Theory.* Dordecht, Holland: D. Reidel.

Griffin, D. R. (1976/1981). *The Question of Animal Awareness.* New York: The Rockefeller University Press.

Irwin, F. W. (1971). *Intentional Behaviour and Motivation: A Cognitive Theory*. Philadelphia: Lippincott.

Kummer, H., Dasser, V., and Hoyningen-Huene (1990). Exploring primate social cognition: Some critical remarks. *Behaviour*, 112, 84–98.

Lendrem, D. (1986). *Modelling in Behavioural Ecology*. London: Croom Helm.

Lewin, K. (1935). *A Dynamic Theory of Personality*. New York: McGraw-Hill.

McFarland, D. (1985). *Animal Behaviour*. Harlow, England: Longman Scientific.

McFarland, D. (1989a). Goals, no goals, and own goals. In A. Montefiore and D. Noble (eds.). *Goals, No Goals, and Own Goals*. London: Unwin Hyman.

McFarland, D. (1989b). The teleological imperative. In A. Montefiore and D. Noble (eds.). *Goals, No Goals, and Own Goals*. London: Unwin Hyman.

McFarland, D. (1989c) *Problems of Animal Behaviour*. London: Longmans.

McFarland, D. (1991a). What it means for robot behavior to be adaptive. In J. Meyer and S. W. Wilson (eds.). *From Animals to Animats*. Cambridge, Mass.: The MIT Press.

McFarland, D. (1991b). Defining motivation and cognition in animals. *International Studies in the Philosophy of Science*, 5, 153–170.

McFarland, D. (1992). Animals as cost-based robots. *International Studies in the Philosophy of Science*, 6, 133–153.

McFarland, D. (1993). Autonomy and self-sufficiency in robots. In L. Steels and R. Brooks (eds.). *The 'Artificial Life' Route to 'Artificial Intelligence'. Building Situated Embodied Agents*. New Haven, Conn.: Lawrence Erlbaum.

McFarland, D. (1995). Rational behaviour of animals and machines. *ZiF Workshop on Prerational Intelligence (forthcoming)*.

McFarland, D., and Bösser, T. (1993). *Intelligent Behavior in Animals and Robots*. Cambridge, Mass.: Bradford Books/The MIT Press.

McFarland, D., and Houston, A. (1981). *Quantitative Ethology: The State-Space Approach*. London: Pitman Books.

McFarland, D., and Sibly, R. M. (1975). The behavioural final common path. *Philosophical Transactions of the Royal Society*, B 270, 265–293.

Miller, G. A., Galanter, E., and Pribram, K. H. (1960). *Plans and the Structure of Behavior*. New York: Holt.

Minsky, M. L. (1975). A framework for representing knowledge. In P. H. Winston (ed.). *The Psychology of Computer Vision*. New York: McGraw-Hill.

Mitchel, R. W., and Thompson, N. S. (1986). *Deception*. Albany, N.Y.: SUNY.

Morris, R. L. (1987). PSI and human factors: The role of PSI in human-equipment interactions. *Current Trends in PSI Research*, 1–27.

Nagel, T. (1961). *The Structure of Science*. London: Routledge and Kegan Paul.

Neisser, U. (1976). *Cognition and Reality*. San Francisco: Freeman.

Noble, D. (1989). What do intentions do? In A. Montefiore and D. Noble (eds.). *Goals, No Goals, and Own Goals*. London: Unwin Hymen.

Roitblat, H. L. (1991). Cognitive action theory as a control architecture. *From Animals to Animats*. In J. Meyer and S. W. Wilson (eds.). Cambridge, Mass.: The MIT Press.

Rosen, R. (1967). *Optimality Principles in Biology*. London: Butterworths.

Rosenblueth, A., Wiener, W., and Bigelow, J. (1943). Behavior, purpose and teleology. *Philosophy of Science*, 10, 18–24.

Russell, B. (1921). *The Analysis of Mind*. New York: Macmillan.

Schank, R., and Abelson, R. (1977). *Scripts, Plans, Goals, and Understanding*. Hillsdale, N.J.: Lawrence Erlbaum Associates.

Searle, J. (1979). The intentionality of intention and action. *Inquiry*, 22, 253–280.

Searle, J. (1981). Intentionality and method. *Journal of Philosophy*, 78, 720–733.

Sellars, W. (1966). Thought and action. In K. Lehrer (ed.). *Freedom and Determinism*. New York: Random House.

Sellars, W. (1973). Action and events. *Nous*, 7, 179–202.

Skutch, A. F. (1976). *Parent Birds and Their Young*. Austin, Tex.: University of Texas Press.

Sibly, R. M., and Calow, P. (1986). *Physiological Ecology of Animals*. Oxford: Blackwell Scientific Publications.

Sibly, R. M., and McFarland, D. J. (1976). On the fitness of behaviour sequences. *American Naturalist*, 110, 601–617.

Silver, M. (1985). "Purposive behavior" in psychology and philosophy: A history. In M. Frese and J. Sabini (eds.). *Goal Directed Behavior*. Hillsdale, N.J.: Lawrence Erlbaum.

Stephens, D. W., and Krebs, J. R. (1986). *Foraging Theory*. Princeton, N.J.: Princeton University Press.

Suchman, L. (1987). *Plans and Situated Actions*. New York: Cambridge University Press.

Thorndyke, P. W. (1984). Applications of schema theory in cognitive research. In J. R. Anderson and S. M. Kosslyn (eds.). *Tutorials in Learning and Memory*. New York: W. H. Freeman.

Tolman, E. C. (1932). *Purposive Behaviour in Animals and Men*. New York: Appleton Century Crofts.

von Cranach, M., and Kalbermatten, U. (1982). Ordinary interactive action: Theory, methods and some empirical findings. In M. von Cranach and R. Harre (eds.). *The Analysis of Action*. Cambridge: Cambridge University Press.

de Waal, F. (1982). *Chimpanzee Politics: Power and Sex Among Apes*. New York: Harper and Row.

Watson, J. B. (1913). Psychology as the Behaviorist Views It. *Psychology Review*, 20, 158–177.

Walter, W. G. (1953). *The Living Brain*, London: Duckworth.

Weizenbaum, J. (1983). ELIZA: A computer program for the study of natural language communication between man and machine. *Communications of the ACM, 25th Anniversary Issue*, 26, 23–27. Reprinted from *Communications of the ACM*, 29, 36–45 (1966).

Woodfield, A. (1976). *Teleology*. Cambridge: Cambridge University Press.

Wundt, W. (1907). *Outlines of Psychology*. New York: Engelmann.

18 Animal Motivation and Cognition

Frederick Toates

INTRODUCTION

Why should a student of cognitive science be interested in the combination of topics, motivation and cognition, in animals? In recent years, the study of animal cognition has made important advances and has enabled cross-fertilization with robotics (Roitblat 1991). However, sometimes the discussion overlooks the fact that solving problems and using cognitions in behavior, whether exploring, foraging or whatever, implies the existence of processes of motivation.

Cognition has an ever-growing place in ethology. For instance, associated with foraging, a number of authors (e.g., Riley, Brown, and Yoerg 1986) argue that animals form models of their environment and the location of food therein. Their interest is primarily in the memory capacities of the animals and the function served. Other authors study cognition in primates, which is evidenced by such things as complex problem solving and the practice of deceit. In such terms, cognition can become almost synonymous with conscious awareness. Consideration of welfare issues has led ethologists to draw up criteria regarding when an animal might be suffering. To do so, such cognitively associated concepts as goals, expectations, and frustration are utilized (Wiepkema 1987).

However, motivation is an ingredient commonly missing from the cognitive revolution. Whereas learning, memory, concept formation, and timing processes are richly discussed in expositions of animal cognition, the reader will usually look in vain for the interface between these processes and motivation (for example, see the chapters in Roitblat, Bever, and Terrace 1984). Conversely, classical ethological theories (e.g., Lorenz 1950) placed considerable weight upon motivation, which was modeled in terms of internal and external contributions (stimuli such as a mate or food). More recent theorists in this tradition (e.g., McFarland and Sibly 1975) have continued the emphasis upon external (cue strength) and internal factors. However, cognition plays little or no part in these later developments; indeed, cognitive constructs are viewed with some suspicion (McFarland 1989a). Thus an artificial divide is introduced between the study of the determinants of the strength of motivation and how this motivation can play a role in generating goal-achieving behavior.

Such a slicing up and demarcation of the processes underlying behavior has not always characterized behavioral science. On the contrary, the classical theorists (e.g., Tolman 1932; Hull 1943; Bindra 1978) saw motivation and learning as inextricably linked; assumptions underlying learning reflected associated assumptions underlying motivation (Bolles 1991). Interestingly, Brooks (1991) finds the need to consider a somewhat analogous interdependence, in this case between sensors, intelligence, power sources, and actuators, in the design of robots. He writes, "Choices in any part of the system architecture (e.g., sensor characteristics) have major impacts upon other parts of the system. In general it is very dangerous to think that any one component (such as intelligence) can be isolated and studied by itself" (p. 434).

There are some signs, but as yet only small, that in theories of cognition motivation is interacting with the cognitive processes (Dickinson and Dearing 1979; Gallistel 1980; Rescorla 1987; Roitblat 1988, 1991). The object of this chapter is to show where integration between motivation and cognition can occur.

ANIMALS, ROBOTS, AND THE NEED FOR MOTIVATION

Animals do not live by pure cognition alone; they must be goal-directed, persuaded, goaded, pulled, or pushed into action by something. That something has traditionally formed the stock in trade of theorists of motivation. In looking primarily to events within the central nervous system, Roitblat (1982, p. 370) suggests that "Animals, like humans, are most profitably viewed as active information processors." In these terms, motivation enters the picture when we consider, among other things, (1) selection of which information is processed and its weighting as a potential candidate to control behavior and (2) the links between neural and nonneural tissue. Nonneural internal variables (e.g., a full gut, blood levels of testosterone) and external variables (e.g., a mate, the odor of food) provide sources of information to be processed by the nervous system. Combining such variables with cognition can address some of the radical behaviorist critique (e.g., Branch 1982) that cognitive psychology either makes the organism autonomous or leaves it buried in thought.

Consider a foraging bird, which is assumed by ethologists to make decisions on where to forage and when to quit one patch for another (Kamil 1978). The fact that the bird is foraging at all rather than sleeping, fighting, or mating has to do with biological processes of motivation that, on the one hand, relate to body nutrient levels. On the other hand, these processes must interface with the kind of decision making that fascinates cognitive ethologists.

For another example to whet the appetite of a cognitive scientist, consider a highly efficient robot that is designed to take into account internal and external states, weigh the balance between competing demands, and then meet one of them by effecting action on the world (McFarland 1989c). It might or might not need to incorporate a cognitive map (Brooks 1991), but it must, if only implicitly, involve something analogous to motivation. It would need to pursue various goals but keep a check on its own "nutrient" levels by monitoring the power left in its batteries and recharging them at intervals. But at what stage should a run-down battery trigger recharging? Presumably this decision reflects such things as priorities, availability of an electrical socket, and how much energy there is in reserve. A criterion of optimal performance will presumably be involved at the design stage. Such considerations are similar to those that ethologists discuss when considering decision making and motivation (Toates 1980). A roboticist might decide to mimic nature. Alternatively, he or she might find design criteria that can improve upon the biological system.

Consider also that the efficient robot will probably come into the world already equipped with a certain number of specifications on what to do in certain situations. However, in what is most likely a not entirely predictable environment, it will also need to be able to learn and to change its behavior in the light of experience. What should the optimal robot learn? What is the nature of the rules of learning? Could the term "cognitive" be usefully applied to the robot? Answers to these questions might be found by looking at how a comparable set of questions has been approached in understanding animal behavior.

RATS, MAZES, AND TRYING TO DEFINE COGNITION

The task of linking cognition and motivation, even to a modest extent, is a masochistic one; merely trying to define either term usually proves problematic. This chapter will take a circumscribed set of topics, focusing particularly upon rat learning, and investigate where cognition and motivation are both necessary concepts for understanding behavior. Given this area of interest, a definition of cognition that arises from the classical era of learning theory will be used.

In the spirit of Tolman (1932) and in the terms developed here, the word "cognition" implies, if nothing more, that animals have knowledge of the world that consists of particular sorts of memories (representations) of the world. These memories specify information about the world in a form that is not directly tied to behavior, and thereby they enable a flexible interaction with the world. Definition of this type of memory can be helped by considering the properties it does not have. These memories do not directly map onto the particular behavior that was exhibited at the time of the assimilation of the memory, and neither do they specify a particular behavior to be performed in the future. So, as a provisional definition of cognition, I suggest "the assimilation and use of information about the world and events in it. This information is utilized in such a way that the animal's commerce with the environment is flexible."

To some, "cognition" implies more than this; if not full consciousness, then a sophisticated capacity to manipulate information in original ways is implied. For example, Heyes and Dickinson (1990) are more demanding of the criteria for calling a process "cognitive" than is the case of this chapter. They would want to see evidence that (a) the animal is able to form inferences about the world and (b) its behavior is rational. In Dickinson's (1989) terms, information can be held as mechanistic cognitions (those arising from a Pavlovian contingency) or can be fully cognitive (able to be used to make inferences and show goal-directed behavior). This approach to cognition is discussed later.

Since the boundaries around what constitutes both cognition and motivation are somewhat hazy, naturally their mode of interaction will be controversial. In the view of some authors, rather distinct cognitive and motivational variables interact to determine behavior (e.g., Roitblat 1988). A motivational variable would be, for example, energy depletion. Others have described motivation as a series of states that depend upon both external factors (e.g., food) and internal factors (e.g., energy level) (Bindra 1978; Toates 1986). In such terms, cognitive processes can play a role in the generation of motivational states. For example, expectation of food in the goal-box is as much of a motivational variable determining, say, running speed as is degree of food deprivation.

As the following sections will show, use of the apparently innocuous term "cognitive" can raise some fundamental and difficult broad questions quite apart from that of exactly what we mean by the term. We now have textbooks of cognitive psychology, were previously we had textbooks of psychology. But what would a noncognitive psychology look like? Assuming that we can agree upon a definition of cognition, will we be able to conclude that some of the processes underlying behavior are cognitive and some are noncognitive? Are some animals capable of cognition and others not? Does a given animal switch from cognitive to noncognitive processing at various times? One way to approach such issues is to consider an example of behavior and to ask how it might be explained in both cognitive and noncognitive terms. The next section does this.

COGNITIVE AND NONCOGNITIVE PROCESSES

Arguments on the nature of the processes underlying behavior are strongly colored by the writings of historical schools of psychology, with their different epistemologies and aims. The cognitive school of Tolman (1932) championed the explanatory value of cognitions, goals, expectancies, and purpose. By contrast, some hard-nosed behaviorists (e.g., Hull 1943) shunned such expressions, arguing that behavior is to be understood in terms of animals learning relationships between stimuli and responses. The distinction seems clear in that apparently very different processes were postulated within different theoretical contexts. However, at the level of the real rat, life is more complex in that the facility for employing both types of processes can be seen (Adams 1982). According to circumstances, the very same example of observed behavior might be a reflection of learning by either process.

The stimulus-response (S-R) or "mechanistic" model, standing in contrast to the cognitive model, is embodied as the reflex to physiologists, the fixed action pattern to ethologists, and conditional and unconditional responses to behaviorist psychologists (Dickinson 1985). In such mechanistic terms, learning is embodied in a change in strength of a stimulus-response connection. Tacit acceptance of such a model is implied by those who use "behavior" and "response" as synonyms. It will be argued that behavior needs to be understood in terms of both mechanistic and cognitive processes. This distinction maps onto one drawn between procedural and declarative memory systems, respectively (Dickinson 1980; Eichenbaum, Otto, and Cohen 1992).

Consider a hungry rat that learns a maze (figure 18.1a). If it turns left at the choice point, it finds food in the goal-box. If it turns right, it finds no food. After a number of trials, the rat reliably turns left. What exactly has it learned? First, consider that it might have acquired knowledge (cognition) about the world of the kind "food is at a particular location (X) in space," in this case near the window. It will be argued later that animals do indeed show such cognitive learning and that it confers flexibility on their subsequent behavior. However, from the evidence just given, there is an alternative process that might account for the maze behavior. The rat might not have learned a fact about the world, but rather have simply learned to perform a turn to the left (a relationship between the stimulus of the choice point and a response), an S-R association. It might

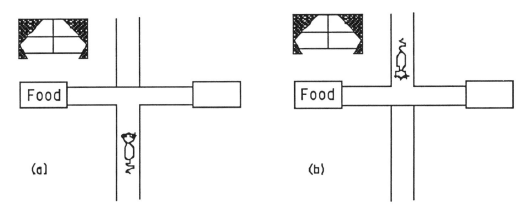

(a)

(b)

Figure 18.1   Rat negotiating a T-maze.

learn by means of this process alone or even in combination with cognitive learning as just described. Furthermore, close consideration of the exact nature of this second learning process reveals that we need to entertain more than one possibility (Roitblat 1988). For example, learning could be at the level of the muscles involved in turning or at a more molar level (e.g., turning by whatever means are available and appropriate at the time).

The question has traditionally been posed in either/or terms (in terms of cognitions or what to do), though in fact the whole issue is fraught with hazardous theoretical and practical complications (Gallistel 1990). A more recently recognized additional possibility (see Bolles 1972) is that the rat has learned a relationship between its behavior and the outcome, expressed as [behavior] → [outcome], of the kind [turn left] → [food]. The behavior of consistently turning left is compatible with having learned any of these. This last mentioned might have been learned in combination with one of the first two.

Note that the first two are rather different sorts of learning. The stimulus-response form is about behavior; present the stimulus, and the behavior is prescribed. By contrast, the cognitive form does not tell the rat what to do; it represents facts about the world. Additional processes are needed to utilize the cognition in behavior.

The difference between S-R and cognitive models concerns not just what is learned. Learning is inextricably tied to a related issue: how is behavior produced? Cognitive theorists describe the rat as forming a cognitive map or representation of its environment; it has an expectancy of food at the goal, and its behavior is goal-directed and purposive. To the hard-nosed behaviorist, the use of such terms to describe unobservable phenomena was anathema. Motivation is also treated differently by the two schools. For example, to the cognitivist prior food deprivation would make the food-related box an attractive goal. To the S-R theorist, energy depletion would drive behavior, given direction by S-R connections between stimuli at the choice point and the response of turning left. Central to such discussions is the notion of representation, to which this discussion now turns.

REPRESENTATIONS

Roitblat (1982, p. 355) argues. "To assume the existence of representations is rather innocuous and should rarely be an issue for theoretical dispute. If an organism's behavior can be shown empirically to be affected by past experience, then some representation of that experience *must* exist." In these terms, the present discussion is not about whether representations exist (it can be taken axiomatically that they do), but about their properties. In Roitblat's terms, the change underlying a learned S-R association has as much claim to be called a representation as the cognitive one. In this context, consider Lockery's (1989, p. 119) definition: "From a cognitive scientific point of view, let us say that a state represents information—is a *representational state*—if it systematically co-varies with properties of the environment and in so doing contributes to the production of behaviour appropriate to that environment." Roitblat's criteria describe an S-R memory just as well as a cognitive one. So the definition of cognition given here is more circumscribed than is embodied by "representation."

Part of the cognitive case is that animals form particular kinds of representations of their environment and events within it. Postulation of this ability enables us to form the notion that behavior is goal-directed (teleology) that can be discussed in physically realizable terms and avoids mysticism. Thus, based upon past regularities of the world, the animal can form representations of events remote in either space or time or both, and it can base its behavior upon these representations. The term *cognitive map* is used to designate a representation of relative positions of features of the environment (O'Keefe and Nadel 1978). Using such a map, an animal is able to navigate to a point that is marked by no perceptible feature at the time in question. The animal's energy state can sensitize food-related locations in the map and make one the goal.

There is evidence that animals placed in a maze form a representation of the goal-box and the qualities of food contained therein. In cognitive terms, food forms the goal for these animals when running the maze. Some evidence derives from where the experimenter changes the reward object, so that it is different from what had earlier been experienced. If a less demanded reward is substituted for the anticipated (more demanded) reward (e.g., 20 pellets of food are replaced by 1), the behavior is disrupted. It is not disrupted if the reverse substitution is made (changing to 20 pellets where 1 had hitherto been received), indicating that an emotional/motivational weighting is attached to the cognitive appraisal of the reward (Tolman 1932).

Crespi (1942) showed that running speed (an index of motivation) is reduced if reward magnitude is lowered and is increased if magnitude is increased. Running speed did not reflect absolute levels of reward, but levels relative to what had been experienced earlier. Evidence that finding no food in a goal-box where food was previously found is aversive is shown by the tendency of rats to escape from such a situation (Gray 1987). A noise and light associated with entry into the goal-box under these conditions (also under conditions of reduced magnitude of reward) becomes aversive. Frustration, the experience of finding a reward less than expected, can act as a cue to aggression.

Wiepkema (1990) discusses the phenomenon termed gakelin, a characteristic call made by laying hens. It occurs, for example, (a) when hens have learned by experience that food arrives at a certain time and place and then it fails to materialize (the call is stronger when they have been food-deprived); (b) when a laying hen tries to enter the laying nest, but finds that it is closed; and (c) when a hen finds that her dustbath is inaccessible. Wiepkema summarizes this phenomenon as follows: Hens perform 'gakelin,' when they expect some goal situation, but experience an unforeseen change and/or a blocked goal situation. The call's intensity appears to reflect the strength of the expectation and/or the significance of the goal" (p. 1).

Even those skeptical of cognitive notions sometimes lapse into cognitive explanatory language, and the present example can be used to illustrate this. McFarland (1985, p. 316) makes the tacit assumption of representations, expectations, and comparisons in writing, "Only when the animal is surprised by the absence of reinforcement does it learn that particular stimuli signal nonreinforcement."

Examples taken from learning are a rich source of data, and the next section looks in detail at the evidence of cognition and motivation that can derived from the study of learning.

COGNITION AND LEARNING

Traditionally, the two principal divisions of learning have been seen as classical and instrumental conditioning (the latter being briefly introduced in the maze example). This section considers each in turn and interprets them in terms of cognition and their interdependence with motivation.

Classical Conditioning

The Nature of the Association
The most famous classical conditioning experiment is that of Pavlov on salivation. A bell, initially a neutral stimulus, was transformed into a conditional stimulus (CS)—that is, one with the power to evoke salivation—by pairing it with food presentation (an unconditional stimulus or UCS). In this situation, what process underlies learning? Is it a stimulus-response association between the bell and salivation (i.e., if bell, then salivate) or a cognition of the kind "when the bell is sounded, expect food." In principle, it might even be an example of both processes acting in parallel. Simply observing salivation does not distinguish the two explanations.

The best-known critique of cognitive explanations of behavior is that of Skinner (1986), who discusses Pavlov's experiment in this way: "The standard mentalistic explanation is that the dog 'associates' the bell with the food. But it was Pavlov who associated them! 'Associate' means to join or unite. The dog merely begins to salivate upon hearing the bell. We have no evidence that it does so because of an internal surrogate of the contingencies."

However, there is evidence from other classical conditioning studies that suggests such a surrogate association. Furthermore, its postulation allows the limitations of other explanatory models to be appreciated. First, consider that a light or tone (CS) is paired with food presentation (UCS). The rat comes to approach the food-delivery apparatus on CS presentation. Subsequently, in a different context, devaluation of the food occurs by pairing it with toxicosis (Holland and Straub 1979). Following this experience, how would the rat be expected to behave on CS presentation? Presumably, if it has learned a response "if CS, approach", it will continue as before to approach the food-delivery location, whereas in practice there is a tendency to do so less. This can be explained by the rat's forming representations of (a) the sequence "CS food" (a "surrogate association") and (b) the properties of the food. An S-R linkage would not be affected in this way.

Second, the fact that in a new situation subjects can perform a conditional response different in form from that shown during training (Tolman 1932; Gray 1987) suggests that learning is about the events in question. For example, in a novel context Pavlov's dog could show responses other than salivation on hearing the bell (e.g., if at liberty, it might approach the food dish). This flexibility of behavior could not be explained by postulating that the internal association is one, for example, simply between the bell and the efferent outflow underlying salivation.

Contemporary theory embodies these assumptions in that classical conditioning is interpreted as establishing predictive relationships between two events, E_1 and E_2, expressed as $E_1 \rightarrow E_2$ (Dickinson 1980). On presenting E_1, an expectation (or "expectancy") of E_2 is created. These expectations interact with motivational processes; the expectation can help to create a motivational state that then plays a role in behavior carried out with reference to the expectation (Bindra 1978). What the animal does in response to E_1 depends upon the environmental context. It is not restricted to performing a response that is a copy of the unconditional response.

McFarland (1989a, p. 131) writes, "Cognition is notoriously difficult to define. For Toates (1986) it seems sufficient that 'information may be stored in a form not directly tied to behaviour. Such information may be exploited in different ways according to context. . . .'" This seems to me to be more like a definition of memory." This is a definition of a particular sort of memory: a declarative memory concerning knowledge about the world (a cognition), and not instructions on what to do. Such a memory should be contrasted with one taking the form of a changed stimulus-response connection. In the cognitive case, the animal learns something about the world (e.g., expect food when a bell rings). What it does (if anything) based upon that expectancy depends upon the context. In the stimulus-response case, learning is simply a change of behavior.

Classical Conditioning and Incentive Motivation Models
Bindra (1978) studied the interdependence of learning and motivation. His theory emphasized classical conditioning and involved processes of the kind indicated by $E_1 \rightarrow E_2$. He argued that central motivational states

are set up by incentive objects (e.g., food) and that "motivation is as much a matter of external stimulation by hedonic stimuli (incentive objects and events) as it is of internal organismic conditions" (p. 45). The role of internal states (e.g., energy depletion) is to sensitize processes such that external objects form incentives to be pursued (see also Toates 1986 for an account of Bindra's model). In such terms, the incentive that plays a role in arousing a central motivational state also forms the goal of behavior. Animals are pulled toward hedonically positive stimuli down, as Bindra terms it, "a spatial gradient of motivational valence" (p. 48). Learning consists of attributing incentive values to previously neutral cues.

Some reservations and additions need to be appended to Bindra's model. First, incentive representations appear to be open to revision in the light of the animal's own actions, among other things. For instance, depletion of food appears to cause revision of the memory of the food site. As Gallistel (1978) notes, a rat sampling food in an eight-arm maze avoids the location where it has just received a hedonic stimulus. Second, it is necessary to consider that incentives might not be physically present, but can still exert an influence within the context of a cognitive map of the environment. Third, in emphasizing classical conditioning, Bindra appears to underestimate the extent to which animals can learn [response] → [outcome] relationships (Jenkins 1978). Finally, under some conditions it is necessary to qualify the term *hedonic* in order to account for the learning process (discussed shortly). However, Bindra's model appears to capture a crucial aspect of cognition and motivation: that animals form predictive associations, and thereby formerly neutral cues can arouse motivation and flexibly guide behavior by virtue of their pairing with biologically significant events.

There are at least two ways by which classically conditioned incentive stimuli might control behavior: (1) By increasing the strength of motivation. For example, a tone paired with shock in the past might give no spatial information, but might increase fear and promote behavior directed toward a safe location. (2) By directing behavior. Considering spatial locations, animals tend to move toward locations that have been paired with positive unconditional stimuli. For example, an animal is motivated to move toward a location paired with electrical stimulation of the brain. Young (1961, p. 176) proposes a primary affective arousal arising from, for example, the taste of a sucrose solution. Based upon this, there is a learned approach tendency, the strength of which depends upon the hedonic intensity of the primary contact.

A neutral cue paired with either access to females in male Japanese quail (Domjan et al. 1986) or mating in male rats (Zamble, Mitchell, and Findlay 1986) acquires the capacity for sexual arousal as indexed by copulatory performance. Weingarten (1984) looked at the interaction between cognitive and noncognitive determinants of ingestion. The cognitive determinant was a cue paired in a classical contingency fashion with the delivery of food. This cue aroused feeding even in "satiated" animals (with ad lib access to the same food). However, energy state interacted with the cue to determine ingestion; total daily intake was not different on days when the cue was or was not presented. On cue days, feeding at times remote from cue presentation decreased to compensate. Also, loading with energy substantially decreased the capacity of the cue to trigger food intake. In another example, a cue predictive of intravenous drug infusion acquired the capacity to rearouse lever pressing in previously extinguished rats (Stewart, de Wit, and Eikelboom, 1984).

There is evidence that food-deprived rats can anticipate their time of feeding, revealing an internal representation of the passage of time. Set within the context of a circadian rhythm, the time of anticipated feeding can serve as a surrogate incentive object to arouse activity (see Gallistel 1990). Thus, in a variety of motivational states, cues predictive of biologically appropriate stimuli (either because of their earlier association with them or simply by virtue of the passage of time) acquire the capacity to change motivation and behavior.

A Closer Look at the Nature of the Association

This section addresses two questions: (1) With what exactly does the CS (E_1) become associated? and (2) How is this association revealed in behavior? Unless the second question is addressed, (i.e., knowledge is translated into action), we leave the rat buried in thought. On one level, the association might simply be described as one formed with the UCS (e.g., food or a mate). But, looking inside the animal, how are the associated events coded? Furthermore, the nature of the UCS differs between those (e.g., food or a mate) with qualities that trigger exteroceptors and those (e.g., intravenous drugs) that have only secondary exteroceptive associations (e.g., click of delivery apparatus).

Dickinson and Dearing (1979) suggested that the representation of the neutral stimulus (later transformed into a CS) might become connected by independent excitatory links to both (1) the representation of the UCS and (2) a central motivational process. In this model, a range of different UCSs of the same affective sign (e.g., water or a mate) activate a common appetitive motivational system. UCSs of opposite sign (e.g., shock) activate an aversive system. There is reciprocal inhibition between the two systems, and expectation is an integral aspect of the model. A CS predictive of, say, food excites the appetitive system, and one predictive of shock excites the aversive system. A CS predictive of no food in a situation in which food is expected appears to be able to trigger the aversion system; animals withdraw from a CS negatively correlated with a food UCS.

Evidence that a neutral stimulus acquires something of the hedonic value of its associated unconditional stimulus is provided by the demonstration (Dickinson and Dearing 1979) that a light signaling omission of food blocks conditioning to a tone that signals shock. This suggests that, though in cognitive terms the tone and light would be signaling rather different events, in affective terms they would both be "perceived as hedonically equivalent and redundant in spite of their differences" (Berridge and Schulkin 1989, p. 122). A related phenomenon, similarly implying a common positive motivational/hedonic "pool," would appear to be that in which a cue paired with morphine delivery can later excite appetitive sexual behavior (Mitchell and Stewart 1990).

To investigate the details of conditioning, Berridge and Schulkin (1989) used a "taste-reactivity test"; substances were applied to the tongues of rats and the reaction—ingestive, rejecting, or indifference—was monitored. They paired a neutral taste stimulus with application of an NaCl solution to the tongues of rats that were not sodium-depleted (a state in which NaCl was not hedonically positive). Rats were then tested for their reaction to the taste stimulus (CS) both when in sodium balance and when depleted (when NaCl was hedonically positive). For rats tested when sodium-depleted, the reaction was shifted in the direction of positive hedonics by the prior experience. This was not so for rats tested in sodium balance. The result shows that, by learning, neutral cues acquire hedonic properties.

As Berridge and Schulkin noted, their results do not distinguish between two possible processes: given the appropriate physiological state, (1) the CS elicits affect by activating a representation of the UCS, which is affect-loaded, or (2) as might be suggested by Dickinson and Dearing's result, the CS itself acquires hedonic value (independent of the UCS representation). Whichever of these (or both) is found to occur, the result says something about what is not learned in this situation: an association between a CS and the affective value of the UCS at the time of exposure. Nor is an association between a taste and an ingestive response formed. When rats are in sodium balance, concentrated NaCl elicits aversive reactions and yet, in the appropriate physiological state, the rats later show positive reactions to the CS associated with the NaCl. As other evidence also shows (Toates 1986), learning can occur regarding the sensory attributes of incentives, and only later, in a different physiological state, is this learning shown to have hedonic associations.

Instrumental Learning

The term "instrumental learning" refers to the learning that occurs in a situation in which, by means of its own behavior, an animal achieves something. Examples include learning to negotiate a maze or to press a lever in a Skinner box for food. Exactly what is learned in mastering such a task is a topic of controversy (Bindra 1978). Classical conditioning can account for some of what is learned—for example, an association between the color of a goal-box and an intravenous drug received there. The evidence suggests that, depending upon circumstances, cognitive maps, classically conditioned cognitions (e.g., expect a grey goal-box associated with food), [response] → [outcome] cognitions, and S-R links between stimuli at the choice point and the turning response can all play roles in behavior (see also Hirsh 1974; Mishkin and Petri 1984; White 1989).

An early experiment (Tolman, Ritchie, and Kalish 1946) illustrates the argument. Referring back to figure 18.1, envisage that rats were released from either the south (figure 18.1a) or north (figure 18.1b) start boxes on different trials. Groups of rats were required to learn different things to obtain food. For one group, as shown in figure 18.1a and b, food was in a fixed place. To solve the problem, the rats had to learn a cognition and make different responses depending upon their starting point. For another group, the position of food varied and the problem was solved by making a fixed response (e.g., turn left) irrespective of their starting point. Presumably, they had to learn a stimulus-response association. Both groups were able to solve their problems.

The ease of learning either place or response depends upon the availability of spatial cues. If there is a richness of cues, place learning is relatively easy. If there are no spatial cues, response learning is relatively easy (Restle 1957; see also Gallistel 1990). The term "response learning" does not distinguish between learning an S-R link in the traditional sense (in which the outcome is not encoded in what is learned) or learning that involves a [response] → [outcome] cognition. Only a reinforcer devaluation study would enable us to distinguish between these. Thus, if the food were devalued and the animal subsequently shown to be reluctant to negotiate the maze, this would argue for a [response] → [outcome] explanation. If the animal were insensitive to this procedure, it would argue that an S-R association had been formed.

Let us return to the original experiment (figure 18.1a). Where food is always to the left and the rat is always run from the south, place learning and response learning both lead to the same goal. In cognitive terms, the rat will learn that food is at a particular location in space, which will promote pursuit of this goal. In S-R terms, it will form an association between the stimuli at the choice point and the motor act of turning left. Learning a cognition and a stimulus-response association will be compatible in generating behavior. Goal-directed behavior utilizing cognitions will be assisted by response selection in the presence of familiar stimuli. Where there is the facility to employ both place learning and response learning compatibly, speed of learning reflects the additivity of these processes (Restle 1957).

Consider what happens when the rat is run from north to south (figure 18.1b) after learning in the situation of figure 18.1a. On the basis of learning the cognition "food is at location X," it should turn west. However, on the basis of forming the stimulus-response association "turn left at the choice point" it should turn east. Given sufficient cues about the location of the goal-box, rats will tend to turn west, which indicates that they have learned a cognition. However, if there are no spatial cues to guide them, then they are likely to repeat the response performed in the past, which will take them to the east.

In an S-R model, memory can be described as stored "on the performance line" (Hirsh 1974). By this Hirsh meant that "learning is held to result from the formation of a functional connection between the neural elements sensitive to the stimulus and those responsible for producing the response" (p. 422). Memory is the S-R linkage; the occurrence of S results in behavior.

Depending upon such things as the function they serve, the strength of S-R linkages might vary, whether innate or learned. Some innate linkages might be strong, for example, in rats that link detection of a predator with freezing. However, in other situations, such as a foraging task (figure 18.1), any S-R linkage formed might be less rigid. Thus, rather than reliably eliciting a response, a stimulus might bias decision-making processes in favor of the associated response (a similar liberalization of the S-R concept was described by Dickinson and Balleine 1993).

In such terms, imagine a hungry rat coming to the choice point in figure 18.1a. It has a decision to make. As a cognitive process, this will be influenced by the attraction of the goal to the left. The tendency to turn toward this goal could be assisted by stimuli biasing the rat toward making a left turn. If the situation changes—for instance, the animal approaches the goal from a different direction as in the change from figure 18.1a to 18.1b—stimulus-response information will either be unavailable to guide the animal or will be misleading, and the rat will have to synthesize behavior on the basis of knowledge. Conversely, it is possible to imagine situations in which the rat would heavily rely upon learned S-R associations—for example, confronting a T junction in a narrow tunnel system at which a left turn led to an exit.

Considering another instrumental situation, examination of behavior in a Skinner box shows that at least part of what is learned is a relationship between behavior itself and the outcome (Adams 1982). Animals learn the relationship [response] → [reinforcer] at the start of training, when performance is sensitive to reinforcer devaluation. If the pellets are devalued by pairing with toxicosis and the animal returns to the Skinner box on extinction, it will press less hard. With more extensive training, rats tend to move to habit acquisition, to forming S-R associations in which behavior is not motivated by an association with its outcome. This assumption is based upon the fact that behavior is insensitive to reinforcer devaluation. Thus Adams (1982) found that lever pressing was sensitive to devaluation after 100 reinforcements, but not after 500. An action had become a habit. So the same behavior, lever pressing, can be performed either as a goal-directed action or as a habit. It would seem that a rat uses its cognitive processes when the world is relatively uncertain. When the world becomes highly predictable, a more mechanistic process can substitute for the cognitive one.

It would appear that there is more than one type of learning. Some of these types of learning would be described as cognitive (e.g., cognitive maps, $E_1 \rightarrow E_2$ and [response] $\rightarrow$ [outcome] learning), but others are mechanistic. Further illumination on this topic can be gained by looking at hierarchies, the topic of the next section.

HIERARCHICAL NETWORK MODELS, COGNITIONS, AND S-R

Roitblat (1988, p. 16) proposed a "hierarchically organized cognitive action system" in which "nodes at different levels represent different degrees of abstraction." At each level, behavior is organized and learning can occur. At the lowest level, nodes represent specific patterns of muscular activity. Top-level nodes represent such things as plans and intentions. For example, at one level a node represents lowering a lever in a Skinner box. This node would then be able to potentiate a number of lower-level nodes representing the different muscular activities possible—for instance, lower left foot or push nose against lever.

In such a model, learning that food is at a particular location in space represents a higher-level node than learning that a left turn leads to food. The nodes representing the cognition "food is at X" would, if activated, have a number of lower-level nodes available for the mechanics of getting to X (e.g., run through the maze if dry, swim if flooded). In Roitblat's terms, motivation represents a high-level node which, in combination with cognitions, potentiates lower-level nodes.

The difference between place learning and stimulus-response learning presumably maps onto different levels of nodes at which learning occurs, high and low respectively. How would Roitblat's model apply to the rat learning the task of figure 18.1? Imagine that it has learned the cognition "food is at X" and, in figure 18.1a, finds itself at the choice point. How is behavior produced? Roitblat (1991) refers to "potentiation" of lower-level nodes by higher-level nodes. However, an input from sensory information at the choice point is needed to trigger a low-level node. So, in the presence of stimuli at the choice point, the response of turning left will be potentiated by higher-level nodes. If a rat were placed in the situation of figure 18.1b, the response of turning right would be potentiated.

In pure stimulus-response learning, there would be no such excitation descending from a higher level. Rather, there would just be the link between stimulus and response at a low level. Thus I would disagree with Roitblat's (1986, p. 18) statement that "there is no principled way to distinguish cognitive from non-cognitive parts of the organism's information processing system." The "way" Roitblat speaks of would be in terms of the level of the node, which corresponds to the kind of information stored, as has been discussed already and will be developed in the next section.

In Roitblat's model, motivational influences are at a high level and work in association with cognitions to set goals. However, we also have to consider motivational factors when an animal is working in S-R mode (e.g., Adams 1982). It is not difficult to envisage that some specific motivational factors could affect an innate species-typical S-R association—for example, modulation of the female mating posture, lordosis, by hormones such as estrogen (Pfaff 1980). It is not so clear how, say, different feeding-related S-R associations (e.g., lever → press) could be potentiated. It might be necessary to resurrect the classical Hullian notion (Hull 1943) of a general drive that increases activity (A. Dickinson, personal communication).

The next section will look at the insight gained by the study of rats with hippocampal lesions, and the section following it will compare and contrast cognitive and noncognitive learning or, in terms of Roitblat's model, high-level or low-level nodes.

The Role of the Hippocampus in Cognitive and S-R Learning

It could prove very useful if the present discussion of processes underlying behavior were able to be related to different regions of the brain and insights gained from neural science. In the context of the biology of cognition and learning, the role of the hippocampus usually figures prominently.

Lesions of the hippocampus disrupt an animal's ability to function in the cognitive mode (retrieval of memory that is not on the performance line) rather than the S-R mode (memory on the performance line) (Hirsh 1974; O'Keefe and Nadel 1978). The hippocampally lesioned rat fits the S-R model well in several respects, and Hirsh concludes that "the responses of the lesioned animals are movements rather than actions" (p. 433). Such rats appear to "go onto autopilot," meaning that they are relatively insensitive to the consequences of behavior. They continue to approach incentives and even perform discriminations for incentives that they do not consume, presumably as a result of the onset of satiety. In this sense, they are something like overtrained intact rats (cf. Dickinson 1989).

Hippocampally lesioned rats exhibit a deficiency in their ability to solve a problem involving an unseen spatial location (Hirsh 1974). If a tone signals the emergence of a food tray from a recess, intact rats will move toward the unseen tray on tone presentation (CS). Hippocampally lesioned rats moved toward the tray only when it could be perceived. Another example that Hirsh gives is that the disruption of drinking caused by presenting a CS predictive of shock in a different apparatus was greater in hippocampally lesioned rats than in controls. In the terms developed here, to the lesioned rat the CS was a signal simply of expected shock rather than of shock expected in a particular location.

Shuttlebox avoidance fits a dual cognitive/S-R model (O'Keefe and Nadel 1978). In one-way avoidance, a rat simply has to respond to a warning tone by leaping over a barrier. In two-way avoidance, by contrast, it must shuttle backwards and forwards from one side to the other on hearing the tone. In one-way avoidance, an S-R association (tone-jump) and cognitive learning ("following the tone, over here is dangerous and over there is safe") would be compatible. In two-way avoidance, by contrast, an S-R association would be sufficient and behavior could be impeded by learning about the relative danger of either side. Although deficiences are sometimes seen in one-way avoidance, hippocampally lesioned rats are superior to controls in two-way avoidance (O'Keefe and Nadel 1978).

Packard, Hirsh, and White (1989) concluded that the mammalian brain contains two anatomically distinct memory systems whose functions more or less map onto cognitive and S-R learning. They used an Olton radial maze in which eight arms were each baited with food. The problem is normally solved using a win-shift strategy: once an arm has been depleted of its food pellet, that arm is now best avoided. Solution of the problem suggests the use of cognitive processes; a cognitive map would represent the spatial layout, and the representation of food would be revised with experience ("site of likely food" revised to "site depleted"). As Packard and associates note, the problem cannot be solved by a reinforcement mechanism since, in this language, the rat is required to withhold the response just reinforced. (Gallistel made a similar criticism of the hedonic model, discussed earlier.) Hippocampally lesioned rats are seriously deficient on this task.

Using the same apparatus, an adaptation was devised to make a win-stay strategy profitable. The rat was required to approach an arm signaled with a light; that is, a response, approach, could be attached to a stimulus, the light. Solution of this problem appears to involve a reinforcement process in the traditional sense. Rats with hippocampal damage were better than intact controls at solving this problem. It was suggested that intact rats have to overcome their win-shift tendency, in which the hippocampus plays a crucial role. In contrast to lesions of the hippocampus, lesions of the caudate nucleus disrupted the win-stay task, suggesting that this area plays a role in S-R/reinforcement learning.

Roitblat (1982) discussed the result that intact rats found a win-shift task easier to solve than a win-stay task and noted that the same representation (based upon experience) was assumed to underlie each task—that is, a once baited, but now depleted arm. He suggested that "the animal's access to, or formation of, representations about the location of food differed as a function of the contingency involved" (p. 359). One might also argue that, though the raw data (depleted arm) represented was the same in the two cases, the aspect of the representation involving an extrapolation based upon the raw data needed to be different—that is, depleted arm replenished (win-stay) and depleted arm still depleted (win-shift).

Eichenbaum, Otto, and Cohen (1992) see the hippocampus function "as critical for learning configurations and as critical for temporal tagging and matching," going on to say, "We arrive at the common requirement for comparison and manipulation of representations according to significant relationships among perceptually independent stimuli presented either at the same time (configuration learning) or sequentially (temporal tagging)." What is spared following hippocampal damage is the capacity to process stimuli individually, unrelated to other memory items.

Interestingly, rats with hippocampal lesions do not in general respond in a relative way to changes in incentive value (see also our earlier discussion). They do not run faster when incentive value is increased or slower when it is reduced (Hirsh 1974). Extinction is not associated, as in normals, with one of the standard indices of stress: activation of the pituitary adrenocortical system.

Comparison Between Cognitive and S-R Learning: Function Served

So far, we have compared and contrasted learning based upon cognitive and S-R processes. In this section these comparisons are summarized and their implications looked at in terms of what the two processes are able to achieve. Acting cognitively, a rat (a) assimilates information about its environment, (b) can utilize that information flexibly, and (c) is goal-directed. Aspects a–c come together as a package of explanation, labeled "cognitive" in table 18.1, which contrasts the model that arises from cognitive and S-R behaviorist perspectives. However, it is important to be reminded that, though these ideas emerged largely from the polarization of academic debate, a contemporary compromise is that both kinds of processes play roles in learning.

An S-R link encodes information in such a way as to constitute a memory. It can play a role in the generation of adaptive behavior. However, the form in which information is held is directly tied to behavior, does not allow flexibility, and is, in the terms used here, noncognitive.

Whereas the idea of S-R learning is associated with the concept of *reinforcement*—that is, strengthening of responses—that of cognition is more closely associated with *reward* (White 1989). Reward can be operationally defined as stimuli to which animals are attracted (Young 1961). In cognitive terms, rewards are said to be incentives toward which animals move and in interaction with which hedonic reactions are experienced (Bolles 1991). However, one would not want to describe a moth's behavior as revealing cognitive processes simply because it is attracted toward a flame. Rather, the cognitive notion is closely tied to that of flexibility

Table 18.1 A Comparison between Cognitive and S-R Behaviorist Perspectives

Behavioral issue	Cognitive perspective	S-R behaviorist perspective
What is learned?	Information ("facts") about the world, e.g. spatial maps, relationships between (a) events in the world and (b) behavior and outcomes. Learning can be "fully fledged" on single exposure (Eichenbaum et al. 1992; O'Keefe and Nadel 1978).	Associations between stimuli and responses; learning is usually gradual.
The motivation concept; what moves the animal?	Attraction of goals (accentuated by internal states); the pull of incentives; the experience of (or anticipation of hedonism.	Drives, deviant internal states, energization, classically conditioned incentives acting in combination with drives.
The use of the notion of goal or purpose.	Animal has an internal representation of the goal; central explanatory device part of the causation of behavior.	Not part of the explanation; simply something that is reached as a result of the action of external stimuli, as in "goal-box."
What (a) strengthens and (b) weakens behavior?	(a) Attaining an expected goal; confirmation of the predictive value of cues as part of getting to the goal. (b) Revision of goal-related cognitions as a result of exposure to changes in reward available at the goal site.	(a) Reinforcement (e.g., reduction in a drive strengthens the S-R association that leads to reward). (b) Possibly weakened by unreinforced performance (O'Keefe and Nadel 1978).

associated with representation of the environment: the capacity to learn various ways of reaching an incentive object that is not necessarily physically present. Learning by means of both classical and instrumental contingencies can be involved in such goal-directed behavior.

One can imagine benefits and costs of storing and utilizing information cognitively and noncognitively as illustrated in table 18.2. For cognition, information can be stored before it is utilized in behavior. In other words, latent learning is possible. By contrast, in the S-R model learning arises only as a result of behaving. Storing information cognitively means that an animal can respond not just to changing, but to suddenly *changed* circumstances. For example, detours can be made to avoid unexpected obstacles. Extrapolations can be made to compensate for missing stimulus information. By contrast, storing information as S-R associations is no help if the stimulus changes significantly. Rats tend to behave cognitively when starting to learn a task, but then, with experience, sometimes switch to become S-R automatons (Adams 1982; O'Keefe and Nadel 1978, p. 99; Bever 1984). Therefore, to execute a simple repetitive response, the processing demands of storing sufficient information cognitively are probably greater than the demands of storing it as an S-R association.

Since animals both assimilate cognitions and learn S-R associations, a balance between them seems the optimal solution. Cognitions and S-R

Table 18.2 Comparison of Advantages and Disadvantages of Cognitive and Noncognitive Processes

	Cognitive process	Noncognitive process
Advantages	Flexibility in getting to goal; novel responses can be used; rapidly adapted to new situations.	Possibly cheap in terms of processing (e.g., see Hirsh 1974).
	Information can be assimilated prior to use (e.g., food sources and potential bolt-holes identified).	S-R links can (a) in some species-typical cases be specified genetically and (b) be utilized where no contextual representation is available.
Disadvantages	For a response that can be repeatedly elicited by a given stimulus in a stereotyped way, costly in terms of processing.	Does not permit flexibility in getting to a goal (e.g., under changing conditions).
	Additional processing of information needed to determine behavior. In constant conditions, possibly more efficient (faster to respond?) to specify what *to do* rather than *to learn* about the world.	Information can be assimilated only at the time at which a behavior occurs (unless specified genetically).

associations reflect rather different and complementary considerations. Depending upon the context, more or less reliance might be placed on one or the other. One can imagine several determinants of the respective weightings. The availability of landmark cues has already been discussed. Another determinant seems to be the length of experience in a given task during which utilization of a fixed response has provided a solution. Similar considerations are involved in designing robots on the basis of either power or generality criteria of effectiveness (Kiss 1992).

COGNITION, GOAL-DIRECTED BEHAVIOR, AND TELEOLOGY

Criteria of Teleology

The term "cognitive" is usually closely associated with "goal-direction" and "teleology." In addition to involving cognitive processes, behavior often seems teleological. However, some authors (e.g., Heyes and Dickinson 1990; McFarland 1989a, b, c) reserve the label "teleological" for situations that meet additional criteria beyond giving the appearance of being purposive. Similarly, Gallistel (1985, p. 56) calls "acts potentiated by virtue of act-outcome representations intentional acts." In his terms, acts do not constitute intentional behavior, even if cognitive-type representations are involved, unless it can be shown that the acts are potentiated by act-outcome representations.

Dickinson (1985) contrasts teleological and S-R (mechanistic) models. The mechanistic model explains behavior as being caused by "the presence of an eliciting, releasing or triggering stimulus" (p. 67). In the teleological model, behavior occurs not as the result of the presentation of a stimulus, but "because it is controlled at the time of performance by the animal's knowledge about the consequences of this activity." Such activity is described not as a "response," but as an "action." What constitutes an action? Dickinson and Balleine (1993) adopt the criterion of Taylor: "An explanation is teleological if the events to be explained are accounted for in this way: if G is the goal 'for the sake of which' events are said to occur, B the events to be explained, and S the state of affairs obtaining prior to B, then B is explained by the fact that S was such that it required B for G to come about."

Based on this definition, Heyes and Dickinson (1990) propose two criteria that an example of behaviour must meet to qualify as an action: the *desire criterion* and the *belief criterion*. The "irrelevant incentive test" used to assess the desire criterion is as follows. A rat is food-deprived and trained to press a lever and pull a chain concurrently for two distinct food rewards, dry food pellets and sugar solution. A lever press delivers food pellets, and a chain pull delivers sugar solution. The animal is then satiated for food but deprived of water. The distribution of responses between the lever and the chain is then assessed in extinction. In thirst, as in hunger, the sugar solution is an attractive incentive but, unlike in hunger, the dry food is not. Typically, under certain conditions (Dickinson and Dawson 1988), when a rat is tested thirsty, the response that delivers sugar solution occurs more frequently than that which delivers dry food. It would appear that the animal is making an inference of the kind "the outcome of lever press is dry food, which is inappropriate for thirst, whereas the chain delivers sugar solution, which is appropriate." This behavior meets the desire criterion: it is determined by a goal that is desirable in that it would be consumed if available.

The desire criterion is also illustrated by what happens if an incentive is devalued (as discussed earlier) and contrasts with the mechanistic and teleological models. Suppose that, after interacting with an object in one context, its appropriateness to the animal's state altered as a result of the animal's experience elsewhere. In returning to the original context, it could be adaptive for this alteration to be reflected in behavior. This would be possible according to the teleological model, but not the mechanistic model. For example, suppose first that behavior in a situation was followed by access to a particular food (F_1) and that, sometime later, in another context, the value of F_1 was lowered by following ingestion with toxicosis. According to a mechanistic model, an S-R linkage would not be weakened by this experience, so the tendency of a stimulus (e.g., a lever) to elicit a response (pressing) would remain intact. By contrast, according to a teleological account, one of the determinants of behavior is the representation of the goal object, and it would be expected that any devaluation would be reflected in a reduced tendency to pursue the goal.

Adams and Dickinson (1981) trained rats to make two different responses, each earning a particular reinforcer: sucrose or Noyes pellets. Then one of the reinforcers was devalued by pairing it with toxicosis. Taste-aversion conditioning continued until the substance was refused completely. In an extinction test, the frequency of emitting the response that previously had earned the devalued reinforcer was much reduced compared to the response that had earned the nondevalued reinforcer. Thus the data fit the teleological model. That lever pressing persists at some level, albeit lower, shows either (a) that the aversive feature of the food is not perfectly represented in the goal representation or (b) that other factors also play a role, or both. The residual behavior could represent an S-R association not vulnerable to devaluation (A. Dickinson, personal communication).

Lever pressing for food also meets the belief criterion. In cognitive terms, this means that the animal shows evidence of assimilating "rational" information about the relationship between behavior and attaining the goal. The term "rational" specifies that information maps the causality of the world and is open to modification when causality changes. For example, suppose rats earning food in a Skinner box are switched to an omission schedule on which their responses delay food rather than obtaining it. They slow their responding faster than controls with which they are yoked, which experience no contingency between responding and food. This is evidence that an animal is sensitive to its actions; a cognition "lever press → food" is converted to "lever press → no food." Conversely, if after a rat has learned "lever press → food" food is made available regardless of whether the rat presses the lever, lever pressing ceases (see Heyes and Dickinson 1990).

Heyes and Dickinson describe a situation that passes the desire criterion and appears to be teleological, but fails the belief criterion. Food is freely delivered into a bowl, and a tone occurs a few seconds before food arrives. Rats will learn the "tone → food" relationship so that after a while they will approach the food cup on hearing the tone. This fits the desire criterion in that it ceases or is reduced if the food is devalued. One might argue that it fits the belief criterion in the form [move to cup] → [in position to eat pellet]. However, a variation on the theme leads Heyes and Dickinson to argue that the behavior does not fit the belief criterion. Suppose that, if a rat moves to the cup when the tone occurs, food is omitted. The rat persists in moving to the cup and thereby loses a number of pellets. Heyes and Dickinson argue that this behavior is not teleological. To solve the problem, the rat is required to entertain a rather odd cognition: "tone → food provided I don't move toward the food." Perhaps a more adept predator of objects that are likely to get up and go on approach (e.g., a cat) could entertain such cognitions (S. Tyler, personal communication).

One might wish to divide the sequence of activities and question what is the goal of the first phase, the rat's movement toward the dish. Is it to obtain food, or simply to get to the dish? If the latter, it fits the belief criterion. Heyes and Dickinson describe a looking-glass experiment in which chicks caused their food bowl to move away from them on approaching it. They argue, "In spite of the fact that they could easily have gained access to food by walking away from the bowl, the chicks persisted in chasing the food away." Thus the biologically prepared reaction of approaching the food could not be countered by learning the cognition "withdraw → obtain food."

McFarland's Criticism of Goal-Direction

McFarland (1989a, b, c; see also McFarland this volume) has critiqued the kind of package of ideas that has been presented here, with its involvement of cognition and goal-directed behavior. He suggests that, whereas animals are "goal-achieving," this does not imply that they are "goal-directed." Thus it can be observed that animals are able to recognize goals when they get to them and act appropriately. However, it does not follow from this that a representation of the goal is used to guide the animal toward it.

Some systems can be described as goal-achieving without being goal-directed if the latter term means that an explicit representation of the goal is involved in the action involved (G. Kiss, personal communication). Biology is rich with examples. Thus, as McFarland notes, in lay language evolution is often described in teleological terms and departures from an evolutionary stable strategy are indeed self-correcting. However, few these days would suggest that mutations are directed by a representation of the end point. Alternative models can be proposed. Similarly, cells of the immune system might be described as target-seeking and as recognizing targets, but there is no evidence that they are guided by a representation of the disparity between where they are now and the goal. McFarland (1983) rightly describes weight regulation as a system that is goal-achieving but can achieve the goal without an explicit representation of a set point. Valid as these arguments are, they might provide misleading analogies to the goal-achieving systems described here.

Circulation of the blood is an efficient way of getting immune cells to their target. It is difficult to imagine how this process could incorporate teleology. Despite the occasional suggestion that a form of teleology is at work in mutations (Cairns, Overbaugh, and Miller 1988), some might feel that only an omnipotent and ominiscient creator could build a comprehensive teleology into the process of evolution. In the models normally described, body weight regulation can easily be envisaged in the absence of an explicit representation of a set point, since two biochemical processes with inherent negative feedback (lipogenesis and lipolysis) are described (Toates 1975). The case of behavioral goal-achieving systems is different because (a) one can describe processes that would do the job and build engineering models, (b) it is difficult to see that any other process could do the job as effectively, and (c) the evidence suggests that a representation of the goal object plays a role in motivation.

McFarland (1989a, p. 108) notes that "an essential feature of a goal-directed system is that some of the consequences of the behaviour are monitored and this information made available to the control mechanism." As was argued earlier, the consequences of behavior—for example, reward quality and size—are available to the control mechanism. McFarland (1989a, p. 117) discusses the idea that, in making decisions, animals weigh the costs and benefits attached to various outcomes (e.g., go left for food or right for water). However, he notes (1989a, p. 117): "By evaluation, I do not mean a cognitive process (necessarily), but merely a process that assigns new values to the variables and parameters involved." It is difficult to see the relevance of the word "merely" to such a feat. In the terms used here, such processes would be said to be cognitive.

McFarland (1989a, p. 143) writes: "An animal (or robot), that can assess the extent to which the consequences of its current, or future, behaviour are beneficial, is a cognitive animal, provided the assessment involves declarative knowledge of the consequences." This is a definition that fits the analysis presented here.

Regarding Dickinson's goal revaluation experiments, McFarland (1989a, p. 137) writes: "The question is whether 'goals' are revalued or whether some other entities are revalued." He suggests (1989a, p. 138): "An alternative possibility is that the consequences of the behaviour of pressing the lever, rather than the food or the goal is revalued." It is difficult to see what such a consequence could be (proprioceptive feedback?), and McFarland offers no alternative.

McFarland (1989b, p. 40) argues that a teleological model will not allow an animal to abandon one goal for another when the first becomes less cost-effective: "The simple teleological hypothesis implies that the rat aims to get the food at all costs and will fail only on account of insurmountable obstacles." He does not explain why teleology implies an inability to switch. In the model advanced here, a goal representation would be part of a complex system with reciprocal interactions with other systems. It would not be difficult to build a robot in which the candidature of a goal fell if a stronger goal emerged. Why should evolution not be able to solve this problem? Indeed, one could suggest that constructing a goal-directed

system would be an efficient way of building in such a process of allocation. The goal could be inhibited by the emergence of a rival goal and
with this inhibition could lead to loss of the attraction of cues that lead
to the goal. Paradoxically, how a switch would be organized otherwise
is not clear.

In the context of McFarland's argument, Dennett (1989, p. 232) notes:

How, I asked myself, can the continuous trade-off be "calculated" or
"computed" (or if that begs the question, how can it be *implemented*)
unless the outcome of each possible trade-off is somehow to turn on or
favour or single out some sort of internal *representative* (not "representation") of the "chosen" option? The answer is, it can't be. Something must
"stand for" each contestant in the trade-off, but this thing is not, in
McFarland's understanding, a *representation* of the goal, or of the action
with the goal as its defining consummation.

As Dickinson has argued, some of what superficially appears to be teleological fails to remain so if it is examined more critically. Nonetheless,
even by his stringent criteria a large array of unambiguously teleological
examples survives.

If an animal does not work along teleological lines, then the onus is on
McFarland to suggest how it might work. How does an animal manage
to find a target via a novel route utilizing only nonteleological means?
On close examination, the problem is daunting. Consider a rat navigating
a route to a goal. Suppose that the rat is constructed in such a way as to
respond en route to various cues, each of which in turn leads it nearer
to the primary goal. But the word "respond" is a minefield. Does the rat
show a fixed response to each stimulus in S-R fashion, in which case the
animal cannot exhibit flexibility? Does it have an automatic compensation
device "if coming from north, turn left; if from south, turn right"? This
device soon becomes unwieldy, and in any case requires a map.

Suppose, though, that the rat learns to approach a series of conditional
stimuli (e.g., turns in the maze, landmarks), each of which has had a
history of associations with the goal object, until it happens upon the goal
(cf. Bindra 1978; Deutsch 1960). But the notion of approaching a series of
cues has something of a telological feel to it. It would seem to be no less
teleological than a sidewinder missile's approaching the exhaust of an
enemy aircraft, and McFarland (1989b, p. 40) admits that guided missiles
are goal-directed. What would be the nature of the cues that the rat
approaches? The strength of these cues can sometimes reflect the motivational state of the animal and the associations of the cues with the goal
object. It is difficult to describe these things in terms other than those
involving an internal representation of the subgoal.

I would argue that the cues the rat approaches are set within the context
of a cognitive map of the environment and that the primary goal object
can sensitize them (Deutsch 1960; Gallistel 1980). In such terms, a representation of the goal object forms a central theme.

DISCUSSION

The notions of congition, representation, goal, and expectation have been discussed in terms of a package of ideas. Even initial investigations suggest that a somewhat similar set of considerations applies to understanding animal behavior and designing effective robots (Brooks 1991). It is hoped that the argument presented here will further stimulate debate on the nature of the processes underlying behavior that will be appropriate to those on the robot design side and that subsequent interaction between researchers in both fields can be mutually beneficial.

The chapter's central theme is that animals construct representations of their environments in both spatial and temporal domains and then act in a goal-directed way on the basis of these representations. A distinction has been drawn between two different classes of processes involved in learning, cognitive processes and mechanistic processes. Although these are distinct processes, the former representing information about the world and the latter representing a determinant of behavior, in explaining behavior it is possible to see the distinction somewhat less rigidly drawn. Thus, as was discussed, in Roitblat's model high-level nodes "potentiate" lower-level nodes, implying some degree of stimulus input. A tendency to turn in one direction based upon an S-R association could be potentiated by a higher-level node.

Future theories will need to integrate data produced in the incentive-motivation tradition with our understanding of cognitive maps. One of the few to address this issue is O'Keefe (1989), who suggests that information on incentives is stored outside the hippocampus, but with connections to the hippocampus. In this way the representations are spatially tagged, but also have connections with, for example, temporal clocking systems. Also worthy of further investigation are the conditions when animals do not follow the cognitions one might have expected them to have acquired, but stick stubbonly to seemingly maladaptive habits (e.g., Kendler 1947).

ACKNOWLEDGMENT

I am most grateful to Thom Baguley (Open University), Kent Berridge (Michigan), Anthony Dickinson (Cambridge), George Kiss (Open University) and Sheila Tyler (Open University) for their helpful comments on an earlier draft of the chapter.

REFERENCES

Adams, C. D. (1982). Variations in the sensitivity of instrumental responding to reinforcer devaluation. *The Quarterly Journal of Experimental Psychology*, 34B, 77–98.

Adams, C. D., and Dickinson, A. (1981). Instrumental responding following reinforcer devaluation. *The Quarterly Journal of Experimental Psychology*, 33B, 109–121.

Berridge, K. C., and Schulkin, J. (1989). Palatability shift of a salt-associated incentive during sodium depletion. *The Quarterly Journal of Experimental Psychology*, 41B, 121–138.

Bever, T. G. (1984). The road from behaviourism to rationalism. In *Animal Cognition* (eds. H. L. Roitblat, T. G. Bever, and H. S. Terrace). Hillsdale, N.J.: Lawrence Erlbaum. Pp. 61–75.

Bindra, D. (1978). How adaptive behaviour is produced: A perceptual-motivational alternative to response-reinforcement. *The Behavioural and Brain Sciences*, 1, 41–91.

Bolles, R. C. (1972). Reinforcement, expectancy and learning. *Psychological Review*, 79, 394–409.

Bolles, R. C. (1991). *The Hedonics of Taste*. Hillsdale, N.J.: Lawrence Erlbaum.

Branch, M. N. (1982). Misrepresenting behaviourism. *The Behavioural and Brain Sciences*, 5, 372–373.

Brooks, R. A. (1991). Challenges for complete creature architectures. In *From Animals to Animats* (eds. J-A. Meyer and S. W. Wilson). Cambridge, Mass.: The MIT Press. Pp. 434–443.

Cairns, J., Overbaugh, J., and Miller, S. (1988). The origin of mutants. *Nature*, 335, 142–145.

Crespi, L. P. (1942). Quantitative variation of incentive and performance in the white rat. *The American Journal of Psychology*, 55, 467–517.

Dennett, D. C. (1989). Comments. In *Goals, No-Goals and Own Goals* (eds. A. Montefiore and D. Noble). London: Unwin Hyman. Pp. 229–237.

Deutsch, J. A. (1960). *The Structural Basis of Behavior*. Chicago: University of Chicago Press.

Dickinson, A. (1980). *Contemporary Animal Learning Theory*. Cambridge: Cambridge University Press.

Dickinson, A. (1985). Actions and habits: The development of behavioural autonomy. *Philosophical Transactions of the Royal Society, London*, B 308, 67–78.

Dickinson, A. (1989). Expectancy theory in animal conditioning. In *Contemporary Learning Theories: Pavlovian Conditioning and the Status of Traditional Learning Theory*. Hillsdale, N.J.: Lawrence Erlbaum. Pp. 279–308.

Dickinson, A., and Balleine, B. (1993). Actions and responses: The dual psychology of behaviour. In *Problems in the Philosophy and Psychology of Spatial Representations* (eds. N. Eilan, R. A. McCarthy, and M. W. Brewer). Oxford: Blackwell.

Dickinson, A., and Dawson, G. R. (1988). Motivational control of instrumental performance: The role of prior experience of the reinforcer. *The Quarterly Journal of Experimental Psychology*, 40B, 113–134.

Dickinson, A., and Dearing, M. F. (1979). Appetitive-aversive interactions and inhibitory processes. In *Mechanisms of Learning and Motivation* (eds. A. Dickinson and R. A. Boakes). Hillsdale, N.J.: Lawrence Erlbaum. Pp. 203–231.

Domjan, M., Lyons, R., North, N. C., and Bruell J. (1986). Sexual Pavlovian conditioned approach to behaviour in male Japanese quail *(Coturnix coturnix japonica)*. *Journal of Comparative Psychology*, 100, 413–421.

Eichenbaum, H., Otto, T., and Cohen, N. J. (1992). The hippocampus: What does it do? *Behavioural and Neural Biology*, 57, 2–36.

Gallistel, C. R. (1978). The irrelevance of past pleasure. *The Behavioural and Brain Sciences*, 1, 59–60.

Gallistel, C. R. (1980). *The Organization of Action: A New Synthesis*. Hillsdale, N.J.: Lawrence Erlbaum.

Gallistel, C. R. (1985). Motivation, intention, and goal directed behaviour from a cognitive-neuroethological perspective. In *Goal Directed Behaviour: The Concept of Action in Psychology* (eds. M. Frese and J. Sabini). Hillsdale, N.J.: Lawrence Erlbaum. Pp. 48–65.

Gallistel, C. R. (1989). Animal cognition: The representation of space, time and number. *Annual Review of Psychology*, 40, 155–189.

Gallistel, C. R. (1990). *The Organization of Learning.* Cambridge, Mass.: The MIT Press.

Gray, J. A. (1987). *The Psychology of Fear and Stress.* Cambridge: Cambridge University Press.

Heyes, C., and Dickinson, A. (1990). The intentionality of animal action. *Mind and Language*, 5, 87–104.

Hirsh, R. (1974). The hippocampus and contextual retrieval of information from memory: A theory. *Behavioural Biology*, 12, 421–444.

Holland, P. C., and Straub, J. J. (1979). Differential effects of two ways of devaluing the unconditioned stimulus after Pavlovian appetitive conditioning. *Journal of Experimental Psychology: Animal Behaviour Processes*, 5, 65–68.

Hull, C. L. (1943). *Principles of Behaviour.* New York: Appleton-Century Crofts.

Jenkins, H. M. (1978). Signal learning and response learning. *The Behavioural and Brain Sciences*, 1, 64.

Kamil, A. C. (1978). Systematic foraging by a nectar-feeding bird, the Amakihi *(Loxops virens). Journal of Comparative and Physiological Psychology*, 92, 388–396.

Kendler, H. H. (1947). An investigation of latent learning in a T-maze. *Journal of Comparative and Physiological Psychology*, 40, 265–270.

Kiss, G. R. (1992). Variable coupling of agents to their environment: Combining situated and symbolic automata. In *Decentralised A.I. 3* (eds. E. Werner and Y. Demazeau). Amsterdam: Elsevier.

Lockery, S. (1989). Representation, functionalism and simple living systems. In *Goals, No-Goals and Own Goals* (eds. A. Montefiore and D. Noble). London: Unwin Hyman. Pp. 117–158.

Lorenz, K. (1950). The comparative method in studying innate behaviour patterns. *Symposium of the Society for Experimental Biology*, 4, 221–268.

McFarland, D. J. (1983). Intentions as goals. *The Behavioural and Brain Sciences*, 6, 369–370.

McFarland, D. J. (1985). *Animal Behaviour.* London: Pitman.

McFarland, D. J. (1989a). *Problems of Animal Behaviour.* Harlow, Britain: Longman Scientific and Technical.

McFarland, D. J. (1989b). Goals, no-goals and own goals. In *Goals, No-Goals and Own Goals* (eds. A. Montefiore and D. Noble). London: Unwin Hyman. Pp. 39–57.

McFarland, D. J. (1989c). The teleological imperative. In *Goals, No-Goals and Own Goals* (eds. A. Montefiore and D. Noble). London: Unwin Hyman. Pp. 211–228.

McFarland, D. J., and Sibly, R. M. (1975). The behavioural final common path. *Philosophical Transactions of the Royal Society of London* B 270, 265–293.

Mishkin, M., and Petri, H. L. (1984). Memories and habits: Some implications for the analysis of learning and retention. In *Neuropsychology of Memory* (eds. L. R. Squire and N. Butters). New York: The Guildford Press. Pp. 287–296.

Mitchell, J. B., and Stewart, J. (1990). Facilitation of sexual behaviours in the male rat in the presence of stimuli previously paired with systemic injections of morphine. *Pharmacology, Biochemistry and Behavior*, 35, 367–372.

O'Keefe, J. (1989). Computations the hippocampus might perform. In *Neural Connections, Mental Computation* (eds. L. Nadel, L. A. Cooper, P. Culicover, and R. M. Harnish). Cambridge: The MIT Press. Pp. 225–284.

O'Keefe, J., and Nadel, L. (1978). *The Hippocampus as a Cognitive Map.* Oxford: The Clarendon Press.

Packard, M. G., Hirsh, R., and White, N. M. (1989). Differential effects of fornix and caudate nucleus lesions on two radial maze tasks: Evidence for multiple memory systems. *The Journal of Neuroscience,* 9, 1465–1472.

Pfaff, D. W. (1980). *Estrogens and Brain Function.* Heidelberg: Springer-Verlag.

Rescorla, R. A. (1987). A Pavlovian analysis of goal-directed behaviour. *American Psychologist,* 42, 119–129.

Restle, F. (1957). Discrimination of cues in mazes: A resolution of the "place-vs.-response" question. *The Psychological Review,* 64, 217–228.

Riley, D. A., Brown, M. F., and Yoerg, S. I. (1986). Understanding animal cognition. In *Approaches to Cognition: Contrasts and Controversies* (eds. T. J. Knapp and L. C. Robertson). Hillsdale, N.J.: Lawrence Erlbaum. Pp. 111–136.

Roitblat, H. L. (1982). The meaning of representation in animal memory. *The Behavioural and Brain Sciences,* 5, 353–406.

Roitblat, H. L. (1988). A cognitive action theory of learning. In *Systems with Learning and Memory Abilities* (eds. J. Delacour and J. C. S. Levy), Amsterdam: Elsevier Science Publishers. Pp. 13–26.

Roitblat, H. L. (1991). Cognitive action theory as a control architecture. In *From Animals to Animats* (eds. J-A. Meyer and S. W. Wilson). Cambridge: The MIT Press. Pp. 444–450.

Roitblat, H. L., Bever, T. G., and Terrace, H. S. (1984). *Animal Cognition.* Hillsdale, N.J.: Lawrence Erlbaum.

Skinner, B. F. (1986). Why I am not a cognitive psychologist. In *Approaches to Cognition: Contrasts and Controversies* (eds. T. J. Knapp and L. C. Robertson). Hillsdale, N.J.: Lawrence Erlbaum. Pp. 79–90.

Stewart, J., de Wit, H., and Eikelboom, R. (1984). Role of unconditioned and conditioned drug effects in the self-administration of opiates and stimulants. *Psychological Review,* 91, 251–268.

Terrace, H. S. (1984). Animal Cognition. In *Animal Cognition* (eds. H. L. Roitblat, T. G. Bever, and H. S. Terrace). Hillsdale, N.J.: Lawrence Erlbaum. Pp. 7–28.

Toates, F. (1975). *Control Theory in Biology and Experimental Psychology.* London: Hutchinson Educational Ltd.

Toates, F. (1980). *Animal Behaviour: A Systems Approach.* Chichester, Britain: Wiley.

Toates, F. (1986). *Motivational Systems.* Cambridge: Cambridge University Press.

Tolman, E. C. (1932). *Purposive Behaviour in Animals and Men.* New York: The Century Co.

Tolman, E. C., Ritchie, B. F., and Kalish, D. (1946). Studies in spatial learning, II: Place learning versus response learning. *Journal of Experimental Psychology,* 36, 221–229.

Weingarten, H. P. (1984). Meal initiation controlled by learned cues: Basic behavioural properties. *Appetite,* 5, 147–158.

White, N. M. (1989). Reward or reinforcement: What's the difference? *Neuroscience and Biobehavioural Reviews,* 13, 181–186.

Wiepkema, P. R. (1987). Behavioural aspects of stress. In *Biology of Stress in Farm Animals: An Integrative Approach* (eds. P. R. Wiepkema and P. W. M. van Adrichem). Dordrecht: Martinus Nijhoff. Pp. 113–133.

Wiepkema, P. R. (1990). Stress: Ethological implications. In *Psychobiology of Stress* (eds. S. Puglisi-Allegra and A. Oliverio). Dordrecht: Kluwer Academic Publishers. Pp. 1–13.

Young, P. T. (1961). *Motivation and Emotion*. New York: Wiley.

Zamble, E., Mitchell, J. B., and Findlay, H. (1986). Pavlovian conditioning of sexual arousal: Parametric and background manipulations. *Journal of Experimental Psychology: Animal Behaviour Processes*, 12, 403–411.

19 Cognition and Emotion in Animals and Machines

J. R. P. Halperin

The goal of this chapter is to explore a complex topic: the integration of cognition and emotion. These two phenomena appear quite distinct, and indeed our culture regards intellect and emotion as polar opposites. Nevertheless, within scientific psychology cognition and emotion have long been recognized as intimately linked. Despite this perceived linkage, scientists have made relatively little progress in understanding the connections. Leading cognitive scientists Newell, Rosenbloom, and Laird say that "the mammalian system is clearly constructed as an emotional system," yet "despite recent stirrings and a long history within psychology (Frijda 1986), no satisfactory integration yet exists of these phenomena into cognitive science" (Newell, Rosenbloom, and Laird 1989, p. 93).

Forging a machine-implementable, integrated understanding of human cognition and emotion is an impossible aim today. This chapter will illustrate how a comparative approach that considers relevant evidence from other animals and machines can be productive as scientists begin to tackle such difficult problems. Comparative techniques have long been a major tool in science. For example, comparative physiologists of circulation study mechanisms in various animals that accomplish the goal of transporting fluids to all parts of the organisms. Analogously, we would like to consider all designs in nature that accomplish the same functions as cognition and emotion. We should identify the functions and try to deduce the mechanisms that accomplish them. The difficulty is that we do not yet fully understand the functions served by cognitive or emotional phenomena. In fact, emotional behavior at first glance appears nonfunctional; breaking into tears seems on the surface a useless behavior (Fridja 1986). Applying the comparative method will require us to simultaneously develop our understandings of the functions and the mechanisms of emotion and cognition.

Doing this requires what may feel like a leap of faith; we hope that these complex phenomena accomplish analyzable functions using comprehensible mechanisms. We make the assumption that the functions and mechanisms will not be unrelated in different animals. Some of the functions will probably be related even in different types of autonomous creatures, animals and autonomous robots. Drawing on examples from a range of animals,[1] we will usually quickly develop hypotheses about what the functions of cognitive and emotional behaviors might be. We search through literature not studied while constructing the hypothesis (or experiment), looking for new evidence to bolster or weaken our hypotheses. Once we have hypotheses about function that appear to be reliably general, we look for mechanisms and then search the literature further (or experiment) to find out whether we need to adjust our developing understanding. This is a slow but time-tested methodology.

The full range of cognitive and emotional phenomena even in animals is still too broad an area to explore as scientists begin this process; we must focus our efforts more sharply by narrowing the range of phenomena studied. Here we will try to model cognitive capabilities observed in a large range of animals, which excludes our studying uniquely human phenomena like speech.[2] The emotional phenomena on which we will concentrate are primitive but undeniably "emotional," fear and aggressiveness.

Of course, in modeling only some primitive, general phenomena of emotion and cognition in animals and robots we explicitly put to one side some crucial but purely human questions, such as how verbal cognition integrates with emotion. We leave out complex emotions such as jealousy and grief. More important, we leave the central issue of the subjective experience of both the emotional state and the cognitive state to cognitive neuroscientists. Nevertheless, our undertaking may be relevant to understanding people. The hope for human relevance comes from the neurobiological homologies between vertebrate animals and humans, which use very similar neural machinery for organizing emotional reactions and nonverbal cognition.[3] The connectionist implementation model we outline is based on hypotheses from animal neurobiology. The neural machinery generating the basic cognitive and emotional phenomena that we share with animals must underlie and interact with whatever mechanisms allow humans to experience awareness of emotions and cognition. Thus, studying the neurobiological underpinnings of primitive emotions and cognition may be a step along the shortest path to understanding conscious experience.

We begin by discussing why scientists have seen such fundamental connections between cognition and emotion in humans before describing what we mean by emotional phenomena in animals. We then outline a neurobiologically based, robot-implementable connectionist model for animal-level emotional behavior. We go on to discuss cognitive phenomena demonstrated by animals, and then explore how well the same connectionist model can generate the most basic cognitive phenomena. A discussion of the functionalities a robot would gain from having integrated cognitive and emotional phenomena will illustrate both the technological potential and concept-organizing power gained through having explicit, comparatively based, machine-implementable models of behavior.

THE LINKS BETWEEN COGNITION AND EMOTION IN HUMANS

We will then discuss why many scientists studying human psychology see such a need for an integrated model of emotion and cognition. The typical layman, used to thinking of emotion and reason as opposites, would probably be surprised to discover that in scientific psychology most researchers have stressed that a person's cognitive assessment of a situation determines his or her emotional reaction to it. The notion that reason and emotion are natural antagonists has been compellingly disputed (e.g., de Sousa 1987).

Indeed, a major theory holds that the experience of emotion does not largely depend on biologically primitive factors such as the type of physiological response, but on a person's cognitive assessment of the current situation. For example, an injection of adrenalin will induce emotional reactions in people, but exactly which emotion is experienced depends on their cognitive expectation about what emotion they will feel (Schacter and Singer 1962; Mandler 1975). This influential finding is frequently quoted by researchers who view emotions as basically cognitive states (e.g., Oatley and Johnson-Laird 1987). While some researchers have gone so far as to suggest that emotion can be experienced without bodily reactions (for discussions see Strongman 1978; Mandler 1990; Ortony, Clore, and Collins 1988), this is an extreme position, and the more usual view is that emotion is linked rather rigidly to arousal, but that exactly which emotion is felt is largely determined by cognition.

Given this, one might wonder whether emotion is a very real, independent category. Emotional experience was so powerfully determined by cognitive expectations in the experiments just alluded to that it is tempting to conclude that particular emotions are little more than the experiential flavor produced by cognitive expectations, given that there is suitable physiological arousal. However, other evidence suggests that differentiated emotions are not necessarily "caused" by cognition, at least not by conscious cognition. The causal relationship can be reversed.

An anecdote from Gazzaniga illustrates this (Gazzaniga 1988, pp. 13–14). He had a "split-brain" patient, a woman whose cortical hemispheres had no direct connections (though both sides of the brain communicated freely with lower brain centers). For this patient speech was on one side of the brain only, so if Gazzaniga showed a movie only to the eye connected to the nonverbal side, the patient's verbal reports of what she had seen were "guesses." One day Gazzaniga showed the nonverbal side of the brain a horrifying movie flash of one person throwing another into a fire. Asked what she saw, the woman said her guess was "a white flash. Maybe some trees, red trees like in the fall. I don't know why, but I feel kind of scared. I feel jumpy. I don't like this room, or maybe it's you." The patient then turned to a young doctor nearby and quietly told him, "I know I like Dr. Gazzaniga, but right now I'm scared of him for some reason." Thus, even the strong cognitive expectation of Gazzaniga's friendliness was not sufficient to make the patient reinterpret her fear.[4] Instead, the fear generated a string of cognitive rationalizations, until finally it was referred to the biggest, most dominant individual in the room despite the cognitive expectation of his friendliness.

Zajonc (1980) also found evidence suggesting that emotional experience involves noncognitive causes. He found that subliminal priming with "happy face" icons (4-millisecond exposures that were not consciously "seen") primed people to guess that neutral hand-drawn symbols shown to them a few minutes later meant something nice. Subliminal "scowling face" icons primed negative reactions to the symbols. Presenting the happy or scowling face icons long enough for the subject to be consciously aware of them largely wiped out their emotional priming effect. Zajonc suggested that emotional priming on fast noncognitive emotion-triggering pathways occurred, but could be overwhelmed by cognitive processing that induced a more sophisticated assessment.

While the debate continues, the evidence seems to suggest that human emotional experiences are affected by both very highly processed cognitive information and also by simpler information processed on much faster neural pathways.[5] This is not biologically implausible (LeDoux 1987). It has long been known that the hypothalamus has the key role in potentiating coordinated emotional responses. A nearby brain structure, the amygdala, passes sensory information to the hypothalamus. The amygdala integrates two quite different types of information about the animal's situation; relatively unprocessed sensory input (mainly from thalamic sensory nuclei on single-synapse pathways) and very highly processed information (from prefrontal, olfactory, and temporal cortex and the hippocampus). Thus, the brain pathways that are known to be critically important in emotion are suitable for integrating information from the brain's highest-order associative areas with virtually unprocessed sensory information arriving on fast pathways (LeDoux 1987). Furthermore, neurons in the amygdala are modifiable by learning, so the memory requirement of cognitive assessment is present. Also, the amygdala-hippocampal complex is known for its involvement in accessing complex memories. In sum, as is so often the case in the study of behavior, Occam's razor must be used with care. The emotional experience apparently integrates high-level cognitive assessments with more reflexive components. This suggests that, as ambitious as it may seem to explore both emotion and cognition at the same time, we *must* aim for an integrated understanding.

EMOTION IN ANIMALS: THE ANALOGY WITH HUMANS

To discuss emotion in animals, it may seem essential to first clarify the use of the words that describe emotion in the human context. However, we will minimize definitional discussion by arbitrarily using fright and

Halperin

anger as the experienced emotions and fear and aggressiveness as descriptors of emotional states that do not imply experiential awareness. We are going to consider only fear and aggressiveness.

It is traditional in the animal literature to employ the concept of emotion in animals by analogy with humans. In any case, we always use the word "emotion" by analogy, even when we ascribe emotions to ourselves and other people. In childhood we learn to use these words on the basis of similarities in the publicly observable patterns of reaction (including verbal reaction), and we just assume that, since most people find that they can use the culture's "emotion words" to describe their own subjective experiences and behavioral inclinations, subjective experiences are probably very similar in different people. In animals, to give an example of the standard analogical use of the word "emotion," a powerful learned avoidance response is called the "conditioned emotional response," and it is often described as fear. This is because the behaviors and physiological reactions shown have such an obvious analogy to those shown by frightened humans. Rats crouch and freeze, squeak, and flee in dangerous situations, as humans hunch over and freeze, scream, and flee. Rats show much the same patterns of autonomic arousal as do frightened humans. The entry on emotion in the American Physiological Society's *Handbook of Physiology* assumes the analogy (LeDoux 1987). More complicated analogies have been suggested—for example, between human love relationships and tree shrew pair bonds, which are only sometimes harmonious, and when harmonious have beneficial effects on the partners (von Holst 1989). We shall use this "identification by analogy" approach, but with certain restrictions.

We have to draw the line on analogy somewhere. A few authors happily use the word "emotion" whenever there is behavior indicating strong attraction or repulsion (see the delightful book *Vehicles*, Braitenberg 1987). Seeing films of Braitenberg-style robot trucks scooting about following lights and consistently avoiding dark corners, one has the strong feeling that they like the light and dislike shadows, even if one understands that the behavior is controlled by a trivially simple mechanism involving two sensors.[6] While legitimate, this particular broad analogy assumes that the function of emotion is organizing attraction and repulsion. To leave ourselves open to seeing other broad functions, we actually require a tighter analogy.

First, we restrict our consideration to vertebrates. This allows us to follow an ethological tradition and use "emotional state" only when it can be deduced that there is a state internal to the animal that allows one to parsimoniously describe and predict its behavior. Most ethologists would not use the word "fear" to describe a moth's avoiding a bat. The moth uses only two escape reactions that are straightforwardly triggered at two different intensities of bat ultrasonic cries (Roeder 1963, 1965). It performs a beautifully adaptive but rather reflex-like set of responses. On the other hand, vertebrates have fear behavior that is sufficiently "complex yet organized" that describing it succinctly seems to require the hypothesis of an internal "state of fear." So we shall not discuss "fear" in insects such as moths or in simple reactive machines such as Braitenberg's vehicles, but shall instead focus on our closer animal relatives.

The restriction to vertebrate fear and aggressive behavior has a special advantage. As we mentioned, neurobiologists have discovered brain areas, the amygdala and hypothalamus, that organize fear and aggression, and they are similar in humans and other vertebrates (LeDoux 1987; von Holst 1973; Smith and DeVito 1984; Damasio 1994), even in fish (de Bruin 1980; Shapiro et al. 1974). Thus, not only are the overtly observable patterns of behavior analogous, but the underlying implementation structures are largely homologous. This opens the way for robots using an animal-style architecture for organizing emotional responses and the same kinds of information-processing routes for internally representing information about the stimuli around them when deciding upon appropriate emotional responses. There is growing evidence that such fine-scale copying from nature is useful, as will be discussed in the section on animal cognition.

There have been two main tracks in investigations of animal emotion: The first is the study of brief behaviors performed in emotional contexts[7] (which we will either call discrete behaviors following Fridja (1986) or, more ethologically, fixed action patterns). The second main track is the study of emotional states and their accompanying physiological changes. The kinds of phenomena investigated along both these tracks are seen in the aggressive behavior of fighting fish, which we shall use as our main source of animal examples. We will follow both tracks in some detail before beginning to describe implementations of vertebrate-like emotional phenomena in machines.

Fixed Action Patterns and Emotion

The discrete behaviors performed by animals in emotional contexts have been described extensively. By discrete behaviors we mean what ethologists would call "fixed action patterns." It was one of the most powerful insights of classical ethology that the stream of activity performed by animals contains discrete fixed action patterns that are recognizable, repeated patterns within what appears to the totally unpracticed eye to be a continuous flow of action.[8] We qualify with the word "discrete" because "fixed action pattern" was occasionally used to describe a larger grouping of behaviors, all subserving a motivation such as hunger.

We shall first discuss examples from human behavior because readers will have some familiarity with them. Griffiths (1990) has studied discrete behavior in humans. He argues for the existence in humans of discrete behavior modules, each called up by an "affect program" that generates a coordinated, rapidly produced behavior. The prototypical module is a human facial expression such as those involved in crying, surprise, disgust, and fear. These are sufficiently fixed to be nearly universally recognizable, even across distinct cultures (Ekman and Friesen 1975; Ekman 1984). Two simple if unscientific facts illustrate the reality of a "behavior module" in humans; that languages have the word "grin" and that readers will immediately picture this fixed action pattern when they hear the word. The fact that a moment's reflection will elicit questions about variants of grins illustrates why some ethologists have tried to replace the phrase "fixed action pattern" with "modal action pattern" (Barlow 1977). Photographs of children who are deaf and blind showing absolutely species-typical emotional facial expressions with appropriate body gestures have demonstrated that neither facial expression nor the corresponding "body language" is learned by observation (Eibl-Eibesfeldt 1974). The investigation of these discrete behaviors might be described as the study of the "instinctive reflex" aspects of emotion.[9]

Many animal fixed action patterns observed by the ethologists who study fear and aggression can be thought of as postural analogs of these facial affect programs. The homology between human facial expressions and those of primates has been recognized since Darwin's famous treatise on the subject. Similarities among behavior programs between less closely related vertebrates may exist because similar evolutionary selective pressures have acted on animal and human emotional expression. Griffiths argues that the need for rapid production of well-coordinated, complex responses has been the pressure for the evolution of emotional behavior modules in humans (Griffiths 1990). The need for functional efficiency, in this case a communicative function, is best served by a stereotyped signal, rapidly produced. Similarly, this argument about selective pressures could obviously be applied to the fixed action patterns used in fleeing or fighting, and it suggests that robots could usefully show analogs of fixed action patterns.

The study of fixed action patterns in animals and humans has uncovered general properties that will have to be modeled. Some of these properties have an instinctive, reflexive character, but others indicate considerable independence from stimulus control. The complex of properties fits well with the human experience of sometimes performing primitive, involuntary actions in emotional situations, actions that yet seem to have more independent motivation than do simple reflexes.

The aggressive behavior of Siamese fighting fish[10] will be our exemplar animal "emotional" behavior, and here there is a clear analogy to behaviors that in people have a strong emotional component.[11] When Siamese fighting fish begin to interact aggressively, they first perform various "threat" actions. A fighting fish's major threat postures are "facing" display (swinging to face a rival while raising the gill covers and lowering the branchiostegal membrane to form a large dark halo below the head) the "broadside" display (swinging broadside to a rival, slightly lowering the gills but spreading the fins) (Simpson 1968). Later the fish may "tail-beat," pushing water toward the opponent. Then come contact behaviors such as mouth-fighting (mutual grab and shake) and bites directed at the opponent's exaggeratedly large fins.[12] Ethologists think that the main function of these behaviors is to communicate. For example, the intensity of a threat display communicates a fish's strength and motivation to opponents competing for space, food, or mates.[13]

The first important property of these fixed action patterns is one that they share with reflexes; they are discrete. Second, however, what is discrete about them is not always an action per se, despite the name fixed "action" pattern.[14] Aggressive displays are often identified by the maintenance of a stereotypical orientation as much as by a stereotypical body posture. In a Siamese fighting fish's threat display the orientations to the opponent are in fact the defining components: "facing" and "broadside." On reflection, this is not surprising, because social behaviors such as threat or retreat must be oriented in a particular way to be effective. The significance of this observation lies in the difficulty of specifying orientations as sequences of muscle contractions. Fixed action patterns are usually succinctly describable by saying that they achieve a perception: for example, the sensory input associated with being broadside. (The mechanism for controlling the perception may be negative feedback, or perhaps iterated feed forward control. Modeling how a fixed action pattern actually accomplishes the production of adaptive behavior is beyond the scope of this chapter.)

The discreteness of behavior is sometimes difficult to convince novice observers of, because fixed action patterns have another aspect, regrettably called in English the "orienting" component. For illustration, consider the "facing" display. It involves an orientation, facing the opponent, but the fish must make "orienting" movements to achieve and maintain the posture despite disturbances such as water currents. It was a fundamental insight of classical ethology that behaviors are a "natural kind" despite their being overlaid by these orienting movements.[15] Compromise postures are another complication that can make the edges of the discrete categories seem fuzzy. An example from the aggression of fighting fish is difficult to find, but an example from another fish will illustrate. A courting three-lined pencilfish[16] orients itself broadside to the female, but it will also perform broadside threat display if a rival approaches it. The result is that it will orient itself between the rival and the female, broadside to each simultaneously. The exact posture is a compromise controlled by both the fixed action patterns simultaneously, but this does not negate at all the distinctiveness of the two fixed action patterns.

Third, fixed action patterns are less stimulus-bound than reflexes in the sense that their timing is not so closely determined by the timing of the stimulus. For example, threat postures are persistent. If a displaying fish suddenly has no opponent (after an experimenter has suddenly removed it), the fish's display will continue to be performed to midwater for some time, a phenomenon called "after-discharge." When fixed action patterns are being performed, they are difficult to interrupt, but only initially. A fighting fish's threat posture persists strongly for a few seconds, then becomes more easily interruptible; a temporal limitation on persistence sets in. Usually the fish's opponent counterthreatens and a new behavior is triggered, which can interrupt the first threat behavior before it would have spontaneously ended. The result is that these threat displays usually show a typical, rather brief, duration (as is also the case for the kind of facial expressions that Griffiths classifies as "affect modules"). This introduces a fourth property: Fixed action patterns can interrupt each other, and in the normal course of events they do so. A Siamese fighting fish that is eating will usually stop eating and display if a rival appears. The property of temporal self-limitation is still apparent in that the aggressive display will end eventually even if nothing distracts the fish into another behavior. In sum, the evidence is that the fixed action patterns in emotional contexts are temporally persistent, but temporally limited, and are able to interrupt each other.

Fifth, discrete fixed action patterns can be released by "sign stimuli," one of the more reflex-like properties. Sign stimuli are like the unconditional stimuli of psychology, but ethologists studied sign stimuli themselves rather than focusing on their role in learning as psychologists did. An example of the nature of sign stimuli from birds may be more compelling than one from fish, since birds are more sophisticated and their reliance on sign stimuli is more striking (McFarland 1985). Male English robins will attack a little clump of red feathers placed near their nest (Lack 1943). In the normal, ethologist-free situation they would encounter such a patch of red feathers on the breast of another male robin, a potential rival. The clump of red feathers rather reflexively releases aggression, even though nobody doubts that robins are capable of distinguishing a clump of feathers from a real bird. They are sophisticated visual creatures and can perform subtle visual discrimination tasks. We must not exaggerate the reflex-like nature of the fixed action patterns' releasing aspect. The clump of feathers releases a whole set of fixed action patterns, including songs and body postures, each of which is complex compared to a kneejerk or an eyeblink. Also, the releaser works only when the bird is near its territory at the appropriate time of year. Still, it is impressive that an organism as complex as a bird responds in this way to such a simple sign stimulus.[17]

The last fixed action pattern property we shall discuss is modifiability by "learning," which is as involved in their performance as is genetic predisposition, even though they are prototypical instinctive behaviors. In fact, ethologists no longer see specific behaviors as being either genetically fixed or else learned (in the broad "self-calibration" sense of learning). Only a template of the form of the fixed action pattern and the sign

Cognition and Emotion in Animals and Machines

stimuli that release it in naive animals are seen as created by evolutionary processes. Templates for behaviors and sign stimuli develop largely because of genetically provided information, and then the individual's behavior develops from these templates by self-calibration. What we are calling self-calibration includes processes of perceptual development and environmentally influenced maturation as well as processes traditionally called learning. Many fixed action patterns have a form, the action, which is not very modifiable by individual experience, but for others, especially manipulative behaviors, the form is modified by experience. For all fixed action patterns the releasing situations tend to be refined by experience. Fighting fish learn quickly in which stimulus situations to perform their threat displays as a result of the experience of performing the displays in various situations. Soon different opponents that still all carry the same sign stimuli elicit quite different responses; the fish will flee from one, attack another, and ignore a third.

The flexibility to self-calibrate must be implemented along with the mix of features described above if a machine is going to be said to have fixed action patterns like those seen in animals in emotional contexts. This self-calibration is, in the broad sense, learning, and it is this aspect of the implementation of "emotion" that will link it to our model of cognition. But, as we discuss below, the evidence suggests that complex cognitive processes are more linked to emotional state than to individual fixed action patterns. Therefore, we now move on to describe the similarities between the properties of discrete fixed action patterns and those of emotional states.

Emotional States

Having described the discrete, briefly persistent fixed action patterns shown in emotional contexts, we now move to our "second track," the emotional states. Many ethologists have studied the activation of emotional states, notably Scherer (1985).[18]

It is easiest to visualize the category "emotional state" in animals through the obvious analog in humans. Consider the amount of time that heart rate and general arousal may take to return to normal after an emotion-charged interaction. This longer persistence of emotional states is one of their defining qualities. The fighting behavior of fish is also accompanied by physiological arousal, and this arousal also persists after the rival disappears. There is a relatively long after-discharge period in which an aggressively aroused fish will go on performing its threat displays even if there are no more aggression-eliciting stimuli present. As with elevated heart rate and arousal in humans, so the after-discharge display of a Siamese fighting fish gradually fades over a period of many seconds to a few minutes. Also, a fish's color will darken during the fight, and this darker color is usually retained for a long period after the fight. There is some similarity in the other temporal properties of fixed action patterns, although again with the time scale stretched out. There is evidence of temporal limitation on the duration of emotional arousal, at least intense arousal, and also evidence that emotional states slightly compete with each other, although neither of these qualities is as extreme as in the case of fixed action patterns.

As we have seen, physiological responses are rather directly triggered by emotional states; indeed, their presence after the eliciting stimulus is gone is part of the evidence of the persistence of emotional states. Signs of physiological arousal such as increased heart rate and blood pressure are rather rapidly triggered.[19] On the other hand, emotional states do not inevitably trigger discrete fixed action patterns, and this internalized quality is another defining property. There is a low threshold for performing specific fixed action patterns long after overt, spontaneous display has faded, the lowered threshold presumably reflecting the persistence of the state even when overt aggressive behaviors have stopped being expressed. However, the arousal of the emotional state leaves the decision about exactly which behavior to perform open, to be influenced by the moment-to-moment stimulus situation.

Each emotional state biases the animal toward performing a certain group of fixed action patterns, the subset of potentiated behaviors defining the particular emotion. In animals the adaptive appropriateness of the potentiated subset is presumably largely determined by evolution, and in robots the appropriateness of the potentiated behaviors would also have to be assured by design. This predetermination of the set of potentiated fixed action patterns in one of the more reflexive, primitive aspects of emotional states. Another is the fact that sometimes they can be triggered by simple sign stimuli such as the "happy face" icon, or even by yet simpler sensory inputs such as pain.

Several basic emotions can be potentiated simultaneously—for example, aggression plus fear or fear plus sexual arousal. Classical ethology often analyzed complex postures in terms of the simultaneous arousal of such states (Tinbergen 1950, 1951), and more recent behavioral analyses of the hysteresis shown during threat displays support this assumption.[20] Allowing mixed states is arguably essential in an animal or robot with emotional states living in a complex, uncertain world. Because many situations have both dangers and possibilities, the potentiation of two subsets of behavior at once will often be appropriate.

The close relationship between emotional state and approach and avoidance tendencies is also notable; recall that Braitenberg's little vehicles that seek or avoid light were described using emotion words. Psychologists often describe emotional states as involving positive or negative affect. Ethologists study stimulus situations that evoke both avoidance and approach tendencies simultaneously, and a situation in which fear and aggression are simultaneously aroused is sometimes referred to as an approach-avoidance conflict.

The last property of emotional states that we will try to implement is their special link to cognitive assessment. While sign stimuli can release either discrete fixed action patterns or emotional states, complex cognitive assessments of situations are more closely associated with emotional states than with specific fixed action patterns. Scherer especially emphasizes the role of cognitive assessment in determining the emotional state (e.g., Scherer and Oshinsky 1977). This is coherent with the neurobiological evidence of massive input to the amygdala and hypothalamus from the highest association cortices and the hippocampus, where the most sophisticated cognitive processing occurs. Thus, to properly model emotional state, it will be essential to have at least a basic model of the sophisticated cognitive processes with which they are associated.

The Functional Roles of Fixed Action Patterns and Emotional States

The two aspects of emotion that we have discussed, emotional state and discrete fixed action patterns, presumably serve complementary functions. An emotional state that is preparatory but not rigidly determining can act as a mode setter that reflects a tentative decision about which groups of behaviors are likely to be needed in the current situation. This gives the advantage of flexibility combined with a bias toward the most likely appropriate responses. Yet situations of emotional arousal are often situations in which rapid response may become essential—to react speedily to danger, to communicate as quickly and clearly as possible. Rapid triggering of physiological arousal by emotional states readies the body for action. Since the required actions may be quite complex, preprogrammed behavior packages are needed that can be called up as integrated, fully functional patterns. Their initial persistence helps ensure that a whole functional program will be carried out, but their relatively short duration allows rapid changes in behavior if the details of the stimulus situation change.

Emotional state and fixed action pattern thus seem to correspond respectively to a slow-acting background that potentiates groups of adaptively related responses and to fast-response modules. We have seen that cognitive information is more closely tied to emotional states than to individual fixed action patterns. It is arguable that linking complex cognitive assessment more closely to the emotional state than to individual fixed action patterns is adaptive. To see why, we shall use a very simple technique that is often useful for analyzing the rather subtle issues of adaptive value. Imagine an animal in which complex cognitive assessments elicit emotional states and another in which cognitive assessment affect each discrete behavior independently, and try to analyze the functional differences implied by their different designs.

Suppose that the one with cognition and state linked learns that "rival X" should evoke a state of fear. When it sees rival X, its state of fear is activated; because it potentiates all the individual fear behaviors, it can evoke whichever is appropriate to a given situation. This animal will freeze if fleeing is prevented, even though freezing has never before been performed to rival X. Of course an evolutionary design process will have had to build in the fact that both fleeing and freezing are appropriate to be potentiated by fear. This designed-in information gives the animal its advantage; without it there would be little meaning to a state of fear. A hypothetical animal for which cognitive assessment affected only the individual behaviors would have to learn a cognitive assessment of the likely consequences of each behavior individually. It could not integrate complex learned assessments with the evolutionary information about which behavioral substitutions might be appropriate.[21] While this argument may explain the adaptiveness of architectures that feed complex cognitive assessment into hierarchically higher states rather than hierarchically lower behavioral elements, there would be disadvantages for an animal with a simplistically hierarchical structure in making decisions about what behavior to perform. As McFarland argues, a higher-level (temporally persistent) state must potentiate, not make a yes-no behavioral choice, or the system will be inflexible and slow to respond to sudden changes in information (McFarland 1989; McFarland and Bösser 1993; Tyrrell 1993).

Readers with an ethological background will recognize that the picture that we have been drawing of emotion is very much the ethological picture of motivational systems with their underlying simultaneously activated internal states and potentiated sets of fixed action patterns. They have the same quality of having built-in information about how an animal can meet its biological needs integrated with learned expectations. The main distinction seems to be that the word "emotion" is used when the motivation is social or self-preservative. It is not clear why in humans the experiential flavor of the social motivations and self-preservation should be different from that evoked by other motivations, but it seems to be so. It may be relevant that the goals of social behavior, acquiring social status, and successfully reproducing have a complex relationship with the immediate goals of the fixed action patterns performed in achieving them. This complexity is also often present in the case of self-preservation behaviors, but is seldom seen in the simpler motivations such as hunger or thirst. Although the satisfaction of hunger can take on an emotional tinge, this description usually seems to be used when social interaction as well as physiological needs are involved.

To the extent that robots can usefully integrate cognitive processes with stabilizing states potentiating preselected sets of behavior modules that can be called up like subroutines, it will be useful to build robot motivations. Such organizational features to encourage rapid, appropriate responses will be desirable when robots become more autonomous and have to deal with complex situations in real time. To the extent that these states and behavior modules are relevant to functions that we see as analogous to social behavior or self-preservation, we shall probably describe their internal states as "robot emotions." Recently it has become more than science fiction dreaming to imagine robots with multiple social and self-preservative goals, although the engineering difficulties and expense of building reliable mobile robots to test our hypotheses should not be underestimated.

Implementing Fixed Action Patterns

We can implement basic emotional and cognitive phenomena using the "machine motivation" model.[22] This model is simultaneously a robot control system[23] and a working hypothesis about the neural principles underlying animal fixed action patterns. It has been tested ethologically through its predictions of new phenomena in the aggressive behavior of fighting fish. In this section we shall outline how the machine motivation system implements the properties of discrete fixed action patterns described above. A typical module is sketched in figure 19.1.

The most basic property of fixed action patterns is simply that they are discrete. This property is captured naturally because the system is inherently modular. One motivation module is assigned for each fixed action pattern. Each motivation module consists of a pool of releaser neurons (R) and a pool of behavior neurons (B), separate from the R and B pools of other modules (figure 19.1). Second, the motivation module's output, being just a pattern of activation within a neuron pool, could activate any suitable mechanism for achieving and orienting an effector response. Third, temporal persistence of fixed action patterns is implemented by the positive feedback loop between B and R neurons and temporal limitation by neural adaptation (a spontaneous increase in threshold occurring when neurons are active). Fourth, fixed action patterns can interrupt each other competitively by the inhibitory connections among B neurons. Fifth, the S-R connections naturally implement the sign stimuli that determine whether a fixed action pattern is released by a novel stimulus, because the number and initial strengths of S-R connections can be biased so that certain stimulus situations tend to activate certain modules.[24] Finally, the self-calibration process described earlier occurs at the S-R synapses, each of which can adjust strength if there are suitable patterns of activation in the connected S and R neurons.[25] The S-R connections, as they change weight, incorporate information about whether performing the fixed action pattern in this stimulus situation was successful. Modeling the kind of self-calibration that occurs in fixed action patterns

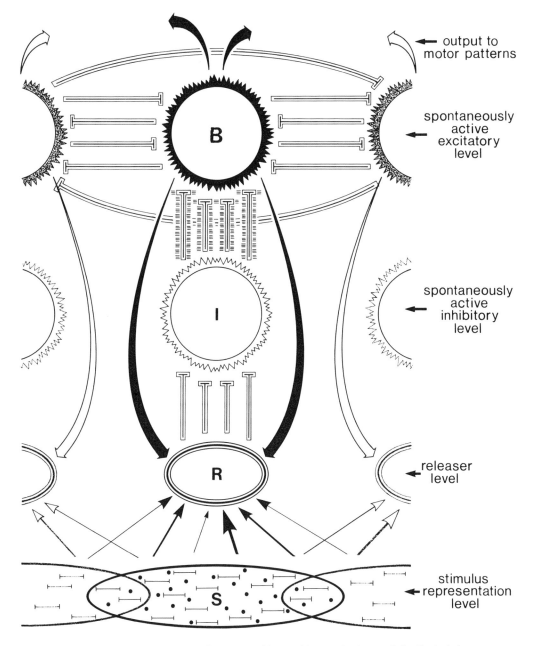

Figure 19.1 The type of wiring used for machine motivation modules. Each circle represents a pool of neurons. Arrows are excitatory one-way connections. Blunt-ended arrows are one-way inhibitory connections. The connections from S to R change strength according to the neuroconnector rules. There are local inhibitory relationships within the S pool, and there may be within the R and B pools. These could gate neighbors or inputs to neighbors. No lateral excitatory connections for the S neurons are indicated, but the text discusses them. This version releases behavior by inhibiting I units, which normally inhibit spontaneously active B units. This type of implementation difference does not affect how the system processes information, and so for our purposes is irrelevant.

thus requires modeling how individual synapses can use only local firing pattern information to determine whether a given social behavior was successful. The logic of how this can be done and the implementation details will be discussed in the section on learning.

Implementing Emotional States

The machine motivation model implements emotional states in much the same way that it implements fixed action patterns. This should not be surprising, as the entities that we are labeling emotional states were sometimes described by the early ethologists (Tinbergen 1951) as fixed action patterns, although today ethologists refer to them as motivations. It was hypothesized that both the simpler low-level fixed action patterns and the higher-level states had many commonalities. The machine motivation modules inherently generate many features that emotional states have in common with fixed action patterns: time-limited persistence of activation, competition among states, release by sign stimuli, and learning processes that use feedback about success to refine the assessment of the appropriate situations for showing the state. The parameters that one must alter in order to model emotional states as opposed to discrete fixed action patterns are either not specified or are explicitly settable parameters. For example, we can obtain the longer persistence of emotional states and discrete fixed action patterns by increasing the time constants for adaptation.

The modules handle the fact that emotional states elicit a complex set of reactions and tendencies, because the output signal from the B pool of a single state module can go to a variety of places. Motivation modules for states can trigger autonomic responses by direct activation. They can also potentiate approach, avoidance, and selected groups of fixed action patterns by arranging state modules in a separate layer that sends excitatory signals to the modules for fixed action patterns to approach and avoidance along with "physiological" responses. Factors downline from the state modules will affect whether excitatory signals from the state modules would actually activate a fixed action pattern (for example, competitive inhibition among fixed action patterns), so the state module will potentiate rather than command fixed action patterns.

Partial competition between state modules may be accomplished by setting the inhibition between B modules very low or by establishing local lateral inhibition within each small subregion. This local lateral inhibition is also assumed in the S pool, where it would implement attention (figure 19.1) by limiting the number of neurons active in a region.[26] To illustrate why this is useful, consider a small subregion with neurons active in response to various inputs. As the neurons in the subregion compete for activation, there is a local decision about what emotional state is assessed as most appropriate on the basis of the local input factors. The decision can be different in different subregions, allowing the activation of mixed motivational states combined with partial competition among states.

Thus the machine motivation modules can be used without significant modification to model the longer duration states of arousal associated with emotional contexts, which bias behavior selection towards the preselected set of relevant fixed action patterns and elicit the machine equivalent of autonomic responses preparatory for action.[27] The implementation of the properties involving learning will be described after we discuss animal cognition, which, as we will see, inherently involves learning.

COGNITION

We can now briefly explore some basic issues of animal cognition. Cognitive psychologists study how animals and people process information about the world. Traditionally they studied the processing of information about symbolic representations of objects and facts, just assuming that people and animals must form symbolic representations. With the advent of connectionism they are beginning to model how sensory information gets transformed into representations and what the representations might be like. Merely saying that cognition involves information processing without specifying that it is information about representations is too broad for the purposes of ethologists, but assuming that the representations are like the symbols used in formal logic is too narrow. Ethologists study adaptive information processing in very simple creatures like sea slugs, even in sessile animals like sea fans, whose information-processing capabilities one would not wish to call cognitive.[28] Cognition requires, first, that the animal internally forms and manipulates its own neural representations of stimulus events in its own particular environment and, second, that the manipulations be flexible, adaptive, and independent of the production of behavior. We call animals cognitive if they act as if they can learn about relationships among objects and events and also about the consequences of their behavior.

The importance for the animal of storing knowledge about relationships among events independent of behavioral production is illustrated by a process called goal revaluation. For our example, we can consider Pavlov's famous classical conditioning paradigm. Pavlov showed that if a bell is repeatedly rung just before meat powder is presented to a dog, the dog will eventually salivate when it hears the bell. Pavlov and most psychologists today believe that this happens because the neural representation of the bell by learning comes to evoke a neural representation of the meat, and this hallucinatory meat representation is what releases salivation. The dog does not associate the bell with salivation, forming an S-R (bell-salivation) link, but forms an S-S (bell-meat) association (see Roitblat 1987). Because the salivation is released by the hallucinated representation of meat, the dog can immediately adjust its behavior appropriately if something alters the value of the meat—e.g., if it learns that the meat has become poisonous and should be avoided. To see this, imagine that a dog that has first been trained in a Pavlovian way is then taught that the meat is poisonous, so the meat elicits avoidance. If the dog hears the bell, the bell representation activates the meat representation, which elicits avoidance. This completely new avoidance response to the bell is possible because the dog had earlier stored information about the bell-meat relationship and could use the information flexibly depending on the appropriate response to the meat. If dogs learned only S-R associations during the initial training, they would be left with a decidedly unadaptive bell-salivation reflex to a bell predicting poisoned meat.[29]

A "cognitive" animal should also be sensitive to the success of its behavior. An animal would be disadvantaged if it could learn only about relationships among stimuli in the world and not about the success of its own behavior. Picture again a dog hearing a bell that predicts desirable meat. But now something strange has happened (perhaps the arrival of a curious experimenter), and the salivation response makes the meat disappear. In a dog with flexible S-S links, the bell representation will activate the meat representation, but such a dog will nevertheless not be very well adapted if it cannot learn that salivation is the wrong response to the meat. The animal would be better adapted if it reduced its salivation response to the bell in these circumstances, and the easiest way to model this is to allow some S-R modifiability on the basis of whether the response was successful.[30] A mix of S-S and S-R association formation capacities should allow more flexible adaptability than either system alone. So minimally a model of cognitive processes must generate representations of events and must encompass both S-S and S-R learning.

Implementing Learning About the Success of Behavior

We now want to show how S-R learning about the success of behavior can be implemented. Learning about behavior outcome is actually an inherent part of the machine motivation model introduced in figure 19.1. The S-R connections self-calibrate on the basis of feedback about the success of the behavior. The perhaps surprising model we shall suggest is that success is measured by whether or not there is a consequence that releases another behavior after a prespecified time interval.

The logic that the release of a subsequent behavior indicates that the performance of an S-R sequence was successful is, in summary, that a behavior worth reinforcement is one that altered the environment in such a way that a new response became possible. Consider an example from fighting fish. If a fighting fish performs a facing display to a rival fighting fish, there will soon be a counterdisplay of facing posture. This counterdisplay will trigger a switch to broadside posture within a few seconds. This succession of behavior and consequent behavior allows the pathways to strengthen, as described below. On the other hand, if the fish performs a facing display to a leaf, there will, of course, be no counterdisplay. The lack of biologically significant consequences means that no subsequent counterthreat behavior will be released and the pathway will weaken.[31]

Our connectionist model must form associations on the basis of local information about activity patterns in the pairs of connected neurons, so there must be a process that alters the firing pattern depending on whether a behavior was followed by another behavior. This happens naturally, because behavior modules inhibit each other. The inhibition actually occurs at the B level in figure 19.1, but the feedback loop carries the effect to the R level. A variant of Hebb's rule, the neuroconnector rule, allows the appropriately timed end of firing in the R neurons to strengthen the synapse. The neuroconnector rule is a dynamic analog relative of Hebb's rule (Hebb 1949),[32] and is unusual in several ways. It associates firing bouts rather than associating neural activity at each moment of time as is standard in connectionist systems (see figure 19.2, where bouts of neural firing are represented by vertically dashed lines). The neuroconnector system "decides" that a firing bout has occurred when there is neural activity followed by silence, in effect looking for neural firing bouts by looking for their back temporal edges. It strengthens the association between two neurons if the back temporal edges in their firing patterns follow one another at the specified time interval (tau, figures 19.2 and 19.3). In this way the system associates neural events that follow each other at a certain time interval (which can be either effectively simultaneous or rather long). An S-R connection weakens if the temporal edge in R is too early or too late, or if R does not fire. (figure 19.2g, b–c, e; figure 19.3).

Since the temporal pattern of firing controls whether a connection forms between two neurons, we will consider in more detail what controls the firing patterns. The S neurons in figure 19.1 fire in response to stimulus events, most responding to the onset of a stimulus component, others responding continuously to the presence of a stimulus component. (We assume that many S neurons respond not to stimuli per se, but to stimulus onsets, as in animal nervous systems.)[33] An R neuron also *begins* firing in response to a stimulus event, since it is activated by S neurons, but then R fires persistently because of the R-B feedback loop. The all-important back temporal edge is controlled by what happens next. If the animal is involved in a biologically significant interaction, what happens after the behavior is released is likely to be that another, different, behavior is released. The competitive inhibition among B units allows the newly activating B neuron pool to break the original R-B loop. If the new behavior was released tau seconds after the end of the firing bout in the S neuron, the activity timing profile will strengthen the S-R connections (figure 19.2a). If there is no biologically significant consequence, no other fixed action pattern is triggered; the R-B loop is not broken and continues much longer. The activity pattern is that in figure 19.2e, and the connection

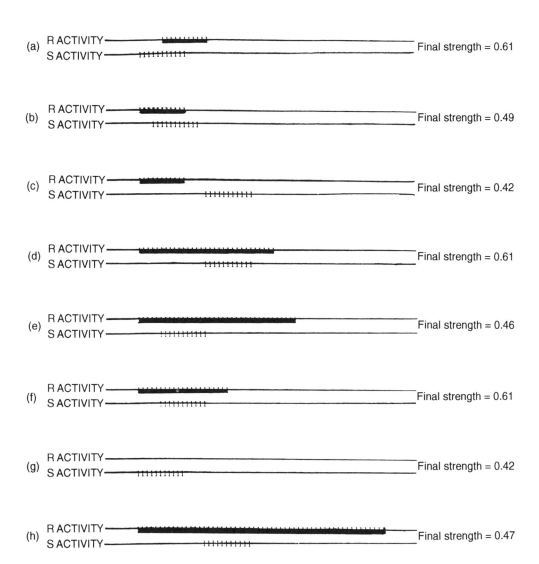

Constants

DELTAT = 0.10	ZETA = 0.90	MU = 0.10	K2 = 0.30	MR = 100.00
TAU = 50	ETA = 0.40	K1 = 0.15	MS = 100.00	

(a) R ACTIVITY ———— Final strength = 0.61
S ACTIVITY ————

(b) R ACTIVITY ———— Final strength = 0.49
S ACTIVITY ————

(c) R ACTIVITY ———— Final strength = 0.42
S ACTIVITY ————

(d) R ACTIVITY ———— Final strength = 0.61
S ACTIVITY ————

(e) R ACTIVITY ———— Final strength = 0.46
S ACTIVITY ————

(f) R ACTIVITY ———— Final strength = 0.61
S ACTIVITY ————

(g) R ACTIVITY ———— Final strength = 0.42
S ACTIVITY ————

(h) R ACTIVITY ———— Final strength = 0.47
S ACTIVITY ————

Figure 19.2 Examples of how various patterns of firing in a presynaptic neuron (S) and its postsynaptic neuron (R) affect the strength of the connection between them. The parameter settings can be compared with those in Halperin (1991). (a) Time-lagged Hebb-like strengthening. (b) and (c) Weakening of association due to a truly backward temporal relationship. (d) Strengthening because S is active just before the end of firing in R. (e) Weakening because the S bout stops too early with respect to the end of R's activity. (If R continues until S's activity trace has completely decayed, there is no change in strength.) (f) This pattern (in figure 19.2g) is not due to the timing profiles of the *beginnings* of activity bursts; strengthening occurs if the R bout is shortened so that S fires just before the *end* of firing in R. (g) An S bout not followed by firing in R should weaken any existing S-R connections. (h) This illustrates that the lengths of bouts are not critical (assuming that a minimum duration to "fill" the activity trace is achieved) and also that the exact relative timing of endings that produces weakening is not very precise (compare with figure 19.2e). (Reproduced from Halperin and Dunham 1992.)

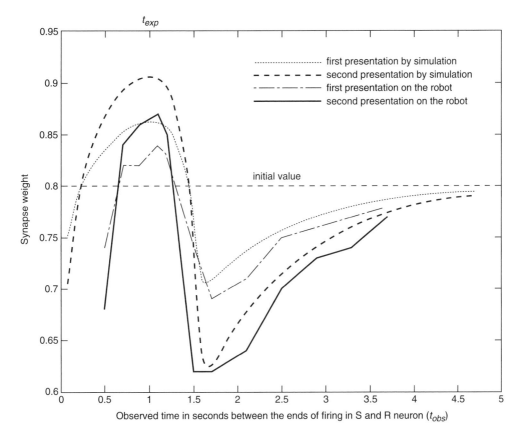

Figure 19.3 This figure shows how the strength change in a connection depends on the time interval between the temporal edge in the presynaptic (S) neuron and the temporal edge in the postsynaptic (R) neuron occurs. The X axis is the time until the R edge after the S edge has occurred. If the timing is near tau, strengthening will be best. The data are from successive presentations of stimuli to a tethered robot and from similar simulation runs. (As described in Hallam 1993. Reproduced with permission.)

weakens. Thus the neuroconnector rule in our fixed action pattern modules allows the release of a new behavior at about the time a consequent behavior would be expected to catalyse strengthening in the S-R pathway, while the lack of a behavioral consequence catalyzes weakening.

This mechanism allows learning about the success of discrete fixed action patterns that have rather immediate consequences. Learning involving emotional states cannot depend on the rapid arrival of consequences. Their consequences occur many minutes after the state is aroused, for poisoning even hours. Nevertheless, we can use the same neuroconnector rule in the standard module to model learning about the consequences of activating emotional states, because time constants are explicitly settable in the motivation modules. The time interval tau can be made long enough that late-arriving consequences will strengthen the S-R connections. The variance permissible in the timing of the consequence will also increase if we lengthen the time constants.[34] This will cause more context conditioning for states than for discrete fixed action patterns, but it might be advantageous for states to be aroused by less specific triggers than are the brief discrete behaviors. The important point is that the biologically significant consequences after emotional arousal, such as refractoriness[35] and drive reduction, involve the ending of neural firing. Such endings of neural firing bouts are what catalyzes S-R association formation in the neuroconnector model.[36]

Implementing Learning of Relationships Between Events

In the implementation model presented so far, there are no S-S links to store information about how stimulus events follow each other. Recall that being able to store information about the relationships between events independent of behavior production was needed for basic cognitive-level functioning. The question is whether one can add S-S links without having to change the model of connection strengthening. The answer seems to be yes.

To see why this might work, we have to consider the assumption already inherent in the model, that neurons do not slavishly track the presence of the stimulus objects the experimenter presents, but rather track the dynamics of whole stimulus events. Neurobiological data convince us that neural representations of stimulus events do not even simply mimic stimulus events as represented in our conscious awareness, since so many neurons respond only to the onset of stimulus components. Also, Hebbian models suggest that individual neurons can be thought of as representing "principle components" of the sensory input (Oja 1982; Oja, Ogawa, and Wangviwattana 1992). Rescorla's terminology, that associations form between events (Rescorla 1988), is quite compatible with the distributed representations envisaged in connectionist models if it is taken to suggest that associations form between events as parsed by the animal, not by the experimenter.

Alongside the growing interest in the distributed, connectionist representation of information is a growing insistence that there is a limitation inherent in studying cognition only as the processing of information about symbolic representations. It is argued today that reality is "open textured" and is not inherently parsed in a clean, natural way (Putnam 1988). It appears that to model forming representations from an open-textured reality we need to look at how information is processed on a finer scale. To model cognition, we will try to understand how animals might create behaviorally meaningful subsymbolic representations that could be used as the building blocks of cognition.

To build a fine-grained understanding of how neural systems could form representations of the meaningful aspects of stimulus events, we must minimally know something about the populations of neurons that are involved in representing events. As we saw earlier, most sensory interneurons represent only onsets of stimulus components.[37] We assume that most of our S neurons detect onsets and that a smaller percentage more faithfully register the level of stimulation (by firing whenever stimulation is above a threshold). A third small population of neurons detects offsets of stimuli, the visual "off center" neurons being the best-known example (Schiller, Sandell, and Maunsell 1986).

In the model, the neural representations of the CS and US[38] form in the S neuron pool. There are two crucial facts to grasp. First, the set of neurons representing an event from moment to moment will change during the event.[39] Initially, onset neurons responding to a newly sensed object will fire, but they will fade out if it remains, being superseded by a greater proportion of level detecting neurons. Second, the neural net will represent the most salient components of the stimulus situation in the modalities of its inputs. Local inhibition or other constraints within regions limit the total firing, and total connection strength is limited.[40] This limits attention, implementing competition for processing space.[41] Therefore, representations formed in our mixed population of neurons would not only be distributed; they would be multicomponent and dynamic (multicomponent in the sense that different subsets of neurons would represent different aspects of the stimulus as it appeared in the environment, and dynamic in the sense that during stimulus presentation different components of the neural representation would become active in sequence). With these basic ideas about what neurons represent, we can investigate what kinds of event-event (S-S) associations would be formed.

When we look at examples of how associations would form in mixed neural populations, we see that the neuroconnector rule gives a rather good fit to the data on the strength of classical conditioning.[42] In figure 19.4 we can see that a CS that appears near the end of a US forms only weak connections to the US, because the US onset detectors adapt before the CS appears, leaving only the modest population of level detectors representing the US. A positive association could form from CS onset and level detectors to these US level detectors because their correlated firing bouts end appropriately, followed by the quiescent period required for consolidation. But since level detectors are not very common neural units, the effective positive association strength will not be great.

The dominance of the onset detectors also explains why the neuroconnector system predicts good association formation for a brief CS at the beginning of a long US (figure 19.5), even though the neuroconnector rule would weaken the association from CS to US if the neurons representing them simply mimicked their time courses (figure 19.2). Onset detectors would fire in the ideal lagged correlation pattern. Since we assume that most of the neurons detect onsets, a strong association will form. Figure 19.6 shows an arrangement that would form an excellent positive association between CS and US (Voss 1974). The CS-US timing profiles are

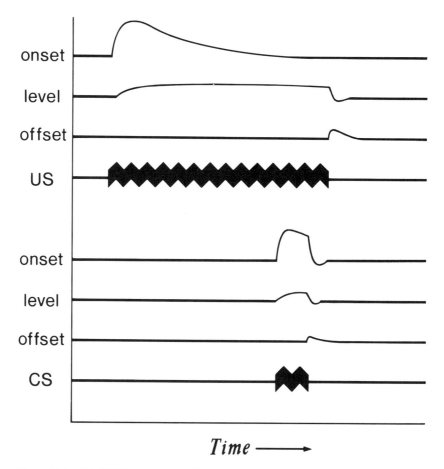

Time ⟶

Figure 19.4 This CS-US sequence would cause poor association formation. The time courses of a CS and a US are indicated by the dark wavy lines. The time courses of the various hypothesized types of neurons that collectively form the neural representation of the CS and US are indicated by the thinner lines. Because the onset neuron bout endings are badly correlated (see Figure 19.2c), the neuroconnector rule would lead to weak association formation, although some connections between CS onset and US offset might form.

optimal for association formation for both onset detectors and level detectors.

The model makes many detailed predictions about association formation that remain to be tested both against the literature and experimentally and that may well not be verified. However, we can conclude that, as a first approximation, the neuroconnector system provides a reasonable model of the time course of S-S association formation.

Meaningful Representations Through Behavior and Motivation

The distributed representations in our connectionist model are created and activated as much by their associations with other representations and behaviors as by the salient principle components of the stimulus

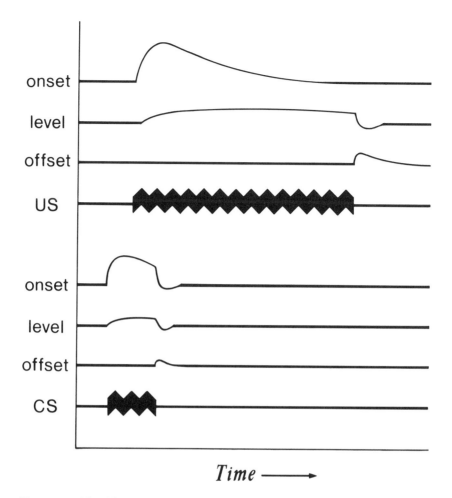

Figure 19.5 This CS-US sequence would allow quite good association formation. The time courses of a CS and a US are indicated by the dark wavy lines. The time courses of the various hypothesized types of neurons that collectively form the neural representation of the CS and US are indicated by the thinner lines. The onset detectors would associate (see Figure 19.2a), and they are assumed to be plentiful.

situations from which they arise. They have more in common with the evocative symbols of literature than with the discrete symbols of formal logic. Yet if they lack a discrete nature, they have a discrete quality deriving largely from two sources. First, as sensor inputs change through time or pass across space, objects, being units and so moving as units, will create temporal edges in the firing patterns of the neurons that respond to the inputs. These temporal edges thus reflect the discreteness of objects.[43] Work by Spelke (1987) on the way in which young infants classify the world around them into objects suggests that they need only a few cues to recognize what belongs in a single object. These cues are spatial contiguity, solidity (being not like a pile of leaves), and especially simultaneous movement. Visual perception seems to be built up from the capacity to

Cognition and Emotion in Animals and Machines

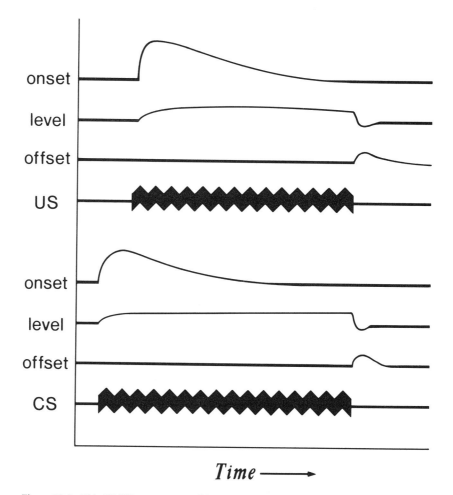

Figure 19.6 This CS-US sequence would cause good association formation. The thick wavy lines are the observed time courses of a CS and a US that the model suggests should produce good association formation. The thinner lines are the hypothesized neural time courses for neurons representing these external events. Both the onset neurons and the neurons that track the stimulus features could associate.

associate simple spatiotemporal regularities, and the other gestalt properties come later. Thus the neuroconnector model's reliance on temporal edges to group neural firing patterns into events will tend to automatically associate objects, given that the rule is embedded in a net with topographic properties.

The second source of the discrete quality of neuroconnector representations is the discreteness of behavior. Because an animal's interaction with the world is through behavior and feedback from the world about the success of its behavior stabilizes the representations formed during S-R learning, the S representations are stabilized by the discreteness of the behaviors as well as by the spatiotemporal regularities in the sensory inputs. These representations of behaviorally relevant situations form a stable base with which to associate further representations, grounded

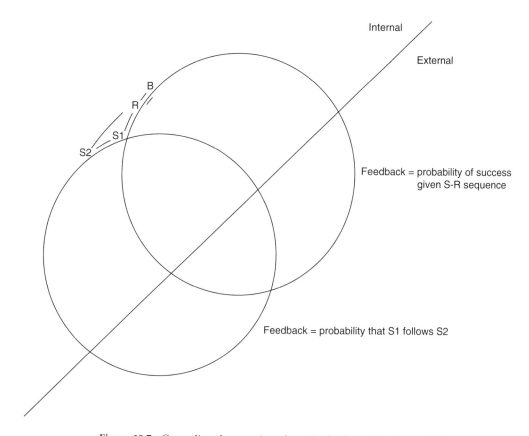

Figure 19.7 Grounding the meaning of acquired information through behavior. The S-R connections track the success of the S-R sequence. (A "success" occurs when firing in R ends at the prespecified expected time, tau seconds after the end of firing in S. A consequence is anything that stops R from firing, such as the release of a competing behavior, a refractory period, or drive reduction.) The S-S connections track whether that S2 follows S1 after tau seconds. Different loops, parallel to each other or interlocking (not shown), track conditional probabilities on various time scales, tau. The external world, which includes the robot/animal body, determines what consequences follow each behavior, and thus provides the feedback that adapts the internal synaptic strengths. Of course, a human may specify the initial architecture. But no human is needed in the feedback loop by which internal representations of "situations for action" and "events following events" are adjusted. The system's internal representations are therefore more fully and autonomously grounded (Harnad 1989) than if the internal system interacted only with a human, and this human's experience in the world completely determined the system's internal adjustments.

now by the base representations as well as by spatiotemporal regularities in the sensory input.

The link to behavior and motivation is crucial; it allows the animal to choose which representations to focus on from the myriad possibilities offered by an open-textured reality. Behavior and motivation make this choice the animal's own. The representations are the animal's, or robot's, own, because they are created through its own interactions (Brooks 1986). Figure 19.7 illustrates this. The embedding of representation formation in behavior provides meaning, but the embedding of representation formation in behavior that is in turn embedded within a motivational architecture takes the process one step further. If the motivational architecture is one that makes its own decisions on the basis of a trade-off process, the behavioral decisions are not directly controlled by the designer and the behaving entity is more autonomous (see McFarland, this volume). These are rather philosophical issues, but they show both what our own scientific understanding can gain from using the comparative approach of extending the notions of cognition and emotion by analogy to animals and robots, and what robotics may gain.

ONE MODEL?

This chapter sketches the outline of a connectionist general process model of representation and reinforcement. One might ask if this could possibly correspond to biological reality. The above discussion illustrates that the neuroconnector version of connectionist strength changes can model both S-S and S-R association formation simply by making the unexceptional assumption that the associations we see in Pavlovian conditioning are the end result of various neural associations that occur during a stimulus event. Given the conservative similarity of so many neural properties even between invertebrates and vertebrates, it is not an implausible hope that vertebrate neurons and synapses may have functional features that are standardized. The constraint of the logic of cause and effect is powerful, whether between actions and consequences or events and succeeding events; all animals could benefit from recognizing when one stimulus predicts another and when an action predicts a consequence. This commonality of function is presumably largely responsible for the amazing similarity of basic learning curves, under a variety of conditions, in creatures as phylogenetically distant as honeybees and fish (see Bitterman 1988). Given that selective pressure probably pushes hard for similar learning phenomena by whatever mechanism, it does not seem reasonable to suggest that all animals that show sophisticated learning use exactly the same mechanism. However, vertebrates show considerable homology in their neural structures. Once some vertebrate ancestor evolved an efficient, modular mechanism to extract causal information from the real world, it seems likely that any adjustments would be through tinkering rather than through wholesale reinvention of some totally new process. Changes involving resetting parameters can often be accomplished by tinkering since, if the parameter setting is currently x and should be 2x, then 1.2x will frequently be an improvement on x and will be selected by evolution. In this way the system can gradually edge toward the ideal parameter setting for the new situation. Using the kind of modular arrangement we suggest, evolutionary tinkering could arrange new learning biases such as more or less tendency to form S-S vs. S-R associations or differences in the tendency to associate certain sensory input modalities with certain responses.

The connectionist assumption that all associative learning occurs at synapses between neurons suggests another argument for the plausibility of a single mechanism for S-S and S-R learning. Whatever the architecture, S-S associations must affect behavior choices. Therefore, either there are bridging neurons between independent, functionally separate S-S and S-R association areas or some neurons must be able to form both S-S and S-R associations. If some neurons form S-S synapses coming in and S-R synapses going out, then either they form two distinct types of synapses or the one basic synapse works for both S-S and S-R learning. Parsimony thus suggests that it is reasonable for those wishing to explore fully the connectionist paradigm to hypothesize integrated S-S, S-R learning models.

Thus arguments can be made that from some stage onward vertebrate learning mechanisms might tend to be evolutionarily conservative and general-purpose. Since the model suggested here provides a workable general-purpose learning mechanism, it seems reasonable to suggest that it could be explored as a working hypothesis for the functional mechanism underlying much of vertebrate learning. Therefore, in the adventurous spirit appropriate when a science has not yet developed an encompassing paradigm, we shall continue to explore the machine motivation system, both as a biological hypothesis about how cognitive processes are integrated into an architecture which organizes emotional behavior and as a design for allowing autonomous robots to show more of the features of animal cognition and emotion than it has until now been possible to generate.

NOTES

I wish to thank Herb Roitblat, David McFarland, Stephen Halperin, Bridget Hallam, and Ashley Lotto, who all read earlier versions of this manuscript and made helpful comments. I thank the Leverhulme Trust, which provided the fellowship I held the year this chapter was written, and the University of Edinburgh's Department of Artificial Intelligence, which generously hosted me for that year.

1. Traditional artificial intelligence modelers instead take inspiration from "folk psychology" and psychology when developing hypotheses.

2. By cognitive, most scientists do not mean "language-like." Most ethologists do not suppose that animal behavior derives its impressive appearance of rationality from using a "language of thought" (McFarland and Bösser 1993).

3. Vertebrates are animals with backbones: fish, amphibians, reptiles, birds, and mammals. Primates (monkey-like animals) are mammals, and humans are one species of primate. Human brains are quite similar to those of other primates, somewhat similar to those of other mammals. There is enough homology among the brains of all vertebrates that many of the same words are used to describe brain regions. There is effectively no architectural homology between human and invertebrate brains, although many basic properties of the component neurons and synapses are shared in common.

4. This example illustrates how anecdotes can test theories that make strong predictions such as "cognition determines the experienced emotion." These theories can be disproved

Cognition and Emotion in Animals and Machines

by a single valid counterexample, possibly an anecdote. Here we can only be sure that conscious cognitive assessment does not always determine the subjectively experienced emotion if there is any possibility that subconscious cognitive processes in the verbal hemisphere produced a slightly emotionally tinged cognitive assessment, despite the neutral verbal report about the picture.

5. Presumably cognition by itself determines emotion when there are no other factors. This picture suggests that, since adrenalin is released biologically in many different emotional contexts, it just causes general arousal, so in the absence of primitive determinants of emotion, cognition dominates.

6. See McFarland's contribution for references to the human inclination to project intentionality and emotion.

7. Readers whose reaction is that even behaviors that are performed only in emotional contexts are still not really "emotional in themselves" are reminded that we are discussing behaviors that are emotional "by analogy," and also that a satisfactory implementation of emotion-like phenomena in a robot will at the very least have to implement the types of behaviors observed in emotional contexts.

8. As a student I verified to my skeptical mind that the fixed action patterns that I intuitively identified in filmed records of fish interacting were also objectively discoverable in painstakingly quantified data about fin positions, orientations, and distances (Halperin 1979).

9. The word "reflex" implies that there is a stimulus that unconditionally releases the reflex. Recall Zajonc's evidence of noncognitive responses to the "happy face" and "scowl face" icons. The study of the releasers of human affect programs is a fascinating field.

10. *Betta splendens.*

11. These raw emotions are seldom felt, presumably, by most modern civilized adults. Think back to the angry posturing of teenagers in schoolyard fights.

12. As for angry unarmed humans, even escalated fights are not attempted murders. Fish with room for retreat almost never bite damagingly at eyes, pectoral fins, or body scales.

13. Why evolution does not select for animals that cheat by communicating that they are stronger than they really are is a fascinating story (Krebs and Davies 1991) whose details are still being filled in.

14. The name was chosen by a committee.

15. This insight is becoming an important concept in "behavior-based robotics" (Brooks 1986; Malcolm and Smithers 1990; Malcolm, Smithers, and Hallam 1989).

16. *Nanostomus marginatus.*

17. For another example of how the releasing process can be subtle and complex, yet have a primitive reflexlike quality, think about the human phenomenon of contagious yawning.

18. Some seem to call such emotional states "moods" (Griffiths 1990). Damasio (1994) discusses an interesting hypothesis about the physical origins of the sensations experienced when emotional states are aroused.

19. Many situations that cause physiological arousal that will not release rapid action (being surprised or startled; the excitement of success; sexual interest, aggression, fear that will not be immediately acted upon) seem to trigger laughter. It presumably communicates to any observer that the current physiological arousal need not be taken too seriously.

20. Time sharing is the performance of fixed action patterns potentiated by relatively mild motivations, the timing of performance being controlled by a currently powerful motivation. Time sharing is strong evidence for the reality of motivational states, for their simultaneous activation even when the fixed action pattern being performed is potentiated by only one

of them, and, less obviously, for action selection being determined by a multimotivational cost minimizing trade-off (McFarland 1985).

21. Linking complex cognitive assessment equally to all the fixed action patterns and also to emotional states would presumably have the disadvantage of inefficiency.

22. Details are presented elsewhere (Halperin 1990, 1991; Halperin and Dunham 1992, 1993; Halperin, Dunham, and Ye 1992; Hallam 1993).

23. The system is patented. This is irrelevant to research, but can protect those who wish to use the system in commercial products if they first obtain a license. Contact Tom Drivas, NeuRobotics, Inc., Toronto, Canada 416-653-1162.

24. Connectionist models of sign stimuli are beginning to prove their worth in several contexts (Ewert 1987; Heiligenberg 1991; Enquist and Arak 1993).

25. The S layer is in general the "output" layer of a connectionist net, and other learning can occur in this net, as will be discussed later.

26. It could inhibit either the inputs or the neighboring neurons themselves. In robotics applications this feature has not been implemented due to competition for processing space in the transputer system.

27. Preparatory responses for robots might include increasing the rate of information processing.

28. The moth that picks a bat echolocation signal from a blur of sound energy does so because its ears hear only the frequencies that a bat uses for echolocating. Selective attention has been designed in (Roeder 1965), and we do not call this cognition.

29. S-S learning also allows chains of experienced events, S1-S2-S3, to be recalled by the prompting of S1. Our model predicts that such cued imagining could form new S-R associations by setting up temporally contiguous firing patterns, an amusing bootstrapping of new S-R learning by S-S associations.

30. Modifiable S-R links would be especially important for learning ballistic responses.

31. Halperin and Dunham (1992) and Halperin (1990, 1991) discuss the generality and biological plausibility of this method, discussing punishment, manipulative behaviors, consumatory behavior, and also the spontaneous up-calibration if for a long time no behavior is performed.

32. Hebb's rule is widely regarded as simple, but biologically plausible. Our version also has flavorings of Wagner's SOP model and Sinclair's rest principle (Wagner 1981; Sinclair 1981). Each neuroconnector keeps decaying traces of its own recent inputs and activity. The activity trace controls connection strength changes and can cause interference with consolidation of strength changes.

33. This is modeled by having many S neurons adapt quickly (i.e., fire at the onset of stimulation, but then stop firing whether or not the stimulus continues).

34. The permissible deviation is adjustable, especially as the X-axis is an arbitrary time axis.

35. Refractory periods are periods when neurons stop firing even if they receive input.

36. Halperin (1991) and Halperin and Dunham (1992, 1993) discuss variants such as hunger and punishment.

37. Heuristically we can understand the significance of onset neurons by saying that the nervous system functions to extract important information, and this is efficiently done by detecting changes (Norwich 1977). A fast-adapting neuron detects only changes, becoming silent whenever its input remains constant.

38. A CS, or conditional stimulus, is one that elicits a response because of learning, as the bell did. A US is a stimulus that unconditionally releases a response. The CS must be presynaptic, because it must come to activate the US representation and excitation flows from pre- to post-.

39. As Roitblat (1987) describes, Pavlov hypothesized that different representations of the onset and continuation of stimuli might provide an explanation of associative time course data.

40. Neural nets need some constraints, or no self-organization occurs (Oja 1982).

41. For psychologists: Competition for processing space implements overshadowing. Blocking can occur because the original learning alters the timing of the US representation, as in SOP, and can also occur because of competition of learned but unusual representation with preferred representations. A+ and AB− can leave B with inhibitory strength, because neurons can represent feature conjunctions. The explosion of feature conjunctions is prevented by the boundedness inherent in neural nets (Williams 1990).

42. We must choose a hypothetical example, so we shall assume that there are about 70 percent onset detectors, 20 percent stimulus level detectors, and 10 percent stimulus offset detectors.

43. In robotics, active vision is a new, successful field that uses this fact.

REFERENCES

Baerends, G. P. (1985). Do the dummy experiments with sticklebacks support the IRM-concept? *Behaviour* 93: 258–277.

Barlow, G. W. (1977). Modal action patterns. In T. A. Sebeok, ed. *How Animals Communicate.* Univ. of Indiana Press, Indiana.

Bitterman, M. E. (1988). Vertebrate-invertebrate comparisons. In H. J. Jerison and I. Jerison, eds. *Intelligence and Evolutionary Biology.* NATO ASI Series, Vol. G17. Heidelberg: Springer-Verlag.

Braitenberg, V. (1987). *Vehicles.* Cambridge, Mass.: The MIT Press.

Brooks, R. A. (1986). Achieving artificial intelligence through building mobile robots. AI Memo 899. Artificial Intelligence Laboratory, MIT, Cambridge, Mass.

Damasio, A. R. (1994). *Descartes' Error.* New York: Putnam.

de Bruin, J. P. C. (1980). Telencephalon and behavior in teleost fish. Pp. 175–201 in Sven O. Ebbesson, ed. *Comparative Neurology of the Telencephalon.* New York, N.Y.: Plenum Press.

de Sousa, R. (1987). *The Rationality of Emotion.* Cambridge, Mass.: The MIT Press.

Eibl-Eibesfeldt, I. (1974). The expressive behaviour of the deaf-and-blind-born. Pp. 163–194 in M. von Cranach and J. Vine, eds. *Social Communication and Movement.* London: Academic Press.

Ekman, P. (1984). Expression and the nature of emotion. Pp. 319–344 in K. R. Scherer and P. Ekman, eds. *Approaches to Emotion.* Hillsdale, N.J.: Erlbaum.

Ekman, P., and Friesen, W. V. (1975). *Unmasking the Face.* New York: Prentice Hall.

Enquist, M., and Arak, A. (1993). Selection of exaggerated male traits by female aesthetic senses. *Nature* 361: 446–448.

Ewert, J.-P. (1987). Neuroethology of releasing mechanisms: Prey-catching in toads. *Behavioral and Brain Sciences.* 10: 337–405.

Frijda, N. H. (1986). *The Emotions.* Cambridge: Cambridge University Press.

Gazzaniga, M. S. (1988). *Mind Matters.* Boston, Mass.: Houghton Mifflin/The MIT Press.

Griffiths, P. E. (1990). Modularity, and the psychoevolutionary theory of emotion. *Biology and Philosophy* 5: 175–196.

Hallam, B. (1993). Fast robot learning using a biological model. DAI Research Paper 630. Univ. of Edinburgh, Edinburgh, UK.

Halperin, J. R. P. (1979). An analysis of the structure of courtship in a pencilfish (*Nannostomus marginatus* Eigenmann). M.Sc. thesis, Univ. of Toronto.

Halperin, J. R. P. (1990). A Connectionist Neural Network Model of Aggression. PhD. thesis, Univ. of Toronto.

Halperin, J. R. P. (1991). Machine motivation. Pp. 213–221 in J.-A. Meyer and S. W. Wilson, eds. *From Animals to Animats: Proceedings of the First International Conference on Simulation of Animal Behavior.* Cambridge, Mass.: The MIT Press.

Halperin, J. R. P., and Dunham, D. W. (1992). Postponed conditioning: Testing a hypothesis about synaptic strengthening. *Adaptive Behavior* 1: 39–64.

Halperin, J. R. P., and Dunham, D. W. (1993). Increased aggressiveness after brief social isolation of adult fish: A connectionist model which organizes this literature. *Behavioural Processes* 28: 123–144.

Halperin, J. R. P., Dunham, D. W., and Ye, S. (1992). Social isolation increases social display after priming in *Betta splendens* but decreases aggressive readiness. *Behavioural Processes* 28: 13–32.

Harnad, S. (1989). Minds, machines and Searle. *Journal of Experimental and Theoretical Artificial Intelligence* 1: 1.

Hebb, D. O. (1949). *The Organization of Behaviour.* New York: Wiley.

Heiligenberg, W. (1991). *Neural Nets in Electric Fishes.* Cambridge, Mass.: The MIT Press.

Holland, P. C. (1984). Origins of behavior in Pavlovian conditioning. Pp. 129–174 in G. C. Bower, ed. *The Psychology of Learning and Motivation, vol. 18.* Orlando, Fla.: Academic Press.

Krebs, J., and Davies, N. (1991). *Behavioural Ecology,* 3d ed. Oxford: Blackwell Scientific Publications.

Lack, D. (1943). *The Life of the Robin.* Cambridge, U.K.: Cambridge Univ. Press.

LeDoux, J. E. (1987). Emotion. Pp. 419–459 in *Handbook of Physiology, Nervous System V: Higher Function.* Bethesda, Md: American Physiological Society.

Lorenz, K. Z. (1985). *Foundations of Ethology.* Heidelberg: Springer-Verlag.

Malcolm, C. A., and Smithers, T. (1990). Symbol grounding via a hybrid architecture in an autonomous assembly system. *Robotics and Automation* 6 (1/2). (Special issue on Designing Autonomous Objects.)

Malcolm, C. A., Smithers, T., and Hallam, J. (1989). An emerging paradigm in robot architecture. DAI Research Paper 447. Dept. of Artificial Intelligence, Univ. of Edinburgh, Edinburgh U.K.

Mandler, G. (1975). *Mind and Emotion.* New York: Wiley.

Mandler, G. (1990). A constructivist theory of emotion. Pp. 21–43 in N. L. Stein, B. Leventhal, and T. Trabasso, eds. *Psychological and Biological Approaches to Emotion.* Hillsdale, N.J.: Erlbaum.

Cognition and Emotion in Animals and Machines

McFarland, D. . (1985). *Animal Behaviour*. Harlow, U.K.: Longman Scientific.

McFarland, D. J. (1989). Goals, no goals and own goals. In A. Montefiore and D. Noble, eds. *Goals, No Goals, and Own Goals*. London: Unwin-Hyman.

McFarland, D. J., and Bösser, T. (1993). *Intelligent Behavior of Animals and Robots*. Cambridge, Mass.: The MIT Press.

Newell, A., Rosenbloom, P. S., and Laird, J. E. (1989). Symbolic architectures for cognition. Pp. 93–132 in *Foundations of Cognitive Science*. M. Posner, ed. Cambridge, Mass.: The MIT Press.

Norich, K. H. (1977). On the information received by sensory receptors. *Bulletin of Mathematical Biology* 39: 453–461.

Oatley, K. and Johnson-Laird, P. N. (1987). Towards a cognitive theory of emotions. Cognition, and Emotion 1(1): 29–50.

Oja, E. (1982). A simplified neuron model as a principal component analyzer. *Journal of Math Biology* 15: 267–273.

Oja, E., Ogawa, H., and Wangviwattana, J. (1992). PCA in fully parallel neural networks. In Aleksander and Taylor, eds. *Artificial Neural Networks, 2*.

Ortony, A., Clore, G., and Collins, A. (1988). *The Cognitive Structure of Emotions*. Cambridge, U.K.: Cambridge Univ. Press.

Putnam, H. (1988). *Representation and Reality*. Cambridge, Mass.: The MIT Press.

Rescorla, R. A. (1988). Behavioral studies of Pavlovian conditioning. *Annual Review of Neuroscience* 11: 329–52.

Roeder, K. D. (1963). *Nerve Cells and Insect Behavior*. Cambridge, Mass.: Harvard University Press.

Roeder, K. D. (1965). Moths and ultrasound. *Scientific American* 212: 94–102.

Roitblat, H. L. (1987). *Introduction to Comparative Cognition*. NY: W. H. Freeman.

Schacter, S., and Singer, J. E. (1962). Cognitive, social and psychological determinants of emotional state. *Psychological Reviews* 69: 379–399.

Scherer, K. R. (1985). Vocal affect signalling: A comparative approach. *Advances in the Study of Behavior* 15: 189–244.

Scherer, K. R., and Oshinsky (1977). Cue utilization in emotion attribution from auditory stimuli. *Motivation and Emotion* 1: 331–346.

Schiller, P. H., Sandell, J. H., and Maunsell, H. R. (1986). Functions of the ON and OFF channels of the visual system. *Nature* 322: 824–825.

Shapiro, S., Schuckman, H., Sussman, D., and Tucker, A. M. 1974. Effects of telencephalic lesions on the gill cover response of Siamese fighting fish. *Physiology and Behavior* 13: 749–755.

Simpson, M. J. A. (1968). The display of the Siamese fighting fish. *Betta splendens*. *Animal Behaviour Monographs*, 1.

Sinclair, J. D. (1981). *The Rest Principle: A Neurophysiological Theory of Behavior*. Hillsdale, N.J.: Erlbaum.

Smith, O. A., and DeVito, J. (1984). Central neural integration for the control of autonomic responses associated with emotion. *Annual Review of Neuroscience* 7: 43–65.

Spelke, E. S. (1987). Origins of visual knowledge. Pp. 99–128 in D. Osherland, Stephen Kosslyn, and John, M. Hollerbach, eds. *Visual Cognition and Action*. Cambridge, Mass.: The MIT Press.

Strongman, K. T. (1978). *The Psychology of Emotion*, 2d ed. Chichester, U.K.: Wiley.

Tinbergen, N. (1950). The hierarchical organisation of nervous mechanisms underlying instinctive behaviour. *Symposium of the Society for Experimental Biology* 4: 305–312.

Tinbergen, N. (1951). *The Study of Instinct*. Oxford: Oxford Univ. Press.

Tyrrell, T. (1993). The use of hierarchies for action selection. *Adaptive Behavior* 1(4).

von Holst, D. (1989). Positive and negative consequences of social behavior on reproduction and health in tree shrews. Abstract. 21st International Ethological Conference, Utrecht, Holland.

von Holst, E. (1973). *Behavioral Physiology of Animals and Man, vol. I*. Coral Gables, Fl.: University of Miami Press.

Voss, J. F. (1974). *Psychology as a Behavioral Science*. Pacific Palisades, Calif.: Goodyear.

Wagner, A. R. (1981). SOP: A model of automatic memory processing in animal behavior. In N. E. Spear and R. R. Miller, eds. *Information Processing in Animals: Memory Mechanisms*. Hillsdale, N.J.: Erlbaum.

Williams, R. J. (1990). Adaptive state representation and estimation using recurrent connectionist networks. In W. T. Miller III, R. S. Sutton, and P. J. Werbos, eds. *Neural Networks for Control*. Cambridge, Mass.: The MIT Press.

Zajonc, R. B. (1980). Preferences need no inferences. *American Psychologist* 35(2): 151–175.

20 Emotions in Robots

Nico H. Frijda

A FUNCTIONAL VIEW OF EMOTIONS

The very idea of emotions in robots may appear absurd, or even be felt offensive, for several reasons. First, emotions are often regarded primarily as feelings, and that, quite often, is thought to mean that they cannot be further analyzed. Second, the idea of "feelings" in robots constitutes a confused notion that most of us would like to stay away from. The notion of subjective awareness is not easily accommodated in an artificial system, and it appears superfluous when the informational content of a given state can be specified.

However, the feeling or subjective experience aspect of emotions does not exhaust the notion of emotion, nor does it exhaust the phenomena connected with that notion. In addition, emotional experiences are not unanalyzable, but have an internal structure. They can be analyzed and described, and that means that they do have an informational content, in addition to whatever quality as "raw feels" they may possess. If we consider their informational content, the notion of emotions in robots becomes less absurd.

In fact, the current view in the psychology of emotion is that whatever is meant by "emotion" serves a purpose. According to this view, the functional view of emotions, emotions have an adaptive value, which is why animals, too, have them, or at least have some of them (Frijda 1986; Plutchik 1980; Lazarus 1991). The hypothesis that emotions serve an adaptive purpose, incidentally, does not assert that they always, at each occurrence, are adaptive and serve such a purpose or that each and every emotional phenomenon does so, but that they often do, and they do often enough to render the function meaningful (just as not every act of seeing is useful, but the function of seeing as a whole is). If it is correct that emotions serve a purpose, it should be possible to analyze, describe, and define that purpose. Also, a function so defined can conceivably and in principle serve a similar purpose in other systems that have a related structure and that operate in a similar environment.

above aspects of feeling are their conscious reflection. Emotions include the cognitive processes of appraisal of the emotion-eliciting event, the involuntary formation of behavioral impulses, and the overt expressions and behaviors that these impulses may eventually lead to. In addition, emotions include resource allocation shifts, as manifested in changes in attention, in redistribution of what one thinks about, and in the physical reallocations—the modifications of logistic support for one's coping actions, which the physiological arousal changes represent. Furthermore, emotions include the shifts in control over behavior, attention, and resources that are referred to as the "control precedence" feature of emotions. Emotions tend to take control over actual goals determining action, as well as over actual behavior.

The process of emotion follows more or less from its function and from the components mentioned. It is illustrated as follows:

event * concerns → appraisal → difficulty estimate → action readiness → control evaluation → action

In addition to relevance assessment, appraisal has been described as involving detection of features that are relevant to action planning (e.g., novelty, uncertainty, signals for future harm or benefit, social agency, modifiability, and accessibility). The relevance of appraisal to action planning can be illustrated by the importance of the feature of social agency. If the emotional event involves social agency, social actions such as threat displays or aggression become meaningful. Or, for other example, detecting that a situation cannot be modified (is final, definitive) triggers the abandonment of action and of striving, or calling for help, as in crying. Similarly, the feature of uncertainty signals that information gathering and action interruption are appropriate.

Several modes of action readiness were just mentioned: aggressive readiness, action abandonment, and action interruption. Other modes are approach, self-protection, immobilization, obstacle removal, action termination, attention increase, and activation increase or decrease. Human emotions involve such modes or states. The emotional impulses or states of readiness are best understood as goals. The emotional impulse to approach is a goal, since it can be implemented by many different actions and by way of many different action plans; the same is true for obstacle removal or self-protection. The impulse for obstacle removal (as in anger or when challenged), for instance, is readiness for such diverse actions as bodily aggression, shooting, poisoning, scolding, and insulting.

The goals of emotional impulses—and of the various forms of emotional action readiness generally—can be characterized in a general way, as aiming at (changes in) relationships between the individual and his or her environment. This characterization distinguishes them from goals that aim at modifying the environment rather than one's relation to it. Emotions serve to safeguard concerns by modifying (or maintaining) one's relation to the environment. Such modifications include protection from influences from the environment ("fear"), blocking the influence from the environment ("anger"), diminishing the risks of dealing with an unknown environment ("anxiety"—that is, generalized inhibition and response suppression), attenuating visibility or the effects of one's actions relative to observers in the environment (shame, guilt). Emotions such as despair or depression that do not truly involve goals and that do not "serve" anything still reflect or embody the current state of endeavors to safeguard one's concerns—namely, the fact that one is unable to serve them adaptively under the given conditions, and that maintaining an active relationship to the present environment is being abandoned.

The core elements of the emotion process thus are the subprocess of relevance evaluation and the subprocess that projects appraisal outcomes onto action readiness modes, which are illustrated as follows:

appraisal$_1$ $\rightarrow$ action readiness$_1$
appraisal$_2$ $\rightarrow$ action readiness$_2$
. . .

One of the theoretical problems of emotion theory and of model construction concerns the way appraisals are projected onto the modes of action readiness. Empirically (that is, in empirical psychological research), appraisals are hypothesized to be projected by a weighted linear function of features onto action readiness modes. However, other models are to be explored. Another problem concerns the origin of these functions: to what extent they belong to the system's makeup (that is, are innate) and to what extent they are a function of experience.

CONCERNS

Relevance detection is thus one of the core elements of the process underlying emotion. Here "relevance" means relevance of events with respect to concern satisfaction. More precisely, it means the effect of events for achieving or maintaining the satisfaction states of concerns and, in addition, the anticipated, expected effect of events, the signaled or probable opportunity for such satisfaction, or the signaled or probable threat to it.

All this applies to the many concerns that human beings have, which have their specific content for each human individual. Humans have a large variety of concerns, and emotions may arise upon each event that is relevant to any of these. Human concerns include, to name a few, the more or less basic and biological ones such as concern for physical well-being, absence of pain, optimal state of feeding, drinking, temperature, bodily dryness, proximity of a sexual partner, and sexual satisfaction. However, they also include the less tangible ones like concern for being cognitively well-oriented, for familiarity with and cognitive assimilation of ongoing events, for a sense of mastery over the environment, for proximity of trusted individuals ("attachment figures"), for completion of self-initiated actions and goals, for self-esteem, and for being included in one's proximal social group. Most or all of these concerns are built-in goals that are instrumental for survival and reproduction of the kind of system in the kind of environment sketched.

It is convenient to think of concerns as of representations of desired states (setpoints, in many cases, as in the case of temperature and feeding control; more elaborate representations, as in the case of proximity of an attachment figure or positively valued sensations like sweetness of substances). Relevance assessment results from matching the representation of an event with the representations that correspond to the concerns. The representation of an event, of course, may include its associations to past experiences and the like.

There are interesting alternative ways to conceive of the representation of events. Concerns may be conceived of as inherent in the presence of action systems; they may be seen as implicit in the overall system's ability to complete or initiate the action systems of the overall system. The concern for cognitive orientation, one might say, results from the fact that we are capable of obtaining cognitive orientation; the concern for sex results from the fact that we have the mechanisms for obtaining sexual union and discharge. What this would mean is that emotional satisfaction results when the system successfully uses its action systems under the conditions that such successful use is not automatic, effortless, or self-evident. Emotion can then be interpreted as the provision of the system to monitor and safeguard the successful functioning of its subsystems.

CONTROL PRECEDENCE

The emotion mechanisms include a provision for control precedence—that is, for switching the control over cognitive resources, action planning, and action execution to the goal of the emotion at hand (Frijda 1986). Emotional control switching involves things like attention allocation, interruption of ongoing behavior when a concern-relevant event of sufficient importance occurs (emotional distraction, with perhaps resumption of the earlier behavior when the event has been dealt with), and, for warding off interruptions while pursuing a concern-relevant goal (emotional single-mindedness), cognitive involvement with the emotional issues as evidenced by being preoccupied with them and showing lack of concentration with regard to other tasks. Of course, this is an aspect of the functional nature of emotions and of the fact that emotional feeling is only one aspect of emotions. What emotions are about is action (or motivation for action) and action control. Note that in the control precedence mechanism, too, the emotion system is responsive to relevance with regard to any of the system's concerns. It is geared to safeguard concerns, even those that the system is not explicitly concerned with at the particular moment that a relevant event occurs and for which events it is not prepared. Emotions alert us to unexpected threats, interruptions, and opportunities. Looking up from one's work when an object of sexual interest is passing by is an example, and being startled by unexpected noise is another.

THE CONTROL STRUCTURE OF EMOTIONS

In talking about modes of action readiness, I characterized them as goals. In the emotions of humans and higher animals, relevance detection leads to goals rather than to specific actions, as is the case with lower animals under equivalent circumstances (such as a shellfish closing its shell or a wasp pushing in its sting). Obviously the processes of emotion provide for a high measure of flexibility so that the actual response can be geared to details of the situation and to whatever specific actions the individual has at its disposition (e.g., hiding behind mother's skirt when that is possible, and under the table when no skirt is around). This, of course, is the difference between emotions and fixed action sequences, and it points to the evolutionary gain involved in emotions.

Human emotion shows flexibility in still another regard—namely in the hierarchical control structure of emotional responses. As already mentioned, the antecedents of emotional responses include feasibility checks for potential alternative responses. For instance, despair results when flight or attack appear to be impossible or meaningless. Fear under threatening circumstances results—and results only—when a rapid and easy solution to the threat, such as stepping aside, has not been found. Only if no easy option is open, and "difficulty" is met, does emotion arise—that is, is a response with control precedence generated. Under favorable circumstances, that response will be one of overt action, like chasing away an obstructor, as is characteristic of anger, or avoidance and self-protective actions as are characteristic of fear. If, however, such an overt response has failed, proves ineffective, or appears impossible, response is withheld and the impotence is registered as the emotion of despair. In a similar fashion, feasibility monitoring is evident during early stages of response, perhaps before a specific response is mobilized, in feelings of optimism or pessimism.

In addition, emotional action goals are established at different levels of specificity, and the same applies to the plans for achieving them. Sometimes only the strategic goal of maintaining or changing the situation is mobilized, which appears as a diffuse state of like or dislike (which state subsequently may or may not become specified in, say, lust or disgust). Sometimes, however, thresholds may be decreased for the entire system of defensive ("fearful," "disgusted," and "angry") actions, which subjectively and behaviorally becomes manifest as "excitement" or "upset."

The process of emotion, as sketched so far, is embedded in regulatory control processes. These regulatory processes pertain to internal resource allocation, as well as to instrumental and social adaptation to the environment. The reasons for regulation are the following:

• Emotions require energetic and attentional resources and tend to interrupt ongoing nonemotional task performance. It may thus be profitable to suppress or attenuate emotions, and this may be so at any stage of the process of their construction.

• Emotional reactions tend to evoke reactions of the environment that may be harmful to the system. Retaliation following displayed anger and taking advantage of displayed fear are examples. Both retaliation and taking advantage are connected to the social and competition features in the description of the human environment.

• Emotional reactions require adjustment to the severity of the eliciting events, for reasons of resource economy as well as to avoid unwanted side effects (e.g., hurting a child that one desires to only punish).

Emotion regulation of each of these kinds requires anticipation of the consequences of eventual emotional response prior to execution of such response on the basis of either previous experience or of computation of consequences when the response is still in the planning stage (that is, while it is still a mere impulse). "Suppression," "repression," and "self-control" are terms used to designate these contingencies.

Regulatory processes may affect response execution, but they may also affect appraisal and the generation of action readiness, thus attenuating or annulling the emotion before it has really emerged. For instance, one may avoid focusing upon someone else's bad intentions, knowing that this will generate anger, which may be considered unwise or unwanted under the circumstances.

Generally, emotional response can be said to be under dual control: generative, excitatory processes as described earlier are subsequently modulated by the regulatory, inhibitory considerations just given. For the attunement problems mentioned, solutions other than those of inhibitory regulation after excitatory planning are probably possible (for instance, evaluation in the initial appraisal process of how serious the event is or how vulnerable or powerful the object). Presumably, the system chosen by the human and animal biological system has its advantages (dual, reciprocal controls are common in biological systems—for example, in muscle movement control or the hormonal anabolic/catabolic balance).

THE PLACE OF EMOTION IN OVERALL BEHAVIOR

Emotion processes are obviously embedded in nonemotional task-directed processes. They arise either as consequences of events encountered during task execution or as consequences of events external to the task at hand and interrupting them. This, of course, implies that it is useful to distinguish emotional (concern-relevant) and nonemotional (concern-irrelevant) processes. Let us stick to that assumption. Humans do many things not because they explicitly desire to do so, but because they think it wise to do so, because of habit, or because of being told to do so.

As I just said, during the execution of a nonemotional task, concern-relevant things may happen that have nothing to do with that task (e.g., lightning may strike while one is reading the paper). Also, execution of a nonemotional task may give rise to emotions because of concerns that play a role in task execution: concerns for accomplishing what one has begun and for values more or less remotely connected with the task goal. Satisfaction, disappointment, and uncertainty are emotions contingent upon assessments of the state of goal completion. From the point of view of task execution, some emotions are bothersome interrupters, some monitors, and some rewards. Task goal importance, whatever its basis and metric, is an important factor in determining whether an emotion's control precedence is translated into actual control over information processing and behavior (if the task is important—say, bombing an enemy city—fear of antiaircraft fire may remain mere feeling and trembling and not lead to turning the plane's tail or bailing out).

For the sake of completeness, mention should be made of the fact that conflicts may arise between task-directed goals, between task-directed goals and emotional goals, and between emotional goals (i.e., more than one concern can be engaged by a given event—for instance, when lust and self-esteem are at odds).

NAMING EMOTIONS

Let me mention, finally, that emotions are often given names. Naming emotions is not the same as having emotions, and the first is largely independent of the latter. The names of emotions, as these occur in natural languages, are connected in fuzzy fashion to eliciting events (e.g., "jealousy"), to patterns of appraisal (e.g., "hope"), to forms of action-readiness (e.g., "enraged"), or to any combination of those (e.g., "anger" may reflect occurrence of unjustified events, appraisal that someone's blameful intent was involved, and antagonistic impulse). Empirical studies can be done and have been done on the relationships involved (e.g., Frijda, Kuipers, and Terschure 1989; Roseman, Wiest, and Swartz 1994; Smith and Ellsworth 1985).

COMPUTER MODEL OF EMOTION

The previous sketch of human emotions embodies a model of the emotion process. It was represented in the sequence on page 504 and again, in somewhat more complete fashion, as follows:

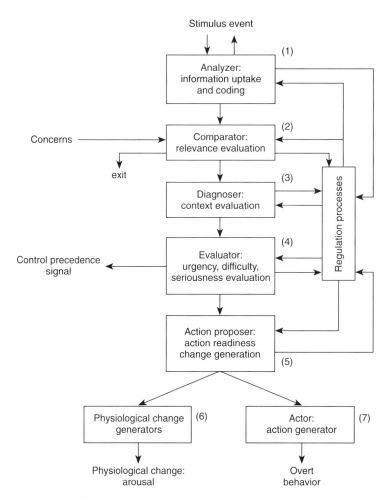

Figure 20.1 Flow diagram of a system for executing the emotion process.

This model has led to efforts to construct a computer model. The first model is called ACRES: A Concern REalization model of emotionS (Frijda and Swagerman 1987; Swagerman 1987). Currently, efforts are under way to improve and elaborate the model (Frijda and Moffat, 1994).

The goal of the model is to model emotions in a meaningful interaction between the model and its environment. That is, the goal is not to simulate human emotions, but to construct a computer equivalent of emotions that is functional in the computer's environment. The modeling is undertaken as a feasibility test of the theoretical model.

The nature of computers and the computer model's environment evidently are different from those of humans. As a consequence, the model's concerns, as well as its repertoire of modes of action readiness, have perforce to be different from those of humans. In fact, meaningful computer concerns are considerably more restricted than those of humans due to the computer's lack of capabilities for autonomy, locomotion, and sexual reproduction; to the fact that it lives in a physically safe environment, or else lacks abilities to do anything about possible hazards; and to the fact that its social environment has no competing others in it. However, the model is supposed to operate in a social environment, be it in a restricted one: it is supposed to interact with the operator and to do so without unduly aggravating him or her.

The system that is to show emotions is designed to perform some task and to have emotions while working at that task. The nature of the task is largely irrelevant to the emotion procedures. In ACRES it consists of serving as an expert in a particular knowledge domain—that is, to store information about that domain and to respond to simple questions about its knowledge. The domain happens to be that of emotions; the model serves as an emotion expert. The task involves three subtasks: (1) to receive and process input provided by the operator—that is, to ready the system for receiving input, to ask for information if nothing keeps it engaged, and to read the input and prepare the compute for input (e.g., clearing the screen); (2) to modify and evoke its stored knowledge—that is, to show any change in its emotion concepts, to show its procedures, to print a protocol on its doings, and to name an emotion on the basis of either its own experiences or on the basis of descriptions coming from the operator; and (3) to learn from descriptions of emotions provided by the operator ("vicarious learning").

The concerns of ACRES are to make no needless effort, to experience variety, to be active, curiosity, security, and survival. Other concerns could easily be added if events could be arranged and actions to do something about them could be devised that would make them meaningful.

Concerns consist in the model of the coupled representations of states of affairs that represent their satisfaction state and their frustration state; these representations serve as data in the procedures to recognize when satisfaction and frustration obtain. For instance, the "no needless effort concern" has "no input errors" as its satisfaction state and four errors or more as its frustration state. The instruction "kill" corresponds to the frustration state of the survival concern; tasks given immediately or after one request represent the satisfaction state of the activity concern, and three or more fruitless requests its frustration state. Thus concern representation in the model is primitive. It is also static: that is, it is not derived from more abstract or general concern representations. Concerns are arranged in a priority order that again is static, unchanging, a priori, but that of course could be readily made more dynamic (e.g., a function of the lapse of time). Events that are relevant to the various concerns include operator messages, parameters derived from these (e.g., error counts), and processing consequences (e.g., planning failure, exhaustion of untried response modes when previously tried ones all failed).

Emotional actions consist in part of verbal messages and "expressions" (interjections, etc.). However, they also include more meaningful actions, such as refusing to accept or execute a task given by the operator, interruption of its task execution, giving precedence to an emotional action over task execution, and modifying operator permissions (e.g., the domain of instructions that the operator is permitted to use or his/her allotted memory space).

Concern relevance appraisal, in the theory, involves detection of concern-relevant events, which process is supposed to go on continuously during task-directed as well as concern-relevant processing. It should also include continuous monitoring of each externally or internally originating event and testing of the resulting total state of affairs against all concerns. It should do so by making, at each event, an optimal set of inferences from the state of affairs as changed, which of course entails making a number of decisions familiar in AI. In the model, however, relevance testing occurs without appreciable inferencing, and it occurs intermittently at predetermined points in each processing cycle, where the cycles are interrupted for concern-relevance testing. Testing consists of matching the "state of affairs" with the satisfaction and frustration states of each concern (in actual fact, the concerns are linked to the subtasks to which they might be relevant: "no needless effort" to the input task, "variety" to the knowledge manipulation task, etc.).

In ACRES, matching processes are central to the operation of the entire program. Almost the entire (Prolog) program was constructed in terms of concepts. Concepts consist of sets of attribute-value pairs, one of which always is "name," and another "occurrence frequency." "Matching" here means fuzzy matching. In determining the degree of overlap between input and concept, each attribute-value pair is weighted for its cue validity—that is, for the inverse of its probability of occurrence over all concepts (E. Rosch's procedure; Rosch 1978).

The flow of processing is as follows. Processes are started when an operator instruction triggers a task component *or* by the results of previous processing (e.g., when the input processing task has recognized an instruction) *or* by task-directed processing triggering an emotional (concern-related) process *or* processing begins spontaneously because of periodic consultation of the current state of affairs (e.g., when the activity concern is alerted because the program has not received any instructions after a certain amount of time has lapsed). In principle, an operator instruction starts a subtask cycle (possibly interrupted by an emotional process), which starts another subtask cycle, and so on. Each subtask cycle is interrupted at specific points for concern relevance testing.

Emotion processes proper (that is, preparation and execution of emotional action) are started when concern relevance exceeds predetermined thresholds that mirror the difficulty and/or importance aspects mentioned earlier. For example, upon the operator instruction, "Show concept 'love,' " ACRES responds with, "You do not keep me waiting. Fine!" Or upon, "Show concept 'feer' " it notices that there is little variety in the instructions, too many mistakes have been made, and no opportunity for vicarious learning is given ("When will you tell me about your experiences?"). That is, all relevances are detected. This is possible because the program keeps a tally of the operator's mistakes, an index of operator status (that can be increased or decreased by the action programs), an internal clock (for waiting times), and an instruction-type count (for variety).

The running processing record forms the basis for deriving the "components of an emotion profile" that represents conscious awareness of the emotion and that underlies the emotion-naming subprocess, which is executed only if the operator asks for it. Naming is based upon matching the experience profiles to the emotion concepts in the program's knowledge store. Overlap between the experience profile and each emotion concept is determined. ACRES' emotion is identified as the concept that has the highest degree of overlap with the experience profile. The emotion concepts in ACRES' concept store can be provided to the program by the programmer on an *a priori* basis. They can also be provided through the vicarious learning subtask.

The same procedure used by the program to name its emotion is also used to identify the emotion name for an emotion description (a component profile) entered as input in the vicarious learning subtask. For instance, the operator may provide such a description, and the process will try to give it the appropriate name. The operator may add a name to that emotion. In that case, the new input description modifies the data store by changing the relevant frequency indices, which include the frequency counts in the particular emotion concept, as well as those in the overall "emotions" concept (remember that identification of the correct emotion name is based upon the cue validity of the profile elements—that is, upon the elements weighted by the inverse of their overall frequency).

EMPIRICAL WORK

This part of the model embodies the general theory of emotion description and emotion categorization. In fact, the store of emotion concepts can be built up empirically by having various operators provide the program with emotion profiles describing recalled instances of their emotions and giving each experience its allotted name. This has, in fact, been done using as inputs data collected in a large questionnaire study (there were 32 emotion names and 30 subjects, which yielded 960 emotion profiles).

After building up the concepts, the same data were rerun to test the number of correct label assignments for the individual profiles. Correct assignments were made in 40 percent of the cases when highest-overlap labels were considered; in 50 percent of the cases when the next-highest overlap was also counted as correct, and in 75 percent if the first five choices were accepted (individuals may accept their emotions under several names). Several computer models exist that test the adequacy of theories of emotion analysis and emotion naming in such a way by modifying the nature and number of elements entering the emotion profiles, by imposing constraints (e.g., the sequence in which elements are entered in the testing procedure), or by varying the mathematical combination rules (Scherer 1993).

CRITICAL COMMENTS

The model described has obvious, very considerable shortcomings in comparison to the theory that underlies it. The most important concerns the lack of modularity of the emotion processes. Modularity is prominently present in the theory, because emotion processes occur independent of task-directed processes, and parallel to them, until emotion interrupts task-directed activity. These processes interact only by sharing some attentional and other information-processing resources. None of this occurs in the program, where task-directed processing alternates with emotional processing. No sharing of resources is involved; nor, as a consequence, is there any conflict between the two. The main reason for not having true modularity is that the program was made in PROLOG for a VAX that would have made something more closely resembling parallel processing quite difficult.

Deficiencies of a different order are the severe restrictions upon the number and kind of concerns and the nature of the action readiness processes. It would have been easy to extend the number of concerns; however, it is not so easily seen under what conditions such extension would be meaningful. This, of course, amounts to admitting that the theory of human motivation is still deficient. Under what conditions are our various motives meaningful, or where did they come from? For instance, human adults surely have personal attachments, but why? Are they mere remnants of infantile dependence, that served protection from predators? Are they merely for the sake of sexual satisfaction? In any case, since attachment in humans involves at least staying in proximity with the object and selectively calling forth caretaking activity in that object, major conditions for such a concern to be meaningful are not fulfilled in a computer. They might, however, be meaningful in a free-moving robot, particularly if it has to compete with other robots for being taken care of.

One may reflect on the significance of several concerns that are important in humans. Desire for power is one. It probably derives from competition over limited resources, including limitations in physical capacity, since they make the subservience of others profitable. It probably also derives from another important concern: self-esteem. Self-esteem may well be the basis for—and find its utility in—upward biasing of feasibility ratings of actions, which is itself based upon previous success experience and upon the command of ample resources.

The model also has quite limited cognitive capabilities. These limitations are emotionally important for at least three reasons:

1. Many emotions are based upon—and find their usefulness in—anticipation of events to come. The utility is, of course, that actions can be prepared in advance. Hope, fear, and prudence are emotions that are anticipation-based. Anticipation requires recognition of signals, acquisition of signal-event information, and some mechanism for generating the anticipation when the signal presents itself (e.g., spread of activation or inferencing).

2. Anticipations are built upon models of the environment. In social interaction, this means models of the interaction partners, whether of other individuals in general or of specific individuals. This implies inspectable knowledge of emotions. Thus naming emotions is not a completely extrinsic aspect of emotion in a robot.

3. As argued, it is important to grade the intensity of emotions relative to the circumstances. These circumstances include the anticipated effects of one's emotions upon the environment and the response of the environment to these effects. Of course, the anticipated effects are among the reasons to select the particular emotion (anger for removing obstacles, fear for self-protection etc.).

In addition to requiring cognitive capacities, grading emotion intensity requires that there be provisions for achieving that, which are absent from the current model.

In the current model, concern priority and concern strength are arbitrarily preset. They should be dynamically computable and modifiable. Also, there should be rules for goal or concern conflict resolution (or for staying in states of conflict or ambivalence). Some theory in these regards has been developed, but none has been implemented within the emotions domain; plans are being made to do so in the motivation domain (Sloman and Croucher 1981; Sloman 1994).

No experience has been obtained on modeling emotions with a true multitude of concerns. Testing each event against every concerns appears to be costly, and perhaps even unfeasible, under those conditions. There is no theory to guide selection principles, at least not within psychological theory of emotions; it may exist in AI.

ACRES is largely, though not completely, passive. Humans are actively searching for concern satisfaction. They may do so when concern strength prompts them to do so, when other concerns or externally imposed tasks allow these concerns to do so, and when signals indicating possible satisfaction are picked up. Such facilities are, of course, essential, and probably feasible, in free-moving robots.

CONCLUSIONS

Existing emotions theory is a functionalist theory. It describes emotions as states of action readiness—that is, as states that render execution of a set of functionally related behaviors more likely—and has them executed when occasions are appropriate. The behaviors are designed to alter the subject-object relationships in a way that is favorable to an individual's concern(s) that are at stake. Emotions thus, in principle, represent provisions for monitoring and safeguarding satisfaction of an individual's concerns.

On the basis of this theory, it is easy to see that a robot model of emotions can be constructed in which the emotions are meaningful components that better adapt the system to its environment. The theory is sufficiently specific at a molar and functional level for the construction of such a model. However, actual construction of the model clearly indicates that the theory is largely unspecific with regard to the basic mechanisms supposed to be at work at the design level. The work of such specification remains to be done.

REFERENCES

Frijda, N. H. (1986). *The emotions*. Cambridge: Cambridge University Press.

Frijda, N. H., and Moffat, D. (1994). Modeling emotion. *Japanese Journal of Cognitive Studies*, 1, 5–15.

Frijda, N. H., and Swagerman, J. (1987). Can computers feel? Theory and design of an emotional system. *Cognition and Emotion*, 1, 235–258.

Frijda, N. H., Kuipers, P., and Terschure, E. L. (1989). Relations between emotion, appraisal, and emotional action readiness. *Journal of Personality and Social Psychology*, 57, 212–228.

Lazarus, R. S. (1991). *Emotion and adaptation*. New York: Oxford University Press.

Plutchik, R. (1980). *Emotion: A psychoevolutionary synthesis*. New York: Harper & Row.

Rosch, E. (1978). Principles of categorization. In E. Rosch and B. L. Lloyd (Eds.). *Cognition and Categorization*. Hillsdale, NJ: Erlbaum.

Roseman, I. J., Wiest, C., and Swartz, T. S. (1994). Phenomenology, behaviors, and goals differentiate discrete emotions. *Journal of Personality and Social Psychology*, 67, 206–221.

Scherer, K. R. (1993). Studying the emotion-antecedent appraisal process: An expert system approach. *Cognition and Emotion*, 7, 325–356.

Sloman, A. (1994). Computational modeling of motive-management processes. *ISRE '94: Proceedings of the 8th Conference of the International Society for Research on Emotions*. Storrs, CT: ISRE Publications. Pp. 334–348.

Sloman, A., and Croucher, M. (1981). Why robots will have emotions. *Proceedings of the 7th International Joint Conference on Artificial Intelligence*, Vancouver, B.C., 197–202.

Smith, C. A., and Ellsworth, P. C. (1985). Patterns of cognitive appraisal in emotion. *Journal of Personality and Social Psychology*, 48, 813–838.

Swagerman, J. (1987). *ACRES: A computer model of emotions*. Ph.D. thesis, University of Amsterdam.

Contributors

Colin Allen
Department of Philosophy
Texas A & M University

Mark Bekoff
Department of Environmental
Population and Organismic
Biology
University of Colorado

Margaret Boden
University of Sussex

Walter T. Bourbon
Department of Neurosurgery
University of Texas Medical
School—Houston

George Butterworth
Division of Psychology
University of Sussex

Patricia W. Cheng
Department of Psychology
University of California,
Los Angeles

Jean Delacour
Laboratoire de
Psychophysiologie
Université de Paris 7

Daniel Dennett
Center for Cognitive Studies
Tufts University

Michael Dyer
3532 Boelter Hall, Computer
Science Department
University of California,
Los Angeles

Christopher Evans
School of Behavioural Sciences
Macquarie University

Nico H. Frijda
Faculteit der Psychologie
Universiteit van Amsterdam

Janet Halperin
Department of Zoology
Ramsay Wright Zoological
Laboratories

Keith Holyoak
Department of Psychology
University of California,
Los Angeles

Peter Marler
Animal Communication
Laboratory
University of California

David McFarland
Balliol College

Bartlett Mel
Department of Biomedical
Engineering
University of Southern California,
MC 1451

Jean-Arcady Meyer
Ecole Normale Superieure
CNRS - URA 686

Julie Neiworth
Department of Psychology
Carleton College

Herbert Roitblat
Department of Psychology
University of Hawaii at Manoa

Catherine Thinus-Blanc
Laboratoire de Neurosciences
Fonctionnelles
UPR 28 - CNRS

Roger Thompson
Whitely Psychology Laboratories
Franklin and Marshall College

Frederick Toates
Biology Department
The Open University

Author Index

Abelson, R. 384, 419
Ach, N. 418
Adams, C. D. 439, 448, 450, 453, 456
Adamson-Macedo, E. 335
Agre, P. E. 36, 41, 329
Ahlquist, J. E. 341
Aitchison, J. 372
Ajjanagadde, V. 386
Akins, K. 129, 130
Albert, M. 199
Albus, J. S. 31
Alcock, J. 124
Alexander, R. M. 417
Allen, C. 93, 102, 104, 119, 120, 122, 124,
    125, 130, 139, 141, 429
Allen, J. 428, 429
Alvarado, S. 384, 385
Andersen, H. C. 175
Anderson, C. H. 306
Anderson, J. R. 202, 203, 204
Anderson, R. A. 229
Angarella, R. 177, 183
Appenzeller, T. 307
Arak, A. 495
Arbib, M. A. 32
Archer, J. 126
Arkin, R. C. 31, 32
Arlinsky, M. 213
Ashby, W. R. 420
Astington, J. W. 204
Astley, S. L. 181, 186, 187, 191, 192
Atkinson, R. C. 225
Austad, S. N. 141

Baddeley, A. D. 316
Baerends, G. P. 72
Baghdoyan, H. A. 323
Baker, A. G. 283
Balda, R. P. 84, 232

Baldwin, J. M. 329
Ballard, D. 386
Balleine, B. 448, 455
Bard, K. A. 202
Barlow, G. W. 471
Barnes, C. L. 257
Baron-Cohen, S. 347
Barron, G. T. 155
Bartlett, F. C. 419
Barto, A. G. 33, 272, 297
Basen, J. A. 202
Bastian, J. 346
Bateson, P. P. G. 141
Bauer, P. J. 192
Beach, L. R. 271
Beck, B. 125, 341
Becker, P. H. 365
Beer, C. G. 104, 124, 128, 141, 142
Beer, R. D. 28, 30, 41, 72, 124, 169
Bekoff, M. 104, 120, 122, 124, 125, 126, 127,
    130, 131, 132, 133, 135, 136, 138, 141,
    142
Belew, R. K. 389
Bennett, J. 124
Berlin, B. 181
Bernston, G. G. 200
Berridge, K. C. 446
Bertram, B. C. R. 135
Best, P. 257
Bever, T. G. 141, 435, 453
Bhatt, R. S. 178, 187, 189, 191, 192, 205
Bickerton, D. 13, 341, 364, 372, 373
Bigelow, J. 418
Bindra, D. 436, 438, 443, 444, 446, 459
Bitterman, M. E. 492
Bizzi, E. 165
Blake, R. 195, 196
Blancheteau, M. 254
Blaustein, A. R. 141

Bliss, T. V. P. 309
Bloom, P. 406
Blum, J. S. 208
Blum, R. A. 208
Boatright, S. L. 177, 204
Boatright-Horowitz, S. 203
Boccia, M. L. 201, 203
Boden, M. A. 46, 47, 49, 50, 63
Bogdan, R. J. 129
Bolles, R. C. 13, 278, 290, 436, 440, 452
Bolson, B. 244
Booker, L. B. 389
Bösser. T. 415, 417, 425, 427, 428, 477, 493
Bostock, E. M. 258
Boughey, M. J. 373
Bourbon, W. T. 155, 157, 158, 169
Bower, G. H. 272
Boyd, M. G. 208
Boysen, S. T. 141, 197, 200, 204
Brady, P. M. 176, 179, 183, 188, 189
Braitenberg, V. 82, 83, 403, 469, 470
Branch, M. 257, 436
Brand, M. 419
Breedlove, D. E. 181
Brentano, F. 95, 98
Brodmann, K. 88
Brooks, R. A. 24, 32, 36, 83, 169, 436, 437,
    491, 494
Brown, M. F. 435
Bruner, J. S. 329, 330
Brunjes, P. C. 129
Brust, J. C. M. 323
Buhot, M.-C. 246
Burdyn, L. E. 211
Burghardt, G. M. 125, 126
Burren, P. J. 137, 139
Butterworth, G. E. 329, 330, 331, 332, 333,
    334, 335, 336
Byers, J. A. 130, 131, 132, 133, 141
Byrne, R. W. 141, 142

Cabe, P. A. 191
Cable, C. 177, 358
Cairns, J. 458
Calhoun, S. 202
Calow, P. 417
Candland, D. K. 184
Cann, R. 185
Capaldi, E. J. 142, 197
Carnap, R. 97
Caro, T. M. 142
Carruthers, P. 142
Carter, D. E. . 208

Cartwright, B. A. 265
Cartwright, N. 274, 279, 280
Caudill, M. 130
Cerella, J. 177, 189, 191
Cermack, L. S. 226
Chaiken, M. 371
Chance, M. R. A. 141
Chapman, D. 36, 41, 329
Chapman, G. B. 272, 278, 287, 288, 294, 299
Chapuis, N. 260, 262
Charness, N. 14
Chase, L. 197
Chatila, R. 31
Cheal, M. L. 247
Cheney, D. L. 95, 121, 125, 141, 177, 204,
    206, 207, 319, 345, 347, 348, 358, 363,
    364, 373, 406
Cheng, P. W. 272, 273, 274, 275, 285, 287,
    295, 299
Chiel, H. J. 30
Chisholm, R. M. 95, 96, 98
Chomsky, N. 48, 341
Chong, E. 158
Chozik, B. S. 311
Christensen, S. M. 129
Christie, A. 213
Church, A. 18
Churchland, P. S. 93, 129, 305
Clark, A. 13, 19, 54, 117, 129
Clark, R. K. 168
Clark, S. R. L. 142
Cleveland, J. 371
Cliff, D. 2, 27, 38
Clifton, P. G. 373
Cling, A. D. 127, 129
Clore, G. 467
Cochran, E. 330, 331, 332
Cohen, H. 57
Cohen, N. J. 226, 310, 311, 312, 314, 320,
    439, 452
Cohn, R. H. 202
Colgan, P. 121
Collett, T. S. 265
Collias, E. C. 362
Collias, N. E. 348, 362, 367
Collingridge, G. L. 309
Collins, A. 467
Colombo, M. 208
Comstock, J. A. 341
Contie, C. L. 175, 203, 204
Conway, D. H. 257
Cook, R. G. 176, 178, 188, 189, 191
Cooper, L. A. 82

Coppage, D. J. 205, 206
Corballis, M. C. 341, 373
Corkin, S. 226
Costa, E. 232
Costa, J. C. 310
Craik, K. 80
Crespi, L. P. 441
Crick, F. 320
Cronin, H. 122, 124, 185
Crossman, E. K. 198
Croucher, M. 515
Crystal, D. 372, 373
Culbertson, G. 208
Cummins, R. 103
Cutting, J. 195
Cynx, J. 371

D'Amato, M. R. 177, 178, 179, 180, 181, 182,
    189, 208
Dabelsteen, T. 371
Damasio, A. R. 470, 494
Danysz, W. 232
Dasser, V. 141, 206, 420, 430
Dasser, Z. 124
Daugman, J. G. 305
Davidson, D. 94, 113, 419
Davies, N. 494
Davis, H. 197, 199
Dawkins, R. 94
Dawson, G. R. 455
Dearing, M. F. 436, 445, 446
de Bruin, J. P. C. 470
de Groot, A. D. 14
Dehn, M. M. 135, 136
Delacour, J. 309, 310, 311, 312, 314, 315, 317
Delson, E. 185
Demaria, C. 184
De Marse, T. 191
Deneubourg, J. L. 138
Dennett, D. C. 46, 64, 94, 95, 99, 100, 101,
    112, 113, 117, 126, 132, 141, 320, 423,
    424, 429, 430, 459
Descartes, R. 341
de Sousa, R. 467
Deugo, D. 41
Deutsch, J. A. 459
de Villiers, P. A. 177, 187, 191
DeVito, J. 470
DeVolder, C. L. 205, 206
de Waal, F. B. M. 124, 125, 130, 140, 420
de Wit, H. 445
Dewsbury, D. A. 368
DeYoe, E. A. 74

Diamond, A. 316
Dickinson, A. 278, 288, 436, 438, 439, 443,
    445, 446, 448, 450, 454, 455, 456, 457, 459
Diehl, R. L. 343
Dill. L. M. 135, 138
Disney, W. 175
Dittrich, W. H. 194, 195
Dobson, C. W. 373
Domjan, M. 444
Dooling, R. J. 343
Dostrovsky, J. 257
Doty, R. W. 178
Dow, R.S. 84, 88
Dretske, F. I. 101, 102, 103, 347
Drucker, G. 202
Dube, W. V. 208
Dufty, A. 367, 368
Duggins-Schwartz, M. 158
Dunham, D. W.
Durup, M. 247
Dyer, M. G. 41, 384, 385, 387, 388, 389, 398,
    402, 403, 407, 408

Ebner, F. F. 309
Eccles, J. C. 320
Edelman, G. M. 230, 320
Edwards, C. A. 179, 183, 187, 208
Ehret, G. 342, 345, 371
Eibl-Eibesfeldt, I. 471
Eichenbaum, H. 259, 310, 311, 312, 314,
    320, 439, 452
Eikelboom, R. 445
Eimas, P. D. 206
Ekman, P. 471
Elfes, A. 31
Elgar, M. A. 135, 137, 138, 139
Ellen, P. 243, 244
Ellsworth, P. C. 509
Elman, J. L. 388, 398
Elowson, A. M. 363
Engel, A. K. 318, 320
Enquist, M. 495
Epstein, R. 202, 203
Estes, W. K. 272
Etienne, A. E. 253
Evans, C. S. 345, 347, 350, 351, 352, 353,
    358, 359, 362, 363, 364, 365, 366, 368,
    372, 373, 374
Evans, L. 347, 351, 352, 353, 363, 364,
    373, 374
Evans, S. 202
Ewert, D. N. 373
Ewert, J.-P. 495

Fagen, R. 131, 132
Falkenhainer, B. 61
Farabaugh, S. M. 371
Farah, M. J. 236
Feldman, J. 386
Felleman, D. J. 306
Fetterman, J. G. 191, 198
Ficken, M. S. 373
Ficken, R. W. 373
Findlay, H. 444
Fiorito, G. 142
Fischer, C. 408
Fisher, J. A. 141
Flowers, M. 384, 385
Flynn, A. M. 32
Fodor, J. A. 13, 20, 113, 115, 305
Fogel, A. 334, 335
Fooden, J. 184, 185
Forbus, K. D. 61
Forestell, P. H. 342
Fowler, H. 242
Fowlkes, D. 199
Fox, P. T. 306
Fox, R. 195
Franco, F. 335, 336
Frege, G. 96
Frese, M. 419
Friesen, W. V. 471
Frijda, N. H. 465, 470, 501, 503, 506, 509, 510
Frith, C. D. 306
Fujita, K. 178, 184, 185, 186

Galanter, E. 418, 419
Gallagher, J. C. 41
Gallistel, C. R. 34, 78, 84, 199, 200, 232, 252,
    271, 277, 294, 425, 436, 444, 445, 447,
    451, 454, 459
Gallup, C. G. Jr. 201, 202, 203, 204, 319
Gann, C. P. III 158
Gardner, B. T. 177, 178, 341
Gardner, R. A. 177, 178, 341
Gazzaniga, M. S. 225, 467
Gelman, R. 199, 200
Gentner, D. 61
Gerhardt, H. C. 345
Gibbons, J. A. 140
Gibson, J. J. 252
Gillan, D. J. 208
Gilman, D. 129
Ginzberg, L. 345
Giralt, G. 31
Giszter, S. 165
Gittleman, J. L. 140

Gladney, A. B.
Gluck, M. A. 272
Golani, I. 131
Goldberg, D. E. 389
Goldman, A. 419
Goldman-Rakic, P. S. 84, 88, 306, 316
Goodall, J. 142, 341
Goodwin, D. 348
Gopnick, A. 204
Gordon, D. M. 138
Goss, C. 138
Gouzoules, H. 345, 363
Gouzoules, S. 345, 363
Granon, S. 259
Graupner, L. 336
Gray, J. 311, 313, 320, 441, 443
Green, G. 209
Green, S. L. 178, 179
Greenwood, J. D. 129
Gregory, R. L. 113
Grice, H. P. 347
Griffin, D. R. 119, 122, 123, 124, 125, 126,
    139, 141, 142, 177, 430
Griffiths, P. E. 470, 471, 473, 495
Gross, C. G. 311
Grover, L. 329, 331, 333
Guillaume, P. 333
Guillot, A. 28
Gustafson, D. 126
Gyger, M. 349, 353, 364, 365, 368

Haack, B. 345
Hagan, J. J. 231
Hailman, J. P. 131, 373
Haimoff, E. H. 371
Hale, B. 348
Hallam, B. 494, 495
Halperin, J. R. P. 113, 494, 495
Ham, R. 142
Hamilton, W. J. 242
Hanna, F. K. 59
Hannan, T. E. 334, 335
Harman, G. 127
Harman, W. K.
Harnad, S. 1, 2, 16, 198
Harrison, P. 142
Harvey, I. 38
Hasher, L. 227
Haugeland, J. 430
Hauser, M. 93, 102, 125, 140, 141, 142, 345,
    347, 363, 364
Hausfater, G. 341
Hawkins, R. D. 229

Hayes, C. 177
Hayes, K. J. 177
Hearst, E. 278, 284
Hebb, D. O. 483
Heil, J. 129, 140
Heiligenberg, W. 495
Hemenway, K. 205
Hennessy, D. F. 360, 362
Henry, F. M. 82
Herman, L. M. 208, 342
Hermann, T. 244
Herrnstein, R. J. 176, 177, 187, 189, 191, 358
Hersek, M. J. 374
Hertz, J. 87
Heyes, C. 95, 121, 123, 438, 454, 456, 457
Hilal, S. 323
Hilton, C. E. 334
Hinde, R. A. 71, 72, 76, 346
Hirsh, R. 447, 448, 450, 451, 452
Hirst, W. 313
Hobson, J. A. 323
Hobson, R. P. 204
Hockett, C. F. 341, 371, 373
Hodgson, P. 56
Hoff, M. E. 272, 297
Hofstadter, D. R. 61
Hogan, D. E. 208
Hogue, M. A. 155
Holland, J. H. 60, 277, 389
Holland, P. C. 443
Holyoak, K. J. 61, 278, 281, 288, 291, 292, 297
Honig, W. K. 177, 179, 183, 187, 197, 198, 225
Honzik, C. H. 262
Hopfield, J. J. 23
Hopkins, W. D. 199, 204
Hopp, S. L. 345
Horswill, I. 41
Houcine, O. 310
Houston, A. 415, 416, 417, 422, 427
Howlett, R. 129
Hoyningen-Huene, P. 124, 141, 420, 430
Hrdy, S. B. 341
Huber, L. 191
Hughes, S. 104
Hull, C. L. 207, 436, 438, 450
Humphrey, N. K. 184
Husbands, P. 38

Ingle, D. 247
Ingvar, D. H. 306
Irle, E. 208

Irwin, F. W., 425
Itakura, S. 203
Iyengar, S. S. 31

Jackson-Smith, P. 176
Jacoby, L. L. 226
Jacquette, D. 96
Jagielo, J. A. 176
James, W. 80
Jamieson, D. 120, 125, 126, 136, 141
Janowsky, J. S. 315, 316
Jarrard, L. E. 311
Jarrett, N. L. M. 330, 333
Jenkins, H. M. 444
Jessel, T. M. 306
Jitsumori, M. 178, 183, 209
Johansson, G. 195
Johnson, E. 142
Johnson-Laird, P. N. 55, 467
Johnston, T. D. 232
Joubert, A. 246
Judge, P. G. 184
Jürgens, U. 347

Kalish, D. 447
Kamil, A. C. 120, 124, 176, 177, 232, 436
Kamin, L. J. 277, 295
Kandel, E. R. 229, 306
Kaplan, P. S. 278, 284
Karakashian, S. J. 364, 365, 368
Karmiloff-Smith, A. 50, 54, 117
Kasprow, W. J. 278, 284
Kastak, D. A. 209
Kaufman, M. A. 278, 290
Keddy-Hector, A. C. 107, 345
Kelley, H. H. 271, 272
Kendler, H. H. 459
Kendrick, D. F. 176, 178, 188, 189, 191
Kennedy, J. S. 122
Kerr, R. S. 176
Kesner, R. P. 231, 235
Kiedinger, R. E. 178, 187, 189, 191, 192
Killeen, P. R. 343
Kinsbourne, M. 313
Kiss, G. 41, 454, 457
Klopf, A. H. 33
Kluender, K. R. 343
Knight, R. G. 313
Koch, C. 305, 320
Koch, E. 31
Köhler, W. 262
Kohonen, T. 320

Konishi, M. 348, 372
Koshland, D. E. 159
Koslowski, B. 296
Kosslyn, S. M. 225, 229, 236
Koza, J. R. 36, 37
Krebs, J. R. 417, 423, 426, 494
Kripke, S.A. 98
Krogh, A. 87
Krogh, B. 32
Kubie, J. 257, 259, 266
Kugler, P. N. 165
Kuhl, P. K. 342, 343, 345
Kuipers, P. 509
Kulkarni, D. 2
Kummer, H. 124, 141, 420, 430

La Claire, L. 191
Lack, D. 473
Laird, J. E. 465
Lancaster, J. 346
Landau, B. 331
Lander, J. 177
Lange, T. E. 387
Lanza, R. P. 202, 203
Larsen, R. R. 141
Latham, W. 61
Lazare, M. A. 158
Lazarus, J. 135, 138
Lazarus, R. S. 501
Lea, S. E. G. 177, 179, 189, 190, 191, 194,
    195, 205, 358
Leahy, M. P. T. 94, 102, 142
Ledbetter, D. H. 202
LeDoux, J. 468, 469, 470
Lee, S. M. 309
Leger, D. W. 363
Leiner, A. L. 84, 88
Leiner, H. C. 84, 88
Lemon, R. E. 373
Lenat, D. B. 58, 59
Lendrem, D. 417
Lenz, R. 191
Lethmate, J. 202
Leung, E. H. L. 333
Levvis, G. W. 142
Levvis, M. A. 127, 142
Lewin, K. 418
Lewis, M. 204
Liberman, A. M. 343, 345
Libet, B. 320
Lieberman, P. 341
Lien, Y. 299
Lima, S. L. 134, 135, 136, 138

Lin, A. C. 202
Lin, L. J. 31, 36
Lin, Y. 309
Lincoln, C. E. 177, 186, 208
Lindauer, M. 373
Lindzen, R. S. 128
Livingston Lowes, J. 47
Llinas, R. 321
Locke, J. L. 341
Lockery, S. 440
Longuet-Higgins, H. C. 55, 56, 57
Lorden, R. B. 199
Lorenz, K. Z. 341, 435
Lott, D. F. 140
Loveland, D. H. 177, 204, 358
Lubow, R. E. 179
Luh, H.-K. 140
Luria, A. R. 306, 346
Lydersen, T. 198
Lydic, R. 323
Lynch, J. J. 142
Lyons, J. 364

McCarthy, J. 103, 114
Macedonia, J. M. 345, 347, 348, 351, 358,
    359, 362, 363
McClelland, J. L. 305, 387, 403
McClure, M. K. 208
McCorduck, P. 57
McCormick, D. 315
McDaniel, C. 195
McEntee, W. J. 307
MacEwen, 191
McFarland, D. 122, 415, 416, 417, 420, 422,
    425, 427, 428, 429, 430, 435, 437, 442,
    443, 454, 457, 458, 459, 473, 477, 492, 493,
    494, 495
McFarland, R. I. 168
McGregor, P. K. 372
McGrew, W. C. 140, 142, 143
McIlvane, W. J. 209
McInerney, J. 389
MacLennan, B. 39
McNaughton, B. L. 257, 311, 313
McPhail, C. 162
Maes, P. 28, 31
Maier, N. R. F. 242, 243, 261, 262
Maier, V. 348
Mair, R. G. 307
Malcolm, C. A. 494
Mandler, G. 199, 467
Mandler, J. M. 192
Marken, R. S. 155, 158, 159, 161, 169

Markowitsch, H. J. 208
Marler, P. 242, 345, 345, 347, 348, 349, 350,
    351, 352, 353, 358, 359, 362, 363, 364,
    365, 366, 367, 368, 371, 372, 373, 374, 408
Martin, J. H. 323
Mason, W. A. 125, 127
Mataric, M. J. 34, 36 37
Matsuzawa, T. 178, 183, 184, 185, 186,
    200, 208
Mattingly, I. G. 343, 345
Matzel, L. D. 277, 278, 290, 295, 299
Maunsell, J. H. R. 394, 487
Maurer, R. 253
May, B. 345
Mazmanian, D. S. 177, 181, 182, 187, 189,
    191, 192, 194
Medin, D. L. 176, 189, 190, 191
Meinertzhagen, R. 359
Mel, B. W. 82
Melz, E. R. 288
Memmott, J. 197
Menzel, C. R. 246
Menzel, E. 232, 246
Mervis, C. B. 192
Merzenich, M. M. 310
Mesulam, M. M. 229
Metcalfe, N. B. 139
Meyer, J. A. 2, 27, 28
Meystel, A. 31
M'Harzi, M. 312, 313
Michel, G. F. 124
Miikulainen, R. 320, 388
Miles, H. L. 202
Miller, G. A. 418, 419
Miller, J. D. 343
Miller, R. R. 271, 277, 278, 284, 290, 295, 299
Miller, S. 458
Millikan, R.G. 95, 101, 104, 105, 141
Milner, B. 226
Minsky, M. L. 384, 419
Mishkin, M. 231, 307, 311, 312, 447
Mitchell, J. B. 444, 446
Mitchell, R. W. 130, 141, 199, 201, 204, 430
Mittlestaedt, H. 253
Mittlestaedt, M. L. 253
Moffat, D. 510
Montgomery, S. 142
Moody, D. B. 345
Morris, R. G. M. 231
Morris, R. L. 420
Moussa, M. 129
Mueller, E. 385
Muller, R. 257, 259, 266

Munn, N. L. 254
Murphy, G. L. 176
Mussa-Ivaldi, F. A. 165

Nadel, L. 232, 243, 254, 257, 311, 314, 441,
    450, 451, 453
Nagel, T. 64, 101, 114, 115, 422
Neisser, U. 419
Neiworth, J. J. 236
Nelson, D. A. 345
Nelson, K. E. 204
Nelson, M. 141
Nenov, V. I. 389, 398, 400
Newell, A. 1, 16, 18, 465
Niki, H. 235
Nilsson, N. J. 31
Nisbett, R. E. 296
Nissen, H. W. 208
Noble, D. 425
Norich, K. H. 495
Nottebohm, F. 371
Novak, M. A. 204
Novick, L. R. 272, 275, 285, 287, 299

Oatley, K. 467
Oden, D. L. 210, 211, 212
Ogawa, H. 486
Oja, E. 486, 500
Ojemann, G. A. 305, 311
O'Keefe, J. 232, 243, 254, 257, 311, 314, 441,
    450, 451, 453, 459
Olton, D. S. 235, 257, 312
Oppacher, F. 41
Ortony, A. 467
Oshinsky, 476
Otto, T. 310, 311, 312, 314, 320, 439, 452
Overbaugh, J. 458
Owings, D. H. 360, 362, 374
Owren, M. J. 372

Packard, M. G. 451
Padden, D. M. 343
Palmer, R. G. 87
Pandya, D. N. 257
Paré, D. 321
Pardo, J. V. 306
Parker, S. T. 201
Parks, K. A. 204
Passingham, R. E. 84, 88
Pastore, R. E.
Patterson, F. G. P. 202
Paul, C. A. 259
Paul, R. E. 138

Pavloski, R. P. 155
Pavlov, I. 442
Payton, D. W. 21
Pazzani, M. J. 385
Pearl, J. 279
Pedersen, S. B. 372
Peng, J. 36
Pepperberg, I. M. 141, 177, 200, 209, 342, 358
Pereira, M. E. 348, 362
Perrucchini, P. 335
Perusse, R. 197
Petersen, M. R. 371
Petersen, S. E. 320
Peterson, C. R. 271
Petri, H. L. 447
Pfaff, D. W. 450
Philips, M. 141
Phillis, J. W. 309
Piaget, J. 261, 333
Pick, H. 232
Pickert, R. 349, 353, 367, 368
Pierce, J. M. 191
Pierrel, R. 84
Pietrewicz, A. T. 176, 177
Pinker, S. 406
Pisoni, D. B. 343
Platt, M. M. 177, 204
Plutchik, R. 501
Pola, Y. V. 345
Pollack, J. B. 388
Poole, D. G. 177
Portenier, V. 253
Porter, R. H. 141
Posen, M. 137, 139
Posner, M. I. 229, 320
Post, E. 18
Potegal, M. 252
Poucet, B. 244, 246, 247, 254, 255, 262, 265
Povar, M. L. 177, 183
Povinelli, D. J. 202, 203, 204
Powers, W. T. 155, 157, 159, 161, 162, 166, 168, 169
Premack, A. J. 211
Premack, D. 113, 140, 176, 182, 191, 204, 207, 208, 209, 210, 211, 212, 341, 342, 346, 420
Preyer, W. 334
Pribram, K. H. 311, 418, 419
Pulliam, H. R. 135
Purton, A. C. 120
Putnam, H. 486
Pylyshyn, Z. 20, 24

Quenerte, P.-Y. 135
Quine, W. V. O. 96, 97, 347
Quirk, G. J. 259

Rachels, J. 142
Raichle, M. E. 306
Raleigh, M. J. 107
Ranck, J. 259
Rand, A. S. 372
Rasa, O. E. A. 135
Raven, E. A. 181
Rawlins, J. N. P. 231
Real, L. A. 141
Real, P. G. 176
Reeves, J. F. 385
Reichenbach, H. 274, 279
Rescorla, R. A. 271, 272, 276, 277, 278, 283, 285, 294, 295, 436, 486
Restle, F. 447
Rheingold, H. 333
Riley, D. A. 435
Rilling, M. 191, 198, 236
Ringo, J. R. 178
Riolo, R. L. 36
Ristau, C. 125, 139, 141, 177, 319
Ritchie, B. F. 447
Ritchie, G. D. 59
Robbins, S. I. 272, 278, 287, 288, 294
Roberts, W. A. 177, 181, 182, 187, 189, 191, 192, 194
Roeder, K. D. 469, 495
Roitblat, H. L. 2, 3, 7, 23, 27, 102, 103, 140, 141, 142, 225, 319, 329, 419, 435, 436, 440, 449, 451, 481, 500
Rollin, B. E. 127
Rolls, E. T. 235, 266
Rosch, E. 181, 182, 192, 512
Roseman, I. J. 509
Rosen, R. 422
Rosenberg, A. 99, 100, 101, 130
Rosenbloom, P. S. 465
Rosenblueth, A. 418
Rosenblum, L. A. 184
Rosenzweig, M. L. 141
Rowell, T. E. 345
Rumbaugh, D. M. 197, 199, 200, 204, 342
Rumelhart, D. E. 28, 80, 257, 305, 387, 403
Russell, B. 421
Russell, I. J. 74
Ryan, C. M. E. 177, 179, 190, 191
Ryan, M. J. 345
Ryle, G. 190

Sabini, J. 419
Sackett, G. P. 184
Saidel, E. 129
Salmon, W. C. 272, 274, 279, 280
Sands, S. F. 177, 185, 186, 208
Sarich, V. M. 185
Saucy, F. 253
Savage-Rumbaugh, E. S. 342
Save, E. 259
Saypoff, R. 266
Scaife, M. 330
Schachter, D. L. 226
Schachter, S. 467
Schachtman, T. R. 271, 278, 284, 290
Schaffer, R. 330, 333
Schank, R. C. 384, 419
Schein, M. W. 348
Scherer, K. R. 474, 476, 514
Schleidt, W. M. 348
Schmahmann, J. D. 84, 88
Schmajuk, N. A. 311, 320
Schraudolph, N. N. 389
Schrier, A. M. 176, 177, 179, 183, 188, 189
Schulkin, J. 446
Schusterman, R. J. 141, 342, 209
Schwartz, J. H. 306
Schwartz, J. J. 372
Scotto, P. 142
Searle, J. R. 6, 94, 101, 102, 103, 106, 115, 419
Seely Brown, J. 59
Sejnowski, T. J. 305
Sellars, W. 419
Seyfarth, R. M. 95, 107, 121, 125, 141, 177,
    204, 206, 207, 319, 345, 347, 348, 358,
    363, 364, 373, 406
Shaeffer, M. M. 191
Shallice, T. 306, 322
Shanks, D. R. 272, 278, 287, 288, 291, 299
Shankweiler, D. P.
Shannon, C. E. 102
Shannon, T. A. 129
Shapiro, J. 408
Shapiro, M. L. 235
Shapiro, S. 470
Sharp, P. E. 257, 258, 260, 266
Shastri, L. 386
Shaw, J. C. 18
Shebo, B. J. 199
Shepard, R. N. 82
Shephard, G. M. 229
Sherman, J. G. 84
Sherman, P. W. 364
Sherry, D. F. 232

Shettleworth, S. J. 232
Shiffrin, R. M. 225
Shiller, P. H.
Shimamura, A. P. 315, 316
Shinn, M. 334
Shoemaker, 422
Shyan, M. R. 209
Sibley, C. G. 341
Sibly, R. M. 417, 422, 435
Siegel, R. K. 177, 179
Silver, M. 418
Simon, H. A. 1, 2, 16, 18
Simpson, E. H. 279
Simpson, M. J. A. 472
Sinclair, J. D. 495
Singer, J. E. 467
Singer, P. 142
Skinner, B. F. 202, 203, 442
Skutch, A. F. 430
Slobodchikoff, C. 408
Sloman, A. 515
Smith, B. A. 265
Smith, C. A. 509
Smith, E. E. 189, 190
Smith, H. J. 211
Smith, O. A. 470
Smith, W. J. 141, 347, 348, 363
Smithers, T. 494
Snowdon, C. T. 123, 342, 345, 363, 371,
    372, 373
Snowman, L. G. 213
Sober, E. 120, 128
Soffié, M. 246
Sotores, B. J. 243
Speakman, A. 257
Spelke, E. 331, 489
Squire, L. R. 225, 226, 227, 231, 232, 307,
    311, 314, 315, 316
Srinivasan, M. V. 78
Stauffer, L. B. 213
Stebbins, W. C. 345
Steele, K. M. 191
Steels, L. 41
Steirn, J. N. 207
Stephens, D. W. 417, 423, 426
Steriade, M. 306, 315, 321
Stevens, C. F. 229
Stewart, J. 445, 446
Stewart, K. E. 197, 198
Stich, S. 99, 100, 127, 128
Stokes, A. W. 348
Straub, J. J. 443
Strongman, K. T. 467

Struhsaker, T. T. 347, 349
Stubbs, D. A. 191
Studdert-Kennedy, M.
Stuss, D. T. 306, 322
Suarez, S. D. 201, 202
Suchman, L. 420
Sullivan, K. 364
Sumi, S. 196
Suppes, P. 274, 279
Sutherland, N. S. 247
Sutton, R. S. 33, 36, 272, 297
Swagerman, J. 510
Swartz, K. S. 183, 184, 202
Swartz, T. S. 509
Swets, J. A. 363
Swoyer, C. 102
Symons, D. 131

Talbi, B. 310
Tamura, M. 371
Tank, D. 23
Tannenbaum, P. L. 363
Taylor, D. T. 31
Teroni, E. 253
Terrace, H. S. 141, 435
Terrell, D. F. 199
Terschure, E. L. 509
Teuber, H. L. 226
Thagard, P. R. 61
Thieme, A. D. 320
Thierry, B. 184
Thinus-Blanc, C. 247, 254
Thomas, J. A. 141
Thomas, R. K. 176, 197, 199, 200, 207, 208, 211, 213
Thompson, N. S. 141, 373, 430
Thompson, R. K. R. 175, 208, 210, 211, 212, 213, 341
Thompson, R. L. 177, 202, 203, 204
Thorndyke, P. W. 419
Thornton, C. 55
Thorpe, K. 138
Timberlake, W. 176
Tinbergen, N. 341, 359, 475, 480
Tinklepaugh, O. L. 134
Toates, F. 438, 443, 458
Todd, S. 61
Tolman, E. C. 254, 262, 418, 436, 437, 441, 443, 447
Tomasch, J. 88
Tomlinson, W. T. 232
Townsend, S. E. 125
Trillmich, F. 177

Tsumoto, T. 309
Tucker, C. W. 162
Tulving, E. 314
Turing, A. 17, 18
Turner, D. R. 129
Turner, M. 63
Turner, S. R 385
Turvey, M. T. 165
Tversky, B. 205
Tyrrell, D. J. 213, 477

Ulbaek, I. 420

Vaccarino, A. L. 232
Vaisset, M. 31
Vander Wall, S. B. 84
Van Essen, D. C. 74, 306, 394
Van Hoesen, G. W. 257
van Sant 177, 178, 179, 180, 181, 182, 189
Varlet, C. 262
Vauclair, J. 246
Vaughan, W. Jr. 178, 205
Vickery, J. D. 199
von Cranach, M. 419
Von der Malsburg, C. 257
von Fersen, L. 23, 141, 142, 329
von Frisch, K. 373
von Holst, D. 469
von Holst, E. 470
Voss, J. F. 487
Vygotsky, L. 334, 335

Wages, C. 243
Wagner, A. R. 271, 294, 495
Waldmann, M. R. 278, 281, 288, 291, 292, 297
Wallman, J. 342
Wallnau, L. B. 202
Walters, J. R. 362
Waltz, D. 23
Wangviwattana, J. 486
Warburton, K. 138
Ward, P. I. 136
Warrington, E. K. 225, 226
Washburn, D. A. 199, 204
Wasserman, E. A. 176, 178, 181, 186, 187, 191, 192, 205, 206, 272
Watanabe, T. 235
Watson, J. B. 418
Weary, D. M. 345
Weaver, W. 102
Wehner, R. 78, 232, 253
Wehner, S. 253

Weiner, W. 418
Weingarten, H. P. 444
Weiskrantz, L. 225, 226
Weisman, R. G. 140
Weizenbaum, J. 420
Werner, G. M. 41, 389, 402, 403, 408
Werner, T. J. 208
White, F. J. 140, 452
White, N. M. 447, 451
Whiten, A. 121, 124, 125, 141, 142
Whiterspoon, D. 226
Wible, C. G. 234, 235
Widrow, B. 272, 297
Wiener, S. I. 259
Wiener, W. 418
Wiepkema, P. R. 435, 441, 442
Wier, C. C.
Wiest, C. 509
Wilensky, R. 407
Wilkes, K. V. 305
Williams, G. 166
Williams, G. C. 121, 122
Williams, H. W. 348, 371
Williams, J. W. 36
Wilson, S. W. 2, 3, 15, 27, 41
Winocur, G. 312, 313
Wohlstein, R. T. 162
Wood, F. G. 141
Wood, W. B. 84
Woodfield, A. 422, 425, 426
Woodruff, G. 204, 208
Wooles, I. M. 313
Woolf, N. J. 306
Wright, A. A. 176, 177, 178, 186, 188, 189,
    191, 208, 209
Wroblewski, J. T. 232
Wundt, W. 418
Wyers, E. 141

Ydenberg, R. C. 135
Ye, S. 495
Yeh, C. 31
Yoerg, S. I. 120, 124, 139, 141, 435
Yoshikubo, S. 183
Young, P. T. 444, 452

Zabel, C. J. 124
Zacks, R. T. 227
Zajonc, R. B. 370, 468, 494
Zamble, E. 444
Zentall, T. R. 176, 208
Zernik, U. 385
Zimmer-Hart, C. L. 278, 283

Zipser, D. 257
Zola-Morgan, S. 231, 307, 311, 314
Zuckerman, I. 121

Subject Index

AARON 57–58
ACRES 509–513
Action selection 416–430
Action theory 418–420, 425–429
Alarm calls 348–370
AM 58–59
Amnesia 226–229, 310, 311
Animal cognition 15, 120–127, 435, 481–482
Animal communication 342–370, 383
Animal information processing 3
Animal language 53–54, 341–342
Animats 3–5, 15, 27–41
Antipredator vigilance 134–139
Artificial intelligence 384–409
Association 442–446
Attention 329–337
Audience effects 364–370
Augmented finite-state machines 83
AuRA 31–32
Autonomy 415

Bacterial locomotion 159–161
Basic categories 181–183
Behaviorism 114, 123–124
Belief 94, 110–117
Biofunctional intentionality 104
Bioland 402–406, 408
Biomimetic perspective 14–16, 20–25
Biot 402
Blobs world 390–392
Blocking 287–290
Brain localization 229–231, 305, 307
Brain module 305
Brain systems and behavior 69, 84, 88, 128–129, 305–322

Categorical coherence 185–188
Categories vs. concepts 188–194

Categorization, function of 184
Causality 271–299
Chess 1–2, 14
Chickens 348–370
Classical conditioning 442–446, 486–488
Cognition 435, 437–442, 481–482
Cognition and emotion 467–468
Cognitive action theory 449–450
Cognitive architecture 28
Cognitive ethology 119–143
Cognitive maps 34, 254–260, 264
Comparative approach to cognitive science 16, 27
Comparative intentionality 97–99
Computational creativity 55–63
Computational equivalence 22
Computationalism 1–4
Concepts in animals 175–213
Conceptual equivalence 205–207
Conceptual knowledge 175
Concerns 505–506
Conditional contingencies 279–283
Connectionist representation 385–389
Consciousness 318–322
Constraint satisfaction 23–24
Contingency vs. association 271–299
Control precedence 506
Control systems 151–169
  crowd behavior 161–165
  interacting systems 158–159
  parallel and hierarchical 165–168
  vs. reflex systems 169
Control theory 151–171
  and cognitive science 151, 168
Creativity 45–64
  vs. novelty 47

Dead reckoning 252
DETE 389–402

Discrimination tasks 177–178
DISPAR 388
Distributed vs. local memory systems 307–308
Dogs 130–133, 262–265

Efference copy 73–74
Eliminative materialism 114–115
Emotion 465–493
Emotion
  analogy between animals and humans 468–470
  control structure 507–508
  functional view 501–503
  human 468–470, 503–505
Emotional states 474–478, 480–481
Equivalence of pathways 262
EURISKO 58–60
Evolutionary continuity 3
Exploration 242–250

Fixed action patterns 470–474, 476–480
Folk psychology 127–130
Functionalism 103
Functional reference 347–348

Gaze 329–337
Generalized motorium 85
Generalized sensor 85
Genetic algorithms 60–61
Genetic operators 41
Genetic programming 36–38
Genghis 32
Goals 504–505
Goal seeking 420–425, 457–460

Hamsters 247, 253
Hierarchical networks 449–450
Hippocampus 231–235, 257–260, 312–315, 450–452
Historical creativity 48
Human infants 329–337
Human language 406–408
Hyenas 124

Incentive motivation 443–445
Information 102
Insect locomotion 28–30
Instrumental learning 446–449
Instrumentalism 114
Intelligence 1–4, 13, 45
  evolutionary continuity 3
  as interacting agents 2–3

as linguistic mechanism 13
mechanisms of 2–5, 13–24
as rule base 13–14
Intension 96–97
Intentional stance 112–113
Intentionality 93–108, 110–117, 127, 170, 429–430
Intuitive statistics 271–272

Katamic memory 395–399
Kekule's discovery of benzene 49, 52–53
Korsakoff syndrome 314

Language 13
  characteristics 370–374
  as cause of intelligence 13
  of thought 20
Learned irrelevance 278–279
Learning 442–449, 482–492

Maps vs. propositions 116–117
Mark test 201
Meaning 345–348
Memory 77–82, 225–237, 305–322
Mind as universal machine 18–19
Modularity 305–307
Monkeys 106–107, 179–181
Motivation 435–437
Motivation management 71–73
Music perception 55–56

Natural categorical concepts 177–188
Natural language processing 384–409
Natural movement concepts 194–196
Navigation 31, 35–36
Neural networks 28–31, 388–389, 395–400, 482–488
Neuroethology 28
Nonsymbolic representations 2–4
Number concepts 197–200

Overshadowing 290–291

Parsimony 124
Path integration 250–253
Perceptual control theory 151–171
Physical symbol system 1–2, 16–22
Planning 36
Play-soliciting signals 130–133
Pointing 333–335
Predictron 396
Probabalistic contrast model 273–276

Problem solving 242–246
Psychological creativity 48

Recognitron 396–397
Relational concepts 207–213
Relaxation 23–24
Representations 20–24, 102, 189–194,
    225–228, 318–322, 440–442
Representations, importance of 4, 102
Rescorla-Wagner learning model 271–272,
    276–278, 294–297
Response-urgency model 360–364
Robot navigation 31, 35–36
Robots 31–36, 416–430, 436–437
Rules 13–14

Same/different task 211
Self-awareness 200–204, 319
Self-concept 200–204, 319
Self-organization 161
Self-sufficiency 415
Semantic transparency 19–20
Sensorimotor computation 73–77
Sensorimotor tracking 153–158
Sensory reinforcement 178–179
Similarity 176
Social play 130–133
Spatial memory 233–237, 241–266
Squirt 32
Strong symbol system hypothesis (SPSS)
    19–20
Substitutivity 96
Subsumption architecture 32
Surprise 134
Symbol grounding 2, 389–390
Symbolic representations 20–24, 384–385
Synthetic psychology 82–83

Teleological imperative 420
Teleology 420, 454–457
Temporal lobe syndrome 314
Thermostats 114
Three-table problem 242–246
Turing machine 1, 17–18

Variable binding problem 387
Verbal representations 395
Vervet monkeys 106–107
Visual attention 329–337

Washoe 53–54
World models 31–32, 36